How to access the supplemental web study guide

We are pleased to provide access to a web study guide that supplements your textbook, *Life Span Motor Development, Sixth Edition.* This resource offers lab activities and video clips that the learner will use for application of key concepts and for hands-on assessment using the guidelines presented in the book.

Accessing the web study guide is easy! Follow these steps if you purchased a new book:

1. Visit **www.HumanKinetics.com/LifeSpanMotorDevelopment.**

2. Click the <u>sixth</u> link next to the corresponding sixth edition book cover.

3. Click the Sign In link on the left or top of the page. If you do not have an account with Human Kinetics, you will be prompted to create one.

4. If the online product you purchased does not appear in the Ancillary Items box on the left of the page, click the Enter Key Code option in that box. Enter the key code that is printed at the right, including all hyphens. Click the Submit button to unlock your online product.

5. After you have entered your key code the first time, you will never have to enter it again to access this product. Once unlocked, a link to your product will permanently appear in the menu on the left. For future visits, all you need to do is sign in to the textbook's website and follow the link that appears in the left menu!

→ Click the Need Help? button on the textbook's website if you need assistance along the way.

How to access the web study guide if you purchased a used book:

You may purchase access to the web study guide by visiting the text's website, **www.HumanKinetics.com/LifeSpanMotorDevelopment,** or by calling the following:

800-747-4457 . . . . .U.S. customers
800-465-7301 . . . . .Canadian customers
+44 (0) 113 255 5665 . . . . European customers
08 8372 0999 . . . . Australian customers
0800 222 062 . . . . .New Zealand customers
217-351-5076 . . . . .International customers

For technical support, send an e-mail to:
support@hkusa.com . . . . U.S. and international customers
info@hkcanada.com . . . . Canadian customers
academic@hkeurope.com . . . . European customers
keycodesupport@hkaustralia.com . . . . . Australian and New Zealand customers

HUMAN KINETICS
The Information Leader in Physical Activity & Health

Product: Life Span Motor Development, Sixth Edition, web study guide

Key code: HAYWOOD-V64E2G-OSG

This unique code allows you access to the web study guide.

Access is provided if you have purchased a new book. Once submitted, the code may not be entered for any other user.

LIFE SPAN MOTOR DEVELOPMENT

SIXTH EDITION

Kathleen M. Haywood, PhD

University of Missouri–St. Louis

Nancy Getchell, PhD

University of Delaware

Human Kinetics

Library of Congress Cataloging-in-Publication Data

Haywood, Kathleen, author.
 Life span motor development / Kathleen M. Haywood, Nancy Getchell. -- Sixth edition.
     p. ; cm.
 Includes bibliographical references and index.
 I. Getchell, Nancy, 1963- author. II. Title.
 [DNLM: 1. Motor Skills. 2. Human Development. WE 103]
 RJ133
 612.7'6--dc23
                                    2013044126

ISBN: 978-1-4504-5699-9 (print)

Acquisitions Editor: Myles Schrag; **Developmental Editor:** Christine M. Drews; **Managing Editor:** Susan Huls; **Assistant Editor:** Melissa J. Zavala; **Copyeditor:** Amanda M. Eastin-Allen; **Indexer:** Nancy Ball; **Permissions Manager:** Dalene Reeder; **Graphic Designer:** Nancy Rasmus; **Graphic Artist:** Kathleen Boudreau-Fuoss; **Cover Designer:** Keith Blomberg; **Photograph (cover):** © Stockdisk; **Photographs (interior):** © Human Kinetics, unless otherwise noted; **Photo Asset Manager:** Laura Fitch; **Visual Production Assistant:** Joyce Brumfield; **Photo Production Manager:** Jason Allen; **Art Manager:** Kelly Hendren; **Associate Art Manager:** Alan L. Wilborn; **Art Style Development:** Joanne Brummett; **Illustrations:** © Human Kinetics; **Printer:** Courier Companies, Inc.

Printed in the United States of America   10 9 8 7 6 5 4 3 2 1

The paper in this book was manufactured using responsible forestry methods.

Human Kinetics

Website: www.HumanKinetics.com

United States: Human Kinetics
P.O. Box 5076
Champaign, IL 61825-5076
800-747-4457
e-mail: humank@hkusa.com

Canada: Human Kinetics
475 Devonshire Road Unit 100
Windsor, ON N8Y 2L5
800-465-7301 (in Canada only)
e-mail: info@hkcanada.com

Europe: Human Kinetics
107 Bradford Road
Stanningley
Leeds LS28 6AT, United Kingdom
+44 (0) 113 255 5665
e-mail: hk@hkeurope.com

Australia: Human Kinetics
57A Price Avenue
Lower Mitcham, South Australia 5062
08 8372 0999
e-mail: info@hkaustralia.com

New Zealand: Human Kinetics
P.O. Box 80
Torrens Park, South Australia 5062
0800 222 062
e-mail: info@hknewzealand.com

E5970

To the many motor development researchers
(past, present, and future)
who continue to push our field forward.
Your work inspires ours.

Contents

Preface

Every day, you move. This doesn't happen in a vacuum, though. Every movement you make occurs within your surrounding environment, whether you are at home, in the gymnasium, or on a ball field. You also move for a reason; the activities or tasks you perform have specific requirements or rules. The way you move has changed a great deal from when you were an infant, and it will keep changing throughout your entire life. This is the essence of the study of motor development: observing changes in movement across the life span, then determining why these movements change in the ways they do.

In this edition, we focus on the model of constraints to help you understand why movements change. The model of constraints accounts for several factors: the individual or mover, the environment in which he or she moves, and the task that he or she has undertaken as well as the interactions between these constraints. It also accounts for why movement changes as the body and individual characteristics change over the life span. It allows us to anticipate how we might change movements by altering the environment, the task, or both (something that future physical educators, physical and occupational therapists, and other practitioners will find quite useful). Using the model of constraints will help you gain a more complete view of motor development across the life span and a means for solving motor development problems long after you finish your course. In fact, understanding life span motor development will assist your progress in all movement-related fields. You will learn what motor development is as well as the theoretical and historical roots of the field. You will also observe many factors related to development of movement skills, such as growth, aging, and perception. In addition, you will discover how constraints and other factors can encourage or discourage various movements—perhaps in ways you hadn't thought about yet!

Who can benefit from reading this text? Many people interested in movement can benefit. Educators at all levels—from early childhood educators to gerontologists—can enhance their teaching by becoming aware of various systems of the body and how they change over time. Persons in the health sciences, such as physical and occupational therapists, will find tools that assist them in observing patterns of movement. Readers in exercise science will receive guidance from the descriptions and explanations of developmental physical fitness and of processes underlying change. However, you don't need extensive experience in movement studies to profit from this text. Because all people go through these developmental changes during their lives, all people can benefit from understanding more about motor development. In fact, parents and future parents will gain understanding of the motor development of their children and how to foster healthful motor development. Thus, many readers of this text will be able to use the information personally no matter how extensively they use it in their professional roles.

eBook
available at
your campus bookstore
or HumanKinetics.com

What's New in the Sixth Edition

The sixth edition of *Life Span Motor Development* and its ancillaries further emphasize the use of motor development information in the real world. For example, each chapter begins with an example of a common experience related to motor development, and this experience is revisited at the end of the chapter, giving the reader the opportunity to consider the experience in light of the material covered in the chapter. Application questions throughout the chapters engage readers in considering how parents or professionals in various roles might use the material discussed. The number and variety of lab activities, delivered on the website, has been increased, and more than 130 new videos are included to provide more opportunities for student-centered learning and, in some cases, to choose projects related to their career goals.

The content in the sixth edition has been updated to reflect new research in the field. The material added to chapter 18 is intended to help practitioners bridge the gap between the model of constraints and structuring learning environments to help their students and clients progress. Readers are shown how to expand the model of constraints to focus on key constraints for a given skill or task and how to scale that constraint to make a learning environment more or less challenging to fit the individual. Readers are also shown how to relate the constraints models to ecological task analyses and how these analyses can be used to assess learners and clients.

Features of the Book

The sixth edition of *Life Span Motor Development* continues several important features of previous editions.

- **Motor development in the real world.** To remind you that motor development is a common part of our human experience, we begin each chapter with a real-life experience—something that is a common experience for many of us or something we see reported frequently in the media.
- **Chapter objectives.** The chapter objectives list the most important concepts you should learn and understand in each chapter.
- **Running glossary.** A running glossary appears in the margins throughout each chapter. The **running glossary words** are highlighted in the text with a second color so that you know to check the margin definition. Some terms don't require a margin definition because they are defined sufficiently in the text. Those words are boldfaced to help you locate them.
- **Application questions.** We distribute application questions as shown here, throughout the chapters. These questions challenge you to consider how parents or professionals could use the material under discussion in a real-world situation.

 Who can benefit from learning about motor development?

- **Key points.** Key points appear periodically throughout the chapter to point out the theme of a discussion or a broad conclusion amidst chapter details. These key points are identified by the icon to the left.

This is an example of a **running glossary word**; it is highlighted in color in the text and is defined in the margin.

KEY POINT
Key points look like this and can be found in the margins of the text.

- Cues to go to the web study guide for lab activities. Each chapter includes cues, such as the example below, to the lab activities in the web study guide. If you purchase a print book, you received access to the web study guide via a key code. If you purchased a used print book or an e-book that does not provide access to the web study guide, you will want to purchase the web study guide so that you have access to the lab activities and videos.

 WEB STUDY GUIDE Gain experience in observing movement by doing Lab Activity 1.1, Observation as a Tool of Inquiry, in the web study guide. Go to www.HumanKinetics.com/LifeSpanMotorDevelopment.

- **Assessment elements.** Most chapters contain an assessment element that will aid you in observing and assessing some aspect of motor development. These elements also help you understand how researchers and other professionals measure certain aspects of motor development.
- **Summary.** This section appears toward the end of a chapter and offers a concise wrap-up of the material presented in the chapter.
- **Reinforcement of chapter content.** To help you integrate the concepts you've learned throughout the chapter into a constraints perspective, each chapter ends with a section titled "Reinforcing What You Have Learned About Constraints." Here you'll find subsections that encourage you to
  - take a second look at the real-life experience that opened the chapter,
  - test your knowledge by answering questions about the material, and
  - complete learning exercises that provide hands-on ways to apply what you have learned.
- **Assistance in meeting national standards.** The sixth edition continues to assist students in meeting national standards. The text and the approach are consistent with the revised guidelines for minimum competencies drafted by the Motor Development Academy of the National Association for Sport and Physical Education, which is part of SHAPE America (formerly the American Alliance for Health, Physical Education, Recreation and Dance). For those preparing to teach, the sixth edition provides guidelines for constructing developmentally appropriate activities and designing learning activities to help your students meet grade-level expectations.

Organization

Part I contains three chapters of fundamental concepts. Key to part I is the introduction of Newell's constraints model, around which the entire text is organized. Chapter 1 defines terms and methods of study in motor development. Chapter 2 offers a historical and theoretical overview of the field. Chapter 3 introduces the principles of motion and stability that underlie all movements and guide motor development.

Part II examines two important individual constraints—physical growth and aging—of the body as a whole and of specific body systems as well as how they change over the life span.

Part III describes changing motor patterns over the life span. Chapter 6 explores motor development during infancy. Chapter 7 examines the development of locomotor skills, chapter 8 the development of ballistic skills, and chapter 9 the development of manipulative skills. These chapters provide much detail related to the specific sequence of changes one sees through development.

The remaining parts focus on additional constraints that influence the movement arising from the interaction of these constraints, emphasizing those that change over the life span. Part IV focuses on sensation and perception as they interact with action, and part V focuses on social, cultural, and psychosocial influences as well as the effect of knowledge on movement. Part VI looks at four important components of physical fitness and how these constrain movement as individuals change over the life span. Many professionals apply adult training principles to children, youths, and older adults without appreciating their unique constraints. These chapters present developmentally appropriate guidelines. For those concerned about the obesity epidemic among children and youths, part VI contains useful information.

The concluding chapter encourages readers to apply what they have learned about changing constraints and their interactions to actual people and situations. We expanded this chapter to provide enhanced opportunities for readers to reflect on all they have learned about motor development over the life span and use that knowledge in specific cases.

Ancillaries

The sixth edition of *Life Span Motor Development* includes a web study guide for students as well as an instructor guide, presentation package plus image bank, test package, and chapter quizzes for instructors.

The *web study guide* contains learning exercises and lab activities for every chapter. These exercises and activities might be done during class, in the laboratory, or as homework assignments. We modified the existing lab activities so that the instructions are easier to understand and more streamlined. New to this edition, lab activity record sheets and questions are available as fillable documents so that students can complete and submit them electronically, resulting in increased efficiency and reduced paperwork for instructors. The lab activities include video clips so that instructors whose classes cannot perform live observations will still be able to use all of the labs. Clips include footage of infants and toddlers; additional footage of people performing the fundamental motor skills; and context-specific, constraint-rich video for chapters 1 through 18.

The *instructor guide* includes an overview, list of major concepts, suggested class activities, and suggested readings for each chapter. It has been revised to provide more information to guide the instructor through the laboratory activities and learning exercises. Answers are provided for the lab activities that require students to assess performers in video clips.

The *test package*, created with Respondus 4.0, includes a bank of more than 490 questions created especially for this edition of *Life Span Motor Development*. Question types include true-false, fill in the blank, short answer, essay, and multiple choice.

Answers are provided for some of the short-answer and essay questions, although you will likely want your students' answers to these questions to reflect the particular discussions held by your class. With Respondus LE, a free version of the Respondus software, instructors can create print versions of their own tests by selecting from the question pool; create, store, and retrieve their own questions; select their own test forms and save them for later editing or printing; and export the test forms into a word-processing program.

Chapter quizzes provide ready-made quizzes for each chapter. The chapter quiz will help instructors assess students' comprehension of the most important concepts in the chapter. Each quiz contains 10 questions.

The *presentation package* includes a comprehensive series of PowerPoint slides for each chapter. The slides highlight the most important concepts from the book and include selected video clips from the lab activities. We have tried to include something from every section of each chapter. Depending on the particular emphasis an instructor wants to give the chapter—or on the background and expertise of the students—instructors may want to delete some slides or embellish others.

The *image bank* includes most of the text's art, photos, and tables. A blank PowerPoint template is also provided so that instructors can customize or create a PowerPoint presentation if they so choose. Easy-to-follow instructions are included.

The web study guide, instructor guide, test package, chapter quizzes, and presentation package plus image bank are all accessible at www.HumanKinetics.com/LifeSpanMotorDevelopment.

Acknowledgments

The *Life Span Motor Development* project began in 1983. Each edition and each addition to what has now become an instructional package reflect the contributions of many. We acknowledge all of those contributions here. Any undertaking this ambitious could be completed only with the help and support of those contributing their unique expertise and talents. This sixth edition continues to expand on the previous editions, and contributions anywhere along the way have made this work what it is today.

First, we extend our appreciation to those who have appeared in photographs or video clips over the years: Jennifer, Douglas, and Michael Imergoot; Laura, Christina, and Matthew Haywood; Anna Tramelli; Cathy Lewis; Jules Mommaerts; Connor Miller; Franklin McFarland; Rachel Harmon; Jessica Galli; Charmin Olion; Chad Hoffman; Stephanie Kozlowski; Julia and Madeleine Blakely; Valeria Rohde; Ian Stahl; Amelia Isaacs; Reese and Nicholas Rapson; Janiyah Bell; Parker Lehn; Logan Allen; Jane Laskowski; Rachel and Jessica Wiley; Diane Waltermire; Jase Elliott; Susan Allen; Susan and Lisa Miller; Emily and Jeremy Falkenham, Sarah Poe; Alex Mitsdarfer; Lyna Buzzard; Blair Mathis; Parker, Addison, Zander, and Willow Burk; Robert, James, and Lillian Hall; Susan Outlaw; Julie and Johnathan Lyons; Grace and Dylan Taylor; Emily and Abram George; Reid and Madi Henness; Kaleb Curry; Kelly Taylor; Luci and Lynette Morris; Tony and Mary Graham; William Gingold; Anna Clark; Sarah, Mary, and Grace White; Neil Hollwedel; Daniel Fishel; Cole and Logan Hasty; Marcia Siebert; and Joshua, Shagna, and Holden Stone; among others.

Next, we acknowledge friends who took or donated some of the photographs in this or previous editions: Brian Speicher, William Long, Rosa Angulo-Barroso, Susan Miller, Dale Ulrich, Mary Ann Roberton, Ann VanSant, John Haubenstricker, B.D. Ulrich, and Jill Whitall, contributed film tracings from which some of the art was drawn. Additional thanks to Mary Ann Roberton for supplying a great picture of Hal in action.

The content of *Life Span Motor Development* touches many subdisciplines and specialty areas of study. We extend our thanks to John Strupel, the late Elizabeth Sweeney, Bruce Clark, Jane Clark, Maureen Weiss, Kathleen Williams, Ann VanSant, and Mary Ann Roberton, who were all kind enough to read sections of the text or contribute information. Thanks to Paul M. Spezia, of St. Peters Bone and Joint Surgery, who provided wrist X rays for the laboratory exercise on skeletal age.

Ann Wagner and Cynthia Haywood Kerkemeyer helped by keyboarding and checking parts of the earlier editions, and the late Lynn Imergoot, Linda Gagen, Patricia Hanna, and Cathy Lewis were kind enough to help with the index of an earlier edition.

We especially thank our many colleagues in motor development who have made suggestions along the way. Their dedication to helping students of motor development appreciate this area of study is always an inspiration. Last but not least, we appreciate the patience and dedication of our team at Human Kinetics for keeping us on track through the many facets of the sixth edition in the face of a tight schedule, and Judy Wright, who helped nurture early editions of *Life Span Motor Development*.

We also acknowledge our families and friends, who have prevailed through many revisions of this textbook. Their continued support over the years makes our work possible.

Credits

Figure 1.2 KMSP/DPPI/Icon SMI.

Figure 1.3 Reprinted from A. Maclaren, ed., 1967, *Advances in reproductive physiology*, Vol. 2 (London: Elek Books). By permission of Jonathan Michie.

Figure 2.1 Courtesy of the authors.

Figure 2.2 Courtesy of the authors.

Figure 2.3 Adapted, by permission, from E. Thelen, B.D. Ulrich, and J. L. Jensen, 1989, The developmental origins of locomotion. In *Development of posture and gait across the life span*, edited by M.H. Woolacott and A. Shumway-Cook (Columbia, SC: University of South Carolina Press), 28.

Chapter 3 Opener Anthony Stanley/Action Plus/Icon SMI.

Text 3.1 Based on www.aimeemullens.com.

Figure 3.2 Reprinted from J.E. Donnelly, 1990, *Living anatomy*, 2nd ed. (Champaign, IL: Human Kinetics), 32. Permission by J.E. Donnelly.

Table 4.1 Adapted, by permission, from P.S. Timiras, 1972, *Developmental physiology and aging* (New York; Macmillan), 63-64.

Figure 4.3 Reprinted, by permission, from P. Rhodes, 1969, *Reproductive physiology for medical students* (London: J. & A. Churchill Ltd.), 191.

Figures 4.4a and b Data from the National Center for Health Statistics in collaboration with the National Center for Chronic Disease Prevention and Health Promotion 2000. Adapted from www.cdc.gov/nchs/about/major/nhanes/growthcharts.clinical_charts.htm.

Figures 4.5a and b Data from the National Center for Health Statistics in collaboration with the National Center for Chronic Disease Prevention and Health Promotion 2000. Adapted from www.cdc.gov/nchs/about/major/nhanes/growthcharts.clinical_charts.htm.

Figure 4.7 Adapted, by permission, from P.S. Timiras, 1972, *Developmental physiology and aging* (New York: Macmillan), 284.

Figures 4.8a, b, and c Reprinted from A. Maclaren, ed., 1967, *Advances in reproductive physiology*, Vol. 2 (London: Elek Books). By permission of Jonathan Michie.

Figure 4.10 Reprinted, by permission, from W.W. Spirduso, 1995, *Physical dimensions of aging* (Champaign, IL: Human Kinetics), 59. Adapted, by permission, from A.R. Frisancho, 1990, *Anthropometric standards for the assessment of growth and nutritional status* (Ann Arbor: University of Michigan Press), 27.

Figure 4.12 Reprinted, by permission, from W.W. Spirduso, 1995, *Physical dimensions of aging* (Champaign, IL: Human Kinetics), 59. Adapted, by permission, from A.R. Frisancho, 1990, *Anthropometric standards for the assessment of growth and nutritional status* (Ann Arbor: University of Michigan Press), 27.

Figure 5.1 Printed in U.S.A. © Carolina Biological Supply Company. Reproduction of all or any part of this material without written permission from the copyright holder is unlawful.

Figure 5.3 Printed in U.S.A. © Carolina Biological Supply Company. Reproduction of all or any part of this material without written permission from the copyright holder is unlawful.

Figures 5.4a and b Reprinted, by permission, from S.I. Pyle, 1971, *A radiographic standard of reference for the growing hand and wrist* (Chicago: Year Book Medical), 53, 73. Copyright Bolton-Brush Growth Study-B.H. Broadbent D.D.S.

Figure 5.8 From R.M. Malina and C. Bouchard, 1988, Subcutaneous fat distribution during growth. In *Fat distribution during growth and later health outcomes*, edited by C. Bouchard and F.E. Johnston (New York: Liss), 70. Copyright © 1988 by Alan R. Liss, Inc. Reprinted by permission of Wiley-Liss, a division of John Wiley and Sons, Inc.

Text 6.1 Reprinted, by permission, from livescience. Available: www.livescience.com/23572-assistive-robotics-aide-young-children-nsf-bts.html

Figure 6.2a Geoff Kirby/Press Association Images.

Figure 6.2b © D.A. Weinstein / Custom Medical Stock Photo.

Figure 6.4 Photo courtesy of Dale Ulrich.

Figure 6.7 Reprinted from B.I. Bertenthal, J.L. Rose, and D.L. Bai, 1997, "Perception-action coupling in the development of visual control of posture," *Journal of Experimental Psychology: Human Perception and Performance* 23: 1631-1634, fig. 1. Copyright © by the American Psychological Association. Reprinted with permission.

Figures 7.2a, b, and c Parts a and c are drawn from film tracings taken in the Motor Development and Child Study Laboratory, University of Wisconsin-Madison and now available from the Motor Development Film Collection, Kinesiology Division, Bowling Green State University. © Mary Ann Roberton. Part b is adapted from R.L. Wickstrom, 1983, *Fundamental motor patterns*, 3rd ed. (Philadelphia: Lea & Febiger), 29. © Mary Ann Roberton and Kate R. Barrett.

Figures 7.4a and b Part a is drawn from film tracings taken in the Motor Development and Child Study Laboratory, University of Wisconsin-Madison and now available from the Motor Development Film Collection, Kinesiology Division, Bowling Green State University. © Mary Ann Roberton. Part b is redrawn from R.L. Wickstrom, 1983, *Fundamental motor patterns*, 3rd ed. (Philadelphia: Lea & Febiger). © Mary Ann Roberton and Kate R. Barrett.

Figure 7.5 Adapted, by permission, from R.L. Wickstrom, 1983, *Fundamental motor patterns*, 3rd ed. (Philadelphia: Lea & Febiger), 29. © Mary Ann Roberton and Kate R. Barrett.

Table 7.2 Reprinted, by permission, from R.L. Wickstrom, 1983, *Fundamental motor patterns*, 3rd ed. (Philadelphia: Lea & Febiger) 68. © Mary Ann Roberton and Kate R. Barrett.

Table 7.3 Reprinted, by permission, from R.L. Wickstrom, 1983, *Fundamental motor patterns*, 3rd ed. (Philadelphia: Lea & Febiger) 68. © Mary Ann Roberton and Kate R. Barrett.

Table 7.4 Adapted, by permission, from V. Seefeldt, S. Reuschlein, and P. Vogel, 1972, *Sequencing motor skills within the physical education curriculum*. Paper presented to the annual conference of the American Association for Health, Physical Education and Recreation. © Vern D. Seedfeldt.

Table 7.5 Adapted, by permission, from J.E. Clark and S.J. Phillips, 1985, A developmental sequence of the standing long jump. In *Motor development: Current selected research*, Vol. 1, edited by J.E. Clark and J.H. Humphrey (Princeton Book), 76-77. Copyright 1985 by Princeton Book Company, Publishers.

Figure 7.7 Adapted, by permission, from R.L. Wickstrom, 1983, *Fundamental motor patterns*, 3rd ed. (Philadelphia: Lea & Febiger), 74. © Mary Ann Roberton and Kate R. Barrett.

Figure 7.8 Drawn from film tracings taken in the Motor Development and Child Study Laboratory, University of Wisconsin-Madison and now available from the Motor Development Film Collection, Kinesiology Division, Bowling Green State University. © Mary Ann Roberton.

Figure 7.10 Adapted, by permission, from R.L. Wickstrom, 1983, *Fundamental motor patterns*, 3rd ed. (Philadelphia: Lea & Febiger), 77. © Mary Ann Roberton and Kate R. Barrett.

Figure 7.13 Drawn from film tracings taken in the Motor Development and Child Study Laboratory, University of Wisconsin–Madison and now available from the Motor Development Film Collection, Kinesiology Division, Bowling Green State University. © Mary Ann Roberton.

Figure 7.14 Drawn from film tracings taken in the Motor Development and Child Study Laboratory, University of Wisconsin–Madison and now available from the Motor Development Film Collection, Kinesiology Division, Bowling Green State University. © Mary Ann Roberton.

Table 7.6 Reprinted, from M.A. Roberton and L.E. Halverson, 1984, *Developing children: Their changing movement* (Philadelphia: Lea & Febiger), 56-63. By permission of Mary Ann Roberton.

Figure 7.15 Drawn from film tracings taken in the Motor Development and Child Study Laboratory, University of Wisconsin–Madison and now available from the Motor Development Film Collection, Kinesiology Division, Bowling Green State University. © Mary Ann Roberton.

Figure 7.16 Drawn from film tracings taken in the Motor Development and Child Study Laboratory, University of Wisconsin–Madison and now available from the Motor Development Film Collection, Kinesiology Division, Bowling Green State University. © Mary Ann Roberton.

Figure 7.17 "Development sequences for hopping over distance: A prelongitudinal screening." L. Halverson and K. Williams, *Research Quarterly for Exercise and Sport*, 56:38, 1985, reprinted by permission of the American Alliance for Health, Physical Education, Recreation and Dance (www.AAHPERD.org).

Figures 7.19a and b Adapted, by permission, from J.E. Clark and J.Whitall, 1989, Changing patterns of locomotion: From walking to skipping. In *Development of posture and gait across the life span,* edited by M.H.Woollacott and A. Shumway-Cook (Columbia, SC: University of South Carolina Press), 132.

Figure 7.20 Adapted, by permission from J.E. Clark and J. Whitall, 1989, Changing patterns of locomotion: From walking to skipping. In *Development of posture and gait across the life span,* edited by M.H. Woollacott and A. Shumway-Cook (Columbia, SC: University of South Carolina Press), 132.

Figure 8.1 Drawn from film tracings taken in the Motor Development and Child Study Laboratory, University of Wisconsin–Madison and now available from the Motor Development Film Collection, Kinesiology Division, Bowling Green State University. © Mary Ann Roberton.

Figure 8.2 Drawn from film tracings taken in the Motor Development and Child Study Laboratory, University of Wisconsin-Madison and now available from the Motor Development Film Collection, Kinesiology Division, Bowling Green State University. © Mary Ann Roberton and Kate R. Barrett.

Table 8.1 Reprinted from M.A. Roberton and L.E. Halverson, 1984, *Developing children: Their changing movement* (Philadelphia: Lea & Febiger), 103, 106-107, 118, 123. By permission of Mary Ann Roberton.

Figure 8.3 Drawn from film tracings taken in the Motor Development and Child Study Laboratory, University of Wisconsin–Madison and now available from the Motor Development Film Collection, Kinesiology Division, Bowling Green State University. © Mary Ann Roberton.

Figure 8.4 Drawn from film tracings taken in the Motor Development and Child Study Laboratory, University of Wisconsin–Madison and now available from the Motor Development Film Collection, Kinesiology Division, Bowling Green State University. © Mary Ann Roberton.

Figure 8.5 Drawn from film tracings taken in the Motor Development and Child Study Laboratory, University of Wisconsin–Madison and now available from the Motor Development Film Collection, Kinesiology Division, Bowling Green State University. © Mary Ann Roberton.

Figure 8.6 Drawn from film tracings taken in the Motor Development and Child Study Laboratory, University of Wisconsin–Madison and now available from the Motor Development Film Collection, Kinesiology Division, Bowling Green State University. © Mary Ann Roberton.

Figure 8.7 The line drawings within this Observation Plan are: Drawn from film tracings taken in the Motor Development and Child Study Laboratory, University of Wisconsin–Madison and now available from the Motor Development Film Collection, Kinesiology Division, Bowling Green State University. © Mary Ann Roberton.

Figure 8.8 Drawn from film tracings taken in the Motor Development and Child Study Laboratory, University of Wisconsin–Madison and now available from the Motor Development Film Collection, Kinesiology Division, Bowling Green State University. © Mary Ann Roberton.

Figure 8.9 Drawn from film tracings taken in the Motor Development and Child Study Laboratory, University of Wisconsin–Madison and now available from the Motor Development Film Collection, Kinesiology Division, Bowling Green State University. © Mary Ann Roberton.

Figure 8.10 Drawn from film tracings taken in the Motor Development and Child Study Laboratory, University of Wisconsin–Madison and now available from the Motor Development Film Collection, Kinesiology Division, Bowling Green State University. © Mary Ann Roberton.

Figure 8.11 Drawn from film tracings taken in the Motor Development and Child Study Laboratory, University of Wisconsin–Madison and now available from the Motor Development Film Collection, Kinesiology Division, Bowling Green State University. © Mary Ann Roberton.

Figure 8.12 Drawn from film tracings taken in the Motor Development and Child Study Laboratory, University of Wisconsin–Madison and now available from the Motor Development Film Collection, Kinesiology Division, Bowling Green State University. © Mary Ann Roberton.

Table 8.2 Reprinted from M.A. Roberton and L.E. Halverson, 1984, *Developing children: Their changing movement* (Philadelphia: Lea & Febiger), 103, 106-107, 118, 123. By permission of Mary Ann Roberton.

Figure 8.14 Drawn from film tracings taken in the Motor Development and Child Study Laboratory, University of Wisconsin–Madison and now available from the Motor Development Film Collection, Kinesiology Division, Bowling Green State University. © Mary Ann Roberton.

Figure 8.16 Drawn from film tracings taken in the Motor Development and Child Study Laboratory, University of Wisconsin–Madison and now available from the Motor Development Film Collection, Kinesiology Division, Bowling Green State University. © Mary Ann Roberton.

Figure 8.17 Drawn from film tracings taken in the Motor Development and Child Study Laboratory, University of Wisconsin–Madison and now available from the Motor Development Film Collection, Kinesiology Division, Bowling Green State University. © Mary Ann Roberton.

Table 8.4 The preparatory trunk action and the parenthetical information in Step 3 of Racket Action are reprinted, by permission, from J.A. Messick, 1991, "Prelongitudinal screening of hypothesized developmental sequences for the overhead tennis serve in experienced tennis players 9-19 years of age," *Research Quarterly for Exercise and Sport* 62: 249-256. The remaining components are reprinted, by permission, from S. Langendorfer, 1987, Prelongitudinal screening of overarm striking development performed under two environmental conditions. In *Advances in motor development research*, Vol. 1, edited by J.E. Clark and J.H. Humphrey (New York: AMS Press), 26.

Figure 9.3 Reprinted, by permission, from L. Hay, 1990, Developmental changes in eye-hand coordination behaviors: Preprogramming versus feedback control. In *Development of eye-hand coordination across the life span*, edited by C. Bard, M. Fleury, and L. Hay (Columbia, SC: University of South Carolina Press), 235.

Figure 9.5 Drawn from film tracings taken in the Motor Development and Child Study Laboratory, University of Wisconsin–Madison and now available from the Motor Development Film Collection, Kinesiology Division, Bowling Green State University. © Mary Ann Roberton.

Table 9.1 "Developmental sequences for catching a small fall: A prelongitudinal screening," H.S. Strohmeyer, K. Williams, and D. Schaub-George, *Research Quarterly for Exercise and Sport*, Vol. 62: 249-256, 199, reprinted by permission of the American Alliance for Health, Physical Education, Recreation and Dance (www.AAHPERD.org).

Figure 9.7 Illustrations are drawn from film tracings taken in the Motor Development and Child Study Laboratory, University of Wisconsin—Madison and now available from the Motor Development Film Collection, Kinesiology Division, Bowling Green State University. © Mary Ann Roberton.

Figure 9.8 From P. McLeod and Z. Dienes, 1996, "Do fielders know where to go to catch the ball or only how to get there?" *Journal of Experimental Psychology: Human Perception and Performance* 22: 541. Copyright © 1996 by the American Psychological Association. Adapted with permission.

Figure 9.9 Redrawn from Lenoir et al. 1999.

Figure 10.1 Reprinted, by permission, from G.H. Sage, 1984, *Motor learning and control: A neuropsychological approach* (Dubuque, IA: Brown), 111. ©The McGraw-Hill Companies.

Figure 10.4 From *Perception: The world transformed* by Lloyd Kaufman, copyright (1979) originally from "Sight and Mind" by Kaufman, L. (1974) by Oxford University Press. Used by permission of Oxford University Press, Inc.

Figures 10.5a and b Selected material from the *Sensory Integration and Praxis Tests-Figure-Ground Perception Test* © 1972 by Western Psychological Services. Reprinted by Human Kinetics Publishing Inc. by permission of WPS, 625 Alaska Avenue, Torrence, California, 90503, U.S.A., rights@wpspublishi.com. Not to be reprinted in whole or in part for any additional purposes without the expressed written permission of the publisher. All rights reserved.

Figure 10.10 Reprinted from T.G.R. Bower, 1977, *A primer of infant development* (San Francisco: W.H. Freeman). Copyright 1977.

Figure 10.11 Based on B.A. Morrongiello 1988, The development of auditory pattern perception skills. In *Advances in infancy research*, Vol. 6, edited by C. Rovee-Collier and L.P. Lipsitt (Norwood, NH: Ablex).

Figure 10.12 © Gg/age footstock.

Figure 11.1 From R. Held and A. Hein, 1963, "Movement-produced stimulation in the development of visually guided behavior," *Journal of Comparative and Physiological Psychology* 56: 872-876, fig. 1. Copyright © 1963 by the American Psychological Association. Reprinted with permission.

Figure 12.1 Jacob De Golish/Icon SMI.

Figure 12.2 Based on Kenyon and McPherson 1973.

Figure 12.3 © Rainer Martens.

Coaching Self-Report Form Reprinted, by permission from J. Williams, 2001, *Applied sport psychology: Personal growth to peak performance*, 4th ed. (New York: McGraw-Hill Companies). © McGraw-Hill Companies, Inc.

Chapter 13 opener © Rainer Martens.

Figure 13.1 Based on Horn 1987.

Figure 13.2 © Rainer Martens.

Figure 13.5 Reprinted from J.L. Duda and M.K. Tappe, 1989, Personal investment in exercise among adults: The examination of age and gender-related differences in motivational orientation. In *Aging and motor behavior*, edited by A.C. Ostrow (Dubuque, IA: Benchmark Press), 246, 248. By permission of J.L. Duda.

Figure 14.2 Data from French and Thomas 1987.

Figure 14.4 Data are from Colcombe and Kramer 2003.

Figures 15.1a and b Reprinted, by permission, from R.M. Malina, C. Bouchard, and O. Bar-Or, 2004, *Growth, maturation, and physical activity*, 2nd ed. (Champaign, IL: Human Kinetics), 259.

Figures 15.2a and b Reprinted, by permission, from O. Bar-Or, 1983, *Pediatric sports medicine for the practitioner* (New York: Springer), 4, 5.

Figures 15.3a and b Data from Shephard 1982.

Figures 15.5a and b Reprinted, by permission, from B.A. Stamford, 1986, Exercise and the elderly. In *Exercise and sport sciences reviews*, Vol. 16, edited by K.B. Pandolf (New York: Macmillan), 344. © The McGraw-Hill Companies.

Figure 15.6 Reprinted, by permission, from L.D. Zwiren, 1989, "Anaerobic and aerobic capacities of children," *Pediatric Exercise Science* 1: 40.

Figure 15.7 Reprinted, by permission, from W.W. Spirduso, K. Francis, and P. MacRae, 2005, *Physical dimensions of aging*, 2nd ed. (Champaign, IL: Human Kinetics), 108.

Figure 16.1 Based on Shepard 1982.

Figure 16.2 Based on Shepard 1982.

Table 16.1 Reprinted, by permission, from W.W. Spirduso, 1995, *Physical dimensions of aging* (Champaign, IL: Human Kinetics), 127.

Figure 16.3 Reprinted from A. Aniansson, M. Hedberg, G.B. Henning, and G. Grimby, 1986, "Muscle morphology, enzymatic activity, and muscle strength in elderly men: A follow-up study," Muscle & Nerve 9: 588. Copyright © 1986 by John Wiley & Sons. Reprinted by permission of John Wiley & Sons, Inc.

Figure 16.4 Reprinted, by permission, from W.W. Spirduso, K. Francis, and P. MacRae, 2005, *Physical dimensions of aging*, 2nd ed. (Champaign, IL: Human Kinetics), 112.

Figure 16.6 Reprinted, by permission, from R.M. Malina, C. Bouchard, and O. Bar-Or, 2004, *Growth, maturation, and physical activity*, 2nd ed. (Champaign, IL: Human Kinetics), 495.

Figure 16.7 Reprinted, by permission, from R.M. Malina, C. Bouchard, and O. Bar-Or, 2004, *Growth, maturation, and physical activity*, 2nd ed. (Champaign, IL: Human Kinetics), 498.

Figure 16.8 "The specificity of flexibility in girls, F.L. Hupprich and P.D. Sigerseth, *Research Quarterly for Exercise and Sport*, 21: 25-33, reprinted by permission of the American Alliance for Health, Physical Education, Recreation and Dance (www.AAHPERD.org).

Figure 16.9 Reprinted, by permission, from W.K. Hoeger et al., 1990, "Comparing the sit and reach with the modified sit and reach in measuring flexibility in adolescents," *Pediatric Exercise Science* 2: 156-162.

Figure 16.10 Reprinted, by permission, from J. Simons et al., 1990, *Growth and fitness of flemish girls* (Champaign, IL: Human Kinetics), 118.

Chapter 17 opener © Rainer Martens.

Figures 1.17a and b From J. Parizkova, 1977, *Body fat and physical fitness* (The Hague, The Netherlands: Martinus Nijhoff B.V.). By permission of J. Parizkova.

Figure 17.2 From J. Parizkova, 1977, *Body fat and physical fitness* (The Hague, The Netherlands: Martinus Nijhoff B.V.). By permission of J. Parizkova.

Figure 17.4 Drawn from data contained in the National Health and Nutrition Examination Survey III, as modified in Kotz, Billington, and Levine 1999; from Flegal et al. 1998.

Chapter 18 opener Joe Toth/BPI/Icon SMI.

Figure 18.1 Jack Terry/Action Plus/Icon SMI.

Figure 18.7 Reprinted, by permission, from J. Herkowitz, 1978, Developmental task analysis: The design of movement experiences and evaluation of motor development status. In *Motor development*, edited by M.V. Ridenour (Princeton, NJ: Princeton Book), 141.

Figure 18.8 Reprinted, by permission, from J. Herkowitz, 1978, Developmental task analysis: The design of movement experiences and evaluation of motor development status. In *Motor development*, edited by M.V. Ridenour (Princeton, NJ: Princeton Book), 149.

Figures A.3a and b Adapted from www.cdc.gov/nchs/about/major/nhanes/growthcharts/clinical_charts.htm. Developed by the National Center for Health Statistics in collaboration with the National Center for Chronic Disease Prevention and Health Promotion, 2000.

Figures A.4a and b Reprinted from www.cdc.gov/nchs/about/major/nhanes/growthcharts/clinical_charts.htm. Developed by the National Center for Health Statistics in collaboration with the National Center for Chronic Disease Prevention and Health Promotion, 2000.

Introduction to Motor Development

When you begin to learn any new area of study, you must start out by deciphering the lingo used by the area's professionals. In motor development, the professionals include physical educators, athletic trainers, coaches, physical and occupational therapists, and professors. This is quite a variety! It may not surprise you, then, to hear that the first part of this text is dedicated to providing a sound base of information—terms, theories, concepts, and important historical notes—on which you can build your knowledge of motor development. You must learn basic terms so that you can read about motor development and converse with others about this field of study. You must learn the scope of the field and how it goes about researching the developmental aspects of motor behavior. It benefits you to learn how information is pictured or presented in the field of study. All of these topics are addressed in chapter 1.

You also need to know the various perspectives that professionals in the field of motor development have adopted to view motor behavior and interpret studies of that behavior. Often, what is known in a discipline of study is a function of the perspectives adopted by those studying in the field. Chapter 2 introduces you to these perspectives.

In chapter 3, you will learn about the principles of motion and stability that influence all of your movements at all times. Understanding these principles will help you see patterns in the way motor skills change over time (addressed in the following chapters). The goal of chapter 3 is to help you understand in a general way how these principles work.

Most important, part I introduces you to a model that will be used to guide your study of motor development. The model, pictured on page 6, is Newell's model of constraints (Newell, 1986). Chapter 1 describes the model's parts and what it depicts. This model gives you a way of organizing new pieces of information. Right now, the most important notion you can gain from this model is that motor development does not focus only on the individual; it also examines the importance of the environment in which an individual moves and the task the individual is trying to accomplish. Moreover, the model gives you a way to analyze and think about issues and problems in motor development. Thus, it will be useful not only in the short term of your study of motor development but also in the long term as you move into a professional position or interact with family and friends regarding their motor skills.

Suggested Reading

Adolph, K., & Robinson, S. (2008). In defense of change processes. *Child Development, 79,* 1648–1653.

Clark, J.E. (2005). From the beginning: A developmental perspective on movement and mobility. *Quest, 57,* 37–45.

Gagen, L., & Getchell, N. (2004). Combining theory and practice in the gymnasium: "Constraints" within an ecological perspective. *Journal of Physical Education, Recreation and Dance, 75,* 25–30.

Gagen, L., & Getchell, N. (2008). Applying Newton's apple to elementary physical education: An interdisciplinary approach. *Journal of Physical Education, Recreation and Dance, 79,* 43–51.

Getchell, N., & Gagen, L. (2006). Interpreting disabilities from a 'constraints' theoretical perspective: Encouraging movement for all children. *Palaestra, 22,* 20–53.

Jensen, J. (2005). The puzzles of motor development: How the study of developmental biomechanics contributes to the puzzle solutions. *Infant and Child Development, 14*(5), 501–511.

Thelen, E. (2005). Dynamic systems theory and the complexity of change. *Psychoanalytic Dialogues, 15*(2), 255–283.

Fundamental Concepts

 CHAPTER OBJECTIVES

This chapter

- defines motor development,
- distinguishes developmental issues from other concerns,
- describes some of the basic tools used by researchers in motor development,
- explains why development occurs over a life span, and
- introduces a model that guides our discussion of motor development.

The *Up* Series

In 1964, director Paul Almond filmed a group of 14 British children, all 7 years old, from diverse socioeconomic backgrounds and created a documentary about their lives titled *7 Up!* In 1971, Michael Apted followed up with *7 Plus Seven*, and he has brought out a new installment of the series every 7 years since, following these same individuals through childhood and adolescence, into adulthood, and now into middle age. Apted hoped to explore the influence of the British class system over time and see if the Jesuit motto "Give me a child until he is seven and I will give you the man" held true. The latest installment, *56 Up*, premiered on British television on May 14, 2012, and was released in the United States in January 2013. In total, the *Up* series will show the lives of the participants over the course of 49 years, from childhood into middle adulthood, thus providing a window into the group and individual development.

If we developed a series of documentaries addressing motor development, who might watch? Many professionals might be interested. Educators, especially physical and early childhood educators, might be interested in which practices work best and whether they are developmentally appropriate. Therapists would want to know the factors that affect movement abilities. Engineers and designers might be interested in changes throughout adulthood in order to make appropriately sized and arranged living spaces, control panels, work equipment, sport gear, and vehicles. Health care providers might want to determine how movement and exercise early in life affect health status later on. Clearly, then, motor development interests many people for many reasons. Indeed, we can learn a great deal by examining change in movement patterns—and why it occurs—from birth until old age. Movement is an integral part of our lives, and its change is inevitable.

Defining Motor Development

Our imaginary documentary series might give you a rough idea of what motor development is. Let's now be more exact and give the field some boundaries, much as a producer would do in order to decide which segments are appropriate for the motor development film and which are not.

Development is defined by several characteristics. First, it is a continuous process of change in functional capacity. Think of functional capacity as the capability to exist—to live, move, and work—in the real world. This is a cumulative process. Living organisms are always developing, but the amount of change may be more noticeable, or less noticeable, at various points in the life span.

Second, development is related to (but not dependent on) age. As age advances, development proceeds. However, development can be faster or slower at different times, and rates of development can differ among individuals of the same age. Individuals do not necessarily advance in age and advance in development at the same rate. Further, development does not *stop* at a particular age but rather continues throughout life.

Third, development involves sequential change. One step leads to the next step in an orderly and irreversible fashion. This change results from interactions both within the individual and between the individual and the environment. All individuals of a species undergo predictable patterns of development, but the result of development is always a group of unique individuals.

Individuals function in a variety of arenas, including the physical, social, cognitive, and psychological. Hence, we use terms such as **cognitive development** or **social development** to address the process of change in particular arenas. Social scientists often specialize in the study of one aspect of development.

We use the term **motor development** to refer to the development of movement abilities. Those who study motor development explore developmental changes in movements as well as the factors underlying those changes. Such study addresses both the process of change and the resultant movement outcome. Not all change in movement constitutes development. For example, if a tennis teacher elicits a change in a student's forehand stroke by changing the student's grip on the racket, we do not view the change as motor development. Rather, we use the term **motor learning**, which refers to movement changes that are relatively permanent but related to *experience* or practice rather than age. We use the term **motor behavior** when we prefer not to distinguish between motor learning and motor development or when we want to include both.

Motor control refers to the nervous system's control of the muscles that permits skilled and coordinated movements. In recent years, researchers in motor development and in motor control have found much in common. Understanding how the nervous system and movement abilities change with age expands our knowledge of motor control, and we now see much overlap in motor development and control research.

 Scan news websites such as MSNBC.com or CNN.com for stories related to motor development. What key words did you select to search for stories on this topic besides *motor* and *development* in order to focus in on this topic?

Undoubtedly, you have heard the term *development* paired with the term *growth*, as in "growth and development." **Physical growth** is a quantitative increase in size or magnitude. Living organisms experience a period of growth in physical size. For humans, this growth period starts with conception and ends in late adolescence or the early 20s. Changes in the size of tissues after the physical growth period (e.g., an increase in muscle mass with resistance training) are described with other terms. Thus, the phrase *growth and development* includes change in both size and functional capacity.

The term *maturation* is also paired with the term *growth*, but it is not the same as development. **Maturation** connotes progress toward physical maturity, the state of optimal functional integration of an individual's body systems and the ability to reproduce. Development continues long after physical maturity is reached.

Physiological change does not stop at the end of the physical growth period. Rather, it can occur throughout life. Physiological change tends to be slower after the growth period but nevertheless remains prominent. The term **aging** can be used in a broad sense to refer to the process of growing older regardless of chronological age; it can also refer specifically to changes that lead to a loss of adaptability or function and eventually to death (Spirduso, Francis, & MacRae, 2005).

Motor development refers to the continuous, age-related process of change in movement as well as the interacting constraints (or factors) in the individual, environment, and task that drive these changes.

Motor learning refers to the relatively permanent gains in motor skill capability associated with practice or experience (Schmidt & Lee, 2005).

Motor control is the study of the neural, physical, and behavioral aspects of movement (Schmidt & Lee, 2005).

Physical growth is an increase in size or body mass resulting from an increase in complete, already formed body parts (Timiras, 1972).

Physiological **maturation** is a qualitative advance in biological makeup and may refer to cell, organ, or system advancement in biochemical composition rather than to size alone (Teeple, 1978).

Aging is the process, occurring with the passage of time, that leads to loss of adaptability or full function and eventually to death (Spirduso, Francis, & MacRae, 2005).

The physiological processes of growth and aging fall on a continuum of life span development. For many years, researchers examined motor development almost exclusively from early childhood through puberty. However, the population across the globe has aged. In many countries—including the United States, China, Russia, Australia, Canada, and the majority of the European Union's nations—by 2030 at least 13% of the population will be aged 65 years or older (Kinsella & Velkoff, 2001). This change brings more urgency to the need for better understanding of motor development in the later years. Although some motor development students might be particularly interested in one portion of the continuum, motor development as a field still concerns change in movement across the life span. Understanding what drives change in one part of the life span often helps us understand change in another part. This process of examining change is part of adopting a developmental perspective.

Constraints: A Model for Studying Motor Development

It is useful to have a model or plan for studying the change in movement that occurs over the life span. A model helps us include all the relevant factors in our observation of motor behavior. This is particularly true as we think about the complexity of motor skills and how our skills change over the life span. For this textbook, we adopted a model associated with a contemporary theoretical approach known as the ecological perspective (see chapter 2). We find that this model helps us make sense of developmental changes by providing a framework for observing change. We believe this model—Newell's constraints model—will help you better understand motor development across the life span.

Newell's Model

Karl Newell (1986) suggested that movements arise from the interactions of the organism, the environment in which the movement occurs, and the task to be undertaken. If any of these three factors change, the resultant movement changes. We can picture the three factors as points on a triangle with a circle of arrows representing their interaction (figure 1.1). Because we are concerned only with human movement here, we use the term *individual* instead of *organism*. In short, to understand movement, we must consider the relationships between the characteristics of the individual mover, his surroundings, and his purpose or reasons for moving. From the interaction of all these characteristics, specific movements emerge. This model reminds us that we must consider all three corners of the triangle in order to understand motor development.

Picture the different ways in which individuals can walk—for example, a toddler taking her first steps, a child walking in deep sand, an adult moving across an icy patch, or an older adult trying to catch a bus. In each example, the individual must modify his or her walking pattern in some way. These examples illustrate that changing one of the factors often results in a change in the interaction with one or both of the other factors, and a different way of walking arises from the interaction. For example, whether you are barefoot or wearing rubber-soled shoes might not make a difference when you're walking across a dry tile floor, but your walk might change notably if the floor were wet and slippery. The *interaction* of individual, task, and environment changes the movement, and, over time, patterns of interactions lead to changes in motor development.

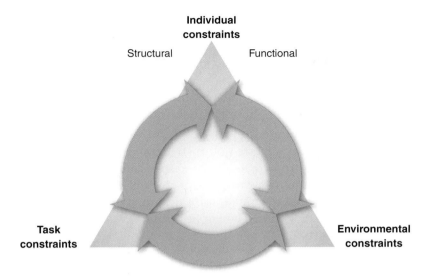

Structural   **Individual constraints**   Functional

Task constraints   **Environmental constraints**

FIGURE 1.1   Newell's model of constraints.

Why is Newell's model so helpful in studying motor development? It reflects the dynamic, constantly changing interactions in motor development. It allows us to look at the individual and the many body systems that constantly undergo age-related changes. At the same time, the model emphasizes the influence of where the individual moves (environment) and what the individual does (task) on individual movements. Changes in the individual lead to changes in his or her interaction with the environment and task and subsequently change the way the individual moves. For example, a young child may enjoy tumbling on mats in his preschool. His parents may put him in a gymnastics class (change in environment); at that class, the instructors may focus on equipment rather than tumbling stunts (change in task). Over time and through his experience focusing on specific equipment in the gymnastics class, the boy may become proficient at the pommel horse. Another example is an older adult who, because of hip arthritis, chooses to walk only when absolutely necessary and stops attending her walking group. Changes in her social environment lead to disengagement in exercise, which in turn leads to loss of strength, flexibility, and mobility and, ultimately, to more hip pain. In both of these examples, the individual, environment, and task influence—and are influenced by—each other.

Newell calls the three factors we placed on the points of our triangle **constraints**. A constraint is somewhat like a restraint: It *limits* or *discourages* (in this case, movement) but at the same time it *permits* or *encourages* (in this case, other movements). It's important not to consider constraints as negative or bad. Constraints simply provide channels from which movements most easily emerge. A riverbed acts as a constraint: It restrains the river water from flowing anywhere and everywhere but it also channels the water to follow a specific path. Movement constraints are characteristics that shape movement. They restrain and channel movement to a particular time and place in space; that is, they give movement a particular form.

Individual constraints, the top point on our triangle, are a person's unique physical and mental characteristics. For example, height, limb length, strength, and motivation can all influence the way an individual moves. Consider the swimmer with a disability in figure 1.2. The disability constrains, but does not prevent, this

A **constraint** is a characteristic of the individual, environment, or task that encourages some movements while discouraging others.

Individual constraints are a person's or organism's unique physical and mental characteristics.

individual's ability to swim; it simply modifies the way in which the swimmer performs her strokes. Individual constraints are either structural or functional.

- **Structural constraints** relate to the individual's body structure. They change with growth and aging; however, they tend to change slowly over time. Examples include height, weight, muscle mass, and leg length. As we discuss these changes throughout the text, you will see how structural factors constrain movement.

- **Functional constraints** relate not to structure but to behavioral function. Examples include motivation, fear, experiences, and attentional focus. Such constraints can change over a much shorter period of time. For instance, you might be motivated to run several miles in cool weather but not in hot, humid weather. This functional constraint shapes your movement to running, walking, or even sitting.

For many professionals, it is important to know whether the student's or client's movement is being shaped by structural or functional constraints. Such information can help one understand how much a movement could change in a short time and whether a change in an environmental or task constraint would be in order to modify the resultant movements. For example, knowing that young volleyball players cannot block a ball at the net because they are not yet at their

FIGURE 1.2   This swimmer's truncated limb is a structural constraint that gives rise to a swimming movement that is different from that of someone without a truncated limb.

adult height would lead a youth sports organizer to change the task by using a lower net height.

Environmental constraints exist outside the body, as a property of the world around us. They are global rather than task specific and can be physical or sociocultural. Physical environmental constraints are characteristics of the environment, such as temperature, amount of light, humidity, gravity, and the surfaces of floors and walls. The example of a runner not feeling motivated to run in humidity represents the functional constraint of motivation interacting with two environmental constraints—temperature and humidity—to constrain movement.

One's sociocultural environment can also be a strong force in encouraging or discouraging behaviors, including movement behaviors. One example is how change in the sociocultural environment in Western society has changed the involvement of girls and women in sport over the past three decades. In the 1950s, society did not expect girls to participate in sport. As a result, girls were channeled away from sport.

Task constraints are also external to the body. They include the goals of a movement or activity. These constraints differ from individual motivation or goals in that they are specific to the task. For example, in basketball the goal is to get the ball in the hoop—this is true for any individual playing the game. Second, task constraints include the rules that surround a movement or activity. If we think about basketball, players could get down the court much more quickly if they could simply run with the ball rather than dribble it. However, the rules dictate that players *must* dribble while running with the ball, meaning that the resultant movement is constrained to include bouncing the ball. Finally, the equipment we use is a task constraint. For example, using a strung racket rather than a wood paddle changes the game played on an enclosed (racquetball) court. Recall also the case of the youth sports organizer, who by lowering net height used the interaction of a structural individual constraint (body height) and a task constraint to allow a certain movement (blocking) to emerge in the game played by young volleyball players. You can probably imagine many of the task constraints in the depicted situation. The basketball player must pass the ball to a teammate while protecting the ball from a defender.

Throughout this discussion of motor development we demonstrate how changing individual, environmental, and task constraints shape the movement that arises from their interaction. Newell's model guides us in identifying the developmental factors affecting movements, helps us create developmentally appropriate tasks and environments, and helps us understand individual movers as different from group norms or averages.

Changing Views on the Role of Constraints

It is important to recognize that in the history of motor development research certain researchers and practitioners focused primarily on individual factors to the exclusion of others. For example, in the 1940s it was assumed that an individual constraint—specifically, the structural constraint of the nervous system alone—shaped movement in infants and children (see chapter 2 for a discussion of this concept). Later, in the 1960s, developmentalists commonly believed that environmental and task constraints, more than individual constraints, shaped movement. Only recently have motor developmentalists begun focusing on all three types of constraints simultaneously as well as carefully examining how constraints interact with and influence each other over time.

Environmental constraints are constraints related to the world around us.

Task constraints include the goals and rule structure of a particular movement or activity.

When one or two types of constraints are deemphasized, so is the rich effect of the three constraints interacting to shape movement. Thus, such an approach limits the resulting view of the emerging movement. In our survey of motor development we identify the effects of these various viewpoints on the importance of the three constraints. Sometimes what we know about an aspect of motor development is influenced by the perspective of the researcher who studied that behavior. It is much like seeing the color of a flower change as we try on sunglasses with lenses of different colors. We might "color" our conclusions about motor development as we emphasize one type of constraint and deemphasize other types.

 Imagine you are a physical educator or a coach. Knowing how height and body size change with growth, how would you adapt the game of basketball (especially the task, through the equipment used) so that movements (shooting, dribbling, passing) remain nearly the same during the growth years?

Newell's model is more global than most models previously used in the study of motor development. We can better account for the complexity of age-related change in movement with this model through the interactions of individual, environment, and task. Keep the model in mind throughout our survey of motor development.

Constraints and Atypical Development

To understand the basics of constraints, we explain concepts using typical motor development. That is, we use examples that describe what we might expect in people with average individual constraints (strength, height, motivation), who move in typical environments (gymnasiums, playgrounds, grocery stores), and who perform normal tasks (sport, activities of daily living). Essentially, this is motor development "on average." People can develop in different ways and still be considered to be in an average range. However, individuals can deviate from the average developmental course in a variety of ways. In some instances, development is advanced (motor skills appear sooner than expected) or delayed (motor skills appear later than expected). In others, development is actually different (the person moves in unique ways). When we discuss constraints and atypical development, we focus on delayed and different development, particularly in individuals with disabilities. Interacting constraints lead to movement changes over individuals' lives. Therefore, we know that differences in structural and functional individual constraints can lead to atypical developmental trajectories. For example, a child with cerebral palsy may be delayed in the acquisition of fundamental motor skills due to muscle spasticity, or an adult with multiple sclerosis will see motor proficiency diminish as a function of deteriorating myelin sheaths in the brain and spinal cord. In certain conditions, people may exhibit motor coordination delays that can be overcome with enhanced practice or experience. In the language of constraints, enhanced practice represents a change in task constraints. Movement practitioners must keep in mind how movement can change as a result of changing constraints and thereby adjust environment and task constraints to accommodate differences in individual constraints. Throughout the text we provide examples of research related to atypical development.

How Do We Know It Is Change?

We've established that age-related change is fundamental in the study of motor development and the developmental perspective. Developmentalists are focused on change. How do we know, though, that a change is age related and not a fluctuation of behavior (a good or bad day on the court, for example) or a product of our measuring instrument (a radar gun versus video motion analysis)? One way to discern developmental change is to carefully observe individuals' movements and then describe differences between people of different age groups or instances of observation.

 WEB STUDY GUIDE   Gain experience in observing movement by doing Lab Activity 1.1, Observation as a Tool of Inquiry, in the web study guide. Go to www.HumanKinetics.com/LifeSpanMotorDevelopment.

In addition, behavioral scientists use statistical techniques that can identify significant change. We sometimes discuss these techniques in the context of a research study. For now, let's focus on the straightforward technique of picturing change by graphing an aspect of development over time. We can then see whether a trend is emerging.

Picturing Change

When we picture age-related measurements by graphing, we traditionally put time or age on the horizontal axis. Time can be measured in days, weeks, months, years, or decades, depending on our frame of reference. A measurement of interest in infancy might be plotted in days or weeks, whereas a measurement of interest over the life span might be plotted in years or decades.

The measurement is plotted on the vertical axis. We usually arrange the measurements so that "more," "faster," or "more advanced" is higher on the scale. Figure 1.3 shows a typical graph of the measurement of growth in childhood. It is common to take a measurement periodically and plot its value at selected chronological ages. We assume that change has occurred consistently in the time between our measurements, so we often connect our data points to make a line. When we graph change using a developmental perspective, we should not make the assumption that more is always better.

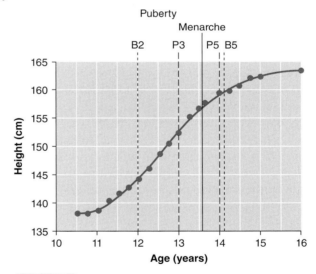

FIGURE 1.3   A typical graphical representation of growth in childhood.

Reprinted by permission from Maclaren 1967.

Individuals move in a variety of ways that are qualitatively different. Some ways of moving may result in longer throws or faster runs, but that does not imply that children who do not move this way are in error or are wrong. It simply means that these children move at a different or lower developmental level.

 WEB STUDY GUIDE   Practice graphing to help picture change in Lab Activity 1.2, Graphing Developmental Data, in the web study guide. Go to www. HumanKinetics.com/LifeSpanMotorDevelopment.

Researching Developmental Change

A **longitudinal research study** is one in which the same individual or group is observed performing the same tasks or behaviors on numerous occasions over a long time.

In the study of development, we ideally watch an individual or group change with age for the entire length of the period we are interested in. This is termed a **longitudinal research study**. The difficulty here comes when our frame of reference is years or decades. For example, a teacher may be interested in the changes in locomotor skills across childhood. We can see that an individual researcher might be able to do only a few such studies in his or her lifetime. This approach would not inform us about motor development very quickly!

A **cross-sectional research study** is one in which developmental change is inferred by observing individuals or groups of varying ages at one point in time.

Researchers have several ways of learning more in a shorter time. One of these techniques is termed a **cross-sectional research study**. In a cross-sectional study, researchers select individuals or groups at chosen points in the age span of interest. For example, researchers interested in change during adolescence might measure a group of 13-year-olds, a group of 15-year-olds, a group of 17-year-olds, and so on. When the measurements of each group are plotted, we assume that any observed change reflects the same change we would observe in a single group over the whole time period. The advantage of this method is that researchers can study development in a short time. The disadvantage is that we never really observe change; we merely infer it from age group differences. If something else were responsible for the age group differences, we could be fooled into thinking the differences were caused by developmental change.

Consider the example of tricycles. At one time, all tricycles were metal and shaped so that the seat was relatively high off the ground. Children under 3 years of age had difficulty just getting on the tricycle. Then someone invented the Big Wheel tricycle, with the large front wheel and the seat only inches off the ground. Toddlers can easily sit on this vehicle.

Can You Tell It's Developmental? A Litmus Test

Armed with definitions of motor development and motor learning, you still might find it difficult to distinguish whether a particular behavior is a matter of learning or development. Mary Ann Roberton (1988, p. 130) suggests that the answers to three questions help us distinguish developmental issues and topics.

1. Are we interested in what behavior is like now and why the behavior is the way it is?
2. Are we interested in what behavior was like before our present observation, and why?
3. Are we interested in how the present behavior is going to change in the future, and why?

Students of both motor learning and motor development answer yes to the first question, but only developmentalists answer yes to the second and third questions. Motor learning specialists are concerned with making changes that bring about a relatively permanent change in behavior within a short time. Motor developmentalists focus on a longer time during which a sequence of changes occurs. Developmentalists might introduce a change in task or environmental constraints to make either or both age appropriate while realizing that the task or environment will have to change again and again as individuals age and change.

Let's pretend that a researcher did a cross-sectional study on coordination of the cycling motion of the legs in toddlers at the ages of 1.5, 2.0, 2.5, and 3.0 years. The study was done just 1 year after the Big Wheel tricycle came on the market (note: as a piece of equipment, the Big Wheel is a task constraint). The researcher observed that toddlers 2.5 and 3.0 years of age could coordinate this movement and concluded that approximately 2.5 years was the age at which toddlers could coordinate the cycling movement of the legs. But what if the researcher had done the study a year earlier, before any of the children would have been on a Big Wheel? The researcher might have observed that *none* of the children could coordinate the cycling movement because none would have been able to ride the high-seat tricycle. The researcher would then have concluded that this coordination developed after the age of 3.0 years.

The invention of the Big Wheel gave a **cohort**, or mini-generation, of toddlers earlier practice in coordinating the cycling movement. Older cohorts could not practice the movement until they were big enough to get up on the higher tricycle. Thus, one cohort had an experience that another did not. Such a cohort difference can fool researchers in a cross-sectional study, leading them to associate performance differences between age groups with age alone and not factors such as exposure to new inventions. Researchers must be particularly aware of cohort differences when examining aging populations due to rapidly changing technologies. For example, many older adults may not own or frequently use computers. Let's say a researcher wants to examine differences in driving techniques among drivers of different age groups and uses a computer simulation in which the car is controlled by a joystick. Older adults may show differences in performance because they are unfamiliar with computer joysticks rather than because of true differences in driving technique. (In fact, children who are not yet eligible to drive may perform better because of their experiences with video games.) Researchers must take care to control for cohort differences.

Researchers have, however, devised a clever way to identify cohort influences while at the same time conducting developmental research in less time than required by a longitudinal study. They do it by combining longitudinal and cross-sectional studies. In effect, they conduct several small longitudinal studies with subjects of different ages of the period of interest. For example, in the first year they would measure three groups of children, one at 4 years of age, one at 6 years of age, and one at 8 years of age. Notice that if the researchers stopped here they would have a cross-sectional study. Instead, a year later they measure all the children again. This time the children are 5, 7, and 9 years of age. They do the same thing another year later, when the children are 6, 8, and 10. In the end they have done three small longitudinal studies: one cohort that was the original 4-year-olds at 4, 5, and 6; one cohort that was the original 6-year-olds at 6, 7, and 8; and one cohort that was the original 8-year-olds at 8, 9, and 10.

Thus, information is made available about ages 4 through 10, but only 2 years were needed to obtain it. What about the possibility of cohort differences? Note that the mini-longitudinal studies cover overlapping ages. Two groups were tested at age 6 and two groups were tested at ages 7 and 8. If performance of the different cohorts is the same at a given age, then it is likely that cohort differences are not present. If the cohorts perform differently at the same age, cohort influences might well be present. This type of design is called a **mixed-longitudinal,** or **sequential, research study**.

New students of motor development can tell whether a research study is developmental by considering the design of the study. The study is developmental if the

A **cohort** is a group whose members share a common characteristic, such as age or experience.

In a **mixed-longitudinal**, or **sequential**, **research study**, several age groups are observed at one time or over a shorter time span, permitting observation of an age span that is longer than the observation period.

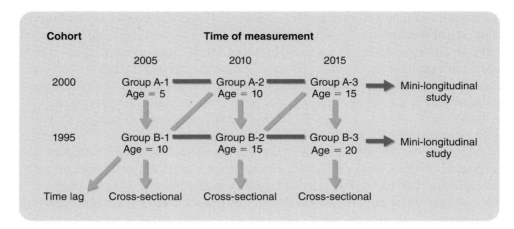

FIGURE 1.4 A model of a sequential research design. Note that each row is a short longitudinal study and that each column is a small cross-sectional study. The time-lag component of sequential research design, shown by the diagonal lines, allows comparison of groups from different cohorts but at the same chronological age, thus identifying any cohort differences. Ages 5 to 20 can be studied in 10 years—1990 to 2000.

design is longitudinal, cross-sectional, or sequential (figure 1.4). Research studies that focus on one age group at one point in time are not developmental.

A Developmental Paradox: Universality Versus Variability

Picture yourself in a gymnasium filled with preschool students. Many children move similarly: They begin to display rudimentary catching and throwing; they walk and run with proficiency but have difficulty skipping. On average, the children perform many of the same motor skills. Yet if you look at an individual child, he or she may move in more or less advanced ways than a child standing a foot away. This difference highlights the paradox of universality of development as opposed to individual differences (Thelen & Ulrich, 1991). Individuals in a species show great similarity in their development in that they go through many of the same (stereotypical) changes. You have heard reference to "stages of development." Stages, of course, describe the emergence of universal behaviors. Those who anticipate working with individuals in a particular age range are often interested in the behaviors typical of those in that range.

However, individual differences in development do exist. Any individual we observe is more likely to be above or below average, or to achieve a milestone earlier or later than average, than he or she is to be exactly average. In addition, children can arrive at the same point in development by very different pathways (Siegler & Jenkins, 1989). All individuals, even identical twins, have different experiences, and people who work with any group of individuals supposedly at the same stage of development are usually amazed by the variability in the group.

Thus, developmentalists, educators, parents, and health professionals must consider an individual's behavior in the context of both universal behaviors and individual differences. It is also important to recognize when others are using a perspective that focuses on the universality of behavior and when they are focusing on variability in behavior. Systematic and controlled observation—that is, *research*—helps us distinguish between behaviors that tend to be universal and behaviors that reflect human variability. Research also helps us identify the role of constraints such as the environment and individual experiences in creating variability of behavior.

As much as possible, the ideas presented in this text are based on research studies; the information comes from an objective source. Keep in mind that this is not the same as saying that any one or two research studies provide us with all the answers we need. Individual research studies do not always rule out all the other possible explanations for the results—to do that, additional research might be required.

Deriving the principles and theories from research to guide educational and health care practice is a *process*. Although practitioners are sometimes frustrated to see that researchers are only in the middle of the process, it is better to recognize that this is the case than to take all research results as the final word. Our goal here is not only to use available research information to make insightful conclusions and decisions about the motor development of individuals but also to learn how to obtain and analyze further research information as it becomes available.

 Think of generalizations we tend to make about people, such as "tall people are thin," and then think of at least one person you know who is an exception to this "rule." What is the consequence of expecting a student or patient to follow a generalization?

Summary and Synthesis

Now that we understand the developmental perspective, it is easy to see why a documentary series on motor development spanning several decades would be of interest to many viewers. At the present moment each of us is a product of "what we were like before," and each of us will change to become something different in the future. We are all developing, and our individual constraints constantly change! Add changing environmental and task constraints and you have a very interesting mix related to motor development.

Many professions involve relationships with people at critical points of the life span—points at which the change taking place influences life thereafter. This is especially true in regard to the physical being and physical skills. As a result, your knowledge of motor development and the constraints related to it will help you and those around you throughout life. If you choose a profession such as teacher, coach, or therapist, this knowledge will help you help others by providing developmentally appropriate activities.

Your study of motor development will be easier if you equip yourself with a few basic tools. Most important is a framework or model to which you can relate new information, and we use Newell's model of constraints throughout this text. Another important tool is knowledge of how research in motor development is designed, which helps you understand how researchers address developmental issues.

Yet another important tool, which we have yet to discuss, is knowledge of the various perspectives that developmentalists adopt as they approach their research. Because the same problem can be approached from many perspectives, it is valuable to know which approach is taken. The next chapter explores various approaches and discusses the theoretical roots of motor development.

Reinforcing What You Have Learned About Constraints

TAKE A SECOND LOOK

At the start of this chapter you learned about the *Up* series, which has been very successful in Great Britain and the United States. Viewers are interested in how the participants change over time as well as how they stay the same and in what factors (or constraints, as we now call them) influence their life trajectories. In other words, they want to see how the lives of these children (and later adults) develop. Just like viewers of these films, readers of this text will examine motor development interactively, considering the influences that individual, environmental, and task constraints have on an individual's movement skills over his or her entire life. It is important that the documentaries do not end (nor do they become less interesting) once childhood ends; rather, they continue because individuals continue to develop and change across the entire life span. For this reason, we adopt a life span perspective for motor development.

TEST YOUR KNOWLEDGE

1. How does the field of motor development differ from that of motor learning? What key perspective separates the two?

2. How do physical growth and physiological maturation differ?

3. Think of your favorite physical activity, exercise, or sport. Describe some of the individual (both structural and functional), environmental, and task constraints of this activity.

4. Why might a person planning a career in teaching children choose also to study older adults?

5. What are the differences between longitudinal research studies and cross-sectional research studies? What characteristics of each are used in sequential, or mixed-longitudinal, research studies?

6. What does it mean if a physical educator uses "developmentally appropriate" teaching practices? Provide some examples using constraints.

LEARNING EXERCISE 1.1

Searching the Internet for Information on Motor Development

The Internet can be a valuable resource for any practitioner. Many organizations and advertisers provide information that anyone with a computer can access. It is important, however, to keep in mind that there are few regulations on the Internet; anyone can make almost any claim (whether it is based on research, opinion, or something else). You, as an informed consumer, must examine websites carefully and determine the usefulness and accuracy of their information, just as you would with library research. In this learning activity you will determine the theoretical assumptions and underpinnings of various websites.

1. Enter the term *motor development* into the search engine of your choice (e.g., Google, Bing). How many hits are there using these two words? Do any of the websites surprise you? How so?

2. Find a website that sells motor development products. Pick a product. What is it, and what is its purpose? How is it developmental, according to the advertiser? Based on what you've learned, is it *really* developmental?

3. Repeat your Internet search, adding the term *infancy* to *motor development*. From the resulting list, examine at least three types of websites (e.g., academic,

sales, medical). Identify some unusual or particularly interesting sites. If you were a parent searching for information, what could you learn from these websites?

Theoretical Perspectives in Motor Development

Changing Interpretations of Constraints

 CHAPTER OBJECTIVES

This chapter

- describes the theories currently used to study motor development,
- illustrates how various theories explain changes in motor behavior, and
- describes the history of the field of motor development.

The Birth of Your First Nephew

Imagine that you visit your older sister in a neighboring state just after she has had her first child. You see the infant as a newborn, just 1 week old. He does not really respond to you unless you place a bottle in his mouth or your finger in his hand. His movements include seemingly random flapping of the arms and legs—unless he is hungry, in which case he flails his limbs and cries! When you leave you think, "He seems pretty uncoordinated and weak." After 9 months, you visit your sister and nephew again. What a change! He sits up on his own, reaches for toys, and has started to crawl. He can even stand when you hold him. He begins to coordinate his actions so that he can move purposefully. Now, let's say you visit again, another 9 months later. Your nephew is no longer an infant but a full-fledged toddler. He can now walk—pretty quickly when he wants to—and has no problem with reaching and grasping. He is beginning to respond to language, particularly with the word *no*. He seems so very different from the newborn you met a mere 18 months before!

In this scenario it would be natural to wonder, "What happened during the past year and a half that resulted in these changes?" In other words, how can you (or anyone else) explain the changes seen across development? Given that there appear to be similarities in the development of different people (universality, described in chapter 1), how do we organize and understand these changes so that we can explain them and predict future development? Certain facts exist. How can we make sense of them? We must look at the different theoretical perspectives on motor development. Theories provide a systematic way to look at and explain developmental change.

Theories of motor development have roots in other disciplines, such as experimental and developmental psychology, embryology, and biology. Contemporary research in motor development often uses what is called an ecological perspective to describe, explain, and predict change. To interpret developmental "facts," it is important to understand the different theoretical perspectives from which the supposed facts emerge. Knowing these theoretical perspectives will help us understand the explanations and form interpretations when several explanations conflict.

Maturational Perspective

KEY POINT
Maturationists believe that genetics and heredity are primarily responsible for motor development and that the environment has little effect.

In a nutshell, the maturational perspective explains developmental change as a function of maturational processes (in particular, through the central nervous system, or CNS) that control or dictate motor development. According to the assumptions of this theory, motor development is an internal or innate process driven by a biological or genetic time clock. The environment may speed or slow the process of change but it cannot change one's biologically determined course.

The maturational perspective became popular during the 1930s, led by Arnold Gesell (Gesell, 1928, 1954; Salkind, 1981). Gesell believed that the biological and evolutionary history of humans determined their orderly and invariable sequence of development (i.e., each stage of development corresponds with a stage of evolution). The rate at which people pass through that developmental sequence, however, can differ from one individual to another. Gesell explained maturation as a process controlled by internal (genetic) factors rather than external (environmental) factors. He believed that environmental factors would affect motor development only temporarily because hereditary factors were ultimately in control of development.

Using identical twins as subjects, Gesell and his associates introduced the co-twin control strategy to developmental research (figure 2.1). What better way to test the effects of environment and heredity than to look at twins? In this strategy, one twin receives a specific training (the experimental treatment) while the other receives no special training (the control treatment). Thus, the control develops naturally, as any child would without special training. In this manner, Gesell examined the effects of the environment on development.

After a certain period of time, the twins were measured and compared with previously determined developmental criteria to see whether the enhanced experience affected the experimental child in any way. Co-twin research provided significant contributions to the study of motor development. In particular, these studies allowed developmentalists to begin identifying the sequence of skill development and noting variations in the rate of skill onset. Gesell concluded from his research that children develop in an orderly fashion (i.e., developmental change came in a predictable, predetermined order over childhood).

Another prominent researcher at the time, Myrtle McGraw, used twins to examine the influence of enhanced experience on motor development (Bergenn, Dalton, & Lipsett, 1992; McGraw, 1935). In her classic study, *Growth: A Study of Johnny and Jimmy*, McGraw started observing the twins several months after their birth.

FIGURE 2.1   Using twins in studies allowed researchers such as Gesell and McGraw to "control" genetics while manipulating the environment.

Courtesy of the authors.

She provided one twin (Johnny), at around 12 months of age, with challenging environments and unique tasks such as climbing a ramp at a progressively higher incline and roller skating. The tasks often required both motor and problem-solving skills. Johnny did excel in certain motor skills but not in others, which did little to resolve the nature-versus-nurture debate prominent in psychology at the time. McGraw's results were equivocal, which may have been due (at least in part) to the fact that the twins were fraternal rather than identical.

In addition to describing the course of motor development, many maturationists were interested in the processes underlying development. McGraw (1943), for example, associated changes in motor behavior with development of the nervous system. She considered maturation of the CNS to be the trigger for the appearance of new skills. McGraw was also interested in learning (and therefore not strictly a maturationist), but those who followed in the study of development generally overlooked this aspect of her work (Clark & Whitall, 1989a).

Use of the maturational perspective as a research tool in motor development began to wane by the 1950s, but the theory's influence is still felt today. For example, the focus on maturation as the primary developmental process led researchers and laypersons alike to assume that basic motor skills will automatically materialize. Hence, even today, many researchers, teachers, and practitioners feel it is unnecessary to facilitate development of basic skills. In addition, the maturationists' emphasis on the nervous system as the *one* system triggering behavioral advancement evolved to almost single-minded emphasis on that system—to the point that no other system was believed to have much significance. The cardiovascular, skeletal, endocrine, and even muscular systems were not deemed of primary importance to motor development. By the mid-1940s, developmental psychologists began to change the focus of their research, and their interest in motor development waned. At that point, physical educators took up the study of motor development, influenced by the maturational perspective. From then until about 1970, people studied motor development by describing movement and identifying age group norms (Clark & Whitall, 1989a). During this period, motor developmentalists from the physical education discipline focused their attention on school-age children. Researchers still used the maturational perspective, and their task therefore was to identify the naturally occurring sequence of changes.

KEY POINT
People have interpreted the maturationist perspective to mean that motor skills will automatically emerge regardless of differing environments. This assumption has influenced many teaching, parenting, and research concepts during the 20th and 21st centuries.

Normative Descriptive Period

Anna Espenschade, Ruth Glassow, and G. Lawrence Rarick led a normative description movement during this era. In the 1950s, education became concerned with standardized tests and norms. Consistent with this concern, motor developmentalists began to describe children's average performance in terms of quantitative scores on motor performance tests. For example, they described the average running speed and jumping and throwing distances of children at specific ages. Although motor developmentalists were influenced by the maturational perspective, they focused on the *products* (scores, outcomes) of development rather than on the developmental *processes* that led to these quantitative scores.

Biomechanical Descriptive Period

Ruth Glassow also led another descriptive movement during this era. She made careful biomechanical descriptions of the movement patterns children used in performing fundamental skills such as jumping. Lolas Halverson (figure 2.2) and

FIGURE 2.2 Lolas Halverson paved the way in the 1960s and 1970s for contemporary research in motor development.
Courtesy of the authors.

others continued these biomechanical descriptions with longitudinal observations of children. As a result, the developmentalists were able to identify the course of sequential improvement that children followed in attaining biomechanically efficient movement patterns. The knowledge obtained from the normative and biomechanical descriptive periods was valuable in that it provided educators with information on age-related changes in motor development. Because description prevailed as the primary tool of these researchers during this time, motor development was labeled as descriptive. Interest in the processes underlying age-related changes, which had been so meticulously recorded before this period of history, seemed to disappear.

Information Processing Perspective

Another theoretical approach focuses on behavioral or environmental causes of development (e.g., Bandura's social learning [Bandura, 1986] and Skinner's behaviorism [Skinner, 1938], among others). The perspective most commonly associated from the 1960s to the 1980s with motor behavior and development is called **information processing**. According to this perspective, the brain acts like a computer, taking in information, processing it, and outputting movement. The process of motor learning and development, then, is described in terms of computer-like operations that occur as a result of some external or environmental input.

This theoretical perspective appeared around 1970 and became the dominant perspective among experimental psychologists, developmental psychologists, and motor learning scientists specializing in physical education during the 1970s and 1980s (Schmidt & Lee, 2005; Schmidt & Wrisberg, 2008). This perspective emphasized concepts such as the formation of stimulus–response bonds, feedback, and knowledge of results (for more detailed information, see Pick, 1989; Schmidt & Wrisberg, 2008). Although some motor developmentalists continued with the product-oriented work of the normative and biological descriptive era, many others adopted the information processing perspective. Researchers studied many aspects of performance, such as attention, memory, and effects of feedback, across age levels (French & Thomas, 1987; Thomas, 1984). Motor learning researchers and experimental psychologists tended to study the perceptual-cognitive mechanism in young adults first. Then, developmentalists studied children and older adults, comparing them with the young adults. In this way, they could identify the processes that control movement and change with development (Clark & Whitall, 1989a). Today, the information processing perspective is still a viable approach to the study of motor development.

Within the framework of information processing, some developmentalists continued to study perceptual-motor development in children. This work began in the 1960s with proposals that linked learning disabilities to children's delayed perceptual-motor development. Early research focused on this link; by the 1970s, researchers had turned their attention to the development of sensory and perceptual abilities, adopting information processing research strategies (Clark & Whitall, 1989a). Therefore, much of what we know about perceptual-motor development resulted from researchers working within an information processing and mechanistic theoretical framework.

Ecological Perspective

KEY POINT
The ecological perspective takes into account many constraints or systems that exist both in the body (e.g., cardiovascular, muscular) and outside the body (e.g., ecosystem related, social, cultural) when observing the development of motor skills across the life span.

A new perspective on development appeared during the 1980s and has become increasingly dominant as the theoretical perspective used by motor development researchers today. This approach is broadly termed the **ecological perspective** because it stresses the interrelationships between the individual, the environment, and the task. Does this sound familiar? It should—it's the perspective adopted by this text! We adopted this perspective because we feel it best describes, explains, and predicts motor development. According to the ecological perspective, you must consider the interaction of all constraints—for example, body type, motivation, temperature, and ball size—in order to understand the emergence of a motor skill—such as kicking (Roberton, 1989). Although one constraint or system may be more important or may cast a larger influence at any given time, all systems play a role in the resultant movement. This point makes the ecological perspective very appealing: At any given moment, how you move is related not only to your body or your environment but also to the complex interplay of many internal and external constraints.

The ecological perspective has two branches, one concerned with motor control and coordination (dynamical systems) and the other with perception (perception–action). The two branches are linked by several fundamental assumptions that differ notably from the maturational and information processing perspectives. In contrast to the maturational perspective, the ecological perspective considers motor development to be the development of multiple systems rather than only one (the CNS). In other words, many constraints change over time and influence motor development. Because these constraints or systems change throughout one's life, motor development is considered a life span process. This contrasts sharply with the view of maturationists, who felt that development ended with the end of puberty (or at adulthood). Another difference relates to the cause of change. In information processing theory, an executive function is thought to decide all action, based on calculations of perceptual information resulting in hundreds of commands to control the individual muscles. That is, the executive directs all movement and all change. The ecological perspective maintains that a central executive would be overwhelmed by the task of directing all movement and change. In addition, this is a very inefficient way to move. Rather, perception of the environment is direct, and muscles self-assemble into groups, reducing the number of decisions required of the higher brain centers (Konczak, 1990). Let's look more closely now at each branch of the ecological perspective.

Dynamical Systems Approach

One branch of the ecological systems perspective is called the **dynamical systems approach**. In the early 1980s, a group of scientists—working at Haskins Laboratory in New Haven, Connecticut, whose mission was and remains to research spoken and written language, and in the psychology department at the University of Connecticut—began to question the effectiveness of understanding motor control through the then-dominant information processing perspective. Peter Kugler, Scott Kelso, and Michael Turvey (1980, 1982), along with others from UConn and Haskins Laboratory, introduced a new approach, called dynamical systems, as an alternative to existing motor control and coordination theories. Following the writings of Soviet physiologist Nikolai Bernstein, they suggested that the very organization of physical and chemical systems constrains behavior. Think about it: Your body can move in many different ways. However, because of the structure of your hip joints and legs (part of your skeletal system), you, as an adult, tend to walk (as opposed to crawl, scoot, or squirm) as a primary mode of transportation. Thus, the structural organization of your body encourages—constrains—you to walk. In other words, your body's structure removes some of the movement choices your CNS might have to make (i.e., among crawling, scooting, squirming, or walking). It's not that you cannot perform these movements; it's just that because of your body structure, you are more attracted to (or constrained to) walking.

 Imagine that a human infant is born in a space station on the moon. Predict the types of movements you would see during the first 2 years of life. In particular, how would you expect the infant to get around?

Unlike the maturational and information processing perspectives, the dynamical systems approach suggests that coordinated behavior is softly assembled rather than hardwired, meaning that the interacting constraints in your body act together as a functional unit to enable you to walk when you need to. By *not* having a hardwired plan, you have greater flexibility in walking, which allows you to adapt your walk to many different situations. This process is called spontaneous self-organization of body systems. As we state in chapter 1, movement emerges from the interaction between constraints (individual, environmental, task). The resultant behavior emerges or self-organizes from these interrelationships. If you change any one of them, the emergent movement may change (Clark, 1995). This is the concept of constraints in the dynamical systems approach.

An important motor development concept produced by the dynamical systems approach is the notion of **rate limiters**, or **controllers**. The body's systems do not develop at the same rate; rather, some might mature quickly and others more slowly,

A **rate limiter**, or **controller**, is an individual constraint or system that holds back or slows the emergence of a motor skill.

and each system should be considered a constraint. Consider the hypothetical example graphed in figure 2.3. The development of four hypothetical systems is pictured in each of the small graphs numbered 1 to 4. As time passes, the development of system 1 remains at a constant value. System 2 plateaus, advances in a large step, then plateaus again. System 3 advances gradually and more continuously, whereas system 4 alternately advances and plateaus in a steplike fashion. The exhibited behavior, represented in the large graph, is affected by all the individual systems as they interact among themselves and with the task and environment.

An individual might begin to perform a new skill, such as walking, only when the slowest of the necessary systems for that skill reaches a certain point. Any such system or set of systems is known as a rate limiter, or controller, for that skill because that system's development controls the individual's rate of development at that time. In other words, the system acts as a constraint that discourages the motor skill until the system reaches a specific, critical level. Suppose that system 4 in figure 2.3 is the muscular system. Perhaps an infant's muscular strength must reach a certain level before the legs are strong enough to support the infant's weight on one leg in order to walk. Hence, muscular strength would be a rate limiter, or controller, for walking. Until the infant reaches a critical level of leg strength (enough to support the body), strength discourages walking and encourages other forms of transportation, such as creeping, crawling, or rolling. The notion of rate limiters fits well in the model of constraints.

These tenets of the dynamical systems approach differ significantly from those of the maturational perspective. Maturationists tend to focus on the CNS as the only system relevant to development and the only rate controller. The dynamical systems approach focuses on many systems and acknowledges that different systems might act as rate controllers for different skills (Thelen, 1998).

 In your experience, what rate limiters have affected your motor behavior? How have these changed at different times in your life?

Another feature of the dynamical systems approach is that it allows for the study of development across the life span. The concept of a system acting as a rate limiter, or controller, for a movement behavior applies into older adulthood as well.

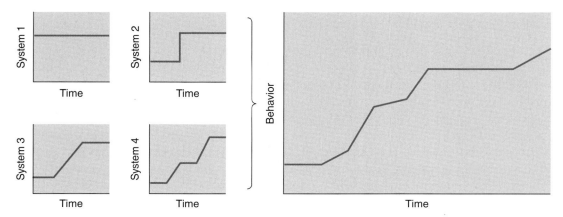

FIGURE 2.3 Four developing systems are depicted as contributing to behavior in an environmental context and for some particular task. The horizontal axis is time, and the vertical axis represents several parallel systems (which act as constraints) developing in different ways.

Adapted by permission from Thelen, Ulrich, and Jensen 1989.

The maturational perspective does not address aging because the predetermined endpoint of motor development is maturation, which occurs in the first several decades of life. In contrast, the dynamical systems approach accounts for changes in older adults as well as advancement in youths. When one or more of an individual's systems has declined to a critical point, a change in behavior might occur. This system is a rate controller; because it is the first to decline to some critical point, it triggers the reorganization of a movement to a less-efficient pattern. For example, if an individual's shoulder joint deteriorates as a result of arthritis and loses flexibility, at some point that individual might have to use a different overhand throwing motion or even throw underhand. The dynamical systems approach is appropriate for explaining developmental changes because changes do not necessarily occur in all systems over the entire span of older adulthood. Disease or injury may strike one system, and systems may be differentially affected by lifestyle. An active older adult who maintains a regular and balanced exercise program may experience fewer declines in many of the systems than a sedentary peer does.

Perception–Action Approach

The second branch of the ecological perspective is the **perception–action approach**. J.J. Gibson proposed this model in his writings during the 1960s and 1970s (1966, 1979), but those who study movement have only recently adopted this approach. Gibson proposed that a close interrelationship exists between the perceptual system and the motor system and emphasized that these systems evolved together in animals and humans. In this approach, we cannot study perception independent of movement if our findings are to be *ecologically valid*—that is, applicable to real-world movement behavior. Likewise, the *development* of perception and the *development* of movement must be studied together. In addition, we cannot study the individual while ignoring the surrounding environment. Gibson used the term **affordance** to describe the function an environmental object provides to an individual; this is related to the size and shape of the object and the individual in a particular setting. For example, a horizontal surface affords a human a place to sit, but a vertical surface does not. A squirrel can rest on a vertical tree trunk, so a vertical surface affords a squirrel a resting place. A baseball bat affords an adult, but not an infant, the opportunity to swing. Hence, the relationship between individual and environment is so intertwined that one's characteristics define objects' meanings, which implies that people assess environmental properties in relation to themselves, not according to an objective standard (Konczak, 1990). For example, an individual perceiving whether he or she can walk up a flight of stairs with alternating footsteps considers not just the height of each stair alone but also the height of each stair in relation to the climber's body size. A comfortable step height for an adult is not the same as that for a toddler. The use of intrinsic (relative to body size) rather than extrinsic dimensions is termed **body scaling**.

When a person looks at an object, he or she directly perceives the function that the object will allow, based both on his or her body and on the object's size, shape, texture, and so forth. This function is called an **affordance**.

Body scaling is the process of changing the dimensions of the environment or an environmental object in relation to the structural constraints of a performer.

 WEB STUDY GUIDE   Create body-scaled contexts for individuals with different disabilities by doing Lab Activity 2.1, Equipment That Affords Action, in the web study guide. Go to www.HumanKinetics.com/LifeSpanMotor Development.

The implications of these ideas for motor development are that affordances change as individuals change, resulting in new movement patterns. Growth in size, for example, or enhancement in movement capabilities, might allow actions not previously afforded. When an infant first faces stairs, her perception of their function is not likely to be one of "climbability" because of her small size and relative lack of strength. As a toddler, though, she grows to a size that makes climbing stairs with alternating footsteps easy. Scaling environmental objects to one's body size permits one to conceive of actions that otherwise seem impossible. Body scaling also applies to other age periods. For example, steps that are an appropriate height for most adults might be too high for an older adult with arthritis to climb comfortably with alternating footsteps. A wall-mounted light switch might be at a comfortable height for most adults yet rest a frustrating inch too high for someone sitting in a wheelchair. At any age, achievement of a movement goal relates to the individual, who is a certain shape and size, and to environmental objects, which afford certain movements to that individual.

Viewed another way, body scaling represents an excellent example of the interaction or interface between individual and task constraints. When walking up stairs, individuals must relate the length of their legs, their strength, and their dynamical range of motion (individual constraints) to the height of the stairs they are about to step on (task constraint). Changes in constraints, such as an ankle sprain, high-heeled shoes, or an icy staircase, will result in changes in the way an individual steps on the stairs. In physical education settings, instructors often assist children in body scaling by providing them with smaller equipment that is more appropriate for their smaller body size. By doing so, instructors manipulate the interaction between individual and task constraints to encourage a more advanced movement pattern (Gagen & Getchell, 2004).

 What activities would a 10-speed bicycle afford an infant, a typically able adult, an individual with paraplegia, or a chimpanzee? What individual constraints affect the activities afforded to each?

Gibson also rejected the notion of a CNS executive that performs almost limitless calculations on stimulus information to determine the speed and direction of both the person and the moving objects. The information processing perspective holds that such calculations are used to anticipate future positions so that we can, for example, reach up to catch a thrown ball. Instead, according to Gibson, individuals perceive their environment directly by constantly moving their eyes, heads, and bodies. This activity creates an optic flow field that provides both space and time information. For example, the image of a baseball approaching a batter not only indicates the ball's location but also expands on the eye's retina, and the batter uses the rate of image expansion to time his swing—that is, the rate of expansion gives the batter's CNS direct information about when the ball will be in range. Likewise, the expansion rate of the image of an oncoming car on a driver's retina yields the time to collision. From Gibson's perspective, an individual can perceive time to collision directly and does not need to perform a complicated calculation of speeds and distances to predict where and when collisions and interceptions will occur.

The ecological perspective has been taking hold in motor development research throughout the past two decades. Developmentalists are asking different types of questions: How does an infant's immediate environment affect her motor behavior? What constraints act as rate limiters to children's throwing? How will changing specific individual constraints in a rehabilitation setting alter motor patterns? Concurrently, they have developed types of research studies, such as examining the relationship between infant reflexes and adult movements (Thelen & Ulrich, 1991). The ecological perspective encourages professionals to view developing individuals in a very different way than before. As a result, these perspectives will excite and challenge students in the field. In many sections of this text, we examine the maturation and dynamical systems approaches on a particular issue and highlight the differences between these perspectives.

Summary and Synthesis

This chapter reviews the history and theoretical viewpoints specific to motor development—the maturational, information processing, and ecological perspectives. The maturational perspective emphasizes biological development, specifically maturation of the CNS. The information processing perspective sees the environment as the main force driving motor development. Unlike followers of the previous perspectives, ecological theorists stress interaction between all body systems (or, as Newell called them, constraints) as well as the inseparable factors of individual, environment, and task. In the ecological perspective, two related approaches to research exist: dynamical systems and perception–action approaches. This textbook adopts an ecological perspective and focuses on how individual, environmental, and task constraints interact to encourage or discourage movements. The concepts of rate limiters, or controllers, and body scaling exemplify how a motor developmentalist must consider the individual's performance of a particular task in a given environment in order to fully understand individuals' motor development over the course of a lifetime.

Diametrically opposed perspectives cannot be merged, but students of motor development are free to view behavior from different perspectives. It is important to remember that these theoretical viewpoints often focus only on specific aspects of development; that is, developmentalists with a particular perspective tend to study certain behaviors or age spans. Maturationists focus on infancy, whereas descriptive developmentalists focus on late childhood and adolescence. Information processing theorists search for age differences, whereas those studying from an ecological perspective observe transitions from one skill to another (e.g., from crawling to walking).

 Reinforcing What You Have Learned About Constraints

TAKE A SECOND LOOK

Let's revisit the first 18 months of your hypothetical nephew's life from an ecological perspective. Thinking about his first week of life, what constraints most influence his motor behavior? That is, what rate limiters keep him moving the way he does? As we suggest in chapter 1, in order to understand developmental change, we should think about where he was, where he is, and where he will be. The first big change, therefore, would be moving from an aqueous environment (his mother's womb) to one where gravity's full force can be felt. Keeping this in mind, part of the reason your nephew may move his arms in a seemingly uncoordinated fashion may relate to his strength (or lack thereof). As his environment changes, a need is created for greater strength to move his arms (individual–environmental constraint interaction). Over time, he builds strength, which interacts with other developing systems. When you see him at 9 months, all the systems have converged to allow him to use his arms more effectively. In terms of the rate limiter of strength, he has reached a critical level that allows him to move more functionally. He has sufficient strength to sit up, move his arm toward a toy, grasp it, and bring it to his mouth. He even has enough strength to stand on both legs and support his weight (with a little help from you).

Consider his next objective: moving independently around his environment. He might eye a chair (which to you affords sitting), scale the height of the seat to the length of his trunk, and pull himself up to a standing position. Can he walk yet? Probably not, as another rate limiter—balance—prevents him from standing alone unsupported. We could go on and on, examining the different ways in which your nephew uses affordances and body scaling, and you can think of examples on your own. Hopefully the interactions between the various constraints become clearer and clearer to you, and by the end of the text you will naturally evaluate the influence of different constraints on motor development.

TEST YOUR KNOWLEDGE

1. List the key researchers in the field of motor development from the maturational, information processing, and ecological perspectives.
2. How can a physical educator or physical therapist use the concept of body scaling to help individuals develop motor skills?
3. Why should physical educators be interested in affordances?
4. Explain, based on the different theoretical perspectives, how an infant learns to walk. What are the most important influences on the infant, according to each perspective?

LEARNING EXERCISE 2.1

Body Scaling to Design Sport Equipment

You have been hired by Haywood's Tennis Supplies to design a line of body-scaled tennis rackets. Because the company would like to distinguish its product line from others on the market, you must prepare an initial report addressing important aspects of the new rackets, available product lines from other companies, and how your rackets will be different. Develop this report; you can use the following questions as a guide.

1. What are the important individual constraints to consider when body scaling tennis rackets?
2. How have other companies body scaled their rackets? On what individual constraint or constraints do they scale?
3. What are some novel ways to scale Haywood's new rackets? What have other companies overlooked?

LEARNING EXERCISE 2.2

Hunting for Rate Limiters in Everyday Situations

Physical educators, physical therapists, parents, and many others want to encourage proficient motor skills in those with whom they interact. One important consideration in working to improve motor skill performance is this: What is holding a person back, or limiting the rate at which he or she acquires a skill? In this exercise you will determine the key rate limiter for a particular skill, given the constraints described.

1. An 11-month-old infant can use furniture to pull himself upright, can cruise the length of the couch if he keeps one hand in contact, and can push a toy shopping cart down the hall. However, when placed standing in the center of the room, he does not walk but rather gets down on all fours and crawls. What is his primary rate limiter for walking?

2. A stroke patient has control over her limbs and has little difficulty walking. She can lift a pencil and write lists and letters. She can comb her hair and brush her teeth. She experiences problems, however, when she tries to lift cans and jars overhead onto shelves. What is her primary rate limiter for reaching?

3. A 5-year-old can easily walk, run, jump, and hop. She plays games with other children on the playground and is very attentive in physical education class. She has problems, however, with galloping and skipping; she cannot seem to master the asymmetrical rhythms of these skills. What is her primary rate limiter for galloping and skipping?

Principles of Motion and Stability

Mechanical Laws Guiding Constraint Interactions

 CHAPTER OBJECTIVES

This chapter

- outlines the principles of motion and stability that lead to proficient motor performance,
- discusses the relationships between these principles and motor behaviors of individuals of various skill levels, and
- explains how skilled performers take advantage of principles.

Running to the Best of Her Abilities

In 1976, Aimee Mullins was born with fibular hemimelia, a congenital condition that results in malformed or absent fibula bones. As a result, she had both her legs amputated below the knee by her first birthday, and doctors believed she would never be able to walk. To some, pursuing an athletic career with this condition may seem daunting or even impossible. Not to Aimee. Early in her childhood, she began walking with prosthetic limbs. By her high school years, she participated in a variety of sports, including softball, downhill skiing, and track. In fact, Aimee was so fast she competed against able-bodied athletes while attending NCAA Division I Georgetown University, becoming the first amputee ever to do so. Aimee also competed in the 1996 Atlanta Paralympics, setting three world records in track events. For Aimee, running at the best of her abilities means running very, very fast.

Aimee Mullens, a world-class athlete, model, and actor, has never let physical differences become obstacles to success. Rather, she challenged conventional wisdom by finding a way to excel in athletics against extreme odds. Both beautiful and eloquent, Aimee discussed the different designs of her prosthetics in the 2009 Technology, Entertainment, Design talk titled "My 12 Pairs of Legs." Her use of a mechanically efficient design in the 1996 Paralympics helped revolutionize the use of "cheetah" polycarbon-fiber sprinting legs, which are more biomechanically efficient than other legs and are the gold standard for athletes today. Such a design takes advantage of certain principles of motion and stability in order to improve the energy efficiency of the runner.

As we note in chapter 1, many elements of motor development tend to occur similarly in different people. That is, humans change patterns of motor behavior in a somewhat predictable fashion. This similarity is not surprising when you consider that most humans share similar individual constraints (two arms, two legs, and upright posture). Similarities also occur because humans operate under a system of rules or principles that dictate how constraints interact in the context of life on this planet. Humans on Earth live in a context that features certain predictable characteristics, such as gravity. Part of the process of developing motor skill involves learning how the human body works within the boundaries of these physical laws. During early life this is not a simple task because individuals must learn to refine their movements while experiencing changes in physical parameters. Furthermore, they must learn to calibrate their movements to the environment while performing specific tasks based on these principles. (Think, for example, of picking up an empty box you thought was full. You must quickly recalibrate your movements in order to maintain your posture or you will fall over.) The process of calibrating movements to task and environment in accordance with mechanical principles can also be difficult for individuals who develop atypically or who must relearn skills after an injury. This chapter considers the physical and mechanical principles under which humans move. In the context of motor development, these are known as the principles of motion and stability.

How would you describe the movements of early, inexperienced movers? Often, their initial attempts at performing skills seem to be inefficient and jerky. They may move the body in separate, discrete steps rather than in a whole movement. They often try to optimize one aspect of the movement (e.g., balance) at the expense of another (e.g., speed) to increase the likelihood of success. As individuals become more proficient at skills, their movements become smoother and more efficient; indeed, their movement patterns often change entirely. Many of children's improvements are due to increases in body size and strength and therefore in their ability to produce force. Yet size and strength alone do not account for how children progress from unskilled to skilled performance. Another part of the process of change involves mastering and exploiting the principles of motion and stability. In fact, all individuals can use these principles to their advantage, in athletic performances as well as in activities of daily living.

Understanding the Principles of Motion and Stability

Movements occur in a context that is governed by certain principles of motion and stability; that is, certain physical laws of motion limit your movements. Consider gravity as an example of a rule that dictates how constraints interact and objects move. The simplest way to think about gravity is that all objects are attracted to each other and that the amount of attraction depends on the objects' masses. Because the mass of the earth is so large, objects on its surface are drawn toward its center. If you jump up, you don't continue to rise. Instead, you come back toward the earth as a result of gravity. What goes up must come down (figure 3.1). The force of gravity exists all around us, dictating that each of us must eventually return to Earth after jumping. Now, let's look at this rule as it applies to constraints. Given that all objects eventually return to Earth, people must calibrate their movements based on their individual constraints (e.g., overall body mass and strength), acting in an environment governed by specific task rules. The interaction of constraints in this context encourages certain motor patterns while eliminating others. What are some of the behaviors encouraged by gravity? An individual must activate certain postural muscles to assume and maintain a position, even while executing a skilled movement. Furthermore, she must work

KEY POINT
Principles of motion and stability act on all movements and movers. As movers become more proficient at skills, they often use these principles to their advantage.

FIGURE 3.1   Because gravity acts on the long jumper equally and at all times, his flight path resembles a parabola, or semicircle

against gravity to become airborne. If a person projects herself or an object at an angle (as opposed to straight up and down), then the force of gravity will ensure that the flight path is parabolic. As you can see, then, principles of motion influence the interaction of constraints.

At the same time, the individual constraints or characteristics of the performer influence the movement pattern undertaken. People throw using a movement pattern that is dictated by the shape and structure of the human body and limbs. Consider the shape and structure of the bones in the shoulder (figure 3.2). Muscles also have particular functional shapes and sizes, and they connect bones to each other. In addition, the nervous system coordinates muscular contractions. Furthermore, individuals use their bodies to move with a particular task goal in mind, which also acts to constrain movements. Here lies the interconnectedness of constraints: The individual, with a task goal in mind, acts in the environment to perform a skill. Thus, individual, environment, and task interact to shape or constrain a movement pattern.

Clearly, some movement patterns optimize the product of skill performance whereas others do not. Given the task of throwing a rock as far as possible, an individual can produce a variety of motor patterns that will move the rock, but only one will move the rock as far as possible. To develop their skills, children and adults must learn to use movement patterns that optimize performance. The changes taking place in children's bodies complicate this process because growth alters an individual's overall size and proportions.

As children grow and mature, their skeletal, muscular, and nervous systems allow them to produce greater force. Changing bodies mean changing individual constraints, and the individual must recalibrate the interactions between individual and environmental constraints. By taking advantage of the principles of motion and stability, children discover qualitatively different movement patterns that improve the outcome of their skill performance. Thus, young children, given their body size, shape, and strength, might execute what is for them the most successful or efficient movement

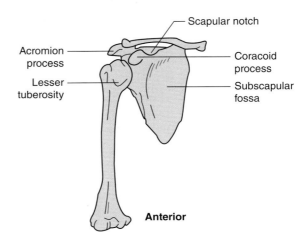

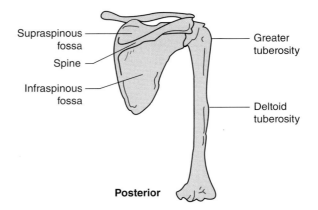

FIGURE 3.2 The structure of the articulating bones in the shoulder joint encourages movement in some directions while preventing it in others. For example, the acromion process prevents movement of the upper arm past 90° without movement of the scapula.

Reprinted from Donnelly 1990.

pattern possible. However, as they grow, mature physiologically, and gain experience, other movement patterns become possible that allow them to execute skills with greater proficiency (Gagen & Getchell, 2008).

Injury or disability can change individual constraints for either short or long periods. Affected individuals must relearn how to use mechanics of movement given their unique body structure and function. Adults can also take advantage of these principles of motion and stability. Just as with children, an adult might execute the movement pattern that affords the greatest success, but with time and experience (and, in some cases, with technologically advanced equipment) new patterns may emerge that provide for more adept performance (Getchell & Gagen, 2006).

Understanding the principles of motion and stability is critical in observing motor performance. These principles help us determine which movement patterns are likely to produce optimal results. Knowledge of the principles also helps us focus on critical aspects of movement that often distinguish skilled movement patterns from unskilled ones. Thus, taking advantage of these principles can help us get much more out of our movements. For these reasons, this chapter reviews and evaluates the principles of motion and stability—the physics of movement—as they apply to basic skill performance. Only some of the more salient principles are discussed here; a more complete analysis of the physics of movement falls in the domain of biomechanics—the mechanics of muscular activity—which is an area of study in itself and which lies beyond the scope of this text. A more detailed explanation of these principles can be found in any biomechanics text (Hall, 2006; Knudson, 2007; McGinnis, 2005).

KEY POINT
Observations of developmental change in basic skill performance benefit from application of the principles of motion and stability.

Moving Against Gravity: The Application of Force

To move either themselves or objects, individuals must produce force; a stationary object or individual will not move until some force is applied to it. You may recognize this as **Newton's first law of motion:** An object at rest stays at rest, or an object in motion stays in motion, until acted on by a force (McGinnis, 2005). You probably understand Newton's first law without ever thinking about it. Or perhaps if you were a messy teen, your parents told you, "If you leave your socks on the floor, they will be there when you get back!" This is an excellent example of Newton's first law. Simply put, to move something, you must apply force to it.

 Lie on the floor on your back and then stand up. What are some of the different ways you can achieve this task goal? Do some movements seem more comfortable or efficient than others? Why?

According to **Newton's first law of motion**, you must apply force to a stationary object to move it and apply force to a moving object to change its movement. Newton's first law is relatively simple and straightforward: It takes force to move something standing still and force to change the direction of something moving. **Newton's second law of motion** is related to force production, acceleration, and mass. Basically, the amount of acceleration an object has when you apply force to it is proportional to the force and inversely proportional to its mass. This relationship is easier to understand when described with examples. It takes more force to "put" or throw a shot (which has more mass) than to throw a baseball (which has less mass) at the same speed. Also, if you kick a soccer ball harder (more forcefully), it will accelerate faster and thus go farther. Understanding Newton's second law is important when attempting to move proficiently.

Newton's second law of motion states that the acceleration of a person or object is proportional to the force applied to it and inversely proportional to its mass.

You can use these laws with other principles related to force to understand how to maximize performance (Gagen & Getchell, 2008). First, a relationship exists between force applied and the distance over which you apply it. You can improve your performance by applying force over a greater distance. For example, a young child throwing a ball may throw the ball without moving her legs. By keeping her feet in place, she can reduce compromises to her balance; however, the ball will not travel as far. An experienced thrower will take a step forward with her opposite leg, thus increasing the linear (straight-line) distance over which the force is applied. Try throwing a ball with and without a step and you will discover how much increasing your linear distance with a step aids your performance.

We can also consider rotary or angular distance in addition to linear distance. When you throw a ball, your arm rotates around a joint; hence, it moves a certain number of degrees, or a certain angular distance. By increasing their range of body motion, individuals can increase the rotary distance over which force is applied and therefore maximize their performance. Using a preparatory windup puts the performer in a position to maximize the linear and rotary distances of force application. The preparatory positioning also stretches the muscles the performer will use, thus readying them for maximal contraction. These actions permit the person to project the object at a greater velocity than could be accomplished without a windup and a full range of motion.

 Imagine you are a physical educator. Throw a ball with and without using a contralateral (opposite side) step. What differences do you find in several quantitative measures (e.g., distance, accuracy)? What differences do you find in movement form? What might be the reason for these changes?

KEY POINT
To improve movement performance, individuals must find the optimal relationship between force and distance in a given movement. Two important phases in this process are preparation (preparatory movement) and the application of force through a full range of motion.

It is important to note that in most movement skills an optimal relationship exists between force and distance. That is, simply increasing linear or angular distance for a given force will not automatically result in an improved performance. The performer must first recognize what is a complete or full range of motion for a given skill. By observing children during movement, you will see them begin to explore relationships between force and distance (Gagen & Getchell, 2008). The changes in movement patterns related to the application of force often allow for a greater velocity and may come at the expense of stability. You can imagine that although a soccer player generates a lot of force in her leg and therefore in a kick, it would not take much effort for another person to move her from her spot on the field (figure 3.3).

 Imagine you are the coach of a wheelchair basketball team. How could a wheelchair basketball player take advantage of Newton's first and second laws and the related principles of motion?

Moving Against Gravity: Action and Reaction

Newton's third law of motion, the law of action–reaction, states that for every force you exert on an object, the object exerts an equal force back on you in the opposite direction.

When observing changes in motor behavior across the life span, we also notice that performers take advantage of **Newton's third law of motion:** To every action there is an equal and opposite reaction. This means that if you exert a force on an object, it exerts a force (equal and opposite) back on you. This may seem confusing at first, but an example may make it clearer. As you walk, you push down on the floor or surface you walk on. What would happen if the floor did not "push" back up on you? If you guessed that your foot would go through the floor, you

FIGURE 3.3   When trying to optimize performance of a skill, athletes must learn the proper relationship between force and distance. This soccer player takes a step to increase distance; any longer step would lead to instability.

are right. Perhaps you have experienced this situation when walking on thin ice or unstable floorboards.

How does the law of action–reaction affect movement patterns? To move forward while walking, an individual must push down and back so that the surface can push up and forward. Watch the movement pattern of newly walking toddlers. Much of their force is directed downward, not backward. This allows them to move without compromising their balance; however, forward progression is slow. With more walking experience, individuals begin to exert more force backward and therefore move forward faster.

Consider the implications of Newton's third law: If every action that a performer makes results in an equal and opposite reaction, then any forces that are applied outside of the plane of motion will lead to undesired reaction forces. These forces will in turn detract from the performance (Gagen & Getchell, 2008). For example, if you want to move forward, then any force exerted in other directions will make your walk less efficient. Athletes attempting maximal performance, such as kicking for the maximal force possible, want to exert as much force as possible in one plane of motion. In a skill such as kicking, maximal effort is characterized by full extension (straightening) of the striking limb.

We can also see the law of action–reaction applied among parts of the body. For example, in locomotor skills such as running, the lower body twists one way and the upper body twists the opposite way. One leg swings forward and the arm on that side of the body swings backward in reaction; thus, the leg on one side of the body and the arm on the opposite side swing forward and back in unison. This familiar pattern is termed **oppositional arm and leg movement** and is a characteristic of skilled locomotor movements.

Imagine the result of several everyday movements if the law of action–reaction did not exist. Have you ever experienced a situation in which you expected a reaction force and it did not occur? What happened?

Relationship Between Rotating Limbs and Projected Objects

As we discussed previously, individuals move when their limbs rotate around one or several joints. This is called rotational movement. In essence, when projecting an object (e.g., throwing or kicking), an individual's limb traces part of a circle—the arm travels in an arc in throwing, and the leg does so in kicking. Releasing or striking an object causes it to fly away from this curved path in a straight line from the release or impact point. A relationship exists between the velocity of the rotating arm and the velocity of the projected object. For example, if a baseball player throws a ball from the outfield, the velocity of the ball as it leaves the player's hand is dependent on how fast the player's arm moves and on the length of his arm at the release point. In more scientific terms, an object's linear velocity is the product of its rotational velocity and its radius of rotation.

What does this mean in terms of optimizing performance? First of all, as children grow, their limb length increases, which should lead to changes in projectile velocity (and consequently distance) that may appear even without changes in movement form (Gagen & Getchell, 2008). Increases in rotational velocity also cause these changes. However, at any given time, people cannot increase their absolute limb length or rotational velocity. What if an athlete already rotates his limb as fast as possible? There is one other way to increase a projected object's velocity. The athlete must extend his limb—and thus increase the radius of rotation—by straightening it out just before the point of release or contact. Consider a tennis server trying to get the most velocity possible on his first serve (figure 3.4). At the point of contact, the player's arm is extended as far as it can be, which will increase the ball's release velocity.

At this point, you may wonder why skilled athletes do not keep their limbs extended as far as possible during the entire movement. If an extended limb leads to greater velocity, why do athletes often begin their movements in a bent or cocked position and not straighten the limb throughout? The answer lies in another law of

KEY POINT
Individuals can increase the velocity of an object they project (throw, kick, hit) by extending the rotating limb as much as possible at the point of release.

FIGURE 3.4 To increase the velocity of a tennis ball, a tennis player extends his arm (thereby increasing his radius of rotation) as much as possible at the moment of contact.

motion: that of inertia. You have probably heard the term *inertia*; it refers to an object's resistance to motion, and it is related to the mass of the object. When dealing with rotating objects (e.g., arms and legs) in sports and physical activities, resistance to motion depends not only on mass but also on limb length. As the limb length increases for a given mass, so does the resistance to motion. As the resistance to motion increases, so does the amount of energy required to move the object. In short, bending the limb decreases the energy necessary to move the limb.

Let's consider several skills in which athletes take advantage of these two principles to maximize performance. First, consider sprinters competing in the 100 m dash (figure 3.5). Just before contact with the ground, the sprinters fully extend their legs to maximize their projected velocity. However, the sprinters bend these limbs as they recover and swing forward. This conserves energy and effort in that limb. Another example is that of batters swinging at pitched balls. The batters conserve effort at the beginning of the swing by keeping their elbows bent. Just before the point of contact, the batters extend their arms as fully as possible.

 Imagine you are a physical educator. In which sports and physical activities, besides tennis, do athletes extend their limbs to increase the velocity of a projected object? Try to think of three obvious examples and three not-so-obvious examples.

Open Kinetic Chain

A person can toss or kick an object a short distance with a flick of the wrist or a tap of the toe. But a maximal ballistic effort must involve not only more body parts but also sequential movement of those parts. The sequence must be timed

FIGURE 3.5 A sprinter changes relative leg length during the course of a stride. The leg is bent to decrease momentum and energy requirements; it is then extended to increase force production.

Open kinetic chain refers to the correctly timed sequence of movements an individual uses to successfully perform a skill.

KEY POINT
One of the most significant changes we see in the skill development of children and beginners is the transition from using a single action to executing skills in a pattern of efficient, properly timed sequential movements.

so that the performer applies the force of each succeeding movement just after the previous movement to accelerate the object. For example, recall that an effective thrower steps forward and rotates the pelvis, then rotates the upper trunk as the throwing arm comes forward, extends, and rotates inward. We term a movement sequence such as this an **open kinetic chain** of movements.

 Imagine you are a physical therapist. How important is sequencing and timing to activities of daily living? What results from changing either sequence or timing in a given movement?

Two elements are essential to the open kinetic chain of movements. First, an optimal sequence of movements exists. Equally important is the timing of events in this sequence. For example, we have discussed how taking a step before a throw increases the amount of work done; however, the step must occur immediately before the throw in order to provide benefit. You may have observed individuals—particularly children—learning to throw who take a step but do not time the step and throw together. In fact, beginners often use single actions or movements when executing motor skills. As they continue to perform these skills, they begin to link together and time these single movements; as a result, they become more proficient movers.

Force Absorption

Have you ever landed from a jump without bending your knees? If so, you understand the concept of action–reaction firsthand: The earth immediately returned the force of your landing body back to you. Obviously, you do not want to land this way every time you jump because injury will surely ensue. To decrease the impact of the landing, you simply bend your knees. Bending your knees during landing increases the time and distance of the landing. This brings us to our next principle of motion, related to force absorption. Simply put, to decrease the impact of a reaction force, you must either increase the amount of time in which the impact occurs or increase the area over which the impact occurs (Carr, 1997).

KEY POINT
To absorb forces transmitted to their bodies, individuals must increase the amount of time of the impact (by allowing the limbs to flex) or increase the area over which the force is absorbed.

You can observe individuals using this principle to decrease impact force in a wide variety of motor activities. When catching a ball, a softball player extends the arms in front of the body, then brings the glove, hand, and arm into the body; this sequence helps absorb the force of a hard-driven ball. Gymnasts are experts at landings, bending their hips, knees, and ankles as fully as possible. Individuals practicing judo increase the time and area of their falls, rolling from the arms to the back (Gagen & Getchell, 2008). Using this principle of motion is important to preventing injury when attempting a maximal performance.

Stability and Balance

We have discussed principles of motion, but principles of stability are equally important. Most people would have difficulty optimizing their movements from an unstable position. That is, stability and balance are essential elements of many sports and other physical activities. Some activities, such as powerlifting and golf, require maximum stability. In others, such as judo and wrestling, athletes try to maintain their stability while disturbing that of their opponents. Still other activities, such as gymnastics and ice skating, require athletes to maintain balance in relatively unstable positions.

Based on the previous examples, you can see that **stability** and **balance** do not refer to exactly the same concept. A stable object or person is one that resists movement. You would have a difficult time tipping over a large, wide, heavy box—it is very stable. Balance, on the other hand, relates to the ability of an object or person to maintain equilibrium. If you can stand on one foot while closing your eyes, you exhibit great balance in an unstable condition.

In most cases, increasing stability ensures balance; however, maintaining balance does not guarantee stability. In fact, a person may not want stability because it will inhibit mobility. People can readily become more stable by increasing the size of their base of support—for example, by spreading their legs when standing or by spreading their hands when doing a handstand. Individuals can add to their stability by keeping their **center of gravity** low and inside their base of support. In the example of a handstand, individuals must keep the legs directly above the trunk to maintain optimum stability; otherwise, they will either move or fall.

In many activities, maximal performance of the skill requires performers to minimize stability in order to increase mobility. In locomotor skills, a person momentarily sacrifices stability (two-footed support base) in order to move by alternately losing and gaining balance (one-footed support base). The body's weight is pushed forward, ahead of the base of support, and the person moves the leg forward to regain balance.

Figure 3.6 shows individuals with varying degrees of stability and balance. In figure 3.6a, the individual is very stable and has a wide base of support and a low center of gravity. It would be difficult to move him. The athlete in figure 3.6b is less stable but more mobile. Figure 3.6c shows an athlete with great balance in a highly unstable position.

Young children, people with certain disabilities, older adults, and people learning new skills often attempt to improve balance by increasing their stability. In locomotor tasks, they will increase their base of support by planting their feet wide or out-toeing (what would be considered "duck-footing") their feet. They keep their center of gravity well within their base of support by avoiding excessive trunk rotation or limb movement. In reception skills such as catching, they also increase

Balance relates to the ability of an object or person to maintain equilibrium.

Center of gravity is the concentration point of the earth's gravitational pull on an individual (McGinnis, 2005).

KEY POINT
An individual's stability is related to the ability to resist movement or disruption. You can increase your stability by increasing your base of support, lowering your center of gravity, and keeping your center of gravity within your base of support.

KEY POINT
Although increasing stability leads to improved balance, it also leads to decreased mobility. Therefore, a skilled performer uses a base of support just wide enough to provide sufficient stability for his or her activity.

FIGURE 3.6 Different degrees of stability: (a) highly stable, (b) moderately stable, and (c) not very stable.

the base of support and lower their center of gravity. In many cases, if such people gain greater muscle control, more experience, proper training, or confidence, they will narrow the base of support and therefore increase their mobility and ability to move quickly.

Imagine you are a physical therapist. Think of four activities of daily living that range from requiring maximum stability to requiring maximum mobility. What are the consequences of losing balance in each activity?

WEB STUDY GUIDE Compare and contrast motion principles in different movements in Lab Activity 3.1, Searching for Movement Similarities and Differences, in the web study guide. Go to www.HumanKinetics.com/Life SpanMotorDevelopment.

Using the Principles of Motion and Stability to Detect and Correct Errors

Once you understand the principles that underlie human movement, you can use them to recognize and fix mechanical errors in a person's technique. At first, the amount of information may seem overwhelming. However, Carr (1997) has provided a simple five-step process for systematically observing and analyzing skill performance. This process provides you with a straightforward method for noticing and assisting with a person's mechanics.

• **Step 1: Observe the complete skill.** Although this seems self-evident, it is surprising how often novice teachers and coaches put themselves in a position where they cannot see a person's complete movement. Planning before performance of the skill is key, and you should keep several concerns in mind. If you can watch the performance only once or twice, focus on only a few elements. Videotape the performance for future analysis. Make sure the person warms up before the movement and performs in a natural environment, and always ensure the safety of the person and others who may be nearby.

• **Step 2: Analyze each phase and its key elements.** Hone in on specific phases of the skill and their key elements. Break the skill into phases; for example, an overarm throw could be divided into preparatory backswing, force production, and follow-through. Next, look at a person's performance of the skill in these phases. Carr suggests two ways to do this. One is to start with the result and work backward. If a person is trying to serve a tennis ball over a net but continues to hit the net, you concentrate on the action of the racket when it contacts the ball and then work back from that point to identify which part of the performance may be leading to this result. Alternatively, you can watch the movement from start to finish. Watch the person's preparatory stance, balance, and weight shift before movement; then focus on each phase of the skill.

• **Step 3: Use your knowledge of mechanics in your analysis.** You have learned a good deal about mechanics, and now is the time to use it. Observers must focus on how the mover applies muscular force to generate movements. Carr suggests a series of questions to guide your analysis.

  ○ Does the mover have optimal stability when applying or receiving force?
  ○ Is the mover using all the muscles that can make a contribution to the skill?

○ Is the mover applying force with the muscles in the correct sequence?

○ Is the mover applying the right amount of force over the appropriate time frame?

○ Is the mover applying the force in the correct direction?

○ Is the mover correctly applying torque and momentum transfer?

○ Is the mover manipulating any linear or rotary inertia properly?

Use these questions to evaluate skill performance. Remember, you are not determining a right and wrong way to perform a skill; rather, you are looking for elements of the movement that can be modified to make the skill performance more proficient.

• **Step 4: Select errors to be corrected.** Many novice performers do not move in a mechanically efficient manner. This is not necessarily good or bad—it is simply how that person performs a skill. You, as a teacher or coach, can pick out certain aspects of movement that the person can improve to become more proficient at a skill. Keep in mind that there are many different ways that people can successfully perform a skill. However, improving the mechanics in several phases of a skill allows for improved performance. Focus on major errors—a performance that lacks in the areas listed in step 3—and ignore minor problems. Work on one aspect of performance at a time. In many cases, improvement in one area will lead to improvement in several other areas.

• **Step 5: Decide on appropriate methods for the correction of errors.** Educators can have different ideas about how to teach or coach motor skills. It's best to take a class or attend a coaching clinic to learn a variety of activity-specific teaching methods. Regardless of which methods you use, here are some keys to remember. First and foremost, keep safety in mind when attempting to correct errors. Highly complex skills and skills that involve flight can become dangerous if the mover diverts attention from the skill to try to correct errors. Next, communicate with your students in understandable language rather than mechanical terms. Consider also how much time you have with the students to correct errors; this will dictate the number of errors you attempt to correct. Finally, use outside resources, such as textbooks or the Internet, to help you find new and innovative ways to teach movement skills. One such website, the Coaches' Information Service of the International Society of Biomechanics in Sports (www.csuchico.edu/isbs), is filled with helpful biomechanical information for coaches.

 WEB STUDY GUIDE   Uncover motion principles underlying developmental change in three skills (Lab Activity 3.2: locomotor movements; Lab Activity 3.3: ballistic skills; Lab Activity 3.4: manipulative skills) in the web study guide. Go to www.HumanKinetics.com/LifeSpanMotorDevelopment.

Summary and Synthesis

Mechanical principles govern all of our movements. The principles themselves act as constraints in that they dictate how an individual interacts with the environment when performing a task. For example, the force of gravity is an environmental constraint that influences how we move on Earth. These principles include Newton's laws of inertia, acceleration, and action–reaction as well as relationships based on these laws dealing with force production and absorption, open kinetic chain, and stability and balance. These principles define relationships that dictate how we move.

Over time, individuals gain understanding of these principles (either explicitly or implicitly) and can learn to control certain factors that allow them to perform skills more proficiently. The qualitative changes in motor performance that occur during childhood reflect changes in the interaction between the environment and the changing individual constraints in the growing child. The progress of children, beginners, and relearners is characterized by their selection of movement patterns that increasingly optimize the movement product in a manner consistent with the principles of motion and stability. The major mechanical principles involved in efficient, skilled movement include the application and absorption of force as well as action and reaction, linear and rotational velocity, sequentially timed movements, and stability and balance. Knowledge of these principles allows us to generalize across various basic skills. We need not approach developmental changes in each of the basic skills as a completely new study because some aspects of change in skills overlap, especially in the categories of locomotion, ballistics, reception, and skills requiring balance.

 Reinforcing What You Have Learned About Constraints

TAKE A SECOND LOOK

Aimee Mullins has challenged preconceived notions of ability and disability her entire life. While in college, she successfully competed against able-bodied athletes in track and field. In recent years some have argued that "cheetah" legs provide an unfair advantage for the individual using them (most notably, Oscar Pistorius was barred from international competition in 2007). Both during and after her athletic career, Mullins argued that track athletes with and without prosthetics should compete against each other on national and international stages. Focusing on only the idea that "cheetah" legs are mechanically efficient overlooks the fact that the resultant movement comes from an interaction of many constraints. In other words, each athlete must master the different principles of motion and stability with respect to their own individual constraints.

TEST YOUR KNOWLEDGE

1. Describe some characteristics of two different motor skills that indicate that the individual is optimizing stability instead of mobility.
2. List Newton's three laws and explain their relationship to movements.
3. What are some of the ways in which a baseball player can increase the force of a throw?
4. How can a child's growth contribute to greater proficiency at certain motor skills?

LEARNING EXERCISE 3.1

Understanding the Relationship Between Forces and Balance

What are the influences on balance when you stand on one leg? Start by standing and balancing on one leg. Now, move your support foot. How does this affect balance, and what is the ideal position? Next, move your free leg to different positions. How does this affect balance, and what is the ideal position? Repeat this process with your arms and head until you find your own ideal balance position. After you finish, compare your ideal position with that (or those) of a partner (or group).

LEARNING EXERCISE 3.2

Examining Principles of Motion and Stability in Specific Sports Skills

In this exercise you will examine the interplay between force and balance in certain sports skills. Start with the overarm throw. Throw a ball as hard as you can.

1. Where does your balance come from? Examine the specific movements that lead to greater balance.
2. Where does your force come from? Examine the specific movements that lead to greater force production.
3. Now, consider the relationship between force and balance. Describe how you would have to change your movements to create *more* force. What would have to change so that you could maintain balance when doing the movement as revised for more force?
4. Try to make these changes in your movements. What happens?

Try this experiment for different sports skills, such as a volleyball spike, a football punt, or a soccer kick.

Physical Growth and Aging

One reason the model of constraints is so useful to those studying motor development is that it shows how physical growth and aging, as changing individual structural constraints, in turn change individuals' interactions with the environment and with the task—and therefore change movement. The change in individual structural constraints through growth is particularly dramatic, as is evident on a whole-body level and a system level. That is, not only does the whole body change in size and proportion, but the body's systems (e.g., skeletal, muscular, endocrine) also change. Changes are more subtle but still present in aging.

Chapter 4 considers the typical pattern of growth and aging of the body as a whole. It emphasizes body size and proportion as well as maturity. Chapter 5 examines five body systems and how they change over the life span. These are the five systems most related to the performance of motor skills. Taken together, these whole-body and system-specific changes play such a large role in a person's age-related change in skill performance that one must possess a thorough knowledge of physical growth and aging in order to effectively study the course of motor development. As we will see later, movement is influenced by size, mass, and leverage.

Suggested Reading

Lohman, T.G., Roche, A.F., & Martorell, R. (Eds.). (1988). *Anthropometric standardization reference manual.* Champaign, IL: Human Kinetics.

Malina, R.M., Bouchard, C., & Bar-Or, O. (2004). *Growth, maturation, and physical activity* (2nd ed.). Champaign, IL: Human Kinetics.

Nilsson, L. (1990). *A child is born.* New York: Delacorte Press.

Ratey, J.J. (2001). *A user's guide to the brain.* New York: Vintage Books.

Spirduso, W.W., Francis, K.L., & MacRae, P.G. (2005). *Physical dimensions of aging* (2nd ed.). Champaign, IL: Human Kinetics.

Physical Growth, Maturation, and Aging

Changing Individual Constraints Across the Life Span

 CHAPTER OBJECTIVES

This chapter

- describes the course of body growth and aging over the life span,
- reviews the role of genes in the course of early physical growth and development,
- reviews the influence of extrinsic factors on growth and development and the increasing role of extrinsic factors as individuals proceed through the life span,
- identifies typical patterns of growth while recognizing individual differences in the timing of growth, and
- distinguishes between growth and maturation.

We Can Be Fooled By Size

On my desk is a picture of my fifth-grade volleyball team. Of course, the tallest girls on the team are in the back row. They are also the two youngest players—by half a year! You likely have a similar story, perhaps about a team, classmates, or relatives. These stories serve as reminders that there is no single blueprint for the growth and maturation of all individuals. Thus, it is important for teachers, therapists, coaches, doctors, and nurses to understand what factors lead to variations in growth patterns and when those variations are normal or abnormal.

Physical growth and aging are fascinating. Humans, as members of a single species, experience many common steps and processes in growth and aging. One example is the adolescent growth spurt. Genetic factors drive a very orderly and sequenced pattern of growth and aging, so in many respects we know what to expect. On the other hand, individuals each have unique potential and their own timing. When we observe a group of preadolescents of the same chronological age, we find a huge range of sizes. Growth and aging are also affected by a variety of extrinsic factors, such as nutrition and disease.

Genetic and extrinsic factors combine to influence physical growth and aging. We can identify patterns and relationships in the growth and aging of humans (universality), but we are reminded over and over again of the individual differences (variability). It is important for us to know both the expected pattern and the range of variation.

You might wonder why motor developmentalists have any interest at all in physical growth and aging. Recall our triangular model, which pictures the interaction of individual, environmental, and task constraints, and think back to one of the reasons we gave for the usefulness of this model to developmentalists. As individuals grow and age (in other words, as the individual constraints related to the body's structure change), the interactions between the three types of constraints must change, giving rise to different movements. If our goal is to make the same movements possible over a long range of the life span, then we need to constantly change the environment or the task to accommodate the changing physical constraints. For example, if we want players of a variety of ages to be able to dunk a basketball, we have to adjust the task by changing the basket height as the height of the players or their jumping ability changes. We need to be constantly alert to changing the environment and task in order to help each individual achieve a desired movement.

 Imagine for a moment that you are the youth sports coach of a sixth-grade basketball team. How much variation would you expect in the height and weight of your players? Would you assign each player a position (forward, center, or guard) based on size? As your players return for future seasons, would these assignments change? Why or why not?

Understanding the patterns and variations of growth and aging is fundamental to helping individuals develop their motor skills. One goal of educators and health care providers is to make motor tasks developmentally appropriate—that is, achievable by those at any age and with any set of abilities or disabilities. This would be impossible without knowledge of physical growth and aging.

Even for students who anticipate working with people past infancy, a good understanding of growth and aging begins with the study of prenatal growth and development. The talents and limitations that each individual brings to a task are often influenced by the course of prenatal growth and development. So, we begin a review of the growing and aging processes with prenatal development. This brief discussion highlights how sensitive individuals are to extrinsic influences, even in the relatively protective womb.

Prenatal Development

The growth process begins the instant an ovum (egg) and spermatozoon fuse in fertilization. Carried out under the control of genes, early development is astonishingly precise. Genes, then, determine the normal aspects of development and inherited abnormal development. At the same time, the growing embryo (and, later, the fetus) is very sensitive to extrinsic factors, which include the environment in which the fetus is growing—the amniotic sac in the uterus—and the nutrients delivered to the fetus via the mother's circulation and the placenta. Even in the womb, individual genetic factors and extrinsic factors interact in the fetus' development. Some extrinsic factors, such as abnormal external pressure applied to the mother's abdomen or the presence of certain viruses and drugs in the mother's bloodstream, are detrimental to the fetus. Other factors, such as delivery of all the proper nutrients, enhance the fetus' growth.

Prenatal growth is divided into two phases: embryonic growth, from conception to 8 weeks, and fetal growth, from 8 weeks to birth. Let's consider the key features of each phase.

Embryonic Development

Development begins with the fusion of two sex cells: an ovum from the female and a spermatozoon from the male (see figure 4.1). The genes direct the continuous development of the embryo in a precise and predictable pattern.

The number of cells increases, and the cells **differentiate** to form specific tissues and organs. This process occurs in a predictable time line, summarized in table 4.1. At 4 weeks, the limbs are roughly formed and the heartbeat begins. By approximately 8 weeks, the eyes, ears, nose, mouth, fingers, and toes are formed. By this time, the human form has taken shape.

Fetal Development

The fetal stage, from 8 weeks to birth, is characterized by further growth and cell differentiation of the fetus, leading to functional capacity. This continued growth of the organs and tissues occurs in two ways: by **hyperplasia** and by **hypertrophy**. If you examine the landmarks of growth carefully, you will also see that growth tends to proceed in two directions. One direction is **cephalocaudal**, meaning that the head and facial structures grow fastest, followed by the upper body and then by the relatively slow-growing lower body. At the same time, growth is **proximodistal** in direction, meaning that the trunk tends to advance, then the nearest parts of the

KEY POINT
Both genetic and extrinsic factors influence normal and abnormal embryonic and fetal growth.

Differentiation is the process wherein cells become specialized, forming specific tissues and organs.

Hyperplasia is an increase in the absolute number of cells.

Hypertrophy is an increase in the relative size of an individual cell.

Cephalocaudal is the direction of growth beginning at the head and extending toward the lower body.

Proximodistal is the direction of growth proceeding from the body toward the extremities.

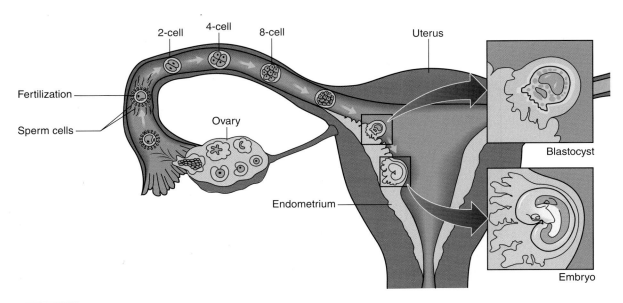

FIGURE 4.1 As the embryo moves through the oviduct, its cells divide and multiply. By the time it implants on the lining of the uterus, it is several hundred cells in size. It is embedded in nutrient cells that nourish it. Implantation in the uterus is facilitated by protuberances of sugar molecules on the surface of the blastocyst.

TABLE 4.1 Landmarks in Embryonic and Fetal Growth

Age (wk)	Length	Weight	Appearance	Internal development
3	3 mm		Head, tail folds formed	Optic vesicles, head recognizable
4	4 mm	0.4 g	Limb rudiments formed	Heartbeat begins; organs recognizable
8	3.5 cm	2 g	Eyes, ears, nose, mouth, digits formed	Sensory organs developing; some bone ossification beginning
12	11.5 cm	19 g	Sex externally recognizable; head very large for body	Brain configuration nearly complete; blood forming in bone marrow
16	19 cm	100 g	Motor activity; scalp hair present; trunk size gaining on head size	Heart muscle developed; sense organs formed
20	22 cm	300 g	Legs have grown appreciably	Myelination of spinal cord begins
24	32 cm	600 g	Respiratory-like movements begin	Cerebral cortex layers formed
28	36 cm	1.1 kg	Increasing development of fat tissue	Retina layered and light-receptive
32	41 cm	1.8 kg	Weight increasing more than length	Taste sense operative
36	46 cm	2.2 kg	Body more rounded	Ossification begins in distal femur
40	52 cm	3.2 kg	Skin smooth with a pinkish tone; at least moderate hair on head	Proximal tibia begins ossification; myelination of brain begins; pulmonary branching two-thirds complete

Adapted, by permission, from P.S. Timiras 1972.

limbs, and finally the distal parts of the limbs (figure 4.2). Body weight increases and the body tissues grow steadily, with the rate of growth increasing at about 5 months and continuing at that rapid rate until birth.

Although cells differentiate during growth to perform a specialized function, some cells have an amazing quality termed **plasticity**, which is the capability to take on a new function. If some of the cells in a system are injured, for example, the remaining cells might be stimulated to perform the role that the damaged cells would ordinarily carry out. The cells of the central nervous system have a high degree of plasticity, and their structure, chemistry, and function can be modified both prenatally and postnatally (Ratey, 2001).

Plasticity is modifiability or malleability; in regard to growth, it is the ability of tissues to subsume functions otherwise carried out by other tissues.

Fetal Nourishment

Many characteristics of the fetal environment have the potential to affect growth, either positively or negatively, and the nourishment system is the extrinsic factor that has the most influence on fetal development. The fetus is nourished by the diffusion of oxygen and nutrients between fetal blood and maternal blood in the placenta (figure 4.3). Carbon dioxide and excretory byproducts also are exchanged and carried away in the mother's blood.

The growing fetus needs energy, nutrients, and oxygen. If these are in short supply, mother and fetus compete for limited resources, possibly compromising the needs of the fetus. Obviously, then, maternal health status plays a role in prenatal development.

A woman who lives in better conditions (with an adequate, safe food supply and a protective, clean environment) and who receives early prenatal health care

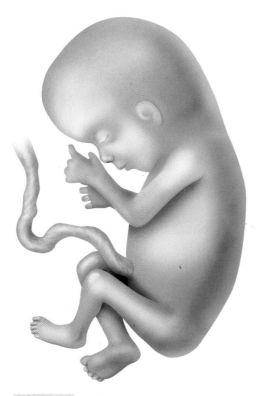

FIGURE 4.2   A fetus at 3 months.

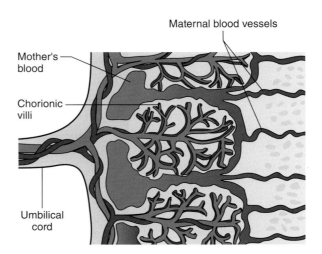

FIGURE 4.3   A diagram of the placenta showing the two circulations—that of mother and that of fetus—which come close enough to each other that substances diffuse from one to the other, though the bloodstreams never mingle.

Reprinted by permission from Rhodes 1969.

is more likely than a woman living in poorer conditions to meet the needs of the fetus. She is also more likely to be at lower risk for illnesses and infections that might compromise the health of the fetus and would result in low birth weight. Consequently, women at lower socioeconomic levels typically give birth to lighter infants than do women at higher socioeconomic levels. This is significant because low-birth-weight infants are at greater risk of disease, infection, and death in the weeks after birth than are normal-weight infants. Some of the differences in birth weight among ethnic groups can be attributed to parental height and are thus largely influenced by genetic factors (Troe et al., 2007). Further research is needed to distinguish the influences on birth weight that are primarily genetic from those that are environmental and thus might be modifiable to promote health in the early postnatal period.

 If you were a doctor, would you have to travel to a poor country with primitive living conditions to treat pregnant women with poor health status? Or would you likely see some poor women in your practice in an affluent country? What groups of pregnant women in an affluent country might be at risk of poor health?

Abnormal Prenatal Development

Abnormal growth may arise from either genetic or extrinsic factors. Genetic abnormalities are inherited and may be immediately apparent or may remain undetected until well into postnatal growth. A host of extrinsic factors can also negatively affect the fetus. Examples include drugs and chemicals in the mother's bloodstream, viruses in the mother's bloodstream, and excessive pressure applied to the mother's abdomen. Let's consider some examples of **congenital defects** in more detail.

Congenital defects are anomalies present at birth, regardless of whether their causes are genetic or extrinsic.

Genetic Causes of Abnormal Prenatal Development

An individual may inherit genetic abnormalities as dominant or recessive (including sex-linked) disorders. Dominant disorders result when one parent passes on a defective gene. Recessive disorders occur in children who inherit a defective gene from each parent.

Genetic abnormalities can also result from a new mutation—that is, the alteration or deletion of a gene during formation of the egg or sperm cell. Researchers suspect irradiation and certain hazardous environmental chemicals of causing genetic mutations, and the potential for genetic damage to sex cells increases with advancing maternal age (Nyhan, 1990). Mutations can also occur spontaneously, without a known cause.

An example of a familiar genetic abnormality is trisomy 21 or Down syndrome. When an egg or sperm cell divides, its 46 chromosomes divide in half. When the sperm cell with 23 chromosomes fertilizes an egg with 23 chromosomes, an embryo ends up with a complete set of 46. Sometimes an egg or sperm cell keeps both chromosome 21s, and every cell in the resulting embryo's body will have an extra chromosome 21. A combination of birth defects can result, including mental retardation, distinctive facial features, visual and hearing impairments, and heart defects.

New mutations and inherited disorders can both result in single or multiple malformations of an organ, limb, or body region; deformations of a body part; or disruptions in development resulting from the breakdown of normal tissue. They can affect one or more of the body systems. Many of these abnormalities ar obvious at birth, but some do not appear until later. Genetic abnormalities vary considerably in appearance and severity.

Extrinsic Causes of Abnormal Prenatal Development

Our earlier discussion of fetal nourishment reveals how dependent the fetus is on the mother for the oxygen and nutrients it needs. Unfortunately, the fetal nourishment system can also deliver harmful substances to the fetus, and various other factors can potentially affect the fetus' physical environment and thereby its growth and development.

Teratogens   In addition to oxygen and nutrients necessary for fetal life and growth, other substances—including viruses, drugs, and chemicals—can diffuse across the placenta and be harmful to the developing fetus. Sometimes even necessary vitamins, nutrients, and hormones can be harmful if their levels are too high or too low. In these cases substances can act as malformation-producing agents, or **teratogens**. The specific effect that a teratogen has on the fetus depends on when the fetus was exposed to the substance as well as the amount of the substance.

There are critical periods of particular vulnerability to change in the growth and development of tissues and organs. Exposure to a teratogen during a critical period has a more significant effect than exposure at another time. For example, the rubella virus is harmful if the embryo is exposed to it during the first 4 weeks of pregnancy. The earlier the infection, the more serious the resulting abnormalities. Very early exposure can result in miscarriage.

Some congenital defects result from the mere presence of a harmful substance in the maternal blood. Whether the fetus is exposed depends on the size of the substance. For example, small virus particles present in maternal blood can cross the placenta and harm the fetus. Drugs with molecular weights under 1,000 also cross the placenta easily, whereas those with molecular weights over 1,000 do not.

Parents can maximize fetal growth and development by avoiding substances that might be teratogenic. Mothers can maintain a diet that supplies adequate but not excessive nutrients; otherwise, the fetus might develop a specific malformation or be generally retarded in growth and small for age at birth. It is important to recognize that these conditions, including low birth weight, can affect postnatal growth and development. For example, a mother's alcohol consumption during pregnancy can result in a condition called fetal alcohol syndrome, which involves a cluster of birth defects that often include mental retardation; heart defects; facial, joint, and limb deformities; slowed growth and small brain size; short attention span; and hyperactivity. Although it is not clear when a small amount of alcohol consumption becomes an amount that affects a fetus, this birth defect is completely avoidable when a mother abstains from using alcohol.

Other Prenatal Extrinsic Factors   Malformation, retarded growth, and life-threatening conditions can also result from external factors affecting the fetus' environment. Examples include

- external or internal pressure on the infant, including pressure from another fetus in utero;
- extreme internal environmental temperature, as when the mother suffers from high fever or hypothermia;
- exposure to X rays or gamma rays;

KEY POINT
Congenital disorders arising from extrinsic factors can affect the potential for postnatal growth and development. When medical professionals and parents are aware of negative influences, they can manage these influences to minimize the risk to the fetus.

A **teratogen** is any drug or chemical agent that causes abnormal development in a fetus upon exposure.

- changes in atmospheric pressure, especially those leading to hypoxia (oxygen deficiency) in the fetus; and
- environmental pollutants.

The precise effects of these factors also depend on the fetus' stage of development. Like teratogens, external factors have the potential to affect present and future growth and development.

Prenatal Development Summary

Prenatal development is influenced by genetic and extrinsic factors. The genes direct an orderly and precise course of development, but extrinsic factors can influence the process either positively or negatively. Many of these extrinsic factors exert their influence through the fetal nourishment system. A fetus that receives appropriate levels of oxygen and nutrients has the best chance of reaching its full genetic potential, including its potential for skill performance.

Prenatal abnormalities can arise from genetic or extrinsic influence. Some abnormal conditions are a product of *both* genetic inheritance and the environment; that is, a tendency for a disease might be inherited, and subsequently the disease will appear under certain environmental conditions (Timiras, 1972). We should view physical growth and development, then, as a continuous process that begins at conception. Individuals are, in part, products of the factors that affected their prenatal growth and development. Hence, the individual structural constraints that educators and therapists consider when planning activities for individuals reflect the course of prenatal development. The process of postnatal development is the continuation of prenatal development.

Postnatal Development

Is an 11-year-old capable of long-distance runs? How about a 60-year-old? We know that no single answer applies to all 11-year-olds or all 60-year-olds because we have acknowledged the coexistence of universality and specificity in development. Educators and therapists benefit from knowing the universal pattern of postnatal growth and physiological maturation as well as the typical pattern of aging in adults. Yet we work with individuals who have their own timing and potential for growth. Therefore, we must be able to evaluate an individual's status and potential in order to help him or her set reasonable personal goals. We must be able to compare an individual with the average and adjust expectations for performance accordingly.

KEY POINT
Postnatal growth proceeds in a precise and orderly pattern, but individual variability, especially in the timing of landmark events, is increasingly obvious as individuals move through infancy, childhood, preadolescence, and adolescence.

Overall Growth

Overall body growth after birth is a continuation of prenatal growth. The growth pattern is predictable and consistent but not linear, no matter which measure of overall growth we choose to study. For example, look at the growth curves for height (figure 4.4, *a* and *b*) and weight (figure 4.5, *a* and *b*). They are characterized by rapid growth after birth, followed by gradual but steady growth during childhood, then by rapid growth during early adolescence, and finally by a leveling off. Thus, the curves are roughly S-shaped. We call this pattern of overall body growth a **sigmoid curve** after the Greek letter for S.

Although a normal growth curve is always sigmoid, the timing of a particular individual's spurts and steady growth periods is likely to vary from the average.

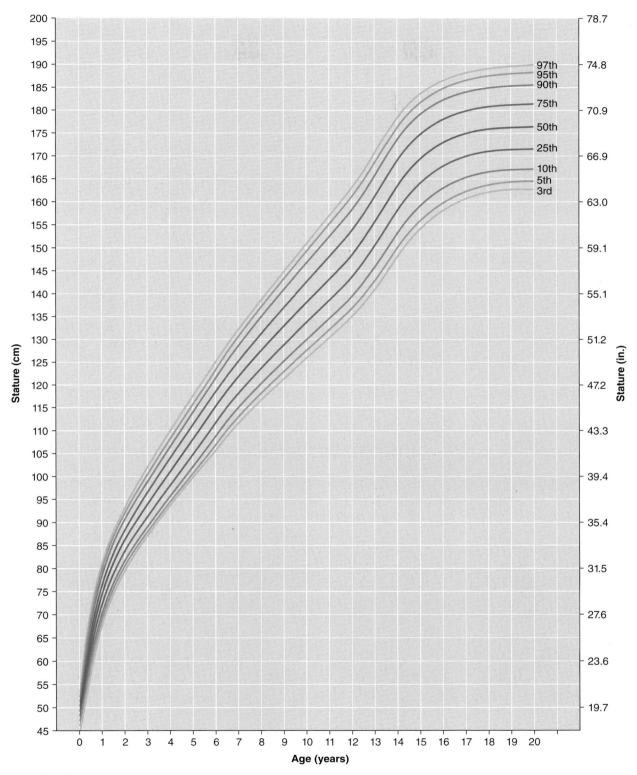

FIGURE 4.4a Stature (standing height) by age percentiles for boys. Note the sigmoid, or S-shaped, form of the curves.

Data from the National Center for Health Statistics in collaboration with the National Center for Chronic Disease Prevention and Health Promotion 2000.

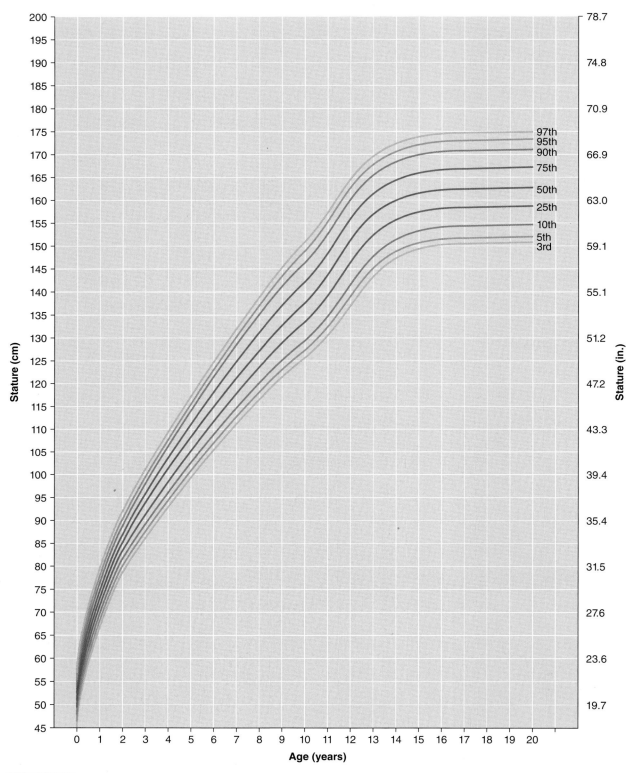

FIGURE 4.4*b* Stature by age percentiles for girls.

Data from the National Center for Health Statistics in collaboration with the National Center for Chronic Disease Prevention and Health Promotion 2000.

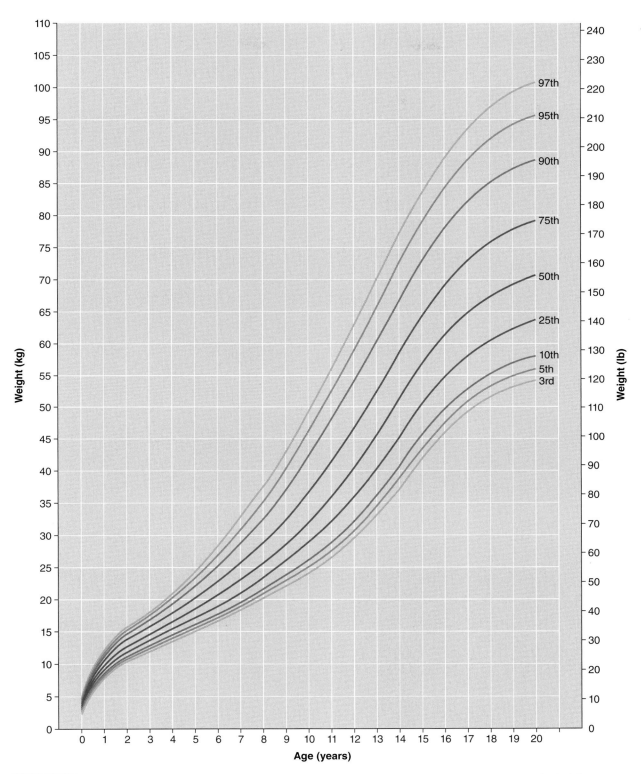

FIGURE 4.5*a*   Weight by age percentiles for boys. Note that the curves are S-shaped, though flatter than the height curves.

Data from the National Center for Health Statistics in collaboration with the National Center for Chronic Disease Prevention and Health Promotion 2000.

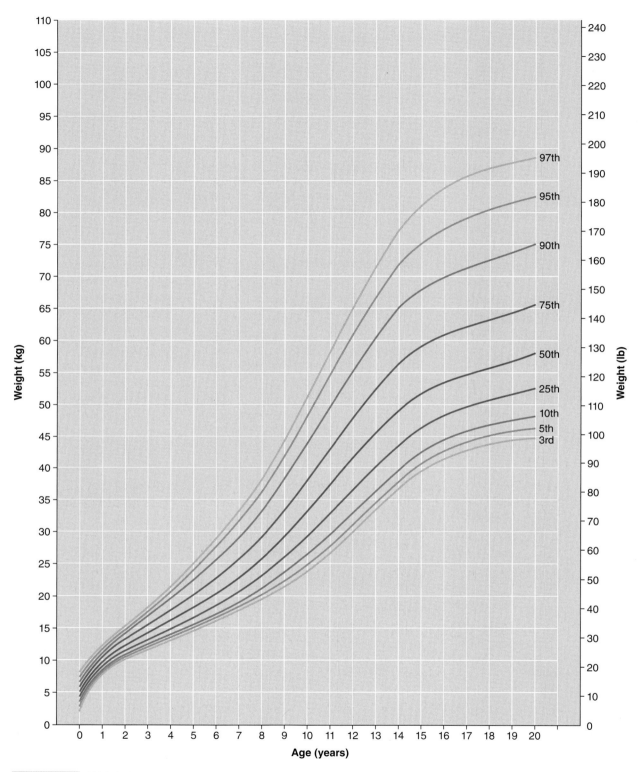

FIGURE 4.5*b* Weight by age percentiles for girls.

Data from the National Center for Health Statistics in collaboration with the National Center for Chronic Disease Prevention and Health Promotion 2000.

For example, one girl might begin her adolescent growth spurt at 8 years, whereas another might begin hers at 10. The slope of the curve can also vary from the average. One girl might grow more rapidly (i.e., have a steeper growth curve) than the other. Note that, on the growth charts, the range of variation—the gap between the 3rd and 97th percentiles—widens with age, especially for weight (Malina & Bouchard, 1991). This is another example of universality and specificity in development. The sigmoid pattern of a graph of overall growth is universal but the timing and steepness of segments of the curve are specific to the individual, and with advancing age the influence of environmental factors increases the variation among individuals.

 WEB STUDY GUIDE   **Learn to graph rate of change in height and weight in Lab Activity 4.1, Graphing a Velocity Curve, in the web study guide. Go to www.HumanKinetics.com/LifeSpanMotorDevelopment.**

Sex

Sex is a major factor in the timing as well as the extent of growth. Sex differences are minimal in early childhood, with boys being very slightly taller and heavier. Throughout childhood, though, girls tend to mature faster than boys, so that at any given age girls as a group are biologically more mature than boys. Important sex differences in growth and development are especially pronounced at adolescence. Girls begin their adolescent growth spurt when they are about 9 years old (often termed the **age at takeoff** because the rate of growth begins to increase), whereas boys begin theirs at about age 11. Note that these ages are group averages. About two-thirds of all adolescents will initiate their growth spurt during the year before or the year after these averages, meaning that approximately one-third will initiate it even earlier or later.

Age at takeoff is the age at which the rate of growth begins to increase.

Height

Height follows the sigmoid pattern of growth: a rapid increase in infancy, tapering off to steady growth in childhood, followed by another rapid increase during the adolescent growth spurt, and finally a tapering off until the end of the growth period. An individual's height can be compared with group norms, and this comparison is often made using a family of height curves plotted against age. The individual curves represent various percentiles, usually the 3rd, 5th, 10th, 25th, 50th, 75th, 90th, 95th, and 97th (as in figures 4.4, a and b). This approach allows us to approximate an individual's percentile for height at a specific age or over time as well as whether he or she maintains position in the group or changes. For example, we might find one individual who remains in the 40th percentile for most of the growth period and another who begins the adolescent growth spurt early and goes from the 60th percentile at age 8 to the 90th percentile at age 10.

Children tend to maintain their relative percentile positions in comparison with group norms after they are 2 or 3 years old; that is, a 3-year-old child in the 75th percentile for height is most likely to be around the 75th percentile throughout childhood. A large fluctuation in relative position could indicate that some extrinsic factor is influencing growth (Martorell, Malina, Castillo, Mendoza, & Pawson, 1988) and that medical examination is warranted.

In addition to the extent of growth, it is interesting to examine the rate, or velocity, of growth (i.e., when individuals are growing rapidly or slowly). By plotting the rate of growth, we can find the age at which one is growing the fastest (**peak velocity**) or the age at which one changes from slow growth to rapid growth (age at takeoff) or vice versa (see the "Assessing the Extent and Rate of Growth" sidebar).

On average, girls reach peak height velocity during the adolescent growth spurt at 11.5 to 12.0 years of age (figure 4.6). Their growth in height then tapers off at approximately age 14, and notable increases in height end around age 16. Boys reach their peak height velocity at 13.5 to 14.0 years. This velocity is somewhat faster than that of girls—approximately 9 cm per year for boys compared with 8 cm per year for girls (Beunen & Malina, 1988). Boys' growth tapers off at 17 years, and notable increases end by age 18. Note that males have about 2 more years of growth than females, amounting to 10 to 13 cm of height. This longer growth period accounts for much of the difference in average absolute height between adult men and women.

Weigh

Growth in weight also follows the sigmoid pattern: a rapid increase in infancy, a moderate increase in childhood, a spurt in early adolescence, and a steady increase that tapers off at the end of the growth period. Weight, however, is very susceptible to extrinsic factors and can reflect variations in the amount of muscle with exercise as well as variations in the amount of fat tissue with diet and exercise. Disease can also influence body weight.

Assessing the Extent and Rate of Growth

In chapter 1, we acknowledge that we often picture growth and development through graphs. This practice is common in describing physical growth. We often see measurements of height, weight, or length plotted against advancing age. These plots are called **distance curves** because they convey the extent of growth; figures 4.4 and 4.5 are examples. If we want to know the distance that growth has progressed at a certain age, we merely read the value opposite that age. For example, from a height curve we can determine how tall an individual was at any age (if using the plot of an individual person) or what the average height for a group was at any age (if using the plot of a group average).

If the line plotted is going up with age, we know that growth is taking place, provided that the axes of the graph are arranged from low (at the origin) to high. We expect growth measurements to increase with age during the growth period. In adulthood, measurements might go up or down as extrinsic factors influence the measurement. Body weight is a good example. If the slope of a distance curve is gradual, the change is moderate for that age period. If the slope is steep, the change is rapid for that age period. Thus, the slope of a distance curve can indicate changes in the *rate* of growth.

The rate of growth can be illustrated more dramatically on graphs of growth speed that are called **velocity curves**. These curves are plotted by first selecting small age spans, such as the time between the 8th and 9th birthdays, the 9th and 10th birthdays, and the 11th and 12th birthdays. Then, for each of these short spans, we find the change in growth as indicated by the distance curve. For example, we might check a distance curve for height and see that the increase in height between the 8th and 9th birthdays is 5 cm. We would then plot a point at 5 cm per year and at 8.5 years

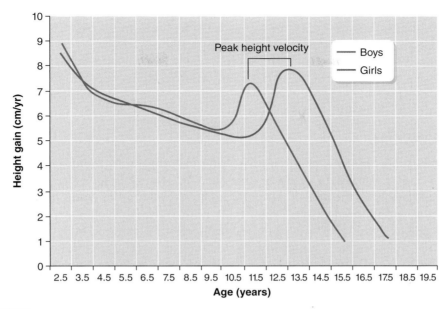

FIGURE 4.6 Velocity curves plotted from figure 4.4*a* and *b*, ages 2 to 18 years. After age 2, the rate of growth slows until the adolescent growth spurt. Note the ages at peak height velocity for boys and girls.

(representing the midpoint of the age span during which the growth was 5 cm). By doing this for a number of age spans and connecting our points with a smooth curve, we produce a velocity curve.

Velocity curves look very different from distance curves. They often have sections where the graphed line is decreasing, indicating that the rate of growth is slowing or decelerating. They also have peaks (i.e., points at which the rate of growth changes from faster to slower). Humans have a peak velocity in their overall growth measurements during early adolescence (termed peak height velocity, peak weight velocity, and so on). This is the age at which growth is the fastest for this portion of the life span. During the downslope of the peak, growth slows, although it may still be quite rapid. For example, a typical peak height velocity for girls is 8 cm per year (figure 4.6), and it typically occurs around 12 years of age. Immediately before this age, the velocity of growth in height increases from 5 to 6 to 7 to 8 cm per year. After this age, growth slows from 8 to 7 to 6 cm per year, and so on. Throughout the age span of 10.5 to 13 years, a fairly rapid increase in height (6–8 cm per year) occurs.

In reading a velocity curve, we must keep in mind that we are reading a rate of growth for a short age span, not the extent of growth. We can say how tall an individual girl is from her distance curve for height but not from her velocity curve. On the other hand, her velocity curve enables us to easily determine the age at which she was growing the fastest.

Readers who have studied calculus will recognize that a velocity curve is the first derivative of a distance curve. The second derivative would provide an acceleration curve, indicating the ages at which growth is accelerating or decelerating.

Peak weight velocity during the adolescent growth spurt follows peak height velocity in adolescents by 2.5 to 5.0 months in boys and 3.5 to 10.5 months in girls. The growth of various segment lengths and breadths can reach peak velocity before or after the individual reaches peak height velocity, but all reach their peak before or at peak weight velocity (Beunen, Malina, Renson, & Van Gerven, 1988). This is the factual basis for the commonly observed pattern of individuals first growing "up," then filling "out."

Relative Growth

Although the body as a whole consistently follows the sigmoid growth pattern, specific body parts, tissues, and organs have differential rates of growth. In other words, each part of the growing individual has its own precise and orderly growth rate. These differential growth rates can result in notable changes in the body's appearance as a whole. Observe how the proportions illustrated in figure 4.7 change dramatically throughout life. Body proportions at birth reflect the cephalocaudal (head to toe) and proximodistal (near to far) directions of prenatal growth. Therefore, a newborn's form is quite different from that of an adult. The head accounts for one-fourth of the total height at birth but only one-eighth of adult height. The legs make up about three-eighths of height at birth but almost half of adult height.

For a newborn to achieve adult proportions, some body parts must grow faster than others during postnatal growth. For example, the legs grow faster than the trunk and head in infancy and childhood, and they undergo a growth spurt early in adolescence. Growth in height results mostly from an increase in trunk length during late adolescence and early adulthood. Boys and girls have similar proportions in childhood, but by the time they are adults, relative growth of some body areas brings about noticeable differences between the sexes. In girls, shoulder and hip breadth increase at about the same rate, so their shoulder-to-hip ratio is fairly stable during growth. Boys undergo a substantial increase in shoulder breadth

KEY POINT
Late maturers have a longer growth period than early maturers and consequently tend to be taller.

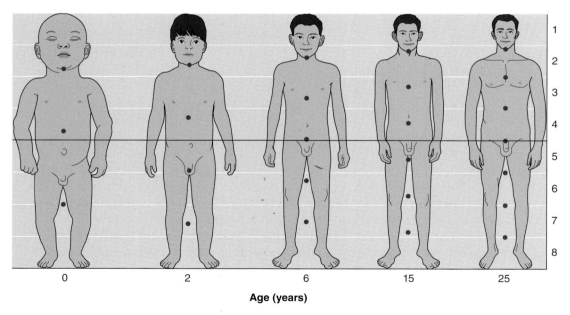

FIGURE 4.7 Postnatal changes in body proportion shown by placing individuals throughout the growth period on the same scale.

Adapted by permission from Timiras 1972.

during their growth spurt, so their ratio changes as they move into adolescence and acquire the typical broad-shouldered shape of adult men.

Teachers, personal trainers, physical therapists, doctors, researchers, and many other professionals take anthropometric measurements. These measurements must be taken with great precision if they are to be used for comparisons with norms or measurements taken at a later date.

Body form might have implications for skill performance in early childhood. For example, even if 5-month-old infants were neurologically ready to coordinate and control the walking pattern, it is unlikely that they could balance their top-heavy bodies on such thin, short legs and small feet. Varying limb lengths and weights can affect balance, momentum, and potential speed in various movements. Recalling Newell's model, we realize that changing individual structural constraints related to body form and proportion could certainly interact with task and environment to produce different movements.

Specific tissues and organs also grow differentially. Although their prenatal growth tends to follow the increase in body weight, the postnatal growth of some tissues and systems follows unique patterns. The brain, for example, achieves more than 80% of its adult weight by the time the individual reaches age 4. Because various tissues of the body grow differentially after birth, our knowledge of individual structural constraints is made more complete by study of the individual body systems. Growth, development, and aging of each of the relevant body systems are discussed in chapter 5.

Physiological Maturation

Tissues of the growing body can advance without necessarily increasing in size. The biochemical composition of cells, organs, and systems can advance qualitatively in what is termed **physiological maturation**. Chronological age, growth in body size, and physiological maturation are related to one another in that as children and youths get older they tend to grow in size and to mature. These dimensions can, however, proceed with their own timing. For example, two children of the same age can be dramatically different in maturation status, with one being an early maturer and the other being a late maturer. Or, two children of the same size can be different ages, and they could be at similar levels of maturation or very different levels of maturation. Thus, it is difficult to infer maturity from age alone, from size alone, or even from age and size considered together. An individual child can appear to be small and slight of build but may actually be relatively mature for his or her chronological age.

Physiological maturation is the developmental process leading to a state of full function.

One indication of maturation status is the appearance of the **secondary sex characteristics** during the adolescent growth spurt. The secondary sex characteristics appear at a younger age in girls and boys who are early maturers and at an older age in those who are late maturers. As noted previously, girls as a group mature at a faster rate than boys; they enter their adolescent growth spurt sooner and their secondary sex characteristics appear sooner. Their breasts enlarge; pubic hair appears; and **menarche**, the first menstrual cycle, occurs. Regardless of the exact chronological age at which a girl begins her growth spurt, menarche typically follows the peak height velocity by 11 to 12 months (figure 4.8, a–c). The average age of menarche therefore is 12.5 to 13.0 years. In boys, the testes and scrotum grow in size and pubic hair appears. Boys have no landmark comparable with girls' menarche for puberty; the production of viable sperm is a gradual process.

Secondary sex characteristics are aspects of form or structure appropriate to males or females, often used to assess physiological maturity in adolescents.

Imagine you are a physical education teacher at an elementary school. What would be wrong with expecting all of the tall children in your class to be the most skilled because you assume they are the most mature? Would you be correct in assuming that the most coordinated children in your fifth-grade class are likely to be those you will see playing on their high school varsity team in 6 years?

Maturation status is relevant as a structural constraint influencing movement. Individuals who are more mature are likely to be stronger and more coordinated than those who are less mature, even at the same chronological age. Parents, educators, and therapists must consider maturation status when designing activities and therapies for youths and when setting performance goals. It is tempting to infer movement performance potential from size alone or age alone, but maturation status is a powerful predictor of performance potential.

KEY POINT
Postnatal growth patterns differ among body parts and body systems.

Measuring Height, Lengths, and Breadths

Frequent measurement of children's growth and comparisons of the values with averages at a given age can help detect abnormal growth. Medical or environmental factors influencing abnormal growth can then be identified and moderated or corrected. Of course, such growth measurements reflect the individual's genetic potential for height and body build (which often correspond to the parents' height and build) as well as the individual's personal growth timing. Therefore, in screening growth measurements, children and teens who measure above the 90th or below the 10th percentile for their age—especially those whose parents are not exceptionally tall or short, respectively—should be referred to medical personnel for examination (Lowrey, 1986).

For growth screenings to be meaningful, measurements must be done accurately using the same measurement techniques used to establish group norms or averages. Descriptions of standard techniques are widely available (Lohman, Roche, & Martorell, 1988, is one example of a standardization manual), and you should refer to these standards if you decide to conduct a screening program. A detailed description of standard techniques is beyond the scope of this text, but let's briefly consider the various measurements used to assess physical growth and body size.

Anthropometry is the science of the measurement of the human physical form.

The measurements used to assess growth and size are known as **anthropometric** measures, and they include height, weight, segment length, body breadth, and circumference. The measurements are sometimes used in ratios to illustrate a particular aspect of size. Standing height is the most common growth measure, but sitting height is an interesting measurement to observe during the growth period. Standing height minus sitting height yields a functional measure of leg length. Infants have relatively long trunks and short legs, so the proportion of standing height to leg length changes over the growth period to reach the typical adult proportion.

Various other segment lengths, such as those of the upper arm and the thigh, can also be measured, as can the breadth of the body at specified locations. Typically, length and breadth measurements are taken where skeletal landmarks can be located so that the measurement reflects skeletal structure and not soft tissues such as fat and muscle that can change with diet and exercise. The most common

Extrinsic Influences on Postnatal Growth

As noted earlier, extrinsic factors can have a great influence on prenatal growth even in the relatively protective environment of the womb. It is no surprise, then, that extrinsic factors have an increased influence on growth and development after birth. Genetics control the timing and rate of an individual's growth and maturation, but extrinsic factors—especially those influencing body metabolism—can have a great effect. During periods of rapid growth, such as just after birth and in early adolescence, growth is particularly sensitive to alteration by environmental factors.

Early diet is a particularly important extrinsic influence. Duijts, Jaddoe, Hofman, and Moll (2010) observed that generation R infants who were breastfed exclusively until 6 months of age had a lower risk of infection than those infants who were exclusively breastfed until 4 months of age and only partially thereafter.

KEY POINT
Extrinsic factors play a larger role as individuals proceed through adulthood, leading to great variability among individuals in older adulthood.

breadth measures are taken at the shoulders and hips, and shoulder width is often divided by hip width to form a ratio. This shoulder-to-hip ratio is also interesting to observe over the growth period because it undergoes dramatic change in boys during the adolescent growth spurt as they reach the typical male body build of broad shoulders and narrow hips.

Circumference measurements can be taken at numerous locations and often represent soft tissue—fat and muscle—as well as bone structure. We expect circumference measurements to increase with growth in size, but a circumference measurement by itself cannot provide information about the amount of fat tissue versus lean body tissue. Pediatricians closely monitor head circumference in infants and toddlers. An abnormally large measurement is associated with hydrocephalus (excess cerebrospinal fluid that could cause brain damage).

Body weight is another common measure of growth and body size. Growth in weight reflects the increase in lean body tissues, which is genetically driven, and the increase in adipose, or fat, tissues, which can be readily influenced by extrinsic factors such as exercise and nutrition. Body weight can be apportioned into lean body mass and fat tissue mass by one of several means described later in this text. The resulting measurement typically is expressed as "percent fat."

In another interesting ratio, body weight (in kilograms) is divided by the square of standing height (in meters). This ratio is called the body mass index (BMI), and it is useful for measuring obesity, especially in adults. The normal range for BMI is 18.5 to 24.9; obesity is defined as a BMI over 30.0.

Many methods exist for measuring physical growth and body size, and each measurement yields a specific type of information. Particularly in combination, these measurements can provide a great deal of information about the course of growth in size. This information can be used by medical professionals to screen for and possibly correct troubling conditions, thereby enabling individuals to reach their growth potential or to maintain good health after the growth period. Such information can also be used to help children and youths understand the changes that their bodies undergo, especially during the adolescent growth spurt.

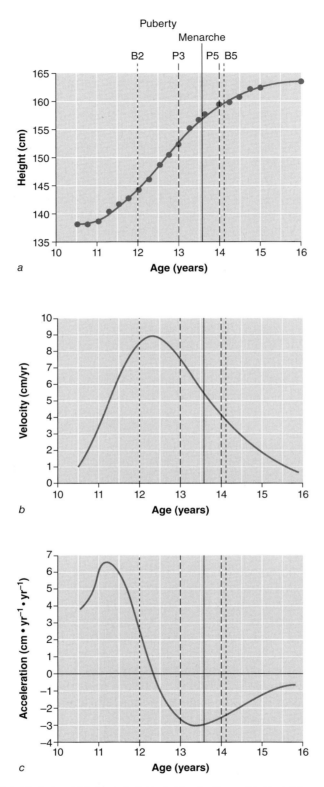

FIGURE 4.8 *(a)* Height attained (distance), *(b)* height velocity, and *(c)* height acceleration curves for a girl at adolescence. Note that menarche comes after peak height velocity. B2 marks the beginning of breast development and B5 marks adult form. P3 marks the intermediate stage of pubic hair development and P5 marks adult form.

Reprinted by permission from Maclaren 1967.

The phenomenon of **catch-up growth** illustrates the susceptibility of overall body growth to extrinsic influence. A child might experience catch-up growth after suffering a period of severe malnutrition or a bout with a severe disorder such as chronic renal failure (figure 4.9). During such a period, body growth is retarded. After the diet is improved or the child recovers from the disorder (i.e., after a positive environment for growth is restored), growth rate increases until the child approaches or catches up to what otherwise would have been the extent of growth during that period (Prader, Tanner, & von Harnack, 1963). Whether the child recovers some or all of the growth depends on the timing, duration, and severity of the negative environmental condition.

One of the generation R studies (Ay et al., 2008) noted that children with slower prenatal growth in weight, especially during the third trimester, demonstrated catch-up growth in the early months after birth. Children who experienced this period of catch-up growth tended to have a higher percentage of fat weight at 6 months of age than did children who did not experience a period of catch-up growth. The generation R project will continue to follow these children to determine whether this early period of catch-up growth might predispose individuals to higher proportions of fat weight later in life.

Catch-up growth
is relatively rapid physical growth of the body to recover some or all potential growth lost during a period of negative extrinsic influence. It occurs once the negative influence is removed.

 WEB STUDY GUIDE   Collect anthropometric measures to assess children's growth in Lab Activity 4.2, Taking Growth Measures, in the web study guide. Go to www.HumanKinetics.com/LifeSpanMotorDevelopment.

 Imagine you are a parent or, if you are in fact one, put on your "parenting cap." Early maturers are likely to demonstrate better athletic performance than their late-maturing counterparts. If you overlook this and expect your son or daughter who is an early maturer to maintain his or her performance edge over others into adulthood, what could be the repercussions when the late maturers catch up? If you have a late-maturing child, what could be the repercussions of an early assumption that the child has no future as an athlete?

Adulthood and Aging

Growth ends for humans in the late teens or early 20s, but the status and size of the body attained during the growth years are not necessarily maintained in adulthood. Some measures of body size can change in adulthood. These changes reflect the aging of tissues and, probably to a greater extent, the influence of extrinsic factors. For example, a lack of weight-bearing exercise and calcium in the diet could contribute to osteoporosis and a resulting decrease in height. The range of extrinsic factors that might or might not influence an individual, as well as the timing of their influence, are extremely variable over the life span. Naturally, then, we expect to see more and more individual variability in changes of body size as we move through the life span.

Men and women grow slightly in height into their 20s. Trunk length may even increase very slightly into the mid-40s. Aside from these very small increases, height is stable through adulthood. It is common, however, for an individual's stature to decrease slightly over the adult years (figure 4.10). Some of this decrease results from the compression and flattening of the body's connective tissues, especially the cartilage pads between the vertebrae in the spinal column. The result is a compression of the spinal column and a decrease in trunk length. The bones also lose density as a result of progressive modifications in the protein

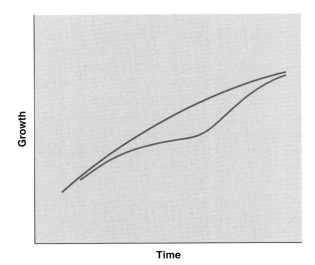

FIGURE 4.9   In this illustration of hypothetical catch-up growth, the blue line represents the course of normal growth as it might have been. The purple line represents actual growth as influenced by a negative extrinsic factor. As the factor exerts its influence, growth slows; however, with removal of the negative factor, growth speeds up in order to catch up to the level that otherwise would have been reached. How close actual growth comes to catching the line representing normal growth depends on the time of occurrence and the length of time the factor exerts its influence, as well as its severity.

matrix of the skeleton (Timiras, 1972). This breakdown is more severe in persons with osteoporosis and can result in the collapse of one or more vertebrae; if this occurs, the loss of stature is pronounced (figure 4.11). Heightened awareness in recent years of the devastating effects of osteoporosis on well-being has led to more

Assessment of Physiological Maturation

Maturation can be assessed directly or indirectly. A direct measurement would be ideal, but direct measures of maturation are not always easy to obtain or applicable to the entire growth period. For example, dental eruption (the appearance of new teeth) indicates maturation status but is restricted to two age spans: between approximately 6 months and 3 years, when the deciduous (baby) teeth first appear, and between approximately 6 and 13 years, when the permanent teeth appear. The appearances of baby and permanent teeth follow a typical order. For early maturers, teeth appear at a younger age than for late maturers.

The appearance of the secondary sex characteristics can also be used to assess maturation. Tanner (Marshall & Tanner, 1969, 1970; Tanner, 1975) devised a system of assessment that separately places boys and girls into one of five stages based on breast, pubic hair, and genitalia development. Stage 1 is the immature, prepubertal state and stage 5 is the fully sexually mature state. The average individual moves through these stages in approximately 4 years, so even with several years of variation in the timing of maturation, this assessment can be used for only about 6 years of the growth period. In addition, there are many individual exceptions to the course of progression. Ratings for axillary hair, voice change, and facial hair are not precise enough for assessing maturation, although these are obvious characteristics of ongoing maturation.

interest in its prevention and treatment, which could at some point lead to less pronounced loss of height in older adulthood.

 Imagine you are a doctor. As your patients enter their 50s, what might you do to decrease the likelihood that they will one day suffer a hip fracture due in part to bones that have lost density?

Adults typically start gaining excess fat weight in their early 20s (figure 4.12). This increase is related to changes in lifestyle. Young adults who begin careers and families commonly take less time to exercise and prepare healthy meals. In contrast, adults who exercise regularly and eat wisely often maintain their weight or even gain muscle and lose fat. Older adults sometimes lose weight, probably as a result of inactivity and a consequent loss of muscle tissue. Loss of appetite accompanying lifestyle changes can also be a factor. Again, active older adults are not as likely to lose muscle weight.

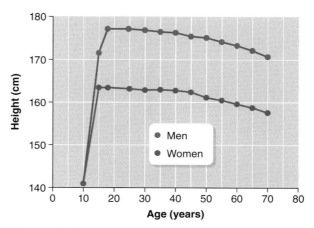

FIGURE 4.10 Body height in adulthood.

Reprinted by permission from Spirduso 1995.

A relatively precise assessment of maturation can be obtained from skeletal maturation. By comparing an X ray of skeletal maturation with a set of standards, developmentalists can assign individuals a skeletal age. In early maturers skeletal age is older than chronological age, and in late maturers skeletal age is younger than chronological age. This maturation assessment is described in more detail in chapter 5.

Given the disadvantages of and difficulty obtaining direct assessments of maturation, many educators and therapists infer maturation status by comparing a set of growth measurements with group norms. That is, if a girl is in the 75th percentile for height, the 70th percentile for weight, the 80th percentile for shoulder breadth, and so on, we could infer that she is an early maturer. Of course, we could be fooled if her genetic potential is to be a large individual. She might be average in maturation status but larger than average for her age because she has inherited the genetic potential to be large. We must always keep in mind the limitations of inferring maturation from growth measurements, yet we still may find it useful to make an inference when considering the movement performance potential of an individual child or youth.

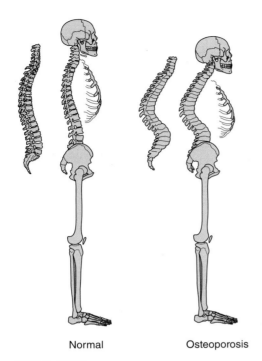

Normal　　　　Osteoporosis

FIGURE 4.11 Loss of height in those with osteoporosis can be pronounced. Compression fractures of the vertebrae lead to kyphosis ("dowager's hump") and pressure on the viscera, causing abdominal distension.

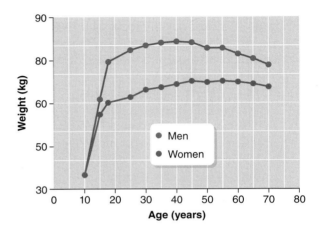

FIGURE 4.12 Body weight in adulthood.

Reprinted by permission from Spirduso 1995; adapted by permission from Frisancho 1990.

Summary and Synthesis

Knowledge of the process of overall postnatal growth provides parents, educators, and therapists with the information they need to see how changing structural constraints affect the movement that arises from individual, task, and environmental constraints. Whole-body growth proceeds in a characteristic pattern known as the sigmoid pattern, but the rate of maturation varies between the sexes and among individuals. Knowing the normal process and the normal variability among individuals helps professionals detect abnormal or retarded growth in individuals.

As individuals move through their growing years and then through their adult years, extrinsic factors contribute more and more to the variability we see among individuals. Because extrinsic factors can usually be manipulated (i.e., accentuated, minimized, or removed), everyone has an interest in knowing what factors have an effect and how they act on individuals.

The individual structural constraints that affect movement often do so at a system level rather than at a whole-body level. For example, muscle growth influences available strength for executing skills. Our understanding of the role of changing structural constraints requires a look at the development of those body systems involved in movement over the life span. This is our task in the next chapter.

Reinforcing What You Have Learned About Constraints

TAKE A SECOND LOOK

Think about that fifth-grade volleyball team mentioned at the beginning of the chapter. The two young but tall players might be early maturers. They might be the stars of the team at this age, but some of the smaller players might pass them in height in a few years or improve their skill level more. It is smart for teachers, coaches, and parents to patiently encourage all children to practice their skills and enjoy activities. It is very difficult to predict who might later pursue participation at an elite level or what activities individuals later find fun and rewarding, especially based on size or maturity at a young age.

TEST YOUR KNOWLEDGE

1. Discuss the differences between measurements of growth and direct measurements of maturation. What does each measure? What are some examples of each?

2. What is the difference between a distance curve and a velocity curve? What does each type of curve tell you about growth? Why are peaks in velocity curves of interest?

3. What areas of a fetus' body advance first? In what directions does growth proceed?

4. Describe how teratogens reach a fetus. What are some factors that determine how a teratogen affects a fetus?

5. Describe sex differences in the course of overall growth from infancy to adulthood. Include the average ages for entering the adolescent growth spurt, peak height velocity, puberty, and the tapering off of growth in height.

6. What body measurements can change in older adulthood? How do they change?

7. What are some environmental factors that could affect middle-aged and older adults and reduce their health or wellness? How? Is it possible to alter these factors? Which ones?

LEARNING EXERCISE 4.1

Secular Trends

A secular trend is a change in a landmark of development over successive generations, usually due to the influence of extrinsic factors. Some researchers have hypothesized current secular trends toward earlier maturity, taller standing height, and greater body weight. Conduct an Internet search to locate information on these possible secular trends. Classify your information as (a) objective research conducted on a large number of participants, (b) anecdotal information about a single case, (c) an author's hypothesis, or (d) opinion. Considering the information altogether, do you find credible evidence that a secular trend exists for any of these three landmarks of development? Support your conclusion with examples.

5

Development and Aging of Body Systems

The Systems as Individual Constraints

 CHAPTER OBJECTIVES

This chapter

- identifies developmental changes in the skeletal, muscular, adipose, endocrine, and nervous systems over the life span;
- notes the interaction of the systems during development and aging;
- discusses the periods when rapid change in the systems makes them particularly sensitive to external influences; and
- identifies a trend of increasing influence of external factors and decreasing influence of genetic factors as individuals proceed through the life span.

Early Attention to Development of the Body's Systems

Someone recently told me of a young woman who was 5 months pregnant but who had not yet seen a doctor. This young woman was from a middle-class household and could afford good medical care. Everyone who heard this account found it hard to believe. The emphasis we place today on good prenatal care reflects our knowledge of what is at stake—not just the overall body growth described in the previous chapter, but also the healthy growth and development of each of the body's systems. We know that the body's systems, just like the body as a whole, are not completely protected in the womb from extrinsic factors. One of the systems most vulnerable to extrinsic factors, such as a mother's nutrition, is the nervous system, and because the body's systems interact, any threat to such an important system has an effect on every system.

Our discussion in chapter 4 of the physical growth, maturation, and aging of the body demonstrates that body size and maturity can be a structural constraint. Thinking about the model of constraints and height, for example, we can see that the movement of dunking a basketball is indeed the interaction of the task (dunking), the environment (the basket height as well as the size and weight of the ball), and the individual structural constraint of height. For individuals of differing heights, dunking success can vary. Yet, as we think about this task, it quickly becomes clear that we must think beyond the body as a whole. We must also consider some of the body's specific systems. In considering how high one might jump, body height is a factor and a product of the body's skeletal system. We should also consider the muscular system, because someone with stronger muscles likely can jump higher than an individual with weaker muscles. The amount of adipose tissue influences body weight and thus how easily one can jump up. Finally, of course, the nervous system must coordinate the muscles to produce the jumping movement. So, we often need to consider one or more body systems, or their interactions, as individual structural constraints to movement.

To understand the role of body systems as structural constraints to movement, we must know how the body systems normally develop, what can influence this development and when, and what effect all of this has on movement. Our discussion of these systems' effects on movement continues throughout this text as we consider how they act as constraints to various aspects of movement.

Development of the Skeletal System

The skeletal system defines an individual's structure. It is not, however, a hard and static structure; it is living tissue. It undergoes considerable change over the life span and reflects the influence of both genetic and external factors.

Early Development of the Skeletal System

Early in embryonic life, the skeletal system exists as a "cartilage model" of the bones. Sites gradually appear in the cartilage model where bone is deposited; these are called ossification centers. About 400 appear by birth and another 400 appear after birth. There are two types of ossification centers. **Primary ossification centers** appear in the midportions of the long bones, such as the humerus (upper arm) and femur (thigh), and begin to form bone cells starting at the fetal age of 2 months (figure 5.1). The bone shafts ossify outward in both directions from these primary centers until, by birth, the entire shafts are ossified.

Postnatal bone growth in length occurs at **secondary ossification centers** at the end of the bone shaft. A secondary center can also be called the **epiphyseal plate**, growth plate, or **pressure epiphysis** (figure 5.2). The epiphyseal plate has many cellular layers (figure 5.3) where cartilage cells form, grow, align, and finally erode to leave new bone in place. Bone is thus laid down at the epiphyseal plates to increase the length of the bone. The process of laying down new bone depends on an adequate blood supply. Any injury that disturbs this blood supply threatens the bone's normal growth in length. In contrast to the long bones, small round bones such as those in the wrist and ankle simply ossify from the center outward.

Growth at the ossification centers ceases at different times in different bones. At the epiphyseal plates, the cartilage zone eventually disappears and the shaft, or diaphysis, of the bone fuses with the epiphysis. Once the epiphyseal plates of a long bone fuse, the length of the bone is fixed. Almost all epiphyseal plates are closed by age 18 or 19.

Recall that girls as a group mature faster than boys. It is no surprise, then, that the various ossification centers appear at younger chronological ages in girls than in boys. Likewise, the epiphyseal plates close at younger chronological ages in girls than in boys. For example, on average, the epiphysis at the head of the

The **primary ossification centers** are areas in the midportion of the shafts of long bones where bone cells are formed so that the cartilage-model bones of the fetal skeleton begin ossifying, from the center outward, to form bone shafts.

The **secondary ossification centers**, or **epiphyseal plates**, are the areas near the ends of long bones where new bone cells are formed and deposited so that the bones grow in length. Active secondary ossification centers are indicated on X rays by a line (an area not opaque) that is a layer of cartilage cells. Such an area is also called a **pressure epiphysis**, especially if it is at the end of a weight-bearing bone.

FIGURE 5.1 A human fetal skeleton at about 18 weeks. Dark areas indicate the ossified portions of the developing skeleton. Spaces between dark areas are occupied by cartilage models.

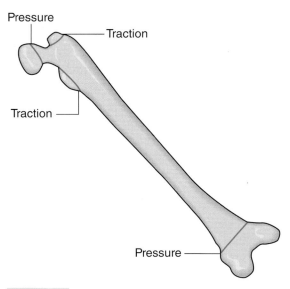

FIGURE 5.2 Pressure epiphyses are located at the ends of long bones, such as the femur (thigh bone) pictured here. Epiphyses also occur at muscle tendon attachment sites, called traction epiphyses.

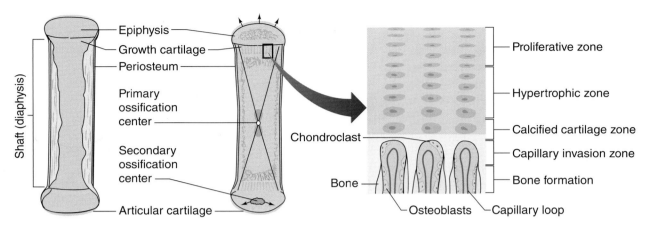

FIGURE 5.3   Development of a long bone in childhood. The epiphyseal growth plate, between the epiphysis and shaft, is enlarged on the right to show the zones in which new cells ossify.

humerus closes in girls at 15.5 years but in boys at 18.1 years (Hansman, 1962). Individuals, of course, have their own unique timing, and a group of children at the same chronological age could easily vary in skeletal age by 3 years or more, demonstrating how variable maturity is in comparison with chronological age during the growth period.

While the long bones are growing in length they also increase in girth, a process called **appositional bone growth**. Girth is increased by the addition of new tissue layers under the periosteum, a very thin outer covering of the bone, much like a tree adds to its girth under its bark.

There are also epiphyses at the sites where the muscles' tendons attach to bones. They are called traction epiphyses. You might have heard of a familiar condition that occurs during the growth period in some youths—Osgood-Schlatter disease. This is an irritation of the traction epiphysis where the patellar tendon attaches to the shin bone below the knee. Pediatricians usually have youths with this condition refrain for a time from vigorous (in particular, weight-bearing and jumping) activities to prevent further irritation of the site. Overuse injuries to traction epiphyses during the growth period can threaten the pain-free movement at a joint in later life. For example, a traction epiphysis near the elbow can be injured by repeatedly and forcefully pronating the forearm, as in throwing.

Ay et al. (2011) found that infants in the generation R study with low birth weight as well as those in the lowest weight groups at age 6 months tended to have a low bone mineral density measure at age 6 months. A positive relationship existed between postnatal growth in weight and bone mineral density as well as bone mineral content. Even infants showing catch-up growth in weight during the first 6 weeks after birth were less likely to have low bone mineral density. As the generation R study continues, it will be interesting to observe the relationship between early levels of bone mineral density and content and later levels so that we might learn whether adults are at risk of bone fractures based on their early growth patterns.

Appositional bone growth involves addition of new layers on previously formed layers so that a bone grows in girth.

KEY POINT
Because linear growth of the body is almost completely the result of skeletal growth, measures of height reflect the increase of bone length.

 WEB STUDY GUIDE   Identify differences in skeletal development in Lab Activity 5.1, Estimating Skeletal Age, in the web study guide. Go to www. HumanKinetics.com/LifeSpanMotorDevelopment.

Imagine you are the parent of a young boy who is the pitcher on his youth baseball team. He already practices once a week and plays a weekly game. The coach wants him to join a second baseball team so that he can get more pitching experience. Would you consent to this? Why or why not?

The Skeletal System in Adulthood and Older Adulthood

The skeletal structure itself changes little in young adulthood, but bone undergoes remodeling throughout the life span. Old bone is replaced by new bone. In youth, new bone is formed faster than older bone is resorbed, allowing for growth. In adulthood, though, bone formation begins to slow and eventually cannot keep pace with resorption. The result is a loss of bone tissue, starting as early as the mid-20s and averaging about 1% of bone mass per year (Smith, Sempos, & Purvis, 1981).

Bone composition also changes over the life span. Children have essentially equal amounts of inorganic and organic components in their bone tissue, but older adults have seven times more inorganic material, making the bone more brittle and subject to microfracture (Åstrand & Rodahl, 1986; Exton-Smith, 1985).

Bone loss with aging occurs in both men and women and is related to changes in certain hormone levels, dietary deficiencies, and decreased exercise. In postmenopausal women, decreased levels of estrogen are implicated in more significant losses of bone mass because estrogen hormones stimulate osteoblastic (bone-forming) activity. Prolonged deficiency of calcium in the diet is another major factor in bone loss, as is shortage of vitamins and minerals. Cumming (1990) demonstrated the importance of dietary calcium by finding that women in early menopause who took a calcium supplement lost less than half the bone mass of women who took no supplement. Exercise probably has an effect on the maintenance of bone by increasing bone formation, whereas calcium and estrogen supplementation lower bone resorption (Franck, Beuker, & Gurk, 1991; Heaney, 1986). When a person engages in physical activity, the mechanical forces applied to the bones help maintain bone thickness and density. In fact, significant increases in bone mass are seen when older adults initiate exercise programs (Dalsky, 1989; Smith, 1982).

Many older adults suffer from a major bone mineral disorder, osteoporosis, which is characterized by a bone mineral density significantly below the average for young adults and, consequently, by a loss of bone strength. The bone becomes abnormally porous through the enlargement of the canals or the formation of spaces in the bone. This condition greatly increases the risk of fractures, especially at the hip, and adds to the difficulty of fracture repair (Timiras, 1972). Osteoporosis can also lead to microfractures of the vertebrae in the spine. Vertebrae eventually may even collapse, resulting in a dramatic change of skeletal structure (refer to figure 4.11) in which the rib cage collapses forward, with the lower edge resting on the pelvis, so that the posture becomes stooped and standing height is notably reduced. The incidence of osteoporosis is higher in older adult women than in men.

It is likely that extrinsic factors, including hormone level, diet, and exercise, work in combination to influence the extent of bone loss and that we do not fully understand how these factors interact. However, it is clear that we can implement certain strategies to minimize the loss of bone tissue in adulthood. Women, for example, can maintain adequate calcium intake during adulthood so that they enter menopause with the highest bone mineral density possible. Widespread attention to the factors that can be manipulated and to early detection and treatment of

The growth status of the bones can be used to assess maturation by comparing an individual's state of development with those depicted in an atlas or standard—that is, a publication picturing skeletal development at many levels, each of which is assigned a skeletal age. The most common bones used for this purpose are the hand and wrist bones (figure 5.4). Thus, from an X ray of a person's hand and wrist, we could determine a skeletal age by finding the picture in the atlas closest to the individual's X ray. For example, a boy might have a skeletal age of 8.5 years because the extent of ossification in his hand and wrist X ray is most similar to that in the standard for 8.5 years. If his chronological age is under 8.5, we would know that he is an early maturer; if it is over 8.5, we

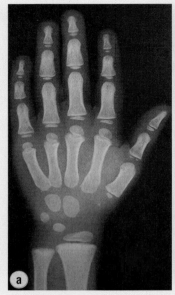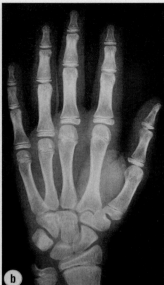

FIGURE 5.4 Hand and wrist X rays are often used to assess skeletal age. The numerous hand and wrist bones provide multiple sites for comparison of a child's X ray with the numerous standard X rays found in an assessment atlas. Here are two X rays from an atlas: *(a)* the standard for boys 48 months old and girls 37 months old, and *(b)* the standard for boys 156 months old and girls 128 months old. Note in the latter image how much more ossification (hardening) has occurred in the small wrist bones and the larger ossified area at the epiphyseal plates of the hand bones and the forearm bones.

Reprinted by permission from Pyle 1971.

would know that he is a late maturer. Skeletal age can easily be a year ahead of or behind chronological age, emphasizing how much variation is possible in maturation status even among those born on the same day.

osteoporosis changes the outlook for many in regard to maintaining bone tissue over the life span.

 WEB STUDY GUIDE Learn about different types of children's skeletal injuries in Lab Activity 5.2, Exploring Skeletal Injuries in Youth Sports, in the web study guide. Go to www.HumanKinetics.com/LifeSpanMotorDevelopment.

Development of the Muscular System

Whereas the skeletal system provides the body's structure, the muscular system allows its movement. More than 200 muscles permit a vast number of movements and positions for the human body. Like the skeletal system, the muscular system changes over the life span under the influence of genetic and external factors.

Early Development of the Muscular System

Muscle fibers (cells) grow during prenatal life by hyperplasia (an increase in the number of muscle cells) and hypertrophy (an increase in muscle cell size). At birth, muscle mass accounts for 23% to 25% of body weight. Hyperplasia continues for a short time after birth, but thereafter muscle growth occurs predominantly by hypertrophy (Malina, Bouchard, & Bar-Or, 2004). The sigmoid pattern of growth in weight reflects the growth of muscle tissue.

Muscle cells grow in both diameter and length. The amount of increase in muscle fiber diameter is related to the intensity of muscle activity during growth. Naturally, muscles must also increase in length as the skeleton grows, and this increase is accomplished through the addition of sarcomeres (the contractile units of muscle cells; figure 5.5) at the muscle–tendon junction as well as through the lengthening of the sarcomeres (Malina et al., 2004).

Sex differences in muscle mass are minimal during childhood; muscle mass constitutes a slightly greater proportion of body weight in boys. During and after adolescence, however, sex differences become marked. Muscle mass increases rapidly in boys up to about age 17 and ultimately accounts for 54% of men's body weight. In sharp contrast, girls add muscle mass only until age 13, on average, and muscle mass makes up 45% of women's body weight (Malina, 1978). The large sex differences in muscle mass involve upper body musculature more than leg musculature. For example, the rate of growth in arm musculature is nearly twice

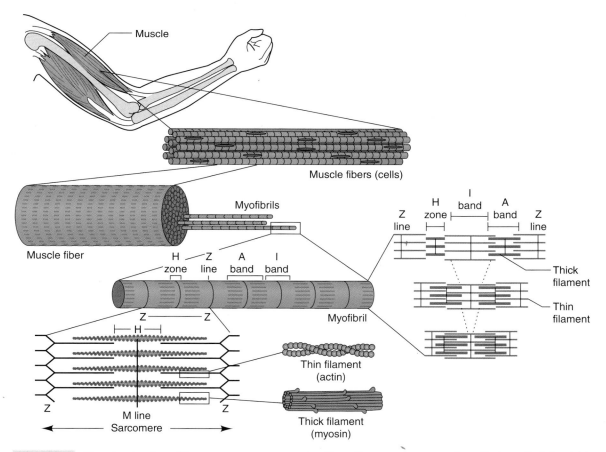

FIGURE 5.5 Muscle structure. The sarcomeres, or contractile units, compose muscle cells (myofibrils), which in turn make up a muscle fiber. Bundles of fibers compose the muscle.

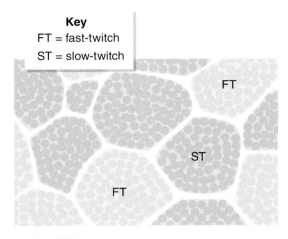

Key
FT = fast-twitch
ST = slow-twitch

FIGURE 5.6   A cross section of muscle showing that fast-twitch (FT) and slow-twitch (ST) fibers are intermingled.

A **twitch** is a brief period of contraction of a muscle fiber (cell) followed by relaxation. Muscles can be classified as **slow twitch** or **fast twitch**. Slow-twitch muscles have a slower contraction–relaxation cycle and greater endurance than do fast-twitch muscles.

as high for males as for females, but the difference in calf muscle growth is relatively small. These sex differences in the addition of muscle mass are related to hormonal influences.

Human muscle consists of two main types of fibers: **slow-twitch** (type I) fibers, which are suited to endurance activities, and **fast-twitch** (types IIa, IIx, and IIb) fibers, which are suited to intense short-duration activities (figure 5.6). At birth, approximately 15% of muscle fibers have yet to differentiate into slow- or fast-twitch fibers (Baldwin, 1984; Colling-Saltin, 1980) and 15% of type II fibers cannot be clearly categorized. These observations have led to speculation that an infant's early activities might influence the ultimate proportion of the different types of fibers, but the issue remains unresolved.

During the first postnatal year the number of undifferentiated fibers decreases, and by 1 year of age the distribution of muscle fiber types is similar to that in adults (Malina et al., 2004). The exact proportions of fiber types for any given muscle vary among individuals (Simoneau & Bouchard, 1989).

The heart is muscle tissue too. Like skeletal muscle, it grows by hyperplasia and hypertrophy. The right ventricle (lower chamber) is larger than the left ventricle at birth, but the left ventricle catches up after birth by growing more rapidly than the right, and the heart soon reaches adult proportions (figure 5.7). The heart generally follows the sigmoid pattern of whole-body growth, including a growth spurt in adolescence, such that the ratio of heart volume to body weight remains approximately the same throughout growth. One of the generation R studies (de Jonge et al., 2011) noted that left ventricular mass was already greater in overweight and obese children than in normal-weight children at 2 years. Future research will focus on whether this greater mass is related to a greater risk of cardiovascular disease in later life.

Early in the 20th century, some researchers thought that the large blood vessels around the heart developed more slowly than the heart itself, which implied that children who engaged in vigorous activity might be at risk. Later, it was shown that this myth had resulted from a misinterpretation of measurements taken in the late 1800s. In fact, blood vessel growth is proportional to the growth of the heart (Karpovich, 1937).

The Muscular System in Adulthood and Older Adulthood

Body composition begins changing in young adulthood. The proportion of lean body weight decreases, most often as a result of fat weight increasing. The change in muscle mass during adulthood is small. Only 10% of skeletal muscle mass is lost on average between the mid-20s and age 50. Changes in diet and physical activity level are probably responsible for this shift in body composition; poor diet promotes increased fat weight, and lack of physical activity leads to decreased muscle weight.

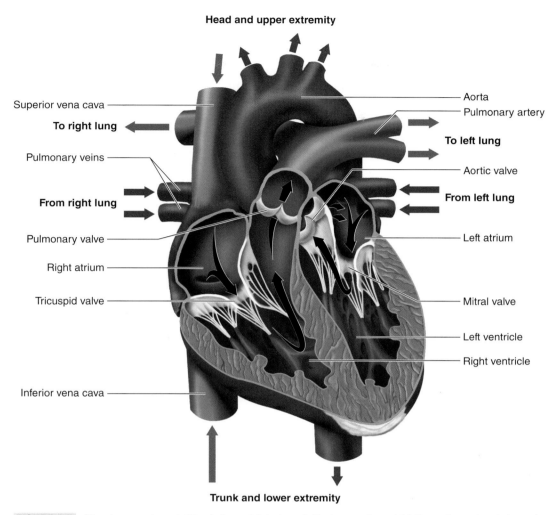

Head and upper extremity

Superior vena cava

To right lung

Pulmonary veins

From right lung

Pulmonary valve

Right atrium

Tricuspid valve

Inferior vena cava

Aorta

Pulmonary artery

To left lung

Aortic valve

From left lung

Left atrium

Mitral valve

Left ventricle

Right ventricle

Trunk and lower extremity

FIGURE 5.7   The human heart. The left ventricle is relatively smaller at birth and must catch up in growth in the early postnatal weeks.

After age 50, individuals begin to lose muscle mass at a greater rate. The extent of loss varies greatly. Individuals who maintain a good diet and participate in resistance exercise lose far less muscle than others do, but on average an additional 30% of muscle mass is lost by age 80. By very old age, sedentary individuals with poor nutrition can lose as much as 50% of the muscle mass they possessed in young adulthood.

Both the number and the diameter (size) of muscle fibers appear to decrease (Green, 1986; Lexell, Henriksson-Larsen, Wimblad, & Sjostrom, 1983). The loss in number of fibers is small before the 50s—only about 5% of the adult number (Arabadjis, Heffner, & Pendergast, 1990)—but more rapid thereafter, amounting to approximately 35% (Lexell, Taylor, & Sjostrom, 1988). Fibers do not seem to decrease in size until the 70s (McComas, 1996). Debate continues about whether the loss in muscle mass involves all three types of muscle fibers or whether type II fibers undergo a greater loss than type I fibers do (Green, 1986; Lexell, 1995).

In relation to cardiac muscle, in old age, the heart's ability to adapt to an increased workload declines. This might relate in part to degeneration of the heart muscle, a decrease in elasticity, and changes in the fibers of the heart valves

(Klausner & Schwartz, 1985; Shephard, 1981). The major blood vessels also lose elasticity (Fleg, 1986). Most changes in the heart muscles of individuals, however, are related to changes in lifestyle and resulting pathology rather than aging of the cardiac muscle fibers.

Bone and muscle mass are related to one another throughout the life span. Use of the muscles probably stimulates the bones to respond with increased bone formation, but many other factors certainly contribute to this relationship. Decline in bone and muscle mass is a constraint in the movement of older adults, and any loss of muscle strength accompanying decreases in muscle mass with aging can lead to a decrease in physical activities that are important to cardiovascular health or that the individual finds enjoyable. Such a loss also places an older individual at risk of falls, which increases the risk of bone fracture. We discuss muscle strength more extensively in chapter 16.

 If you were a personal trainer, would the sex of your clients be the only consideration in their potential to maintain or increase muscle mass? Would psychological, social, or cultural factors influence your approach to training them?

KEY POINT
It has been difficult for researchers to distinguish the changes that are an inevitable result of age from those that reflect the average older adult's lack of fitness or poor diet.

Development of the Adipose System

A common misconception about adipose (fat) tissue is that its presence in any amount is undesirable. In reality, adipose tissue plays a vital role in energy storage, insulation, and protection.

Early Development of the Adipose System

The amount of adipose tissue increases in early life. It first appears in the fetus at 3.5 months and increases rapidly during the last 2 prenatal months. Despite this late prenatal increase, adipose tissue accounts for only 0.5 kg (1.1 lb) of body weight at birth. A rapid increase of fat occurs in the first 6 months after birth, and the highest peak weight velocity occurs in the first month. Greater-than-average peak weight velocities were associated with increased risk of overweight and obesity at age 4 years in the generation R study group (Mook-Kanamori et al., 2011). After this rapid increase in the first 6 months, fat mass increases gradually until age 8 in both boys and girls. Girls tend to have slightly more fat mass than boys at age 2 (Ay et al., 2008). In the generation R study group, individual children tended to maintain their relative position in the group for amount of subcutaneous fat mass, especially in the trunk, throughout the first 2 years of life. In boys, adipose tissue continues to increase gradually throughout adolescence, but girls experience a more dramatic increase. As a result, adult women have more fat weight than adult men, with averages of 14 kg (30.9 lb) and 10 kg (22 lb), respectively. Fat weight during growth increases by both hyperplasia and hypertrophy, but cell size does not increase significantly until puberty.

Individual fatness varies widely during infancy and early childhood. A fat baby will not necessarily become a fat child. After 7 to 8 years of age, though, it is more likely that individuals maintain their relative fatness. An overweight 8-year-old has a high risk of becoming an overweight adult.

The distribution of fat in the body changes during growth. During childhood, internal fat (fat around the viscera) increases faster than subcutaneous fat (fat under the skin), which actually decreases until age 6 or 7. Boys and girls then show an increase in subcutaneous fat until they are 12 or 13. This increase in subcutaneous fat continues in girls, but boys typically lose subcutaneous fat in midadolescence. Adolescent boys also tend to add more subcutaneous fat to their trunks than to their limbs, whereas girls have increased subcutaneous fat at both sites. Note that in figure 5.8 skinfold measurements for boys' extremities (top blue line) actually decrease, except during the growth spurt. Trunk skinfolds tend to hold steady but also increase during the growth spurt. Girls' skinfold measurements (purple lines) increase steadily for both trunk and limbs, especially after age 7. Girls usually add more subcutaneous fat to their legs than to their arms.

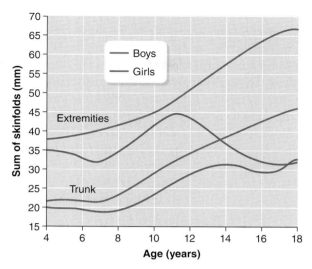

FIGURE 5.8 Changes in fat distribution during growth are illustrated by plotting the sum of five trunk skinfold measurements and five extremity skinfold measurements. Note the increase in both types of measurement in girls, contrasting with a decrease in extremity subcutaneous fat in boys during adolescence.

Reprinted by permission from Malina and Bouchard 1988.

 What are the life span implications of individuals adding too much fat during the periods of increase in fat tissue?

There is much that we don't know about adipose tissue development and obesity. Researchers are currently examining many topics, including maternal weight gain during pregnancy, early infant feeding, and genetic factors. Of particular interest are the two periods when the number of adipose cells increases—during the first 6 postnatal months and around puberty. Increases in cell number are significant because adipose cells persist once they are formed, even with malnutrition; that is, the cells may be empty of fat, but they still exist. Therefore, these two periods may be critical in the control of obesity.

Adipose Tissue in Adulthood and Older Adulthood

Both sexes tend to gain fat weight during the adult years, reflecting changes in nutrition and activity level. The average American woman gains 11.8 kg (26 lb) and the average American man gains 8.2 kg (18 lb) between 20 and 50 years of age (Hellmich, 1999). Total body weight begins to decline after age 50, but this reflects loss of bone and muscle, as body fat continues to increase.

Body fat redistributes with aging. Subcutaneous fat on the limbs tends to decrease, whereas internal fat in the abdomen tends to increase (World Health Organization, 1998; World Health Organization Expert Subcommittee, 1998). This pattern is significant because abdominal obesity has been associated with a higher risk of cardiovascular disease.

It is difficult to identify typical patterns of adipose tissue gain or loss in older adults. Because obese individuals have a higher mortality rate, either lighter individuals survive to be included in studies of older adults, whereas obese individuals do not, or thinner adults are more eager to participate in research studies. It appears that an increase in fat weight with aging is not inevitable. For example, such gains are not found in lumberjacks in Norway who have a very active lifestyle as a result of their profession, persons from undernourished parts of the world, and master athletes (Shephard, 1978b; Skrobak-Kaczynski & Andersen, 1975). Typically, though, most older adults add some fat weight as they age, and active older adults add less than their sedentary peers. Overweight and obesity can be a constraint to movement at any age. Movement must be more effortful with greater weight, joint movement can be restricted, and social pressure related to body image and self-esteem can discourage participation in physical activities.

Development of the Endocrine System

The cells of a living being must be precisely regulated for their content and temperature. The control systems regulating the cells of the body are the nervous system and the endocrine system, and it is not surprising that they play a major role in growth and maturation. The endocrine system exerts its control over specific cellular functions through chemical substances called **hormones**. Those secreted by the hypothalamus in the brain regulate the pituitary gland, which, in turn, regulates the adrenal gland, the thyroid gland, and the release of sex hormones.

Hormones
are chemical substances secreted into body fluids by a gland. These substances have specific effects on the activities of target cells, tissues, or organs.

Early Development of the Endocrine System

The endocrine system's regulation of growth is a complex and delicate interaction of hormones, genes, nutrients, and environmental factors. In fact, hormone levels must be delicately balanced. Either an excess or a deficiency of hormones may disturb the normal process of growth and development. A detailed discussion of how the hormones influence growth and maturation is beyond the scope of this text, so we will just mention three types of hormones here. All three promote growth in the same way: They stimulate protein anabolism (constructive metabolism), resulting in the retention of substances needed to build tissues. There are specific times in the growth period when one of these hormones may play a critical role in growth.

Growth Hormone

Growth hormone (GH) influences growth during childhood and adolescence by stimulating protein anabolism so that new tissue can be built. Under the control of the central nervous system, GH is secreted by the anterior pituitary gland (figure 5.9). The body needs this hormone for normal growth after birth. A deficiency or absence of GH results in growth abnormalities and in some cases the cessation of linear growth.

Thyroid Hormones

The thyroid hormones are secreted by the thyroid gland, located in the anterior neck region. Two types of thyroid hormones influence whole-body growth after birth, and a third plays a role in skeletal growth.

The pituitary gland secretes a thyroid-stimulating hormone that regulates the thyroid hormones secreted by the thyroid gland. Thyroid-stimulating hormone excretion is, in turn, increased by a releasing factor found in the brain's hypothalamus. Thus, two systems act in concert: a pituitary–thyroid system and a nervous system–thyroid system. This is one example of how the nervous system and endocrine system work together.

Gonadal Hormones

The gonadal hormones affect growth and sexual maturation, particularly during adolescence, by stimulating development of the secondary sex characteristics and the sex organs. The androgens, specifically testosterone from the testes and androgens from the cortex of the adrenal glands, hasten fusion of the epiphyseal growth plates in the bones. Thus, these hormones promote skeletal maturation (fusion) at the expense of linear growth; this explains why early maturers tend to be shorter in stature than later maturers.

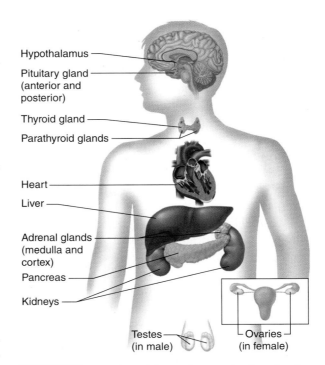

FIGURE 5.9 Location of the various endocrine glands.

Androgens also play a role in the adolescent growth spurt of muscle mass by increasing nitrogen retention and protein synthesis. This spurt is more pronounced in young men than in young women because men secrete both testosterone and adrenal androgens whereas women produce only the adrenal androgens. In women, the ovaries and the adrenal cortex secrete estrogens. Increased estrogen secretion during adolescence, as with androgens, speeds epiphyseal closure, but estrogen also promotes fat accumulation, primarily in the breasts and hips. Men and women both have estrogen and testosterone but in very different proportions.

 Teenage boys sometimes take steroid supplements in order to add muscle mass and look older. Increased secretion of androgen (a steroid) at puberty, though, hastens fusion at the epiphyseal plates. What unintended effect might these supplements have on growing boys?

Insulin

The hormones we have discussed up to this point all play a major and direct role in growth and development. Another familiar hormone, insulin, has an indirect role in growth. Produced in the pancreas, insulin is vital to carbohydrate metabolism, stimulating the transportation of glucose and amino acids through membranes. Its presence also is necessary for the full functioning of GH. A deficiency of insulin can decrease protein synthesis, which is detrimental at any time in life but especially during growth.

The Endocrine System in Adulthood and Older Adulthood

Earlier, we acknowledged that the nervous system and the endocrine system work in concert to regulate cellular functions and organ systems. It is no surprise, then, that the continued functioning of these integrating systems is important to good health throughout the life span. In fact, one group of theories about the cause of aging, called gradual imbalance theories, suggests that over time the nervous system, endocrine system, and immune system gradually fail to function (Spirduso, Francis, & MacRae, 2005). This gradual failure might occur at different rates in the three systems, leading to imbalances between them. Imbalances and reduced effectiveness within systems leave older individuals at increased risk of disease.

Thyroid function is an example; it tends to decline with aging, and thyroid disorders are more prevalent among older adults. A long-term increase in thyroid hormone levels can be related to congestive heart failure. It is therefore important for older adults to be screened for hyperthyroidism. On the other hand, insufficiency of thyroid hormone, or hypothyroidism, is associated with acceleration of aging systems.

Gonadal hormone levels also decrease with age. Hormone replacement therapy may counteract many of the effects of aging. For example, prescribing androgen supplements has been successful in countering muscle wasting and osteoporosis. We need more information about the side effects of hormone replacement therapies, as evidenced by the eventual finding that women receiving hormone replacement therapy at menopause were unfortunately at increased risk of some types of cancers.

Older adults maintain secretion levels of insulin comparable with those of younger adults, but the incidence of type 2 diabetes (non-insulin-dependent diabetes mellitus, which is caused by insulin deficiency) increases markedly with age. It is possible that older adults do not utilize insulin as effectively as younger adults to promote glycogen storage, thus retarding the mobilization of fuel for exercise. All of these examples show that gradual declines or imbalances in the nervous, endocrine, and immune systems can lead to increased risk of disabilities or diseases that in turn can both threaten good health and serve as constraints to physical activity.

Development of the Nervous System

No single system is as much the essence of an individual as the nervous system. We need only observe an individual with severe brain injury to know this. The nervous system controls movement and speech. It is the site of thinking, analysis, and memory, and its development is important to social, cognitive, and motor development.

Early Development of the Nervous System

Much of neurological development occurs very early in the life span. The course of neurological development is a prime example of the interplay of genetic and extrinsic factors. Genes direct the development of the nervous system's structures and its main circuits. The trillions of finer connections between nervous system cells, however, are fine-tuned by extrinsic factors. Let's consider neurological development in more detail, including the role of extrinsic factors.

Prenatal Growth of the Nervous System

Neurons are the cells of the nervous system that receive and transmit information.

In general, the formation of immature **neurons**, their differentiation into a general type, and their migration to a final position in the nervous system occur prenatally. Neurons proliferate in the early prenatal period at an astonishing rate of 250,000 per minute. As many as 200 billion are formed. During the third and fourth prenatal months, almost all the neurons that the individual human brain will ever have are formed, although it seems that genes direct an overproduction of cells so that the system can later be pruned (Ratey, 2001). Neurons contain a cell body, which carries out functions to keep the cell alive; up to 100,000 dendrites, which receive impulses from other neurons; and an axon, which transmits impulses to other neurons, glands, organs, or muscles (figure 5.10).

The new neurons also travel to a final destination during the prenatal period. Some form the brain stem, which controls heartbeat and breathing; some the cerebellum, which controls posture; and some the cerebral cortex, where perception and thought take place. Generally, neurons are in their final location by the sixth prenatal month. Neurons specialize. For example, visual neurons are specialized as a function of both their genes and the location to which they migrate, in this case a part of the brain where visual information arrives. The migration process is vital to normal brain development (Ratey, 2001).

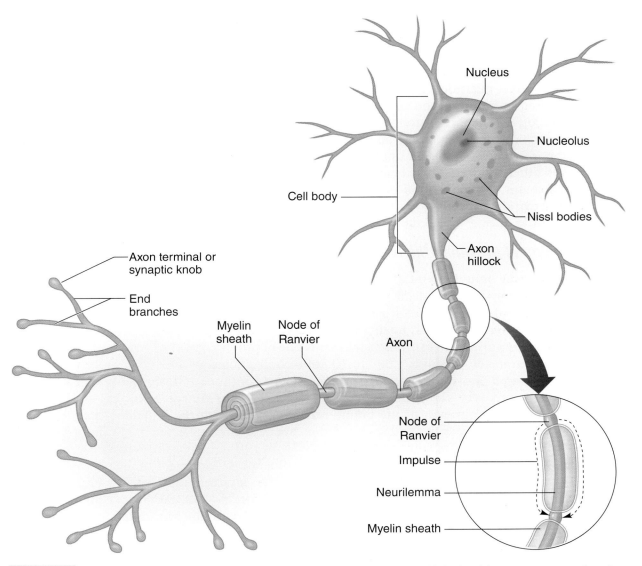

FIGURE 5.10   The structure of a nerve cell, or neuron. Note that there can be multiple dendrites to carry nerve impulses to the cell body, but only one axon emerges to carry an impulse to other neurons, glands, or muscles. The axon can, however, branch extensively.

Once the neurons are in place, they grow an axon along a chemical trail to a general destination in order to connect to other neurons, forming the brain's circuitry of about 100 trillion connections, or **synapses**. Because of the overproduction of neurons, axons compete for the chemical trails. Some axons and their neurons die off. The neurons fire electrical impulses that strengthen some of the connections between neurons. The firing is somewhat random prenatally but more organized as the fetus, and later the infant, receive input from the environment (Ratey, 2001). Thus, a natural pruning occurs of both neurons (reducing the number to approximately 100 billion at birth) and their branches and connections. Weak or incorrect connections are sacrificed to make the neural network more efficient.

A **synapse** is a connection between two neurons; it is made by the release of chemicals called neurotransmitters from an axon. These neurotransmitters cross a small gap between neurons, then permeate the cell wall at the dendrite, or cell body, of a receiving neuron to trigger an electrical impulse.

 Assume you have just found out you will be a new mother. What substances would you avoid consuming until your baby is born? Why?

The migration of neurons and the branching of their processes are susceptible to effects of environmental factors delivered via the fetal nourishment system described in chapter 4. Growing evidence shows that some disorders, such as epilepsy, autism, and dyslexia, are caused at least in part by faulty migration of neurons (Ratey, 2001). Nicotine that is introduced to a fetus by a mother's smoking might affect migration, branching, and pruning of the neurons, and we know that children of mothers who smoked while pregnant are at increased risk of mental retardation. Alcohol introduced by a mother's alcohol consumption can cause improper neuron migration, and babies with fetal alcohol syndrome are known to later exhibit lower IQs and more prevalent reading and mathematics disabilities than other children. There are many examples of fetal exposure to illicit drugs and toxins and of malnutrition influencing development of the nervous system. It is clear that the nervous system is one of the systems most susceptible to teratogenic exposure during the prenatal period.

Postnatal Growth of the Nervous System

At birth the brain is about 25% of its adult weight. Brain growth increases rapidly after birth and reaches 80% of adult weight by age 4. Then it enters a period of steady growth through adolescence. The rapid early growth reflects an increase in the size of the neurons, further branching to form synapses, and an increase in **glia** and **myelin**. The first postnatal year is one of prolific synaptic formation, and each neuron can establish 1,000 to 100,000 connections.

This rapid growth of the early postnatal period continues to make neurological development very susceptible to extrinsic factors. Poor nutrition, for example, could stunt the growth of the brain, a deficit from which the individual might never recover. Injury to the left side of the **cerebral cortex** (figure 5.11) early in life leads to deficits in language ability (Witelson, 1987). Increasing evidence also shows that an infant's early life experiences influence development of the nervous system. Greenough and colleagues (Comery, Shah, & Greenough, 1995; Comery, Stamoudis, Irwin, & Greenough, 1996; Greenough et al., 1993; Wallace, Kilman, Withers, & Greenough, 1992) found that rats raised with much stimulation grew significantly more synapses than those raised without stimuli. The same pattern holds for humans. Learning is one of the most significant extrinsic factors influencing postnatal development of the nervous system. We now know that the brain restructures itself with learning. Magnetic resonance imaging documents that areas of the brain corresponding to frequently used body parts expand as the synaptic

Glia are the cells of the nervous system that support and nourish the neurons. **Myelin** is an insulating sheath around the axons.

The **cerebral cortex** is the wrinkled surface of the brain containing millions of neurons and regulating many human functions and behaviors.

KEY POINT
The brain demonstrates enormous plasticity during all phases of the life span, and its 100 trillion connections change constantly.

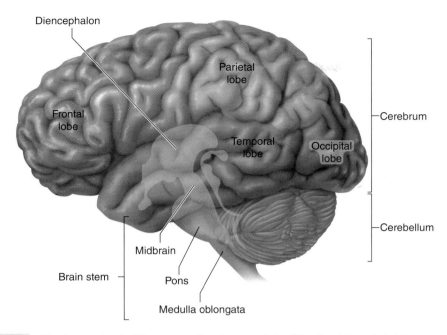

FIGURE 5.11   The human brain. The cerebral cortex consists of the frontal, parietal, temporal, and occipital lobes.

connections in those areas expand. From the early weeks of life and continuing over the life span, neural connections and pathways that are stimulated are strengthened whereas those not used are weakened.

The Genome Project has determined that 30,000 to 50,000 of the 100,000 genes in the human genome are designated for the brain. Even that number probably does not fully control our 100 trillion synapses; there is room for variation resulting from experience, and most of our traits reflect the interaction of genes and our environment.

Brain Structures

The spinal cord and lower brain structures are more advanced at birth than are the higher brain structures. Lower brain centers involved in vital tasks, such as respiration and food intake, are relatively mature. Lower brain centers also mediate many reflexes and reactions. These automatic movement responses dominate the fetus' and newborn's movements, so it makes sense that lower brain centers are relatively more advanced than higher brain centers at this time.

For many years, researchers have interpreted the onset of goal-directed movements in infants as evidence that higher brain centers are maturing. The cortex is involved in purposeful, goal-directed movement. The first clear evidence of successful intentional movement (reaching) occurs at 4 to 5 postnatal months (Bushnell, 1982; McDonnell, 1979). Hence, early researchers assumed that this behavior signaled the first functioning of the cortex at about 4 months of age, even though the cerebral hemispheres are formed at birth. More recently, researchers have used positron emission tomography (PET) scans to study the infant brain. The scans show little activity in the frontal cortex at 5 days of age, increased activity at 11 weeks, and adult levels at 7 to 8 months (Chugani & Phelps, 1986). Clearly, then, the process whereby the frontal cortex becomes functional is gradual. In fact, specialization of areas of the cortex continues well into adulthood.

The development of myelin in the nervous system contributes to speedy conduction of nerve impulses. Myelin cells, comprising mostly fat, wrap themselves around the outgoing neuron cell process, or axon (refer to figure 5.10). Myelinated axons can fire nerve impulses at higher frequencies for longer periods than those not myelinated (Kuffler, Nicholls, & Martin, 1984).

Axons that are as yet unmyelinated in the newborn are probably functional, but **myelination** improves the speed and frequency of firing. The function of the nervous system in movements requiring or benefiting from speedy conduction of nerve impulses, such as a series of rapid movements or postural responses, might be related to the myelination process during development. The importance of myelin is evident in multiple sclerosis, a disease that strikes young adults and breaks down the myelin sheath, resulting in tremor, loss of coordination, and possibly paralysis.

The spinal cord is relatively small and short at birth. A cross-sectional view of the spinal cord (figure 5.12) shows a central horn-shaped area of gray matter and a surrounding area of white matter. The central area contains tightly packed neuron cell bodies. Note the roots that lie just outside the cord; they contain the axons of the cord's neurons and, in the case of the sensory roots, nerve cell bodies. Fibers from the dorsal and ventral roots merge to form the peripheral (spinal) nerves outside the cord. A marked increase in the myelination of these peripheral nerves occurs 2 to 3 weeks after birth, and this process continues through the second or third year of life.

Two major motor nerve pathways, or **nerve tracts**, carry impulses from the brain down the spinal cord to various parts of the body. One pathway, the **extrapyramidal tract**, is probably involved in delivering the commands for both the random and the postural movements made by the infant in the first days after birth. The other, the **pyramidal tract**, myelinates after birth; it is functioning by 4 to 5 months and controls the muscles for finger movements.

The myelination pattern that the spinal cord and nerve pathways undergo might have implications for motor development. Myelination proceeds in two directions in the cord: first in the cervical portion, followed by the progressively lower portions, and then in the motor (ventral) horns, followed by the sensory (dorsal)

Myelination is the process whereby the axons of the neural cells are insulated when insulating myelin sheaths formed by Schwann (glial) cells wrap themselves around the axon.

Nerve tracts are major neurological pathways. There are two major motor tracts: the **extrapyramidal** and the **pyramidal**.

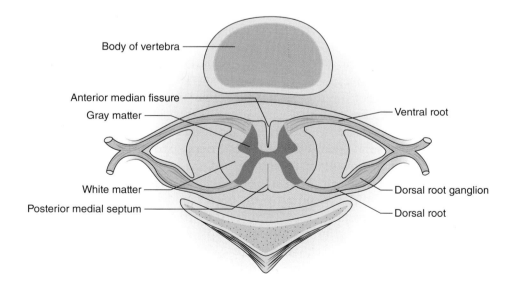

FIGURE 5.12   Cross section of the spinal cord.

horns. The direction of myelination tends to be away from the brain in the motor tracts. In contrast, the direction of myelination is toward the brain in sensory tracts, occurring first in the tactile and olfactory pathways, then in the visual pathways, and finally in the auditory pathways. Sensory pathways mature slightly faster than motor pathways, except in the motor roots and cerebral hemispheres. Higher-level functioning might be possible only when the neurons involved in a behavior are myelinated, allowing faster and more frequent conduction of nerve signals.

The Nervous System in Adulthood and Older Adulthood

The traditional view of the nervous system has been that after adolescence the only changes in the system would be losses, including a loss of neurons, thinning of the dendritic branches, a decline in the number of synapses, changes in the neurotransmitters, and reductions of myelin. This traditional view was based largely on observing behavior, especially slowing motor responses to stimuli as aging proceeds. Now, however, with the use of new imaging techniques that allow researchers to better see what is actually happening to brain tissue, we know that there are significant exceptions to the trend of losses. Our new picture is one of enormous plasticity. **Neurogenesis** has been observed in some areas of the brain (Verret, Trouche, Zerwas, & Rampon, 2007), and the 100 trillion connections among the neurons are constantly changing over the life span.

> **Neurogenesis** is the division and propagation of neurons.

The repercussions of age-related losses in the nervous system are widespread. Slowing of responses can affect movements in recreational activities as well as activities of daily living. Response slowing also affects the performance of cognitive tasks. Several theories have been advanced to explain how physiological changes result in slowing of responses. One of these theories is the neural network model. In this model, the nervous system is seen as a neural network of links and nodes. To respond to a stimulus, a signal begins at the input end of the individual's nervous system and travels through the network to the output end. With aging, links in the network are thought to break at random so that the neural signal must detour, increasing the time before the response is made. With advancing age, more links break and the processing time for a signal gets longer and longer (Cerella, 1990). Clearly, the loss of neurons, dendrites, and synapses, as well as the decline in neurotransmitters, are physiological changes that would result in broken links in the neural network.

> **KEY POINT**
> Regular vigorous exercise can play a key role in minimizing the loss of neurons and synapses with aging.

As in young people, extrinsic factors play a role in nervous system changes, and one of the most important factors is exercise. The very same exercise that benefits the cardiovascular system has positive effects on the nervous system, including reduced risk of stroke, increased branching of dendrites, and maintenance of the neurons' metabolism. Regular vigorous exercise maintains the level of blood flow to the brain, lessens the loss of dendrites, stimulates neurogenesis, and promotes new synaptic connections. These effects can result in improved cognitive function in older adulthood (Weuve et al., 2004).

Summary and Synthesis

A major theme in this discussion of body systems is that systems do not develop and age independently of one another; rather, they develop in concert, with one system often stimulating change in another. For example, growth of the long bones may stimulate the muscles to grow in length. In addition, the neurological system directs secretion of the pituitary hormones, which have their own effects (decreasing estrogen levels, for instance, affect bone strength in older women). Thus, a system can have its own timing or pattern of development but also interact with other systems in the bigger picture of the individual's development. Even when we want to focus on the development or aging of one body system, we should do so in the context of the other systems changing as well.

In addition, there are periods when change in a system is more rapid. These are often referred to sensitive periods because we expect extrinsic factors to be more influential in times of greater change than in times of gradual change. Of course, the extrinsic influence could be positive (facilitating growth or slowing aging) or negative (slowing growth or accelerating aging).

Last, extrinsic factors can influence development at any point in the life span but have more influence in development as individuals move through the life span. Genes are also influential throughout the life span but have their greatest influence in transforming a tiny embryo of a few cells to a complex individual, all in less than 20 years. Extrinsic factors can affect a fetus, but the fetus is protected in the womb from many extrinsic factors. After birth, though, numerous extrinsic factors can influence many aspects of development at the levels of cell, system, and organism. These extrinsic factors can have transient or long-lasting effects. For example, resistance exercise promotes muscle strength, but when an individual stops exercising, the muscles begin losing strength. On the other hand, an active lifestyle in preadolescence may promote bone density that provides a lifelong benefit. This accumulating effect of extrinsic factors explains the great variation in health status that we can observe across individuals toward the end of the life span.

The structural constraints influencing movement can operate at the system level. So, when we consider how the changing individual interacts with the task and environment to give rise to movement, it will most often be in the context of change in a system. We now know more about changes in the systems that make up an individual's structure. Of course, other characteristics of the individual change with growth and aging; vision, hearing, and self-confidence are just a few examples. Our knowledge of change in structural constraints, however, allows us to consider the course of motor development.

The model of constraints offers a deeper understanding of motor development than simply a description of the interaction of changing individual, task, and environmental factors. It also explains why certain movements can arise when they do. This is so because often a particular structural constraint shapes movement at a particular point in the life span. For example, consider a 4-month-old who can hold his head up but can't sit or stand on his own. Why not? We might suggest that the infant needs to undergo an improvement in balance, an increase in trunk muscle strength, an increase in leg muscle strength, an increase in bone density, an increase in leg length to offset the large size of the upper body, or other changes. Which system is the limiting one? The balance system? The muscle system? The skeletal system? That is, which system is the rate limiter, or the system limiting the rate of development?

We have come a long way in knowing more about some of the structural changes that accompany growth and aging. We can better predict how specific changes might influence movement, and because we know more about the course of physical development we can better predict when structural changes might change the movement. We also know more about when an individual is subject to greater or lesser influence from extrinsic factors. This knowledge can inform us about changes in extrinsic factors that could bring about changes in movement. Part III considers the course of motor development as the individual, changing in structure over the life span, interacts with the task to be done and the surrounding environment.

 Reinforcing What You Have Learned About Constraints

TAKE A SECOND LOOK

The concern about the young woman described at the beginning of this chapter is real. Insufficient nutrition in the months before and after birth can have a limiting and lasting effect on development of the nervous system. It is important that the growth of the body's systems get off to a good start and that the health of each system be fostered throughout the life span. For example, adults who consume a diet rich in calcium can forestall loss of bone density. We benefit from knowing the course of growth and aging in the individual systems because we can then identify the points in the life span where the individual is most susceptible to extrinsic influence, for better or for worse.

TEST YOUR KNOWLEDGE

1. What is the epiphyseal growth plate? What is the difference between a pressure epiphysis and a traction epiphysis? Why would an injury to the growth plate in a young child be of concern?

2. What is osteoporosis? Who does it affect, and what are the repercussions for health and for participation in activities?

3. Discuss sex differences in the growth of muscle tissue. How does the growth of cardiac muscle compare with that of skeletal muscle?

4. Do adults necessarily gain fat tissue as they age? What is the evidence for your answer?

5. How does the distribution of fat change over the growth period? How does the amount and distribution of fat change in adulthood? What distribution pattern in adulthood is associated with greater risk of cardiovascular disease?

6. What are the major types of hormones involved in growth? How do the hormones influence growth?

7. What contributes to the rapid gains in brain weight during the first year after birth? What part of the brain is most advanced at birth?

8. How has the view of what happens in the nervous system with aging changed with the use of new imaging techniques? What lifestyle factors could spur changes in the nervous system, and how?

9. Choose one extrinsic or environmental factor and describe how it might influence the growth of various systems.

LEARNING EXERCISE 5.1

System Changes in Older Adults

Throughout our discussion, we describe the average or typical course of aging for each system. It is often useful to consider how a particular person either matches or varies from the typical. Locate an adult who is 60 years of age or older and willing to discuss what he or she remembers about changes in his or her skeletal structure, muscle tissue, and adipose tissue. You might ask, for example, about osteoporosis screenings, changes in body weight during middle and older adulthood, and changes in fat versus muscle weight as the person changed body shape. Write a short paper summarizing your conversation, indicating what matched and what varied from the norm described in this chapter.

LEARNING EXERCISE 5.2

Human Growth Hormone

Human growth hormone, or GH (or a releasing factor that stimulates GH secretion), is available for sale on the Internet. Yet the use of GH is banned by many sport governing bodies, some of which test their athletes for use of GH as a supplement. Research the use of GH, then answer the following questions.

1. Why would athletes want to use GH? What effect does it have in individuals who have reached maturity? How does it produce these effects?

2. Are there known risks of using GH supplements? If yes, explain your findings.

3. Even if little research has been conducted on the long-term effects of using GH as a supplement, what are some of the suspected risks of long-term GH supplementation?

4. Based on your findings, what would you recommend to a teenage athlete who is tempted to use GH? Why?

Development of Motor Skills Across the Life Span

In part III, the pieces of the motor development puzzle begin to come together as we examine motor development over the life span and consider the associated constraints influencing the course that development takes. This part of the book discusses the changes in skill performance observed from birth to older adulthood; it also identifies the individual, environmental, and task constraints that may bring about these changes.

Chapter 6 discusses early motor development. During the first year of life, infants rapidly acquire new motor skills, progressing toward the ability to move adaptively in their environment. Because of the scope and speed with which young children change, the entire chapter is devoted to the time period between birth and the onset of walking (at approximately 11 to 15 months of age). This is a critical time in atypical development as well because small differences in individual constraints early on can evolve into large differences later in life.

Chapter 7 discusses changes in locomotor skills from approximately 1 year of age through the life span. These skills include the most commonly used locomotor patterns—walking and running—as well as skills used in play and sport contexts, such as jumping, hopping, and galloping. You should begin to see similarities in developmental trajectories, which are known as developmental sequences, given the similarity in individual constraints and the guiding principles of motion and stability. You will also see how the development of specific individual constraints influences developmental sequences.

Chapter 8 addresses ballistics skills, such as throwing, striking, and kicking. Again, you will see many similarities in the developmental sequences for various ballistic tasks. Finally, chapter 9 covers manipulative skills—both fine motor skills, such as reaching and grasping, and gross motor skills, such as catching.

Suggested Reading

Adolph, K.E., & Robinson, S.R. (2013). The road to walking: What learning to walk tells us about development. In P. Zelazo (Ed.), *Oxford handbook of developmental psychology* (Vol. 1, pp. 403–443). New York: Oxford University Press.

Galloway, J.C. (2004). The emergence of purposeful limb movement in early infancy: The interaction of experience, learning and biomechanics. *Journal of Human Kinetics, 12*, 51–68.

Gagen, L.M., Haywood, K.M., & Spaner, S.D. (2005). Predicting the scale of tennis rackets for optimal striking from body dimensions. *Pediatric Exercise Science*, 17, 190–200.

Mally, K.K., Battista, R.A., & Roberton, M.A. (2011). Distance as a control parameter for place kicking. *Journal of Human Sport and Exercise*, 6(1), 122–134.

Stodden, D.F., Fleisig, G.S., Langendorfer, S.J., & Andrews, J.R. (2006). Kinematic constraints associated with the acquisition of overarm throwing. Part I: Step and trunk actions. *Research Quarterly for Exercise and Sport*, 77, 417–427.

Whitall, J. (2003). Development of locomotor co-ordination and control in children. In G.J.P. Savelsbergh, K. Davids, J. Van der Kamp, & S. Bennett (Eds.), *Development of movement coordination in children: Applications in the fields of ergonomics, health sciences and sport* (pp. 251–270). London: Routledge.

Early Motor Development

Fundamental Individual Constraints

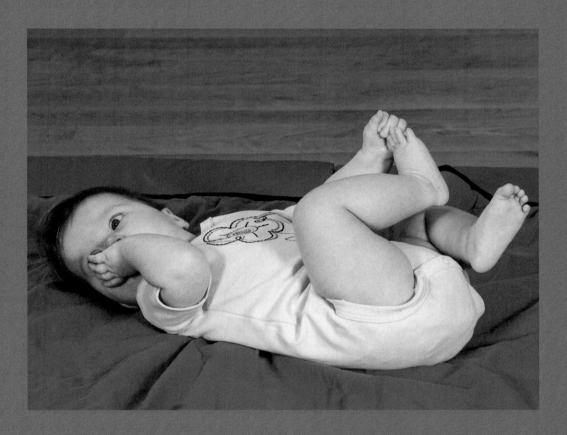

 CHAPTER OBJECTIVES

This chapter

- describes types of movement that occur in infancy,
- lists infantile reflexes and postural reactions,
- explains the relationship between infants' earlier and later movements,
- describes motor milestones,
- explains how early movements are shaped by a variety of constraints, and
- examines postural development and balance in infancy.

Innovative Interventions for Infants: Babies Driving Robots

Children born with severe mobility impairments, such as those associated with cerebral palsy, are at increased risk for mobility-related developmental delays in cognition, language, and socialization. Providing daily mobility between the ages of 1 and 5 years is critical, given that significant learning, brain, and behavioral development is dependent on mobility during this time. The National Science Foundation-funded project, affectionately called "Babies Driving Robots and Race-cars," began at the University of Delaware when Sunil Agrawal, a professor in the department of mechanical engineering, approached Cole Galloway, a professor in the department of physical therapy. Galloway explains, "Dr. Agrawal told me, 'We have small robots, and you have small infants. Do you think we can do something together?'" Soon after, the researchers created the first prototype, UD1. This robotic car featured a joystick and infrared sonar sensors with obstacle-avoidance software. The researchers tested the prototype in the university's early learning center, a research facility that accommodates 250 children with varying abilities.

In the initial group study, normal 6-month-olds sat in UD1 and pulled the joystick, and away they would go. The children began to understand the cause-and-effect relationship between the joystick's movement and the car's movement. Once the children made this breakthrough, the researchers would train them in how to control the direction of their driving. Galloway and his team began to quantify the results of the children's mobility. The children had increased cognitive and language scores as well as better motor skills. Follow-up case reports on infants and toddlers with spina bifida and cerebral palsy noted improvements in driving skill and developmental scores.

Reprinted, by permission, from livescience. Available: www.livescience.com/23572-assistive-robotics-aide-young-children-nsf-bts.html.

In the past few years, researchers have taken a careful look at the relationship between movements that infants make and their developing minds. It appears as though this link is much stronger than originally believed. In other words, it is becoming clear that in order to understand cognitive development in infancy, we need to understand motor development and, eventually, determine the interactions and transactions between them. Such an approach fits with the ecological perspective as well as the constraints model. This chapter provides you with information about the motor behaviors exhibited by infants, which is the first step toward understanding how motor development is related to cognitive and perceptual development during infancy. There are also important practical reasons for knowing about infant motor development. In typically developing infants, many movements occur in fairly predictable order and timing. It is essential to learn about and understand typical development in order to be able to recognize deviance—either progression or regression—from the typical pattern.

In terms of motor development, most newborn infants exhibit spontaneous and reflexive movements. As infants move toward becoming toddlers, they begin to attain motor milestones. These gross movements slowly become more refined throughout infancy and early childhood. In addition, infants gain the ability to lift their heads, sit up, and eventually stand with minimal support. In the past, parents and educators alike have thought of this process as maturation. In other words, maturation of the central nervous system was the sole individual constraint guiding early motor behavior. This notion, discussed in chapter 2, comes out of the maturational perspective. However, current research from an ecological perspective suggests that the interplay of many systems (cognitive, perceptual, motor) leads to the movement adaptations seen in infancy. Therefore, this chapter presents the concept that many constraints in addition to maturation encourage or discourage early motor behavior.

How Do Infants Move?

If you watch newborns, you will notice that some of their movements seem to be undirected and without purpose. For example, infants often kick their legs while lying on their backs. These spontaneous movements appear without any apparent stimulation. At other times, infants will move in a specific way every time they are touched in a certain place. Who can resist an infant "holding your hand"— that is, grabbing your finger when you touch her palm? An infant is born with a variety of reflexes that seem to disappear slowly as she ages, and she appears to move with discrete, purposeless actions that have little to do with future voluntary movements. However, there is more to infant motor behavior than meets the eye. Those seemingly random infant movements have an important relationship with intentional movements that occur later in life. After the first few months of life the infant will begin to attain motor milestones, which are particular movement skills that eventually lead to locomotion, reaching, and upright posture.

Newborn movements, then, have been classified into two general categories: random or spontaneous movements, and infantile reflexes (Clark, 1995). These two types of movement are very different from each other.

Spontaneous Movements

People give much attention to the study of infantile reflexes; however, reflexes represent only a small portion of early motor behavior. How else do newborns move? If not eating or sleeping, newborns most likely will squirm, thrust their legs or arms, stretch their fingers and toes, or make other **spontaneous movements** (also termed stereotypies). These spontaneous movements seem very different from walking or reaching, and pediatricians, parents, and others have believed that they had no particular purpose or relationship to the future movements the child would someday choose to make. However, this may not be the case.

Spontaneous movements are infants' movements that occur without any apparent stimulation.

Supine Kicking and Walking

If a child is laid on his back (the supine position), he will likely spontaneously thrust his legs. This is called supine kicking. Thelen and her colleagues (Thelen, 1985, 1995; Thelen & Fisher, 1983; Thelen, Ridley-Johnson, & Fisher, 1983) studied the nature of supine kicking in infancy. In analyzing the position and timing of leg segments in these kicks as well as muscular activity in the leg muscles, they discovered some surprising results. The supine kicking was not random but rhythmical, and the kicks had a coordinated pattern. The ankle, knee, and hip joints moved cooperatively with each other, not independently from one another. It seems amazing that these supine kicks during infancy have a coordinated pattern. What is more remarkable is that the coordination of these kicks resembles the positioning and timing of an adult walking step (figure 6.1). The pattern of muscle use in infant supine kicking is also coordinated. Sometimes an infant kicks only one leg, but at other times an infant will kick both legs alternately, just as an adult alternates legs in walking. Even premature infants perform coordinated supine kicks (Geerdink, Hopkins, Beek, & Heriza, 1996; Heriza, 1986; Piek & Gasson, 1999).

 What might account for some of the differences in infant kicking and adult walking? Think in terms of individual, environmental, and task constraints.

Though an infant's supine kicks are similar to an adult's walking steps, they are not identical. Infants' timing is more variable from kick to kick, and they tend to move the joints in unison rather than in sequence. Infants also tend to activate both

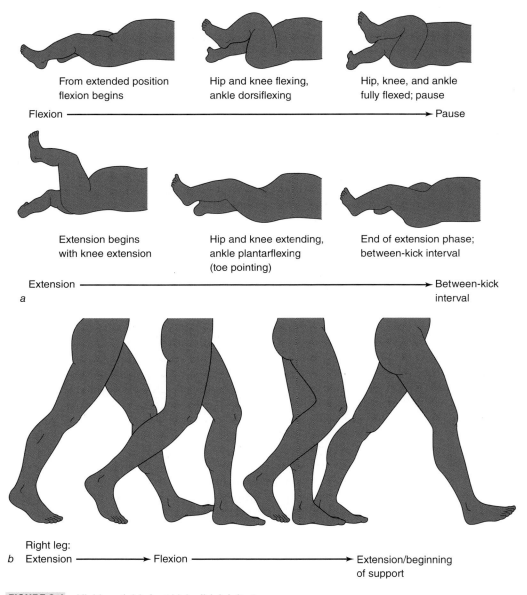

FIGURE 6.1   Kicking. *(a)* Infant kick. *(b)* Adult step.

the muscles for flexing the limb (flexors) and the muscles for extending the limb (extensors). This is called cocontraction. In contrast, adults move by alternating flexor and extensor muscles. However, by the end of their first year, infants begin to move the hip, knee, and ankle sequentially rather than in tight unison. Both alternating and synchronous (i.e., with both legs in unison) kicks are evident after 6 months, indicating that infants are developing more ways to coordinate the two limbs (Thelen, 1985, 1995; Thelen & Fisher, 1983; Thelen et al., 1983).

 WEB STUDY GUIDE   **Observe an infant throughout the first six and a half months of his life in Lab Activity 6.1, Identifying Rate Limits During the First 6.5 Months, in the web study guide. Go to www.HumanKinetics.com/LifeSpan MotorDevelopment.**

Spontaneous Arm Movements

Infants also move their arms, and newborns' spontaneous arm movements show well-coordinated extension of the elbow, wrist, and finger joints. In other words, the fingers do not extend independently, or one at a time, but rather in unison with the hand, wrist, and elbow (just as with the kick). Arm movements are not as rhythmical and repetitive as leg kicks, though (Thelen, 1981; Thelen, Kelso, & Fogel, 1987). As with the kick, early arm thrusts are not identical to adult reaching movements. It takes infants several months to begin opening their fingers independently of the other joints in anticipation of grasping objects as adults do (Trevarthen, 1984; von Hofsten, 1982, 1984). In addition, these spontaneous movements appear to be influenced by environmental constraints, as Kawai, Savelsbergh, and Wimmers (1999) found when they placed newborn infants in four environmental conditions and discovered differences in frequency and activity of spontaneous arm movements.

As mentioned previously, the rhythmic flapping of arms and kicking of legs have been termed stereotypies because of the underlying temporal structure of the movements (Thelen, 1979, 1981). Other stereotypies exist, which Thelen identified according to specific regions of the body, such as legs and feet (e.g., alternating leg movements), head and face (e.g., head banging), and fingers (e.g., flexing fingers). What does the existence of stereotypies suggest? First, newborns may be weak and unable to produce intentional, precise, goal-directed movements, but even at a young age they exhibit underlying rhythmic coordination within limbs or pairs of limbs (Piek, Gasson, Barrett, & Case, 2002). Second, these coordination patterns resemble the coordination patterns we see in later voluntary movement, which suggests some relationship between random and voluntary movement. Perhaps spontaneous movements are part of the fundamental building blocks of voluntary, functional movement (Jensen, Thelen, Ulrich, Schneider, & Zernicke, 1995).

Infantile Reflexes

Reflexive movements are often visible in young infants. Unlike random movements, reflexes are involuntary movements that an individual makes in response to specific stimuli. Sometimes these responses occur only when the body is in a specific position. An infant does not have to think about making reflexive movements; they occur automatically. Some reflexes, such as eye blinking, occur throughout the life span, but others are present only during infancy (**infantile reflexes**). We can categorize those seen during infancy into three types of movements: primitive reflexes, postural reactions, and locomotor reflexes (table 6.1). Let's define each of these categories and discuss their purposes.

KEY POINT
Infants' movements, though not always goal directed or goal achieving, can be coordinated, and the coordination patterns may resemble patterns seen in adults.

An **infantile reflex** is an involuntary, stereotypical movement response to a specific stimulus; the term refers specifically to such responses seen only during infancy. There are three types of infantile reflexes: the primitive and locomotor reflexes and the postural reactions.

Primitive Reflexes: Around From the Beginning

When a newborn infant grasps an object placed in her hand, she does so automatically and without conscious thought. This is an example of a primitive reflex, an involuntary response to specific stimulation that is often mediated by lower

TABLE 6.1   Infantile Reflexes

Reflex or reaction	Starting position (if important)	Stimulus	Response	Time	Warning signs
Primitive reflexes					
Asymmetrical tonic neck	Supine	Turn head to one side	Same-side arm and leg extend	Prenatal to 4 mo	Persistence after 6 mo
Symmetrical tonic neck	Supported sitting	Extend head and neck; flex head and neck	Arms extend, legs flex; arms flex, legs extend	6 mo to 7 mo	
Doll-eye		Flex head	Eyes look up	Prenatal to 2 wk	Persistence after first days of life
Palmar grasping		Touch palm with finger or object	Hand closes tightly around object	Prenatal to 4 mo	Persistence after 1 yr; asymmetrical reflex
Moro	Supine	Shake head, as by tapping pillow	Arms and legs extend, fingers spread; then arms and legs flex	Prenatal to 3 mo	Presence after 6 mo; asymmetrical reflex
Sucking		Touch face above or below lips	Sucking motion begins	Birth to 3 mo	
Babinski		Stroke sole of foot from heel to toes	Toes extend	Birth to 4 mo	Persistence after 6 mo
Searching or rooting		Touch cheek with smooth object	Head turns to side stimulated	Birth to 1 yr	Absence of reflex; persistence after 1 yr
Palmar-mandibular (Babkin)		Apply pressure to both palms	Mouth opens; eyes close; head flexes	1 to 3 mo	
Plantar grasping		Stroke ball of foot	Toes contract around object stroking foot	Birth to 12 mo	
Startle	Supine	Tap abdomen or startle infant	Arms and legs flex	7 to 12 mo	

Reflex or reaction	Starting position (if important)	Stimulus	Response	Time	Warning signs
Postural reactions					
Derotative righting	Supine	Turn legs and pelvis to other side	Trunk and head follow rotation	From 4 mo	
	Supine	Turn head sideways	Body follows head in rotation	From 4 mo	
Labyrinthine righting	Supported upright	Tilt infant	Head moves to stay upright	2 to 12 mo	
Pull-up	Sitting upright, held by 1 or 2 hands	Tip infant backward or forward	Arms flex	3 to 12 mo	
Parachute	Held upright	Lower infant toward ground rapidly	Legs extend	From 4 mo	
	Held upright	Tilt forward	Arms extend	From 7 mo	
	Held upright	Tilt sideways	Arms extend	From 6 mo	
	Held upright	Tilt backward	Arms extend	From 9 mo	
Locomotor reflexes					
Crawling	Prone	Apply pressure to sole of one foot or both feet alternately	Crawling pattern in arms and legs	Birth to 4 mo	
Stepping	Held upright	Place infant on flat surface	Walking pattern in legs	Birth to 5 mo	
Swimming	Prone	Place infant in or over water	Swimming movement of arms and legs	11 days to 5 mo	

brain centers (Peiper, 1963). Generally, newborns exhibit strong reflexes at birth; these reflexes tend to lose their strength over time until they disappear around the fourth month. How can we tell primitive reflexes from spontaneous movements?

- Reflexes are responses to specific external stimuli, whereas spontaneous movements do not result from any apparent external stimuli.
- Reflexive movements are specific and often localized, whereas spontaneous movements tend to be nonspecific and generalized.
- The same stimulus will elicit a specific reflex over and over again (McGraw, 1943).

The palmar grasp and the asymmetric tonic neck reflex are shown in figure 6.2. The labyrinthine righting reflex and the stepping reflex are shown in figure 6.3.

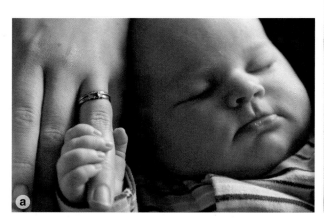

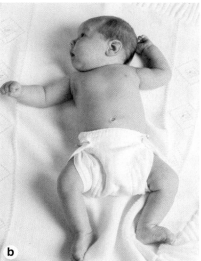

FIGURE 6.2 *(a)* Palmar grasp. The reflex is stimulated by touching or stroking the palm of the hand. *(b)* Asymmetrical tonic neck reflex. Note the "fencer's" position, which is one way to identify and describe this reflex.

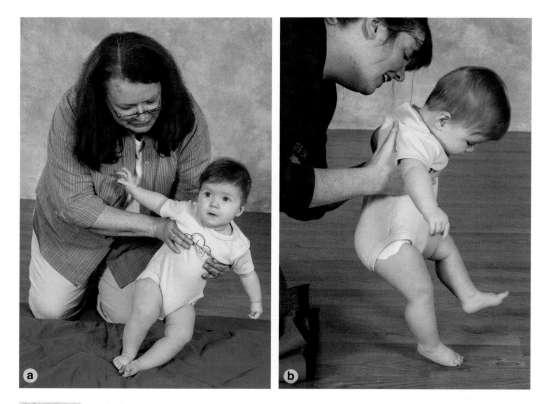

FIGURE 6.3 *(a)* Labyrinthine righting reflex. The infant rights the head when tipped backward. *(b)* Stepping reflex.

Postural Reactions: Moving Upright in the World

As their name implies, postural reactions, or gravity reflexes, help the infant automatically maintain posture in a changing environment (Peiper, 1963). Some of these responses keep the head upright, thereby keeping the breathing passages open. Others help the infant roll over and eventually attain a vertical position. Postural reactions generally appear after the infant is 2 months old. For example, an infant can roll over only after derotative righting appears after 4 months of age. By late in the first year or early in the second year of life, these isolated reactions requiring specific postures and stimuli drop out of the infant's repertoire of movements. However, these reflexes don't literally disappear. Children and adults react to being thrown off balance with specific muscle responses intended to bring the body back to balance. If you have recently tried in-line skating or snowboarding for the first time, you probably know this all too well! As you start to fall, you automatically extend your arms, and this automatic response results in many broken wrists—and unbroken skulls.

Locomotor Reflexes: Moving in Place

For a while in the 1980s, infant swim classes were all the rage. In these classes, parents placed their newborns in the water and the infants could actually swim! Precocious newborns? Perhaps, but more likely the infants were exhibiting the swim reflex, which, like other locomotor reflexes, gets its name because it appears similar and related to a voluntary movement (in this case, swimming). The locomotor reflexes appear much earlier than the corresponding voluntary behaviors and typically disappear months before the infant attempts the voluntary locomotor skill. There are three such locomotor reflexes: stepping, swimming, and crawling.

Appearance and Disappearance of Reflexes

In typically developing infants, infantile reflexes gradually show a less specific response with time; eventually, you can no longer stimulate these reflexes. In fact, the primitive reflexes start to weaken or become modified after about 2 weeks (Clark, 1995). Infants learn to adapt their reflexes after 2 weeks in order to modify the movement outcome (e.g., faster sucking leads to a faster supply of milk). Those who work with infants sometimes use the pattern of reflex appearance and disappearance to assess an individual infant's development. If the reflexes appear and disappear at an age close to the average, they consider the infant's development typical, whereas deviation from the typical pattern and typical execution of the response may signal a problem. An individual may deviate from typical in two ways:

- Exhibiting a reflex when the individual should not
- Not exhibiting a reflex when the individual should

A reflex that persists well after the average age of disappearance may indicate a pathological cerebral condition (Peiper, 1963). A nonexistent or very weak response on one side of the body compared with the other also could reflect a pathological condition.

In the popular television program *ER*, the doctors often check an incoming patient by running a probe along the bottom of the patient's foot. This is a real technique, called the Babinski test (see table 6.1 for a description of the Babinski reflex). This test is used to check for neurological problems in patients with head injuries. A positive Babinski sign indicates that the Babinski reflex as seen in infancy has returned—and that the patient most likely has an injury to the central nervous system.

Be careful when attempting to assess the neurological status of an infant (Bartlett, 1997). Remember that each individual develops as a result of interacting individual, environmental, and task constraints. This means that one infant may continue exhibiting reflexes after another of the same age has stopped without any pathological condition being involved. Most infants are ahead of or behind the average ages represented in normative data or scales. In addition, it is difficult to establish the exact time a reflex disappears. Only when the reflex persists for several months past the average might it constitute a warning sign of a pathological condition. You should also be aware that reflexive responses are very sensitive to environmental conditions. If you change an infant's body position or provide him with a stimulus that is different from those in table 6.1, you won't get a response. It is easy for an untrained person to overlook some aspect of the environment and thus fail to elicit a response; as a result, he or she may incorrectly conclude that a pathological condition exists. Therefore, trained professionals should be consulted for such assessments.

Why Do Infants Move? The Purpose of Reflexes

Ask any mother and she will tell you that infant movements start well before birth! In fact, several reflexes appear as soon as 2 to 3 months in utero. But why are infants born with reflexes? Some, like the rooting reflex, seem to have an obvious purpose: to help an infant survive. Others, such as the asymmetrical tonic neck reflex or swimming reflex, seem to have no clear relevance to the infant at birth. Perhaps some reflexes are important before birth.

Researchers have explained the role of reflexes in three general ways: structural, functional, and applied. The structural explanation views reflexes as a byproduct of the human neurological system. That is, some theorists believe that reflexes merely reflect the structure of the nervous system—in other words, the way humans are wired. The functional explanation suggests that reflexes exist to help the infant survive—to eat, breathe, and grasp (Clark, 1995). Milani-Comparetti (1981; Milani-Comparetti & Gidoni, 1967) suggests that the fetus uses reflexes to position itself for birth, then to assist in the birthing process. Both the structural and functional explanations consider reflexes at birth but do not suggest anything about their purpose past birth. Applied theories, in contrast, examine the role of reflexes in future volitional movements. (Once again, we see some very different ideas depending on the theoretical viewpoints of the researchers.) Others take the view that reflexive movements lead to coordinated limb movements (Peiper, 1963), thus giving the infant the opportunity to practice coordinated movements before the higher brain centers are ready to mediate such actions.

 Look at table 6.1 again. How do you see each reflex fitting into a role for future movements?

Relationship of Reflexes to Voluntary Movement

Ideas about the relationship between reflexes and later movement have changed dramatically over the past 50 years as a result of some unique experiments. Early researchers such as McGraw (1943) believed that infants could not move voluntarily until reflexes had been inhibited by the central nervous system—a theory termed motor interference. As time went on, researchers began to question this view. A relatively simple experiment by Zelazo, Zelazo, and Kolb (1972a,b) challenged the notion that reflexes and voluntary movements are not related. They elicited the stepping reflex daily in a small number of infants during their first 8 weeks. This daily practice not only increased the stepping reflex in these infants but also resulted in the earlier onset of voluntary walking in the trained infants compared with infants who did not practice the reflex. The investigators concluded that the involuntary walking reflex could be transformed into voluntary walking (see also Zelazo, 1983). They proposed that the disappearance of the reflex was due to disuse, that the period of reflex inhibition before onset of the voluntary skill was unnecessary, and that the systematic stimulation of a locomotor reflex could enhance infants' acquisition of voluntary locomotion.

Esther Thelen (1983, 1995; Thelen & Ulrich, 1991) also questioned whether reflexes had to be inhibited before voluntary movement could occur. With her colleagues, she proposed that other constraints, rather than strictly maturation, may be related to the disappearance of the stepping reflex. Thelen examined the changing individual constraints during early childhood and noticed that infants have a dramatic increase in leg weight, primarily from fat, during the first 2 months of life. She reasoned that this great increase in leg weight, along with the absence of a corresponding increase in muscle strength, may cause the stepping reflex to disappear because the infant has insufficient strength to lift the now-heavier legs. In other words, strength may be a rate limiter for stepping after 2 months or so of infancy.

To test this idea, Thelen and her associates took a group of 4- to 6-week-old infants who were still reflex-kicking and added small weights, equal to the amount of weight gain the infants were to experience, to their ankles. The amount of reflex stepping decreased, suggesting that the weight gain might be a viable explanation for the disappearing reflex. However, studies of these very young infants showed only half the picture. Thelen had to demonstrate that reflex stepping still existed in older infants if she accounted for the constraint of strength. To do so, she took older infants (who no longer reflex-stepped) and submerged them to their chests in a small tank of water. The water had the effect of buoying the legs (simulating an increase in strength), and these infants began to step with greater frequency. This result is similar to that of Zelazo's, whose training may have made the infants' legs strong enough to step despite weight gain. Finally, Thelen (1985; Thelen & Ulrich, 1991; Vereijken & Thelen, 1997) found that infants who did not reflexively step at 7 months *did* step when held over the moving belt of a motorized treadmill. The sum of these studies suggests that several individual constraints (rather than simply maturation) play a strong role as rate limiters on movement patterns during infancy. These studies have inspired several other infant research studies that utilized treadmills. Figure 6.4 illustrates the ongoing research that uses treadmills to elicit stepping in infants with Down syndrome.

KEY POINT
The increase and decrease of stepping with changes in environmental and task constraints (e.g., addition of a moving treadmill belt, manipulation of leg weight) indicate that systems other than the nervous system must be involved in this aspect of motor development.

Motor Milestones: The Pathway to Voluntary Movements

Compare the movements of a newborn with those of the same child 12 months later. Somehow, those spontaneous and reflexive movements give way to complex, coordinated, purposeful activities such as walking, reaching, and grasping. What happens to the infant in the intervening months? Clearly, the infant does not suddenly acquire a complex skill; rather, he must learn how to coordinate and control the many interacting parts of his body. He must attain certain fundamental skills that

A **motor milestone** is a fundamental motor skill, the attainment of which is associated with the acquisition of later voluntary movements. The order in which an infant attains these milestones is relatively consistent, although the timing differs among individuals.

lead to skilled performance. We call these fundamental skills **motor milestones** (figure 6.5), and each one is a landmark or turning point in an individual's motor development. Think of them this way: To walk, you must be able to stand; to stand, you must be able to hold your trunk upright; and to hold your trunk upright, you must be able to hold your head erect. Each skill is associated with a preceding milestone. Individual infants vary in the time at which they reach a motor milestone, but they acquire these rudimentary skills in a relatively consistent sequence. Table 6.2 gives the timing and sequence of selected motor milestones.

Bayley (1936, 1969), Shirley (1931, 1963), and other researchers observed infants

FIGURE 6.4 To improve the onset and quality of independent walking, an infant with Down syndrome is trained on a motorized treadmill.

Photo courtesy of Dale Ulrich.

and determined a sequence of motor milestones as well as the average ages at which the infants achieved them. This progressive pattern of skill acquisition can be related to predictable changes in individual constraints that occur in typically developing infants. These include

- maturation of the central nervous system,
- development of muscular strength and endurance,
- development of posture and balance, and
- improvement of sensory processing.

After reading this chapter, students may wonder whether the motor milestone research from Bayley and Shirley is still relevant. Haven't improvements in nutrition and child-rearing practices—as well as innovations in infant toys and equipment—led to quicker attainment of motor milestones? Or perhaps improvements in experimental methods and observation have resulted in more precise age-range windows? The World Health Organization set out to answer these questions with its Multicentre Growth Reference Study (MGRS; de Onis et al., 2004, 2007; Wijnhoven et al., 2006; WHO Multicentre Growth Reference Study Group, 2006). The entire study involved six nations and thousands of children; for assessment of gross motor development, the group observed a total of 816 children from five countries (Ghana, India, Norway, Oman, and the United States). The groups focused on six motor milestones: sitting without support, creeping, standing with assistance, walking with assistance, standing alone, and walking alone. Children were observed longitudinally from the age of 4 months until they could walk on their own. The fieldworkers making observations were highly trained, and high levels of interobserver reliability were set to ensure that all fieldworkers identified the milestones correctly and similarly.

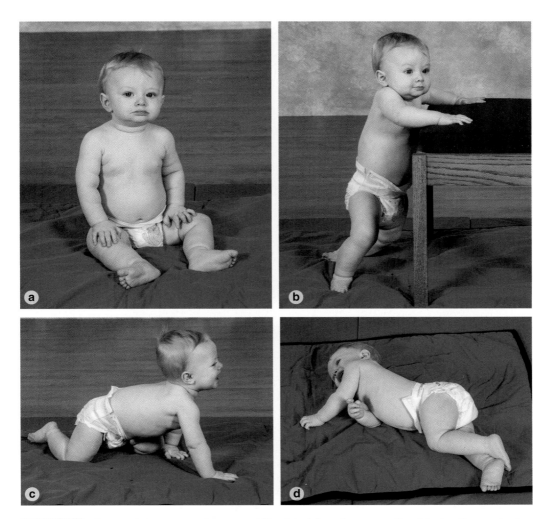

FIGURE 6.5   Some of the motor milestone skills: *(a)* sitting alone steadily, *(b)* standing up by furniture, *(c)* creeping, *(d)* rolling from back to front.

What did the WHO Multicentre Growth Reference Study find in terms of age of attainment for the motor skills? The results for the 50th percentile ranking for the MGRS were remarkably similar to those found by Bayley in 1936 and within the ranges found by Shirley in 1963. The greatest discrepancies occurred in the earliest motor milestones; however, Bayley's average ages never differed from the ages found in the MGRS by more than 3 weeks. For example, the MGRS reported that the 50th percentile of infants sat without support at 5.9 months, whereas Bayley reported an average of 6.6 months and Shirley reported 7.0 months. Similarly, the MGRS reported that 50% of the infants attained the skill of standing with assistance at 7.4 months, whereas Shirley reported 8.0 months and Bayley reported 8.1 months. From this point on, however, the data from the MGRS and Bayley match closely. Shirley's average ages vary more and are always later than MGRS ages; however, her age ranges are still within the contemporary ranges found by the MGRS.

What can we conclude from all of this? First, based on the MGRS, it appears that a secular trend in milestones does not exist. That is, infants are currently attaining motor milestones at about the same age as infants did more than 80

TABLE 6.2 Selected Motor Milestones

Average age (mo)	Age range (mo)	Milestone (Bayley Scales of Infant Development)	Milestone (Shirley Sequence)
0.1		Lifts head when held at shoulder	
0.1		Lateral head movements	
0.8	0.3–2.0	Arm thrusts in play	
0.8	0.3–2.0	Leg thrusts in play	Chin up (lifts head in prone)
0.8	0.3–3.0	Retains (i.e., grasps) red ring	
1.6	0.7–4.0	Head erect and steady	
1.8	0.7–5.0	Turns from side to back	
2.0			Chest up (lifts head and chest in prone position)
2.3	1.0–5.0	Sits with slight support	
4.0			Sits with support
4.4	2.0–7.0	Turns from back to side	
4.9	4.0–8.0	Partial thumb opposition	
5.0			Sits on lap; grasps object
5.3	4.0–8.0	Sits alone momentarily	
5.4	4.0–8.0	Unilateral reaching	
5.7	4.0–8.0	Rotates wrist	
6.0			Sits in chair; grasps dangling object
6.4	4.0–10.0	Rolls from back to front	
6.6	5.0–9.0	Sits alone steadily	
6.9	5.0–9.0	Complete thumb opposition	
7.0			Sits alone
7.1	5.0–11.0	Prewalking progression	
7.4	6.0–10.0	Partial finger prehension	
8.0			Stands with help
8.1	5.0–12.0	Pulls to standing	
8.6	6.0–12.0	Stands up by furniture	
8.8	6.0–12.0	Stepping movements	
9.0			Stands holding furniture
9.6	7.0–12.0	Walks with help	
10.0			Creeps
11.0	9.0–16.0	Stands alone	Walks when led
11.7	9.0–17.0	Walks alone	
12.0			Pulls to stand
14.0			Stands alone
14.6	11.0–20.0	Walks backward	
15.0			Walks alone
16.1	12.0–23.0	Walks up stairs with help	
16.4	13.0–23.0	Walks down stairs with help	
23.4	17.0–30.0+	Jumps off floor, both feet	
24.8	19.0–30.0+	Jumps from bottom step	

years ago. Second, the observation techniques that Bayley and Shirley used were both valid and reliable. Finally, we can still use the Bayley and Shirley scales with confidence that the age ranges represented indicate where typically developing infants should, on average, be.

 WEB STUDY GUIDE Observe babies move in Lab Activity 6.2, Assessing Motor Milestones, in the web study guide. Go to www.HumanKinetics.com/ LifeSpanMotorDevelopment.

Constraints and the Attainment of Motor Milestones

Remember that individual constraints can act as rate limiters, or controllers. That is, for an infant to exhibit a certain skill, she needs to develop a certain system to a particular level. For example, in order to lift her head while lying on her belly, an infant must have sufficient strength in her neck and shoulders (figure 6.6). Because different systems advance earlier in some infants than in others, the rate of achievement of motor milestones varies. Experience and environmental constraints also play a role in individual variability (Adolph, Vereijken, & Denny, 1998). Culturally defined parental handling practices can alter the rate at which an infant attains motor milestones (Clark, 1995). For example, an infant born to a new mother may experience "first child syndrome," which is not a disease but a cultural phenomenon in the United States wherein first-time mothers hold their infants for long periods and avoid putting the infants on their stomachs for a long time. These periods of prolonged holding result in delayed onset of certain motor milestones such as crawling; the infant does not have the opportunity to strengthen her neck muscles when lying prone. Once again, we see that motor development arises from the interaction of individual, environment, and task.

Recent research suggests that the attainment of certain milestones themselves can act as rate limiters for other skills. Corbetta and Bojczyk (2002) looked at the reaching and nonreaching movements and hand preferences of nine infants from the age of 3 weeks until the time at which they could walk independently. The most striking finding was that when the infants attained certain motor milestones—such as sitting, crawling, or walking—they changed their hand preference and even reverted back to an earlier form of reaching (with two hands). In the attainment of walking, the change back to two-handed reaching is likely the result of the infants' balance acting as a rate limiter; this type of reach is less likely to compromise the infants' newfound ability to walk. The

FIGURE 6.6 In order to crawl, an infant must first be able to lift her head and shoulders in a prone position, which requires neck and shoulder strength.

It is clearly necessary and beneficial to assess individual children and groups of children. Assessment can, for example, help professionals identify children who need special attention, chart individual and group progress, and choose appropriate educational tasks. Professionals must recognize, though, that testing instruments have specific purposes and are best used when the purpose matches a particular need. For instance, we can broadly classify testing instruments as either norm referenced or criterion referenced.

The purpose of norm-referenced scales is to compare an individual or group with previously established norms. Such a comparison indicates where a person falls in a group of like individuals matched on relevant factors, such as age, sex, and race. The value of norm-referenced scales in identifying slowly developing children is obvious; at the same time, such scales give professionals no information about the nature or cause of a delay or about what educational experiences to prescribe to facilitate future development.

Criterion-referenced scales indicate where a child falls on a continuum of skills that we know are acquired in sequence. The developmentalist administers the criterion-referenced scale periodically and compares individuals with their own previous performances rather than with a population norm. Often, criterion-referenced scales indicate what skills the individual has mastered and what skills are just emerging. Educators can prescribe education and practice activities based on those emerging skills, thus guaranteeing that the educational task is developmentally appropriate for the individual.

fluctuation in hand preference provides more evidence to suggest that many interacting constraints influence the development of motor skills.

Motor Milestones and Atypical Development

Because of their sequential nature, motor milestones may provide clues for trained professionals, such as doctors and physical therapists, about an infant's neurological health. In a study of 173 high-risk preterm infants, Allen and Alexander (1994) evaluated six motor milestones on sequential visits to screen for cerebral palsy. They found that they could predict cerebral palsy accurately when looking for a 37.5% delay on each of the six motor milestones on subsequent evaluations. This finding underscores two important points. First, the milestone sequence is fairly predictable in typically developing infants. Second, although variability exists in the acquisition of milestones, substantial delay in several milestones may indicate a developmental problem. Of course, it's always best to check with a professional before assuming that an infant has such a problem.

Other conditions can lead to differences in the onset of motor milestones. For example, early in development, infants with Down syndrome often experience hypotonia, which is best described as a lack of muscle tone. In fact, infants with Down syndrome have been characterized as "floppy." Hypotonia often improves later in development. However, this lack of muscle tone usually results in delayed acquisition of motor milestones, such as grasping, sitting, rolling, and pulling to stand, throughout infancy (Jobling & Virji-Babul, 2004). Because these milestones require a certain degree of strength, hypotonia can be considered a rate-limiting factor in the acquisition of these milestones. Furthermore, infants acquire many of these milestones in a sequence that leads to the ability to maintain an upright

Most of the scales developed for infants are of the norm-referenced type. (Typically, more expertise is needed to administer a criterion-referenced scale than a norm-referenced scale.) The Bayley Scales of Infant Development, discussed in this chapter, are norm referenced (Bayley, 1969). The complete Bayley Scales consist of a mental scale (163 items), a motor scale (81 items), and a behavior record for social and attentional behaviors. Users of these scales can compare infants and toddlers from 2 months to 2.5 years with mental and motor norms.

Another well-known norm-referenced scale is the Denver Developmental Screening Test (Frankenburg & Dodds, 1967). This test can be used from birth to 6 years of age to assess four areas:

1. Gross motor performance (31 items)
2. Fine motor performance (30 items)
3. Language development (21 items)
4. Personal–social skills (representing age-appropriate social skills; 22 items)

A third well-known norm-referenced scale is the Gesell Developmental Schedules (Gesell & Amatruda, 1949). All these instruments are well standardized, but their motor scales are less reliable and valid than is desirable. In this sense they are useful but limited in the information they provide about motor development.

posture. Therefore, delays in milestones lead to delays in the attainment of fundamental motor skills, such as walking, and activities of daily living, such as eating (Reid & Block, 1996; Ulrich, Ulrich, & Collier, 1992).

Because infant mobility appears to be important to early development, any condition that delays or impedes infant mobility may negatively affect cognitive development. Motor development and early movement influence both social and cognitive development. For example, an infant begins to explore his environment by reaching and grasping objects; this allows for a human–object interface that involves multiple sensory systems (e.g., vision, tactile, and, if the object is placed in the infant's mouth, taste). Such movements help create neural pathways in the brain, which are critical in the first 3 years of life (Kail & Cavanaugh, 2010; Ulrich et al., 1992). If infants are significantly delayed in these experiences, they will miss out on some or all of these opportunities to learn to integrate sensory information (Ulrich, Lloyd, Tiernan, Looper, & Angulo-Barroso, 2008). Part of this learning is discovering cause–effect relationships in their surroundings. Further, independent locomotion provides infants and toddlers with a way to control and explore their environment as well as an opportunity to interact socially (Lynch, Ryu, Agrawal, & Galloway, 2009). Therefore, delayed acquisition of motor skills can have a far more profound effect than simply the inability to move; it can influence the entire developmental process, leading to greater cognitive disabilities than would exist if the same child had had movement opportunities (Ulrich et al., 2008).

 If you were a physical therapist, what types of delays would you expect to see if you were working with infants who had low muscle tone or muscle spasticity? Consider how the delay in one milestone would affect later milestones.

WEB STUDY GUIDE   Use a criterion-referenced scale to assess toddlers in Lab Activity 6.3, Assessing Toddler Motor Behavior, in the web study guide. Go to www.HumanKinetics.com/LifeSpanMotorDevelopment.

Development of Postural Control and Balance in Infancy

Many of the motor milestones of the first year of life involve the attainment of certain postures, of which sitting and standing are the most obvious examples. Once infants can maintain a posture, they are balancing. As a result, developmentalists have been interested in whether postural control and balance make up the rate-limiting system in the onset of certain milestone skills. They have also been interested in whether infants rely on the same cues for balance that adults do.

Some evidence shows that newborns make postural adjustments of the head in response to a visual display of optical flow, or the change in optic patterns that occurs while one moves (Jouen, 1990; Jouen, Lepecq, Gapenne, & Bertenthal, 2000). This finding might indicate that the rate-controlling factor is not the perception of optical flow but rather the making of appropriate postural responses. Researchers have studied this question using the moving-room technique (figure 6.7). Pope (1984) held infants in a seated position on a stationary platform and observed their muscular responses through electromyograph recordings when the walls and ceiling of the small room surrounding them were moved. The effect was to provide visual information that made it seem as if the body, not the room, were moving, while kinesthetic information from the vestibular and somatosensory receptors indicated that the body was not moving. Thus, the visual information and the kinesthetic information were in conflict. The 2-month-olds reacted to the visual information rather than the kinesthetic information. That is, they responded as if their bodies were swaying and activated muscle to regain their starting posture.

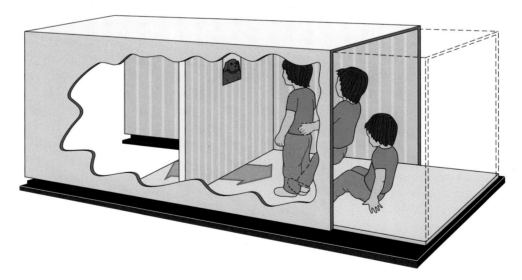

FIGURE 6.7   A moving room. In this drawing, the small "room" (made up of four walls and a ceiling) is moved toward the child, and the child falls backward. This response would occur if the child perceived the optical flow produced by the room movement as forward sway rather than as room movement.

Bertenthal, Rose, and Bai (1997) observed 5-, 7-, 9-, and 13-month-olds sitting in a moving room when the room moved at two different speeds. This age span included some infants who could sit alone and some who could not. The investigators found that all the infants, even those not yet capable of sitting alone, responded to room movement (they believed the visual information more than the kinesthetic information), and their action was linked to the movement speed. Investigators also observed that infants' responses improved with sitting experience; those with experience made postural responses sooner, more accurately, and more consistently.

When infants who have just begun standing are placed in a moving room, they often sway, stagger, or fall—unlike adults, who can keep their balance (Bertenthal & Bai, 1989; Butterworth & Hicks, 1977; Lee & Aronson, 1974; Woollacott & Sveistrup, 1994). Newly standing children take longer than adults to use their postural muscles when thrown off balance and sway more before attaining stability (Forssberg & Nashner, 1982). The moving-room effect diminishes in children after their first year of standing.

It seems, then, that visual perception of self-motion is not the rate-controlling factor in infant posture and balance. Rather, the rate-controlling factor may be a *coupling* of the sensory information with the appropriate motor response. The refinement of this coupling occurs for every task, such as sitting and standing. This view is consistent with research on the neurological system, suggesting that vision must be linked to specific motor response loci (Goodale, 1988; Milner & Goodale, 1995). Once refined, these perception–action couplings provide very sensitive and rapid adjustments to the environment. As infants move, their environments change. As the environments change, infants must regulate and refine their movements based on continuous sensory information. In other words, infants must continuously calibrate their sensorimotor coupling (Chen, Metcalfe, Jeka, & Clark, 2007; Metcalfe et al., 2005). As systems develop and change, the sensorimotor coupling must change as well, requiring a recalibration to the environment.

Barela, Jeka, and Clark (1999) observed touch control in infants as they reached four important stages: pulling to stand, standing alone, beginning to walk, and reaching 1.5 months of walking experience. As the infants acquired standing experience, both their body sway and the force they applied to a nearby contact surface decreased. In the first three of these stages (pulling to stand, standing alone, and beginning to walk), the infants responded to body sway by applying force to the surface. After the infants gained walking experience, they used the touch information to control posture rather than simply react to sway. Somatosensory information certainly plays an important role in posture and balance. Infant research has established the important role of perceptual information from the various systems in actions that maintain our posture and balance, and more research is needed on how these various sources of information are integrated in the maintenance of posture and balance.

Summary and Synthesis

A newborn infant moves in a variety of ways. She may kick her legs and wave her arms in a seemingly random fashion; we call these spontaneous movements or stereotypies. She may also respond to a touch with a specific movement pattern; these responses are called infantile reflexes. During the first year she will begin to lift her head and sit alone. Such skills, which appear in a fairly well-defined sequence, are called motor milestones. She will sit, crawl, and stand, all of which demand postural control. In a typically developing infant, these motor behaviors come forward in a relatively predictable sequence and time frame, owing to rapidly changing individual constraints (both structural and functional). Differences among infants in sequence and timing do exist, however. The difference may simply indicate that for this particular infant, the interactions between individual, environmental, and task constraints encourage motor behaviors in a unique way. On the other hand, some infants may have some underlying condition, such as cerebral palsy or Down syndrome, that leads to a delay in the attainment of motor milestones.

What do the movements we see during infancy tell us about the infant himself? Developmentalists still debate the purpose of reflexes and spontaneous movements. However, several things are becoming clear. First, these movement patterns are not random; rather, they are coordinated (if not purposeful). Second, early movement patterns play some role in future movement, most likely creating the foundations of future movements. In any case, we cannot separate early movements from later skills. The infant's experiences—along with his physical characteristics, the environment, parental handling, and other constraints acting in the context of his infancy—all interact in the development of movement skill.

 Reinforcing What You Have Learned About Constraints

TAKE A SECOND LOOK

Referring back to the anecdote about babies and robots at the start of the chapter, some people may ask, "Why let an infant drive a robot?" Others may wonder why, if interested in teaching kindergarten through 12th grade or rehabilitating adults, one would study infancy at all. Two important reasons exist. First, infant motor behavior appears to form the basis of later voluntary behavior, as shown by a variety of researchers, such as Thelen and colleagues. Second, a positive relationship appears to exist between motor and cognitive behavior. As Galloway, the researcher who studied babies and robots, explained about infancy, "As soon as you're reaching, as soon as you're walking, your cognition explodes." For infants and children who are developing atypically, observing developmental delays early on may allow for early intervention and a reduction in later deficits. Therefore, it is important to understand infant development because infancy provides an important piece of the motor development puzzle.

TEST YOUR KNOWLEDGE

1. For four of the infantile reflexes listed in table 6.1, describe either a survival function or a purpose later in life.
2. Consider the individual, environmental, and task constraints interacting during infancy, then give several reasons why an infant might be delayed in attaining a motor milestone.
3. Describe how both task and environmental constraints can have a profound effect on the emergence of motor skills.
4. On what perceptual system do young infants seem to rely for balance information?

LEARNING EXERCISE 6.1

Identifying Constraints During Infancy and Toddlerhood

The attainment of a milestone indicates a unique interaction of various constraints that allow the particular behavior to emerge. The rate at which motor milestones appear (and to a certain extent, the type of milestone) for one infant can differ from that for other infants. This suggests that particular constraints may act as rate limiters, or controllers, for a given infant and that when a critical value of that rate limiter is at last reached, the infant will achieve the motor milestone or skill.

One of the best ways to observe constraints in action is to watch a group of infants whose ages vary. Visit a local infant center and carefully observe the infants as their caretakers interact with them. Given your knowledge of infant development from this chapter, make a list of the constraints that affect the motor behavior of individual infants. Find individual, environmental, and task constraints in the context of the infant center. For individual constraints, explain which might act as rate limiters for motor milestones. For environmental and task constraints, explain how these either encourage or discourage different motor behaviors.

Development of Human Locomotion

![Chapter objectives icon] **CHAPTER OBJECTIVES**

This chapter

- defines the concept of locomotion in humans,
- describes the types of locomotion,
- discusses the development of specific locomotor patterns, and
- explains the individual constraints that affect development of locomotor patterns.

Who Says Growing Old Means Slowing Down?

As the world's population continues to gray, more and more older adults defy popular stereotypes of frailty and weakness by participating in physical activity at an elite level. One such athlete is Philippa "Phil" Raschker, who was selected as Female World Masters Athlete of the Year by the World Masters Athletics Association. Raschker, competing in the 60-to-64-year-old age group, has amassed an amazing 71 gold, 19 silver, and 7 bronze medals at the World Masters Athletics Championships (many in running events, such as the 100 m dash and the 300 m hurdles) since 1983. These include three she won at the championships in 2011. She has twice been a finalist for the Amateur Athletic Union Sullivan Award, given annually to the country's top amateur athlete of *any* age group. Other finalists have included superstar athletes LeBron James, Apolo Ohno, Michael Phelps, and Diana Taurasi. The 2004 documentary *Racing Against the Clock* featured Raschker and four other senior women who are still competing successfully in track and field. Phil Raschker exemplifies the fact that aging does not necessarily preclude one from maintaining, or even developing, considerable locomotor abilities.

People interested in motor development often focus on early acquisition of locomotor skills. Our introduction demonstrates, however, that locomotion is a lifelong movement activity. Changes do, of course, occur in walking, running, galloping, and other motor skills as individual, environmental, and task constraints change. This chapter examines various locomotor skills across the life span, how they change systematically, and how individual constraints act as rate controllers.

Locomotion is the act of moving from place to place.

Locomotion is the act of moving, or the capability to move, from place to place. Moving around, getting from here to there: Locomotion is something we do each day without much thought at all. However, this seemingly simple definition may hide the fact that moving from place to place is actually a complex activity that involves many interacting systems and constraints. The study of locomotion falls within many fields, from medicine to psychology, and includes many movements, from squirming to swimming. Across the life span, individuals use various methods of locomotion. Of course, the type of locomotion they use depends on interacting constraints. During the childhood years, height, weight, and lengths change dramatically and may act as rate controllers. During much of the life span, other types of constraints, such as motivation or even the perceived gender association of a skill (e.g., "skipping is for girls"), may encourage or discourage behavior. As one approaches old age, structural constraints such as physical characteristics may return as important rate controllers. However, functional constraints, such as fear of falling or loss of balance capability, may act just as strongly to discourage locomotion, as can environmental constraints, such as weather changes (e.g., snow and ice). As a result, we must examine many changing constraints to understand locomotion across the life span.

The First Voluntary Locomotor Efforts: Creeping and Crawling

What does it take for an infant to move from one place to another for the first time? Certain motor milestones must be achieved, such as lifting the head in the prone position. The infant must also have enough strength to support and move himself and must uncouple his limbs, which have primarily moved in unison and in the same direction. In addition to these individual constraints, the environment must allow for infant locomotion, and the infant must evaluate the environment to see how well it matches his or her individual constraints. Adolph (1997) suggests that the environment must afford the infant several things:

> The surface must provide a continuous path to support the body, must be large enough to allow passage as the body moves forward, must be sturdy enough to support body weight, and must be firm enough, flat enough, and have sufficient friction to maintain balance as weight shifts from limb to limb. (p. 6)

Certain systems act as rate limiters, or controllers, that hold an infant back from the initiation of locomotion. Once critical levels are reached in these systems, an infant can begin to move. The first types of locomotion that infants exhibit are usually **creeping** (moving on hands and knees) (figure 7.1) and **crawling** (moving on hands and stomach, in a "combat crawl"). The following progression of skills leads to creeping and crawling:

1. Crawling with the chest and stomach on the floor
2. Low creeping with the stomach off the floor but the legs working together (symmetrically)
3. Rocking back and forth in the high creep position
4. Creeping with the legs and arms working alternately

Although not typically seen, another form of quadrupedal gait exists in infants: walking on hands and feet. Burton (1999) reviewed the work of Hrdlicka, who published a book in 1931 called *Children Who Run on All Fours*, and interpreted it using a dynamic systems approach. He concluded that the emergence of this gait pattern resulted from infrequently occurring interactions between constraints. First, environmental constraints related to crawling surface may make knee support

Creeping and **crawling** occur when all four limbs are in contact with the supporting surface. In crawling, the infant's chest and stomach also touch the surface. In creeping, only the hands and knees touch the surface.

FIGURE 7.1 Infant creeping. Balance and strength must be sufficient for infants to support themselves, first on three limbs and eventually on one arm and the opposite leg.

uncomfortable (e.g., gravel, asphalt); thus, the infant changes to feet support. Next, the reinforcement or response of the parent or caregiver may encourage further use of this gait. Finally, average- or above-average strength and health of the infant must interact with these environmental factors to allow the hands-and-feet gait pattern to appear. Because these factors (and perhaps others that haven't been explored) often do not exist and interact to encourage the hands-and-feet gait pattern, we hardly ever see "running on all fours" in infants.

Walking Across the Life Span

Typically, a developing human can look forward to a long career as a walker. It's easy to assume that once people can walk, they won't change their walking technique much over the life span. As with other motor behaviors, however, people continually change the way they walk as constraints change. What remains the same across one's lifetime is the underlying timing of **walking**, which is 50% phasing between the legs (Clark, Whitall, & Phillips, 1988). In other words, individuals alternate their legs so that the left leg is halfway through its motion as the right leg begins its own. Also, there is a period of double support, when both feet contact the ground, followed by a period of single support. These are the relative timing relationships (coordination) that appear early in life, and they don't seem to change much (Clark, 1995). However, as an individual's body or the environment changes, the absolute timing (i.e., slower or faster) and placement (i.e., step height or length) can change substantially.

> **Imagine you are a parent. What sort of rate controllers might keep your crawling infant from creeping?**

First Steps: Characteristics of Early Walking

Most people—especially parents—know what a toddler's first solo steps look like. In fact, researchers have studied and described these first steps (Adolph, Vereijken, & Shrout, 2003; Burnett & Johnson, 1971; Clark et al., 1988; Sutherland, Olshen, Cooper, & Woo, 1980). At first, each step tends to be independent of the next. The toddler takes short steps with little leg and hip extension. She steps with flat feet and points her toes outward. The toddler spreads her feet wide apart when planted to improve her lateral balance. She doesn't use any trunk rotation. The toddler holds her arms up in high guard; that is, her hands and arms are carried high in a bent position. All of the characteristics in early walking lead to improved balance for the new walker (figure 7.2, *a* and *b*). As the child continues to develop, her arms will drop to about waist level (middle guard) and later to an extended position at the sides (low guard; figure 7.2*c*), but they still will not swing. When children do begin to use the arm swing, it frequently is unequal and irregular; both hands might swing forward together (Roberton, 1978b, 1984).

Rate Limiters in Early Walking

Infants have the ability to move their legs in an alternating pattern from birth onward, yet they cannot walk for at least 7 months after birth. Clearly, several individual constraints must develop to certain critical levels before the infant can support and move his own weight. His legs must be able to move alternately, and he must have enough strength to support himself on a single limb. He must also

Walking is defined by a 50% phasing relationship between the legs as well as a period of double support (when both feet are on the ground) followed by a period of single support.

KEY POINT
After infancy, most humans move from place to place using upright bipedal locomotion. A particular pattern of locomotion is called a gait. Upright bipedal gait patterns include walking, running, galloping, skipping, and hopping.

KEY POINT
Rate limiters in early walking are muscular strength and balance.

FIGURE 7.2 *(a)* A beginning walker. Note the short stride and high-guard arm position. *(b)* To maintain balance, beginning walkers often plant their feet wide apart, with the toes out. *(c)* Rather than swing the arms in time with the legs, beginning walkers often hold their arms in high-, middle-, or low-guard position.

Parts a and c © Mary Ann Roberton; Part b © Mary Ann Roberton and Kate R. Barrett.

balance on one leg while transferring his weight to his other foot. These requirements suggest specific rate-controlling factors. Thelen, Ulrich, and Jensen (1989) suggest that infants must have muscle strength in the trunk and extensor muscles to allow them to maintain an upright posture on a small base of support. They must also develop balance, or an erect posture or body position, to the point where they can compensate for the shift of weight from one leg to the other (Adolph et al., 2003; Clark & Phillips, 1993; Clark et al., 1988).

Addressing Atypical Walking Development in Down Syndrome

As we mention in chapter 6, children with Down syndrome often experience delays in motor milestones. The cascading effect of delayed early milestones leads to delayed onset of walking, sometimes significantly. As part of a series of studies investigating the use of a treadmill intervention to promote earlier onset of walking, Ulrich, Ulrich, Angulo-Kinzler, and Yun (2001) examined a group of infants with Down syndrome. On average, infants began the study at 10 months of age (±1.5 months) and began participating when they could sit independently for 30 s. All participants received physical therapy that infants with Down syndrome typically receive. In addition, the intervention infants received in-home practice stepping on a small motorized treadmill. During the intervention, the parents held the infants over the treadmill, which moved at 0.46 mile per hour. If the infants did not step, the parents repositioned them. This process was performed for 8 min a day (starting at 1 min of intervention followed by 1 min of rest) 5 days per week until the infant began independent walking. Further, the research team visited participants on a biweekly basis and carefully monitored motor development and growth.

The results indicated that the experimental protocol was successful. Before independent walking, the intervention group could rise to a standing position as well as walk with assistance sooner than the control group could (the former not significant at $p = .09$ and the latter difference significant at $p = .03$). In addition, the group with treadmill training learned to walk with assistance sooner and to walk independently significantly sooner (at 19.9 months vs. at 23.9 months) than the control group. The researchers concluded that the treadmill intervention was successful in encouraging the emergence of independent walking in this sample of infants with Down syndrome.

 Imagine you are a parent. What environmental or task constraints might limit the rate at which walking develops in your infant?

An instructor of motor skills must be able to critically observe children's skill patterns. The instructor needs to give students feedback, provide further practice experiences, and formally assess their skills. The observation process requires a disciplined, systematic focus on the critical features of a skill pattern rather than on the outcome, or product, of a skill. The observer must learn observation techniques and practice them like any other skill in order to make them automatic.

Barrett (1979) provided a guide for improving the observation skills of instructors and coaches based on three principles:

1. Analysis
2. Planning
3. Positioning

To analyze developmental movement, the observer must first know the developmental sequences of the skill, including the critical features that characterize a given developmental step and the mechanical principles involved in proficient performance.

Observers must also organize and plan their observations in order to prevent their attention from wandering once activity begins. They may find it helpful to have written observation guidelines, many of which can be based on the developmental sequences suggested by researchers. One can, however, design suitable observation guidelines by simply listing the critical features of the skill to be watched. It might also be a good idea for observers to watch a given feature of a skill many times (two or three tries, or more).

The third principle is positioning. Many new observers rivet themselves to one location and attempt to watch everything from there. However, some critical features of motor skills can be seen only from the side; others are best seen from the front or back. It is important, then, for the observer to move about and to watch the performer from several angles.

Proficient Walking Patterns

Part of becoming a proficient walker involves taking advantage of the principles of motion and stability discussed in chapter 3. For example, new walkers optimize balance by widening their stance, which increases their base of support. However, stability is not always desirable, especially because it comes at the expense of mobility. Thus, once an infant's balance improves, she must decrease her base of support to become more mobile. Many of the characteristics of proficient walking relate to exploiting biomechanical principles as body dimensions change—in other words, recalibrating the body to the environment. Consider these developmental changes in walking that lead to a proficient level:

- Absolute stride length increases, reflecting greater application of force and greater leg extension at push-off. Also, as children grow, increased leg length contributes to a longer stride.
- Planting the foot flat on the ground changes to a heel-then-forefoot pattern, which results from an increased range of motion.
- The individual reduces out-toeing and narrows the base of support laterally to keep the forces exerted in the forward–backward plane.

The process of motor skill observation demands focused attention. New observers must plan ahead, know the critical features of the skill to be watched, position themselves properly, and practice observing.

You can see the key features that distinguish developmental levels by simply watching skill performance, but often there is a need to conduct a more formal assessment. Teachers, therapists, and researchers typically need to record an individual's development level in order to track progress, design activities, or make comparisons. Conducting a more formal assessment requires several tools:

- A description of the movements and positions that are characteristic of each step in a developmental sequence
- A plan for observing movement so that an individual can be quickly and accurately placed into a developmental step or level
- A recording sheet so that observations can be quickly recorded for future use

These tools are provided for many of the fundamental motor skills discussed in the next several chapters. A developmental sequence table lists the developmental steps as well as a description of the movements or positions characteristic of each step. They are organized by a body component, such as the legs or arms, or by a phase of the skill, such as the backswing. An observation plan follows. For each component, the observation plan directs you, by means of a question, to watch for one specific movement or position at a time. By indicating what you observe, you move through the observation plan until you arrive at the performer's developmental level. This information can be placed on a record sheet, much like the ones used in the lab activities for chapters 7 – 9.

- The skilled walker adopts the **double knee-lock** pattern to assist the full range of leg motion. In this pattern, the knee extends at heel strike, flexes slightly as the body weight moves forward over the supporting leg, and then extends once more at foot push-off. Because the knee extends twice in one step cycle, we call this pattern a double knee-lock.
- The pelvis rotates to allow the full range of leg motion and oppositional movement of the upper and lower body segments.
- Balance improves, and forward trunk inclination is reduced.
- The skilled walker coordinates oppositional arm swing (with the arms extending at the sides) with the movement of the legs. This pattern is consistent with the principle of action and reaction; that is, the opposite arm and leg move forward and back in unison. The arm swing must become relaxed and move from the shoulder, with a slight accompanying movement at the elbow.

Developmental Changes in Walking During Early Childhood

Children usually achieve developmental changes in walking by an early age; by age 4, most children have the essential ingredients of an advanced walk (Sutherland,

1997). Adolph and her colleagues provide an excellent overview of the development of infant walking in a 2003 paper, aptly titled "What Changes in Infant Walking and Why." Children exhibit pelvic rotation at an average age of 13.8 months, knee flexion at midsupport at 16.3 months, foot contact within a trunk-width base of support at 17.0 months, synchronous arm swing at 18.0 months, and heel-then-forefoot strike at 18.5 months (Burnett & Johnson, 1971). The length of time for which one foot supports body weight while the other swings forward increases, especially from 1.0 years to 2.5 years of age (Sutherland et al., 1980).

Stride length increases throughout midadolescence, partly because of the fuller range of motion at the hips, knees, and ankles and partly because of the increase in leg length resulting from growth. The velocity of the walk also increases, especially between 1.0 and 3.5 years of age (Sutherland et al., 1980). The rhythm and coordination of a child's walk improve observably until age 5 or so, but beyond this age, pattern improvements are subtle and probably not detectable by the novice observer.

Developmental Changes in Walking During Older Adulthood

We do not wish to imply that no development occurs between early childhood and older adulthood. However, the changes that do occur represent individual (rather than universal) differences, as discussed in chapter 1. Individuals may change their walking patterns over time due to weight gain or loss, changes in strength or balance, injury, or gait training. Any of these changes will change the constraint interactions during walking. Therefore, we cannot make generalizations about any specific developmental trends in walking in the late teens or early 20s. As for middle adulthood, we cannot predict developmental changes for these years as we can for early childhood because change is individualized and based on changing individual constraints. As individuals enter older age, they will again tend to change in a more predictable way as certain individual constraints tend to change more (figure 7.3).

FIGURE 7.3 Walking patterns in adulthood tend to change as a result of changing individual constraints.

Again, the changes in walking patterns seen in older adults represent a recalibration to the environment and the task based on changes in individual constraints.

A number of research studies have focused on walking patterns in adults over 60 years old. Murray and coworkers (Murray, Drought, & Kory, 1964; Murray, Kory, Clarkson, & Sepic, 1966; Murray, Kory, & Sepic, 1970) conducted a series of studies on gait patterns in older men and women in which they measured the linear and rotary displacements and the velocity of the limbs during walking. They found that the older men walked in a pattern similar to that of younger men but with these differences:

- Step length of the older men was approximately 3 cm shorter.
- Older men toed out approximately 3° more than younger men.
- Older men had a reduced degree of ankle extension.
- Pelvic rotation was diminished in older men.

Similarly, older women showed greater out-toeing, shorter stride length, and less pelvic rotation than younger women.

Another common finding is that older adults walk more slowly than younger adults (Drillis, 1961; Gabel, Johnston, & Crowninshield, 1979; Molen, 1973). Schwanda (1978) confirmed the finding of a shorter stride length among older men and further demonstrated that most other aspects of the walking pattern (stride rate, swing time of the recovering leg, time of support, and vertical displacement of center of gravity) remain similar to those of middle-aged men.

You may recall that new walkers also had greater out-toeing and a shorter stride length to assist in balance. Could balance be the reason older adults demonstrate similar movement characteristics? That possibility exists because balance can be affected by the aging process. On the other hand, researchers have associated some of these changes with differences in walking speed. When younger adults walk slowly, they too shorten their strides and decrease joint rotation (Craik, 1989; Winter, 1983). Gabell and Nayak (1984) observed walking in a group of 32 older adults, aged 66 to 84 years, who were selected from a group of 1,187. (The researchers repeatedly screened members of the large group for various types of pathology in order to select the small healthy group.) They found no significant differences between walking patterns of the 32 older adults and those of younger adults. Thus, some of the changes in older adults' movement patterns might relate to disease and injury in the various body tissues, especially those that result in loss of muscle strength. Even so, these and other studies (Adrian, 1982) indicate that the changes in older adults' walking patterns are minor.

KEY POINT
Rate controllers in walking during older adulthood may be caused by factors such as disuse and fear of falling and therefore may be altered and improved.

Rate Controllers in Later Walking

Any of the changes associated with the aging process can act as rate controllers in the task of walking. Structural constraints may result from osteoarthritis in the joints or from a decline in muscle mass. However, as noted previously, older adults do not necessarily change their gait in a drastic way. A disease state must progress to a critical level before it will discourage all walking. More often, older adults modify their gait to accommodate pain or changes in balance. Functional constraints, such as balance and fear, can also affect walking patterns. Often, two types of individual constraints will interact and their sum will act as a rate controller. If older adults fall, they may develop a fear of falling. That fear of falling results in a gait designed to assist with balance (wide base of support, short step length). If these factors are combined with pain from osteoarthritis, older adults may be less inclined to walk long distances. Unfortunately, a decrease in walking (and other physical activities) leads to a decrease in muscle mass and flexibility, which in turn affects walking patterns. What results is a sequence of events that eventually discourages walking—a sequence that can be altered if one or several individual constraints are actively manipulated.

Running Across the Life Span

Picture this scenario: You leave your house late and must rush to catch the bus to get to class. As you approach the bus stop, you notice the bus pulling away from the curb. What do you do? This is not a trick question; of course you run to catch the bus. Humans often run when they need to get from one place to another quickly. **Running** is a more advanced motor skill than walking, but the two motor patterns have many similar features. For example, in both patterns an individual's legs move symmetrically but in an alternating pattern with each other. Walking and running also have distinct differences. Walking has a period of double support when both feet are in contact with the ground. This never occurs in running; in fact, running has a flight phase, during which neither foot is on the ground.

Children typically start to run about 6 to 7 months after they begin to walk (Clark & Whitall, 1989b; Whitall & Getchell, 1995). Remember, for a gait to be considered a run it must include a flight phase. That means that an infant's earliest attempts to run are actually fast walks. Infants running for the first time may exhibit some of the characteristics of an early walk, even though the infant no longer uses these characteristics in her walk (Burnett & Johnson, 1971). When first learning to run, the child may adopt a wide base of support, a flat-footed landing, leg extension at midsupport, and the high-guard arm position. This regression probably reflects an attempt by the child to simplify the task (e.g., by eliminating the arm swing) until she acquires more experience. As the child practices the running stride and gets used to its balance demands, she will put the swing back into the movement pattern.

Running, like walking, has a 50% phasing relationship between the legs. Unlike walking, running has a period of flight, during which neither foot is in contact with the ground.

Characteristics of Early Running

Imagine toddlers attempting to run for the first time. All prior attempts at upright locomotion involved at least one limb on the ground at all times. Now they must propel themselves into the air with one leg and then catch themselves with the other. For a toddler, this feat takes tremendous strength and balance.

Early characteristics of running reflect the changes in speed (task constraint) between walking and running (see table 7.1 for the developmental sequence). Some of these characteristics are pictured in figure 7.4a. Notice the leg action. You see a brief period of flight, but the legs still have a limited range of motion. The rear leg does not extend fully as the child pushes off the ground. As the swinging leg comes forward, the recovering thigh moves with enough acceleration that the knee bends but without too much acceleration, which would carry the thigh to a position parallel to the ground at the end of the leg swing. Therefore, the range of motion is limited and the stride length is short.

Next, examine the arm swing and note the opposition of the arms to the legs. The arms swing to accompany the trunk's rotation rather than drive forward and back as they would in a skilled sprinter's movement. The elbows extend when they swing back, which is unnecessary movement; the arms swing out slightly to the side,

TABLE 7.1   Hypothesized Developmental Sequence for Running

	Action
	Leg action
Step 1	Minimal flight. The running step is short and flat-footed. On the recovery swing forward, the leg is rather stiff.
Step 2	Crossover swing. The stride is long, and the knee of the recovery leg flexes to at least a right angle. The leg action, though, has lateral movements wherein the legs swing out and in during the recovery.
Step 3	Direct projection. The stride is long, and the recovery leg tucks to swing forward. The legs project directly backward on takeoff and swing directly forward for the touchdown.
	Arm action
Step 1	High or middle guard. Both of the arms are held up between waist and shoulder level and move very little as the legs stride forward and back.
Step 2	Bilateral arm swing. The arms swing but are coupled, moving forward and backward together.
Step 3	Opposition, oblique. The arms drive forward in the opposition pattern, each moving forward and backward with the opposite leg, so that one arm is moving forward while the other is moving backward. The arms, though, swing across the chest or out to the side in a plane oblique to the plane of movement.
Step 4	Opposition, sagittal. The arms swing forward and back in the opposition pattern and stay nearly in the sagittal (or forward–backward) plane of movement.

wasting energy. Beginning runners sometimes swing their arms horizontally, across the body, rather than forward and back, probably to aid their unsteady balance.

Figure 7.4b portrays some characteristics of early running that one can observe from the rear. As the child swings the recovering thigh forward, it inefficiently rotates to the side rather than moving straight forward. The arm swings to the side and away from the body, probably to assist with balance, but, again, this movement pattern wastes energy that could be directed toward running forward.

Rate Limiters in Early Running

To understand the rate limiters in early running, we must review similarities and differences between walking and running. First of all, the coordination patterns are quite similar; both have a 50% phasing relationship between the legs. Therefore, coordination is not likely to be a rate limiter for running. However, running requires a

FIGURE 7.4   A beginning runner. (a) The legs have a limited range of motion. The arms extend at the elbows and swing slightly to the side rather than driving forward and back. (b) The thigh and arms swing out rather than forward and back.

Part a © Mary Ann Roberton; Part b © Mary Ann Roberton and Kate R. Barrett.

flight phase. To propel themselves into the air, toddlers must have sufficient strength in each leg to lift themselves off the ground. Clearly, then, strength is a very important rate limiter in running (Clark & Whitall, 1989b). Also, once in the air, infants must catch themselves on the other leg and then balance on that leg while shifting their weight forward. Thus, balance is another important rate limiter for running.

Proficient Running

Like walking, proficient running requires effective use of the biomechanical principles discussed in chapter 3. When running, you must optimize movement forms that allow you to move quickly, even at the expense of balance. Keeping this in mind, we can identify the developmental changes that beginning runners make to optimize their performance, as pictured in figure 7.5, as follows:

- Stride length increases, indicating that the runner is applying greater force. As greater force is used, several characteristics of mature running emerge: the rear leg is fully extended at push-off; the heel is tucked close to the buttocks and the thigh swings forward with greater acceleration; and the thigh comes parallel to the ground before foot strike. When the recovery leg is swung forward in a tuck position, the runner's effort is conserved.
- The runner eliminates lateral leg movements so that forces are kept in the forward–backward plane.
- For extended running, each foot strikes the ground with the heel first and then the forefoot or strikes the ground in an approximately flat pattern.
- The runner eliminates out-toeing and narrows the base of support.
- The runner's support leg flexes at the knee as the body's weight comes over the leg.
- Trunk rotation increases to allow for a longer stride and better arm–leg opposition. The trunk leans slightly forward.
- The arms swing forward and back, with the elbows approaching right angles, and move in opposition to the legs.

 Imagine you are a spectator at an Olympic track meet. Most elite sprinters look very similar—their form is almost identical. However, the form of marathon runners differs greatly among individuals. What can you speculate about why sprinters have similar running forms but distance runners have different ones?

FIGURE 7.5   An advanced runner. Note the full range of leg motion.
© Mary Ann Roberton and Kate R. Barrett.

Developmental Changes in Early Running

As children grow, these qualitative changes in running pattern, together with increased body size and strength and improved coordination, typically result in improved quantitative measures of running speed and time in flight. Such changes have been well documented in several University of Wisconsin studies of children between ages 1.5 and 10 years (Beck, 1966; Clouse, 1959; Dittmer, 1962) and in other studies (Branta, Haubenstricker, & Seefeldt, 1984; Roberton, 1984). Therefore, we can expect improvement in the process and product of running performances as children grow, and improvements in the product—increased speed, for example—certainly may continue throughout adolescence. However, not every individual achieves all of the improvements in running pattern during childhood. Most teenagers continue to refine their running form, and it is not uncommon to observe inefficient characteristics in adults' running, especially out-toeing, lateral leg movements, and limited stride. Perhaps these tendencies reflect skeletal and muscular imbalances in individual runners. Thus, age alone does not guarantee perfect running form; adolescents and adults may have inefficient running patterns.

Developmental Changes in Later Running

Some research exists on the developmental changes that occur as people age. Nelson (1981) studied the walking and running patterns of older women (aged 58 to 80). She asked the participants in her study to walk normally, walk as fast as possible, jog, and then run as fast as possible. Average speed, stride length, and stride frequency all tended to increase over this sequence, but individuals varied greatly in how they changed from walking to jogging. The older women generally increased their walking speed by lengthening their stride, but they increased their running speed by increasing stride frequency, as do young women. However, major differences were found between younger and older women in the pattern used for fast running:

- Older women did not tuck their recovering leg as completely.
- Older women had a shorter stride length.
- Older women took fewer strides than younger women.

The absolute speeds of jogging and running also differed between the age groups. Older women jogged more slowly (1.85 vs. 3.93 m/s) and ran more slowly (2.60 vs. 6.69 m/s) than a group of 20-year-old women (Nelson, 1981).

Rate Controllers in Later Running

Many of the rate controllers mentioned for later walking also affect running. However, because running requires greater generation of force and greater ability to balance, considerably smaller changes in these constraints may lead to the disappearance of this skill. Furthermore, one may have the ability to run but not the desire or the opportunity; in other words, an older adult may run only in an urgent situation, such as escaping a burning house. However, as more and more seniors discover that maintaining fitness levels can postpone undesired changes associated with aging, more and more opportunities for running exist. The Senior Games (formerly known as the Senior Olympics) have expanded greatly in the past decade; many states have statewide games, and the Huntsman World Senior

Games are held in Utah each year. The running events range from the 100 m dash to the half-marathon and even the triathlon. Age categories for runners range from 50 to 85 or 90-plus for men and women. Still, participants in the Senior Games represent a small portion of the population over 50. In fact, it is still noteworthy when an older adult participates in athletics.

 Not all of the constraints that discourage running in older adults are structural. Imagine you are a physical therapist and think of at least two other constraints in each of the constraint categories.

Assessment of Running: Observation Plan

Assessing motor skills using developmental sequences can seem like a daunting task to a novice observer. Fortunately, using an observation plan can make the task much simpler (see figure 7.6 "Observation Plan for Running"). In a nutshell, an observation plan allows you to make quick judgments about the developmental level of a particular runner by completing a flow chart of quick yes or no checkpoints. By observing a runner and making decisions about movements, you can establish developmental levels very efficiently and effectively.

 WEB STUDY GUIDE   Identify developmental differences among runners in Lab Activity 7.1, Assessing the Developmental Levels of Runners, in the web study guide. Go to www.HumanKinetics.com/LifeSpanMotorDevelopment.

Other Locomotor Skills

Most other locomotor skills have not received the amount of empirical attention given to walking and running. However, many researchers, teachers, and therapists have observed these skills, and we can gain valuable insights from their observations. The skills we discuss here are jumping, hopping, galloping, sliding, and skipping, and like many of the observers, we focus primarily on the childhood years.

Jumping

Jumping occurs when individuals propel themselves off the ground with one or both feet and then land on both feet.

Hopping occurs when individuals propel themselves with one foot and then land on the same foot.

Leaping occurs when individuals propel themselves with one foot and then land on the other foot.

Typically, children attempt jumping tasks at a young age and often achieve the simplest forms before age 2. In **jumping**, individuals propel their bodies from a surface with either one or both feet and land with both feet. Children also acquire specialized forms of jumping during childhood, such as hopping and leaping. **Hopping** requires taking off and landing on the same leg, often repeatedly. **Leaping** involves a run with a projection forward from one foot to a landing on the other (increased flight time). Table 7.2 outlines several examples of jumping, hopping, and leaping. Let's first look at jumping.

Characteristics of Early Jumping

We can gauge developmental changes in jumping in various ways:

- The age at which a child can perform certain kinds of jumping (age norms)
- The distance or height of a jump
- The jumping form or pattern

Early developmentalists determined age norms for jumping achievements in preschool children (Wickstrom, 1983). These norms appear in table 7.3, which indicates that children learn to step down off of a higher surface from one foot to the other before jumping off the floor with both feet. Children then learn to jump down from progressively greater heights onto both feet. Later, they master forward

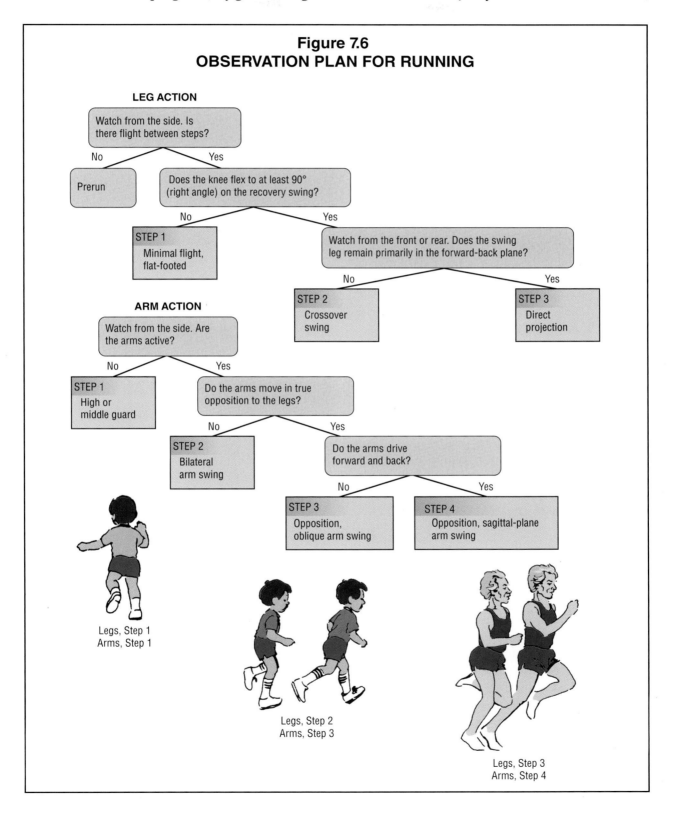

Figure 7.6
OBSERVATION PLAN FOR RUNNING

TABLE 7.2   Types of Jumps Arranged by Progressive Difficulty

Jump down from one foot to the other foot.
Jump up from two feet to two feet.
Jump down from one foot to two feet.
Jump down from two feet to two feet.
Run and jump forward from one foot to the other.
Jump forward from two feet to two feet.
Run and jump forward from one foot to two feet.
Jump over object from two feet to two feet.
Jump from one foot to same foot rhythmically.

© Mary Ann Roberton and Kate R. Barrett.

TABLE 7.3   Jumping Achievements of Young Children

Achievement	Motor age (mo)	Source
Jump from 12 in. (30 cm) height; one foot	24	M & W
Jump off floor; both feet	28	B
Jump from 18 in. (46 cm) height; one foot	31	M & W
Jump from chair 10 in. (26 cm) high; both feet	32	B
Jump from 8 in. (20 cm) height; both feet	33	M & W
Jump from 12 in. (30 cm) height; both feet	34	M & W
Jump from 18 in. (46 cm) height; both feet	37	M & W
Jump from 12 in. (30 cm) height; both feet	37.1	B
Jump forward 4 to 14 in. (10–35 cm) from 12 in. (30 cm) height; both feet	37.3	B
Hop on two feet 1 to 3 times	38	M & W
Jump over rope 8 in. (20 cm) high; both feet	41.5	B
Hop on one foot 1 to 3 times	43	B

Note: Adapted from information in studies by Bayley (1935) (B) and McCaskill & Wellman (1938) (M&W).

© Mary Ann Roberton and Kate R. Barrett.

jumps, jumps over objects, and hopping a few times on one foot. By school age, children can usually perform all of these jumps.

Because of a secular trend, the exact ages at which children today can perform the various jumps might be younger than those in table 7.3, but the order in which they acquire those skills is the same. Developmentalists frequently use product assessments—that is, they measure the horizontal or vertical distance jumped—to assess jumping skill after children have refined the movement process. We focus here on the movement pattern because the measurement of distance jumped is rather self-explanatory and straightforward.

Basic skill development in children is a gradual process of refining skills. Oftentimes, this process includes a qualitative change in the skill, such as taking a step forward when throwing. Authors have described development of a particular skill through successive steps, or developmental sequences, based on qualitative changes in critical features of the skill. Two types of developmental sequences exist. The whole-body approach describes all characteristic positions of various body

TABLE 7.4   Developmental Sequence of the Standing Long Jump for the Whole Body

	Action
Step 1	Vertical component of force may be greater than horizontal; resulting jump is then upward rather than forward. Arms move backward, acting as brakes to stop the momentum of the trunk as the legs extend in front of the center of mass.
Step 2	The arms move in an anterior–posterior direction during the preparatory phase but move sideward (winging action) during the in-flight phase. The knees and hips flex and extend more fully than in step 1. The angle of takeoff is still markedly greater than 45°. The landing is made with the center of gravity above the base of support, with the thighs perpendicular to the surface rather than parallel as in the reaching position of step 4.
Step 3	The arms swing backward and then forward during the preparatory phase. The knees and hips flex fully before takeoff. On takeoff the arms extend and move forward but do not exceed the height of the head. The knee extension may be complete, but the takeoff angle is still greater than 45°. On landing, the thigh is still less than parallel to the surface, and the center of gravity is near the base of support when viewed from the frontal plane.
Step 4	The arms extend vigorously forward and upward on takeoff, reaching full extension above the head at liftoff. The hips and knees extend fully, and the takeoff angle is 45° or less. In preparation for landing, the arms are brought downward and the legs are thrust forward until the thighs are parallel to the surface. The center of gravity is far behind the base of support on foot contact, but at the moment of contact the knees are flexed and the arms are thrust forward to maintain the momentum to carry the center of gravity beyond the feet.

Note: Degrees are measured from horizontal.

Adapted by permission from Seefeldt, Reuschlein, and Vogel 1972.

components in a step (table 7.4). The component approach follows each separate body component through whatever number of steps accounts for the qualitative changes observed over time (table 7.5).

Several published developmental sequences help us examine the developmental changes that occur in jumping movement patterns. Such sequences identify the steps that children achieve in making the transition from inefficient to proficient movement patterns. The advancements reflect the children's adoption of movements that take advantage of the principles of motion. We can see improvements in both the vertical jump and the horizontal (standing long) jump, but the developmental sequences that researchers have suggested thus far are based on the standing long jump (Clark & Phillips, 1985; Roberton, 1978b, 1984; tables 7.4 and 7.5).

We first identify some of the characteristics of beginning jumpers in both the vertical jump and the standing long jump. Most young jumpers begin by executing a vertical jump, even if they intend to jump horizontally. Look at the beginning jumpers in figures 7.7, 7.8, and 7.9. A vertical jump is shown in figure 7.7 and a horizontal jump in figures 7.8 and 7.9. Note that in all three jumps, the preparatory crouch is slight and the legs are not fully extended at liftoff. In fact, the vertical jumper in figure 7.7 tucks the legs to leave the ground rather than extend them at takeoff to project the body up. In this example, the head is no higher at the peak of the jump than at takeoff.

Another characteristic of beginning jumpers is that they do not use a two-foot (symmetrical) takeoff or landing, as shown in figure 7.7, even when they intend to do so. A one-foot takeoff, or step-out, is the lowest level of leg action in the

TABLE 7.5   Developmental Sequence
of the Standing Long Jump Takeoff for Body Components

Action
Leg action

Step 1	One-foot takeoff. From the beginning position, the jumper steps out with one foot. Usually there is little preparatory leg flexion.
Step 2	Knee extension first. The jumper begins to extend the knee joints before the heels come off the ground, resulting in a jump that is too vertical to achieve maximum horizontal distance.
Step 3	Simultaneous extension. The jumper extends the knees at the same time the heels come off the ground.
Step 4	Heels up first. The jump begins with the heels coming off the ground, then the knees extend; the jumper appears to start the takeoff by tipping forward.

Arm action

Step 1	No action. The arms are stationary. After takeoff, they may "wing" (shoulder girdle retracts).
Step 2	Arms swing forward. The arms swing forward at the shoulder from a starting position at the sides. The arms might also swing out to the side (abduct at the shoulder).
Step 3	Arms extend, then partially flex. The arms extend back together during leg flexion, then swing forward together at takeoff. Arm swing never reaches a position overhead.
Step 4	Arms extend, then fully flex. The arms extend back together during leg flexion, then swing forward to a position overhead.

Adapted by permission from Clark and Phillips 1985.

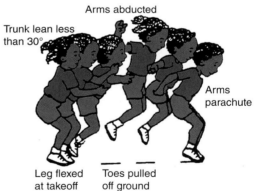

FIGURE 7.7   Sequential views of a vertical jump. The form here is inefficient. The legs are tucked up under the body rather than fully extended to project the body off the ground. Notice that one foot touches down first. The arms do not assist in the jump; the jumper holds them in the winging posture.
© Mary Ann Roberton and Kate R. Barrett.

FIGURE 7.8   A beginning long jumper. As the jumper's weight shifts forward, the toes are pulled off the floor to "catch" the body at landing. The trunk lean at takeoff is less than 30° from the vertical. The arms are used at takeoff but are in an abducted position, laterally rotate in flight, and "parachute" for the landing.
© Mary Ann Roberton.

developmental sequence of the standing long jump takeoff. The legs may also be asymmetrical during flight. To improve this leg action, the jumper needs to (1) make a symmetrical two-foot takeoff, flight, and landing and (2) fully extend the ankles, knees, and hips at takeoff after a deep preparatory crouch. The knees and hips flex together in the flight phase of the standing long jump after a full and forceful extension of the legs at takeoff.

To jump a long distance, the skilled performer leans the trunk forward at least 30° from the vertical. By age 3, children can change their trunk angle at takeoff to make either a vertical or a horizontal jump (Clark, Phillips, & Petersen, 1989). However, beginning jumpers often keep the trunk too erect during a horizontal jump. When a skilled jumper leans the trunk forward to facilitate jumping for distance, the heels usually come off the ground before the knees start to extend (Clark & Phillips, 1985). Skilled jumpers appear to tip forward at the start of the takeoff. The leg action in which "heels up" begins the takeoff is the most advanced step in the developmental sequence for the leg action of the horizontal jump.

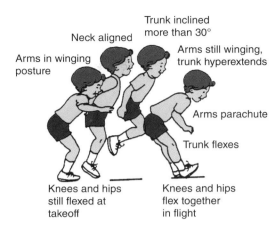

FIGURE 7.9 A beginning jumper. The leg action is in step 3 (table 7.5) at takeoff, as the knees extend at the same time the heels leave the ground. The knees and hips flex together during flight, and the knees then extend before landing. The trunk is somewhat erect at takeoff; it hyperextends in flight, then flexes for landing. The arms wing at takeoff (step 1) before parachuting for the landing.

Lack of coordinated arm action also characterizes beginning vertical and horizontal jumpers. Rather than use their arms to assist in the jumping action, they may use their arms asymmetrically, hold them stationary at the side, or keep them in a high-guard position as a precaution against falling. Arms may wing (extend backward) ineffectively during flight (figure 7.7) or parachute (extend down and out to the side) during landing (figure 7.8). To achieve a proficient jump, the jumper must use the arms symmetrically to lead the jump from a preparatory extended position to an overhead swing. The developmental sequence for the arm action of the standing long jump progresses from no arm action to limited arm swing; to extension, then partial flexion; and finally to extension, then complete arm swing overhead.

Proficient Jumping

Through these developmental changes, performers can develop a proficient jumping pattern, as shown in figures 7.10 and 7.11. To execute proficient jumps, they do the following:

- Get into a preparatory crouch that will stretch the muscles and allow the legs to apply maximal force as they fully extend at the moment of liftoff.
- Take off for a horizontal jump with the heels coming off the ground and with both feet leaving the ground at the same time.
- Extend the arms backward, then initiate the takeoff with a vigorous arm swing forward to a position overhead.

In jumping for height, proficient jumpers do the following:

- Direct force downward and extend the body throughout flight. If they are to strike an object or touch something overhead, the dominant arm reaches up and the opposite arm swings down. They gain height through a lateral tilt of the shoulders.

- Keep the trunk relatively upright throughout the jump.
- Flex the ankles, knees, and hips on touchdown to allow the force of landing to be absorbed.

In jumping for distance, proficient jumpers do the following:

- Direct force down and back by beginning the takeoff with the heels leaving the ground before the knees extend. The trunk appears to tip forward.
- Flex the knees during flight, then bring the thighs forward to a position parallel with the ground.
- Swing the lower legs forward for a two-foot landing.
- Let the trunk come forward in reaction to the thigh flexing, putting the body in a jackknife position.
- Flex the ankles and knees when the heels touch the ground to absorb the momentum of the body over distance as the body continues to move forward.

 WEB STUDY GUIDE   **Identify developmental differences among long jumpers in Lab Activity 7.2, Assessing the Developmental Levels of Long Jumpers, in the web study guide. Go to www.HumanKinetics.com/LifeSpanMotor Development.**

Developmental Changes in Jumping

With practice, then, children can eventually make refinements in their jumping pattern as described. Continuous growth in body size and strength also contributes to quantitative improvements in how far children can jump. During the elementary school years, children average increases of 3 to 5 in. (~8 to 13 cm) a year in the horizontal distance they can jump and approximately 2 in. (5 cm) a year in vertical distance (DeOreo & Keogh, 1980). Qualitative improvements in jumping vary among children. For example, Clark and Phillips (1985) observed that fewer than 30% of the 3- to 7-year-olds they filmed had the same level of leg and arm action. Most had more advanced leg action than arm action, but some had more

One arm swings down as other arm reaches up

Arms swing to begin the jump

Trunk is straight during crouch

Full leg extension

Preparatory crouch

FIGURE 7.10   An advanced vertical jump for the purpose of reaching high. From a preparatory crouch, this basketball player swings his arms forward and up to lead the jump. The hips, knees, and ankles extend completely at takeoff. Near the peak of the jump, one hand continues up while the other comes down, tilting the shoulder girdle to assist in the high reach. Note that the trunk tends to remain upright throughout.

© Mary Ann Roberton and Kate R. Barrett.

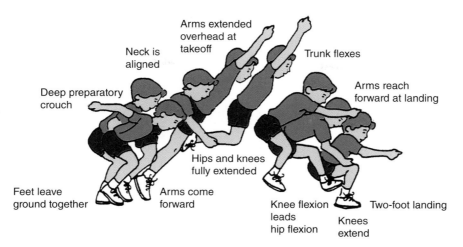

Deep preparatory crouch

Neck is aligned

Arms extended overhead at takeoff

Trunk flexes

Arms reach forward at landing

Hips and knees fully extended

Feet leave ground together

Arms come forward

Knee flexion leads hip flexion

Knees extend

Two-foot landing

FIGURE 7.11 An advanced long jump. The feet leave the ground together and touch down together. The legs fully extend at takeoff, beginning with heels up. The knees then flex in flight, followed by hip flexion and finally knee extension to reach forward for landing. The trunk is inclined more than 30° at takeoff, and the jumper maintains this lean in flight until the trunk flexes for landing. The arms lead the jump and reach overhead at takeoff, then lower to reach forward at landing.

advanced arm than leg action. If one component was more advanced than the other, it was usually by only one step, but some children were two steps more advanced in one component than in the other. Thus, we see many movement patterns among developing children.

The differences between a vertical jump and a standing long jump involve position and movement speed. For example, in the standing long jump, the hips are more flexed than in the vertical jump as the jumper makes the transition from the preparatory crouch to the takeoff. The hips extend faster in the standing long jump, whereas the knees and ankles extend faster in the vertical jump. Other characteristics of jumping remain stable across developmental steps and type of jump. Clark et al. (1989) found that 3-, 5-, 7-, and 9-year-olds and adults all used the same pattern of leg coordination. In addition, all used that same pattern for both standing long jumps and vertical jumps. Specifically, the timing of hip, knee, and ankle joint extension at takeoff was similar in all groups. Perhaps this similarity reflects the mechanics involved in propelling the body's mass off the ground. The neuromuscular system must use a leg coordination pattern that gets the body off the ground, but limb positions and movement speeds change as the jumper is better able to optimize jumping distance or adapt the jump to a specific task, such as shooting a jump shot in basketball.

It is clear that not all persons master jumping in childhood or even in adolescence. Zimmerman (1956) found many inefficient jumping characteristics in college women, including limited arm swing and incomplete leg extension at takeoff. For children and teens to receive assistance from their instructors in perfecting an advanced jumping pattern, instructors must be able to critically observe and analyze jumping performance. Use figure 7.12 "Observation Plan for the Standing Long Jump" to assess the developmental level of the standing long jump takeoff.

Rate Limiters in Jumping

For children to perform a two-foot jump, they must be able to develop enough force to bring their bodies into the air from a still position. Unlike in walking and

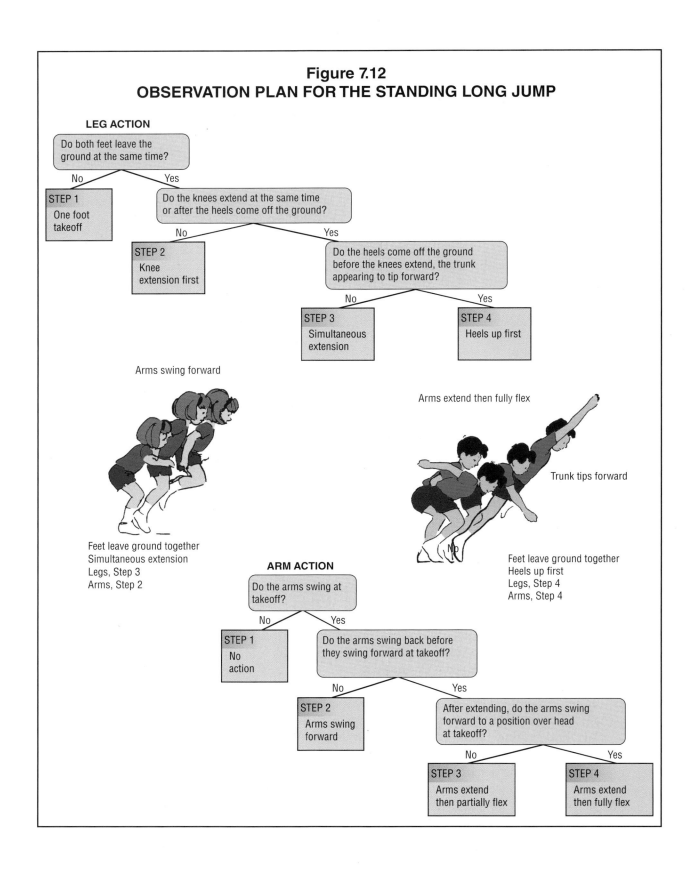

Figure 7.12
OBSERVATION PLAN FOR THE STANDING LONG JUMP

LEG ACTION

Do both feet leave the ground at the same time?

No — STEP 1 One foot takeoff

Yes — Do the knees extend at the same time or after the heels come off the ground?

No — STEP 2 Knee extension first

Yes — Do the heels come off the ground before the knees extend, the trunk appearing to tip forward?

No — STEP 3 Simultaneous extension

Yes — STEP 4 Heels up first

Arms swing forward

Arms extend then fully flex

Trunk tips forward

Feet leave ground together
Simultaneous extension
Legs, Step 3
Arms, Step 2

Feet leave ground together
Heels up first
Legs, Step 4
Arms, Step 4

ARM ACTION

Do the arms swing at takeoff?

No — STEP 1 No action

Yes — Do the arms swing back before they swing forward at takeoff?

No — STEP 2 Arms swing forward

Yes — After extending, do the arms swing forward to a position over head at takeoff?

No — STEP 3 Arms extend then partially flex

Yes — STEP 4 Arms extend then fully flex

running, they cannot take advantage of a "fall and catch" motion but rather must project their entire bodies into the air.

Hopping

Adults rarely use hopping to move around, yet to become a skillful mover, an individual should develop hopping skills during childhood. To hop, especially repeatedly, one must project and absorb body weight with just one limb and maintain balance on the small base of support that one foot provides. Complex sport and dance skills often incorporate these movement abilities.

Characteristics of Early Hopping

Children may move through the levels of arm action and leg action at different rates. Look at the two early hoppers shown in figures 7.13 and 7.14. The leg action of the hopper in figure 7.13 is ineffective as a force producer. The child momentarily lifts the support leg from the floor by flexing it rather than projecting the body up by leg extension; the swing leg is inactive. The arms are also inactive, and the child's leg and arm actions fall into the first developmental step (see table 7.6 for the developmental sequence). The hopper in figure 7.14 has achieved some leg extension; this child is in step 2 of leg action but still in step 1 of arm action.

Proficient Hopping

To become proficient hoppers, children need to make the following improvements:

- The swing leg must lead the hip.
- The support leg must extend fully.
- The arms must move in opposition to the legs.
- The support leg must flex at landing to absorb the force of the landing and to prepare for extension at the next takeoff.

The hopper in figure 7.15 has made one of these improvements by moving the arm opposite the swing leg in opposition, but the other arm does not move in a consistent way. The advanced hopper in figure 7.16 assists the hop by moving both arms in opposition to the legs. In terms of leg motion, the hopper in figure 7.15 extends the support leg at takeoff, reflecting good force application, and uses the swing leg, but not vigorously. The hopper in figure 7.16 has made this improvement—the swing leg leads the takeoff, allowing the momentum of several body parts to be chained together, and then swings back behind the support leg to lead the next takeoff.

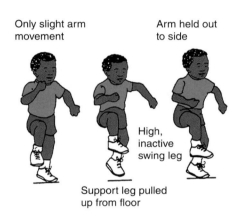

Only slight arm movement

Arm held out to side

High, inactive swing leg

Support leg pulled up from floor

FIGURE 7.13 An early hopping attempt exhibiting step 1 leg action and step 1 arm action. The support leg is pulled off the floor to produce only momentary flight. The arms are high and are not working in opposition.

© Mary Ann Roberton.

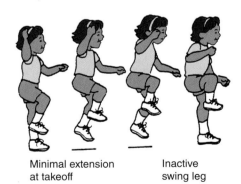

Minimal extension at takeoff

Inactive swing leg

FIGURE 7.14 This girl uses some leg extension to leave the ground, but her swing leg is still inactive. She is in step 2 of the developmental levels for leg action.

© Mary Ann Roberton.

TABLE 7.6   Developmental Sequence for Hopping

Action
Leg action

Step 1	Momentary flight. The support knee and hip quickly flex, pulling (instead of projecting) the foot from the floor. The flight is momentary. Only one or two hops can be achieved. The swing leg is lifted high and held in an inactive position to the side or in front of the body.
Step 2	Fall and catch; swing leg inactive. Forward body lean allows minimal knee and ankle extension to help the body "fall" forward of the support foot, then quickly catch itself again. The swing leg is inactive. Repeat hops are now possible.
Step 3	Projected takeoff; swing leg assists. Perceptible pretakeoff extension occurs in the hip, knee, and ankle in the support leg. There is little or no delay in changing from knee and ankle flexion on landing to extension before takeoff. The swing leg now pumps up and down to assist in projection. The range of the swing is insufficient to carry it behind the support leg when viewed from the side.
Step 4	Projection delay; swing leg leads. The weight of the child on landing is now smoothly transferred along the foot to the ball before the knee and ankle extend to takeoff. The support leg nearly reaches full extension on the takeoff. The swing leg now leads the upward-forward movement of the takeoff phase, while the support leg is still rotating over the ball of the foot. The range of the pumping action in the swing leg increases so that it passes behind the support leg when viewed from the side.

Arm action

Step 1	Bilateral inactive. The arms are held bilaterally, usually high and out to the side, although other positions behind or in front of the body may occur. Any arm action is usually slight and not consistent.
Step 2	Bilateral reactive. Arms swing upward briefly, then are medially rotated at the shoulder in a winging movement before takeoff. It appears that this movement is in reaction to loss of balance.
Step 3	Bilateral assist. The arms pump up and down together, usually in front of the line of the trunk. Any downward and backward motion of the arms occurs after takeoff. The arms may move parallel to each other or be held at different levels as they move up and down.
Step 4	Semi-opposition. The arm on the side opposite the swing leg swings forward with that leg and back as the leg moves down. The position of the other arm is variable, often staying in front of the body or to the side.
Step 5	Opposing assist. The arm opposite the swing leg moves forward and upward in synchrony with the forward and upward movement of that leg. The other arm moves in the direction opposite to the action of the swing leg. The range of movement in the arm action may be minimal unless the task requires speed or distance.

Note: This sequence has been partially validated by Halverson and Williams (1985).

Reprinted from Roberton and Halverson 1984.

Developmental Changes in Hopping

Few children under age 3 can hop repeatedly (Bayley, 1969; McCaskill & Wellman, 1938). Developmentalists often cite the preschool years as the time when children become proficient hoppers (Gutteridge, 1939; Sinclair, 1973; Williams, 1983). Yet Halverson and Williams (1985) found that more than half of a group of 63 children (3-, 4-, and 5-year-olds) were at step 2 in the arm and leg action. They observed few attempts that they could classify at the advanced levels, and hopping on the

Arm opposite swing leg comes forward with that leg

Range of swing leg is larger

Takeoff leg is extending

Swing leg pumps up and down

FIGURE 7.15   A more advanced hop: step 3 in the developmental sequence of leg action, step 4 in arm action. The swing leg leads the hop. Although the range of the swing leg is larger, it could increase even more.

© Mary Ann Roberton.

nonpreferred leg was developmentally behind hopping on the preferred leg. Figure 7.17 shows that many more children were at the lowest developmental step when hopping on their nonpreferred leg than when hopping on their preferred leg. Few children were beyond step 2 when hopping on either leg. If the children in this study are representative of this age group, hopping continues to develop well past the age of 5.

Why do children advance from one developmental level of hopping to another? Several researchers attempted to answer this question by examining the force and stiffness of landing in hopping (Getchell & Roberton, 1989; Roberton & Halverson, 1988). Note that in step 2 the

Support leg will fully extend at takeoff

Swing leg is seen fully behind support leg

Swing leg leads

FIGURE 7.16   This boy demonstrates step 4 leg action in that the range of the swing is sufficient to carry the swing leg completely behind the support leg. Both arms move in opposition to the legs.

© Mary Ann Roberton.

hopper lands flat-footed and holds the swing leg still. By step 3 the hopper uses a softer landing (more leg flexion to cushion the landing, followed by extension to the next takeoff) and swings the nonhopping leg. Researchers confirmed that the force of landing in a step 2 hop rises sharply on landing, whereas in a step 3 hop it rises gradually. To achieve a soft landing, the neuromuscular system probably prepares ahead of time (ahead of the landing) to moderate the force of landing by allowing the leg to "give" (flex). Perhaps, then, once children achieve a step 2 hop, their ability to project the body higher and travel faster—and perhaps their increasing body weight—increases the force of the landing. Once that force reaches a critical value that could cause a damaging, jarring landing, the neuromuscular system changes children's hopping movements to allow a softer, more cushioned landing. Hence, children advance to the next developmental level.

WEB STUDY GUIDE   Identify developmental differences among hoppers in Lab Activity 7.3, Assessing the Developmental Levels of Hoppers, in the web study guide. Go to www.HumanKinetics.com/LifeSpanMotorDevelopment.

Part of the rehabilitation process for some injuries to the lower limbs includes hopping on the injured leg (generally later in the rehabilitation process). Imagine you are a physical therapist and a patient has asked the following question: If adults do not hop regularly, why is hopping so important in rehabilitation? Consider your answer in terms of constraints.

An Integrated Approach to Understanding Hopping

If we dig deeper into understanding the change in developmental levels in the hop, we reveal the remarkable interaction of individual constraints in the body and within the framework of the principles of motion. Let's consider a child who hops with step 2 action. The swing leg is held in front; therefore, it simply reacts rather than contributes to the hop. For a lightweight child who needs to produce little force to move, a stationary swing leg does not prevent hopping. The child produces force, primarily downward, from the stance leg. As the child grows she adds body weight and size, which increase her inertia (which, in turn, increases the force required to overcome inertia). Projecting force downward from the stance leg no longer suffices for a hop; she adds swing leg movement to provide additional force, as the movement of the swing leg helps push the body down and back. The ground responds by pushing the body up and forward (Newton's third law), and the child hops into the air. What goes up, however, must come down—and the child returns to earth with a greater amount of force (due to her increased weight and the height of the hop) than in a step 2 hop. To break the fall, the child must "give" to

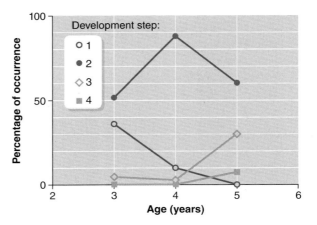

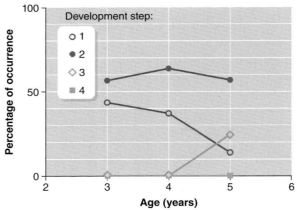

FIGURE 7.17   The developmental level of leg action in 3-, 4-, and 5-year-old hoppers on their preferred leg (top) and nonpreferred leg (bottom). Note that more children were at step 1 when hopping on their nonpreferred leg than when hopping on their preferred leg. Only at age 5 were any notable number of the children at step 3.

Reprinted by permission from Halverson and Williams 1985.

land softly. This illustrates one way in which the body recalibrates and changes movement patterns to account for changing individual constraints. The changes in the swing leg in step 3 are complemented by changes in the stance leg, both of which lead to a higher, safer hop.

Observing Hopping Patterns

As with the other locomotor skills, a novice observer must practice hopping assessment. Halverson (1983; see also Roberton & Halverson, 1984) suggests a systematic pattern of observation that focuses on the body parts one at a time. As a novice observer, you should observe leg action from the side. Initially, pay attention to the swing leg. Is it active? If so, does it move up and down or swing past the support leg? Next, observe the support leg. Does it extend at takeoff? Does it flex on landing and extend during the next hop? Look at arm action from the side and the front. Watch first to see whether the arm movement is bilateral or opposing. If it is bilateral, you can then categorize arm movement as inactive, reactive, or backward in direction. If arm movement is opposing, note whether one or both arms move synchronously with the legs. Use figure 7.18 "Observation Plan for Hopping" to assess the developmental levels of hoppers.

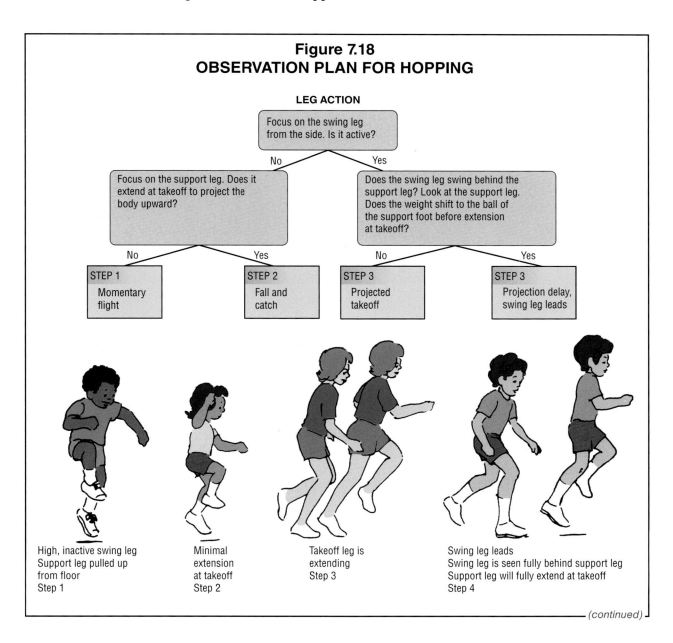

Figure 7.18
OBSERVATION PLAN FOR HOPPING

LEG ACTION

Focus on the swing leg from the side. Is it active?

No — Focus on the support leg. Does it extend at takeoff to project the body upward?

Yes — Does the swing leg swing behind the support leg? Look at the support leg. Does the weight shift to the ball of the support foot before extension at takeoff?

No — STEP 1 Momentary flight

Yes — STEP 2 Fall and catch

No — STEP 3 Projected takeoff

Yes — STEP 3 Projection delay, swing leg leads

High, inactive swing leg
Support leg pulled up from floor
Step 1

Minimal extension at takeoff
Step 2

Takeoff leg is extending
Step 3

Swing leg leads
Swing leg is seen fully behind support leg
Support leg will fully extend at takeoff
Step 4

(continued)

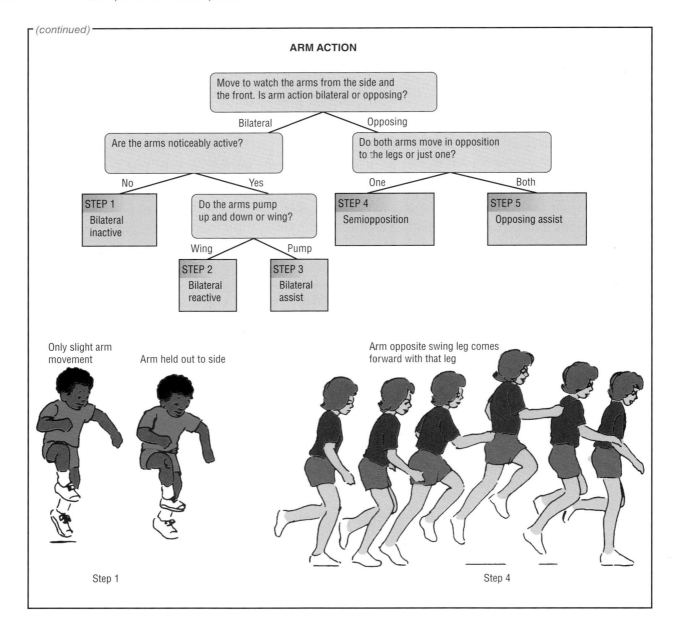

(continued)

ARM ACTION

Move to watch the arms from the side and the front. Is arm action bilateral or opposing?

Bilateral — Opposing

Are the arms noticeably active?

Do both arms move in opposition to the legs or just one?

No — Yes

One — Both

STEP 1 Bilateral inactive

Do the arms pump up and down or wing?

STEP 4 Semiopposition

STEP 5 Opposing assist

Wing — Pump

STEP 2 Bilateral reactive

STEP 3 Bilateral assist

Only slight arm movement

Arm held out to side

Arm opposite swing leg comes forward with that leg

Step 1

Step 4

Rate Controllers in Hopping

Hopping likely depends on the postural system's ability to balance the body on one limb for a succession of hops. Also, to hop repeatedly, the individual must be able to generate enough force to lift the body with one limb, recover, and quickly generate enough force to hop again. Running also requires projection and acceptance of weight on one limb; however, in running, legs alternate and are able to regain energy as they swing in a flexed position. In the hop, the leg stays extended—thus, hopping requires more effort than running. Therefore, the ability to generate force can act as a rate controller.

Galloping, Sliding, and Skipping

Galloping, **sliding**, and **skipping** involve the fundamental movements of stepping, hopping, or leaping. Galloping and sliding, both asymmetric gaits, consist of a step on one foot, then a leap-step on the other foot (Roberton & Halverson, 1984; Whitall, 1988). The same leg always leads with the step. The difference between galloping and sliding is the direction of movement. In galloping, the individual moves forward; in sliding, the individual moves sideways. Skipping is a step and a hop on the same foot, with alternating feet: step-hop on the right foot, step-hop on the left foot, step-hop on the right foot, and so on. The movement is usually forward (figure 7.19, *a* and *b*).

 Consider situations or contexts in which locomotor skills other than walking and running are socially acceptable. Do not limit yourself to sport and dance applications.

Characteristics of Early Skill Patterns

Children's early attempts at these skills are usually arrhythmic and stiff, as shown in figure 7.20. The arms are rarely involved in projecting the body off the floor. Children might hold their arms stiffly in the high-guard position or out to the side to aid their balance. Their stride or step length is short, and they land flat-footed. Little trunk rotation is used, and they exaggerate vertical lift. In early galloping attempts, a child's trailing leg may land ahead of the lead leg.

Proficient Skill Patterns

In contrast, children who are proficient at galloping, sliding, and skipping move in a manner that is rhythmical and relaxed, as seen in figure 7.21. Proficiency in these skills includes the following characteristics:

- The arms are no longer needed for balance.
- In skipping, the arms swing rhythmically in opposition to the legs and provide momentum.

FIGURE 7.19 *(a)* Galloping is a step on the lead leg and a leap-step on the trailing leg. *(b)* Skipping is a step and then a hop on the foot that just stepped followed by a step and a hop on the other foot, and so on, continuing alternatingly (e.g., step-hop left foot, step-hop right foot, and so on).

Adapted by permission from Clark and Whitall 1989.

FIGURE 7.20 A beginning galloper. The arms are held stiffly, the stride length is short, and vertical movement is exaggerated.

Adapted by permission from Clark and Whitall 1989.

FIGURE 7.21 An advanced galloper. The arms move in opposition to the legs. Movements are rhythmic and landings are not flat-footed.

- The child can use the arms for another purpose during galloping and sliding, such as clapping.
- Forefoot or heel-to-forefoot landings prevail.
- The knees "give" on landing, remaining flexed while they support the body's weight, and then extend at takeoff, especially when the child is traveling quickly.

Developmental Changes

Galloping is the first of these three bipedal patterns to emerge. It develops sometime between 2 and 3 years of age, after the child has firmly established the running pattern (around age 2) and usually before hopping, which occurs at age 3 or 4. Galloping is the first asymmetrical locomotor pattern a child learns. As noted earlier, walking and running have 50% phasing—the legs make the same movement, but the cycle of one leg is halfway behind the cycle of the other. Galloping, in contrast, is uneven. The steps take longer than the leap-steps. Gallopers, regardless of age, tend to use one of two timing patterns: the step takes either approximately twice as long as the leap-step (a 66% to 33% phasing) or 3 times as long (a 75% to 25% phasing) (Clark & Whitall, 1989b; Whitall, 1988). Children master sliding next, and in both galloping and sliding they develop the ability to lead with the nondominant leg much later than the ability to lead with the dominant leg.

Skipping is usually the last of the locomotor patterns to emerge, usually between 4 and 7 years of age. A little more than half of 5-year-olds demonstrate skipping (Branta et al., 1984). At first, a child might perform a unilateral step-hop—that is, a skip with the dominant leg and just a running step with the other leg. When the child begins to skip with both legs, occasional breaks, with a step or gallop interjected, are common (Gutteridge, 1939; Wickstrom, 1987).

Though no one has validated developmental steps for skipping, several changes are apparent. A beginning skipper uses a high hop and knee lift. The skip appears jerky, which perhaps reflects the need for much effort to project the body off the ground for the hop. Eventually, the child partially extends the leg on the hop and uses a lower but smoother knee lift, making the skip smoother and more rhythmic. Perhaps greater leg strength allows the child to get the body off the ground with only partial leg extension.

Several changes occur in arm action. Beginners use the arms inconsistently, often swinging one or both arms up to the side. Skippers then begin to use the arms bilaterally, swinging them sometimes forward and back in circles, sometimes forward and down. Skilled skippers can use their arms in opposition to their legs (Wickstrom, 1987).

It is easy to speculate about why skipping is the last fundamental locomotor skill that children develop. The coordination between the legs is symmetrical, but in each leg the pattern of movement is asymmetrical. Girls typically perform these locomotor skills at an earlier age than do boys, perhaps reflecting their slight edge in biological maturity for chronological age, their imitation of other girls, or encouragement from family and friends.

Observing Galloping, Sliding, and Skipping Patterns

While observing galloping, first take a side view and note where the trailing foot lands in relation to the lead foot. The extent of vertical lift is also clearly visible from the side. Arms can be viewed from any angle. In proficient galloping the trailing foot lands alongside or behind the lead foot, the flight pattern is low, and the arms are free to swing rhythmically, clap, or engage in another activity. Note whether a child can lead with the dominant leg only or with either leg.

Sliding is best observed from the front. Focus on the knees to see if they are stiff, as in early sliding, or relaxed so that the child's steps have the spring characteristic of proficient sliding. Note whether the arms are in an inefficient guard position or are relaxed and free to be used for another task. As with galloping, you should see if a child can slide to the dominant side only or to both sides.

When watching skipping, observe whether the child skips with one leg and runs with the other or skips with both. If the child skips with both legs, look at the height of the hop and the knee lift from the side. Lower height and knee lifts characterize a more proficient, smoother skip. Finally, watch the arm pattern to see if it is bilateral or, in a more proficient skipper, in opposition to the leg movement.

Rate Limiters for Galloping, Sliding, and Skipping

Galloping generally follows running in the development of motor skills. What rate limiters exist for galloping? To gallop, individuals must uncouple their legs from the 50% phasing they use when walking and running. To do so requires rhythmic or coordination changes. At the same time, the two legs are performing different tasks (step vs. leap-step); therefore, they require different amounts of force, which requires changing force coordination (Clark & Whitall, 1989b). Thus, coordination appears to be a rate limiter for galloping. To slide, individuals must also turn to one side. The neuromuscular system may limit the rate at which these two skills required for galloping and sliding develop.

The emergence of skipping does not appear to be limited by generation of force for the hop because children hop before they skip. Nor is balance a probable rate limiter because it is more difficult to balance while hopping than while skipping. As mentioned earlier, skipping is the most complex fundamental locomotor pattern. Skipping might not appear until the individual's neuromuscular system can coordinate the two limbs as they alternately perform asymmetric tasks.

Summary and Synthesis

Transporting ourselves from here to there is an important part of human life. We consider locomotion to be one of the first signs of an infant's independence. Infants may creep, crawl, or move on hands and feet as their initial means of getting around. Not long after, they develop the ability to walk, which is the most basic form of upright bipedal locomotion. Walking involves alternating leg motion, with a period of single-foot support following a period of double-foot support. Next, toddlers run. Running is similar to walking, with alternating foot strikes, but has a period of flight rather than double support. Children then develop the ability to jump, gallop, hop, slide, and skip. All of these more complex locomotor patterns have different constraints that affect the timing and sequence in which they emerge. We can trace the changes in these motor skills throughout individual life spans as the forms of the movements change with the changing constraints of adolescence, adulthood, and older adulthood.

From crawling through skipping, children acquire fundamental locomotor skills as their bodies and the world around them change. Many individual constraints act as rate limiters to these emerging skills. After an individual acquires these skills, the form of the skills changes as the child becomes more proficient at them. If you look across locomotor skills, you can see similar patterns of change. For example, in all of the locomotor skills, individuals narrow their base of support to increase mobility and widen it (as in infancy and older adulthood) to increase stability. The developmental changes described in this chapter can be used to generally estimate an individual's developmental status. Of course, the developmental sequences provide specific characteristics of these changes.

It is perhaps not surprising that researchers tend to focus on childhood when studying locomotor skills. Not only do children acquire the skills rather quickly, they also use the skills regularly, which is not the case for most adults. Try to remember the last time you galloped. If you can, you will probably remember that you galloped for some purpose, such as performing a dance. Adults generally do not use the entire range of fundamental locomotor patterns, at least not in the United States. What constrains these patterns from emerging? Farley (1997) describes the energetic inefficiency of human skipping; because skipping is "slow, jolting, and tiring," it makes an unlikely candidate for adult locomotion. In addition, sociocultural attitudes suggest that these motor skills are not appropriate for adults. The question remains: Do adults and older adults hop, gallop, jump, slide, and skip the same way that children do?

Reinforcing What You Have Learned About Constraints

TAKE A SECOND LOOK

Phil Raschker, mentioned at the beginning of the chapter, is not the only senior athlete with exceptional locomotor skills. In 2005, Ginette Bedard ran a marathon in 3:46:18, a time that is within 6 min of qualifying for the Boston Marathon in the 18- to 34-year-old age group. Ginette was 72 years old at the time. Male senior athletes are no slouches either. Ed Whitlock qualified for the Boston Marathon in the 18- to 34-year-old male category in 2004 by running a marathon in 3:08:35 at the age of 73. These athletes demonstrate that people can avoid or delay declines in individual constraints commonly associated with aging (e.g., strength or endurance) for a substantial period of time. Furthermore, once they obtain locomotor skill, adults can improve on performance long into adulthood.

TEST YOUR KNOWLEDGE

1. Describe the constraints that may act as rate controllers for specific locomotor activities.

2. How can a teacher or therapist manipulate task constraints to help a child acquire the skill of galloping?

3. What are some of the ways in which humans can move from place to place (without equipment)? Which ones are not currently observed in adults? Why are these locomotor forms rarely used?

4. What movement characteristics might you see in an older adult who is galloping? Why?

LEARNING EXERCISE 7.1

Comparing Preferred and Nonpreferred Hopping Legs

What individual constraints could be involved in determining the developmental level of hopping?

1. Observe three people (try to include at least one child). Ask each person to hop on his or her preferred leg (i.e., whichever foot he or she naturally chooses). Assess each hopper's developmental level using the observation plan provided in chapter 7.

2. Now, ask each person to hop on his or her opposite, or nonpreferred, leg. What happens to the person's developmental level?

3. A difference of one developmental level often exists between the preferred leg and the nonpreferred leg, particularly in children. Generate a list of possible reasons to account for the difference.

Development of Ballistic Skills

 CHAPTER OBJECTIVES

This chapter

- identifies developmental changes in throwing, kicking, punting, and striking movements;
- compares the characteristics of early performers across the various ballistic skills; and
- notes similar characteristics of proficient performance of ballistic skills.

Tennis' Grande Dame Is Still Winning at Age 97

Dorothy "Dodo" Cheney, daughter of women's tennis pioneer May Sutton and doubles champ Thomas Bundy, is a tennis star in her own right. In 1938 she won the Australian Open, and she hasn't stopped winning since. In fact, she has won more than 300 senior titles—a record in the United States Tennis Association—since the time she turned 40 years old in 1956. In 2004, she was inducted into the International Tennis Hall of Fame, and in 2010, she received a lifetime achievement award from the San Diego Hall of Champions. In 2011, she won her 381st national championship at age 95. Dodo Cheney is proof that ballistic skills can be executed—and executed well—over the life span.

Ballistic skills are those in which a person applies force to an object in order to project it. The ballistic skills of throwing, kicking, and striking have similar developmental patterns because the mechanical principles involved in projecting objects are basically the same. The ballistic skill that researchers have studied most is the overhand throw for distance. Much of the discussion on throwing also applies to kicking and striking, which we examine later in this chapter.

Overarm Throwing

Throwing takes many forms. The two-hand underhand throw (with windup between the legs) and the one-hand underhand throw are both common in young children. There is also a sidearm throw and a two-hand overarm throw. The type of throw that a person uses, especially among children, often depends on task constraints, particularly rules and the size of the ball. Our focus, though, is on the one-hand overarm throw, which is the most common type of throw in sport games and has been studied more widely than other types. Many of the mechanical principles involved in the overarm throw apply to other types of throws as well.

Researchers often make product assessments to gauge throwing skill development; that is, they measure the end product, or result, of the throwing movement, such as the accuracy, distance, or ball velocity. However, product measures have several drawbacks. Researchers must often change an accuracy assessment task when working with children of different ages. Young children need a short distance over which to throw to reach the target, but a short distance makes the task too easy for older children, who might all achieve perfect scores. Thus, researchers must either increase the distance or decrease the target size for older groups. In addition, scores on throws for distance often reflect not just throwing skill but also factors such as body size and strength. Two children may have equal throwing skills but quite different distance scores because one child is bigger and stronger. Finally, measuring ball velocity at release requires specialized equipment that may not be readily available. Thus, we could argue that product scores are not as useful to teachers, parents, and coaches as knowing how a child throws. Let's now turn our attention to the quality of the throwing pattern.

Characteristics of Early Overarm Throwing

It is helpful to contrast children's early attempts to throw with an advanced overarm throw. Young children's throwing patterns, especially those of children under 3 years, tend to be restricted to arm action alone (Marques-Bruna & Grimshaw, 1997). The child depicted in figure 8.1 does not step into the throw or use much trunk action. This child merely positions the upper arm, often with the elbow up or forward, and executes the throw by elbow extension alone. Figure 8.2 shows more movement but little gain in mechanical efficiency. These children demonstrate minimal throwing skill.

Proficient Overarm Throwing

By studying the characteristics of a proficient throw, we can identify the limitations in early throwing attempts. An advanced, forceful throw for distance involves the following movement patterns:

- The weight shifts to the back foot; the trunk rotates back; and the arm makes a circular, downward **backswing** for a windup.
- The leg opposite the throwing arm steps forward to increase the distance over which the thrower applies force to the ball and to allow full trunk rotation.
- The trunk rotates forward to add force to the throw. To produce maximal force, trunk rotation is "differentiated," which means the lower torso leads the upper torso, resulting in a movement that looks like the body "opens up."
- The trunk bends laterally, away from the side of the throwing arm.
- The upper arm forms a right angle with the trunk and comes forward just as (or slightly after) the shoulders rotate to a front-facing position. This means that from the side, you can see the upper arm within the outline of the trunk.
- The thrower holds the elbow at a right angle during the forward swing, extending the arm when the shoulders reach the front-facing position. Extending the arm just before release lengthens the radius of the throwing arc.

The **backswing** is the backward, or takeaway, movement to put the arm, leg, or racket in a position to move ballistically forward to project an object.

FIGURE 8.1 A beginning thrower simply brings the hand back with the elbow up and throws by extending the elbow without taking a step.
© Mary Ann Roberton.

FIGURE 8.2 A beginning thrower. Note the trunk flexion, rather than rotation, with the throw.
© Mary Ann Roberton and Kate R. Barrett.

- The forearm lags behind the trunk and upper arm during the forward swing. While the upper trunk is rotating forward, the forearm and hand appear to be stationary or to move down or back. The forearm lags until the upper trunk and shoulders actually rotate in the direction of the throw (the front-facing position).
- The follow-through dissipates the force of the throw over distance. The greater portion of wrist flexion comes during follow-through, after the thrower releases the ball.
- Dissipating force after release allows maximal speed of movement while the ball is in the hand.
- The thrower carries out the movements of the body segments sequentially, progressively adding the contributions of each part to the force of the throw. Generally, the sequence is as follows:
  - Forward step and pelvic rotation
  - Upper spine rotation and upper arm swing
  - Upper arm inward rotation and elbow extension
  - Release
  - Follow-through

Developmental Changes in Overarm Throwing

Now that we have discussed the characteristics of an advanced, forceful throw, we can examine how an individual progresses through the developmental steps from initial throwing attempts to advanced throwing skill. Several developmental sequences of overarm throwing have been proposed, beginning with a sequence outlined by Wild in 1938 and including that of Seefeldt, Reuschlein, and Vogel in 1972. Later, Roberton proposed a developmental sequence for the overarm throw using the body component approach. Two of the component sequences, arm action and trunk action, are **validated developmental sequences** (Roberton, 1977, 1978a; Roberton & DiRocco, 1981; Roberton & Langendorfer, 1980). In fact, Roberton and Konczak (2001) determined that changes in developmental sequences (i.e., a change from level 2 to level 3) accounted for more than half the change in velocity in throwing among 39 children studied over 7 years. Carefully studying the developmental overarm throw sequence outlined in table 8.1 will help you compare these steps with the characteristics of early throwers depicted in figures 8.1 and 8.2 and those of the more advanced throwers shown in figures 8.3 through 8.6.

Validated developmental sequences are sequences of advances in the performance of a skill that have been determined by longitudinal study and shown to fall in the same fixed order for all individuals.

FIGURE 8.3 A thrower with stage 2 arm action. The forearm reaches its farthest point back before the shoulders rotate to front-facing, but the humerus then swings forward before the shoulders; the elbow is consequently visible outside the body outline. Note the right angle between the humerus and the trunk.

© Mary Ann Roberton.

 If you were a physical education teacher, what factors would you expect to increase the likelihood that a developing child would reach the advanced steps in each component of throwing?

TABLE 8.1   Developmental Sequence for Throwing

Action

Trunk action in throwing and striking for force

Step 1	No trunk action or forward or backward movements. Only the arm is active in force production. Sometimes the forward thrust of the arm pulls the trunk into a passive left rotation (assuming a right-handed throw), but no twist-up precedes that action. If trunk action occurs, it accompanies the forward thrust of the arm by flexing forward at the hips. Preparatory extension sometimes precedes forward hip flexion.
Step 2	Upper trunk rotation or total trunk ("block") rotation. The spine and pelvis rotate away from the intended line of flight and then simultaneously begin forward rotation, acting as a unit, or "block." Occasionally, only the upper spine twists away, then toward the direction of force. The pelvis, then, remains fixed, facing the line of flight, or joins the rotary movement after forward spinal rotation has begun.
Step 3	Differentiated rotation. The pelvis precedes the upper spine in initiating forward rotation. The child twists away from the intended line of ball flight and then begins forward rotation with the pelvis while the upper spine is still twisting away.

Backswing, humerus, and forearm action in the overarm throw for force
Preparatory arm backswing component

Step 1	No backswing. The ball in the hand moves directly forward to release from the arm's original position when the hand first grasped the ball.
Step 2	Elbow and humeral flexion. The ball moves away from the intended line of flight to a position behind or alongside the head by upward flexion of the humerus and concomitant elbow flexion.
Step 3	Circular, upward backswing. The ball moves away from the intended line of flight to a position behind the head via a circular overhead movement with elbow extended, or an oblique swing back, or a vertical lift from the hip.
Step 4	Circular, downward backswing. The ball moves away from the intended line of flight to a position behind the head via a circular down-and-back motion, which carries the hand below the waist.

Humerus (upper arm) action component during forward swing

Step 1	Humerus oblique. The upper arm moves forward to ball release in a plane that intersects the trunk obliquely above or below the horizontal line of the shoulders. Occasionally, during the backswing, the upper arm is placed at a right angle to the trunk, with the elbow pointing toward the target. It maintains this fixed position during the throw.
Step 2	Humerus aligned but independent. The upper arm moves forward to ball release in a plane horizontally aligned with the shoulder, forming a right angle between humerus and trunk. By the time the shoulders (upper spine) reach front-facing, the upper arm and elbow have moved independently ahead of the outline of the body (as seen from the side) via horizontal adduction at the shoulder.
Step 3	Humerus lags. The upper arm moves forward to ball release horizontally aligned, but at the moment the shoulders (upper spine) reach front-facing, the upper arm remains within the outline of the body (as seen from the side). No horizontal adduction of the upper arm occurs before front-facing.

Forearm action component during forward swing

Step 1	No forearm lag. The forearm and ball move steadily forward to ball release throughout the throwing action.
Step 2	Forearm lag. The forearm and ball appear to lag (i.e., to remain stationary behind the child or to move downward or backward in relation to the child). The lagging forearm reaches its farthest point back, deepest point down, or last stationary point before the shoulders (upper spine) reach front-facing.
Step 3	Delayed forearm lag. The lagging forearm delays reaching its final point of lag until the moment of front-facing.

> continued

TABLE 8.1 > continued

Action
Foot action component in forceful throwing and striking
Step 1	No step. The child throws from the initial foot position.
Step 2	Homolateral step. The child steps with the foot on the same side as the throwing hand.
Step 3	Short contralateral step. The child steps with the foot on the opposite side of the throwing hand.
Step 4	Long contralateral step. The child steps with the opposite foot over a distance of more than half the child's standing height.

Note: Validation studies support the trunk sequence (Langendorfer, 1982; Roberton, 1977, 1978a; Roberton & DiRocco, 1981; Roberton & Langendorfer, 1980). Validation studies also support the arm sequences for the overarm throw (Halverson, Roberton, & Langendorfer, 1982; Roberton, 1977, 1978a; Roberton & DiRocco, 1981; Roberton & Langendorfer, 1980), with the exception of the preparatory arm backswing sequence, which was hypothesized by Roberton (1984) from the work of Langendorfer (1980). Langendorfer (1982) believes the humerus and forearm components are appropriate for overarm striking. The foot action sequence was hypothesized by Roberton (1984) from the work of Leme and Shambes (1978); Seefeldt, Reuschlein, and Vogel (1972); and Wild (1937).

FIGURE 8.4 A relatively advanced thrower. Arm, leg, and preparatory action are characteristic of the most advanced step, but the trunk action is characteristic of stage 2, or block rotation, rather than differentiated rotation.

FIGURE 8.5 From the rear you can see that this advanced thrower flexes the trunk laterally away from the ball at release.

FIGURE 8.6 This still drawing of a baseball pitcher captures the forward movement of the hips while the upper trunk is still back. This is called differentiated trunk rotation because the hips and upper trunk rotate at different times.

Just as with locomotor skills, you can more easily assess the developmental sequences of throwing using an observation plan (see figure 8.7 "Observation Plan for Throwing").

Begin the comparison by focusing on the trunk action component. In the first step of the developmental sequence, you do not see trunk action or forward or backward movements before the thrower releases the ball (figures 8.1 and 8.2). In the second step, the thrower proceeds to a **block rotation** of the trunk. Block rotation occurs between the third and fourth positions in figure 8.4. Distance throwers typically flex the trunk laterally (figure 8.5). The most advanced trunk action—**differentiated trunk rotation**—is often observable in pictures of baseball pitchers. In figure 8.6, the pitcher has started to rotate the lower trunk toward the direction of the throw while the upper trunk is still twisting back in preparation to throw. Specific parts of the trunk start rotating forward at different times.

To analyze the complexity of arm movements in throwing, first study the preparatory backswing, then the upper arm (humerus) motions, and finally the forearm motions. An unskilled thrower often does not use a backswing (figure 8.1). At the next step in the developmental sequence, a thrower flexes the shoulder and elbow in preparation for elbow extension, as in figure 8.2. A more advanced preparation involves using an upward backswing, but the most desirable backswing for a throw for distance is circular and downward. The thrower pictured in figure 8.4 is using this pattern.

As an unskilled thrower begins to swing the upper arm forward to throw, he or she often swings it at an angle oblique to the line of the shoulders—that is, with the elbow pointed up or down. A desirable advancement is to align the upper arm horizontally with the shoulders, forming a right angle with the trunk, as seen in figure 8.3. Even so, the upper arm may move ahead of the trunk's outline, which results in a loss of some of the momentum the thrower gains from moving the body parts sequentially for a forceful throw. In the most advanced pattern, the upper arm lags behind so that when the thrower reaches a front-facing position, you can see the elbow from the side within the outline of the trunk, as in figure 8.4.

It is also desirable for the forearm to lag behind. The thrower in figure 8.3 has some forearm lag, but the deepest lag comes before rather than at the front-facing position. The thrower in figure 8.4 demonstrates the advanced pattern of delayed forearm lag.

Most unskilled throwers throw without taking a step, like the child in figure 8.1. When a child learns to take the step, he or she often does so with the homolateral leg—the leg on the same side of the body as the throwing arm—which reduces the extent of trunk rotation and the range of motion available for a forceful throw. When the child acquires the advanced pattern of a contralateral step, he or she may initially take a short step, as in figure 8.2. A long step (more than half of the thrower's height) is desirable.

The body component analysis of overarm throwing demonstrates that individuals do not achieve the same developmental step for all body components at the same time. For example, the thrower in figure 8.2 is in step 1 of trunk, humerus, and forearm action but in step 3 of foot action. The thrower in figure 8.4 is in step 3 of humerus, forearm, and foot action but in step 2 of trunk action. Children who are the same age may be moving at various levels of the body component sequences, so they look different from one another as they advance through the developmental sequence.

However, not every possible combination of steps within the components is observed. In considering the trunk, humerus, and forearm components, Langendorfer

Block rotation of the trunk is forward rotation of the lower and upper trunk as a unit.

In **differentiated trunk rotation**, the lower trunk (hip section) rotates forward while the upper trunk (shoulder section) is rotating backward, still preparing to rotate forward.

KEY POINT
Letting distal body sections lag behind more proximal ones allows momentum to be transferred and distal sections to increase speed, providing the movements are well timed.

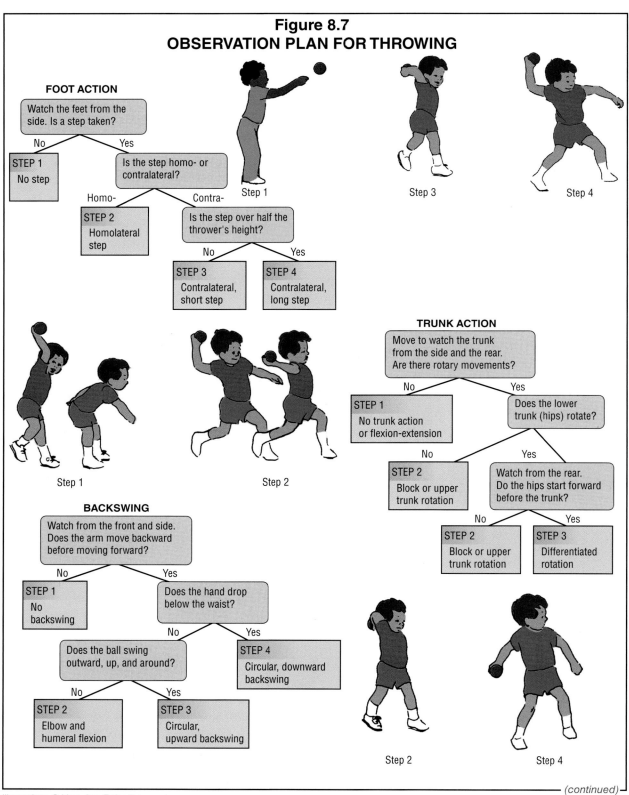

Figure 8.7
OBSERVATION PLAN FOR THROWING

FOOT ACTION

Watch the feet from the side. Is a step taken?

No → STEP 1 — No step

Yes → Is the step homo- or contralateral?

Homo- → STEP 2 — Homolateral step

Contra- → Is the step over half the thrower's height?

No → STEP 3 — Contralateral, short step

Yes → STEP 4 — Contralateral, long step

Step 1

Step 3

Step 4

Step 1

Step 2

TRUNK ACTION

Move to watch the trunk from the side and the rear. Are there rotary movements?

No → STEP 1 — No trunk action or flexion-extension

Yes → Does the lower trunk (hips) rotate?

No → STEP 2 — Block or upper trunk rotation

Yes → Watch from the rear. Do the hips start forward before the trunk?

No → STEP 2 — Block or upper trunk rotation

Yes → STEP 3 — Differentiated rotation

BACKSWING

Watch from the front and side. Does the arm move backward before moving forward?

No → STEP 1 — No backswing

Yes → Does the hand drop below the waist?

No → Does the ball swing outward, up, and around?

No → STEP 2 — Elbow and humeral flexion

Yes → STEP 3 — Circular, upward backswing

Yes → STEP 4 — Circular, downward backswing

Step 2

Step 4

(continued)

(continued)

HUMERUS ACTION

Watch from the side. Do the elbow and upper arm move forward at shoulder level (humerus forms a right angle with the trunk)?

No

Yes

STEP 1

Humerus oblique

At the moment of front-facing, is the elbow pointed toward you at the side, or is it seen outside the outline of the body?

Outside

To side

STEP 2

Humerus aligned but independent

STEP 3

Humerus lags

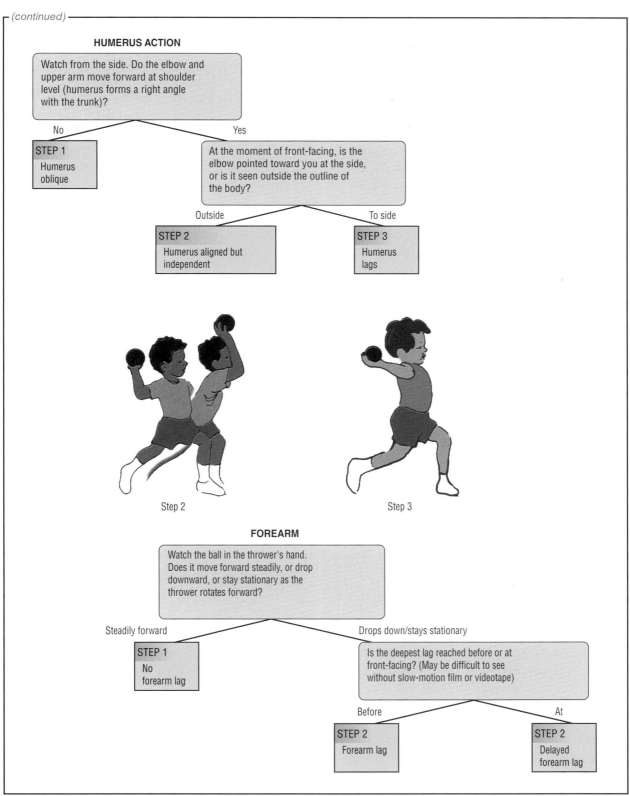

Step 2

Step 3

FOREARM

Watch the ball in the thrower's hand. Does it move forward steadily, or drop downward, or stay stationary as the thrower rotates forward?

Steadily forward

Drops down/stays stationary

STEP 1

No forearm lag

Is the deepest lag reached before or at front-facing? (May be difficult to see without slow-motion film or videotape)

Before

At

STEP 2

Forearm lag

STEP 2

Delayed forearm lag

and Roberton (2002) observed just 14 of the possible 27 combinations of developmental steps for these three components. It is likely that structural constraints limit the movements that some body sections can make while other body sections are moving in a particular way. When you observe throwing, then, you will tend to see certain common combinations and you probably will not see others at all. Langendorfer and Roberton (2002) also studied the common combinations of steps within components as children develop. They found a tendency for children to change from no trunk rotation to trunk rotation before the upper arm and forearm advanced to intermediate levels. The shift of the humerus to an advanced level occurred after both the upper arm and forearm advanced to the intermediate level. It is likely that mechanical constraints and neurological development are responsible for these trends; that is, they are likely to be rate controllers in the development of throwing.

It is desirable for all individuals to move through the various developmental steps during childhood in order to achieve an advanced throwing pattern that they can use in a number of physical activities, from softball to football to team handball. In fact, several authors noted that children can develop a skillful throwing pattern by age 6 (DeOreo & Keogh, 1980; McClenaghan & Gallahue, 1978; Zaichkowsky, Zaichkowsky, & Martinek, 1980). At least two studies, however, present contradictory results. Halverson, Roberton, and Langendorfer (1982) filmed a group of 39 children in kindergarten and first, second, and seventh grades and classified them according to Roberton's developmental sequence. Their analysis of upper arm action demonstrated that most of the younger boys were already at step 2 of humerus action, and by the seventh grade, more than 80% of boys had achieved the most advanced level (step 3). In contrast, approximately 70% of the girls were still in step 1 of humerus action when initially filmed. By the seventh grade, only 29% of the girls had reached step 3.

This trend was also apparent for forearm action. Almost 70% of the boys demonstrated step 2 forearm action when initially filmed. Some were still at this level by the seventh grade, but considerably more—a total of 41% of the boys—had reached step 3. More than 70% of the girls began in step 1, and the majority—71% of all the girls—were only at the second level in the seventh grade. Sex differences in developmental throwing progress were even more apparent for trunk action. Almost all the boys started in step 2, and 46% advanced to step 3 by the seventh grade. Similarly, almost 90% of the girls were in step 2 in kindergarten, but by the seventh grade all the girls remained in step 2; none had advanced to step 3.

Another study (Leme & Shambes, 1978) focused on throwing patterns in adult women. The 18 women were selected because they had very low throwing velocities. All demonstrated inefficient throwing patterns, including block rotation, lack of a step forward with the throw, and lack of upper arm lag. Although these women were unique because of their low throwing velocities, the study certainly demonstrates that not all adults achieve an advanced throwing pattern. Perhaps these women lacked practice opportunities or good instruction in childhood. Together, these two studies suggest that progress through the developmental levels is not automatic and may not ever be completed.

Observing Overarm Throwing Patterns

Overarm throwing is complex and difficult to observe in detail. The best procedure is to focus on a small number of components, or even a single component, at any one time. Some characteristics are best observed from the front or back:

- Trunk-to-upper-arm angle
- Elbow angle
- Lateral trunk bend

Others are best observed from the throwing side:

- The step
- Trunk rotation
- Upper arm and forearm lag

Videotaping is particularly valuable in helping you learn to observe the overarm throw. By videotaping, one can go back and review the different arm actions separately and in slow motion.

 WEB STUDY GUIDE Identify developmental differences among throwers in Lab Activity 8.1, Assessing the Developmental Levels of Overarm Throwing, in the web study guide. Go to www.HumanKinetics.com/LifeSpanMotor Development.

Throwing in Adulthood

As we have seen, throwing is a complex skill that requires the coordination of many body segments. To execute a maximum throw, the thrower must move many joints through a full range of motion with precise timing. This makes throwing an interesting skill to study in older adults. For example, we can ask whether older adults coordinate their movements for throwing just as young adults do or use different movement patterns. If they use the same patterns, we can ask whether older adults control those movements as young adults do or vary the extent or speed of movements in ways different from the movements of young adults.

Let's begin with observations of older adults that tell us what movement patterns older adults use. Williams, Haywood, and VanSant (1990, 1991) used the developmental steps in table 8.1 to categorize active older adult men and women between the ages of 63 and 78. Although the developmental steps were identified to monitor change in children and youths, they can be used to describe the movement patterns of throwers at any age.

The older adults were active in a university-sponsored physical activity program but did not practice throwing or participate in activities with overarm movement patterns. The investigators found their throwing movements to be only moderately advanced on the developmental sequences. Most older throwers took a short contralateral step (step 3) and were categorized at step 1 or 2 of humerus action and step 1 or 2 of forearm action. Almost all used block rotation of the trunk (step 2). Sex differences similar to those in children existed; that is, men generally had better form. However, qualitative throwing status also related to childhood and young adult experiences. Those who had participated in sports with overarm movement patterns at younger ages had better throwing form.

The ball velocities generated by the older adults were moderate (similar to velocities generated by 8- to 9-year-olds). The men averaged 54.4 ft/s (16.6 m/s), and the women averaged 39.1 ft/s (11.9 m/s). Hence, the older adults also confirmed the sex differences in velocity noted in youths.

KEY POINT
In comparing younger and older adult throwers, we can observe both the movement patterns used and how the movements are controlled.

Because actions during the backswing in ballistic skills generally are related to ball velocity, Haywood, Williams, and VanSant (1991) closely examined the backswing used by older adults. Those who used a circular, downward backswing threw faster than those using an upward (therefore shorter) backswing. Many older adults used backswing movement patterns that seemed different from those that children use. For example, many started the circular, downward backswing (step 4) but did not continue the circle. Instead, they bent the elbow to bring the ball up behind the head. A possible reason for this could be a change in the musculoskeletal system, such as decreased shoulder flexibility or a loss of fast-twitch muscle fibers. Possibly the throwers could not continue arm movement at the shoulder joint, or would experience pain in doing so, and thus they reorganized the movement.

The older adults in these studies were not observed when they were young adults, so we do not know whether any or all of them reached the highest developmental level in all the body components when they were younger. We can only hypothesize that their moderate status as older adults reflects at least some change from the movement patterns of their youth.

A commonly held notion of skill performance in older adulthood is one of consistent decline with advancing age. To observe throwing with advancing age, Williams, Haywood, and VanSant (1998) observed eight older adults over a period of 7 years. One individual was in her 60s, but most were in their late 70s. In contrast to what many would predict, throwing movements were relatively consistent over the years. Participants were placed in the same sequential step in 80% of the possible observations of body components over all the years. In cases where individuals changed, the change often (though not always) involved a decline. Increased variability was associated with change; that is, if a participant changed their developmental level from a previous session, they would often be inconsistent over the five trials, showing a variety of developmental levels. Williams and colleagues also observed small changes over the years that did not necessarily result in a change in developmental step. These small changes included decreased range of motion and slower movement speeds. This longitudinal observation shows that throwing performance in older adulthood is relatively stable. Small changes are more typical of performance than are large declines.

It's clear that older adults coordinate their throwing movements as do young adults of moderate throwing skill. Few older adults are observed to use the same movement patterns as the most advanced young adults, but this could reflect the limited number of observations of older adults as well as the constraints imposed by rate-controlling systems. The change observed over time in older adulthood is most likely to be change in the control of movements, especially a slowing of speed or a decrease in range of motion.

Though we need more research and more longitudinal observation of older adults, the model of constraints can guide our study of older adult performance. One or more body systems might regress, causing a slowing or limitation of movement, then reach a critical point at which the movement pattern must change. For example, advancing arthritis in the shoulder joint could cause the musculoskeletal system to act as a rate controller for throwing movements. Some movement patterns might be unique to older adulthood because declines in the various body systems that occur with aging might not be exactly the opposite of the advances that occur with physical growth. Others might well be the same

KEY POINT
Throwing movements of older adults are characterized more by stability in the developmental steps than by rapid decline. Change is more often typified by increased variability from throw to throw, a slight slowing of movement, or a more limited range of movement.

movement patterns seen in children and youths as they advance through the developmental sequence.

Throwing for Accuracy

The developmental sequences constructed for overarm throwing specifically address a throw for distance rather than for accuracy. The model of constraints would lead us to predict that changing the task from throwing for distance to throwing for accuracy results in a change in the movement pattern, and Langendorfer (1990) demonstrated this to be the case. He had young adults and 9- to 10-year-olds throw for distance and accuracy. The accuracy task was to hit an 8 ft (2.4 m) circular target at a distance of 11 yd (10 m) for adults and 6.6 yd (6 m) for children. Male throwers were categorized at significantly lower developmental steps when throwing for accuracy than for distance. Female throwers tended toward lower steps but were not significantly different in the two task conditions. Langendorfer felt that the distance for the accuracy throw for females resulted in a forceful task condition, which suggests that under true accuracy conditions throwers use movement patterns that are different from those for distance conditions.

KEY POINT
If the developmental sequences for forceful throwing are used to describe a short throw for accuracy, even the most proficient throwers might not use the most advanced movement patterns.

 Think of throwing as it is required in three or four sports or games. Do these activities emphasize distance, accuracy, or a combination of both? In which of these conditions would it be appropriate to use the developmental sequences with the perspective that the most proficient throwers would place in the upper steps?

Williams, Haywood, and VanSant (1993, 1996) replicated Langendorfer's study with older adults, asking them to throw for distance and for accuracy to a target 11 yd (10 m) away. Throwing velocity was measured for both task conditions, and the observers found that throwers used a slower velocity in the accuracy condition. As a group, the older adults changed little from one condition to the other, but most individuals adapted their movements in at least one body component. As with Langendorfer's female throwers, the older adults likely found the 11 yd distance of the accuracy throws to require relatively more force than young men would perceive was necessary. An accuracy condition at a shorter distance might have elicited more differences in the movements used.

Of course, in sports and games, throws are rarely made for distance without some accuracy constraint, or for accuracy without the need for force. What this research demonstrates is that different movement patterns arise for different task constraints, even for the same person in the same environment. When we compare movement patterns, then, by using either developmental categories or some other description of a movement pattern, we must recognize that the comparisons are valid only when the task constraints are identical. Even then, the person–task interaction influences the movement. For example, a strong individual could throw a given distance without the need for a step of the contralateral foot, whereas a weaker individual needs a step to reach that same distance. Parents, coaches, teachers, and recreational leaders must keep such factors in mind when comparing throwers.

 WEB STUDY GUIDE Compare throwing for force versus for accuracy by doing Lab Activity 8.2, Comparing Throws for Force With Throws for Accuracy, in the web study guide. Go to www.HumanKinetics.com/ LifeSpanMotorDevelopment.

Kicking

Like throwing, kicking projects an object; unlike throwing, however, the kicker strikes the object. Thus, children must have sufficient perceptual abilities and eye–foot coordination in order to execute a **kick** and consistently make contact with the ball. Teachers and parents can simplify the task for young children by challenging them to kick a stationary ball.

A **kick** is a ballistic strike from the foot.

Characteristics of Early Kicking

As with throwing, unskilled kickers tend to use a single action rather than a sequence of actions. As you can see in figure 8.8, there is no step forward with the nonkicking leg, and the kicking leg merely pushes forward at the ball. The knee of the kicking leg may be bent at contact, and an unskilled kicker may even retract the leg immediately after contacting the ball. The trunk does not rotate, and the child holds the arms stationary at the sides. The child in figure 8.9 demonstrates more advanced kicking skill by stepping forward with the nonkicking foot, thus putting the kicking leg in a cocked position.

KEY POINT
Just as young children throw with arm action alone, young kickers use only leg action.

FIGURE 8.8 A beginning kicker simply pushes the leg forward.
© Mary Ann Roberton.

Proficient Kicking

Compare the characteristics of early kicking with the critical features of advanced kicking shown in figure 8.10. The advanced kicker does the following:

- Starts with a preparatory windup. The kicker achieves this position, with the trunk rotated back and the kicking leg cocked, by leaping or running up to the ball. As a natural consequence of the running stride, the trunk is rotated back and the knee of the kicking leg is flexed just after the push-off of the rear leg. Hence, the kicker is able to apply maximal force over the greatest distance. Running up to the ball also contributes momentum to the kick.

- Uses sequential movements of the kicking leg. The thigh rotates forward, then the lower leg extends (knee straightens) just before contact with the

FIGURE 8.9 This kicker has made some improvements compared with the beginning kicker. He steps forward, putting the leg in a cocked position, but the leg swing is still minimal. The knee is bent at contact, and some of the momentum of the kick is lost.
© Mary Ann Roberton.

FIGURE 8.10   An advanced kicker. Note the full range of leg motion, trunk rotation, and arm opposition.

© Mary Ann Roberton.

ball to increase the radius of the arc through which the kicking leg travels. The straightened leg continues forward after contact to dissipate the force of the kick in the follow-through.

- Swings the kicking leg through a full range of motion at the hip.

- Uses trunk rotation to maximize the range of motion. To compensate for the complete leg swing, the kicker leans back at contact.

- Uses the arms in opposition to the legs as a reaction to trunk and leg motion.

Developmental Changes in Kicking

The study of kicking development in children has not been as extensive as educators would like. Although we know the overall changes children must undergo to perform an advanced kick, the qualitative changes that each body part makes are not well documented. Haubenstricker, Seefeldt, and Branta (1983) found that only 10% of the 7.5- to 9.0-year-old children they studied exhibited advanced kicking form. So we have reason to speculate that, as with throwing, children do not automatically achieve proficient kicking.

What other factors can modify the movement pattern used in kicking? Recently, Mally, Battista, and Roberton (2011) investigated the effect of distance on kicking form. Using a dynamical systems perspective (see chapter 2), they postulated that distance acts as a control parameter for kicking, much as the way speed, when scaled up or down, changes a walk to a run or vice versa. Following this logic, individuals will change their kicking pattern once a critical kicking distance is reached. Mally and colleagues tested 19 children at an average age of 8.1 years. The children kicked at five randomly ordered distances (approximately 1.5, 3, 6, 9, and 12 m). They kicked three times each while being videotaped. The authors analyzed the kicks based on key features of kicking, such as the final foot position in the approach, arm position on the final step, and leg and arm action during the forward swing of the leg. Of these features, four changed significantly as a function of distance (number and type of forward steps in the approach, position of the shank in the forward leg swing, leg action in the follow-through). The fact that significant differences existed suggests that distance may act as a control parameter for kicking. This also offers clues into the basis of developmental change in the kick, in that the pattern of changes resembles that seen in prelongitudinal screening of other skills. In other words, children changed movement form when asked to kick longer distances much in the way children improve proficiency over their childhood. This suggests that the ability to generate force may be a key component driving developmental change in kicking.

Observing Kicking Patterns

To give children adequate instruction in kicking, it is especially important to observe individual children. From the side, a teacher or coach can look for

- placement of the support foot,
- range of motion and precontact extension in the kicking leg,
- range of trunk motion, and
- arm opposition.

Let's now turn to the development of punting—a special form of kicking for which researchers have hypothesized a developmental sequence.

Punting

A **punt** is a form of kicking where an object is dropped from the individual's hands before impact with the foot.

The ballistic skill of punting is mechanically similar to kicking, yet punting tends to be more difficult for children to learn. To **punt**, a child drops the ball from the hands and must time the leg swing to the dropping ball.

Characteristics of Early Punting

A beginning punter tends to toss the ball up rather than drop it and will often release the ball after the support leg contacts the ground, if the child even takes a step at all. The arms drop to the sides. The child might rigidly extend the kicking-leg knee or bend it at a right angle, as in figure 8.11. The child typically holds the foot at a right angle to the leg so that the ball contacts the toes rather than the instep, resulting in an errant punt.

Arms drop to sides

Kicking knee flexed at contact

Short step

FIGURE 8.11 A beginning punter takes only a short step and flexes the kicking-leg knee 90° at contact (step 1). The ball is dropped from waist height (step 3), but the arms drop to the sides at contact (step 1).

© Mary Ann Roberton.

Proficient Punting

To execute a sound punt, as shown in figure 8.12, a child must

- extend the arms forward with the ball in hand before dropping it as the final leg stride is taken;
- move the arms to the side after releasing the ball, then move into an arm opposition pattern;
- leap onto the supporting leg and swing the punting leg vigorously up to contact the ball, such that the body leaves the ground with a hop of the supporting leg; and
- keep the kicking-leg knee nearly straight and the toes pointed at time of contact.

FIGURE 8.12 An advanced punter. The last step is a leap, the ankle is extended (plantar flexed) at ball contact, and the punt is completed with a hop on the support leg (step 3). The ball is dropped early from chest height (step 4), and the arms abduct and move in opposition to the legs (step 3).

© Mary Ann Roberton.

Developmental Changes in Punting

Roberton (1978b, 1984) hypothesized a developmental sequence for punting (table 8.2). Arm action is divided into two sequences, one for the ball-release phase and one for the ball-contact phase. The ball-release sequence outlines progress that moves from tossing the ball up to begin the punt, to dropping the ball late, and finally to timing the drop appropriately. The ball-contact sequence shows that the arms make a transition from nonuse to bilateral movement, then to the arm opposition pattern that characteristically accompanies forceful lower trunk rotation.

The leg action sequence reflects a developmental transition from a short step of the nonkicking leg to a long step and finally to a leap. At contact, the ankle of the kicking leg changes from a flexed to an extended position.

Observing Punting Patterns

Observing a punter from the side offers you a view of the ball drop, the arm position, and the foot position (see figure 8.13 "Observation Plan for Punting"). You can clearly see the degree of foot extension at ball contact from this position.

TABLE 8.2 Developmental Sequence for Punting

	Action
	Arm action: ball-release phase
Step 1	Upward toss. Hands are on the sides of the ball. The ball is tossed upward from both hands after the support foot has landed (if a step was taken).
Step 2	Late drop from chest height. Hands are on the sides of the ball. The ball is dropped from chest height after the support foot has landed (if a step was taken).
Step 3	Late drop from waist height. Hands are on the sides of the ball. The ball is lifted upward and forward from waist level. It is released at the same time as or just prior to the landing of the support foot.
Step 4	Early drop from chest height. One hand is rotated to the side and under the ball. The other hand is rotated to the side and top of the ball. The hands carry the ball on a forward and upward path during the approach. It is released at chest level as the final approach stride begins.

> continued

TABLE 8.2   > continued

	Action
	Arm action: ball-contact phase
Step 1	Arms drop. Arms drop bilaterally from ball release to a position on each side of the hips at ball contact.
Step 2	Arms abduct. Arms bilaterally abduct after ball release. The arm on the side of the kicking leg may pull back as that leg swings forward.
Step 3	Arm opposition. After ball release, the arms bilaterally abduct during flight. At contact the arm opposite the kicking leg has swung forward with that leg. The arm on the side of the kicking leg remains abducted and to the rear.
	Leg action: ball-contact phase
Step 1	No step or short step; ankle flexed. The kicking leg swings forward from a position parallel to or slightly behind the support foot. The knee may be totally extended by contact or, more frequently, still flexed 90°, with contact above or below the knee joint. The thigh is still moving upward at contact. The ankle tends to be dorsiflexed.
Step 2	Long step; ankle extension. Several steps may be taken. The last step onto the support leg is a long stride. The thigh of the kicking leg has slowed or stopped forward motion at contact. The ankle is extended (plantar flexed). The knee has 20° to 30° of extension still possible by contact.
Step 3	Leap and hop. The child may take several steps, but the last is a leap onto the support foot. After contact, the momentum of the kicking leg pulls the child off the ground in a hop.

Note: This sequence was hypothesized by Roberton (1984) and has not been validated.

Reprinted by permission from Roberton and Halverson 1984.

Sidearm Striking

Sidearm striking is a form of striking where the arm remains at or below shoulder level. One example of sidearm striking is a person swinging a baseball bat.

Although many sports and physical activities incorporate striking, research data on the development of striking is sparse. Striking encompasses numerous skills. It can be done with various body parts, such as the hands or feet. People can also use a variety of implements in various orientations, such as swinging a bat sidearm, a racket overhand, or a golf club underhand. In our discussion, we focus on one-hand **sidearm striking** with an implement and one-hand overarm striking with an implement.

Of the basic skills we've discussed so far, striking involves the most difficult perceptual judgment. Success in meeting a moving object is limited in early childhood; therefore, it is difficult to assess striking of a moving object by young children. For this reason, teachers often adapt striking tasks for young children by making the ball stationary. Researchers often base the developmental sequences on striking a stationary ball so that they can describe the changes in young children's movement patterns.

We can apply the mechanical principles and developmental aspects of one-hand striking of a stationary object to other types of striking tasks. Keep this in mind as we examine the development of the striking pattern. Table 8.3 shows the developmental sequence of the sidearm strike.

Characteristics of Early Sidearm Striking

A child's first attempts to strike sidearm often look like unskilled attempts to throw overhand. The child chops at the oncoming ball by extending at the elbow, using

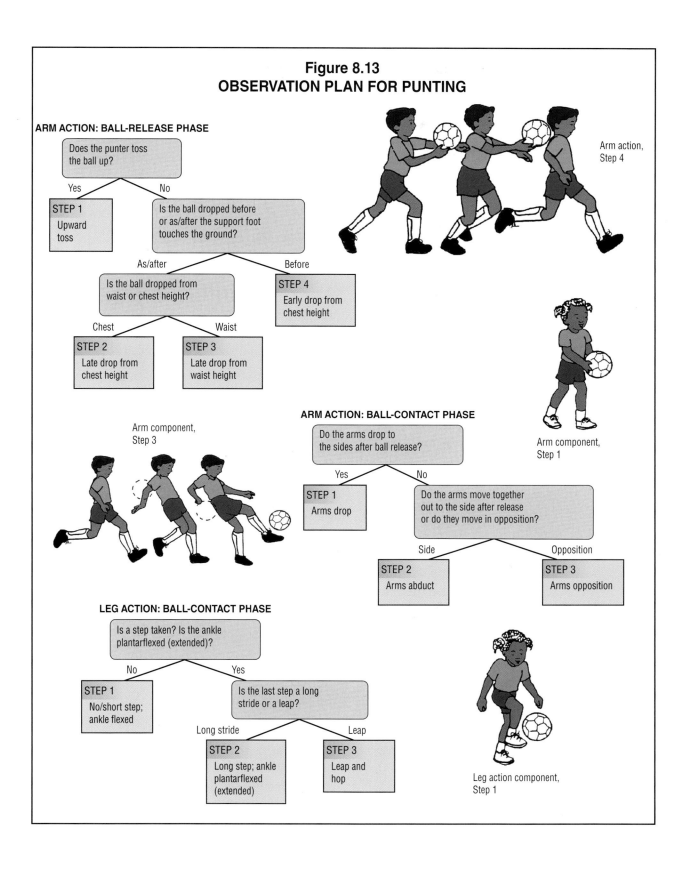

Figure 8.13
OBSERVATION PLAN FOR PUNTING

ARM ACTION: BALL-RELEASE PHASE

Does the punter toss the ball up?

Yes

STEP 1
Upward toss

No

Is the ball dropped before or as/after the support foot touches the ground?

As/after

Is the ball dropped from waist or chest height?

Chest

STEP 2
Late drop from chest height

Waist

STEP 3
Late drop from waist height

Before

STEP 4
Early drop from chest height

Arm action, Step 4

Arm component, Step 3

Arm component, Step 1

ARM ACTION: BALL-CONTACT PHASE

Do the arms drop to the sides after ball release?

Yes

STEP 1
Arms drop

No

Do the arms move together out to the side after release or do they move in opposition?

Side

STEP 2
Arms abduct

Opposition

STEP 3
Arms opposition

LEG ACTION: BALL-CONTACT PHASE

Is a step taken? Is the ankle plantarflexed (extended)?

No

STEP 1
No/short step; ankle flexed

Yes

Is the last step a long stride or a leap?

Long stride

STEP 2
Long step; ankle plantarflexed (extended)

Leap

STEP 3
Leap and hop

Leg action component, Step 1

TABLE 8.3   Developmental Sequence for Sidearm Striking

Action
Racket action component
Step 1   Chop. The racket is swung in the vertical plane.
Step 2   Arm swing only. The racket swings ahead of the trunk.
Step 3   Racket lag. The racket lags behind trunk rotation but goes ahead of the trunk at front-facing.
Step 4   Delayed racket lag. The racket is still lagging behind the trunk at front-facing.
Foot, trunk, and upper arm action component
See the foot, trunk, and upper arm sections in table 8.1.

little leg and trunk action. As in figure 8.14, the child often faces the oncoming ball.

Proficient Sidearm Striking

An advanced sidearm strike incorporates many of the characteristics of an advanced overarm throw. Such characteristics include the following:

- Stepping into the hit, thus applying linear force to the strike. The step should cover a distance more than half the individual's standing height (Roberton, 1978b, 1984). The preparatory stance should be sideways to allow for this step and the sidearm swing.

- Using differentiated trunk rotation to permit a larger swing and to contribute more force through rotary movement.

- Swinging through a full range of motion to apply the greatest force possible.

- Swinging in a roughly horizontal plane and extending the arms just before contact.

- Linking or chaining the movements together to produce the greatest force possible. The sequence is as follows: backswing and forward step, pelvic rotation, spinal rotation and swing, arm extension, contact, and follow-through.

FIGURE 8.14 This young girl executes a striking task with arm action only. She faces the ball and swings down rather than sideways.

© Mary Ann Roberton.

Developmental Changes in Sidearm Striking

Researchers have not validated a completed developmental sequence for sidearm striking, but we can apply the sequences for foot and trunk action in the overarm throw to striking (see figure 8.15, "Observation Plan for Sidearm Striking"). In addition, we know some of the qualitative changes individuals make in the arm action for sidearm striking. The arm action for sidearm striking is distinct from that for overarm and underarm (as in the golf swing) striking, but all three forms share many of the same mechanical principles. We discuss sidearm striking first, but keep in mind that many of the qualitative changes in the arm action for sidearm striking, as well as the mechanical principles involved, apply to overarm striking as well.

The first obvious change in sidearm striking from the technique shown in figure 8.14 occurs when a striker stands sideways to the path of the incoming ball. By

Figure 8.15
OBSERVATION PLAN FOR SIDEARM STRIKING
(for foot, trunk, and humerus components, use the throwing observation)

RACKET/BAT ACTION

Is the racket swung in a horizontal plane?

No → STEP 1 Chop

Yes → Does the racket "lag" (pause in forward motion)?

No → STEP 2 Arm swing only

Yes → Does the racket "lag" occur at the front-facing position?

No → STEP 3 Racket lag

Yes → STEP 4 Delayed racket lag

Step 1   Step 2   Step 4

transferring the weight to the rear foot, taking a step forward, and transferring the weight forward at contact, a striker is able to improve striking skills. The child pictured in figure 8.16 turns sideways but has not yet learned to step into the strike.

A second beneficial change is the use of trunk rotation. In a developmental sequence similar to that for throwing, individuals first use block rotation before advancing to differentiated (hip, then shoulder) rotation. A skilled striker who uses differentiated rotation appears in figure 8.17.

Strikers also progressively change the plane of their swing from the vertical chop seen in figure 8.14 to an oblique plane and finally to a horizontal plane, as seen in figure 8.16. Eventually, they obtain a longer swing by holding their elbows away from their sides and extending their arms just before contact. A beginning striker frequently holds a racket or paddle with a power grip, where the handle

FIGURE 8.16 This girl has made improvements as compared with the beginning striker in that she stands sideways and executes a sidearm strike. However, she does not yet involve the lower body.

© Mary Ann Roberton.

FIGURE 8.17 An advanced striker. The swing arm moves through a full range of motion. The striker steps into the swing and uses differentiated trunk rotation.

© Mary Ann Roberton.

is held in the palm like a club (figure 8.18, *a* and *b*; Napier, 1956). With this grip the striker tends to keep the elbow flexed during the swing and to supinate the forearm, thus undercutting the ball. Although children tend to use the power grip with any striking implement, they most often adopt it when given implements that are too big and heavy for them. Educators can promote use of the proper "shake-hands" grip by giving children striking implements that are an appropriate size and weight (Roberton & Halverson, 1984)—that is, by scaling the size and weight of the implement to the size and strength of the child.

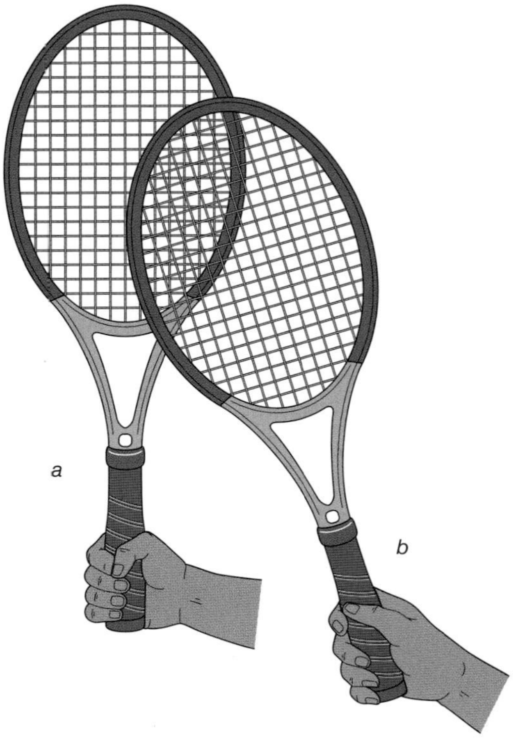

Observing Sidearm Striking Patterns

As with many of the skills we've looked at thus far, studying a child's swing from more than one location yields the most information. From the "pitching" position (i.e., directly in front of the child, at a safe distance away and in a location where you can administer a pitch) you can observe the direction of the step, the plane of the swing, and arm extension. From the side you can check the step, the trunk rotation, and the extent of the swing.

FIGURE 8.18 *(a)* Beginners often use a power grip, causing them to undercut the ball. *(b)* A "shake-hands" grip is desirable for sidearm striking.

Overarm striking is a form of striking where the arm travels above the shoulder level. One example of overarm striking is a person swinging a racket in a tennis serve.

Overarm Striking

One can execute **overarm striking** without an implement, as in the overarm volleyball serve, or with an implement, such as in the tennis serve. We focus on overarm striking with an implement.

Characteristics of Early Overarm Striking

A beginning striker demonstrates limited pelvic and spinal movement, swings with a collapsed elbow, and swings the arm and racket forward in unison, as in figure 8.19. If the striker is receiving a pitched ball, the collapsed elbow leads to a low point of contact between the racket and the ball. The movement pattern of early overarm striking, then, is similar to that of early overarm throwing and early sidearm striking.

Proficient Overarm Striking

A person who is skilled at overarm striking, as depicted in figure 8.20, does the following:

- Rotates both the pelvis and the spine more than 90°.
- Holds the elbow at an angle between 90° and 119° at the start of forward movement.
- Lets the racket lag behind the arm during the forward swing.

Elbow stays bent through swing

Arm and racket swing together

Ball contact is low

FIGURE 8.19 Beginning overarm striking. Trunk movement is minimal. The elbow is collapsed, and the arm and racket move together.

Trunk rotation occurs

Racket lags behind arm

Ball contact is higher

FIGURE 8.20 Proficient overarm striking. Trunk rotation is obvious. The racket lags behind the arm during the swing.

Racket lag is consistent with the open kinetic chain principle, where force is generated by a correctly timed sequence of movements. The humerus and forearm lag is an example of an open kinetic chain: The humerus lags behind trunk rotation, the forearm lags behind the humerus, and the racket lags behind the forearm to create the chain of sequential movements.

Developmental Changes in Overarm Striking

Langendorfer (1987) and Messick (1991) proposed developmental sequences for overarm striking. Both sequences are based on cross-sectional studies; neither has been validated with longitudinal research.

Overarm striking is similar to overarm throwing and sidearm striking, but it also has unique features. Langendorfer identified eight component sequences from a study of children 1 to 10 years old. The trunk, humerus, forearm, and leg sequences are similar to those for overarm throwing (table 8.1). Sequences unique to overarm striking include pelvic range of motion, spinal range of motion, elbow angle, and racket action (table 8.4). Messick observed 9- to 19-year-olds executing tennis serves. She identified elbow angle and racket sequences similar to those that Langendorfer identified, except that extending the forearm and racket up to contact the ball was characteristic of the tennis serves. She also noted a devel-

TABLE 8.4   Developmental Sequence for Overarm Striking

Action	
Preparatory phase: trunk action	
Step 1	No trunk action or flexion and extension of the trunk
Step 2	Minimal trunk rotation (<180°)
Step 3	Total trunk rotation (>180°)
Ball-contact phase: elbow action	
Step 1	Angle is 20° or less, or greater than 120°
Step 2	Angle is 21° to 89°
Step 3	Angle is 90° to 119°
Ball-contact phase: spinal range of motion	
Step 1	Spine (at shoulders) rotates through less than 45°
Step 2	Spine rotates between 45° and 89°
Step 3	Spine rotates more than 90°
Ball-contact phase: pelvic range of motion	
Step 1	Pelvis (below the waist) rotates through less than 45°
Step 2	Pelvis rotates between 45° and 89°
Step 3	Pelvis rotates more than 90°
Ball-contact phase: racket action	
Step 1	No racket lag
Step 2	Racket lag
Step 3	Delayed racket lag (and upward extension)

The preparatory trunk action and the parenthetical information in step 3 of racket action are reprinted, by permission, from J.A. Messick, 1991, "Prelongitudinal screening of hypothesized developmental sequences for the overhead tennis serve in experienced tennis players 9-19 years of age," *Research Quarterly for Exercise and Sport* 62: 249-256. The remaining components are reprinted, by permission, from S. Langendorfer, 1987, Prelongitudinal screening of overarm striking development performed under two environmental conditions. In *Advances in motor development research*, Vol. 1, edited by J.E. Clark and J.H. Humphrey (New York: AMS Press), 26.

opmental sequence of preparatory trunk action in tennis overarm striking. This appears in table 8.4.

Neither Langendorfer nor Messick found the developmental sequences for foot action in throwing to apply to overarm striking, although they observed age differences in weight shifting—older performers shifted their weight more than younger ones. Perhaps overarm striking requires a different sequence that has not yet been identified. This may be especially true in the context of tennis, where the rules specify that the server must not step on or over the baseline before striking the ball.

Observing Overarm Striking Patterns

Observation of overarm striking is similar to that of sidearm striking. You might prefer, though, to watch from behind rather than from the "pitching" position, in addition to watching from the side.

 WEB STUDY GUIDE   Identify developmental differences among strikers in Lab Activity 8.3, Assessing the Developmental Levels of Striking, in the web study guide. Go to www.HumanKinetics.com/LifeSpanMotorDevelopment.

Older Adult Striking

As active middle-aged and older adults such as Dodo Cheney make sports news, we know that ballistic skills can be lifetime skills. The research on active adults performing ballistic skills is limited but likely to increase as larger numbers of seniors maintain an active lifestyle involving sports that require ballistic skills. It is not surprising that tennis and golf are two of the contexts for older adult research because both have a large senior following and established senior programs.

The tempo and rhythm of a short iron shot in golf have been compared in younger (19- to 25-year-old) and older (60- to 69-year-old) males who are experienced golfers (Jagacinski, Greenberg, & Liao, 1997). This task, of course, emphasizes accuracy more than distance. As a group, the older golfers had a slightly faster tempo, or overall speed of the shot. Differences in rhythm also existed. Older golfers reached peak force earlier in the swing, whereas younger players reached it just before impact. Older golfers also had larger force changes in later phases of the swing. This might indicate that the older golfers exert relatively more force to execute this short iron shot than younger golfers. In terms of accuracy, 3 of 12 older golfers made less than 10% of their shots, but the remainder were as accurate as the younger golfers. Increased variability in accuracy among members of the older group was found, then, and many older golfers showed no decrement. We should keep in mind that the strength and flexibility demands of this task were relatively low; thus, losses of strength and flexibility with advancing age would not have constrained the older golfers compared with younger ones.

 What might be the rate controllers causing older adults to reorganize their movement patterns for striking? Would these controllers differ for those who remain active in a "striking" sport, as compared with those who are sedentary?

Haywood and Williams (1995) observed older adult tennis players as they executed an overarm serve. These older adults played tennis an average of 2.7 times per week. They were divided into a younger group (from 62 up to 68 years old) and an older group (69 up to 81 years old). The developmental steps described earlier for preparatory trunk action, elbow action, and forearm and racket action were used to categorize the servers by movement pattern. Ball impact velocity was also measured. The younger and older servers did not differ in any of these measures, nor did male and female servers differ. Most of the servers used moderate-level trunk, forearm, and racket movements, but the older group was somewhat more advanced in elbow action. So, the investigators found little evidence of significant decline for a population continuing to use a striking skill.

The investigators measured static shoulder flexibility in the senior tennis players to determine whether a decline of flexibility might act as a rate controller for overarm striking movements. However, there was no difference in flexibility between the two age groups. Of course, as with the older throwers described earlier, these tennis players were not observed longitudinally, and we do not know whether they ever used more advanced movement patterns. Two of the servers, one man and one woman, were placed into the highest developmental category of each body component observed; both servers were former tennis teaching professionals. This investigation therefore suggests that well-practiced movement patterns tend to be maintained over the older adult years and perhaps even from younger years.

Summary and Synthesis

Proficient performance in the ballistic skills exhibits movements that obey mechanical principles for maximizing force and speed (as discussed in chapter 3). As children and youths improve their performance of ballistic skills, we see changes that make their movements more and more consistent with those mechanical principles. Examples include a forward step that transfers momentum into the direction of the throw or strike; rotary motions of the trunk, usually sequenced as lower trunk followed by upper trunk for arm throws and strikes; and sequential movement of the projecting limb to allow distal body components and striking implements to lag behind larger and more proximal body components so that momentum is transferred and speed is increased. We know that transition to the most efficient movement patterns is not automatic. Some adults continue to use movement patterns that produce moderate results when maximal ones are desired. Because little observation of life span striking performance is available, it is difficult to know the amount of decline in the throwing and striking performance of older adults. Active older adults, however, appear to maintain movement patterns fairly well, especially when the patterns are well practiced.

Task conditions and the interaction between the person and the task are important in determining what movement patterns emerge in performance. In assessing how youths are progressing or whether seniors are declining, we must not only consider the rate controllers possibly influencing those changes but also acknowledge the particular task conditions for the movement observed. An individual throwing a short distance for accuracy would not necessarily need to use the movements characteristic of the most advanced level in each body component.

Reinforcing What You Have Learned About Constraints

TAKE A SECOND LOOK

Dorothy "Dodo" Cheney has integrated changing constraints in order to remain successful at tennis over eight decades. She has adapted to changes in her own body, winning matches in every age group in which she has played. She has also won on every playing surface on which she has competed (environmental constraints) and in singles, doubles, and mixed doubles (task constraints)!

TEST YOUR KNOWLEDGE

1. What distinguishes kicking from punting?
2. Identify four of the major qualitative changes in the development of each of the following ballistic skills: throwing, punting, and overarm striking.
3. What qualitative developmental changes are shared by throwing and overarm striking? Why might both skills change in these ways?

LEARNING EXERCISE 8.1

Overarm Throwing: Changes in Form Related to Changes in the Throwing Arm

What individual constraints could be involved in determining the developmental level of overarm throwing for force?

1. Observe three people (try to include at least one child). Ask each person to throw with his or her preferred arm (i.e., the arm he or she naturally chooses). Assess each thrower's developmental level using the observation plan provided in chapter 8.
2. Now, ask each person to throw with the opposite, or nonpreferred, arm. What happens to the developmental level?
3. There will often be a difference of at least one developmental level between the preferred and nonpreferred throwing arms. Generate a list of possible reasons to account for the difference.

9

Development of Manipulative Skills

 CHAPTER OBJECTIVES

This chapter

- documents a transition in infancy from the use of power grips to pick up objects to the use of precision grips;
- demonstrates how the size of an object, relative to the size of the hand, can influence the grip used to pick up the object;
- examines the role of vision in reaching for objects;
- identifies developmental changes in catching; and
- considers how catchers are able to intercept objects.

Helping Hands

In January of 2013 Matthew Scott celebrated the 14th anniversary of his hand transplant, which was the first in the United States and the most successful in the world to date. Scott, who is left handed, lost his left hand in a firecracker accident in 1985. He received the transplant from a cadaver in a 15 h operation (Handfuls of Happiness, 2000). A year and a half later, Scott was able to sense temperature, pressure, and pain in his new hand as well as turn pages, tie shoelaces, and throw a baseball. At his 8-year checkup he could hold a 15 lb weight with his transplanted hand and pick up small objects.

Those of us who have had an arm or wrist in a cast can probably begin to imagine what it would be like to attempt certain tasks or sports with one hand or without hands. Our hands allow us to perform a wide range of skills, from handling small, delicate objects to steering large ships. Today the use of cell phones to send text messages is commonplace, and most teens probably consider typing text messages to be a fundamental skill!

As with any other movement, we expect limb movements to arise from the interaction of individual, task, and environmental constraints. Consider the task of lifting a heavy crystal bowl from a table, as well as the question of whether an individual should pick it up with one hand or two. The environment plays a role because gravity acts on the object. Crystal is heavier than plain glass. The task is a factor in several ways. Consider the shape of the bowl. Does the shape and the weight—that is, the interaction of environment and task—afford lifting the bowl with one hand, or does it require two? Now consider the person's strength. Does this individual structural constraint interact with task and environment to afford lifting with one hand or two?

With growth and aging, many individual structural constraints change. The length and size of the limbs change with growth, as does strength. On the other hand, when we age, conditions such as arthritis can make manipulative skills difficult or even painful. Thus, just as with other types of skills, the performance of manipulative skills changes with growth and aging.

Grasping and Reaching

When a skilled adult wants to obtain a small object, the arm reaches forward and then the hand grasps the object. The reach and grasp form a smooth movement unit. To simplify our study of the development of reaching and grasping in infancy, however, we'll consider grasping, or **prehension**, first.

Prehension is the grasping of an object, usually with the hand or hands.

Grasping

In 1931, H.M. Halverson published a classic description of grasping development, the 10 phases of which are summarized in figure 9.1. Halverson filmed infants

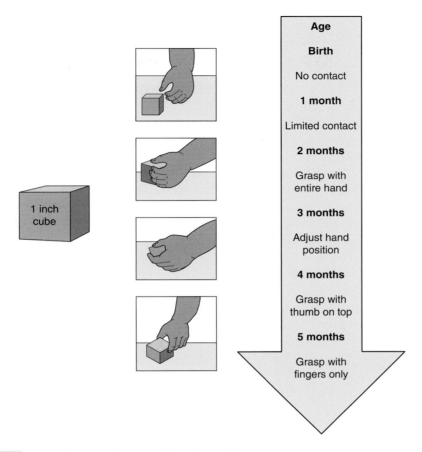

FIGURE 9.1   A developmental progression of grasping.

between 16 and 52 weeks of age grasping a 1 in. (2.5 cm) cube. In early grasping, the infant squeezes an object against the palm without the thumb providing opposition. Eventually, the infant uses the thumb in opposition but still holds the object against the palm. Such grips are collectively called power grips. Halverson observed that after about 9 months of age, infants began to hold objects between the thumb and one or more fingers; these are called precision grips. Thus, the first year is characterized by a transition from power grips to precision grips.

Hohlstein (1982) later replicated Halverson's study, but in addition to the 1 in. cube used in the original study, she provided objects of different sizes and shapes. The transition from power to precision grips was still evident, but shape and size of the object influenced the specific type of grasp used. In fact, by 9 months of age infants reliably shape their hand in anticipation of an object's shape as they go to grasp it (Lockman, Ashmead, & Bushnell, 1984; Piéraut-Le Bonniec, 1985).

Through Halverson's early work, developmentalists viewed prehension as a behavior acquired in steps. Maturationists of Halverson's era viewed these age-related changes in the same vein as motor milestones. They linked each progression to a new stage with neuromotor maturation, especially maturation of the motor cortex. However, the finding that shape and size of the object to be grasped influence the grip used suggests that the individual, the environment, and the task interact in prehension movements. Halverson studied only one set of environment

KEY POINT
The first year sees a transition from power grips to precision grips, but the particular grip used is influenced by the shape and size of the object grasped.

and task characteristics. More variety of movement grips is observed with changing environment and task characteristics in the early months of life.

For example, Newell, Scully, McDonald, and Baillargeon (1989) watched 4- to 8-month-old infants grasp a cube and three cups of different diameters. They found that infants used five types of grip 95% of the time. The specific grip seemed to depend on the size and shape of the object. The investigators even observed precision grips with the smallest cup at a younger age than Halverson observed. Because we can observe this precision grip at such a young age, it's clear that the neuromotor system must be mature enough at this young age to control the precision grip. Lee, Liu, and Newell (2006), who observed prehension longitudinally from age 9 to 37 weeks, also found that the grasp used by infants depended on the properties of the object. Clearly, then, neuromotor maturation is not the only structural constraint involved in grasping.

Newell, Scully, Tenenbaum, and Hardiman (1989) suggested, based on observations of older children, that the grip used to obtain any particular object depends on the relationship between hand size and object size. That is, the movement selected by individuals is related to their hand size compared with an object's size, or movements reflect **body scaling**. Butterworth, Verweij, and Hopkins (1997) tested this idea by having infants between 6 and 20 months of age pick up cubes and spheres of different sizes. They confirmed Halverson's general trend from power to precision grips. By early in the second year, precision grips predominated. Younger infants tended to use more fingers to grasp the objects than older infants did. Object *size* greatly influenced the grip selected, and *shape* had somewhat less influence on the grip. Butterworth and colleagues observed all but Halverson's inferior-forefinger grasp in the youngest infants, 6 to 8 months of age, so infants use a greater variety of grips than we would assume from Halverson's work. Thus, neuromotor development for grasping movements must be more advanced than those in Halverson's day thought. Task and environmental constraints clearly play an important role in infants' adaptations of their movements.

 Think about making and eating your breakfast in the morning. How many objects do you grip, and how does the configuration of your hand change for each one? Have you ever broken your wrist and found it was difficult to do such tasks?

It so happened that the infant boys in Butterworth and colleagues' study had longer hands than the girls had. The hypothesis of Newell, Scully, Tenenbaum, and Hardiman predicted that these boys and girls would use different grips, but this was not the case. Thus, the influence of object size on grip used supports the idea that the ratio between hand size and object size is important, but the lack of a difference between the boys and girls does not. Therefore, more research is needed before we know whether infants do in fact use body scaling in selecting a grip. Still, this work affirms that interactions between the infant, the environment, and the task are important even in early grasping and that changes in movement patterns related to changing structural constraints occur even in infancy.

Is body scaling used at older ages? Do older children and adults use the ratio of hand size to object size in selecting a grip? Newell, Scully, Tenenbaum, and Hardiman (1989) observed 3- to 5-year-olds and adults. They found that a relatively constant ratio of hand size to object size determined when individuals chose to use two hands to pick up an object instead of one, no matter what their age. Thus, the ratio was consistent even though the adults had larger hands. The same has been found to be true in children 5, 7, and 9 years of age (van der Kamp, Savelsbergh, & Davis, 1998). The interaction of the individual's structural constraints with environmental and task constraints, then, gives rise to either a one-hand or a two-hand grasp.

Vision also plays a role in this type of task. From a young age on, we select the grip appropriate for the size, weight, and shape of the object to be obtained (figure 9.2). Butterworth and colleagues (1997) observed that infants often knocked an object before actually grasping it. In contrast, adults configure, or shape, their hands for a particular object *before* making contact with it. Adults also make a decision about whether to reach for an object with one hand or two *before* making contact with it. That is, visual information is used in preparation for the grasp. During childhood, individuals acquire the experience with objects needed to precisely configure the hand. Kuhtz-Buschbeck et al. (1998) noted that 6- and 7-year-olds were more dependent than adults on visual feedback during the reach to shape their hand for the grasp. Similarly, Pryde, Roy, and Campbell (1998) observed 9- and 10-year-olds slowing down more than adults at the end of a reach, presumably taking more time to use visual information for grasping the object. Older children, in the 5- to 10-year-old range, and adults appear to use visual information to anticipate the grasp and optimize accuracy (Smyth, Katamba, & Peacock, 2004; Smyth, Peacock, & Katamba, 2004).

If indeed body scaling determines grip selection starting in childhood, grasping quickly becomes a well-practiced skill, with growing hand size and arm length taken into account in the body-scaled ratio. Grasping doesn't need to be relearned with increases in growth. Thus, we might expect it to be a very stable skill over the life span. Only conditions such as arthritis or a loss of strength in old age would influence hand configuration. Indeed Carnahan, Vandervoort, and Swanson (1998) found that young adults (average age 26 years) and older adults (average age 70 years) accurately adapted the opening of the hand to grasp moving objects of

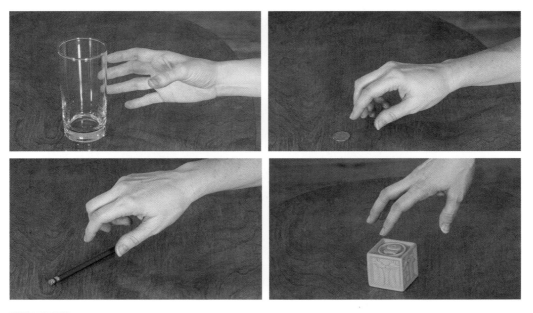

FIGURE 9.2   The type of grip one uses to pick up an object depends in part on the size and shape of the object. An adult configures, or shapes, the hand for the object to be grasped before making contact.

different sizes. Of course, most manipulative tasks are not just a matter of grasping an object but rather of bringing the hand to an object so that it can be grasped. We now examine the development of reaching over the life span.

 Think about your experience in grasping objects. Have you ever said, "This is heavier than it looks"? Or, "This is lighter than it looks"? What does this tell you about the role of vision in grasping?

 WEB STUDY GUIDE   Identify different grasping techniques during infancy in Lab Activity 9.1, Observing Grasping Development, in the web study guide. Go to www.HumanKinetics.com/LifeSpanMotorDevelopment.

Reaching

Infants make a transition during their first year from random arm movements to reaches that allow them to grasp objects. The questions we ask about the developmental processes that bring about this change in reaching are similar to those asked about early leg movements in chapter 6. In the case of reaching, what is it that drives the change from random and reflexive arm movements (prereaching) in the first few months after birth to eventual successful reaching of objects? Beginning with Piaget (1952), many developmentalists proposed that reaching and grasping required seeing both the object and the hand in the visual field so that vision and proprioception could be matched. Bruner (1973; Bruner & Koslowski, 1972) further suggested that infants build a system of visually guided arm movements from initial, poorly coordinated movements. Others considered reaching development to be a process of fine-tuning abilities that are already in place (Bower, Broughton, & Moore, 1970; Trevarthen, 1974, 1984; von Hofsten, 1982).

It now seems, though, that there is not a continuous change from prereaching to reaching—that is, it seems that infants are *not* learning to match vision of the hand and arm with proprioception of the movement (von Hofsten, 1984). Infants are very good from the start at reaching in the dark when they cannot see their hand (Clifton, Muir, Ashmead, & Clarkson, 1993; McCarty & Ashmead, 1999). This is not to say that vision is not important to the task. Infants later rely on vision to refine the path of the reach and, as we said earlier, configure the hand to the object (figure 9.3). Rather, it might be the case that learning to reach is, more than anything else, a problem of learning to control the arm.

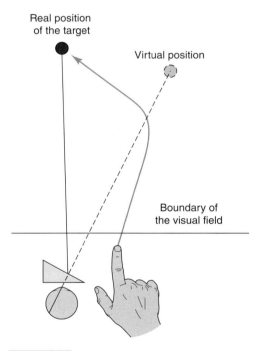

FIGURE 9.3   Displaced vision tasks demonstrate the role of vision in reaching. Prisms placed in front of the eyes shift the apparent location of an object from its real position. Individuals reach but grasp nothing because they reach directly for the location they identified by vision. They do not wait to see their hand in the visual field and then guide it to the location.

Reprinted by permission from Hay 1990.

Thelen et al. (1993) examined this issue by recording the arm movements of four infants longitudinally from 3 weeks to 1 year of age. Their decision to conduct a longitudinal study was important because some of their findings would have been masked in a cross-sectional study that averaged the movement of groups of infants. Thelen et al. observed that infants made the transition from prereaching to reaching at 3 to 4 months of age. The infants began with ballpark reaches—movements of exploration and discovery—but each infant found his or her own means of controlling reaches based on the movements he or she already used. Two of the infants preferred fast, oscillating movements that they had to dampen when they reached to get near a toy. The other two infants had to apply muscle force to their preferred slow movements to reach a toy. After several months of practice, the infants became quite good at reaching for a toy, but each addressed a different biomechanical problem and generated a different solution to make the transition from crude initial reaching attempts to consistently successful reaches. The period of improvement was characterized by times when reaches improved and then regressed before improving again.

Thelen et al. believed their longitudinal study of infant reaching demonstrated that infants learn by doing. Rather than infants' central nervous systems planning a trajectory of arm movement, one that would carry the hand to a toy, infants adjust the tension in the arms and apply muscle energy to get the hand close to the toy. By repeating the reaching, infants found increasingly efficient and consistent reaching patterns, yet they found these movement solutions individually, adapting their actions based on perceptions of their self-generated movements.

Hand–Mouth Movements

Another type of arm movement brings the hand, with or without an object, to the mouth. Between 3 and 4 months, infants become more consistent at bringing the hand to the mouth rather than to other parts of the face. At 5 months, they begin to open the mouth in anticipation of the hand's arrival (Lew & Butterworth, 1997). The role of vision in these movements has not yet been studied, nor has the relationship between hand–mouth movements and reaches for objects in the same infants.

Bimanual Reaching and Manipulation

The reaches we've discussed thus far are unimanual, or one-arm, reaches, but infants also acquire bimanual reaching and grasping (Corbetta & Mounoud, 1990; Fagard, 1990). Skilled performers know to use two hands when grasping objects that are too large for one hand, and they can use one hand to complement the other. For example, they might use one hand to hold a container and the other to open the lid.

Newborns' random arm movements are asymmetrical (Cobb, Goodwin, & Saelens, 1966). The first bilateral movements—extending and raising the arms—are observed at approximately 2 months of age (White, Castle, & Held, 1964). Within a few months, infants can clasp their hands at the body midline. At approximately 4.5 months, infants often reach for objects with both arms (Fagard, 1990), but reaches begun with two hands usually result in one hand reaching and grasping the object first. Corbetta and Thelen (1996) studied the bimanual reaches of the infants described earlier (Thelen et al., 1993). During the first year, reaching fluctuated between periods of unimanual reaching and periods of bimanual reaching (figure 9.4). Infants tended to make synchronized nonreaching arm movements during periods of bimanual reaching but exhibited no pattern during periods of unimanual reaching. The four infants did not necessarily experience shifts from one

KEY POINT
To reach objects, infants learn to control their arms; they learn by doing.

KEY POINT
Infants exhibit bimanual reaching during the first year but cannot perform complementary activities with two hands until the second year.

KEY POINT
Infants in their first year alternate between periods when unimanual reaches predominate and periods when bimanual reaches predominate.

kind of reaching to the other at the same ages. Manual activities might be influenced by postural control, yet it might also be the case that no single factor influences the predominance of unimanual or bimanual reaching. Rather, changing constraints can push infants to particular movement patterns.

After 8 months, infants start to dissociate simultaneous arm activity so they can manipulate an object cooperatively with both hands (Goldfield & Michel, 1986; Ruff, 1984). Late in the first year, infants learn to hold two objects, one in each hand, and often bang them together (Ramsay, 1985). By 12 months, they can pull things apart and insert one object into another. Soon infants can reach for two objects with different arms simultaneously. Not until the end of the second year, however, can infants perform complementary activities with the hands, such as holding a lid open with one hand while withdrawing an object with the other (Bruner, 1970).

FIGURE 9.4 Obtaining large objects necessitates bimanual reaching. In young infants, one hand might reach the object before the other. Infants older than 7 months reach either unimanually or bimanually, depending on the object's characteristics.

Infants early in their second year can use objects as tools. Barrett, Davis, and Needham (2007) noted that infants with prior experience with a tool, such as a spoon, persisted in holding the handle of the spoon even when a task was better accomplished by holding the bowl. Infants could use a novel tool flexibly, though, and could be trained on what end of a tool to hold.

KEY POINT
Early in the second year, infants can use tools flexibly.

The Role of Posture

Postural control is important in reaching. Consider that as adults we often lean forward or twist as we reach for an object. Infants typically sit independently by around 6 to 7 months. Before this, their trunks must be supported for them to achieve a successful reach. Reaching improves when infants are able to maintain postural control (Bertenthal & von Hofsten, 1998). Even at 4 months of age, infants adjust their posture as they reach, and improvements in these adjustments during the first year continue to facilitate reaching (Van der Fits & Hadders-Algra, 1998).

One of the lab activities at the end of this chapter provides an opportunity for you to observe the type of grasp that a particular infant uses to pick up various objects.

Manual Performance in Adulthood

The ability to reach and grasp remains an important motor skill throughout the life span. Many careers involve manipulation, and in older adults the ability to perform some activities of daily living—such as bathing and dressing, preparing meals, and making phone calls—can dictate whether the individual is able to live independently. We discussed earlier some of the changes in individual constraints that accompany aging. It is easy to see that some of these might be a significant factor in the performance of large motor activities, but would they also affect manipulative skills? Would fine motor skills be better maintained over the life span than large motor skills? Let's consider some of the research on manipulation in adulthood.

Kauranen and Vanharanta (1996) conducted a cross-sectional study of men and women between 21 and 70 years of age. A test battery was administered that included reaction time, movement speed, tapping speed, and coordination of the hands and feet. Scores declined on all of the hand measures after age 50; the reaction, movement, and tapping times slowed, and coordination scores declined.

What about manual performance at older ages? Hughes et al. (1997) observed older adults with an average age of 78 over a 6-year time span. Every 2 years, these adults completed the Timed Manual Performance Test and a grip strength measure. The Timed Manual Performance Test consists of 22 manipulative tests, 17 from the Williams board tests of manual ability and 5 from Jebsen's test of hand skills. Each subject's score consisted of the total time in seconds needed to complete the test. Generally, more individuals at older ages went over the time threshold on the performance test, and grip strength declined with advancing age. Declining manual performance was associated with loss of strength and upper joint impairment resulting from musculoskeletal disease. Also, in reaching for objects, older adults slow down more than young adults at the end of the reach, presumably to make more corrections in their trajectory (Roy, Winchester, Weir, & Black, 1993).

Contreras-Vidal, Teulings, and Stelmach (1998) observed younger (20s) and older (60s and 70s) adults making handwriting movements. These movements, of course, do not demand speed, nor do they require great precision. Compared with the younger adults, the older adults could control force well but did not coordinate their finger and wrist movements as well.

Loss of speed in movement with aging is a common finding for large and fine motor movements. Additionally, the research studies reviewed here indicate that movements might not be as finely coordinated with advancing age. We can see, however, that disuse and disease are every bit as important in the loss of manipulative skills as in the loss of locomotor or ballistic skills. Greater loss can be expected among those who curtail manipulative activities as they age, contributing in turn to a loss of strength, which may further hurt performance. In fact, compensatory strategies are adopted by those who continue activities over the life span. One example is that of older transcriptionists who type out documents from shorthand notes. It seems that older, experienced typists look further ahead than younger adults to give themselves more time to respond (Salthouse, 1984).

It is clear that the interaction of individual, task, and environmental constraints is as important in fine, manipulative motor skills as it is in large motor skills. Over the age span, changing individual constraints bring changes in the interaction with environmental and task constraints, thus causing changes in movement.

KEY POINT
Some aspects of older adults' reaches slow down, putting them at a disadvantage in making sequential movements, but accuracy of manipulation is stable, especially on well-known tasks.

 Think about the increased use of e-mail, which involves typing on a standard-size keyboard, and of text messaging, which involves typing on a very small keyboard. Do certain age groups prefer one or the other? Why? Is preference related to experience?

Rapid Aiming Movements

In some complex motor skills, participants make rapid aiming movements. Such arm movements involve an initiation and acceleration phase from the start of the movement to the point when peak velocity of the arm movement is reached, then a deceleration and termination phase from peak velocity to the end of the movement.

Young adults tend to make this movement symmetrically; that is, the acceleration and deceleration phases are equal. In contrast, older adults do not begin the movement as forcefully or travel as far in the acceleration phase. They tend to have a longer deceleration phase to compensate because they need more adjustments in the final phase, especially when the aiming movement needs to be very accurate (Vercruyssen, 1997).

Rapid aiming movements are involved in tasks requiring monitoring and manipulation of complex displays such as cockpits. In critical tasks, many such movements can be required in sequence, and any slowing effects can accumulate. Age differences, then, might not be important in single, simple, or self-paced arm movements but may be critical when many sequential movements are needed in a short time. The interaction of individual and task constraints is evident in this type of skill. Practice is important to older adults. They can compensate for some slowing when they know the location of buttons or levers very well.

Catching

Several manipulative skills are basic to sport performance. In these skills, a performer must gain possession or control of an object by reaching to intercept a moving object or stopping it with an implement. The most common manipulative skill is catching. Fielding in hockey also allows a player to control the ball or puck, such that it remains in the player's control rather than bouncing or rolling away. Of these reception skills, we know the most about the development of catching.

Baseball trivia buffs never tire of recounting great outfield catches. Perhaps the greatest was Willie Mays' over-the-shoulder catch in the 1954 World Series. The score was tied 2-2, with two runners on base and no outs. Vic Wertz hit a long drive to right center field. Mays turned and ran full speed, his back to home plate. Just a few feet from the wall (which was particularly deep at New York's Polo Grounds), he was able to stretch his arms and catch the ball, then make a tremendous throw back to the infield. The Cleveland Indians weren't able to score that inning, and the New York Giants went on to win the game and sweep the series.

Catching is relatively difficult as a developmental task. During early childhood we see children throw and kick, even if their movement patterns are not yet proficient. But if young children catch a ball, it often reflects the skill of the thrower in getting the ball to arrive in outstretched arms. It is the interception aspect of catching that makes it difficult. With this in mind, let's consider how catching develops and then examine interception in catching.

The goal of catching is to retain possession of the object you catch. It is better to catch an object in the hands than to trap it against the body or opposite arm because if the object is caught in the hands, the catcher can quickly manipulate it—usually by throwing it. A child's initial catching attempts involve little force absorption. The young child pictured in figure 9.5 has positioned his hands and arms rigidly. Instead of catching the ball in his hands, he traps it against his chest. It is common to see children turn away and close their eyes in anticipation of the ball's arrival. The next section discusses characteristics of proficient catching and then examines how children typically develop proficient catching.

FIGURE 9.5 Beginning catching. This young boy holds his arms and hands rigidly rather than giving with the arrival of the ball to absorb its force gradually.

© Mary Ann Roberton.

FIGURE 9.6 Proficient catching. The ball is caught with the hands, and the hands and arms give with the ball.

Proficient Catching

In moving from novice to proficient catching skills, as shown in figure 9.6, a child must

- learn to catch with the hands and give with the ball, thus gradually absorbing the ball's force;
- master the ability to move to the left or the right, or forward or back, to intercept the ball; and
- point the fingers up when catching a high ball and down when catching a low one.

Developmental Changes in Catching

It is more difficult to identify developmental sequences for catching skills than for most locomotor or ballistic skills because the sequence is specific to the conditions under which the individual performs the skill. Many factors are variable in catching—for example, the ball's size, shape (e.g., a round basketball vs. a football), speed, trajectory, and arrival point. Haubenstricker, Branta, and Seefeldt (1983) conducted a preliminary validation of a developmental sequence for arm action in two-hand catching. They used progressively smaller balls as children demonstrated better skill. Table 9.1 summarizes the sequence, which was originally outlined by Seefeldt, Reuschlein, and Vogel (1972). At 8 years of age, most of the boys and almost half of the girls tested were at the highest level of arm action. Virtually all of the children had passed through steps 1 and 2 by this time. Slightly higher percentages of boys than girls performed at higher levels at any given age, but overall this group demonstrated well-developed arm action by age 8. Table 9.1 also suggests the key observation points that can help you place performers at a developmental level.

Strohmeyer, Williams, and Schaub-George (1991) proposed developmental sequences for the hands and body in catching a small ball (table 9.1). A unique feature of this work is that it is based on catching balls thrown directly to the catcher as well as balls thrown high or to the side of the catcher. These sequences suggest that as catchers improve, they

KEY POINT
Catching is specific to environmental and task constraints.

TABLE 9.1   Developmental Sequence for Two-Hand Catching

	Action
	Arm action
Step 1	Little response. Arms extend forward, but there is little movement to adapt to ball flight; ball is usually trapped against chest.
Step 2	Hugging. Arms are extended sideways to encircle (hug) the ball; ball is trapped against chest.
Step 3	Scooping. Arms are extended forward but move under (scoop) the object; ball is trapped against chest.
Step 4	Arms give. Arms extend to meet object with the hands; arms and body give; ball is caught in hands.
	Hand action
Step 1	Palms up. The palms of the hands face up. (Rolling balls elicit a palms-down trapping action.)
Step 2	Palms in. The palms of the hands face each other.
Step 3	Palms adjusted. The palms of the hands are adjusted to the flight and size of the oncoming object. Thumbs or little fingers are placed close together, depending on the height of the flight path.
	Body action
Step 1	No adjustment. No adjustment of the body occurs in response to the ball's flight path.
Step 2	Awkward adjustment. The arms and trunk begin to move in relation to the ball's flight path, but the head remains erect, creating an awkward movement to the ball. The catcher seems to be fighting to remain balanced.
Step 3	Proper adjustment. The feet, trunk, and arms all move to adjust to the path of the oncoming ball.

The arm action component is adapted from Haubenstricker, Branta, and Seefeldt (1983), which is based on Seefeldt, Reuschlein, and Vogel (1972). The hand and body action components are reprinted from Strohmeyer, Williams, and Schaub-George (1991).

Reprinted by permission from Strohmeyer, Williams, and Schaub-Gecrge 1991.

- are better able to move their bodies in response to the oncoming ball,
- adjust their hands to the anticipated location of the catch, and
- catch the ball in their hands.

The investigators tested their sequences on a cross section of children between 5 and 12 years old. All of the children over 8 years old made some adjustment in body position in response to the oncoming ball, and 11- to 12-year-olds successfully adjusted their body positions about 80% of the time. In contrast, this older group could properly adjust their hand positions in response to the ball only 40% of the time if the ball was thrown directly to them and less than 10% of the time if it was thrown to various positions around them.

 Think of your own skill level in catching. What kinds of catching tasks do you find easy? Is there a catching task you find difficult?

Catching, like striking, involves anticipating where a ball can be intercepted as well as the ability to complete the movements that position the hands at that location. As we would expect, children better predict the ball flight as they get older, especially when the viewing time (path of the ball) is short (Lefebvre &

Reid, 1998). The anticipatory aspects of manipulative skills are discussed in more detail elsewhere in this chapter.

Observing Catching Patterns

Catching can be observed from the front, allowing you to toss the ball, or from the side. It is easy to assess the product in catching tasks. One can simply record a percentage of balls successfully caught, noting the task constraints, including the size and type of ball used, the throwing distance, and the trajectory of the ball.

Parents, teachers, and coaches often want to know about the movement process used in catching. Figure 9.7 "Observation Plan for Catching" provides a suggested

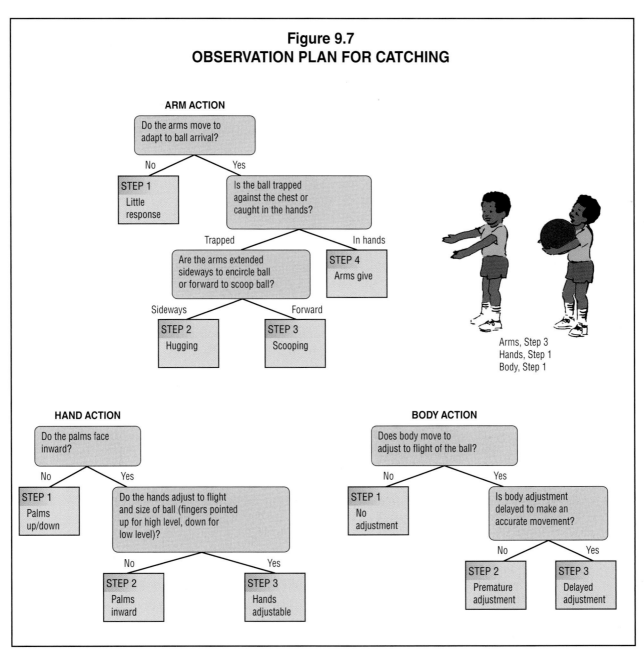

Figure 9.7
OBSERVATION PLAN FOR CATCHING

ARM ACTION

Do the arms move to adapt to ball arrival?

No → STEP 1 — Little response

Yes → Is the ball trapped against the chest or caught in the hands?

Trapped → Are the arms extended sideways to encircle ball or forward to scoop ball?

In hands → STEP 4 — Arms give

Sideways → STEP 2 — Hugging

Forward → STEP 3 — Scooping

Arms, Step 3
Hands, Step 1
Body, Step 1

HAND ACTION

Do the palms face inward?

No → STEP 1 — Palms up/down

Yes → Do the hands adjust to flight and size of ball (fingers pointed up for high level, down for low level)?

No → STEP 2 — Palms inward

Yes → STEP 3 — Hands adjustable

BODY ACTION

Does body move to adjust to flight of the ball?

No → STEP 1 — No adjustment

Yes → Is body adjustment delayed to make an accurate movement?

No → STEP 2 — Premature adjustment

Yes → STEP 3 — Delayed adjustment

Illustrations © Mary Ann Roberton.

developmental sequence that indicates which step the catcher demonstrates for each body component. For example, if you observe a child who extends her arms, palms up, and scoops a large ball thrown to her, trapping it against her chest, all without moving her feet, the developmental levels would be step 3 for arm action, step 1 for hand action, and step 1 for body action.

 WEB STUDY GUIDE   **Identify developmental differences among catchers in Lab Activity 9.2, Assessing the Developmental Levels of Catchers, in the web study guide. Go to www.HumanKinetics.com/LifeSpanMotorDevelopment.**

Anticipation

It is clear that many manipulative tasks and interception skills involve anticipation. The ball or other moving object can approach at different speeds, from different directions, and along different trajectories and may be of varying size and shape. To be successful, performers must initiate movements well ahead of interception so that the body and hands (or implement, such as a hockey stick) can be in the proper position when the object arrives. In fact, the manipulative component of reception skills (e.g., positioning and closing the hands on the ball) is often perfected before an individual develops the ability to be in the right place at the right time.

Coincidence-anticipation tasks are motor skills in which one anticipates the completion of a movement to coincide with the arrival of a moving object.

Some developmentalists have researched this aspect of reception skills through the use of **coincidence-anticipation** tasks. With this approach, it is easy to vary task characteristics and observe the effect on performance. Variations in task characteristics influence not only the product of performance—a hit or catch versus a miss—but also the process, or movement pattern, used in the task. For example, children who are capable of catching *small* balls in their hands may choose to scoop very *large* balls with their arms, perhaps as a surer means of retaining them (Victors, 1961). Thus, a task can be defined as requiring a simpler or more complex movement response, and the characteristics of the ball can be varied to further constrain the movement. Yet many research studies on coincidence anticipation are conducted in a laboratory setting with an apparatus that allows factors such as ball speed, trajectory, and direction to be varied and are not very similar to the real-world task of catching a ball. Therefore, it is important to recognize that these studies might tell us more about the perceptual limits of performers for a specified interception task than for real-world catching.

Let's consider some of the task constraints in coincidence-anticipation tasks. Several researchers have found that coincidence-anticipation performance improves throughout childhood and adolescence (Bard, Fleury, Carriere, & Bellec, 1981; Dorfman, 1977; Dunham, 1977; Haywood, 1977, 1980; Lefebvre & Reid, 1998; Stadulis, 1971; Thomas, Gallagher, & Purvis, 1981). However, the exact pattern of improvement with advancing age depends on task constraints:

• Young children are less accurate as the movement required of them gets more complex (Bard et al., 1981; Haywood, 1977). So, response complexity is one task characteristic that influences how well children perform on interception tasks.

• Children's accuracy decreases if the interception point is farther away. For example, McConnell and Wade (1990) found that the number of successful catches and the efficiency of the movement pattern used decreased if children 6 to 11 years old had to move 2 ft instead of 1 ft, left or right, to make a catch.

• Young children are more successful at intercepting large balls than small balls (Isaacs, 1980; McCaskill & Wellman, 1938; Payne, 1982; Payne & Koslow, 1981).

• A high trajectory also makes interception more difficult for young children because the ball changes location in both horizontal and vertical directions (DuRandt, 1985).

• Some ball color and background combinations influence young children's performance. Morris (1976) determined that 7-year-olds could better catch blue balls moving against a white background than white balls against a white background. The effect of color diminished with advancing age.

• The speed of the moving object affects coincidence-anticipation accuracy but not in a clear pattern. A faster speed makes interception more difficult, especially when the object's flight is short. But researchers often note that children are inaccurate with slow velocities because they respond too early (Bard et al., 1981; Haywood, 1977; Haywood, Greenwald, & Lewis, 1981; Isaacs, 1983; Wade, 1980). Perhaps children prepare for the fastest speed an object might travel and then have difficulty delaying their responses if the speed is slow (Bard, Fleury, & Gagnon, 1990). Also, the preceding speeds might influence young children more than they do older performers. If the previous moving object came quickly, young children judge the next object to be moving faster than it really is (Haywood et al., 1981), just like baseball batters are fooled by a pitcher's "change up" or slow pitch. Educators should be aware, then, that children can have difficulty adjusting their responses when the speed of an object in an interception task varies greatly from one repetition to the next. This is particularly true if the object's flight is short or the response required is complex.

 Imagine you're an elementary school physical education instructor. Recall the sports that involve moving objects, then identify the many ways in which pitchers and servers in various sports change the pitch or serve to make interception of the ball more difficult. In contrast, how would you throw a ball to small children to increase the likelihood that they will catch it?

What underlies these age-related trends in coincidence anticipation? Early studies of these skills took an information processing perspective. That is, performers were thought to receive visual and kinesthetic information and perform "calculations" on that data, much like a computer, to project the future location of the moving object in order to intercept it.

The perception–action perspective, in contrast, holds that all the needed information is in the environment and that no calculations are necessary. Meaningful information in the environment specifies the action or movement possibilities of that environment and for specific events. This relationship is called an **affordance**. For catching, two important characteristics of the person–environment system concern constant patterns of change, called **invariants**, and the expanding **optic array**. The optic array refers to the visual picture falling on our retinas as we approach an object or as a moving object approaches us. That picture expands in size on the retinas with approach and constricts with retreat.

From the perception–action perspective, it is possible that we use the rate of expansion of this image on our retinas to know when arrival or collision will occur (Lyons, Fontaine, & Elliott, 1997). Insects that intercept prey and birds that fold their wings back before diving into water demonstrate perfect timing in these interceptions, and, given their small brains, it is more likely that they perceive aspects of the environment directly than that they perform complex calculations to predict arrival times. Van Hof, van der Kamp, and Savelsbergh (2008) investigated whether infants between 3 and 9 months could act on an approaching ball. They placed a ball on a mechanical apparatus so that the ball came directly over the right shoulder of a seated infant at various speeds. Infants aged 3 to 5 months often did not even reach for the balls and were not very accurate when they did. Individual differences occurred in age of improvement, but by 8 to 9 months the infants were relatively accurate. They also were more likely not to attempt to catch fast-moving balls that they were unlikely to intercept.

Several research teams have recently used the perception–action perspective to study the "real world" task of catching a ball projected in a high trajectory, much like the task faced by an outfielder in baseball. Such researchers are now able to track the position of both the ball and the catcher by using video technology. McLeod and Dienes (1993, 1996) demonstrated that catchers could intercept a directly approaching high-trajectory ball by keeping a ratio, based on the angle of gaze, at or near zero. (For those with a mathematical background, the ratio is the second derivative of the tangent of the angle of gaze.) If the ratio's value is positive, the ball will land behind the catcher; if it is negative, the ball will land in front. By keeping the ratio near zero, the catcher knows whether to move forward or backward and how quickly to move (figure 9.8).

Oudejans and colleagues (Michaels & Oudejans, 1992; Oudejans, Michaels, Bakker, & Dolne, 1996) similarly demonstrated that catchers could keep the vertical optical acceleration of the ball close to zero. Unlike McLeod and Dienes' notion that the catcher focuses on angle of gaze, in this approach the catcher focuses on the ball's acceleration in the vertical plane as the catcher views the ball. Both approaches tell a catcher whether to move forward or backward.

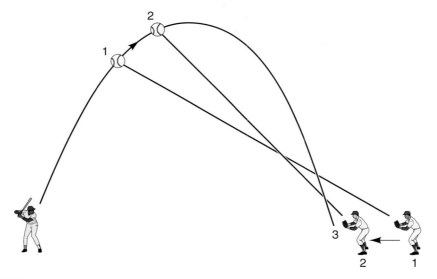

FIGURE 9.8 The catcher might intercept the approaching ball by keeping a ratio, based on the angle of gaze, at or near zero. When the ball and catcher are in position 1, this ratio is a negative number. The catcher must move forward to bring the ratio closer to zero. At position 2 the ratio is closer to zero but still not zero. The catcher continues to move until the ratio is zero, and both the catcher and the ball arrive at position 3.

Adapted by permission from McLeod and Dienes 1996.

Of course, many catches require sideways movement. A strategy proposed for this situation is keeping the lateral position of the ball constant with respect to the catcher. This is called the constant bearing angle strategy (figure 9.9) (Lenoir, Musch, Janssens, Thiery, & Uyttenhove, 1999). For example, a soccer goalie could keep this angle constant by moving sideways to intercept a ball. McBeath and colleagues (McBeath, Shaffer, & Kaiser, 1995; Shaffer, 1999; Shaffer & McBeath, 2002) identified a relationship that incorporates both elevation of gaze and horizontal angle of gaze, as would be important for catching a high-trajectory ball projected to the side of a catcher. If this relationship is kept constant, a catcher can arrive at the correct place to catch the ball. The specific mathematics of the relationship are not important here; what matters for us is that we can see that invariant relationships are available to catchers in the environment and that it is possible to arrive at the correct place without our brains calculating a landing point based on the early part of the trajectory. Practically, a fielder (as long as he or she can move fast enough) can adopt the unconscious strategy of continuously moving to stay under the balls' trajectory as viewed. If the ball's path appears to arc up and past the catcher, the ball will land behind the catcher. If the ball's path appears to arc down, the ball will land in front. So, the catcher can adjust to maintain the proper visual appearance and adapt to changes in the path due to ball spin, air resistance, or wind in order to arrive at the right place.

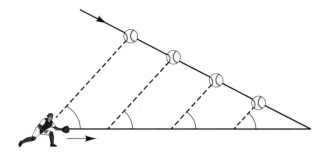

FIGURE 9.9   A catcher moves to the side to intercept a ball by keeping the bearing angle formed by the dashed line constant.

Redrawn from Lenoir et al. 1999.

 Imagine you are a baseball or softball coach. Keeping in mind the perception–action approach, how might you help a young fielder who is having trouble catching fly balls?

How Do Children Learn to Arrive at the Right Place?

From an information processing viewpoint, children must learn to make more precise calculations to become proficient catchers. Errors made in early attempts serve as informative feedback that can be used to refine the calculation process. From a perception–action viewpoint, however, what children need is to subconsciously discover an invariant. When children begin catching by standing still, for example, McLeod and Dienes' ratio is zero for balls that land in their arms and something else for balls that do not land in their arms. With sufficient exposure, children discover the relationship between the ratio and the "catchability" of a ball and eventually use the relationship when they begin moving for a ball.

From the perception–action perspective, then, one role of parents, teachers, and coaches is to help children discover the various sources of perceptual information that constrain movement in interception tasks. They can do so by manipulating informational constraints during the exploratory process of practice. Bennett, Button, Kingsbury, and Davids (1999) recently demonstrated that 9- and 10-year-olds who were asked to practice one-hand catching with a restricted view of the ball later benefited when learning a catching task under new conditions. Thus, highlighting the useful sources of information by varying task constraints during practice can be helpful.

Some attempts to improve anticipatory sports skills with training in novice adults have been ineffective (Wood & Abernethy, 1997). Abernethy, Wood, and Parks (1999) suggest that training must be sport specific (environment and task specific) and must focus on the factors known to limit novice performance. They demonstrated that novice adults can benefit from such training; the novice adults performed a laboratory task similarly to experts after training. It is important to identify the perceptual information that constrains movement. This research suggests that whether the individual is a child or a novice adult, manipulating constraints to help the performer identify the important information in the environment subconsciously facilitates the movements that result in success. More information, however, is needed about the relative merits of simple exploratory practice and instruction.

 Imagine you are a teacher and design an activity that helps children learn to catch fly balls.

Catching in Older Adulthood

Little research-based information is available about catching by older adults. We might suspect that experienced older adults know the invariant patterns that provide information about intercepting balls. Factors that might change, however, could include the quickness with which movement is initiated, the maximum speed that could be achieved in moving to the ball, and the extent of reach if the "catchability" of a given ball were at the limit for an individual's speed in moving. All of these factors might contribute to an older adult being unable to catch as many balls as a younger adult could.

Coincidence-anticipation research provides some information about the anticipatory aspects of skills such as catching. Older adults are somewhat less accurate and more variable in their performance than younger performers, and the differences are greater when the moving object moves faster and when the older adults are sedentary rather than active (Haywood, 1980, 1982; Wiegand & Ramella, 1983). Wiegand and Ramella (1983) observed that older adults improved with practice at the same rate as younger adults. Over a 7-year period, from an average age of 66.9 years to an average age of 73.5 years, active adults demonstrated improvement in performance on a coincidence-anticipation task (Haywood, 1989). Thus, repetition of such skills probably is important for maintaining skill. The task constraints on the movement response in the coincidence-anticipation tasks, however, were minimal. When task constraints are such that larger, more complex movements or movements over distance in a short time are required, a higher number of older adults might be less successful at these tasks given their individual constraints.

Driving and Piloting

Although only a portion of older adults participate in sports involving interception, a large number drive automobiles. In fact, the issue of whether an older adult should continue driving is often an emotional one because driving often represents a considerable degree of independence and freedom. Driving is a complex perceptual-motor skill involving manipulation. Skillful driving depends on vision (and sometimes audition, or hearing), attentional focus, experience, speed, and coordination, all under occasionally stressful conditions.

Older adults have more difficulty than younger adults in dividing their attention and performing two tasks at once in driving situations (Brouwer, Waterink, Van Wolffelaar, & Rothengartter, 1991; Ponds, Brouwer, & Van Wolffelaar, 1988). Older adults also take longer to plan movements and are slower in executing movements, especially when speedy movement is needed (Goggin & Stelmach, 1990; Olson & Sivak, 1986). Goggin and Keller (1996) examined whether aging differentially affects the sensory-cognitive or motor functions in driving. They had older adult drivers take a written test about a videotape of 15 driving situations. The older drivers also made driving responses to the same videotaped situations on a driving simulator. Goggin and Keller reasoned that if older adults had difficulty only on the written test, aging likely affected sensory-cognitive functions, but if they had difficulty only with the simulator responses, aging likely affected motor functions. The adults performed less well on the written test and better on the simulator. Thus, sensory-cognitive factors such as attention and decision making might be more significant factors in poor performance of driving-related motor skills.

 Think about the older adults in your family. How are their driving skills? Do any of them compensate for a loss of driving skill? How?

The effects of aging on airplane piloting performance have also been studied (see Morrow & Leirer, 1997, for a review). Mandatory retirement ages for commercial pilots are also an emotional issue for those involved. Like driving, piloting is affected more as task complexity increases. Perceptual aspects of piloting, attention, and working memory are particularly affected by aging. Expertise on familiar tasks, however, offsets the effects of aging, and highly practiced skills are well maintained.

Applying the model of constraints, we can see that an increased number of constraints on a task adds to its complexity, and when individual constraints change with aging, the interaction of constraints can quickly cause the difficulty of driving and piloting tasks to reach a critical point. As mentioned earlier in regard to rapid aiming tasks, experience with a set of environmental and task constraints allows older adults to compensate for slowing of manipulative movements. Thus, continued practice with tasks, whether sport or driving tasks, is important for maintaining skill. Eventually, however, decrements in sensory-cognitive systems, as well as in speed of movement, lead to a loss of skill.

Summary and Synthesis

Manipulative skills set humans apart from other species. Whether executing sports skills or tasks of everyday living, people need to reach, grasp, and maneuver objects. Infants become skilled at reaching and grasping early in life, during the first year, although using the two hands in complementary ways comes a little later.

Children can become accomplished catchers by 11 or 12 years of age, but in all catching tasks at any age, the farther the catcher must travel, the more difficult the catch. Aging probably affects a catcher's ability to get to a ball more than the ability to know where to be in order to catch the ball. Changing structural constraints influence the speed with which manipulative and locomotor movements can be initiated and completed. When tasks demand great speed, older adults are disadvantaged compared with younger adults.

Children need practice in order to learn, even if subconsciously, the information available in the environment that is important for catching success. Adults need practice in order to maintain their skills, especially in demanding conditions. Thus, at any age, a person's skill in completing challenging manipulative tasks often reflects experience and practice in dealing with the individual, task, and environmental constraints involved.

 Reinforcing What You Have Learned About Constraints

TAKE A SECOND LOOK

As the case of Matthew Scott teaches us, being able to manipulate objects with two hands is important in activities of daily living and many activities that are uniquely human and enjoyable for us. When faced with the loss of manipulative skills, it is worth extraordinary effort to restore the ability to perform those skills. The development of manipulative skills certainly emphasizes the importance of task and environmental constraints in performance. As Matthew Scott undertook the journey to use his transplanted hand, he was challenged by environmental and task constraints that many of us take for granted. With continued therapy, he has been able to use his new hand while dealing with an increasing range of environmental and task constraints.

Manipulative skills are among the fundamental motor skills. The perception–action perspective in particular holds that the environment provides individuals with much of the information they need in order to intercept objects. Thus, manipulative skills such as catching do not improve just because individual constraints change. The changing interaction of individual constraints with task and environmental constraints is an important aspect of the development of manipulative skills. This interaction is equally important in the maintenance of manipulative skills in older adulthood. Experience with numerous interactions of our existing individual constraints and environmental and task constraints gives us the ability, eventually, to successfully manipulate objects even when we have not previously seen a particular ball trajectory and speed—or used a particular keyboard.

TEST YOUR KNOWLEDGE

1. How does the size of an object affect the grip that an infant uses? How might this factor influence where an infant falls on Halverson's prehension sequence? How does the shape of an object affect the grip used?

2. Do infants learn to reach for objects by better matching their hand position to the seen location of the object, or by better controlling their arms? Explain why you chose your answer.

3. How does manipulative skill change in older adulthood, and how can older adults adapt to these changes?

4. What are the major developmental trends we see in children as they become increasingly proficient in catching?

5. When balls do not come directly to the catcher, what situations (environmental and task constraints) make catching success difficult for children? For adults?

6. Explain, from the information processing perspective and the perception–action perspective, how children learn to go to the proper place to catch a ball not traveling directly toward them.

7. What changing individual structural constraints might affect an older adult's skill in driving or piloting?

8. Think about the term *coincidence anticipation*. Explain why someone who prefers the perception–action approach might consider this to be a misnomer for interception skills.

LEARNING EXERCISE 9.1

Investigating Infant Reaching

Place an infant between 6 and 12 months of age in an upright sitting position in front of a table or tray. One at a time, place six small objects in front of the infant; the objects should vary in size, weight, and shape (all should be small enough for an infant to pick up with one hand). Consult figure 9.1 and note the type of grip the infant uses for each object. Be careful not to let the infant put small objects in his or her mouth because they can pose a choking hazard. Next, repeat the process to see whether the infant uses the same grip on each object as in the first round. Finally, prepare a report on the different grips you observed for the various objects; be sure to distinguish between power grips and precision grips. Discuss whether or how the grips changed as the weight or shape of the object changed.

Perceptual-Motor Development

Infants and toddlers experience dramatic changes in perception. Infants learn, for example, the names and locations of their body parts as well as the relationships between objects, such as "in front of" or "behind." Such changes play a large part in the cognitive and physical skills that infants and toddlers can execute. There is no doubt that the perceptual systems, as individual structural constraints, interact with the task and environment to give rise to movement; in fact, the interactions between the perceptual systems and the environment are very rich.

The study of perception and its relationship to movement, or action, has been at least as controversial as any aspect of motor development. Certainly, professionals have adopted varying perspectives on the role of perception in motor development. Perhaps the most recent and significant debate involves the notion that movement drives perceptual development as much as perceptual development permits new movements. On the horizon, too, is a research frontier concerned with movement and exercise facilitating growth in the neurologic system over the life span. Thinking about both of these areas of research, we can see that the model of constraints is useful because it highlights the interaction of individual, environment, and task in giving rise to movement. We begin our discussion by reviewing the age-related changes in sensation and perception in the vision, kinesthetic, and audition systems in chapter 10. Also discussed is the development of integration between and among the sensory-perceptual systems. Then in chapter 11 we examine how the perception and action are linked with special emphasis on how postural control and balance highlight that link.

Suggested Reading

Dent-Read, C., & Zukow-Goldring, P. (Eds.). (1997). *Evolving explanations of development: Ecological approaches to organism–environment systems.* Washington, DC: American Psychological Association.

Gottlieb, G., & Krasnegor, N.A. (Eds.). (1985). *Measurement of audition and vision in the first year of postnatal life: A methodological overview.* Norwood, NJ: Ablex.

Kellman, P.J., & Arterberry, M.E. (1998). *The cradle of knowledge: Development of perception in infancy.* Cambridge, MA: MIT Press.

Konczak, J. (1990). Toward an ecological theory of motor development: The relevance of the Gibsonian approach to vision for motor development research. In J.E. Clark & J.H. Humphrey (Eds.), *Advances in motor development research* (Vol. 3, pp. 201–224). New York: AMS Press.

Lynch, A., & Getchell, N. (2010). Using an ecological approach to understand perception, cognition, and action coupling in individuals with Autism Spectrum Disorder. *International Public Health Journal*, 2(1), 7–16.

Ratey, J.J. (2008). *Spark: The revolutionary new science of exercise and the brain.* New York: Little, Brown.

10

Sensory-Perceptual Development

CHAPTER OBJECTIVES

This chapter

- reviews developmental changes in the vision, audition, and kinesthetic systems;

- discusses changes in visual, auditory, and kinesthetic sensation that occur with aging;

- traces the development of visual perception—in particular, perception of space, objects, and motion;

- provides an overview of the development of kinesthetic perception, especially perception of tactile location, the body, limb movements, spatial orientation, and direction;

- describes the development of auditory perception; and

- studies the process whereby environmental objects and events perceived in different modalities are perceived as the same object or event.

Your Environment

Most of us have had the opportunity to see an IMAX movie on a large surround screen. In recent years, there has been an upsurge in the number of three-dimensional IMAX theaters. With big-budget movies such as *Life of Pi*, *The Hobbit* trilogy, and *The Hunger Games: Catching Fire*, Hollywood filmmakers have embraced the IMAX experience. Many of these movies include the view seen as if flying from the cockpit of an airplane. The visual information is so rich that oftentimes people who tend to get airsick or seasick cannot watch such movies without getting sick. These movies serve as a reminder that sensory and perceptual information—especially visual information—is an important part of our experience in, and interaction with, our environment. We exist only in an environment. How we operate in that environment is a function of how we sense and perceive it.

Sensation is the neural activity triggered by a stimulus that activates a sensory receptor and results in sensory nerve impulses traveling the sensory nerve pathways to the brain.

Perception is a multistage process that takes place in the brain and includes selecting, processing, organizing, and integrating information received from the senses.

In many ways, almost every motor act can be considered a perceptual-motor skill. Human movement is based on information about the environment and one's position or location in it. For example, a softball infielder sees the location of the pitch, the batter striking the ball, and the ball bouncing on the ground; hears the hit and perhaps sees a runner on the base path; and feels the position of her body and arms. The infielder uses this information to decide where and when she can intercept the ball, where to move, and how to position her body. It might seem that not all movements are so dependent on sensing and perceiving the environment. Yet even an experienced platform diver, blindfolded and wearing earplugs, must feel how gravity pulls his body and know where his trunk and limbs are relative to one another to execute his dive.

As the motion sickness effect of a three-dimensional movie demonstrates, sensory information and perceptual information are highly integrated. We typically experience events in multiple sensory systems. We are uncomfortable if the information from one sense contradicts the information from another—we stagger, fall, or feel sick. If we are denied information from one sense we can compensate by attending to information from another, but we might not be as accurate in our perceptions. Moreover, our sensory-perceptual selves and the environment are interactive systems. We do not simply receive information from the environment; rather, we act to obtain information. For example, we turn our ears toward a sound or reach to feel the texture of a surface. Thus, we must keep in mind the highly integrative nature of **sensation**, **perception**, and movement even as we discuss individual systems or types of perceptual discrimination.

Individuals with normally functioning sensory receptors can attach different meanings to the same stimulus, and even the same individual can interpret a single stimulus in different ways. You might remember seeing in a general psychology class some visual displays that have this effect. Remember the one that can be seen as two facial profiles or as a vase (figure 10.1)? Thus, perception is the process whereby we attach meaning to sensory stimuli. How individuals interpret sensory stimuli is the fascinating topic of perceptual development. For individuals to move or act in an environment, they must perceive that environment. In fact, some views of perception and action see them as so interactive as to be inseparable. The environment influences what movements are possible or efficient, and moving through the environment informs us about the nature of the environment and our interactions with it. No study of motor development is complete without the study of the relationship between perception and action.

The sensory-perceptual systems are, of course, individual structural constraints to movement and to other activities such as reading. Ear-

FIGURE 10.1 This drawing can be seen as two facing facial profiles or as a vase.

Reprinted, by permission, from G.H. Sage, 1984, *Motor learning and control: A neuropsychological approach* (Dubuque, IA: Brown), 111. ©The McGraw-Hill Companies.

lier chapters discussed the development of many of the structural systems, such as the skeletal and muscular systems. This chapter discusses the development of visual, auditory, and kinesthetic sensation and perception.

Visual Development

Vision plays a major role in most skill performance. To better understand this role, we need to examine age-related changes in visual sensation and visual perception (figure 10.2).

Visual Sensation

Several aspects of vision determine how clearly one can see objects. Here, we confine our discussion to visual **acuity**. During the first month of life, the visual system provides the infant with functionally useful but unrefined vision at a level approximately 5% of eventual adult acuity, or 20/400 on the Snellen scale of visual acuity (20/20 is desirable) (figure 10.3). The newborn's resolution of detail is such that she can differentiate facial features from a distance of 20 in.; beyond this, she probably cannot see objects clearly (Kellman & Arterberry, 1998).

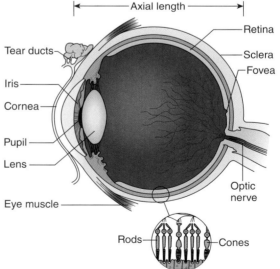

Acuity is sharpness of sight.

FIGURE 10.2 The human eye. An axial length that is too short or too long results in farsightedness or nearsightedness, respectively. An imperfect curvature of the cornea also causes blurred vision, a condition known as astigmatism.

At about 6 months of age, as infants' motor systems are ready to begin self-propelled locomotion, their visual systems perceive adequate detail to assist them in the task. From the ecological perspective, vision is another system that must develop to an adequate level to facilitate locomotion.

Visual sensation continues to improve during childhood. Five-year-olds have visual acuity of about 20/30, and by age 10 children without a visual anomaly score at the desired level of 20/20. It is likely that visual experience is necessary for the development of vision because deprivation of vision during development is known to induce refractive errors in animals (Atkinson & Braddick, 1981).

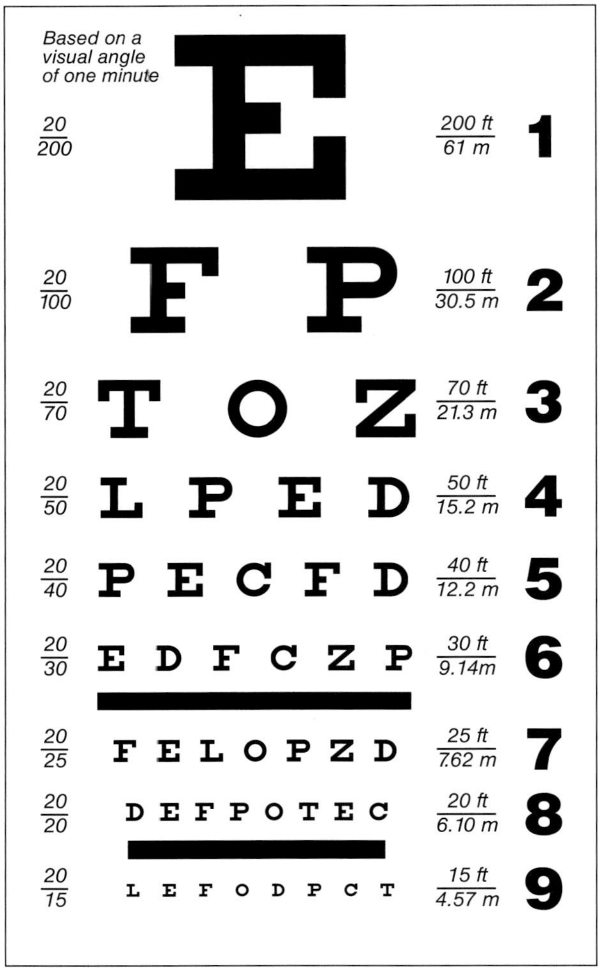

As a person ages, changes in the visual system occur naturally, and some conditions and diseases become more prevalent, especially in older adults. These changes may affect the quality of the visual information that reaches the central nervous system and may have implications for the performance of skills as well as tasks of everyday living.

For example, the condition termed **presbyopia** (from *presbys* for "old man" and *ops* for "eye") becomes clinically significant at around age 40. It affects the ability to see nearby images clearly. The resting diameter of the pupil also decreases with aging, typically reducing retinal illuminance (the amount of light reaching the retina) in a 60-year-old to one-third of that in a young adult. The lens also yellows with age, further reducing the amount of illuminance reaching the eye and making glare a problem for older adults.

Visual disturbances that are more prevalent in older adults include the following:

- Cataracts
- Glaucoma
- **Age-related maculopathy**

KEY POINT
Vision reaches adult levels around 10 years of age, but any refractive errors resulting from imperfections in the axial length of the eye can be corrected with glasses or contacts.

Presbyopia is the gradual loss of accommodation power to focus on near objects. It accompanies advancing age.

Age-related maculopathy is a disease affecting the central area of the retina that provides detailed vision.

FIGURE 10.3 A Snellen chart. Sharpness of sight is measured by whether observers can distinguish letters that differ only by whether a small gap is filled, such as *F* and *P*, or *C* and *O*. Children must know letters to be measured in this manner. Alternative methods are available for testing infants and toddlers.

People who work with children or older adults can look for certain signs that may indicate a visual problem. These include

- squinting,
- under- or overreaching for objects, and
- performing unusual head movements to align one's gaze with a particular object.

Activity leaders should make sure that activity areas are well lit but without glare, and they should encourage performers to wear any corrective lenses prescribed for them (Haywood & Trick, 1990). Because vision provides so much of the perceptual information that people need in order to perform skills successfully, efforts to enhance the visual information that the central nervous system receives should also enhance visual perception and thus skill performance. An excellent way to remind ourselves of how much we rely on sensory information is to close our eyes while trying to perform a routine activity.

Visual Perception

People depend heavily on visual perception in the performance of most skills. The development of visual perception is a topic for texts in and of itself, so only major aspects of visual perception are highlighted here.

Perception of Space

One of the fundamental perceptions is that of three-dimensional space. Almost all movements—reaching and grasping, locomotion, and complex skills such as driving a car or piloting a plane—depend on a perception of three-dimensional space. Visual sensations are received by sensory receptors in the retina in approximately a two-dimensional format. So how do people interpret the world in three dimensions?

To perceive space in three dimensions, individuals must perceive depth and distance. The visual system has numerous sources of information about distance and **depth perception**. One source is **retinal disparity**. Because an individual's two eyes are in different locations, each eye sees the visual field from a slightly different angle (figure 10.4). The information needed for judging depth comes from a comparison of the two slightly different pictures. Depth perception is aided by good visual acuity because a sharper picture from each eye provides more information for the comparison.

Viewers have other sources of information about depth. By moving the head or

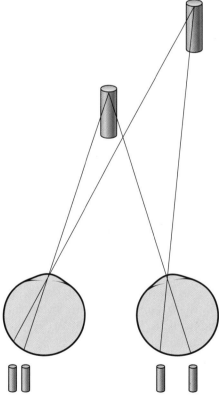

FIGURE 10.4 Retinal disparity. The images on the left retina are closer together than the images on the right retina. The observer sees the two rods in depth.

Reprinted by permission from by Kaufman 1979.

Depth perception is a person's judgment of the distance from self to an object or place in space.

Retinal disparity is the difference in the images received by the two eyes as a result of their different locations.

Motion parallax
is the change in
optical location for
objects at different
distances during
viewer motion.

Optic flow
is change in
the pattern of
optical texture, a
transformation of
the optic array, as
a viewer moves
forward or backward
in a stable
environment.

moving through space, they receive depth cues from **motion parallax**. Objects in space change locations on our retinas, and nearer objects overlap more distant objects as the head moves. Gibson (1966) suggested that this transformation of the optical array, which he called **optic flow**, provides much information about the three-dimensional nature of our environment. This direct means of perceiving the environment likely guides locomotion, controls posture, and helps us anticipate contact with objects and surfaces (Crowell & Banks, 1993; Johansson, von Hofsten, & Jansson, 1980; Warren & Wertheim, 1990).

Viewers with experience in the world also use an assumption of physical equality to judge depth. That is, when two like objects can be expected to have the same size but project different relative sizes on the retina, we assume that the object with the larger retinal size is closer to us. Similarly, if we look down a roadway, we assume it is the same width across even though the curbs appear to get closer to one another (the curbs form converging lines).

 If you were a physical education teacher, what types of activities might you teach that would require depth perception?

Infants have functional vision and, therefore, the mechanics for retinal disparity and motion parallax as sources of depth perception. From about 1 month of age, infants blink more often when shown a display that appears to be approaching than when shown a display that does not (Nanez & Yonas, 1994), demonstrating that they perceive the object to be moving toward them, not merely increasing in size. In the well-known visual cliff experiments of Walk and Gibson (1961; Gibson & Walk, 1960; Walk, 1969), infants between 6 and 14 months of age, placed on one side of an apparent drop-off (a piece of glass over the drop-off prevented it from being a real cliff), stopped at the edge even though their mothers beckoned them from the other side. These studies demonstrate that even young infants have some level of depth perception. Yet, children may err in judging depth until near-adult levels are reached in early adolescence (Williams, 1968).

Behavioral experiments on depth perception are consistent with work on maturation of the visual cortex of the cerebrum. At birth, the cells in layer four of the cortex receive neural input from both eyes. By 6 months of age, these neural inputs separate into alternating columns, receiving input from the right and left eyes, respectively (Held, 1985, 1988; Hickey & Peduzzi, 1987). Disparity information would depend on knowing which eye is sending what information, so this aspect of neurological maturation might well be crucial in the onset of depth perception through retinal disparity.

More older adults than younger adults fail depth perception tests, but thresholds for distinguishing depth change little if at all (Wright & Wormald, 1992; Yekta, Pickwell, & Jenkins, 1989). Higher failure rates probably reflect an increase with advancing age in the number of viewers with visual problems.

Although perception of space is an important aspect of visual perception, our environment also includes objects. Thus, it is equally important to perceive objects, their attributes, and their relationships to oneself and to others.

KEY POINT
Cues about depth
and distance in our
environment are
often derived from
the two eyes being
in different locations
or from movement
of the head.

Perception of Objects

Among the important attributes of objects are size, shape, and motion. The concept of "object" is relative. An airplane pilot might consider a runway to be an object, whereas a person standing on the runway considers it a surface. With growth, what infants initially perceive as a surface might become an object. For example, the floor of a playpen is a surface to an infant, whereas the playpen is an object to an adult, who can fold it and carry it away. Adults use a variety of diverse sources of information in perceiving objects (Kellman & Arterberry, 1998). For example, it is likely that we detect edges (discontinuities in the visual display) and decide whether they are object boundaries. If we see a person standing in front of a car, we assume that the nearer object (in this case, the person) has a boundary and that the car continues behind the person. We do not think the car stops at one edge of the person and then starts again at the other edge. Depth and motion cues help in these perceptions.

The perception of edges and boundaries helps us extract an object or figure from the background environment (figure 10.5). You might recall doing puzzle pages of embedded figures. In these pages, an artist embeds familiar objects such as a ball or candy cane in a line drawing. The type of perception that allows us to find the embedded objects is **figure-and-ground perception**. The perception of edges and boundaries also helps us distinguish whole objects from parts of an object, called **whole-and-part perception**. For example, if you are driving down the street and see half a bicycle tire protruding from a row of parked cars and a child's head above it, you are not puzzled. You immediately perceive that a child on a bicycle is pulling into your path, and you slow down.

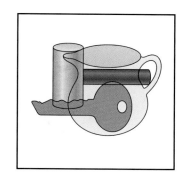

a

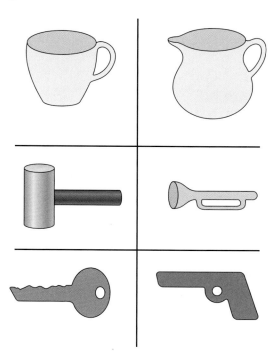

b

FIGURE 10.5 A test plate from the Figure-Ground Perception Test of the Southern California Sensory Integration Test. A child must identify which of the six objects in *(b)* are present, or embedded, in picture *(a)*.

Reprinted by permission from Ayres 1972.

Figure-and-ground perception is the ability to see an object of interest as distinct from the background.

Whole-and-part perception is the ability to discriminate parts of a picture or an object from the whole, yet integrate the parts into the whole, perceiving them simultaneously.

We know little of infant perception of edges and boundaries. Some research indicates that infants rely more on depth and motion cues than on edges in perceiving objects (Granrud et al., 1984; von Hofsten & Spelke, 1985). Children improve in figure-and-ground perception tasks between 4 and 6 years of age (Williams, 1983) and again between 6 and 8 years (Temple, Williams, & Bateman, 1979).

Very young children have difficulty integrating objects that form a whole. For example, you might recall seeing sculptures comprising familiar objects, such as a stick person constructed from nuts and bolts. Pictures of this nature are used to assess whole-and-part perception (figure 10.6). Children under 9 years of age

FIGURE 10.6   A typical picture that could be used to assess whole-and-part perception. Very young children typically report seeing a face or the pieces (e.g., banana, strawberry, pumpkin). Older children and adults typically report seeing a face made from pieces of fruit.

typically report seeing only the person, only the nuts and bolts, or both but at different times. After 9, most children can integrate parts and the whole into the total picture (Elkind, 1975; Elkind, Koegler, & Go, 1964). Realize, though, that adult levels of sensitivity to object perception cues far exceed what is necessary to perceive objects in typical environments (Kellman & Arterberry, 1998). So, infants may still perceive objects fairly well, even though not at adult levels.

Think about driving a car around a busy city. When and how often is space and object perception involved in your actions?

The perception of distances influences our perception of objects in the environment and their properties. We must perceive that an object has constant size even though it might vary in distance from us (figure 10.7). Slater, Mattock, and

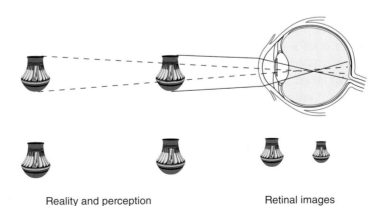

Reality and perception   Retinal images

FIGURE 10.7   Size constancy. The image of an object halves in size with each doubling of the distance of the object from the eye, but the object does not appear to shrink. We assume that the object is constant in size and is changing distance from us rather than changing in size and remaining at a constant distance.

Brown (1990) showed that newborns have **size constancy**. They demonstrated first that infants look more at objects with a larger projection size on the retina. Next they familiarized the infants with cubes (large and small) whose size remained constant but whose distance from the infants was varied. When a familiar object with constant size was shown to the infants along with an object of novel size (at distances to make both projected sizes equal), they looked more at the novel-sized object, indicating that they detected the difference in size (see the "Assessment of Infant Perception" sidebar).

Evidence of newborn sensitivity to shape or form—that is, **shape constancy**—has also been found through the **habituation** method. If a newborn becomes familiar with one shape and is then presented that shape along with a new one, the newborn will spend more time looking at the new shape if shape differences are perceived. One type of form perception is **face perception**, and even 4-day-old infants spend a longer time looking at their mothers' faces than at a female stranger's (Bushnell, 1998; Bushnell, Sai, & Mullin, 1989). They probably use the outer contour of faces to perceive patches of light and dark as faces. To perceive form, viewers must either attend to or ignore the **spatial orientation** of objects, depending on whether this information is relevant to the task at hand. In some cases, it is crucial to recognize that two objects are identical even if one is tipped to one side, upside down, or rotated. In other situations, the differing orientation of an object or symbol is critical to its meaning; such is the case with the letters *d* and *b*.

 Imagine you are an early childhood teacher and identify all the letters that can become another letter if their orientation is changed.

Children seem better able to attend to spatial orientation of an object than to ignore it (Gibson, 1966; Pick, 1979). Children at 3 and 4 years of age can learn directional extremes such as high and low, over and under, and front and back, but they often call intermediate orientations the same as the nearest extreme. By age 8, most children have learned to differentiate obliques (various angles) and diagonals (45°) but may still confuse left and right (Naus & Shillman, 1976; Williams, 1973).

Perception of Motion

Motion perception is of particular interest in the study of motor development. We know that dedicated neurological mechanisms exist for detecting motion. Specifically, individual cortical cells fire according to the direction, location, and speed of an object on the retina, and the medial temporal area of the visual cortex is dedicated to processing motion signals (Kellman & Arterberry, 1998). Therefore, it is not surprising that infants perceive motion.

Early in infancy, however, infants lack adult sensitivity to motion. Direction of motion is not well perceived until 8 weeks of age (Wattam-Bell, 1996a,b). Thresholds for detecting velocity are higher in newborns than in adults; however, by 6 weeks of age, only extremely slow velocities of nearby objects are difficult for the infant to perceive (Aslin & Shea, 1990; von Hofsten, Kellman, & Putaansuu, 1992). Older adults have difficulty perceiving motion at the **detection thresholds** (Elliott, Whitaker, & Thompson, 1989; Kline, Culham, Bartel, & Lynk, 1994). It is not clear whether this has practical significance in real-world conditions; further research is needed.

This discussion of visual perception has been necessarily brief. Overall, however, the evidence discussed here indicates that basic visual perceptions provide

Size constancy is the perception of actual object size despite the size of its image as projected on our retina.

Shape constancy is the perception of actual object shape despite its orientation to a viewer.

Habituation is the state of having adapted to a stimulus.

Spatial orientation is the orientation or position of objects as they are located in space or in a two-dimensional drawing.

KEY POINT
Infants are sensitive to the size and shape of objects.

A **detection threshold** is the point on a continuum at which the energy level is just sufficient for one to register the presence of a stimulus.

Assessment of Infant Perception

Because infants are not able to describe what they perceive, researchers must devise other ways to discover what infants perceive through observing their actions and responses. One of the clever ways this is done is through **preferential looking**. Infants tend to look at objects or events that are new, surprising, or different from those they are familiar with. Similarly, the attention of an infant tends to wander away from objects and events to which they are exposed continuously or repeatedly. In the latter case, we say the infant has habituated to the object or event.

To determine what infants perceive with this method, researchers first expose an infant to an object or event, typically for a certain length of time or number of presentations. When the infant habituates to this stimulus and becomes so used to it that the infant's attention wanders elsewhere, the researcher presents another object or event that is different in some dimension. For example, the researcher changes the size of the object if she is interested in perception of size, or the shape if she is interested in perception of shape. The infant attends to the new stimulus if he perceives it as different. The infant shows little interest if the object is perceived to be the same as the familiar one. The researcher could vary the amount of change to see how much difference the infant perceives.

Researchers also habituate an infant to an object and then present it along with a novel object. Usually, one object is placed on the infant's right and the other on the left. The researcher, positioned directly in front of the infant, records the amount of time the infant looks at each object. The infant presumably prefers the object that is novel, if indeed the infant perceives a difference, hence the term *preferential looking*. If much more time is spent looking at the novel object, the researcher concludes that the infant perceives the new object as different from the familiar one. If there is no difference in looking time, the researcher concludes that the difference is not perceived. To learn more about this method, see Bornstein (1985).

even infants with a great deal of information about the environment. As a child grows, perception at thresholds of detection improves to adult levels. It is likely that attention plays a role in the performance of visual perception tasks and that performance is improved by attention to the important parts of the environment (Madden, Whiting, & Huettel, 2005). However, perception at thresholds will most likely show decrements in older adulthood. Far more information is needed on what significance performance at thresholds has for daily tasks in the real world.

Kinesthetic Development

The kinesthetic system might be described as the system that gives us "body sense." It is certainly vital to our ability to position ourselves and move in our environment. To know that this is true we need only recall walking through a haunted house at a fair or circus, where our visual system and our kinesthetic system are given conflicting information.

Kinesthetic Sensation

The kinesthetic, or proprioceptive, system is important to skill performance because it yields information about the

- relative position of the body parts in relation to each other,
- position of the body in space,
- body's movements, and
- nature of objects that the body comes into contact with.

Unlike the visual system, which relies on the eyes as sensory receptors, kinesthetic information comes from various types of receptors throughout the body called **proprioceptors** (table 10.1). Those proprioceptors located in the muscles, at the muscle–tendon junctions, in joint capsules and ligaments, and under the skin are called **somatosensors**; those located in the inner ear are called the **vestibular apparatus** (figure 10.8).

Many infantile reflexes are stimulated through kinesthetic receptors. Therefore, the onset of a reflex indicates that the corresponding kinesthetic receptor is functioning. The first prenatal reflex that can be elicited is opposite-side neck flexion through tactile stimulation around the mouth at just 7.5 weeks after conception.

Researchers have used tactile stimulation of other body parts to determine that cutaneous receptor development proceeds in an oral, genital–anal, palmar, and plantar (sole of foot) sequence. This developmental sequence follows the cephalocaudal and proximodistal growth directions we discuss in chapter 4.

At birth, infants clearly respond to touch. They can also identify the location of touches, especially in the region of the mouth and the face (Kisilevsky, Stach, & Muir, 1991). We know, too, that the vestibular apparatus is anatomically complete at approximately 9 to 12 weeks of prenatal life, but its functional status before birth is unclear. The labyrinthine righting reflex appears around the second postnatal month (Timiras, 1972), and that fact provides some evidence of vestibular function. Therefore, the system for kinesthetic sensation is functional in early life.

 What are some of the ways parents might use touch to communicate with their infants?

We have anecdotal information but little research data on age-related changes in kinesthetic sensation (Boff, Kaufman, & Thomas, 1986). Indications are that absolute thresholds increase and that at least some older adults experience decreased sensitivity (Kenshalo, 1977). Far more objective research is needed on the aging of kinesthetic receptors.

Proprioceptor is the collective name of the various kinesthetic receptors located in the periphery of the body; the two types of proprioceptors are the somatosensors and the vestibular apparatus.

Somatosensors are the receptors located under the skin, in the muscles, at muscle–tendon junctions, and in joint capsules and ligaments.

The **vestibular apparatus** houses the receptors located in the inner ear.

KEY POINT
Kinesthetic sensation comes from a variety of sensory receptors throughout the body.

TABLE 10.1 Kinesthetic Receptors and Their Locations

Kinesthetic receptor	Location
Muscle spindles	Muscles
Golgi tendon organs	Muscle–tendon junctions
Joint receptors	Joint capsule and ligaments
Spray-type Ruffini endings	
Golgi-type receptors	
Modified Pacinian corpuscles	
Vestibular semicircular canals	Inner ear
Cutaneous receptors	Skin and underlying tissues

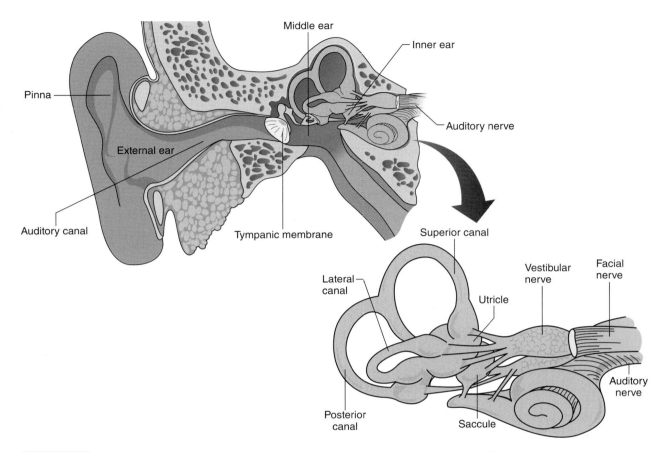

FIGURE 10.8   Structures of the inner ear. Sensory receptors are located in the utricle and saccule.

Tactile Localization

Although newborns feel touches, an individual must know where on the body a touch occurs as well as the nature of that touch; this knowledge is termed **tactile localization**. Making fine discriminations about where one has been touched, sight unseen, and whether the touch involves one point or two in close proximity, is an ability that develops in childhood. Children are less accurate at 4 years of age than at 6 to 8 years in locating a touch on the hands and forearms; performance on this type of task does not improve significantly between ages 6 and 8 (Ayres, 1972; Temple et al., 1979). Based on this limited data, then, the perception of tactile localization on the hands and arms seems to be relatively mature by age 6.

Threshold discrimination—detecting the smallest gap between two points that touch the skin—varies in different areas of the body (figure 10.9); we do not know whether it also varies with age (Van Duyne, 1973; Williams, 1983). Ayres (1966) reported that only half of a group of 5-year-olds could consistently discriminate a touch on different fingers, though average performance improved through 7.5 years of age (the oldest age tested).

Recognizing unseen objects and their characteristics by feeling them with the hands is the kinesthetic perception parallel to the visual perception of objects. In infants, such manipulation is often more accidental than purposeful. Yet by age 4, the average child can handle objects purposefully, and by age 5 a child can explore the objects' major features. Manual exploration becomes systematic—that is, children become more methodical—at about age 6 (Van Duyne, 1973), and in

Tactile localization is the ability to identify without sight the exact spot on the body that has been touched.

KEY POINT
Children improve in their ability to locate touches, but little is known about threshold discriminations for touch.

the next 2 years, haptic (cutaneous) memory and object recognition also improve (Northman & Black, 1976). Research by Temple et al. (1979) indicates that children also increase their speed of tactile recognition during this time.

Perception of the Body (Body Awareness)

To carry out everyday activities and to perform complex skills, it is necessary to have a sense of the body, its various parts, and its dimensions. One aspect of **body awareness** is the identification of body parts. As children get older, more of them can label the major body parts correctly (DeOreo & Williams, 1980), and they can name more detailed body parts (Cratty, 1979). The rate at which an individual child learns body part labels is largely a function of the amount of time parents or other adults spend practicing with the child. Probably two-thirds of 6-year-olds can identify the major body parts, and mistakes are rare in all typically developing children after age 9.

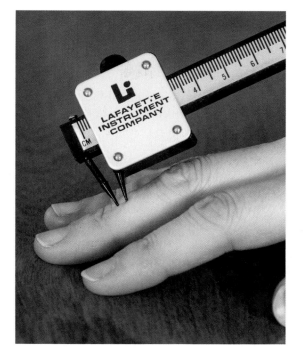

FIGURE 10.9 Tactile point perception includes accurate judgment of the number of simultaneous touches on the skin. As two touch points get closer together, it is more difficult to discriminate between a single touch and two touches.

> **Body awareness** is the recognition, identification, and differentiation of the location, movement, and interrelationships of body parts and joints; it also refers to a person's awareness of the spatial orientation and perceived location of the body in the environment.

 Imagine you are a youth sports coach in one of your favorite activities. What skills in this activity rely at least in part on body awareness? What cues can you use to draw a beginner's attention to body position?

Children also need a sense of the body's spatial dimensions, such as up and down. They usually master the up–down dimension first, followed by front–back, and finally side. A high percentage of 2.5- to 3-year-olds can place an object in front of or behind their bodies, but more of them have difficulty placing an object in front of or behind something else. By about age 4, most children can do the latter task as well as place an object to the side of something (Kuczaj & Maratsos, 1975).

Laterality   Although children typically master up–down and front–back awareness before age 3, they develop an understanding that the body has two distinct sides, or **laterality**, at approximately 4 to 5 years of age (Hecaen & de Ajuriaguerra, 1964). The child comes to realize that even though his two hands, two legs, and so on are the same size and shape, he can position them differently and move them independently. Eventually, the child is able to discriminate right and left sides—that is, to label or identify these dimensions.

An age-related improvement in the ability to make right–left discriminations occurs between age 4 or 5 and age 10; most children respond almost perfectly by age 10 (Ayres, 1969; Swanson & Benton, 1955; Williams, 1973). However, children can be taught to label right and left at younger ages, too, even as young as 5 (Hecaen

> **Laterality** is a component of body awareness—specifically, the awareness that one's body has two distinct sides that can move independently.

& de Ajuriaguerra, 1964). Young children also have difficulty executing a task when a limb must cross the midline of the body, such as writing on a chalkboard from left to right. This ability improves between ages 4 and 10, but some 10-year-olds still have difficulty with such tasks (Ayres, 1969; Williams, 1973).

 Imagine you are an early childhood educator. What activities could you use to help children learn to discriminate between left and right?

Lateral dominance
is the consistent preference for use of one eye, ear, hand, or foot instead of the other, although the preference for different anatomical units is not always on the same side.

Lateral dominance   Interest in **lateral dominance**, especially hand dominance, dates back to Aristotle. Over the centuries, some have favored a nativist view of dominance suggesting that lateral dominance is inborn, especially after Broca's studies suggested asymmetries between the right and left halves of the brain. Broca was a French surgeon who first reported in 1861 that individuals with loss of language abilities had lesions in a specific area on only one side of the brain. This finding first suggested that an entire function, in this case speech, might be controlled by only one side of the brain. Today we know that "Broca's area" is not the only site in the brain involved in speech.

Other behavioral scientists have favored a "nurture" perspective (see chapter 2), holding that preference for writing and tool use can be changed by training. In recent years the study of lateral dominance has been tied to the study of language development, which has hindered rather than helped our understanding of handedness (see Hopkins & Ronnqvist, 1998, for a discussion).

Asymmetries in hand use have been widely observed in infants. Infants younger than 3 months of age grasp objects longer, make a fist longer, and are more active with one hand than the other (Hawn & Harris, 1983; Michel & Goodwin, 1979; Michel & Harkins, 1986). These asymmetries are not consistently predictive of adult hand dominance (Michel, 1983, 1988), but a link may exist between early asymmetries and later hand dominance because the asymmetries tend to follow orientation. Infants who prefer to turn their heads to the right seem to prefer reaching with their right hands, and vice versa. These self-generating experiences may facilitate eye–hand coordination of one hand more than the other (Bushnell, 1985; Michel, 1988).

When infants begin to reach after 3 months, they also demonstrate a hand preference (Hawn & Harris, 1983). Unimanual manipulation appears at approximately 5 months, and by 7 months infants show a preference for manipulating with a particular hand (Ramsay, 1980; table 10.2). A hand preference is evident approximately 1 month after bimanual manipulation first appears, even as both hands hold an object (Ramsay, Campos, & Fenson, 1979). Infants typically prefer the same hand in unimanual and bimanual handling; that is, they use either the right or left hand in both types of manipulation (Ramsay, 1980). Although these early preferences might change, usually the hand that emerges as preferred in early childhood, most often by age 4, remains the dominant hand in youth and adulthood (Sinclair, 1971). It is important to remember that in certain environmental situations children might find it convenient to use their nonpreferred limbs (Connolly & Elliott, 1972). By adulthood, individuals typically use their dominant limbs even if it is more awkward to do so.

 Think about your daily activities and the instruments you use. Do any of them favor right handedness or left handedness?

In addition to hand preferences, we come to favor one of our eyes, ears, and feet over the other. If the favored parts are all on one side of the body, the dominance

TABLE 10.2   Infant Hand Preferences

Nature of hand preference	Approximate age
Fisting and longer grasps	Before 3 mo
Unimanual reaching	After 3 mo
Unimanual manipulation	By 7 mo
Bimanual manipulation	Within 1 mo of emergence of unimanual manipulation
Hand dominance	By 4 yr

is termed pure; otherwise, it is called mixed. In the past, developmentalists have suggested that pure dominance is preferable, the implication being that one side of the brain is clearly dominant. For example, in the 1960s, a popular perceptual-motor theory proposed by Doman and Delacato (Delacato, 1966) held that pure dominance is necessary for proper neurological organization. Those with mixed dominance could anticipate problems in perceptual-motor performance, reading, speech, and other cognitive abilities. Research has never shown this to be the case. Studies have failed to show any real cognitive advantage for individuals with more lateralized brains (Kinsbourne, 1988, 1997).

Limb Movements

You can assess a child's perception of the extent of movement at a joint by asking the child to accurately reproduce a limb movement or to relocate a limb position without looking. Children improve in this task between ages 5 and 8; little improvement is noted after age 8 (Ayres, 1972; Williams, 1983).

Spatial Orientation

Kinesthetic spatial orientation involves perception of the body's location and orientation in space, independent of vision. Temple et al. (1979) tested this perception by asking children to walk a straight line while blindfolded and measuring their deviation from the straight path. Performance improved between 6 and 8 years of age; 8-year-olds were the oldest age group included in the study. Investigations of spatial orientation over a wider age range are necessary.

Direction

Directionality is often linked to laterality, an awareness of the body's two distinct sides. Children with a poor sense of laterality typically also have poor directionality. Although this relationship seems intuitively logical, deficiencies in laterality are not known to be the cause of deficiencies in directionality (Kephart, 1964).

Individuals obtain most information for directional judgments through vision, so these judgments rely on integration of visual and kinesthetic information. Long and Looft (1972) suggested that children improve their sense of directionality between ages 6 and 12. By age 8, children typically can use body references to indicate direction. They are able to say correctly, "The ball is on my right" and "The ball is to the right of the bat." At age 9, children can change the latter statement to "The ball is to the left of the bat" when they walk around to the opposite side of the objects. They can also identify right and left for a person opposite them. Such improvements in directional references continue through age 12. Long and Looft noted that some refinement of directionality must take place in adolescence because

Directionality is the ability to project the body's spatial dimensions into surrounding space and to grasp spatial concepts about the movements or locations of objects in the environment.

many 12-year-olds are unable to transpose left and right from a new perspective, such as when looking in a mirror.

Kinesthetic Changes With Aging

We know very little about how aging affects the kinesthetic receptors themselves, but researchers have identified age-related changes in kinesthetic perception. Some, but not all, older adults lose cutaneous sensitivity, vibratory sensitivity, and sensitivity to temperature and pain (Kenshalo, 1977). Older adults experience some impairment in judging the direction and amount of passive lower limb movement (in which someone else positions the limb) (Laidlaw & Hamilton, 1937). However, they remain fairly accurate in judging muscle tension produced by differing weights (Landahl & Birren, 1959).

Auditory Development

Although it is not as important to skill performance as vision or kinesthesis, auditory information is still valuable for accurate performance. People often use sounds as critical cues to initiate or time their movements.

Auditory Sensation

Hearing involves the external ear, the middle ear, and the cochlea of the inner ear. The inner ear develops first and is close to adult form by the third prenatal month. By midfetal life, the external ear and middle ear are formed as well (Timiras, 1972). Fetuses reportedly respond to loud sounds, but perhaps this response is actually to tactile stimuli—that is, vibrations (Kidd & Kidd, 1966).

A newborn's hearing is imperfect partly because of the gelatinous tissue filling the inner ear. The **absolute threshold** is about 60 decibels higher for a newborn than for an adult. So, a newborn can detect only an average speaking voice when an adult can detect a whisper (Kellman & Arterberry, 1998). Newborns also do not discriminate changes in the intensity of sounds (**differential threshold**) or in sound frequencies as well as adults can.

The gelatinous material in the inner ear is reabsorbed during the first postnatal week so that hearing improves rapidly (Hecox, 1975; Timiras, 1972). By 3 months, infants hear low-frequency sounds (500–1,000 Hz) very well but do not hear high-frequency sounds (4,000 Hz) quite as well. Because human speech generally is under 5,000 Hz, this level of hearing permits the infant to sense speech. In fact, infants might be predisposed to listen to speech (Vouloumanos & Werker, 2007) and process their own mother's voice faster than that of others as early as 4 months of age (Purhonen, Kilpelainen-Lees, Valkonen-Korhonen, Karhu, & Lehtonen, 2005). The infant can hear low- to mid-pitched voices better than high-pitched voices. By 6 months, however, infants' hearing is similar to that of adults, including hearing of high-frequency sounds (Spetner & Olsho, 1990).

More older adults than younger adults suffer from **presbycusis** (from *presbys* for "old man" and *okousis* for "hearing"), but the source of this loss varies among individuals. Some hearing loss might result from physiological degeneration, but hearing loss often results from lifelong exposure to environmental noise (Timiras, 1972).

The absolute threshold for hearing pure tones and speech increases in older adults, meaning that sounds must be louder for older adults to hear them. Differential thresholds also increase for pitch and speech discrimination (Corso, 1977).

Absolute threshold is the minimal detectable sound that a hearer can sense at least half of the time a signal is sounded.

Differential threshold is the closest that two sounds can be yet still allow the hearer to distinguish them at least 75% of the time.

KEY POINT
Infants can hear human speech.

Presbycusis is a loss of hearing sensitivity.

As a person ages, the ability to hear high-frequency sounds is particularly affected. One result is that older adults cannot hear certain consonant sounds well; they might report that they hear someone talking but cannot understand the message. Older adults are also at a distinct disadvantage in adverse listening situations, such as attempting to listen to one person in a room crowded with talking people (Stine, Wingfield, & Poon, 1989).

 Think of your older relatives and acquaintances. What activities of daily living can present difficulties for seniors with presbycusis?

Auditory Perception

It is easy to overlook the amount of information we get from sound. For example, we can determine the location of an event by sound, whether something or someone is leaving or approaching, who or what made a sound, and even the material from which an object is made. Although we think of vision and kinesthesis as more important to skill performance, auditory perception gives us much information about the environment in which we move. The aspects of auditory perception that we discuss here are location, differences between similar sounds, patterns, and auditory figure and ground. Notice that several of these aspects are parallel to types of visual and kinesthetic perception.

Location

We locate a sound by determining its direction and distance from us (figure 10.10). Newborns turn in the direction of a sound, and they rapidly improve in their ability to locate sound during the first year. When presented two sounds, each in a different location, the minimum angle between the two locations that 6- and 7-month-olds can detect as being two different locations is in the range of 12° to 19° (Ashmead, Clifton, & Perris, 1987; Morrongiello, 1988b), compared with 1° to 2° in adults. Infants determine the direction of nearby sounds better than that of distant sounds, but improvement is continuous such that by age 3 children can determine the direction of even distant sounds (Dekaban, 1970). Infants between 4 and 10 months also can distinguish temporal patterns in sounds (Lewkowicz & Marcovitch, 2006).

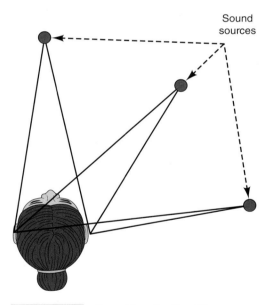

FIGURE 10.10 Sound localization. The more a sound deviates from the straight-ahead position, the greater the time difference in the arrival of the sound at each ear.

Reprinted by permission from Bower 1977.

 Think of your living routines. What are some tasks that involve localizing sound?

It is more difficult to determine how well infants perceive the distance of a sound. Clifton, Perris, and Bullinger (1991) found that 7-month-olds reached for an object that was the source of a sound significantly more often when it was within reach than when it was out of reach. It is possible they choose not to reach because they know it is out of reach. It seems that from birth, individuals have some sense of the location of sounds in the environment and rapidly improve in determining both the direction and distance of sounds.

Older adults with presbycusis show a notable decrement in the ability to localize sound (Nordlund, 1964). This is not surprising given that localization depends on accurate auditory sensations related to the time at which sounds arrive at the two ears and on the intensity differences in sound. In fact, older adults who demonstrate good speech discrimination abilities also show normal sound localization, whereas those with poor speech discrimination show poor sound localization (Hausler, Colburn, & Marr, 1983).

Differences

The perception of sound differences by children is often studied by means of discrimination tasks. For example, children are asked to distinguish two sounds that are similar in pitch, loudness, or speech sound, such as *d* and *t* or *b* and *p*. Infants as young as 1 to 4 months can discriminate between basic speech sounds, such as *p*, *b*, and *m* (Doty, 1974), but children between 3 and 5 years old experience increasing accuracy in recognizing differences in sounds (DiSimoni, 1975). Temple et al. (1979) found a further improvement in auditory discrimination between 6 and 8 years, as did Birch (1976) between 7 and 10 years, in an auditory matching task. A similar trend apparently exists for discrimination of pitch (Kidd & Kidd, 1966). In general, it appears that by 8 to 10 years of age, children have greatly improved their ability to detect differences in similar sounds, but they continue to refine their auditory discrimination skills until they are at least 13.

If we could set aside age-related changes in sensitivity for hearing pure tones, the deficits in hearing speech sounds among older adults would be minimal (Helfer, 1992; Lutman, 1991; van Rooij & Plomp, 1992). Therefore, age deficits in speech perception are largely a function of decline in pure-tone sensitivity. Interestingly, older adults often make better use of context cues to help their recognition of speech than young adults do (Craig, Kim, Rhyner, & Chirillo, 1993; Holtzman, Familant, Deptula, & Hoyer, 1986).

Patterns

For speech and music to be more than just noises, individuals must perceive relationships between sounds. Of course, we perceive patterns in other senses. Visual pattern perception has long interested developmentalists, but attention to auditory pattern perception is more recent.

Auditory patterns are nonrandom, temporally (time-) ordered sound sequences. Three properties of sound give rise to auditory patterns:

1. Time
2. Intensity
3. Frequency (Morrongiello, 1988a)

Speech and music have a temporal pattern, an intensity (loudness or softness) pattern, and a frequency (high pitch or low pitch) pattern simultaneously. Developmentalists usually study one characteristic at a time.

Infants as young as 2 to 3 months old react to changes in the temporal pattern of a tone sequence, showing that they perceive temporal patterns (Demany, McKenzie, & Vurpillot, 1977). Young infants, however, perceive only pattern changes involving the number of groups of tones (e.g., changing nine tones from three groups of three to two groups, one of five and one of four) (Morrongiello, 1984). At 12 months, infants can perceive changes in the number of groups and in the number of tones in each group (figure 10.11). Thus, by the end of the first year, infants can perceive sound on the basis of temporal pattern, which is probably a prerequisite for language development.

Nine tones in three groups of three tones:

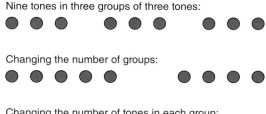

Changing the number of groups:

Changing the number of tones in each group:

FIGURE 10.11 Auditory stimulus patterns presented to infants. Young infants can detect a change in the number of groups from what is familiar to them, but it is not until they are 12 months old that they can detect changes in both the number of groups and the number of tones in a group. Time between tones in a group was 0.2 s, and time between groups was 0.6 s.

Based on Morrongiello 1988, The development of auditory pattern perception skills. In *Advances in infancy research*, Vol. 6, edited by C. Rovee-Collier and L.P. Lipsitt (Norwood, NH: Ablex).

Infants between 5 and 11 months can discriminate intensity changes for vowels in a syllable (Bull, Eilers, & Oller, 1984), but we know little else about infants' intensity perception. Infants younger than 6 months can discriminate frequency relationships in a simple, short sequence. Not until the end of their first year, though, can infants perceive frequency relationships between the tones in a long, complex sequence (Morrongiello, 1986; Trehub, Bull, & Thorpe, 1984). The same is true of speech patterns. Children between 4 and 6 years can discriminate the frequency features of six-tone melodies played at normal speed (Morrongiello, Trehub, Thorpe, & Capodilupo, 1985). Infants progress rapidly in auditory pattern perception during their first year. These advances probably are prerequisites to language development. Preschool children make further progress in perceiving patterns in increasingly longer and more complex contexts.

What systems might limit the development of auditory pattern perception? Obviously, the auditory system must be developed, and, as mentioned earlier, auditory sensation is quite mature within days of birth. The sensory cortex of the brain, however, is still maturing rapidly over the first few years of life. With continuing development, it probably permits conceptualization of patterns and of the identity of transformed patterns (Morrongiello, 1988a)—for example, the same rhythmic pattern played at different tempos. Cognition also must advance because in order to perceive patterns, an individual must be able to remember and process information, especially for long and complex sequences.

In addition, the environment in which infants develop might "tune" the developing auditory system to recognize certain features of language and music. In this way, we might learn to prefer the perceptual patterns prevalent in our native language and the music of our culture (Morrongiello, 1988a; Swingley, 2005; Trehub & Hannon, 2006).

Auditory Figure and Ground

Often a person must attend to certain sounds while ignoring other irrelevant sounds in the background. In this auditory parallel to visual figure-and-ground perception, the figure is the sound of interest and the ground is distracting noises in the background. For example, try listening to someone talk to you on the telephone (figure sounds) while music is playing and several people in your room are talking (background sounds). Young infants can detect sounds amid ambient noise (Morrongiello & Clifton, 1984), but some children have more difficulty than others in separating auditory figures from the background. We would benefit from more research on the processes underlying these differences.

 Think about driving an automobile. What clues for driving safely might you miss if music is playing loudly or you are wearing earphones?

Older adults commonly report difficulty with hearing amid background noise (see Tun & Wingfield, 1993, for a review). It is possible that this problem reflects changes in the sensory system or in parts of the neurological system related to hearing. It may also reflect changes in attention mechanisms—that is, older adults might have more difficulty attending to a particular sound source in the midst of other sounds.

As noted previously, development of auditory perception is rapid. Not long after birth, infants can already perceive the location of and differences in sounds. An individual's ability to make fine discriminations improves in childhood. Perceptions of auditory events in the environment in adulthood are likely disturbed only when age-related changes in sensation, including injury and disease, affect detection of sounds.

Sensation, Perception, and Perceptual-Motor Development Summary

It is clear that some aspects of visual, kinesthetic, and auditory perception exist in infancy. Developmental trends continue throughout childhood, especially in the finer discriminations. By the time children are 8 to 12 years old, aspects of their visual perception have developed to near-adult levels. It seems that kinesthetic perception typically develops to near-adult levels somewhat earlier, usually by about age 8, although this generalization is based on limited research. Young children can perceive the location of sound, and by age 10 they perform at near-adult levels on many auditory discrimination tasks. Refinement of auditory skills continues through the early teens. Some aspects of auditory perception have not been studied in children.

In general, children between the ages of 8 and 12 approach adult levels of performance on many perceptual tasks, and only small refinements in perceptual skills are yet to be made. Assessments of perceptual-motor development have been designed, and educators and therapists sometimes screen young children for deficits in perceptual-motor development.

Some aspects of perceptual development are not well documented; further research is needed. In addition, little is known about what causes changes in perceptual processes as people age, but it is known that decremental changes in the sensory systems reduce the quality of the sensory information reaching the central nervous system, potentially affecting perception. At any age, limited sensory information could serve as a rate limiter to performance by influencing perception of needed information.

The perceptual systems do not operate in isolation of one another. To complete this discussion of perceptual development, the following section explores how information perceived in one sense, or modality, is related to that perceived in other modalities.

WEB STUDY GUIDE Administer some simple perceptual-motor test items in Lab Activity 10.1, Testing Perceptual-Motor Development, in the web study guide. Go to www.HumanKinetics.com/LifeSpanMotorDevelopment.

Intermodal Perception

Events occur in the environment and are often sensed and, therefore, perceived in different modalities, or senses. If a jar slips from our hands while we are trying to open it, we feel it slipping, we see it falling, we hear it hit the floor and break, and we might even smell the released contents. This event can be perceived through vision, kinesthesis, and audition. Developmentalists have considered perception through different modalities from two very different perspectives. From the first, or integrational, perspective, the energy reaching the different senses is of different forms—light, sound, temperature, and so on—and each sensory system yields a unique sensation. The task of a developing infant, then, is to learn how to integrate the separate systems—that is, to learn how those unique sensations are related to one another.

The second, or unified, perspective sees the senses as united in bringing information about events, but through different modalities. The nervous system is structured for multimodal perception so that, from the start, perceptions are coherent in time and space (Damasio, 1989; Stein & Meredith, 1993). The perceptual systems extract patterns; many patterns are similar across the modalities. For example, events occur at a point in time, so the temporal properties of an event are not unique to any one modality. In a sense, these patterns are **amodal invariants**. We see a drummer strike a drum and we hear the drum's sound, but we also perceive the rhythmic pattern that existed across vision and audition. In this model, the central task of development is to learn about events in the world with the information coming through various sensory systems (Kellman & Arterberry, 1998). Research in neurophysiology during the 1980s and 1990s lends some support to this unified perspective of intermodal perception. This research has identified areas of the brain containing neurons that receive input from different modalities (Stein, Meredith, & Wallace, 1994), thus calling into question views of separateness among the sensory-perceptual systems.

The unified perspective is more consistent with the ecological perspective of perception and action. The integration perspective is more consistent with an information processing perspective. Earlier chapters acknowledge that much of the research on perception has been done from the information processing perspective. Keep this in mind as we review research in the following areas of intermodal perception:

- Auditory-visual
- Visual-kinesthetic
- Auditory-kinesthetic
- Spatial-temporal

Amodal invariants are patterns in space or time that do not differ across the sensory-perceptual modalities.

KEY POINT
One view emphasizes the development of infants' abilities to integrate separate perceptual systems. The other emphasizes the perception of patterns about an environment unified across the systems.

Auditory-Visual Intermodal Perception

Newborn infants have been observed to move their eyes in the direction of a sound. Morrongiello, Fenwick, Hillier, and Chance (1994) played a 20 s recording of a rattle to newborns. They placed the loudspeaker at varying angles from the infant's midline. The farther the speaker from the midline, the farther the newborns turned their heads. In some trials, the investigators also shifted the sound from one loudspeaker to another, and the infants adjusted their heads correspondingly. Although this is a rudimentary response, it appears that even newborns seek to match their visual fixation to the spatial origin of a sound.

More challenging auditory-visual perceptions show a developmental trend in childhood (see figure 10.12). Goodnow (1971b) tapped out a sequence [* ***], then asked children to write the sequence using dots and spaces to picture where the taps occurred. She also reversed the auditory-visual (A-V) task by asking children to tap out a pictured sequence (V-A). Children around age 5 did not perform the A-V sequence as well as children at age 7. A trend toward improved performance on the V-A task was also found in children between ages 6.9 and 8.5 years. This and similar studies indicate that visual and auditory intermodal perception improves between ages 5 and 12 (Williams, 1983). Young children find A-V tasks more difficult than V-A tasks, but this difference diminishes after age 7 (Rudel & Teuber, 1971).

 Imagine you are a youth coach in your favorite sport. Is the integration of auditory and visual information involved in any part of the sport? How about kinesthetic and visual information? What might you do to help beginners use this information to improve performance?

Visual-Kinesthetic Intermodal Perception

Visual-kinesthetic perception is the coordination between seen and felt properties of objects. Because infants do not reach for and manipulate objects before 4 to 5 months of age, the study of visual-kinesthetic perception at young ages centers on mouthing of objects. Meltzoff and Borton (1979) found that 1-month-olds looked longer at the type of pacifier that they had mouthed but had not seen, either one that was a cube with nubs or one that was a smooth sphere. At some level, then, infants relate oral and visual information.

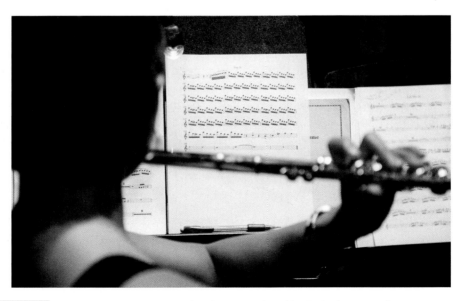

FIGURE 10.12 Musicians play notes in the rhythm notated in their sheet music to create sounds corresponding to the notated pattern.

Visual-kinesthetic perception involving manipulation of objects has been explored at later stages of infancy, and research study outcomes have been variable. Goodnow (1971a) studied visual and kinesthetic integration in children. She presented five shapes (Greek and Russian letters) by either sight or feel to three age groups (5.0- to 5.5-year-olds, 5.6- to 6.8-year-olds, and 9.0- to 10.0-year-olds). She then presented these five shapes, along with five new ones, again by sight or feel, and challenged the children to identify the familiar shapes. Four presentation patterns were possible:

1. Visual presentation–visual recognition (V-V)
2. Kinesthetic presentation–kinesthetic recognition (K-K)
3. Visual presentation–kinesthetic recognition (V-K)
4. Kinesthetic presentation–visual recognition (K-V)

Goodnow found that children, especially the youngest ones, had more difficulty in the K-K pattern than in the V-V pattern. This performance discrepancy narrowed in the older age groups. The K-V task proved more difficult for the children than the V-K task. Goodnow noted that the scores of the youngest group in the kinesthetic conditions were extremely variable. This study and others using similar tasks and different age groups lead us to the conclusion that a developmental trend exists in visual-kinesthetic intermodal perception during childhood. When the kinesthetic task involves active manipulation of an object, 5-year-olds can recognize the shapes relatively well, but slight improvement continues until age 8. If passive movements are involved, performance is not as advanced, and improvements continue through age 11 (Williams, 1983).

Auditory-Kinesthetic Intermodal Perception

The amount of research conducted on auditory-kinesthetic integration is small compared with that involving vision. Temple et al. (1979) included the Witeba Test of Auditory-Tactile Integration in a test battery administered to 6- and 8-year-olds. In this test, an experimenter twice tells a child the name of an object or shape. The child then feels a number of objects or shapes, attempting to select the one that matches the auditory label. The investigators found that 8-year-olds performed this task much better than 6-year-olds did.

This experimental method is based on children understanding the label given to the object or shape. Thus, it is possible that this age-related difference in performance resulted from younger children not knowing, misunderstanding, or not remembering the auditory label in addition to, or instead of, their auditory-kinesthetic intermodal perception. With this limitation in mind, we can tentatively conclude that auditory-kinesthetic integration improves in childhood.

Spatial-Temporal Intermodal Perception

You may recall the earlier discussion of amodal invariants—patterns that might be invariant across modalities—such as space and time. For example, when children viewed the dot pattern in Goodnow's experiment, they were dealing with a spatial stimulus—the arrangement of dots in space. When they listened to an auditory pattern, they were attending to a temporal (time-based) stimulus. They were perceiving, then, a pattern that crossed space and time as well as vision and audition.

Sterritt, Martin, and Rudnick (1971) devised nine tasks that varied the number of perceptual integrations to be made as well as the type of integration, including spatial-temporal characteristics. For example, a child must integrate a short pause between two tones (temporal) with a short space between two dots (spatial). They presented the nine tasks to 6-year-olds. The easiest task for the children was the V-V spatial (intramodality) task. Children had some difficulty with tasks that required them to integrate visual-spatial stimuli with visual-temporal or auditory-temporal stimuli. They had more difficulty integrating two temporal patterns, whether the task was intra- or intermodal. While progressing in intermodal perception, then, children also improve their ability to integrate spatial and temporal stimuli as well as their ability to integrate two sets of temporal stimuli.

Difficult or subtle aspects of intermodal perception might continue to develop during adolescence. Intermodal perception most likely is stable in adulthood and older adulthood. Any decrements are probably a function of changes in the sensory-perceptual systems—changes that affect the amount of information available. For example, if cataracts cause a viewer to miss seeing the details of an object, the visual information for an integration may not be available. On the other hand, older adults might be able to use their experience as a compensatory mechanism and use information from one modality to compensate for information not available in another because of age-related change in the sensory or neurological systems. Certainly, more research is needed on this topic.

 WEB STUDY GUIDE   Observe children's intermodal perception of small objects seen and manipulated in Lab Activity 10.2, Development of Intermodal Perception, in the web study guide. Go to www.HumanKinetics.com/LifeSpanMotorDevelopment.

Intermodal Development Summary

Intermodal coordination begins at birth, but there appears to be a developmental trend in childhood and adolescence for tasks that involve matching and subtle aspects of integration. The accuracy of children's performance is related to the order of presentation. That is, presenting the visual pattern or object first yields better performance than presenting the auditory information first. Also, children first master spatial-spatial integration tasks, followed by mixed spatial and temporal tasks, and finally temporal-temporal tasks.

Summary and Synthesis

The visual, kinesthetic, and auditory systems function at birth and continue to improve throughout infancy and childhood. The level of function in infancy appears adequate for the learning tasks facing infants, and the rate of improvement seems consistent with the learning tasks facing toddlers. By late childhood, the senses function at levels similar to those of adults. Detecting stimuli, however, is not the same as knowing what they mean; sensation is not the same as perception. In chapter 11 we consider the advancement of perception and perceptual-motor behavior.

Aging is accompanied by change in the sensory systems, although we know more about the changes in vision than about those in kinesthesis or audition. Decrements tend to vary widely among older adults. Compensation for some of these losses is possible; for example, seniors can wear eyeglasses or hearing aids.

Conditions that accentuate differences are also helpful to older adults. Examples include the provision of good lighting and the reduction of background noise. Of course, a decrement in sensation can make for difficulty in perception, so just as with the early portion of the life span, it is important to study age-related change in perception.

Traditionally, much of the study of perceptual and perceptual-motor development has focused on the changing capacity of each individual system regardless of the environment. Even study of how the perceptual systems put together information received by each system about the same object or event assumed that integration was a step that followed perceptual processing. More ecological views of perception have been around for some time, but the difficulty of studying a perceptual system and the environment as an ecosystem has limited the data available to inform this perspective.

 Reinforcing What You Have Learned About Constraints

TAKE A SECOND LOOK

When we watch an IMAX movie, the visual sensations and perceptions can be so real that even the kinesthetic system responds as if we were having the real experience. Those inclined to get airsick or carsick might actually do so watching the movie. The interactions of the sensory-perceptual systems are demonstrated even in the somewhat artificial experience of watching an IMAX movie. The model of constraints we use throughout our discussion of motor development stresses interactions. Thus, the ecological viewpoint is a better fit with our model of constraints. If we extend the ecological viewpoint a step further, perceptual and motor or perception–action become inseparable. Each continually informs the other so that there is a continuous interaction of perceiving the world and moving in it. We can see how important it is for teachers, therapists, coaches, and trainers to understand sensory and perceptual systems and how these systems might change over the life span. As the final part of this discussion of perceptual-motor development, chapter 11 explores perception–action from this viewpoint.

TEST YOUR KNOWLEDGE

1. What changes in visual sensation occur during infancy? During childhood?
2. Describe how humans perceive depth in the space around them.
3. Describe the various aspects of visual object perception.
4. What changes in kinesthetic sensation occur during infancy? During childhood?
5. What are the various aspects of kinesthetic perception, and at what age does each likely reach near-adult levels?
6. What changes in auditory sensation occur during infancy? During childhood?
7. What are the various aspects of auditory perception, and what information about the sound source does each provide?
8. What changes occur in the visual, kinesthetic, and auditory receptors in older adulthood?
9. What is the typical method for studying intermodal perception?
10. What are amodal invariants?

Learning Exercise 10.1

LIMITED SENSATION

We can gain an appreciation of the information that comes to us through our sensory-perceptual systems by artificially limiting that information. Working with a partner, try these activities:

1. Play catch in an old pair of sunglasses with tape covering one lens.
2. Walk down a hallway while blindfolded (with your partner guiding you for safety).
3. Facing away from your partner, carry on a conversation while wearing a pair of earplugs as your partner slowly increases the distance between the two of you.

Afterward, discuss what tasks were difficult or impossible and what the implications would be for daily living—for example, attending a university, driving a car, or playing intramural sports.

Perception and Action in Development

 CHAPTER OBJECTIVES

This chapter

- reviews historical perspectives on the role of action in perceptual development;
- surveys contemporary views on perceptual-motor programs and the links between the cognitive, perceptual, and motor systems;
- examines differences in perception between infants with and without experience in self-produced locomotion; and
- studies the interaction between perception and action in maintaining balance after infancy.

Motor Development in the Real World

Redshirt Your Kindergartener?

The term *redshirt* was borrowed from a practice in athletics in which first-year college players are held out of athletic participation for a year in order to give them additional time to grow and mature. The practice has been particularly popular in sports such as football. In a similar vein, a segment on the television show *Today* examined the fact that some parents delay their children's entry into kindergarten for a year (termed an academic redshirt), especially if their children would be among the youngest starting in a given year. Parents have always been concerned about their children's readiness to start school. They want their children to reach a maturity level that will enable them to succeed in school once they start rather than risk them being behind the majority of their classmates.

This parental concern has encouraged some individuals to offer special programs that claim to help children develop the perceptual skills necessary for classroom success. Certainly, success in the classroom depends on a level of perceptual development, and some of the readiness programs promoted to parents emphasize perceptual-motor development. So far, this text has emphasized the sensory and perceptual systems used in motor skills. But might movement actually play a significant role in the development of sensory-perceptual systems? Are perception and movement more tightly coupled than our discussion thus far has acknowledged? Certainly some believe this to be the case, although a variety of views exist on the exact nature of the relationship.

This chapter discusses the interrelationship between perception and movement actions. It begins with the notion that movement has a role in, and perhaps is even necessary for, perceptual development. The chapter then examines an aspect of everyday life in which perception and action are linked: maintenance of posture and balance.

The Role of Action in Perception

Developmentalists have long suspected that movement is extremely important to the development of perception. That is, they suspect that movement through the environment is vital to the coupling of perceptions and purposeful movements in the environment. The exact role of motor activity in the development of perception is difficult for researchers to study. The ideal experiment on this topic, of course, would be to deprive some individuals of movement and compare them with others who were allowed to move through the environment. Because this isn't possible, our information tends to come from animal studies and other research situations in which movement experiences vary through naturally occurring circumstances. Today, however, new research frontiers are being established through the increasing use of imaging technology, such as magnetic resonance imaging and positron-emission tomography scans.

Historical Views

The exact nature of the perception–action link, especially in the early years, is so elusive that it has spawned controversies among developmentalists. During the 1960s, a number of individuals proposed perceptual-motor theories, screening tools, and remedial programs. Many of these developmentalists were interested in perceptual-motor activity because they realized that perceptual development is as important to the development of cognition as it is to the development of skilled movement. For example, individuals must perceive the difference in spatial orientation between a circle and a line when they are arranged to form the letter *d* and when they are arranged to form the letter *b*. If individuals cannot perceive this difference, they will have difficulty reading. Some earlier developmentalists saw perception as a precursor to both movement and cognition, and they proposed that children with learning disabilities had deficits in perceptual development. Further, they hypothesized that perceptual-motor activity programs could remediate deficits. By practicing to improve perceptual-motor responses, children would overcome perceptual deficiencies, and cognitive activities reliant on perception would benefit as much as motor activities.

Among the more popular theories in the mid-20th century were the neurological organization theory of Delacato (1959, 1966); the physiological optics program of Getman (1952, 1963); the visual perception tests and program of Frostig, Lefever, and Whittlesey (1966); the sensory-integration tests of Ayres (1972); the movigenics theory of Barsch (1965); and the perceptual-motor theory of Kephart (1971). Early on, there appeared to be empirical support for these theories and programs as children placed in the remedial programs showed improved classroom performance. The evaluations of these programs, however, were often flawed because they did not account for other factors that could contribute to improvement, such as the increased attention that children received in the remedial programs. Eventually, sufficient information from well-designed evaluations failed to show that participation in a perceptual-motor program produced improvements in readiness skills, intelligence, classroom achievement, or language (Goodman & Hamill, 1973). Perceptual-motor programs did help in the development of motor skills.

Piaget (1952) also recognized the importance of movement. He proposed that reality is constructed by relating action to sensory information in well-defined developmental stages during infancy, childhood, and adolescence. For Piaget, neither perception nor action is well organized in infancy.

Contemporary Views

Today, educators and therapists are cautious about claims that participation in a perceptual-motor program can remediate learning deficiencies. Yet they realize that such participation is beneficial for children with and without learning difficulties. Perceptual-motor programs at least provide valuable experience in performing skills based on key perceptual characteristics of a task. As such, they can contribute to a positive outlook on one's ability to perform. Perceptual-motor activities can also reinforce concepts needed for motor and cognitive tasks, such as shapes and directions. Most current physical education curricula for young children devote significant time to perceptual-motor activities. In addition, supplemental perceptual-motor programs are frequently offered to special groups. A recent hypothesis posits that physical activity triggers brain activity, which facilitates learning for a time after the period of activity (Ratey, 2008).

Let's first consider the nature of perceptual-motor programs, then consider some contemporary views on links between perception, cognition, and motor activity (action). Perceptual-motor programs can be either comprehensive or focused on certain aspects of perception. They can also be designed for young children in general, for groups with a characteristic deficiency, or for individuals (based on their particular deficits). Table 11.1 illustrates this variability among perceptual-motor programs. Parents and educators alike must act as critical consumers in assessing the value of any program and its claim for success. Until we understand more about the links between perception, cognition, and action, the most realistic claims are those focused on the development of motor skills. The best programs do not advocate a single approach to the exclusion of others.

Scanning techniques that allow imaging of the brain and its specific areas are giving rise to new viewpoints. Diamond (2000) reviewed newer evidence of brain function and development to suggest that motor development and cognitive development may be more interrelated than previously thought, even to the extent of being fundamentally intertwined. She pointed to the following findings:

- The prolonged development of the prefrontal cortex (involved in complex cognitive operations) has been emphasized, but the development of the cerebellum (involved in motor functions), which is also prolonged, has not (see figure 5.11).
- Similarly, although many complex cognitive skills are recognized as developing into adolescence, it is overlooked that many complex motor skills also develop into adolescence.
- Functional imaging of the brain (e.g., magnetic resonance imaging while an individual performs a task) has demonstrated that the dorsolateral area in the prefrontal cortex and the neocerebellum in the contralateral hemisphere are coactivated during performance of cognitive tasks.
- Similar task characteristics activate both of these areas, such as difficult (rather than easy) cognitive tasks; a new task; or a task requiring a quick response, concentration, or greater memory demands.
- The prefrontal cortex may play a role in motor activity through connections with the cortical and subcortical areas that are important in motor control.
- The caudate nucleus in the basal ganglia (important in movement control) and dopamine, a neurotransmitter, are involved in neural circuits of both motor and cognitive functions.
- About half of children with attention-deficit/hyperactivity disorder have motor coordination problems, and some studies report that they have smaller cerebella.
- Children with dyslexia or specific language disorders frequently have motor deficits.
- Children with autism frequently have motor impairments.

Recent work has focused on a group of brain proteins called factors, especially brain-derived neurotrophic factor (BDNF), which is involved in building and maintaining the infrastructure of the nervous system. It both stimulates growth of neurons and protects against neuron loss. Moreover, BDNF strengthens connections between neurons. Animal studies have demonstrated increases in BDNF in rodents that exercised; the increase was in the hippocampus, an important center

TABLE 11.1   Stated Features of Various Contemporary Perceptual-Motor Programs

Factor	Typical features
Purpose of the program	Develops the ability to remember patterns of movement, sequences of sounds, and the look and feel of objects via training of the nervous system
	Enhances brain development by stimulating the 5 senses through movement
	Helps children become efficient movers and enhances learning readiness
	Develops gross motor skills and fine motor skills
	Improves self-esteem through success at play
	Replicates early movement experiences required to establish wiring of the brain
Intended participants	Preschool and primary school children
	Preschool children with speech and motor development delays
	Normally developing 2-, 3-, and 4-year-olds
	Special needs students
	Children with neurodevelopmental delays (learning difficulties, attention disorders, behavior problems)
Instructors	Teachers
	Professional-preparation students
	Physiotherapists
	Occupational and speech therapists
Context	Regular school offering
	Fee-based weekend programs
	Fee-based after-school programs
Location	Preschool
	Elementary school
	University
	Clinic
Activities	Gross motor skills
	Fine motor skills
	Swimming skills
	Rhythmic skills
	Visual-spatial skills (tracking objects, matching shapes)
	Ocular control activities (converging, tracking, fixating)
	Eye–hand coordination activities
	Eye–foot coordination activities
	Crossing the midline of the body
	Body awareness activities
	Spatial awareness activities
	Establishment of a preferred hand
	Balance activities
	Directionality activities
	Laterality activities
	Localizing touch
	Body concept activities
	Body image activities
	Clapping to rhythms
	Recognizing sound rhythms and patterns
	Locating a sound source
	Musical games
	Auditory discrimination and figure-and-ground activities

in the brain for learning and memory processes (Cotman & Berchtold, 2002). In addition, group of hormones called growth factors are released when circulation increases, as with exercise. These factors work with BDNF, and one of them stimulates capillary growth in the brain (Ratey, 2008). These growth factors and BDNF have a role in neurogenesis and in strengthening connections between neurons, which in turn is necessary for memory. Production of BDNF and growth factors declines with aging. Chapter 14 discusses a link between aerobic exercise and cognitive function in older adults.

All of these observations indicate greater interdependence of the brain in cognitive and motor tasks than was previously emphasized. Both thinking patterns and movement, once learned, are stored in primitive areas of the brain that were once thought to control only movement. This process allows higher brain centers to continue adapting to new experiences. Ivry and Keele (Ivry, 1993; Ivry & Keele, 1989; Keele & Ivry, 1990) also proposed that the lateral hemispheres of the cerebellum are involved in critical timing functions that are crucial to sensory, cognitive, and motor tasks. It is interesting to note that children with dyslexia have difficulty with bimanual tasks requiring timing precision (Wolff, Michel, Ovrut, & Drake, 1990). Several contemporary educators report success in promoting active learning for both normally developing and exceptional learners. Active learning is the notion that movement activates the brain and facilitates learning, in contrast to passive learning environments that require learners to sit quietly, watching and listening to a teacher (Hannaford, 1995; Jackson, 1993, 1995, 2000). Finally, Sibley and Etnier (2003) conducted a meta-analysis of studies on the relationship between physical activity and cognition in children; these studies included a variety of physical activities and a variety of cognitive assessments. A significant positive relationship was found between physical activity and cognitive functioning; the largest effects for cognitive assessment were seen specifically with perceptual skills tests.

Imagine you are a teacher. As we learn more about the connection between movement and learning, would your approach to instruction include teacher-centered activities that require students to simply follow directions or more student-centered activities such as movement exploration? Why?

Even with their common link to perceptual development, motor development and cognitive development have been studied separately for decades, if not centuries, and have been treated as distinct systems. Their conceptualization mimicked a belief that the brain centers for thought and the brain centers for controlling movement were more separate than, as we now know, they really are. Our thinking has been colored by this view. Momentum is building to approach the study of the cognitive, perceptual, and motor systems in more integrated ways, and we hope this approach will allow us to one day better understand the nature of the links between them.

For now, the ecological view of development embraces the notion of a close link between perception and action (Kellman & Arterberry, 1998). Ecological developmentalists believe that the task of starting with very little perception and poor motor control and matching them through trial and error is too monumental for infants to achieve in a matter of months. Instead, the ecological view holds that the newborn infant perceives the environment and many of its properties before the onset of purposeful movements. Thus, the infant has a somewhat limited perception, which guides a movement, which in turn generates additional perceptions. The cycle is repeated and the infant eventually refines perception. This sequence is termed a perception–action loop (Gibson, 1966, 1979). The difficulty with this view is that

KEY POINT
Exercise increases metabolic substances in the brain that can help build new neurons, especially in brain areas that are important to learning and memory.

KEY POINT
Motor development and cognitive development appear to be fundamentally interwoven.

we don't observe behaviors in infants that appear to be perception–action loops. Developmentalists do not yet know whether we simply have not found a way to measure the behavior or whether these loops do not exist.

Thinking back to our discussion of recent research in perceptual development, a slightly different view emerges: Perception develops ahead of movement skills. In infancy, new motor skills are acquired with guidance from the information obtained through perception. New actions in turn make new information available, and perceptual exploration is further refined (Kellman & Arterberry, 1998; von Hofsten, 1990). With this current perspective in mind, we now examine self-produced locomotion and its role in the refinement of perceptual abilities.

Self-Produced Locomotion

If action facilitates perceptual development, then some types of perception would be evident only after an infant has begun performing a specific action. Researchers typically have observed perception in infants of the same age but with varying loco-motor experience so that differences would be related to experience and not age. As mentioned earlier, researchers must use research paradigms in which experience varies naturally or use animal studies in which they can control conditions. In 1963, Held and Hein studied early motor activity in kittens. These researchers restricted the movements of some newborn kittens and permitted others to move. They kept the visual experience identical for all the kittens by placing them in pairs in a merry-go-round apparatus. One of the pair was harnessed but could walk around (active kitten), whereas the other was restricted to riding in a gondola (passive kitten) (figure 11.1). The passive kittens later failed to accurately judge depth and failed to exhibit paw placing or eye blinking when an object approached. Evidently, self-produced movement is related to the development of behavior depending on visual perception. There is also evidence of more brain growth and more efficient nervous system functioning in young animals when researchers provided them with perceptual-motor stimulation over and above the norm (Williams, 1986).

KEY POINT
Animal studies tend to support the notion that movement is necessary for normal perceptual development.

The visual cliff studies described in chapter 10 suggest that depth perception is present early in life. Other studies have suggested that avoidance of heights develops between 6 months and 1 year as a result of self-produced locomotor experience. Bertenthal, Campos, and Barrett (1984) found that prelocomotor infants given artificial locomotor experience by use of a baby walker (a seat in a frame that has wheels) responded to heights, whereas infants of the same age but without this artificial locomotor experience did not. In addition, one infant whose locomotor skills were delayed as a result of wearing a heavy cast did not respond to the visual cliff until self-produced locomotion began. Finally, infants who averaged 41 days of creeping experience were much more likely to avoid the visual cliff than were infants with 11 days of experience, even at identical ages. Thus, self-produced locomotion appears to facilitate development of depth perception. Once infants learn to avoid the visual cliff drop-off when crawling, they maintain the avoidance when learning to walk (Witherington, Campos, Anderson, Lejeune, & Seah, 2005).

 Imagine you're a therapist working with a toddler who cannot walk. What activities could you do that would facilitate the child's perceptual development?

Kermoian and Campos (1988) also investigated the link between infants' self-produced locomotion and their perception of spatial relationships by studying the infants' strategies in searching for objects. They gave infants a set of progressively

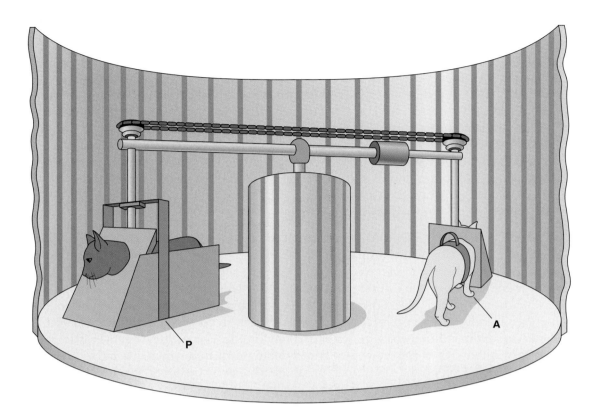

FIGURE 11.1   The apparatus Held and Hein used for equating motion and consequent visual feedback for an actively moving (A) and a passively moved (P) animal.

Reprinted by permission from Held and Hein 1963.

more difficult searching tasks (called object permanence tasks) ranging from retrieving a half-hidden object to retrieving objects under one of several cloths after the passage of time. Three groups of 8.5-month-old infants performed the tasks:

1. Prelocomotor infants
2. Prelocomotor infants with walker experience
3. Locomotor (creeping) infants

The more locomotor experience infants had, the better they scored. Other studies support the suggestion that locomotor experience facilitates development of **spatial perception**. Lockman (1984) found that a basic ability to detour around a barrier is present in 12-month-old infants. By testing infants longitudinally starting at age 8 months, Lockman identified a sequence of improvements in spatial perception:

Spatial perception is the perception that enables one to deal effectively with spatial properties, dimensions, and distances of objects and object relations in the environment.

- Infants first learn to retrieve an object hidden behind a cloth; they become aware that objects still exist even if they are hidden behind a barrier.
- Some weeks after developing this ability, infants can reach around a barrier to obtain their goal.
- Infants can move themselves around a barrier to obtain their goal. On average, several weeks pass between success in reaching around a barrier and success in traveling around it.

- Most infants can successfully detour around an opaque barrier before they can travel around a transparent barrier. Transparent barriers initially puzzle infants because visual and kinesthetic (tactile) cues conflict.

Thus, infants are able to deal with spatial relationships at increasing distances from their bodies. McKenzie and Bigelow (1986) further demonstrated that infants become more efficient by taking the shortest path around a barrier (figure 11.2) and that they can better adapt to a relocated barrier by 14 months of age. Hence, with increasing movement experience in the environment, infants perceive spatial relationships even at a distance from their bodies.

 WEB STUDY GUIDE   **Observe the developmental status of spatial perception in an infant in Lab Activity 11.1, Development of Spatial Perception, in the web study guide. Go to www.HumanKinetics.com/LifeSpanMotorDevelopment.**

Another line of research involves perception of surfaces. In these studies, researchers were interested in how locomotor experience influences the actions of infants when presented with different surfaces. For example, Gibson et al. (1987) presented infants with crawling experience and walking experience with a rigid surface (cloth over plywood) and a "deforming" surface (cloth over a waterbed). All of the infants traversed the surfaces, but the walkers hesitated to cross the deforming surface. They first stopped to explore the deforming surface, through both vision and touch, and eventually crossed the deforming surface by crawling. When presented the opportunity to cross either surface (rigid or deforming), the crawlers showed no preference but the walkers chose the rigid surface.

KEY POINT
Locomotor experience facilitates depth and spatial perception.

KEY POINT
Locomotor experience facilitates perception of surface texture and slope.

Adolph, Eppler, and Gibson (1993) also noted that walkers were more sensitive than crawlers to surface slopes. Crawlers, with less locomotor experience, almost always attempted to crawl up and down slopes even if the slopes were too steep for them. Walkers again tended to explore the surface, by patting it with their hands or feet or by stepping onto the sloped surface and rocking back and forth over their ankles. All walked up slopes of 10°, 20°, 30°, or 40°. They often refused steep descending slopes or used another form of locomotion, such as crawling down backward. Thus, the walkers had enough experience with surface slopes that they could immediately perceive which slopes did not afford walking. They quickly chose another form of locomotion appropriate for the surface slope.

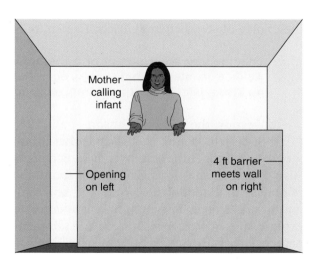

Infant's view

FIGURE 11.2 Room layout for a detour task. Infants can take the most efficient route around a barrier to their mothers (whom they can see over the barrier) by 14 months of age. By this age, they can also adapt when the barrier is relocated against the left wall. Younger infants usually take less efficient routes, such as approaching the barrier, then traveling along it, sometimes turning the wrong way and backtracking, or going to where the opening was before the barrier was relocated.

Perception of Affordances

Recall that the ecological view of perception and action is based on direct perception of the environment rather than indirect perception. Indirect perception is derived from an assessment of environmental characteristics, cognitive calculations, and projections based on those characteristics. Consistent with the notion of direct perception, developmentalists with an ecological perspective believe that we directly perceive what the objects and surfaces in the environment permit us to do, given our own capabilities. That is, we perceive **affordances** (see chapter 2).

Stair climbing provides a good example of an affordance. A set of stairs with an 8 in. (20 cm) rise between steps does not afford alternate-step climbing for an 18-month-old, as it does for an adult. A 24 in. (61 cm) rise does not afford alternate-step climbing for the average adult. As an individual grows and develops, her perception of affordances might change as her action capabilities change, even though an object's physical properties remain the same. Taking action, then, is a critically important aspect of the development of the perception–action system. Interaction with the environment is valuable for the perception of affordances.

If we perceive affordances rather than object characteristics, then individuals must be sensitive to the scale of their bodies. For example, perhaps individuals must be sensitive to their leg length in order to judge the "climbability" of any set of stairs. Warren (1984) tested this notion with adults and found that individuals perceived stairs with a riser height of more than 88% to 89% of their leg length to be "unclimbable" by means of alternate stepping. This model did not apply to older adults, whose affordances for stair climbing related more to strength and flexibility than to leg length (Konczak, Meuwssen, & Cress, 1988, cited in Konczak, 1990). Nor did the model apply to infants and toddlers. Infants in a study chose smaller step heights than did toddlers, but no anthropometric measurements related to the choice of step height (Ulrich, Thelen, & Niles, 1990).

 Imagine you are a parent or a therapist in an average home environment. Aside from stairs, what actions do certain objects or structures afford? How do these differ for older children, older adults, or individuals with disabilities?

Conversely, the work of Gibson et al. (1987) and Adolph, Eppler, and Gibson (1993), described earlier, indicates that infants can perceive affordances. Infants seem to remember the results of their own previous actions with surfaces and slopes. Also, Bushnell and Boudreau (1993) found that infants can perceive the properties of objects in the following order: size and temperature, texture and hardness, and weight and shape. These findings are consistent with infants' manual abilities to explore objects. Perception of size and temperature requires only clutching, whereas perception of texture and hardness requires rubbing and poking, and perception of weight and shape requires finger, hand, and arm movement. This is the same order in which these manipulations are acquired. The perception and the action proceed together.

Lockman (2000) suggested that infant tool use has its origins in perception–action routines repeatedly used by infants during the first year (figure 11.3). Through trial and error, infants gradually explore forms of tool use, relating objects to other objects and surfaces. In so doing, infants detect affordances. These are not affordances of individual tools, but affordances of the relationships between objects, marking a sharp contrast with the approach previously taken on infant tool use. In this still-prevailing perspective, tool use is assumed to be discontinuous,

---

Affordances are the actions or behaviors provided for or permitted to an individual by the places, objects, and events in and of an environment.

KEY POINT
Affordances incorporate our body scale, which is our size relative to the environment.

KEY POINT
If we perceive affordances rather than object characteristics, then the size of one's body in relation to environmental objects plays a role in that perception.

and the initial use of a tool is assumed to reflect a new level of representational thinking by the infant—an insight, so to speak. In the perception–action perspective, on the other hand, potential relationships between objects are detected from information directly perceived in the environment. Tool use depends on properties of both the tool and the surface or another object. So, trial-and-error tool use can be viewed as self-generated opportunity for perceptual learning (Lockman, 2000).

Individuals may use many types of body scales, and the important scales may change throughout life. Perhaps changes in a person's various body systems influence which scale he or she uses. Our sensitivity to body scaling has implications for skill instruction. For

FIGURE 11.3 The ability to reach, grasp, and control objects provides an infant with the opportunity to explore relationships with and detect affordances of these objects.

example, if a child cannot swing a big, heavy, adult tennis racket with one hand, the child cannot use adult technique in the sport. The large racket does not afford the adult style of movement. Either the racket must be scaled down to fit the child or the child might need to use two hands to swing the racket. Gagen, Haywood, and Spaner (2005) found that strength as well as size might be an important consideration in scaling equipment for ballistic tasks.

Body scaling helps us appreciate how important it is for those interested in motor development to understand the course of growth and aging. Continued research is necessary to determine the reference scales that individuals use for particular tasks. Such research would help determine whether it is indeed an affordance or individual characteristics of objects that are perceived.

KEY POINT
Infants have an increasing ability to detect affordances.

 If you were an early childhood or elementary physical education teacher, how would you use knowledge of body scales to select equipment for your students?

Evidence indicates that movement facilitates continued perceptual development. Recall the earlier discussion of neurological development. Greenough, Black, and Wallace (1987) hypothesized that, initially, an excess number of synapses forms among neurons. With continued development, some survive whereas others do not. Connections that are activated by sensory and motor experience survive; unused connections are lost. Synaptic proliferation prepares an organism for experiences—presumably the experiences common to all members of a species. Undergoing experiences during this sensitive period of development both promotes survival of the synaptic connections and strengthens those connections (Ratey, 2008).

KEY POINT
A neurological basis exists for positing the necessity of movement experience to perceptual development.

These theories need more experimental verification, but they provide a plausible explanation for the role of action in perceptual development (Bertenthal & Campos, 1987). They also imply that deprivation of action experience puts an individual at risk of deficient perceptual development.

Another way of looking at the interplay of perception and action is to examine the development of postural control and balance. Action must be coupled with perception so that individuals can deal with events or movements that disturb their posture and balance.

Postural Control and Balance

Postural control and balance are perfect examples of perception and action as an ecosystem. To control our posture in order to sit, stand, or assume any desired position, we must continually change our motor response patterns according to the perceptual information that specifies the environment and our bodies' orientation in it. Several perceptual systems are involved in maintaining posture and balance. Vision tells us how our bodies are positioned relative to the environment. Kinesthetic input from our bodies' proprioceptors tells us how our limbs and body parts are positioned relative to each other. Kinesthetic input from the vestibular system provides information about our head position and movement. Even the auditory system can contribute information about balance (Horak & MacPherson, 1995).

We must maintain posture and balance in an almost infinite number of situations. Sometimes we balance when stationary (static balance) and sometimes when moving (dynamic balance). We must also balance on a variety of body parts, not just two feet. Think of all the body parts on which gymnasts must balance in their various events. Sometimes we need to balance on surfaces other than the ground, such as a ladder. We might even have to balance without all the information we would like—for example, when we have to walk in the dark.

Given the number of perceptual systems involved in balance and the wide range of environmental and task constraints that are possible for any given balance task, the triangular model of constraints provides a good perspective on the development of balance. A developmental trend for a certain set of task and environmental constraints might differ from the trend for another set of constraints. In fact, movement scientists recognized some time ago that performance levels on various types of balancing tasks are specific to that task (Drowatzky & Zuccato, 1967). We discuss postural control and balance in infants in chapter 5. Now let's consider the development of balance in childhood through older adulthood.

Balance in Childhood

Balance performance improves on a variety of balance tasks from 3 to 19 years of age (Bachman, 1961; DeOreo & Wade, 1971; Espenschade, 1947; Espenschade, Dable, & Schoendube, 1953; Seils, 1951; Winterhalter, 1974). The exact nature of the improvement trend depends on the task. For example, on some tasks we might see a plateau in performance for several years. This could reflect the way we measure improvement on that particular task; perhaps the child is improving in a way not detected by our measurement. It is also possible that children begin to rely more on kinesthetic information and somewhat less on visual information for balance. Children 4 to 6 years of age have been observed to regress on moving platform tests, and children 3 to 6 years have shown both adultlike and nonadultlike postural responses to a moving room (Schmuckler, 1997). They take longer to respond than younger children and vary greatly in the way they respond (i.e., in how the various muscles are activated to regain balance). This finding does not seem to be accounted for by changes accompanying physical growth (e.g., changes in limb and trunk proportion and mass), which leads to the suspicion that shifts in reliance on different perceptual systems are perhaps involved (Woollacott, Debu, & Mowatt, 1987). By the time children reach the 7- to 10-year-old range, however, they show adultlike postural responses (Nougier, Bard, Fleury, & Teasdale, 1998; Shumway-Cook & Woollacott, 1985; Woollacott, Shumway-Cook, & Williams, 1989).

Balancing during locomotion is a challenging task. When we walk or run, for example, we must maintain our stability yet propel the body forward in order to travel. To do so, we probably use two frames of reference. One is the supporting surface, and the other is gravity. Another challenge is to control the degrees of freedom of movement at the various body joints. On one hand, individuals might stabilize the head on the trunk in order to minimize the movement they must control. On the other hand, they might stabilize head position in space and use the orientation of the head and trunk to control their equilibrium.

Assaiante and Amblard (1995; Assaiante, 1998) proposed a model to explain the development of balance in locomotion over the life span. The model describes four important periods. The first covers birth to the onset of standing and is characterized by a cephalocaudal direction of muscle control. The second includes the achievement of upright stance to about 6 years of age; during this time, coordination of the lower and upper body must be mastered. The third period, from about age 7 to sometime in adolescence, is characterized by the refinement of head stabilization in balance control. The fourth and last period, which begins in adolescence and extends through adulthood, is characterized by refined control of the degrees of freedom of movement in the neck. Thus, the task of childhood is to learn how the different frames of reference complement one another during movement. This is an intriguing model that may well stimulate future research on the development of dynamic balance.

 Think of your own experience in visiting an amusement park attraction or "haunted house" that used visual displays to confuse you. How did the visual display conflict with your other senses? Which of your systems were put into conflict? How did you maintain your balance (if you did)?

Balance Changes With Aging

In adulthood, individuals standing on a force platform (see the "Assessing Balance" sidebar) show a minimal amount of sway. If the platform is moved repetitively back and forth, adults use visual information to stabilize the head and upper body, and the muscle response to movement occurs in the ankles (Buchanan & Horak, 1999). When adults stand on such a platform and it is moved slightly or slowly but unexpectedly, they use an ankle strategy to regain balance. That is, they use lower leg muscles that cross the ankle joint to bring themselves upright once again. When the movement is larger or faster, a hip strategy is used; muscles crossing the hip and knee joints bring the center of gravity back over the base of support (Horak, Nashner, & Diener, 1990; Kuo & Zajac, 1993).

Older adults experience a decline in the ability to balance. Those over 60 sway more than younger adults when standing upright, especially if they are in a leaning position (Hasselkus & Shambes, 1975; Hellebrandt & Braun, 1939; Perrin,

Jeandel, Perrin, & Bene, 1997; Sheldon, 1963). Age-related changes in balance are also seen with older adults on movable platform tests. In comparison with young adults, slightly more time passes before an older adult's leg muscles respond after a perturbation in order to maintain balance, and sometimes the upper leg muscles respond first instead of the lower leg muscles, a pattern opposite that found in young adults. The strength of the muscles' response is more variable among repetitions in older adults (Perrin et al., 1997; Woollacott, Shumway-Cook, & Nashner, 1982, 1986).

Age-related changes in balance ability could be related to a variety of changes in the body's systems, especially in the nervous system. As mentioned previously, some older adults experience changes in the kinesthetic receptors, and these changes might be more extreme in the lower limbs than in the upper ones. Older adults might also be placed at a disadvantage due to vision changes as well as changes that

Assessing Balance

Balance can be assessed in many ways, both in field settings and in laboratories. Different assessments are used for static balance and dynamic balance. A device used in many laboratory settings is a force plate or force platform. A simple force plate consists of two square plates positioned one over the other with four pressure gauges in between the plates and at the four corners of the plates. The device is placed on the floor, or even set into the flooring to be level with the surface, so that individuals can stand on, walk across, or even jump on or off the plate.

The most basic force plate simply measures vertical force applied in the geometric center of the top plate. More complicated force plates can measure force at, and the location of, a center of pressure. Think about an individual standing on a force plate on one leg. As he or she sways and the body varies from perfect vertical, the center of pressure exerted on the force plate moves. The force plate can detect the location of the center of pressure, how far it moves, and when. The most advanced force plates can break the vector of the force exerted on the force plate into three spatial components. So, force plates can measure changing pressures under the feet as someone stands on or moves across the platform.

When researchers are interested in static balance, they can ask individuals to stand on a force plate and measure both how far the individual sways and the velocity of sway. Individuals can stand on one foot or two feet and in any kind of stance, such as side stride or split stride. Researchers also can ask individuals to lean as far as possible without losing balance to quantify the ability to control the body or the maximum limits of stability.

Computerized dynamic posturography assessments incorporate a force plate. These devices are used to study the reaction of individuals to being slightly thrown off balance by virtue of the force plate tilting. By controlling the surrounding visual field with a three-sided enclosure around the participant, researchers can present conditions with normal vision or no vision and with a surround that is stable or that moves as the individual sways. Researchers can also control whether the force plate moves, and in what direction, by rotating or translating. This allows them to study the visual, vestibular, and somatosensory systems and their interactions in balance, including when balance is perturbed and the person must react to regain or maintain balance. Electromyographs can be used in conjunction with systems such as this to record how the muscles are activated to regain balance.

occur in the vestibular receptors and nerves in adults over 75 (Bergstrom, 1973; Johnsson & Hawkins, 1972; Rosenhall & Rubin, 1975). A decrease in fast-twitch muscle fibers or a loss of strength could hamper an older adult's quick response to changes in stability, as might arthritic conditions in the joints.

Perrin et al. (1997) recorded electromyograph activity in older adults during a backward tilt of a movable force platform. They observed some of the reflexes in the lower legs that were not involved in balance control, as well as the responses necessary for regaining balance. By comparing the time from the balance perturbation with the onset of each of these muscle responses in young and older adults, the investigators determined that nerve conduction speed in both the peripheral and central nervous systems was slower in the older adults. Thus, the declines in balance performance with aging most likely are associated with age-related changes in a variety of systems.

KEY POINT
The difficulties that older adults experience with balance most likely reflect changes in more than one system.

Falls are a significant concern in older adults. In fact, falls are the leading cause of accidental death for people over 75 years old. A common result of falling, especially among older adults with osteoporosis, is fracture of the spine, hip (pelvis or femur), or wrist. Complications of such a fracture can result in death. Even when older adults recover, they experience heavy health care costs, a period of inactivity, and dependence on others. A fear of falling again can make them change their lifestyles or be overly cautious in subsequent activities.

Woollacott (1986) studied the reaction of older adults when a movable platform tipped forward or backward to perturb their balance unexpectedly. Half the older adults she observed lost their balance the first time, but these adults learned to keep their balance after a few more tries. Thus, older adults are more liable to fall on a slippery surface than young adults but are capable of improving their stability with practice. Campbell et al. (1997) and Campbell, Robertson, Gardner, Norton, and Buchner (1999) compared the number of falls over a 1-year period in women over 80 years of age who participated in an individualized exercise program stressing strength and balance with the number of falls in women over 80 who did not participate in an exercise program. The number of falls in the exercise group (88) was significantly lower than the number of falls in the other group (152). Prevention and rehabilitation programs, then, are useful in reducing the risk of falls in older adults, but they must be ongoing. In chapter 15, we discuss the role of aerobic exercise in maintaining the speed of cognitive processes.

KEY POINT
Exercise programs focused on improving strength and balance can reduce the risk of falls in older adults.

 WEB STUDY GUIDE   Test several people on balance tasks and rate the balance tasks in Lab Activity 11.2, Development of Balance, in the web study guide. Go to www.HumanKinetics.com/LifeSpanMotorDevelopment.

 Imagine you have a grandparent who comes to live with you. What types of surfaces and conditions around your house could be more likely to lead to falls for him or her than for a young adult? What steps could you take to reduce the chances of a fall?

Summary and Synthesis

Perception and action are an ecosystem. Actions are coupled to perceptions, as shown by postural and balance responses. There is some disagreement about the exact role of action in the development of perception but little disagreement over its importance. Experience with movement has been shown to facilitate perception of space, including depth, surfaces, and slopes.

Perception–action coupling for posture and balance is evident in young infants. However, it appears that a developmental trend determines which perceptual system gets priority. Young infants depend more on visual information when it conflicts with kinesthetic information. With advancing development, this finding is reversed. Older children, youths, and young adults rarely fall when placed in an environment in which vision and kinesthesis conflict. They have learned to rely more on kinesthetic information. Older adults show changes in their responses to balance perturbations. Although changes in the perceptual system could affect these responses, the changes seem to occur more in the timing and pattern of the muscle responses to perceptual information.

Thelen (1995) summed up the relationship of perception and action: "People perceive in order to move and move in order to perceive. What, then, is movement but a form of perception, a way of knowing the world as well as acting on it?"

 ## Reinforcing What You Have Learned About Constraints

TAKE A SECOND LOOK

Think about the dilemma presented at the beginning of this chapter. It has always been hard for parents and teachers to know when to push children to take on certain learning tasks and when to allow children to put off those challenges. On one hand they want their children to be successful, but on the other they are afraid their children will be behind others in their development. Recent research appears to show that cognitive, perceptual, and motor systems develop together. If development in one system falls behind development in the others, we know from the model of constraints that it can become a rate limiting system that holds back the others. Hopes for artificially controlling the rate of development are generally met with failure. What parents and professionals can do is manipulate the environment and manipulate task goals to set the stage for advances in development when individuals are ready to make those advances.

TEST YOUR KNOWLEDGE

1. What are some reasons that contemporary researchers think cognitive and motor development are more intertwined than previously thought?

2. What seems to be the role of experience with self-produced locomotion in the development of perception? Which aspects of perception are most affected?

3. Considering your answer to the preceding question, what would be the repercussions for perceptual and motor development of depriving an infant of locomotor experience?

4. How did views of perceptual-motor development change in the 20th century?

5. What is an affordance? What does the notion of affordance have to do with adapting equipment size to the size of a performer?

6. On what perceptual systems do children rely for balance, and how does this change with development?

7. What changes in various body systems might lead to a higher frequency of falls in older adults? What might reduce the risk of falling?

LEARNING EXERCISE 11.1

Cognitive and Motor Deficits

Choose one of the following disorders: autism, dyslexia, developmental coordination disorder, or attention-deficit/hyperactivity disorder. Research the characteristics of the disorder to determine whether both cognitive and motor deficits are commonly associated with it. Describe specific characteristics of deficits in each area (cognitive and motor), as appropriate. What accommodations would be necessary for a child with this disorder in a regular physical education class offered at the elementary school level?

Functional Constraints to Motor Development

Part V focuses on the effect of the sociocultural environment—for example, constraints that exist as a function of family influences or cultural belief systems—on individual functional constraints. Functional constraints can include motivation, attitude, self-concept, perception of a gender role, and knowledge about a topic. Especially when working with children, we must wait for individual *structural* constraints to undergo change through growth and maturation. In contrast, *functional* constraints can change more quickly. For example, a teacher could set a task goal that interacts with an individual's high level of motivation to bring about a rather rapid change in motor behavior. Not all functional constraints, however, change quickly. Self-concept is shaped over many years and is influenced by social interactions, and knowledge about a sport is often acquired over several years of experience in playing that sport.

Functional constraints and environmental constraints interact richly. For example, sociocultural norms strongly influence perceived gender roles; in turn, one's perceived gender role influences the types of physical activity that one views as appropriate. Even the popularity of certain sports or dance forms in a culture can influence the knowledge that someone living in the culture possesses about that sport or dance.

This part of the text examines functional constraints and the changes they undergo over the life span. Chapter 12 considers the role of society and culture in influencing individuals' choice of physical activities and play environments. Chapter 13 discusses how environmental constraints influence the functional constraints of self-esteem and motivation and how that interaction influences choices about physical activities. Chapter 14 explores how the amount of knowledge people acquire about a particular activity influences their play and participation in that activity.

Suggested Reading

Coakley, J. (2007). *Sport in society: Issues and controversies* (9th ed.). St. Louis: McGraw-Hill.

Giuliano, T., Popp, K., & Knight, J. (2000). Footballs versus Barbies: Childhood play activities as predictors of sport participation by women. *Sex Roles, 42,* 159–181.

Greendorfer, S.L. (1992). Sport socialization. In T.S. Horn (Ed.), *Advances in sport psychology* (pp. 201–218). Champaign, IL: Human Kinetics.

Heywood, L. (1998). *Pretty good for a girl.* New York: Free Press.

Lorber, J. (1994). Believing is seeing: Biology as ideology. *Gender and Society, 7,* 568–581.

Parish, L.E., & Rudisill, M.E. (2006). HAPPE: Promoting physical play among toddlers. *Young Children, 61*(3), 32.

Valentini, N.C., & Rudisill, M.E. (2004). Effectiveness of an inclusive mastery climate intervention on the motor skill development of children. *Adapted Physical Activity Quarterly, 21,* 285–294.

12

Social and Cultural Constraints in Motor Development

The Effects of Environmental Constraints

 CHAPTER OBJECTIVES

This chapter

- discusses the role of sociocultural constraints in motor development;
- defines the role of specific social agents, such as parents and schools, in individual development; and
- explains the socialization process and how it differs for various groups.

Looking Past the Skirts in U.S. Field Hockey

Most citizens of the United States, if asked to conjure up a group of athletes playing field hockey, would envision women in plaid skirts running around a field whacking a ball with curved sticks. Fans with this picture in their heads might have been surprised to see Andrew Zayac and Jon Geerts playing at the 2006 National Field Hockey League championship or Cornelius Tietze playing at the 2010 Pennsylvania high school, PIAA Field Hockey Championship. The vast majority of field hockey players are women, but Title IX legislation allows men to participate as well. Zayac and Geerts played on the team from the University of Maryland at College Park, which took home the 2006 club crown, and Tietze played on Wyoming Seminary's AA championship team. However, people living Pakistan, India, or the Netherlands might be more surprised by the scarcity of men on the field; in those and other countries, the majority of athletes playing field hockey are men. In fact, both Geerts and Tietze grew up in Europe playing field hockey. Clearly, both males and females can play field hockey. When growing up in a particular culture, people assign an "appropriate" gender (e.g., the notion that field hockey is for girls) to different sports.

When selecting sports in which to participate, people are influenced by the culturally specific gender associations of specific sports. Field hockey is a perfect example. No one would think twice if a boy played field hockey in Europe; in the United States, however, only the occasional boy plays. When we think of this phenomenon in terms of constraints, we can see that no individual constraints discourage or prevent boys (as a group) from playing field hockey. The constraints have more to do with the social or cultural environment. Society as a whole influences the activity choices that individuals make, and girls and boys alike benefit from the addition of new athletic role models. When social or cultural factors influence the types of physical activity in which people get involved, those factors act as sociocultural constraints. You might not have considered sociocultural constraints as important to motor development, but in this chapter you will discover that these ever-present constraints can have a great influence on motor behavior throughout the life span.

The idea that social and cultural aspects can influence motor development may come as a surprise to a maturationist. If you believe that genetics determines development, then you would be hard pressed to think of society as a developmental agent. However, those who follow an ecological perspective believe that social and cultural influences (in the form of environmental constraints) may greatly influence and interact with individual and task constraints. This means that media coverage of events such as women's wrestling and ice hockey may encourage participation in these sports by changing some of the social and cultural stereotypes associated with females in sport.

Social and Cultural Influences as Environmental Constraints

In chapter 1, we introduce the idea of sociocultural influences as environmental constraints—the idea that sociocultural attitudes of groups of people either encourage or discourage certain motor behaviors. These factors are considered environmental constraints because they reflect a general attitude or belief system present either in society at large or in certain subcultures. If such attitudes are pervasive enough, they can modify someone's behavior. They may not be obvious at all, yet they may still exert a powerful influence on how individuals move. Just as temperature and ambient light can fill a room, field, or community, so can attitudes, values, norms, and stereotypes envelop us. Even as late as the 1970s girls were not expected, or in some cases even allowed, to participate in some organized sports, such as baseball and ice hockey. This attitude about girls in sport meant that the opportunity to play organized and even pickup sports was limited. In essence, this attitude discouraged sport participation for many girls, especially after puberty. However, the passage of Title IX (requiring equal opportunity for girls and women in sport) in 1972 drastically changed the landscape of sport in the United States, making it more possible and, in time, socially acceptable for girls and women to participate in sport.

Society and culture can have a profound effect on an individual's movement behaviors, particularly in the area of sport and physical activity (Clark, 1995). Sociocultural elements such as gender, race, religion, and national origin can all direct one's future movement behavior (Lindquist, Reynolds, & Goran, 1998). Even the media encourage and promote different types of physical activities (e.g., those that are gender specific) to mass audiences (Koivula, 2000; Messner, Duncan, & Jensen, 1993; Wigmore, 1996). A simple example illustrates how sociocultural constraints work: Think about who the most successful American athlete was during the past 10 years. Many athletes may come to mind, such as LeBron James, Tom Brady, or Mia Hamm. Most likely, you imagine a trim, muscular individual who plays a professional sport in the United States. However, if we asked this question of someone from Japan, he or she might picture a sumo wrestler (figure 12.1). Most Americans would not even know the names of sumo wrestlers. More important, in the context of motor development, most American children would not aspire to become sumo wrestlers and most American adults would not attempt to participate in sumo wrestling, regardless of individual constraints such as body type (which may actually encourage participation in some cases). In the United States, Sumo wrestling is not encouraged as a sport. Thus, society and culture influence the choice of sport or physical activity in which one participates; that is, they act as environmental constraints, encouraging certain movement activities while discouraging others. The chances that a young American boy or girl would pursue a career in sumo wrestling are slim. As a result, an entire group of movements (those associated with sumo wrestling) are discouraged and may never be performed; over time, this constraint interacts with individual constraints to limit or even prevent the emergence of these movements.

Participating in physical activities contributes to motor development. The benefits of experience in physical activity are well known and include improved physical and emotional health. In addition, sport may influence the behavioral patterns of participants (e.g., by teaching leadership and other skills). Thus, it makes sense to provide opportunities for all people to participate in sport and physical activity from an early age and throughout the life span. However, decisions to participate

KEY POINT
Societal and cultural beliefs, attitudes, and stereotypes can encourage or discourage motor behaviors. These are ever-present environmental constraints.

FIGURE 12.1 While quite popular in Asian countries, sumo wrestling is not followed intently in America.

in sport or maintain a physically active lifestyle can have as much to do with the social milieu as with individual constraints. For example, the individual constraints of most typically developing American children allow them to participate in a wide variety of activities, yet many choose computer and video games and television over playing outdoors. Why?

 What are some of the most important social and cultural elements (people, places, and so on) that have influenced you during your life? How have these influences changed from the time you were an infant to the present?

An individual's early socialization in sport and physical activity is a key factor in motor development and the likelihood of later participation. People and situations continue to influence individuals in their choice of activities throughout their lives. For example, your peers influence your recreational activities and lifestyle choices. These activities can be physical (pickup basketball versus video games), academic (library versus study group), and social (movies versus barhopping), among others. The **socialization process**—as related to sport and physical activities, including the individuals who are influential in the process—deserves attention as a major environmental constraint in one's motor development.

Three major elements of the socialization process lead an individual to learn a societal role, as shown in figure 12.2 (Greendorfer, 1992; Kenyon & McPherson, 1973):

1. Significant others (influential or important people, called socializing agents)
2. Social situations (places where socialization takes place—schools, home, playgrounds)
3. Personal attributes (individual constraints)

> The process by which one learns a social role in groups with certain values, morals, and rules is one's **socialization process**.

We examine the first two of these elements to see their influence and importance in the process of socialization into sport and physical activity. Of course, the third element, personal attributes, represents an interaction between environmental constraints (socializing agents and situations) and individual constraints. Among the socializing agents are family members, peers, teachers, and coaches. This section examines the influences these people provide—and how they might encourage or discourage certain motor behaviors. First, however, we examine a cultural phenomenon that cuts across many contexts: gender typing in sport and physical activities.

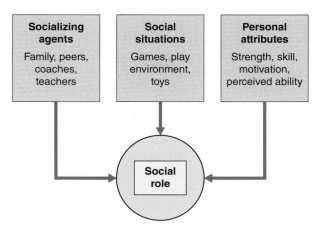

FIGURE 12.2   The three major elements of the socialization process that lead to the learning of a societal role for participation in physical activity.
Based on Kenyon and McPherson 1973.

KEY POINT
Significant others (e.g., parents and friends) and social situations (e.g., school or sports teams) contribute to an individual's socialization process.

Sociocultural Constraints in Action: Gender-Specific Stereotyped Behaviors

Significant others enter any context with socially and culturally prescribed notions of how they and others should act. Examination of one such notion, that of gender-specific stereotyping, shows just how potent sociocultural constraints can be. In general, people are born physiologically either male or female; their biological characteristics determine their **sex**. In contrast, **gender** is a culturally determined sociological construct that differentiates between men ("masculine") and women ("feminine") (Eitzen & Sage, 2003).

Parents and other significant socializing agents often encourage children toward what they perceive as gender-appropriate behaviors, based on each child's biological characteristics (Fagot & Leinbach, 1996; Fagot, Leinbach, & O'Boyle, 1992; Lorber, 1994). In terms of developing motor skills, significant others steer boys toward "masculine" and girls toward "feminine" sports and physical activities (Royce, Gebelt, & Duff, 2003; Shakib & Dunbar, 2004). This practice is often termed **gender typing**, or gender-role stereotyping. Children begin to learn these gender roles early, perhaps as early as their first year (Fagot & Leinbach, 1996).

Traditionally, Western societies gender-type participation in sport and physical activities. Certain sports (e.g., football, baseball, and wrestling) are identified as masculine and others (e.g., figure skating, gymnastics, and field hockey) are identified as feminine. In addition, Westerners consider sport to be important and appropriate for boys; however, that attitude doesn't always carry through for girls. Therefore, adults often permit and encourage vigorous, outgoing, rough-and-tumble play for toddler boys whereas they may be more likely to discourage girls from (or even punish them for) running, climbing, or venturing away from parents (Campbell & Eaton, 2000; DiPietro, 1981; Eaton & Enns, 1986; Eaton & Keats, 1982; Fagot & Leinbach, 1983; Lewis, 1972; Liss, 1983; Lloyd & Smith, 1985; McBride-Chang & Jacklin, 1993). Society reinforces constrained, sedentary

Sex refers to biological characteristics used to determine whether individuals are classified as male or female.

Gender refers to culturally defined sociological characteristics used to differentiate between males and females.

Gender typing, or gender-role stereotyping, occurs when a parent or significant other encourages activities that are deemed "gender appropriate."

types of play for girls, and thus many girls self-select away from vigorous play (Greendorfer, 1983), which leaves a comparatively small number of girls as active participants in vigorous, skilled play. Although the number of girls participating in high school sports has drastically increased since the inception of Title IX, girls still make up less than half the overall number of participants (Stevenson, 2007). Furthermore, girls are more likely to drop out of sport and activity participation after high school.

Why is the issue of gender typing important for girls and boys? For girls, such limited involvement and practice may not allow them to develop their motor skills to their full potential. Even girls who do participate may feel that all-out effort and skilled performance are gender inappropriate. This, in turn, could affect a girl's or woman's motivation for participating, for training, or for striving for high achievement standards that rival those of boys and men. At the same time, boys may feel forced into participating in gender-appropriate sports they dislike. Worse yet, they may drop out of physical activity altogether rather than be subjected to participating in an undesired but gender-typed sport. Thus, this pervasive societal influence on boys' and girls' sport participation may factor into measurements of skill and fitness that compare the sexes. This is an important consideration in the context of an integrated model of interacting constraints. What appear to be fitness or skill differences in boys and girls based on physiological makeup (sex) may in fact be related to a lifetime of stereotyped influences (gender) (Campbell & Eaton, 2000).

Despite a growing awareness during the 1970s and 1980s that these societal roles might limit girls' opportunities to enjoy the many benefits of sport participation, parents did not seem to change their contact patterns with their children. Research studies in the mid-1980s confirmed that parents still tended to interact differently with sons and daughters in play environments (Power, 1985; Power & Parke, 1983, 1986; see Williams, Goodman, & Green, 1985, on "tomboys"). For example, parents tended to direct their girls' play but allowed boys more opportunities for independent, exploratory play (Power, 1985). Although many changes seemed to take place during the 1990s, research still indicates that boys and girls received stereotypical messages about participation in physical activity (Coakley, 1998; Eitzen & Sage, 2003). Some research from the 21st century suggests that these roles have not yet changed. In a 2003 study by McCallister, Blinde, and Phillips, middle-school-age girls were surveyed on their beliefs about and attitudes toward girls and boys in physical activity and sport. Not only did the girls studied perceive boys as more athletic and physically capable and associate being an athlete with being a male, they also perceived athleticism as a negative trait in a girl. Overall, the researchers found that traditional, stereotypical beliefs held true in this sample. Some research indicates that times are changing: In a sample of 565 university-aged students, Royce, Gebelt, and Duff (2003) found that both men and women perceived female athletes as respected. Overall, the sample studied did not see being feminine and being an athlete as mutually exclusive, suggesting a change in negative stereotypes related to women in sport.

What happens to girls who defy gender-role stereotypes? Giuliano, Popp, and Knight (2000) studied 84 Division III female college students, both athletes and nonathletes. They found that as children the athletes tended to play with "masculine" toys and games, were considered "tomboys," and played primarily with boys or mixed-gender groups, whereas the nonathletes did not. This finding suggests that, rather than harming the females in any way, these early "masculine" experiences may have encouraged them to participate in athletics and physical activities throughout college—and perhaps beyond. Given the importance of a physically active lifestyle, then, parents may wish to avoid rigid adherence to gender-typed behaviors for their daughters.

 WEB STUDY GUIDE   Examine television commercials and the packaging of toys for evidence of gender-role stereotyping in Lab Activity 12.1, Examining Gender-Role Stereotyping, in the web study guide. Go to www.HumanKinetics. com/LifeSpanMotorDevelopment.

Significant Others: People's Values Acting as Constraints

Significant others, or **socializing agents,** are the people most likely to play a role in an individual's socialization process—family members, peers, teachers, and

Significant others, or **socializing agents,** are family members, peers, teachers, coaches, and others who are involved in the socialization process of an individual.

Can Laws Change Constraints? Effects of Title IX on Girls' and Women's Sport Participation

Before the passage of Title IX, far more boys than girls participated in high school athletics. In 1971, fewer than 300,000 female athletes participated in high school sports compared with almost 4 million male athletes (Reith, 2004). Some argued that boys were biologically predisposed to sport participation; that is, more boys participate in sport because their sex is an individual constraint that encourages athletics. This argument provided a biological rationale for providing boys with more athletic opportunities than were provided for girls. But was biology the reason for the vast difference in participation numbers, or was this difference socially constructed? Title IX, passed in 1972, provided a unique chance to examine this question. Title IX states, "No person in the United States shall, on the basis of sex, be excluded from participation in, be denied the benefits of, or be subjected to discrimination under any education program or activity receiving federal financial assistance." In terms of its effect on sport, the law mandated that educational programs strive for more gender equity. (For a full description of Title IX and its effect on sport, see Acosta & Carpenter, 2008, or Reith, 2004).

Times have changed since 1971. More than 7 million high school students participated in athletics between 2005 and 2006. Of these, 3 million were girls and 4.2 million were boys (Howard & Gillis, 2007; Stevenson, 2007). These numbers show that participation in high school sports has expanded for both genders. What trends have appeared since 1972 in the types of sports high school students select? It appears that more high school athletes—both boys and girls—select gender-neutral sports, whereas participation in highly gendered sports has tended to increase more slowly (football is the major exception to this trend; Stevenson, 2007). In 1972, boys played football more than any other sport, followed by basketball and track. These remained the most popular sports for boys in 2004 and 2005, although baseball and soccer were increasing in popularity. Girls participate in basketball, track and field, fast-pitch softball, and volleyball in the greatest numbers. The overall increase in athletic participation and the specific increase in participation among girls suggest that the constraints discouraging participation were not individual but rather were related to the sociocultural environment.

FIGURE 12.3   Significant others such as coaches may influence the socialization process throughout childhood.

coaches (figure 12.3). People who act as socializing agents should be considered constraints because they will encourage or discourage certain motor behaviors. This section examines how each of these groups might influence participation in sport and physical activity.

The roles that parents, peers, teachers, and coaches play in the socialization of children can vary with the gender of a child. In addition, the gender of the person serving as a model for behavior may differentially influence the child's internalization of the behavior. The result of such socialization can constrain a child to very specific types of physical activities and virtually eliminate others.

Family Members

A person's family has a major influence in the process of socialization into physical activities, as well as other pursuits, in part because the family's influence begins so early in a child's life (Kelly, 1974; Pargman, 1997; Snyder & Spreitzer, 1973, 1978; Weiss & Barber, 1996). In fact, the family may be the only source of social interaction that an infant has—and therefore the primary source of social constraints. From their very first interactions, family members expose their infants to certain experiences and attitudes. They reinforce the behaviors deemed appropriate through their gestures, praise, and rewards; at the same time, they punish inappropriate behaviors. The process is systematic, but at times it is so subtle that family members may hardly realize what and how they communicate to the infant.

Parents   When someone participates in physical activities after early childhood, he probably reflects his parents' interest and encouragement during the early years. Parents can encourage children to engage in either physical or sedentary activities. This may relate to the participation habits of the parent (DiLorenzo, Stucky-Ropp, VanderWal, & Gotham, 1998). As children become physically active, parents can encourage or discourage games and, eventually, specific sports or physical activities.

Parents' early involvement could lead to a lifetime of participation in physical activities for a child (Weiss & Barber, 1996). About 75% of eventual sport participants become involved in sport by age 8 (Greendorfer, 1979; Snyder & Spreitzer, 1976). In fact, the best predictor of adult sport involvement is participation during childhood and adolescence (Greendorfer, 1979; Loy, McPherson, & Kenyon, 1978; Snyder & Spreitzer, 1976). It follows, then, that a parent's early bias toward or away from physical activities can have lasting consequences. Although Title IX may be opening new doors for girls in terms of parental expectations for gendered activity, things might not have changed much for boys. In a 2007 study, Kane determined that parents perceived gender nonconformity in their preschool children as primarily positive—but only within a limited range for sons. At the same time, the parents in this study reported that it was important for their sons to conform to normative standards of masculinity.

Individual parents may play different roles in socializing children into physical activity. Snyder and Spreitzer (1973) proposed that a child's same-sex parent is most influential in the extent of that child's sport involvement. Further, McPherson (1978) suggested specifically that mothers serve as sport role models for their daughters. This notion was supported by DiLorenzo et al. (1998), who found that for eighth- and ninth-grade girls, their mothers' physical activity and support were predictors for physical activity. Some researchers believe that fathers more strictly reinforce gender-appropriate behavior, which would include sport participation for boys (Lewko & Greendorfer, 1988). Greendorfer and Lewko (1978) identified fathers rather than mothers as a major influence in the sport involvement of both boys and girls. In contrast, Lewko and Ewing (1980) found that fathers influenced boys between the ages of 9 and 11 years who were highly involved in sport and that mothers influenced highly involved girls. In order to become involved, girls seemed to need a higher level of encouragement from their families than boys did, and they needed it from many members of the family. A similar pattern was found in Japanese children (Ebihara, Ikeda, & Miyashita, 1983). Although the research does not definitively indicate a differential role for mothers and fathers, parents clearly influence and affect the choices their children make in physical activities.

During the 1980s and 1990s, girls' and women's participation in sport and physical activity became more recognized and widespread. Furthermore, it has become far more socially acceptable for women to participate in sports (e.g., soccer and ice hockey) that have been gender-typed as male in the past. For example, in 2006 and 2007, more than 5,000 high school girls participated in wrestling, more than 4,000 participated in flag football, and more than 7,000 participated in ice hockey (Howard & Gillis, 2007). Sports leagues for both genders have begun to include divisions for adults of different ages and skill levels, reflecting an increased interest in sport past high school and college. In addition, more opportunities exist for women and men to participate in nonsport physical activities ranging from spinning to step aerobics to cardio kickboxing. This increase in both types and opportunities of activities for parents will likely have a positive effect on the socialization of children into physical activity.

Siblings   Siblings form an infant's first playgroup and thus may act as important socialization agents into physical activity. For example, both brothers (Weiss & Knoppers, 1982) and sisters (Lewko & Ewing, 1980) can influence girls' sport participation. Studies suggest that African American boys see athletes as their role models and that their male siblings shape their idea of a role model (Assibey-Mensah, 1998). On the other hand, some children and teens report that older siblings were not important in their sport involvement (Greendorfer & Lewko, 1978; Patriksson, 1981). Thus, it is possible that for most children siblings merely reinforce the socialization pattern into physical activity established by parents rather than act as a major socializing force in themselves (Lewko & Greendorfer, 1988).

How Do Race, Ethnicity, and Other Factors Affect the Role of the Family in Physical Activity Socialization?   Various investigators have reached different conclusions about the influence of family members on socialization into physical activity. Greendorfer and Lewko (1978) attempted to clarify these various conclusions by questioning children from a broad range of social backgrounds. They found some differences in the patterns of significant influences. The significant other who exerted the most influence on socialization into physical activity varied somewhat among children according to sex, social background, race, and geographic location. For example, fathers were influential in socializing Caucasian American but not African American boys into sport (Greendorfer & Ewing, 1981). In contrast, Lindquist et al. (1998) found few differences in children's physical activity based on ethnicity when they controlled for social class and family background. This finding suggests that the roles of race, ethnicity, social background, and other factors in family socialization are more complex and difficult to characterize on a group basis. In fact, this complexity supports our notion of motor development: Socially and culturally specific agents constrain motor behaviors of individuals in different ways, leading to the emergence of different motor behaviors. We should not generalize about social agents but rather keep in mind that diverse patterns of influence may exist.

Peers

A child's peers have the potential to reinforce or counteract the sport socialization process begun in the family (Bigelow, Tesson, & Lewko, 1996; Brown, Frankel, & Fennell 1990; Greendorfer & Lewko, 1978; Weiss & Barber, 1996). If a peer group tends to participate in active play or sport, its individual members are drawn to such activities. If the group prefers passive activities, its individual members tend to follow that lead. Adult athletes typically report that peer groups or friends influenced the extent of their sport participation when they were in school, although the strength of this influence varies by sport. The first peer group that a child encounters is typically a playgroup. Children typically become involved in such groups from a very young age (some playgroups begin when children are still in infancy) and continue in them during their early school years.

Boys and girls from several countries, including the United States, Japan, and Canada, have reported that peers influenced their childhood sport participation (Ebihara et al., 1983; Greendorfer & Ewing, 1981; Greendorfer & Lewko, 1978; Yamaguchi, 1984). During preadolescence, children enter more formalized peer groups, such as cliques. These peers continue to be influential during adolescence (Brown, 1985; Brown et al., 1990; Butcher, 1983, 1985; Higginson, 1985; Patrick et al., 1999; Patriksson, 1981; Schellenberger, 1981; Smith, 1979; Weiss & Barber, 1996; Yamaguchi, 1984). In fact, among the women she questioned, Greendorfer (1976) found that the peer group was the only socializing agent that influenced sport involvement throughout all phases of the life cycle studied: childhood, adolescence, and young adulthood. Other socializing agents were important at some ages but not at others. For example, the family, so important to young children, probably is less influential for adolescents.

Peers often provide a stronger influence for participation in team sports than for participation in individual sports during childhood and adolescence (Kenyon & McPherson, 1973). Children's and adolescents' supportive peer groups are usually made up of others of the same sex. For adults, especially women, and particularly after marriage, spouses and friends of the opposite sex become more influential in either encouraging or discouraging involvement in certain activities (Loy et al., 1978). As individuals leave school and enter new social environments as members of the workforce, they often leave their peer groups. If a peer group was sport oriented, a reduction in sport involvement might follow. On the other hand, new peer groups at the workplace could stimulate sport involvement; the individual might, for example, join a team in a recreational sport league or perhaps participate in company-sponsored exercise and recreational programs (Loy et al., 1978).

It is likely that the typical middle-aged adult, even one who was involved in sport as a young adult, reduces sport involvement. A study by Ebrahim and Rowland (1996) found that of 704 women aged 44 to 93 years, only 25% took part in vigorous activity during the week before the study. This trend might be due in part to a lack of programs aimed specifically at middle-aged and older adults. However, this has been changing in recent years as the emphasis on fitness that began in the late 1970s has led to greater availability of exercise and recreation programs for members of these age groups. In addition, adult participation in sport and exercise programs has become acceptable and even desirable in Western societies. Peer groups appear to be essential for adherence to exercise, so they may be part of the initial reason for joining a recreational group. Once involved, adults keep participating to be part of a peer group.

Despite the strong influence of peer groups on sport participation throughout life, it is still not clear that membership in a sport-oriented peer group always precedes participation—that is, that a person is drawn to an activity because of a desire to associate with peers. It is possible that individuals first select groups that fit their interests, including an interest in sport (Loy et al., 1978). Although it is unclear which comes first, the interest in sport and the desire to be a part of a peer group make it likely that an individual will continue to participate and to select membership in active groups. Peers apparently play just as important a role in sport socialization as the family plays (Lewko & Greendorfer, 1988).

Coaches and Teachers

Coaches and teachers can also influence an individual's involvement in sport and physical activity (Greendorfer & Lewko, 1978). Male athletes consistently report that coaches and teachers influenced both their participation in and their selection of sports, particularly when they were adolescents and young adults (Ebihara et al., 1983; Kenyon & McPherson, 1973). Female athletes report that teachers and coaches influenced them during childhood (Greendorfer & Ewing, 1981; Weiss & Knoppers, 1982) and adolescence (Greendorfer, 1976, 1977). In contrast, Yamaguchi (1984) found that schoolteachers and coaches were not influential. Participants rarely name teachers and coaches as the most influential agents in their sport involvement. Perhaps the role of teachers and coaches is to strengthen the sport socialization process begun earlier by family and friends.

KEY POINT
An individual's peer group may either encourage or discourage physical activities. As socializing agents, peer groups can be as important as family.

Adults who dislike physical activity often report that they had poor movement experiences, particularly in physical education, when they were children. Keeping this in mind, how could you, as a physical educator, manipulate different types of constraints to make the gymnasium a more positive learning environment?

Nevertheless, teachers and coaches should not overlook their potential to influence their students' sport involvement. They can introduce children and adolescents to exciting new activities and stimulate them to learn the skills and attitudes associated with sport. Conversely, teachers and coaches must also recognize the potential they have to turn their students away from sport and physical activity. Bad experiences in school can have lifelong consequences for a person's overall

Assessing Youth Sports Coaching Behaviors: Coaches as Socializing Agents

Participation in youth sports has grown steadily over the past several decades (Smoll & Smith, 2001), and this growth has led to a demand for coaches who understand the needs of young participants. Remember, coaches can act as socializing agents for young children. Many of the feelings, values, and behaviors that people have about physical activity come from their experiences in youth sports. A good coach can facilitate a lifetime of positive experiences, just as a poor coach can drive young people away from sport and physical activity.

Frank Smoll and Ron Smith (2001) suggest that youth sports coaches adopt a four-part philosophy to enhance the enjoyment and benefits of children's participation in sport. They posit that the primary objective of youth sports is to have fun. Here are the four points:

1. Winning isn't everything, nor is it the only thing.
2. Failure is not the same thing as losing.
3. Success is not synonymous with winning.
4. Children should be taught that success is found in striving for victory (i.e., success is related to effort).

How do coaches evaluate their ability to make physical activity a fun, positive experience for kids? Coaches can understand their own coaching behaviors better through self-monitoring. To aid in this process, Smoll and Smith developed the Coaching Self-Report Form, which the coach should complete soon after each practice or game. This form helps coaches assess the frequency of desired behaviors in sport situations. Along with feedback from knowledgeable sources such as other coaches or teachers, use of the form can enhance a coach's ability to be a positive socializing agent for participants in youth sports.

lifestyle (Snyder & Spreitzer, 1973). Such negative experiences, known as **aversive socialization,** can occur when teachers or coaches embarrass children in front of their peers, overemphasize performance criteria at the expense of learning and enjoyment, or plan class activities that result in overwhelming failure rather than success. Children who experience aversive socialization naturally avoid physical activities and fail to learn skills well; consequently, any attempts they make to participate frustrate and discourage them.

 WEB STUDY GUIDE   Reflect on how your life was shaped by socializing agents in Activity 12.2, Significant People in Your Life, in the web study guide. Go to www.HumanKinetics.com/LifeSpanMotorDevelopment.

KEY POINT
It is essential that coaches and teachers understand their potential influence in promoting or deterring physical activity participation among their athletes and students.

Coaching Self-Report Form

Complete this form as soon as possible after a practice or game.
For items 1, 2, and 3, think not only about what you did but also about the kinds of situations in which the actions occurred and the kinds of athletes who were involved.

1. Approximately what percentage of the time did you respond to good players' actions with reinforcement?

2. Approximately what percentage of the time did you respond to players' mistakes or errors with each of the following communications?

    a. Encouragement only

    b. Corrective instructions given in an encouraging manner   (Sum of *a* and *b* should not exceed 100%)

3. About how many times did you reinforce athletes for showing effort, complying with team rules, encouraging teammates, showing team spirit, and exhibiting other good behaviors?

4. How well did your team play tonight? (Circle one.)

    very poorly   not very well   average   quite well   very well

5. How positive an experience *for the kids* was this practice or game?

    very negative   somewhat negative   neutral

    somewhat positive   very positive

6. How positive an experience *for you* was this practice or game?

    very negative   somewhat negative   neutral

    somewhat positive   very positive

7. Is there anything you might do differently if you had a chance to coach this practice or game again? (If so, briefly explain.)

Social Situations

The situations in which children spend their formative years are a part of the socialization process. Play environments, games, and the toys children use can all influence their later activities.

Play Environments and Games

An adequate environment for play, such as a backyard or playground, can provide the social situation and environment that a child needs in order to begin involvement in sport and physical activity. Play spaces probably also influence activity selection. A child who lacks an adequate play space has a diminished opportunity to get involved in activities and practice skills. These environmental constraints thus discourage participation in sport and gross motor activities. Children who grow up in urban areas with limited play space are typically exposed to sports and activities that require little space and equipment, such as basketball. Colder climates provide children with an opportunity to learn ice skating; warmer climates encourage swimming.

Play environment may also act as a sociocultural constraint, especially if the play space has gender-associated values, which can influence boys and girls to participate in gender-typed activities. For example, double-dutch rope jumping falls in the "feminine" domain; a boy might be labeled a "sissy" for rope jumping and thus be discouraged from participating in that activity. A girl might be told that a certain sport (e.g., football) is inappropriate for girls or labeled a "tomboy" if she does participate. Western society has traditionally considered certain types of games appropriate for boys but not for girls and vice versa. This labeling is particularly apparent as children enter adolescence.

The pressure to participate in gender-appropriate games has implications for children's opportunities to practice skills. Traditional boys' games are typically complex and involve the use of strategy; participants are encouraged to work hard in pursuit of specific goals and to use negotiation to settle disputes over rules. Traditional girls' games, on the other hand, are typically noncompetitive, and rather than encouraging interdependence among group members, they involve waiting for turns to perform simple repetitive tasks, such as jumping rope or playing hopscotch. Such games rarely give girls opportunities to increase game complexity or to develop increasingly more difficult skills. In fact, the games often end because the participants lose interest, not because they achieve a goal (Greendorfer, 1983).

These days, more and more children are participating in activities that are not "gender appropriate" (Giuliano et al., 2000). Further, some sports and activities, such as soccer and aerobics, are losing their gender-specific associations. Gender typing of sports and activities still exists, however, and it acts as a strong constraint on movement activities. Educators should keep in mind that a play environment that channels boys and girls into gender-typed games perpetuates a situation in which boys can better develop complex motor skills but girls cannot.

Play With Toys

Imagine walking into a toy store as a child. What do you experience? Bright colors and loud sounds beckon you toward toys that promise to enlighten, engage, and excite you. As a child (or even an adult), you may not realize that these toys act as part of the socialization process. That's right; even toys are constraints! Toys can encourage children to be active or inactive. For example, a Frisbee or Koosh ball encourages a child to throw, catch, and develop an accurate shot. On the other hand, a board game or doll encourages sedentary play. Toys can also stimulate children to emulate sports figures; among others, one can find basketball, soccer, and cheerleader Barbies as well as World Wrestling Entertainment action figures. At the same time, video and computer games may simulate sport without promoting any physical activity at all. Each kind of toy has its advantages, but certain toys facilitate children's socialization into sport and physical activity more than others do.

 Consider a toy that is popular today, such as Easy Bake Real Meal Oven, Webkinz (stuffed animals with virtual counterparts in a game on the company's website), or Nerf N-Strike Disk Shot (a shooting game that uses soft projectiles and moving targets). How might these toys encourage certain behaviors and discourage other behaviors in a child?

Toys are also a means by which gender typing can occur in the socialization process. For example, toys marketed to boys tend to be more complex and encourage more vigorous activity than those marketed to girls. The typical girls' toy, such as a doll or kitchen set, promotes quiet indoor play (Greendorfer, 1983; Liss, 1983). Gender typing through toys is well entrenched in society, and even children under 2 years old may be aware of the gender associations of toys (Levy, 2000). In a series of studies published in 2005, Blakemore and Centers interviewed undergraduates to determine their perceptions of the gender suitability of certain toys and to find out how they rated the characteristics of the toys. The participants associated girls'

toys with physical attractiveness, nurturance, and domestic skill and associated boys' toys with violence, competition, excitement, and, to some degree, danger (Blakemore & Centers, 2005). Manufacturers often use gender-typed strategies to advertise their products. For example, commercials or packaging for sports equipment, racing-car sets, and action-oriented video games feature boys, and those for dolls picture girls (figure 12.4). Watch carefully for television advertisements during daytime television—most target either boys or girls but not both. These marketing ploys influence children as well as their parents.

Parents also enjoy giving their children the same kinds of toys they played with as children, thus tending to perpetuate traditional gender typing. For example, a father might buy a Lincoln Logs set for his son, remembering the hours he spent with one as a child—despite the more modern, complex, and potentially less gender-stereotyped

FIGURE 12.4 Advertising for children's toys is often gender typed.

toys on the market. Moreover, parents can promote gender typing by negatively reinforcing play with toys they judge to be gender inappropriate (Fagot, 1978), such as telling boys not to play with dolls. In a study of gender typing, toys, and preschoolers, Raag and Rackliff (1998) found that many of the boys thought their fathers would perceive cross-gender-typed toys as "bad." Raag (1999) also found that children who had a parent or significant other who viewed gender-neutral toys as "bad" were somewhat influenced by gender-typed toy labels. Such gender typing through toys is slow to change, and there is little evidence of change over the past several decades (Blakemore & Centers, 2005; Campenni, 1999; Eisenberg, Welchick, Hernandez, & Pasternack, 1985; Lloyd & Smith, 1985; Marcon & Freeman, 1999). In a unique study, Pennell (1999), disguised as Santa's head elf, questioned 359 males and 417 females of various ages and ethnic backgrounds about their toy choices. Pennell found that both girls and (to a greater extent) boys had strong gender-typed toy preferences.

In recent years, society has become more aware of the many ways in which children are gender typed and the implications of this process. Yet there is little evidence of any substantial change away from gender typing (Banerjee & Lintern, 2000; Blakemore & Centers, 2005; Pennell, 1999; Turner & Gervai, 1995; Turner, Gervai, & Hinde, 1993; Weisner, Garnier, & Loucky, 1994). Teachers must realize that they influence this aspect of socialization (Fagot, 1984). Again, the evidence shows that teachers still behave differently toward the play of boys than toward that of girls (Fagot, 1984; Oettingen, 1985; Smith, 1985). They can reinforce early gender typing by continuing to label certain activities as more important or appropriate for one sex than for the other. They can choose different activities for boys' and girls' achievements. Or they can make every attempt possible to eliminate such distinctions and allow each individual to explore his or her full potential. It is likely that such day-to-day decisions and expectations accumulate over time to reduce differences in boys' and girls' motor development by channeling their practice opportunities (Brown et al., 1990; Brundage, 1983; Giuliano et al., 2000; Greendorfer & Brundage, 1984).

Other Sociocultural Constraints: Race, Ethnicity, and Socioeconomic Status

Earlier in this chapter we describe some constraints related to gender as socially constructed rather than biologically defined. For example, the notion that girls are weaker than boys is firmly established in Western culture even though little biological evidence backs it up. (Recall that few physiological differences exist between boys and girls before puberty.) Socially constructed notions also go beyond gender differences into the realms of race, ethnicity, and socioeconomic status (SES). Oftentimes, it's difficult to distinguish between sociocultural constraints (e.g., prevailing cultural attitudes) and individual constraints (e.g., physiological functioning) because research may not be completely clear-cut on how race, class, or ethnicity is defined. For example, race and ethnicity are often used together, but they are not equivalent. Racial characteristics are biologically based and relate to genetic similarities within groups, whereas ethnic characteristics are culturally based and relate to cultural similarities that connect groups. Race and ethnicity can coincide (biologically similar individuals who live in a particular geographic locale likely share culture), which makes their independent study very difficult.

Consider ways in which low socioeconomic status might encourage certain behaviors and discourage others.

Furthermore, social class and SES are associated with certain characteristics that may cut across race and ethnicity. Given that all of these factors interrelate, it is hard to identify constraints as strictly sociocultural or individual when considering SES. It may be best to consider the relationship of SES to other factors when looking for the influence of constraints. For example, children who come from a lower SES background may have less access to organized sports and physical activities, particularly those that require expensive equipment (e.g., ice hockey) or lessons (e.g., figure skating or tennis) and extensive time commitments from at least one parent. As a result, these children may not gain experiences and practice related to these particular activities.

We should consider the research on race, ethnicity, and SES from a slightly different point of view—one that examines differences among groups without suggesting a priori that differences are biological in nature. This approach allows us to examine the potential influence of a variety of constraints without limiting our interpretation to "biological fact" (which might actually be a cultural assumption). Malina, Bouchard, and Bar-Or (2004) provide an extensive review of historical and contemporary research related to physical differences based on race, ethnicity, and SES.

Summary and Synthesis

Humans are social beings. That is, individuals constantly interact with and depend on others as a part of everyday life. People form groups that can be small (family), medium (sports teams, town membership), or large (United States citizens). These groups often feature distinct values, morals, rules, and other factors that create a social atmosphere in which group members live. Thus, different groups and group members act as socializing agents who, along with social situations, encourage what is viewed as socially and culturally appropriate motor development. As you might expect, these sociocultural constraints interact with functional individual constraints to influence motivation, self-esteem, and feelings of competence for a task. Such constraint interactions are explored in chapter 13.

 Reinforcing What You Have Learned About Constraints

TAKE A SECOND LOOK

We should not overlook the effects of our social and cultural environment, or the influence of gender typing, on motor development. Back in the early 1970s, boys participated in sports such as field hockey, gymnastics, volleyball, and softball in far greater numbers than they do today. After Title IX passed, girls began to participate in these sports in large numbers. Perhaps the increase in girls' participation led to gender stereotyping of these sports as "feminine" and, in turn, to a drop in boys' participation. However, with the participation of Andrew Zayac, Jon Geerts, and others in sports such as field hockey, sociocultural constraints will likely change again, eventually encouraging a broader range of individuals to play more sports.

TEST YOUR KNOWLEDGE

1. Who are the socializing agents most likely to influence children's socialization into sport and physical activity?

2. How might gender-role stereotyping result in fewer women participating in sport and physical activity?

3. Describe how toys are part of the socialization process.

4. What is the difference between "sex" and "gender," and why does this distinction matter in the context of motor development?

5. Describe the changing roles of significant others across childhood and adolescence.

6. How do sociocultural constraints work in regard to our model of motor development? Provide specific examples.

LEARNING EXERCISE 12.1

Observing Sociocultural Constraints on the Internet

One of the benefits of the Internet is that we have immediate access to information about many societies and cultures. After a little web browsing, it becomes clear that various societies and cultures promote varying activities for their members—sports, for example, or the age at which a certain activity is deemed appropriate, or the roles viewed as proper for males and females, and so on. In this learning activity you will use the Internet to explore several countries and identify sociocultural constraints specific to those places.

1. Have you ever wondered what your motor development might be like if you had grown up in a different society and culture? In this exercise you will imagine in turn that you are a college-age individual from each of six continents: Africa, Asia, Australia, Europe, North America, and South America. To get started, select a country from each continent. Do not choose the country in which you reside.

2. Next, visit at least two websites *from* each country as well as two websites *about* each country (e.g., from an encyclopedia or travel guide). Remember to record the URLs of these websites for future reference. The more websites you visit, the more information you will have to work with.

3. For each country, identify sociocultural constraints specific to that society or culture.

4. For each country you choose, develop a biographical portrait of yourself as you might be if you had been born and raised there. Focus on sociocultural constraints. What would you be like? How would your life and motor development differ from country to country? How might your motor development there compare with your actual motor development in your real home country? Would similarities exist between your lives in the various countries?

Psychosocial Constraints in Motor Development

Individual–Environment Constraints

CHAPTER OBJECTIVES

This chapter

- explores the relationship between social influences and an individual's feeling of self-esteem,
- discusses the effect of self-esteem on motivation to participate in sport and physical activity,
- investigates why individuals continue participation or drop out of sport, and
- examines children's attributions of success or failure in physical activity.

Motor Development in the Real World

Project ACES and the World's Largest Exercise Class

May 1, 2013, marked the 25th anniversary of Project ACES (All Children Exercise Simultaneously). On that day, millions of schoolchildren all over the globe exercised at the same time (10 a.m. in each locality) in a symbolic gesture of fitness and unity. This noncompetitive program has proven to be educational, motivational, and fun. When Len Saunders created Project ACES in 1989, he had no idea that it would reach the magnitude and success it enjoys today. The program has been praised by U.S. presidents Barack Obama, Bill Clinton, George H.W. Bush, and Ronald Reagan. The program has also received praise from state governors, senators, and sports and entertainment celebrities and has been endorsed by groups such as the American College of Sports Medicine and the President's Council on Fitness, Sports and Nutrition. Project ACES has reached millions of children, parents, and teachers all over the world, including participants from more than 50 countries. Visit the project's website at www.lensaunders.com/aces/index.html.

The goal of Project ACES is to motivate children to participate in physical activity on a daily basis. The belief is that good experiences with physical activity in childhood lead to continued participation throughout the life span, which in turn allows a lifetime of improved health. In the United States, a government focus on health and physical activity (e.g., Healthy People 2010) may have helped increase the number of citizens who choose to exercise. From 2001 to 2005, more women (up 8.3% to 46.7%) and men (up 3.5% to 49.7%) reported that they exercised on a regular basis; these figures are closing in on the Healthy People 2010 target of an activity rate of 50% (Centers for Disease Control and Prevention, 2007). Still, despite the gains in participation, more than half of the population in the United States does not exercise on a regular basis.

Why do some individuals participate in physical activities on a regular basis whereas others avoid them? We spend much of this text describing motor behaviors that most typically developing individuals exhibit. However, we have yet to discuss one type of constraint—the individual functional constraint—that can drastically alter type and amount of personal physical activity and affect the emergence of movement over time. An individual functional constraint is not a specific anatomical structure but rather a psychological construct, such as motivation, self-efficacy, or emotion. Often, socializing agents such as parents or peers play a strong role in developing an individual's functional constraints. Therefore, we consider the interaction between sociocultural constraints and individual functional constraints.

As noted in the previous chapter, the social or cultural environment can encourage or discourage specific behaviors. Of course, these environmental constraints have different effects on different individuals. One person may not participate in an activity because of parental influences that discourage sport; another person may participate *because of* these same influences, as an act of rebellion. This chapter explores the interaction between social factors and functional constraints such as emotions, perceived ability, motivation, and other personal attributes. One key functional constraint related to physical activity is self-esteem.

Self-Esteem

All individuals evaluate themselves in various areas, such as physical ability, physical appearance, academic ability, and social skills. These self-judgments are called by many names, including self-esteem, self-concept, self-image, self-worth, and self-confidence. This chapter uses the term **self-esteem** to mean one's personal judgment of his or her own capability, significance, success, and worthiness; it is conveyed to others in words and actions (Coopersmith, 1967). Whether your self-evaluations are accurate is not as important to your self-esteem as is your *belief* that they are accurate (Weiss, 1993). Others can identify your level of self-esteem through what you say to them as well as through your nonverbal behaviors in joining or avoiding certain activities. For example, someone with high self-esteem for physical activity is not likely to avoid physical activity. Self-esteem is important because it influences one's motivation to join and sustain particular activities. Researchers have found a high correlation between physical activity and self-esteem (McAuley, 1994; Sonstroem, 1997).

Self-esteem is not just a general sense. It is specific to **domains**—that is, areas or situations. For example, a certain teenage boy may evaluate himself as high in the physical and social domains but low in the academic domain. In each domain, individuals may differentiate their abilities at even more specific levels (Fox & Corbin, 1989). Academic ability may be perceived in terms of ability in mathematics, writing, foreign languages, and so on. This chapter focuses on self-evaluations in the physical domain related to physical skills.

Professionals interested in motivating people to be active must understand self-esteem and the factors that influence people's judgments of their capabilities. Those working with children should know how self-esteem develops, and those working with people of any age should be aware of the criteria that people use as a basis for their evaluations and whether these criteria change as individuals grow older.

Development of Self-Esteem

Children's self-esteem is greatly influenced by verbal and non-verbal communications from those who are significant to them, including parents, siblings, friends, teachers, and coaches (figure 13.1). Verbal comments such as "Good" or "Why can't you do better?" are sources of information, as are facial expressions and gestures (Weiss, 1993). Children are likely to compare themselves with other children as well,

Self-esteem is one's personal judgment of his or her own capability, significance, success, and worthiness; it is conveyed to others through words and actions (Coopersmith, 1967). It involves one's self-evaluation both in general and in specific areas.

A **domain** is an independent area or sphere of influence, such as the social, physical, or academic.

KEY POINT
Self-esteem influences participation in sport and physical activity; it also influences skill mastery. It becomes more accurate as a person ages. Over time, an individual's self-esteem in a given domain more closely matches his or her actual abilities.

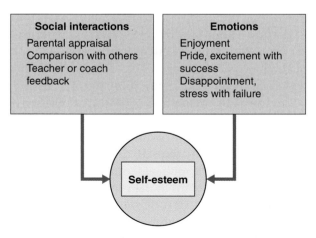

FIGURE 13.1   Emotions and social interactions influence the development of self-esteem for physical performance. Interactions are verbal and nonverbal.
Based on Horn 1987.

Measuring Self-Esteem in Children

It would seem much easier for developmentalists to measure running and jumping, or strength and flexibility, than self-esteem in children. Susan Harter (1985) uses a question format ("Some kids . . . BUT other kids . . .") to measure children's self-perceptions. For example, one pair of statements is, "Some kids feel that they are better than other kids their age at sports BUT other kids don't feel they can play as well." Next to each statement are two boxes, one labeled *really true for me* and one labeled *sort of true for me*. Children check one of the boxes, indicating which kids they perceive as being like themselves and to what extent.

Harter's Self-Perception Profile for Children contains 36 statements for 5 specific domains (scholastic competence, athletic competence, social acceptance, physical appearance, and behavioral conduct) and a global score for self-worth. This profile is appropriate for children aged 8 through early adolescence. For children under age 8, Harter and Pike (1984) designed a pictorial scale. Instead of two statements, two pictures are presented: One shows a competent or accepted child and the other shows an unaccepted child or a child who is unable to do the accepted task. Children say whether they are a lot or a little like the child in the picture. Hence, the scale is made more concrete for young children and can be given to children who cannot read or understand written statements. The pictorial scale assesses four domains: cognitive competence, physical competence, peer acceptance, and maternal acceptance. Scales available for adolescents and adults typically cover many more domains.

and the results of these evaluations influence self-esteem. These appraisals and comparisons do not, however, exert equal influence throughout life. This section examines how the pattern of influence can change.

 Imagine you are a physical therapist. Should improving patients' self-esteem be a primary concern in your work? Why or why not?

Social Interactions

Children as young as age 5 can compare themselves with others (Scanlan, 1988), but under the age of 10 they depend more on parental appraisals and outcomes of contests than on direct comparisons (Horn & Hasbrook, 1986, 1987; Horn & Weiss, 1991). Young children are not as accurate as teenagers in their evaluations of their physical competence. The level of intrinsic motivation and the extent to which children believe they control their lives influence the accuracy of children's perceptions of their physical ability. Children older than 10 rely on comparisons with and appraisals given by their peers. Perceived competence is important: Those with high perceptions of competence tend to have more positive reactions in sport and physical activity than do those who feel less competent (Weiss & Ebbick, 1996).

Feedback and appraisal from teachers and coaches also contribute to the development of self-esteem in the physical domain (Smoll & Smith, 1989). For example, male athletes aged 10 to 15 years show high self-esteem when they play for coaches who give frequent encouragement and corrective feedback (figure 13.2), especially if the athletes begin with somewhat low self-esteem (Smith, Smoll, & Curtis, 1979). Coaches' appraisals and self-perceptions of improvement also influence teenage girls, but the pattern of coaches' influence is interesting. In a study by Horn (1985), self-esteem did not increase when girls received reinforcement from coaches after successful performances. Instead, an increase in perceived competence was associated with criticism. Apparently, the coaches' positive comments were general and did not relate specifically to the girls' performance whereas the criticisms were associated with a skill error and often included a suggestion for improvement. Therefore, teachers and coaches cannot expect global praise to automatically raise a child's self-esteem. Feedback should relate to performance (Horn, 1986, 1987).

Emotions

The development of self-esteem is also related to emotions associated with participation. The pride and excitement associated with success, as well as the disappointment and stress associated with failure, influence a person's self-esteem and motivation to sustain participation (Weiss, 1993). This, of course, relates not just to sport but to physical activity in general. Enjoyment leads to higher levels of self-esteem and motivation to participate. In turn,

FIGURE 13.2 Feedback from a teacher or coach can contribute to the development of an important individual constraint: self-esteem.

perceptions of high ability and mastery, low parental pressure, and greater parent or coach satisfaction lead to enjoyment in preadolescents and young adolescents (Brustad, 1988; Scanlan & Lewthwaite, 1986; Scanlan, Stein, & Ravizza, 1988).

Relationship Between Causal Attributions and Self-Esteem

Self-esteem can influence behavior because people tend to act in ways that confirm their beliefs of themselves; that is, people tend to be self-consistent. If you have low perceived competency and low self-esteem surrounding your ability to perform a skill, then you tend to perform the skill with low competency. These beliefs often are evident in the reasons people give for their successes and failures. These reasons are called **causal attributions**. People of any age with high self-esteem tend to make attributions that are

1. *internal* (believing that they influence outcomes through their own behavior),
2. *stable* (believing that the factors influencing outcome are consistent from situation to situation), and

Causal attributions are the reasons to which people credit their successes and failures. These differ for people with high and low self-esteem.

3. *controllable* (believing that they personally control the factors influencing outcome).

For example, competitors with high self-esteem attribute their success to their talent (internal), think they can win again (stable), and believe they are responsible for their successes rather than merely lucky (controllable). They view their failures as temporary and meet them with renewed effort and continued practice to improve skills.

In contrast, people with low self-esteem attribute success to factors that are

1. *external* (believing that they could not change outcomes),
2. *unstable* (believing that the outcome is a product of fluctuating influences such as good and bad luck), and
3. *uncontrollable* (believing that nothing they do could result in a different outcome).

Competitors with low self-esteem often attribute losing to a lack of ability and attribute winning to luck or to a task so easy that anybody could win.

Examining causal attributions can help us understand adult behavior, but few researchers have studied the causal attributions of children in sport and physical activity. This information is particularly important because children are in the process of developing self-esteem. We have seen that children use various factors in judging themselves as they develop. Therefore, we must be concerned with the accuracy of their self-estimates and the roles that adults play in helping children make appropriate attributions.

Children's Attributions

The sparse information available on age-related changes in children's attributions indicates that children aged 7 to 9 years attribute outcomes to both effort and luck more than older children and teens do (Bird & Williams, 1980). These factors are unstable. The children in this study, however, reacted to stories provided by the researchers rather than to actual outcomes they experienced, and a more recent study failed to find age differences in attributions after actual participation (Weiss, McAuley, Ebbeck, & Wiese, 1990). Because young children might not be able to distinguish between ability and effort very well, more information is needed on age differences.

Differences do exist in the attributions made by children who differ in their perceived physical competence (Weiss et al., 1990). As expected, children with high physical self-esteem give internal, stable, and controllable reasons for their successes. Their attributions for success are more stable and their future expectations for success are higher than those of children with low physical self-esteem. Again, children vary in the accuracy of their physical estimates (Weiss & Horn, 1990), and girls who underestimate (rather than accurately estimate or overestimate) their physical abilities typically choose less challenging skills and attribute outcomes to external factors. Boys who underestimate their physical abilities report little understanding of what is responsible for their successes or failures. Children who both perceive their physical abilities as low and tend to underestimate their abilities probably make inaccurate attributions about the outcomes of their efforts. Their behavior is characterized by

- an unwillingness to try challenging tasks,
- a lack of effort to do well, and
- avoidance of participation.

KEY POINT
Children who perceive their physical abilities as low are not likely to persist in physical activities, therefore missing out on the associated health and psychosocial benefits (Weiss, 1993).

Parents, teachers, and coaches can help children, especially those with low self-esteem, give proper credit to the reasons for success or failure. Adults can help children with low self-esteem retrain their attributions (Horn, 1987; figure 13.3). Rather than let children attribute failure to lack of ability and attribute success to luck, adults can emphasize improvement through effort and continued practice. They can also encourage children to set goals and can provide accurate feedback about the children's progress. Children who come to think their situations are hopeless

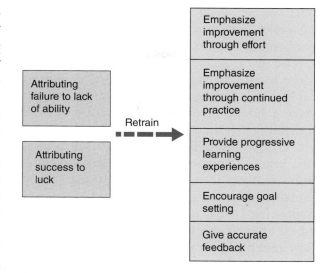

FIGURE 13.3 Adults must help children with low self-esteem for physical performance improve their self-esteem. Retraining can change causal attributions.

(i.e., those with learned helplessness) need challenges that are accurately matched to their abilities and in which difficulty is increased in steps much smaller than those presented to other children. Children with high self-esteem for physical competence probably possess high levels of intrinsic motivation to participate in physical activity. If children with low self-esteem are ever to enjoy physical activity and ultimately realize the benefits of participation, adults must make special efforts to improve their self-esteem (Weiss, 1993).

Adults' Attributions

Self-esteem also influences the motivation of adults. Like children, adults tend to behave according to their beliefs about themselves. Recall that children obtain the information on which they base their self-judgments largely from their significant others and their own comparisons. Adults obtain information from four sources (Bandura, 1986):

1. Actual experiences (previous accomplishments or failures)
2. Vicarious experiences (observing a model)
3. Verbal persuasion from others
4. Their physiological state

An individual's actual experiences are particularly influential, and changing physiological status is a reality for most older adults. For example, failing eyesight lowers an older adult's confidence for participating in racket sports. In contrast, verbal persuasion is a much weaker influence. The models available to older adults vary considerably. Some have opportunities to see others like themselves participating in a wide range of activities; others do not, especially on a personal basis rather than in a magazine or on television. Given these influences, it is clear that a person's self-esteem can increase or decrease throughout life.

A few investigators have related adults' physical self-esteem and their motivation to maintain or improve their fitness. Ewart, Stewart, Gillilan, and Kelemen (1986) involved men with coronary artery disease, aged 35 to 70, in either a walk or jog

KEY POINT
An adult's level of self-esteem affects motivation for physical activity. Like children, adults behave according to their beliefs about themselves, which are acquired from actual and vicarious experiences, others' opinions, and their physiological state.

plus a circuit weight-training program or a walk or jog plus volleyball program for 10 weeks. They measured self-esteem, arm and leg strength, and treadmill-running performance before and after the program.

The researchers found that those with higher pretraining self-esteem improved more in arm strength than those with lower self-esteem, even when accounting for beginning strength level, type of training, and frequency of participation. Self-esteem did improve with training but only when participants received information indicating that their performance was improving. For example, the weight-training group improved their self-esteem for lifting weights but not for jogging, even though they improved on both tests in a postprogram assessment. They could monitor their improvements in weight training during the program but their jogging distance remained constant, so they had no indication they were improving. Hogan and Santomeir (1984) also observed an increase in self-esteem for swimming in older adults after a 5-week swimming class. Thus, older adults' self-esteem can influence how much improvement they realize in a program, and participation can raise self-esteem when participants have information about their actual improvements.

 WEB STUDY GUIDE   Interview sport participants to obtain information about their attributions for success and failure in Lab Activity 13.1, Identifying Causal Attributions in Sport Participants, in the web study guide. Go to www.HumanKinetics.com/LifeSpanMotorDevelopment.

Motivation

The **motivation** to participate in activities of a certain type involves many factors, including those that lead people to initiate or join an activity. Other factors encourage people to persist in an activity and to exert effort in order to improve. Still other factors lead people to end their involvement. In the previous chapter, we discuss factors that encourage children's initial sport involvement or the sport socialization process. Let's turn now to factors that keep children in physical activity and sport or lead them to drop out. We also consider how the factors that motivate people to participate in physical activities change over the life span.

Persistence

Researchers have focused quite a bit of attention on the reasons that children and teens continue to participate in sport (Weiss, 1993). In general, the reasons include the following:

- A desire to be competent by improving skills or attaining goals
- A desire to affiliate with or make new friends
- A desire to be part of a team
- A desire to undertake competition and be successful
- A desire to have fun
- A desire to increase fitness

McAuley (1994) and Sonstroem (1997) found that girls most often cited fun (followed by health benefits) as the reason they participate in physical activity. Most individuals cite not just one or two but several reasons for participating. Harter (1978, 1981) proposed a competence motivation theory to explain this.

According to the theory, children are motivated to demonstrate their competency and therefore seek out mastery attempts, or opportunities to learn and demonstrate skills. Those who perceive that they are competent and believe that they control situations have more intrinsic motivation to participate than others.

Membership in subgroups can also influence a person's motivation to persist in sport. Examples of subgroups include age groups, starters versus benchwarmers, elite athletes versus recreational participants, and so on. Consider age groups. Brodkin and Weiss (1990) studied varying age groups of competitive swimmers: ages 6 to 9, 10 to 14, 15 to 22, 23 to 39, 40 to 59, and 60 to 74. They found that children cited wanting to compete, liking the coaches, and pleasing family and friends as reasons to participate. The 15- to 22-year-olds listed social status, as did young children to an extent, and fitness motives were important to the young and middle adults. Children and older adults did not consider fitness as important. Young children and older adults named fun as the most important reason to participate.

Another investigation of children involved in swimming found that those younger than 11 years were motivated to participate by external factors: encouragement from family and friends, liking the coaches, social status, and activities that they enjoyed (Gould, Feltz, & Weiss, 1985). Teenagers in this study cited more internal factors: competence, fitness, and the excitement of swimming. Thus, different age groups may have different reasons for participating, but more research is needed on other activities and with participants of varying skill levels (Weiss, 1993).

Dropping Out

Withdrawal from sport programs is a very real aspect of youth involvement in physical activity. Changing from one type of activity to another might be part of one's development or might reflect a person's changing interests or desire to try something new, but withdrawing from activity altogether has serious repercussions for health at any point in life. It is often difficult for surveys and research studies to distinguish between participants who switch activities and those who withdraw from activity altogether. In addition, dropouts do not always quit by choice; injuries or high monetary costs, for instance, might force some to withdraw. Thus, the reasons that participants give for quitting deserve further attention.

Some young dropouts cite very negative experiences, such as these, as reasons for withdrawing from sport (McPherson, Marteniuk, Tihanyi, & Clark, 1980; Orlick, 1973, 1974):

- Dislike for the coach
- Lack of playing time
- Too much pressure
- Too much time required
- Overemphasis on winning
- Lack of fun
- Lack of progress
- Lack of success

Such negative reactions come from a small number of dropouts (Feltz & Petlichkoff, 1983; Gould, Feltz, Horn, & Weiss, 1982; Klint & Weiss, 1986; Sapp & Haubenstricker, 1978). The majority of dropouts withdraw to pursue other

KEY POINT
Not all children and adolescents cite negative reasons for leaving sport and physical activity. Often, individuals simply want to pursue different activities that may or may not include physical activity.

interests, to try different sport activities, or to participate at lower intensity levels. Teens often report dropping out to take jobs. Many plan to reenter their sport later. Thus, much of the attrition in youth sports reflects shifting interests and involvement levels rather than negative experiences. Nonetheless, professionals should be concerned about negative experiences because they can be detrimental to a person's psychological development and can lead to a lifelong avoidance of healthful activities.

 WEB STUDY GUIDE   Reflect on activities in your life and what influenced you to persist or end involvement in those activities in Lab Activity 13.2, Motivation to Participate, in the web study guide. Go to www.HumanKinetics.com/LifeSpanMotorDevelopment.

Teacher-Centered Versus Student-Centered Approaches

What motivates a child to learn motor skills? When teaching fundamental motor skills to young children, instructors often attempt to promote change in movement through teacher-centered methods. That is, the instructor designs and presents developmentally appropriate activities in class and then chooses when to progress students to the next task. As a motor skills intervention, the teacher-centered approach has proven successful in various research studies (Goodway & Branta, 2003; Sweeting & Rink, 1999). However, to date, it is unknown whether teacher-centered approaches are the most effective way to improve children's motor skills.

As an alternative to the teacher-centered approach, a group of researchers have examined a different approach toward teaching motor skills to young children. It is called mastery motivational climate (Goodway, Crowe, & Ward, 2003; Parish, Rudisill, & St. Onge, 2007; Valentini, Rudisill, & Goodway, 1999). Fundamental to this approach is the notion that effort and outcome are related; that is, when the learner's environment is both mastery oriented and highly autonomous, children achieve and learn (in this case, improve in fundamental motor skills; Ames, 1992). Several research studies have shown that this approach to teaching and learning leads to improvement in motor skills (Valentini & Rudisill, 2004a,b,c) and in physical activity levels (Parish, Rudisill, & St. Onge, 2007).

How would an instructor develop a mastery motivational climate for young children? Researchers at Auburn University provided a model that follows the principles presented by Ames (1992); they call it HAPPE (high autonomy physical play environment) and describe it as follows (Parish & Rudisill, 2006):

- Toddlers (and young children) engage in a variety of authentic and meaningful tasks that match their skills and abilities. The tasks allow children to make choices according to individual interests and abilities.

- The primary authority in the classroom rests with the teacher, who serves as a facilitator of learning. Toddlers and young children are actively involved in decision making, self-management, and self-monitoring and they have opportunities to develop leadership roles.

- Teachers offer recognition to individual children in response to their effort and engagement in learning. Teachers give feedback and encourage toddlers' attempts to learn a skill.

- Groupings emerge naturally as toddlers and young children choose to play alone or with another child and as they decide which skill they want to practice. More experienced toddlers may choose to play in small groups.

- Toddlers are encouraged to evaluate their own performance, and teachers guide toddlers as they solve problems typically encountered during physical play.
- Toddlers have plenty of time to fully explore and practice physical play.

Researchers have found that motivational climates help young children improve in fundamental motor skills and physical activity (e.g., Goodway & Branta, 2003; Goodway et al., 2003; Parish, Rudisill, & St. Onge, 2007). Still, more research needs to be done in order to determine whether teacher-centered and student-centered approaches differ substantially in the amount and rate at which they enhance motor skill development.

Adult Activity Levels

Both the amount and the intensity level of physical activity decrease as adults grow older, especially among women (Boothby, Tungatt, & Townsend, 1981; Curtis & White, 1984; Ebrahim & Rowland, 1996; McPherson, 1983; Rudman, 1986). In 1996, the U.S. Department of Health and Human Services reported that even when adding together all the different types of exercise in which individuals participate, two-thirds of adults aged 65 and older who did exercise did not achieve recommended levels (U.S. Department of Health and Human Services, 1996). This withdrawal from and reduction in physical activity does not result from changes in physiological health alone (Spreitzer & Snyder, 1983). Psychosocial factors also influence adults' activity levels (McPherson, 1986). These factors include the following:

- Stereotypes of appropriate activity levels
- Limited access to facilities and programs
- Childhood experiences
- Concerns over personal limitations on exercise
- Lack of role models
- Lack of knowledge about appropriate exercise programs
- Belief that exercise is harmful or is ineffective in preventing disease (Duda & Tappe, 1989a)

However, indications exist that adults, especially older ones, are becoming more actively interested in health and in the influence of physical activity on health status (Howze, DiGilio, Bennett, & Smith, 1986; Maloney, Fallon, & Wittenberg, 1984; Prohaska, Leventhal, Leventhal, & Keller, 1985). In fact, the number of women participating in the National Senior Games increased by 110% from 1991 to 1998 (Women's Sports Foundation, 2000).

Duda and Tappe (1988, 1989a,b) proposed that adult exercise participation reflects three interrelated factors (figure 13.4):

1. Personal incentives, such as a desire to demonstrate mastery, compete, be with others, receive recognition, maintain health, cope with stress, or improve physical fitness
2. A sense of self, particularly in regard to one's self-esteem for physical activity
3. Perceived options, or the opportunities a person has in a given situation, such as transportation to various sites where adult programs are offered

If you were to design a physical activity program for older adults, what could you do to encourage your participants first to join and then to continue with the program?

Personal incentive values and self-esteem can change throughout life. For example, as an adult ages, the desire to compete might decrease while the desire to be with others might increase. Older adults can also come to perceive that their physical abilities have declined over time. Duda and Tappe surveyed 144 adults in three age groups (25–39, 40–60, and 61-plus years) who were participating in an exercise program. Personal incentives differed among the age groups and between men and women. Middle-aged and older adults placed more value on the health benefits of exercise than did young adults. For example, figure 13.5 shows the extent to which men and women in each age group valued the stress-reducing benefits of exercise. Young adult men put little emphasis on this exercise benefit, as shown by their low average on the Personal Incentives for Exercise Questionnaire. Men also valued competitive activities more than women did. Exercise leaders, then, might help older adults stick to their exercise programs by emphasizing social interaction, health benefits, and stress reduction (Duda & Tappe, 1989b).

No age group differences in self-esteem were apparent among these older adults, but differences did exist between men and women. The women had lower physical self-esteem and less feeling of control over their health status than the men did. These beliefs are typically associated with less involvement, but the women felt they had more social support for their involvement than did the men, and they continued to participate.

Exercise leaders who adopt strategies targeted at adults who might have low physical self-esteem can improve participants' self-esteem and exercise involvement (Duda & Tappe, 1989b). Another group of adults might not have the same character-

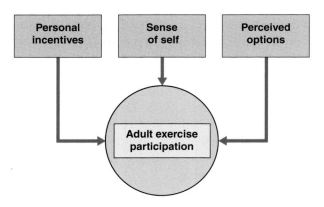

FIGURE 13.4 Three interrelated factors can influence the level of adults' exercise participation.

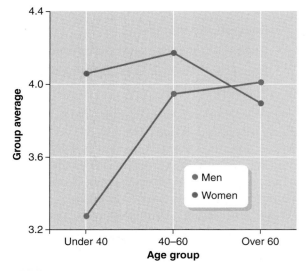

FIGURE 13.5 Personal incentives for adults to exercise differ between age groups and between the sexes. Group averages on the "coping with stress" category of the Personal Incentives for Exercise Questionnaire (a 5-point Likert-type scale) are plotted here.

Reprinted by permission from Duda and Tappe 1989.

FIGURE 13.6   In order to improve self-esteem and other individual functional constraints, exercise leaders should keep in mind the incentives for and perceptions of physical activity that older adults have.

istic incentives and perceptions as those Duda and Tappe surveyed. Yet exercise leaders can encourage older adults to persist in their exercise programs by being aware of the incentives and perceptions of their particular groups (figure 13.6). They can then emphasize the aspects and benefits of exercise that are most important to those participants.

Summary and Synthesis

Individuals' perceptions of their physical abilities can change dramatically across the life span. In turn, these perceptions can affect self-esteem. Maintaining high levels of self-esteem seems to enhance performance as well as perceived competence, which motivates an individual to continue participating in physical activity. This set of dynamics offers an example of how constraints can interact to encourage movement. For example, older adults who desire social interactions with friends, as well as improved fitness levels, may join an exercise program for older adults. This program may involve activities that facilitate both socialization and fitness, which help individuals improve their self-esteem. The higher levels of self-esteem and perceived competence then help motivate the older adults to return to the program, which continues to foster self-esteem, and so on.

At the same time, these constraint interactions can discourage behavior. Consider children who begin participating in a sport such as soccer. They may have joined to be with friends and have fun. Perhaps, however, the coach wants to win and provides criticism and negative feedback to the players if they make a mistake. The players may begin to attribute losses to their lack of ability and believe that they lack competence in that activity. In turn, their self-esteem begins to decrease. Eventually, they may drop out of the sport altogether.

These two examples demonstrate the powerful interplay between sociocultural and individual functional constraints. We all live in a social context and are subject to social opinions. These opinions help fashion and reinforce our beliefs about ourselves. Eventually, we act as we believe. Keeping this in mind, it is essential for those who work with others in physical activity and sport to look beyond the activity to the individuals themselves.

 Reinforcing What You Have Learned About Constraints

TAKE A SECOND LOOK

Think back to project ACES, discussed at the beginning of the chapter. Imagine that you are exercising and that, at the very same moment, millions of other people are doing the exact same thing. Does the thought of all those people joined in simultaneous physical activity motivate you to exercise? Len Saunders designed Project ACES to motivate children to exercise by bringing them together at one point in time. Motivation (an individual functional constraint) can be greatly enhanced by creating a learning environment designed to motivate, such as Project ACES or HAPPE at Auburn University. This interaction of constraints (motivated individuals in a motivational climate) should encourage positive and progressive change in motor skill over time.

TEST YOUR KNOWLEDGE

1. What is self-esteem? Is it general or specific? How is it developed?

2. People tend to attribute their successes and failures to various causes. What are the differences in the causal attributions made by those with high self-esteem and those with low self-esteem? To what do children tend to attribute their performance?

3. What factors are associated with persisting in sport and physical activity? With dropping out?

4. How does perceived competence change with children's causal attributions?

Learning Exercise 13.1

EXPLORING MOTIVATIONS FOR PHYSICAL ACTIVITY AND EXERCISE

What motivates you and other students to be involved in sport and physical activities? If you evaluate a group of students, you will likely discover a diverse array of reasons to participate—or not participate.

1. First, determine your own motivations.
   - Do you participate in sport and physical activities now? Look at the list of reasons for persisting in sport participation in the "Persistence" section of chapter 13. Write down those reasons that apply to you and add any others not included in the list.
   - Have you dropped out of a physical activity? Look at the list of reasons for dropping out of a sport in the "Dropping Out" section of chapter 13. Do any of the reasons listed apply to you?

- Have you persisted in some activities and dropped out of others? What factors are related to these choices?

2. Compare your notes from #1 above with a group of other students.
   - What are the factors most commonly associated with persistence?
   - What are the factors most commonly associated with dropping out?
   - Calculate percentages for easy interpretation (e.g., "Seventy percent of my group dropped out because of lack of time").
   - Reflect on these factors and offer some generalizations about motivational factors and the students in your class.

14

Knowledge as a Functional Constraint in Motor Development

 CHAPTER OBJECTIVES

This chapter

- discusses the benefits to motor performance of knowing about an activity,
- differentiates between the knowledge of novices and that of experts and recognizes that children tend to be novices, and
- identifies trends in the speed of cognitive processing over the life span.

A Little Knowledge Goes a Long Way

Technology has changed sport and dance performance in many ways. Technique can now be analyzed and compared with that of skilled models or that of an athlete's previous performances. Instant replays can confirm or refute referees' decisions. But nothing has become more commonplace than using technology to provide information about tactics. Coaches and athletes alike review video clips and statistics to identify patterns in their opponents' play, and they spend long hours developing strategies to counter those patterns. The cost of using technology is widely accepted as a necessity in order to be competitive. Technology certainly adds to the knowledge that athletes gain from their own experience; at some levels of competition, where athletes are closely matched in skill level, the decisions that athletes make based on their knowledge of a sport can make the difference in the outcome of a competition.

Great performers bring not only their physical talents and conditioning but also their knowledge about a task to the physical performance of that task. Knowledge, then, is an individual constraint that interacts with other constraints to give rise to movement; specifically, it is a functional individual constraint. Individuals and groups have varying amounts of knowledge about a movement task. For example, children have had less time to acquire knowledge than adults, whereas older adults might have the advantage of far more experience than younger adults. This chapter examines how knowledge constrains movement over the life span.

Knowledge Bases

At any age, knowledge about an activity facilitates performance, and increased knowledge facilitates remembering information about that topic (Chi, 1981). Children undoubtedly have a smaller base of knowledge than adults because they have had fewer experiences. Yet children who become experts on a particular topic can outperform adults in that area. Chi (1978) observed that child experts in chess recalled significantly more chess positions than adult novices in chess. Why would performance be related to size of the **knowledge base**? There are at least three reasons:

1. Increased knowledge reduces the need to remember a great deal of information in the short term (Chase & Simon, 1973).
2. Increased knowledge allows more effective use of the cognitive processes (Ornstein & Naus, 1984, cited in Thomas, French, Thomas, & Gallagher, 1988).
3. Increased knowledge reduces the amount of conscious attention needed to perform some tasks (Leavitt, 1979).

A **knowledge base** is the amount of information a person has on a specific topic, consisting of declarative knowledge and possibly procedural and strategic knowledge.

Thus, knowledge is a functional constraint that interacts with other constraints, especially task constraints, to give rise to movement. Performance is facilitated not only by practice of physical skills but also by increased knowledge of the sport or activity.

Types of Knowledge

Before considering the development of knowledge about sport, we must identify the types of knowledge and the differences between experts and novices. Chi (1981) has defined three types of knowledge:

1. Declarative knowledge—knowing factual information
2. Procedural knowledge—knowing how to do something in accordance with specific rules
3. Strategic knowledge—knowing general rules or strategies that apply to many topics

KEY POINT
Experts have more declarative and procedural knowledge, and they structure that knowledge differently than do novices.

Declarative and procedural knowledge are specific to a certain topic; strategic knowledge can be generalized. The give-and-go is an example of strategic knowledge that can be generalized. An athlete who understands how to execute a give-and-go (in which a player passes to a teammate, then advances toward the goal or basket for a return pass) in basketball can execute a give-and-go in hockey or soccer, provided she has the physical skills to do so. Experts have more declarative and procedural knowledge about an activity than do novices (Chi, 1978; Chi & Koeske, 1983; Chiesi, Spilich, & Voss, 1979; Spilich, Vesonder, Chiesi, & Voss, 1979). Experts independently organize the information they know in a similar way (Chiesi et al., 1979; Murphy & Wright, 1984)—that is, experts structure knowledge, whereas novices do not. By organizing their information in a methodical **knowledge structure**, such as a hierarchy, experts facilitate their memory recall and, therefore, their use of information.

Thomas and colleagues (1988, adapted from Berliner, 1986) identified other sport-specific ways in which experts and novices differ. Those pertinent to our discussion follow:

A **knowledge structure** is the manner in which a person organizes information about a topic, typically expressed in hierarchical fashion. Experts structure information in ways similar to other experts.

- Experts make more inferences about objects and events. In sport, this helps experts predict upcoming events and anticipate the most likely occurrences.
- Experts analyze problems at a more advanced level. For example, expert athletes probably think of offensive plays as concepts rather than as lists of individual players' movements.
- Experts quickly recognize patterns. For example, expert athletes quickly recognize defensive configurations.
- Experts preplan their responses for specific situations. Softball infielders, for example, do so before the batter hits by choosing the base to which they will throw given the runners on base and the number of outs.
- Experts tend to organize knowledge in relation to the goal of the game. For example, an expert basketball player thinks of offensive strategies not in terms of a long list of individual offenses but in terms of those that successfully attack, say, a zone defense versus those that attack a player-to-player defense.
- Experts spend much time learning about their topics. Sport-specific expertise in particular requires hours of practice and experience, especially if a player wants to develop procedural how-to knowledge.

Keep in mind that expertise is specific. For sport and dance, this means that individuals become experts in specific sports (tennis, basketball) or dance forms (modern, ballroom). In addition, expert performers in sport and dance have a high level of physical skill. Both skill and the knowledge of how to use skills in specific situations are necessary for success (Thomas et al., 1988).

 From the perspective of a coach, identify three or four team sports, as well as a particular position for each, that would require an athlete to have skill *and* knowledge in order to perform well.

Development of a Knowledge Base

Let's consider how individuals, especially children, develop a knowledge base in a particular sport. First, they must acquire declarative knowledge, which provides a foundation for procedural knowledge (Chi, 1981). Young children often lack declarative knowledge of a sport (figure 14.1); typically, they are novices who must learn game rules, goals, and patterns of play before they can exhibit procedural knowledge and make appropriate decisions regarding which action to perform. Strategic knowledge is the last to develop. It requires experience with many types of tasks, which then enables children to generalize across topics.

French and Thomas (1987) conducted one of the first studies of knowledge development in sport with children. They proposed that children need declarative knowledge of both basketball and basketball skills in order to make appropriate decisions while playing basketball. Coaches classified the 8- to 12-year-old boys in a youth basketball program based on their skills, knowledge of the game, and ability to make good judgments in a game. The best third of the group was designated the expert group and the bottom third the novice group. The boys in these two groups were then tested on their basketball knowledge and skills. In individual interviews, they were asked to give the appropriate action for each of five basketball game situations described to them. The researchers also observed the players during games and graded their decisions as appropriate or inappropriate. The experts scored much

FIGURE 14.1   These novice soccer players are just beginning to develop a knowledge base about soccer.

better than the novices on both the knowledge and skill tests. More importantly, the experts chose the appropriate action in game situations more often than novices. During their situation interviews, experts were more likely to give answers dependent on the action of the opponents and to identify more alternatives, indicating more basketball knowledge.

French and Thomas observed some of the 8- to 10-year-old boys from their first study over the course of a season along with a group of boys who did not play basketball. By the end of the season, both expert and

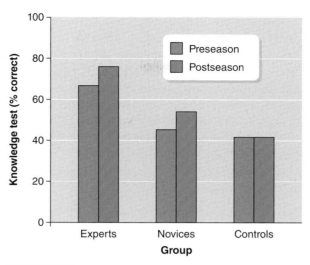

FIGURE 14.2 Both expert and novice boys scored better on a postseason basketball knowledge test than on a preseason test. A control group did not improve.

Data from French and Thomas 1987.

novice players were making better decisions about actions and scored better on the knowledge test (figure 14.2). The control group made no significant progress. Interestingly, none of the children improved in physical skill over the season, either on skill tests or in game play. This initial study, then, indicates that basketball knowledge is related to children's skill performance and that children might acquire knowledge faster than they improve their physical skills. Professional tennis players were shown in turn to have more tactical concepts than varsity players (McPherson & Kemodle, 2007) or other tennis players (Nielsen & McPherson, 2001).

French, Nevett, and colleagues (French et al., 1996; Nevett & French, 1997) also examined expertise in youth baseball players. In their first study, they hypothesized that players with more declarative and procedural knowledge solve game situation problems better whereas those with less knowledge exhibit more errors in solving those problems. The researchers gave youth baseball players 7 to 8 years old and 9 to 10 years old five baseball situation problems to solve. The players' coaches categorized the players for skill level. In three of the problem situations, the players who coaches categorized as more skilled solved the problem better, regardless of age. Overall, though, these 7- to 10-year-olds were still developing their knowledge base regarding baseball. They had difficulty quickly predicting base runners' actions and failed to monitor some critical game conditions.

Nevett and French (1997) followed up this initial study with 8-, 10-, and 12-year-old and high school baseball shortstops. They trained players to use a talk-aloud procedure between pitches. Although players were told to verbalize any of their thoughts, the researchers were particularly interested in information about possible plays that could be made if the batter hit the ball. Players who were 12 years of age and under did not develop advanced defensive plans, rehearse the plans, or update the plans as well or as frequently as high school players did. It is likely that frequent and repetitive responses to game situations through experience help in the development of procedural knowledge structures. Even though declarative knowledge can be acquired at young ages, experience in game situations is necessary in order to develop a knowledge structure that is beneficial to skilled performance.

McPherson (1999) expanded work on knowledge bases in sport to adults. She posed six tennis situation problems to six novice tennis players and six college varsity experts, all of who were women aged 18 to 22 years. Compared with youth experts in previous research, adult experts generated a greater number, variety, and level of sophistication of condition-and-action concepts. Adult novices were similar to youth novices in that they had weak representations of the game situation problems and offered few solutions. The adult novices generated fewer tactical concepts than did youth tennis experts in previous studies. Thus, years of experience—from practicing, being coached, and playing—are influential in developing a knowledge base, and youths with more experience can have a more advanced knowledge base than adult novices.

KEY POINT
Experience in playing is important in developing a knowledge structure.

 WEB STUDY GUIDE   Explore how the speed of recognizing defensive and offensive configurations in basketball is related to one's knowledge base in Lab Activity 14.1, Examining Knowledge and Decision Making in Physical Activities, in the web study guide. Go to www.HumanKinetics.com/LifeSpan MotorDevelopment.

Assessing Cognitive Decision Making

The more knowledge an athlete has, the more quickly and accurately that athlete can decide on an action. So, in assessing decision making, the speed and accuracy of decisions in sport provide information about the size of an athlete's knowledge base.

In their study of knowledge development in sport, French and Thomas (1987) needed to assess the decisions that young basketball players made during games. The written knowledge test and interview yielded useful information, but it was not certain that the players who gave good answers to questions away from the court would make good decisions in a fast-moving, demanding game situation.

To assess decision making in games, French and Thomas designed an observational instrument based on a typical offensive sequence in basketball: When a player catches the ball, he or she must decide whether to hold the ball, pass, dribble, or shoot. The researchers identified all the decisions a player could make, then categorized them as appropriate or inappropriate for a given situation.

French and Thomas videotaped youth basketball games. A trained basketball expert watched each player in each game for one quarter of playing time and coded each decision the player made when he or she received a pass. A second expert watched independently and coded some of the players to ensure that an expert observer would code each decision the same way at least 90% of the time. The observer gave a player a score of 1 for an appropriate decision and a score of zero for an inappropriate decision. For example, a player received 1 point for passing to an open teammate but no points for passing to a closely guarded teammate. In this way, the researchers could measure the players' decision making in game play.

Observational instruments are an excellent means of measuring behavior. Performers can be observed in real situations rather than in artificial laboratory conditions. Note, however, that French and Thomas had to develop a coding system that included all of the decisions a player could make, then locate experts and train them to use the assessment instrument. Finally, the observers coded from videotape so that they could stop the tape to record their judgments, thereby ensuring that they missed no action. This is a tedious procedure, but it provides an interesting and accurate measure of decision-making behaviors in sport.

Teachers and coaches would benefit from continued study of knowledge development in sport. Educators may be able to improve children's skill acquisition in sport and dance by using appropriately timed instruction of and emphasis on rules, formations, strategies, and goals. Increased knowledge enhances memory.

 If you were a physical education teacher at a middle school, what is one activity you would use in your classes? What knowledge about the activity could you teach as you introduce the physical skills of the activity?

Sex differences in sport performance might be attributable in part to differences between boys' and girls' knowledge of sport. Society makes it easier for boys to acquire sport knowledge by targeting sport-related merchandise to them—board and electronic games, books, collector cards, and so on. Girls' use of these items could be viewed by some as less appropriate to their gender role, and companies tend to market nonsport items such as dolls or crafts to girls. This difference could contribute to a persisting performance gap between boys and girls. Also, children who practice more probably acquire more knowledge, so unequal opportunities to participate might also widen the performance gap between most boys and at least some girls (Thomas et al., 1988).

Knowledge bases in older adults have not been widely studied. Langley and Knight (1996) conducted a case study of a single senior adult competitive tennis player, a 58-year-old man. The investigators conducted interviews and observations and analyzed narrative information with coding techniques. They found that the senior player had a rich knowledge of tennis situations, which centered on performance capabilities and opponent limitations. The player knew how his opponent's actions in a particular setting affected his own capabilities in that setting. He realized that his physical conditioning had declined somewhat as he aged but felt that his better skill in executing a number of shots more than compensated. Langley and Knight used Gibson's (1979) notion of affordances to suggest that experienced players perceive the game play environment in terms of the actions that environment affords. Experience allows the player to perceive affordances that are opportunities for success against an opponent.

Working with adults only, Gygax, Wagner-Egger, Parris, Seiler, and Hauert (2008) applied a method for studying mental representations from the field of psycholinguistics. Focusing on soccer players' mental representations as they encountered playing situations, the researchers observed differences in focus of attention—tending to include or not include other players—that were associated with varying expertise. The pattern of association, though, was not simply related to increasing expertise. Gygax et al. also explored the emotional elements of mental representations. These cognitive aspects of motor performance need more research attention.

We can speculate that older adults with expertise in a sport have an advantage in performance because superior knowledge might offset a loss of physical skill or speed (figure 14.3). Also, older adults learning new sports can expect to improve as they acquire knowledge of the sport.

KEY POINT
Older adults can have a rich knowledge base in a sport or dance form through extensive experience. This knowledge may allow older adults to compensate for slight declines in physical performance.

Memory

Knowledge and memory are inseparable topics. We remember what we understand; at the same time, "coming to understand" is related to our existing base of mental representations, which define our knowledge at that point in time. Sutherland, Pipe, Schick, Murray, and Gobbo (2003) found that providing children with prior information about an event improved their recall of the event and their knowledge acquisition in the event, both soon after the event and 4 months later. So, new experiences are integrated with our existing base of meaning.

The question asked most often about memory development is whether memory capacity changes with development. Yet, how much we remember, no matter what our age, depends on what we already know about a topic. Knowledge is organized or structured in specific content domains (Kuhn, 2000), such as chess, dinosaurs, or baseball. Memorizing, then, is a process of revising our knowledge of a topic. Although much research has been carried out on the topic of memory capacity, the answer to whether it increases with development has been elusive. This probably reflects researchers' approaching the study of memory without regard to one's knowledge context. That is, memory has been studied in isolation. The answer to the question of capacity awaits new research approaches that study memory in the broader context of the developing cognitive system.

FIGURE 14.3　Knowledge can help older adults perform successfully even if physical abilities begin to decline.

People of all ages remember more when they have a reason to do so. Very young children first remember when adults engage them in recounting experiences. With advancing age, children internalize this remembering activity and carry it out on their own. Eventually they remember purposively, for their individual benefit or that of their social group. Again, laboratory research on memory often has involved memorizing items for no particular reason other than completing the research task. Future researchers must study memory in the context of information that is important to people.

Young children typically do not employ strategies for remembering, but they can be taught to use strategies such as rehearsal, labeling, and grouping. Thomas, Thomas, and Gallagher (1981) demonstrated that teaching children a rehearsal strategy along with a skill enhanced their skill acquisition. Gallagher and Thomas (1980) also found that grouping arm movements in an organized order helped children recall and duplicate movements. The difficulty is that children won't necessarily apply the strategies learned in one context to another context. Perhaps the use of memory strategies is related to a broader issue—the development of cognitive strategies such as inference and problem solving—and needs to be studied in that context. Van Duijvenvoorde, Jansen, Bredman, and Huizenga (2012) found that when the demands of long-term and working memory were reduced, children, adolescents, and young adults were all capable of making advantageous decisions. Explicitly providing the pros and cons of options helped children and adolescents make advantageous decisions even in complex situations. Because this research used a cognitive task, additional research in movement settings is needed to see whether the same results are obtained.

Research on memory in adults and older adults tends to find a decline in performance on memory tasks. Yet, as with the research involving children, researchers have tended to study memory in isolation and without regard to adults' knowledge of a topic or motivation to remember. Moreover, a host of environmental factors might affect performance of older adults on memory tasks. Diseases (e.g., hypertension) might impair memory performance. Highly fit older adults have been observed to perform better than unfit adults on memory tasks (Stones & Kozma, 1989), and memory performance has been linked to self-reported health status (Perlmutter & Nyquist, 1990). Improvements on memory tasks have also been noted after exercise interventions, so exercise probably has a small but positive effect on memory performance (Clarkson-Smith & Hartley, 1990; Colcombe et al., 2005).

Alzheimer's disease is one of the most devastating diseases of aging for individuals and their families. Late-onset Alzheimer's disease, the most common form, is characterized by confusion, memory loss, and behavioral problems. As the number of individuals living into older adulthood increases, so too will the number of older adults who develop Alzheimer's. The cause of late-onset Alzheimer's disease is probably both genetic and environmental, but researchers are investigating both genes that might trigger the disease, through production of a specific protein, and genes that might control the timing of onset. The hope is that drugs might be designed that could either block the protein or delay onset of the disease, perhaps past the natural life span.

Although performance on memory tests might show improvement through childhood and decline in older adulthood, it is most important to acknowledge that memory is related to current knowledge and understanding of information in a specific context as well as to the motivation to remember information.

Speed of Cognitive Functions

In addition to differences in individuals' knowledge about specific sports and dance over the life span, general differences exist in the speed with which individuals can access and use that knowledge. That is, a person can have considerable knowledge yet be unable to recall and apply that knowledge as quickly as another person. This would be a more pertinent issue when participating in activities requiring quick decisions and responses. For example, slower cognitive function would not be an issue in deciding how to pick up a spare in bowling because there is sufficient time between deliveries. It would be an issue, however, in the middle of a tennis point when deciding whether a lob is an appropriate shot for the situation.

Let's now consider age-related differences in the speed of cognitive functions. We would do well to begin by acknowledging that most of the research on cognitive speed has been undertaken from an information processing perspective. From this viewpoint, short-term and long-term memory and information retrieval play a major role in movement responses. In contrast, ecological perspectives downplay the role of knowledge and cognitive processes in movement responses. From this perspective, affordances in the environment are perceived. Experience might influence whether an affordance is perceived, but the affordance is always available in the environment. With this in mind, let's first consider cognitive speed in children.

Speed of Cognitive Processing in Children

Children take longer than adults to process cognitive information to be remembered. As children get older, they can eventually process either the same amount of information faster or more information in the same amount of time. This trend is apparent in even the simplest of motor responses, **simple reaction time**. The maximum speed of this response increases from age 3 through adolescence (Wickens, 1974). An improvement with age also occurs in the time required to respond in continuous tracking (Pew & Rupp, 1971). In this type of task, children must continuously match their movement to a target—for example, a video game in which the player controls the image of a car with a joystick to keep the car on a curved road. The slower processing speed exhibited in children appears related to factors considered to be central processes (processes of the central nervous system, or CNS) rather than peripheral ones (Elliott, 1972). One such central process is attention; another is speed of the memory processes.

The speed with which an individual can select motor responses is a function of age (Wickens, 1974). Clark (1982) demonstrated this by manipulating the spatial stimulus–response compatibility of a reaction-time task when testing 6-year-olds, 10-year-olds, and adults. In the compatible condition, participants pressed a key on the right if the right stimulus light came on and a key on the left if the left stimulus light came on. In the incompatible condition, participants pressed a key opposite the direction of the light. Spatial compatibility, then, affects the participant's response selection. Clark found that processing time decreased (performance improved) in the older groups tested in the incompatible condition.

Although these central factors of attention, memory, and response selection influence children's slower processing speeds, peripheral factors do not. For example, nerve impulse conduction speed in the peripheral nerves does not contribute substantially to the speed differences between children and adults. Young children are able to process information faster as they mature because of improvements in central factors such as response selection and speed of the memory process.

 How could slower cognitive processing affect children in sports such as soccer, basketball, and tennis? If you were a coach, how might you structure their tasks for increased success given this limitation?

Speed of Cognitive Processing in Middle-Aged and Older Adults

As is the case with young children, middle-aged and older adults exhibit limitations in the processing of information. These limitations are also apparently related to central rather than peripheral processes. However, researchers have found important differences between performers at opposite ends of the life span. For example, older adults do not exhibit declining performance in all types of skills. They undergo little change in their performance of single, discrete actions that can be planned in advance (Welford, 1977b) or of simple, continuous, and repetitive actions, such as alternately tapping two targets (Welford, Norris, & Shock, 1969). However, in actions requiring a series of different movements, especially when speed is important (Welford, 1977c), older adults show a large decrement in performance. The major limitations on older adults, then, seem to involve the decisions they base on perceptual information and the programming of movement sequences (Welford, 1980). These are central rather than peripheral factors. Let's consider in more detail some of the central components of information processing that are affected by aging.

Older adults apparently learn new tasks, whether cognitive or motor, more slowly than younger adults do. For example, rote learning of cognitive material is slower in older adults because they need more repetitions to reach criterion—that is, to learn the material at a predesignated level. This may reflect the need for more time for the information to register in long-term memory. Similarly, older adults improve more slowly than younger adults in new motor skills, although they maintain well the skills they learned early in life (Szafran, 1951; Welford, 1980).

Attentional factors also play a role in the performance limitations of older adults, who perform their fastest on a reaction-time task when a warning signal is given at a consistent interval before the stimulus and perform their slowest when the signal interval varies from trial to trial. This finding suggests that a fixed interval minimizes distraction by irrelevant associations (Birren, 1964). Rabbitt (1965) also demonstrated that older adults are hampered more than younger adults by the presence of irrelevant stimuli in a card-sorting task. In this task, participants are challenged to sort a stack of cards based on information given on the card face, such as the shape of a symbol or its color. If some information on the card face is not relevant to the sorting task, older adults' performance suffers compared with that of younger adults.

KEY POINT
At any point in the life span, CNS factors play a much larger role in speed of cognitive processing than do peripheral factors.

Many older adults are more easily distracted and attend less well to critical stimuli than when they were younger. The cause of this decline in performance might be a lowered signal-to-noise ratio in the CNS. The neural impulses of the CNS take place against a background of random neural noise such that the effectiveness of a neural signal depends on the ratio between the signal strength and the background noise—the signal-to-noise ratio. As a person ages, signal levels in the CNS decrease because of changes in the sense organs, loss of brain cells, and factors affecting brain cell functioning; at the same time, noise level increases (Crossman & Szafran, 1956; Welford, 1977a). Older adults can compensate for this lower signal-to-noise ratio if they are given extra time to complete a task, but they are at a disadvantage if they must perform a series of movements or make a series of decisions rapidly.

CNS factors also influence the slower speed of processing in older adults. Researchers have consistently documented a slowing of reaction time with aging. Although a slight slowing of neural impulse conduction velocity is associated with aging, it is not great enough to account for the magnitude of lengthened reaction times.

Choice reaction time slows in older adults even more than does simple reaction time. Making a task more complex by increasing the number of signals or by designating responses that are less logical (e.g., pressing the left button in response to the right signal light) disproportionately increases older adults' reaction time when compared with that of younger adults (Cerella, Poon, & Williams, 1980; Welford, 1977a,b).

Choice reaction time is a measure requiring the earliest possible response to more than one stimulus, usually with a different response matched to each of the possible stimuli.

Older adults' movement time also shows a very slight slowing (Singleton, 1955), but older adults maintain the speed of planned, repetitive movements such as tapping (Earles & Salthouse, 1995; Fieandt, Huhtala, Kullberg, & Saarl, 1956; Jagacinski, Liao, & Fayyad, 1995). Because almost all behaviors mediated by the CNS slow down as an adult ages, central factors are assumed to be largely responsible for slower information processing speed (Birren, 1964). However, the schemata of older adults can be particularly complete and refined for skills the adult has had a lifetime of experience with. This experience is particularly helpful when accuracy is more important than speed. When older adults are not pressed to perform as quickly as possible, they demonstrate very accurate performance on well-practiced tasks.

In our discussion to this point, you may have noticed that older adults have been discussed as if they form a homogeneous group. No distinction has been made between subgroups such as healthy adults and clinical populations, or active and inactive adults. Since the 1970s, however, research studies have shown that active older adults are closer to young adults in simple and choice reaction-time performance than are inactive older adults (Rikli & Busch, 1986; Spirduso, 1975, 1980). In 2003, Colcombe and Kramer published a meta-analysis of 18 aerobic fitness intervention studies with older adults. They found that fitness training improved performance on a variety of cognitive tasks. The greatest effect was for executive tasks

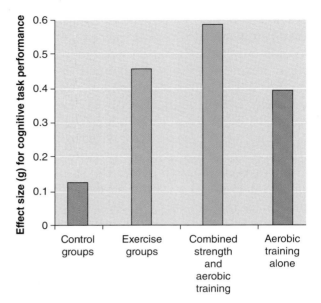

FIGURE 14.4 Stanley Colcombe and Arthur Kramer conducted a meta-analysis showing that cognitive task performance was better at a second testing for both control and exercise groups. Yet, improvement in the exercise groups was much greater than that in the control groups. Among exercisers, groups combining strength and aerobic training improved somewhat more than those using aerobic training only. Four types of cognitive tasks were included: speed, visuopatial, controlled processing, and executive control. The greatest effect was on executive control tasks, but improvement occurred on all cognitive tasks.

Data are from Colcombe and Kramer 2003.

(those involving planning, inhibition, and scheduling of mental processes), but speed, visuospatial, and controlled-process (e.g., choice reaction time) tasks also improved (figure 14.4). The benefits of training were greater if the intervention was a combined aerobic and strength program as compared with aerobic training alone, if the program lasted more than 6 months, if sessions lasted more than 30 min, and if exercisers were "young-old" (55–65 years) or "mid-old" (66–70) rather than "old-old" (71–80).

Great interest exists in learning how exercise exerts its favorable effect on cognitive functions, and researchers in this area can now take advantage of more widely available advanced imaging techniques, such as function magnetic resonance imaging (MRI). Colcombe et al. (2003) used MRI scans to show that aerobic fitness levels moderated loss of nervous system tissue with aging, and Colcombe et al. (2006) used MRI scans to find that brain volume increased in 60- to 79-year-olds who started an aerobic exercise program. So, aerobic fitness has a favorable effect on the brain structure of older adults. Is the same true of brain function? Colcombe et al. (2004) used functional MRI scans to see that fit adults showed greater activity in involved areas of the brain during a cognitive task compared with unfit adults (see also McAuley, Kramer, & Colcombe, 2004). This finding, along with those on training older adults to perform specific tasks (Erickson et al., 2007), suggests that the older adult brain retains more plasticity in functioning than was previously thought. A number of other factors could be involved in the beneficial effect of

KEY POINT
Sufficient aerobic training can improve older adults' performance on a variety of cognitive tasks.

exercise, including improved vascular health in the brain and beneficial effects on insulin resistance and glucose intolerance (Weuve et al., 2004).

 WEB STUDY GUIDE **Observe reaction-time performance in individuals representing many parts of the life span in Lab Activity 14.2, Age-Related Reaction Times, in the web study guide. Go to www.HumanKinetics.com/ LifeSpanMotorDevelopment.**

 If you were a therapist at a residential facility for older adults, what activities might Colcombe and Kramer's meta-analysis lead you to recommend for the residents? Why?

Summary and Synthesis

Knowledge acts as a constraint in performing skills. Those with more knowledge make more appropriate responses in settings requiring decisions. They anticipate situations and actions and think of global strategies more than of specific, single occurrences. Acquiring knowledge takes time and experience. Children need experience to develop an extensive knowledge base, yet expert children can bring more knowledge to a situation than a novice adult can. Older adults with extensive experience can make their knowledge base a great asset in the performance of skills.

Speed of cognitive processing does, however, differ over the life span. Although youth and older adult experts might surpass young adults with their knowledge, they might experience slower processing of that information. On the other hand, older adults who train aerobically at a sufficient level might moderate declines in cognitive function.

 ## Reinforcing What You Have Learned About Constraints

TAKE A SECOND LOOK

We have seen that knowledge is important to the performance of motor skills. It seems that the time and money athletes and teams spend on the technology that increases their knowledge about their own and competitors' performance is well worth it! It is helpful to appreciate that knowledge about an activity is an individual constraint that can be changed quickly. Teachers and coaches who help performers increase their knowledge help their performance by doing so, sometimes at a more rapid rate than the improvement of physical skills.

TEST YOUR KNOWLEDGE

1. Name and define the types of knowledge, and provide an example of each, for one of your favorite sports or dance forms.
2. Describe four sport-specific ways that novices and experts differ in their knowledge of a sport.
3. What can youth athletes do better as they increase their expertise in their sports?
4. What are some factors that can influence performance on memory tasks?
5. Describe the trend in cognitive processing speed over the life span, assuming that middle-aged and older adults become more sedentary with age.
6. How does aerobic training affect cognitive functioning in older adults? What are the implications for activities of daily living and sport participation?

LEARNING EXERCISE 14.1

Teaching Strategies for Older Adult Learners

Older adults may learn new things more slowly than young adults do.

1. Identify two strategies you would adopt to teach a new skill to an older adult.
2. Write a lesson plan for teaching this skill that uses each of your two strategies.

LEARNING EXERCISE 14.2

Compensatory Strategies of Older Adults

Older adults who participate in sport sometimes compensate for limitations in their movement (due, for example, to changes in the skeletal system, muscle strength, or flexibility) by anticipating their next movements based on experience in playing the game. Interview an older adult who participates fluently in a sport such as tennis, racquetball, or volleyball and ask him or her to describe making such adaptations. For example, Dodo Cheney, who won tennis championships into her 80s, recounts learning to position herself closer to the net (when in her younger days she would have positioned herself at the baseline) in order to reach drop shots or short balls.

Interaction of Exercise Task and Structural Constraints

The theme of our study of motor development is that movement arises from the interaction of individual, environmental, and task constraints. We also note repeatedly that within each type of constraint, multiple systems interact. For example, chapter 5 examines individual structural systems—such as the skeletal, muscular, and neurological systems—that interact with growth and aging. Later chapters review perceptual systems, their interaction, and how they constrain movement. In part VI, we explore the interaction of task and structural constraints, focusing specifically on exercise.

Over time, exercise leads to improved levels of physical fitness, which can be measured by changes in different structural constraints. Physical fitness has many systems or components, such as flexibility and strength. A person who is fit in one component is not necessarily fit in another. For example, an individual may be very strong but not very flexible. This part of the book discusses in detail the following structural constraints as components of fitness: cardiorespiratory endurance (chapter 15), strength (chapter 16), flexibility (chapter 16), and body composition (chapter 17).

Some writers view fitness as including additional components, such as agility and power, but the four mentioned here are the essential systems that can be measured to show change in structural constraints. Potentially, a person can improve physical fitness through a systematic program of exercise aimed at these four components. An individual's fitness level in each of the four systems—along with the interaction of these systems—can either permit or restrain movements over the life span. Fitness is important in every part of the life span, but older adulthood is the period when fitness may have the greatest influence on quality of life, through the movements permitted and the positive effect on all of the body's systems. We begin by discussing endurance for vigorous activity.

Suggested Reading

Bar-Or, O., & Rowland, T.W. (2004). *Pediatric exercise medicine: From physiologic principles to health care application*. Champaign, IL: Human Kinetics.

Cahill, B.R., & Pearl, A.J. (Eds.). (1993). *Intensive participation in children's sports*. Champaign, IL: Human Kinetics.

Feltz, D.L. (Ed.). (2004). The Academy papers: Obesity and physical activity. *Quest, 56*, iv–170.

Maud, P.J., & Foster, C. (Eds.) (2006). *Physiological assessment of human fitness* (2nd ed.). Champaign, IL: Human Kinetics.

Rowland, T.W. (Ed.). (1993). *Pediatric laboratory exercise testing*. Champaign, IL: Human Kinetics.

Rowland, T.W. (2005). *Children's exercise physiology* (2nd ed.). Champaign, IL: Human Kinetics.

Spirduso, W.W., Francis, K.L., & MacRae, P.G. (2005). *Physical dimensions of aging* (2nd ed.). Champaign, IL: Human Kinetics.

Taylor, A., & Johnson, M. (2008). *Physiology of exercise and healthy aging*. Champaign, IL: Human Kinetics.

15

Development of Cardiorespiratory Endurance

CHAPTER OBJECTIVES

This chapter

- examines the body's response to short-term vigorous exercise and how this response changes over the life span,
- reviews the effects of short-term exercise over the life span,
- studies the body's response to prolonged exercise and how this response changes over the life span, and
- reviews the effects of endurance training over the life span.

Motor Development in the Real World

Never Leave Your Living Room

A movie trailer showed one person piloting a plane while another person, a passenger, asks, "Where did you learn to fly?" The answer? "PlayStation!" You might recognize the answer as one of the electronic game consoles that can be connected to a television. It seems as though electronic games for television or computer get better and more lifelike every year. You can play games based on all the major sports, both individual and team, and with many of the nuances (e.g., putting spin on your shots) of the real thing. It makes one wonder whether some people will ever leave their living room to actually play the sports! When time spent playing video games is added to the hours spent watching television and using computers, it is easy to see why concern about the fitness level of people in Westernized countries, even children, is so widespread. Components of physical fitness can act as individual constraints to most activities; some components are more important to some kinds of physical activities than others. A lack of fitness can easily serve as a rate limiter to the performance of motor skills and the physical activities of everyday living. Indeed, fitness is related to one's very quality of life. Of course, a relationship exists between the growth and aging of the body and of its systems (structural constraints) and the fitness components, and a relationship exists between functional constraints and training for the maintenance or improvement of fitness. It is important to understand how these various structural and functional individual constraints interact in the performance of skills.

Of all the fitness components, cardiorespiratory endurance has the greatest implications for lifelong health, but its development in children is surrounded by many myths. For many years, experts thought that children's cardiovascular and respiratory systems limited their capacity for extended work. They thought so because measurements of children's blood vessel size were misinterpreted. Even though the mistake was soon discovered, the myth has persisted for decades (Karpovich, 1937). In addition, many parents and teachers think that children automatically get enough exercise to become and remain fit. This belief serves as a social constraint to children's regular and systematic participation in exercise. Recent studies documented a worldwide trend toward reduced fitness (Tomkinson & Olds, 2007; Tomkinson, Olds, Kang, & Kim, 2007), showing that the sedentary lifestyle that many of today's adults have adopted has spilled over to the lives of their children. A high percentage of children and teenagers already exhibit one or more of the risk factors for coronary heart disease, and far too many are obese. Children in poor physical condition are likely to maintain that status throughout their adult lives. Educators and exercise leaders must thoroughly understand development of and potential for cardiorespiratory endurance so that they can challenge children to attain an appropriate level of fitness for vigorous activity.

Cardiorespiratory endurance reflects one's ability to sustain vigorous activity. It is important for two broad reasons. First, participation in many physical activities demands sustained vigorous exertion. Second, the health of the cardiac, vascular, and respiratory systems is related to endurance level, largely because training that improves endurance makes these systems more efficient. In this chapter we review the body's basic physiological responses to both short-term and long-term vigorous activities. We also discuss the changes that occur in these responses with growth and aging.

Physiological Responses to Short-Term Exercise

Vigorous physical activity can be a short burst of intense exercise, a long period of submaximal or maximal work, or a combination of these types. Our bodies meet the differing demands of brief, intense activity and of longer, more moderate activity with different physiological responses. During a brief period (10 s) of intense activity, the body responds by depleting local reserves of oxygen and sources of energy stored in the muscles, thus creating a deficit of oxygen that must eventually be replenished. These are **anaerobic** (without oxygen) systems. Anaerobic system performance can be reflected in measurements of **anaerobic power** and **anaerobic capacity**.

As the period of exercise demand grows longer, the anaerobic systems contribute less to the body's response. Respiration and circulation increase to bring oxygen to the muscles. Ninety seconds into an exercise bout, anaerobic and **aerobic** (with oxygen) energy systems contribute about equally. After 3 min, aerobic processes meet the demands of exercise. The types of exercise that promote anaerobic performance, then, are vigorous but of short duration, whereas those that promote aerobic performance are sustained and consequently less vigorous or intense.

Anaerobic power is the rate at which a person's body can meet the demand for short-term, intense activity.

Anaerobic capacity is the maximum oxygen deficit that a person can tolerate.

Developmental Changes in Anaerobic Performance

At any age, anaerobic performance is related to

- body size, particularly fat-free muscle mass and muscle size;
- the ability to metabolize fuel sources in the muscles; and
- quick mobilization of oxygen delivery systems.

Some of these factors change as a person grows (Malina, Bouchard, & Bar-Or, 2004).

Childhood

Young children have smaller absolute quantities of energy reserves than adults do because they have less muscle mass (Eriksson, 1978; Shephard, 1982). Therefore, children attain less output of absolute anaerobic power than adults do. As children grow their muscle mass increases, as do their energy reserves. They also can better tolerate the by-products of the metabolic process. Thus, mean and peak anaerobic power improve steadily as a person ages (Duche et al., 1992; Falgairette, Bedu, Fellmann, Van Praagh, & Coudert, 1991; Inbar & Bar-Or, 1986). Total work output scores improve over the entire adolescent period in boys but only until puberty in girls, perhaps reflecting the patterns of muscle growth in the sexes (figure 15.1, *a* and *b*) or sociocultural views of appropriate activities for girls.

Accounting for differences in muscle mass, however, does not entirely eliminate the differences in anaerobic performance that favor boys (Van Praagh, Fellmann, Bedu, Falgairette, & Coudert, 1990). Not all of the differences between children and adults are attributable to difference in body size, either. When we divide anaerobic performance scores by body weight, scores still improve with age.

Undoubtedly, better neuromuscular coordination and skill contribute to improved anaerobic performance as children grow older, and the capacity for energy production improves with age (Rowland, 1996). Armstrong, Welsman, and Kirby (1997) found that advancing maturation independent of body mass was related to higher mean and peak anaerobic power. More mature children can be expected to show better anaerobic performance than other children even if they are similar in body size to less mature children (Tomkinson, Hamlin, & Olds, 2006).

Adulthood

Once individuals attain adult body size, their anaerobic performance remains stable throughout young adulthood (Inbar & Bar-Or, 1986). Any improvement in anaerobic power and capacity is achieved through training alone. The anaerobic systems of older adults do not produce energy as quickly as those of younger adults; this decline is likely associated with loss of muscle mass. At the same level of exercise, older adults accumulate by-products of energy metabolism sooner than young adults do (Spirduso, Francis, & MacRae, 2005). The loss of anaerobic power was recorded as 50% by age 75 (Grassi, Cerretelli, Narici, & Marconi, 1991).

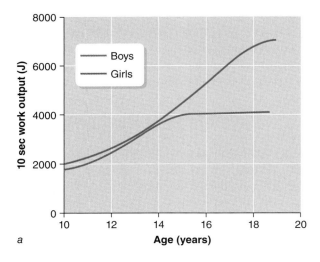

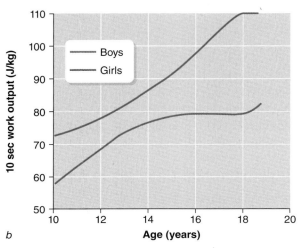

FIGURE 15.1   Anaerobic performance. *(a)* Change in total work output (measured in Joules) on a 10 s all-out bicycle ergometer ride with advancing age. C. Bouchard and J.A. Simoneau (unpublished data) measured a cross-sectional group of French Canadian youths on this task. When anaerobic performance scores are divided by body weight, as in *(b)*, scores still improve with age.

Reprinted by permission from Malina, Bouchard, and Bar-Or 2004.

It is not clear, however, whether anaerobic power and capacity necessarily decline as adults grow older. Those engaged in lifelong intense training showed no deterioration in anaerobic performance (Reaburn & Mackinnon, 1990). These master athletes likely maintained much of their muscle mass. Because any loss of muscle mass in older adults is likely to affect anaerobic performance, a lack of training in anaerobic tasks to maintain conditioning logically would affect performance.

Anaerobic Training

Although the results of training studies are somewhat inconsistent, preadolescent and adolescent boys have demonstrated improved anaerobic power with anaerobic training (Grodjinovsky, Inbar, Dotan, & Bar-Or, 1980; Rotstein, Dotan, Bar-Or, & Tenenbaum, 1986). Improvements are not large, and some cross-sectional comparisons show no anaerobic differences between active and nonactive boys (Falgairette, Duche, Bedu, Fellmann, & Coudert, 1993; Mero, Kauhanen, Peltola, Vuorimaa, & Komi, 1990). Improvements with training might be associated with metabolizing energy reserves more efficiently, therefore improving anaerobic capacity (Eriksson, 1972). Less is known about girls, but McManus, Armstrong, and Williams (1997) found small improvements in prepubescent girls with both cycle and sprint running training.

 Imagine you are a physical education teacher. Which games that students play provide anaerobic training at the elementary school level? At the middle school level?

Little is known about how untrained older adults respond to anaerobic training, although training programs that improve muscle mass are likely to bring about an improvement of anaerobic performance. Reaburn and Mackinnon (1990) studied master athletes over 46 years of age who were training for world swimming competition. After sprint swimming, these athletes produced and removed lactic acid just as well as younger adults. Therefore, long-term training of sufficient intensity might maintain anaerobic performance.

Physiological Responses to Prolonged Exercise

How do our bodies sustain submaximal physical activity for prolonged periods? Unlike in short-term exercise, the energy for prolonged exercise is derived from aerobic systems—the oxidative breakdown of food stores—in addition to the local reserves depleted in the first few minutes of exercise. The success with which we meet the needs of prolonged activity can be indicated by measurements of **aerobic power** and **aerobic capacity**.

Sustained, prolonged activity depends on the transportation of sufficient oxygen to the working muscles for longer periods. The needed oxygen is delivered through

KEY POINT
Anaerobic training improves the anaerobic performance of preadolescent children and maintains that of master athletes.

Aerobic power is the rate at which long-term oxygen demand is met during prolonged activity.

Aerobic capacity is the total energy available to meet the demands of prolonged activity.

Assessing Anaerobic Performance

No direct, noninvasive methods of measuring anaerobic fitness exist, so it is typically studied through short-duration tasks. The Quebec 10 s and the Wingate 30 s all-out rides on a bicycle ergometer and the Margaria step-running test are common laboratory tests that provide scores in total work output, mean power, or peak power. Total work output indicates how much absolute work an individual can do in a 10 or 30 s time period. In contrast, power indicates the rate at which individuals can produce energy—that is, the work they can do per a specific unit of time. Mean power is the average power individuals achieve during the 10 or 30 s period, whereas peak power is the highest rate they achieve. The 50 yd dash and sprinting a flight of stairs are common field tests. Participants must be willing and able to give an all-out effort in order to provide an accurate measure of anaerobic performance. Taking anaerobic measurements can be difficult or even dangerous with older adults, especially those who have been inactive.

increases in heart and respiratory rates, cardiac output, and oxygen uptake. An increased respiratory rate brings more oxygen to the lungs, making it available for diffusion into the bloodstream. Increased cardiac output (the amount of blood pumped into the circulatory system) allows more oxygen to reach the muscles. The body achieves this increased cardiac output through increased heart rate or increased stroke volume. Changes in stroke volume during exercise are relatively small, but one of the long-term benefits of training is greater stroke volume.

The limiting factor to continued vigorous activity is the heart's ability to pump enough blood to meet the oxygen needs of the working muscles. When individuals engage in very heavy activity, their heart rates increase throughout the session until exhaustion ends the activity. When they stop vigorous activity, their heart rates decrease quickly for 2 to 3 min and then more gradually for a time related to the duration and intensity of the activity. Fit individuals regain their resting heart rates more quickly than unfit individuals.

This description is only a brief summary of the physiological responses to exercise. A more detailed treatment is available in exercise physiology textbooks.

Changes in Aerobic Performance During Childhood

Hemoglobin is the protein in the blood that carries oxygen.

KEY POINT
Children's physiological response to endurance activity is very efficient, but children cannot exercise as long as adults can.

KEY POINT
Absolute maximal oxygen uptake increases in boys throughout childhood and adolescence and in girls until age 12, after which it plateaus.

Maximal oxygen uptake is the highest amount of oxygen the body can consume during aerobic work.

KEY POINT
Maximal oxygen uptake per kilogram of body weight is stable in boys and declines slightly in girls throughout childhood and adolescence.

How do children respond physiologically to prolonged activity? Children tend to have hypokinetic circulation (Bar-Or, Shephard, & Allen, 1971); that is, their cardiac output is less than an adult's (cardiac output is the product of stroke volume and heart rate). Children have a smaller stroke volume than adults, reflecting their smaller hearts. They compensate in part with higher heart rates than adults at a given level of exercise, but their cardiac output is still somewhat lower than an adult's. Children also have lower blood **hemoglobin** concentrations than do adults; hemoglobin concentration is related to the blood's ability to carry oxygen.

You might assume that these two factors in children, hypokinetic circulation and low hemoglobin concentration, result in an oxygen transport system that is less efficient than that in adults. However, children can extract relatively more of the oxygen circulating to the active muscles than adults can (Malina & Bouchard, 1991; Shephard, 1982), which seems to compensate for these factors. The result is a comparably effective oxygen transport system. Children also mobilize their aerobic systems faster than adults do (Bar-Or, 1983).

Children do have a lower tolerance than adults for extended periods of exercise, perhaps due to smaller energy reserves in the muscles. As children grow, their hypokinetic circulation is gradually reduced and their response becomes increasingly similar to the adult response.

Longitudinal and cross-sectional studies demonstrate that absolute **maximal oxygen uptake** increases linearly in children from age 4 until late adolescence in boys and until age 12 or 13 in girls (Krahenbuhl, Skinner, & Kohrt, 1985; Mirwald & Bailey, 1986; Shuleva, Hunter, Hester, & Dunaway, 1990). Maximal oxygen uptake is the most common measure of fitness for endurance activities. Figure 15.2a shows this trend between ages 6 and about 18 years of age. Boys and girls are similar in maximal oxygen uptake until about age 12, though boys have a slightly higher average. After this age, maximal oxygen uptake plateaus in girls but continues to increase in boys. The increase with age is related to growth of the musculature, lungs, and heart.

A strong relationship exists between absolute maximal oxygen uptake and lean body mass. In fact, maximal oxygen uptake can be expressed in relative rather than absolute terms, dividing it by body weight, lean body weight, or another body dimension. As figure 15.2b shows, maximal oxygen uptake relative to body weight stays about the same throughout childhood and adolescence in boys. It declines in girls, probably because adipose (fat) tissue increases. When maximal oxygen uptake is related to fat-free mass, scores show a slight decline during and after puberty and small sex differences remain.

Thus, body weight appears to increase slightly faster than maximal oxygen uptake around puberty (Malina & Bouchard, 1991). Maximal oxygen uptake might depend somewhat on maturity in addition to body size; comparisons of maximal oxygen uptake with age show a relationship in adolescents who vary in age but are identical in size (Sprynarova & Reisenauer, 1978). Two adolescents identical in size could differ in maximal oxygen uptake if one were more physiologically mature than the other.

Even though maximal oxygen uptake is the best single measurement of endurance, it might not predict running performance in children as well as it does in adults. Running test performance relates more to anaerobic measures in children than in adults. Caution should be used when inferring maximal oxygen uptake levels from children's running performance.

It is important to recognize the relationship between children's increasing body size and their improving ability to sustain exercise during growth. With body growth come increases in lung volume, heart and stroke volume, total hemoglobin, and lean body mass. These factors foster improved cardiac output and, subsequently, improved exercise capacity and absolute maximal oxygen uptake. Because children vary in size despite their chronological age, evaluations of exercise capacity among children should relate to body size rather than chronological age alone. In the past, educators frequently based evaluation only on age.

Average exercise capacity and average body size of groups of children and adolescents generally increase with age, but exercise capacity is also related to maturation rate. As noted in chapter 4, the relationship between chronological age and

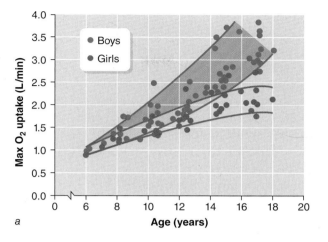

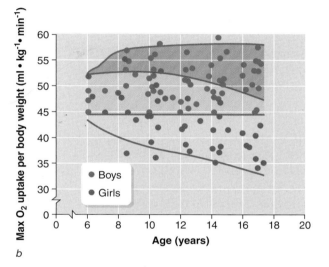

a

b

KEY POINT

Maximal oxygen uptake is related to body size, especially lean body mass, as well as to maturity status.

FIGURE 15.2 The relationship between maximal oxygen uptake and age. (a) Absolute scores. (b) Maximal oxygen uptake values relative to kilograms of body weight. The boys' scores are centered in the shaded area and the girls' scores are centered in the unshaded area.

Reprinted by permission from Bar-Or 1983.

maturation status is imperfect. Therefore, each child's unique size *and* maturity level should be considered when establishing expectations for endurance performance.

In children, body size is a far better predictor of endurance than the child's sex. After puberty, however, boys on average attain a considerable edge over girls in absolute maximal oxygen uptake and have the potential to retain this edge throughout life. Several factors contribute to this sex difference. One is body composition. The average man gains more lean body mass and less adipose tissue during adolescence than does the average woman. Women are similar to men in maximal oxygen uptake per kilogram of fat-free body mass, but when adipose tissue is included, women have a lower maximal oxygen uptake. Another factor in sex differences in oxygen consumption is that women tend to have lower hemoglobin concentrations than men do (Åstrand, 1976).

By the time the average male reaches late adolescence he has an edge over the average female in both oxygen consumption and working capacity (figure 15.3). It must be remembered that environmental factors,

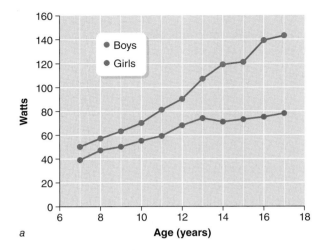

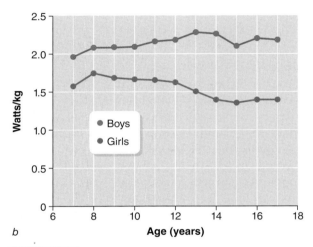

FIGURE 15.3 Physical working capacity with advancing age in childhood and adolescence. Measurements were made in school classrooms (without habituation of the Canadian subjects) at a heart rate of 170 beats per minute. Readings would probably be up to 10% higher given climatic control (20–22 °C) and some familiarization with experimental procedures. Measurements are in *(a)* watts (1 watt = 6 kg·m⁻¹·min⁻¹) and *(b)* watts per kilogram of body weight.

Data from Shephard 1982.

especially training, influence the endurance capacities of individual men and women throughout their lives. Thus, it would not be surprising to find that an active woman has a higher maximal oxygen uptake than a sedentary man.

Laboratory studies tend to conclude that children have greater metabolic requirements for moving their body mass in such activities as walking or running than adults do (Bar-Or, 1983; Rowland, 1996). This finding, which implies that children are at a disadvantage in endurance exercise compared with adults, might actually be an artifact of laboratory studies. When exercise economy is scaled to body mass, differences between boys and men are eliminated (Eston, Robson, & Winter, 1993). That is, laboratory studies tend to compare children and adults at identical workloads when it is likely that they exercise at a metabolic rate scaled to body size (Rowland, 2012). Children, then, are as economical as adults. This finding is interesting in light of our emphasis on the importance of body scaling.

 WEB STUDY GUIDE   Analyze children's scores on a test of prolonged moderate activity and note sex differences in Lab Activity 15.1, Changes in Youth Endurance Performance, in the web study guide. Go to www.HumanKinetics. com/LifeSpanMotorDevelopment.

Aerobic Performance in Adulthood

Average maximal oxygen uptake per kilogram of body weight peaks in the 20s, then decreases throughout the adult years. The loss is approximately 1% per year of life. The decline is found in both cross-sectional and longitudinal research and among athletic, active, and sedentary adults (Spirduso, 1995). Athletic and active adults, however, maintain a higher maximal oxygen uptake than sedentary adults. This section discusses the structural and functional changes in the cardiovascular and respiratory systems that contribute to this decline.

Cardiovascular Structure and Function

Cardiovascular function is related to the structure of the heart and blood vessels. The major structural changes in a nondiseased heart with aging include a progressive loss of cardiac muscle, a loss of elasticity in cardiac muscle fibers (Harrison, Dixon, Russell, Bidwai, & Coleman, 1964), a thickening of the left ventricular wall, and fibrotic changes in the valves (Pomerance, 1965). The major blood vessels also lose elasticity (Fleg, 1986). It remains unclear whether these changes are unavoidable in aging or reflect a chronic lack of oxygen. The effects of these structural changes on cardiovascular function are numerous.

•   **Maximum heart rate.** Whereas resting heart rate values of older adults are comparable with those of young adults, the maximum achievable heart rate with physical exertion gradually declines with aging (Lipsitz, 1989). The difference is about 188 beats per minute for persons in their 20s and 168 for persons in their 50s and 60s (Spirduso, 1995). Decreased maximum heart rate may be the major factor in reduced maximal oxygen uptake with aging (Hagburg et al., 1985).

•   **Stroke volume.** The stroke volume of older adults may or may not decline with aging; research studies have yielded both results (see Stamford, 1988, for a review). Asymptomatic ischemic heart disease (affecting blood supply to the heart) may account for the equivocal results. Investigators using rigorous screening for heart disease may find no decrease in stroke volume, whereas researchers whose studies include participants with undetected disease may find a decrease (Safar, 1990).

•   **Cardiac output.** Cardiac output is the product of heart rate and stroke volume. Healthy older adults experience a decline in cardiac output during heavy activity with a decline in maximal oxygen uptake, and those with ischemic heart disease experience even greater decline as maximum heart rate and stroke volume decrease. Cardiac output at rest or with submaximal work is unchanged with aging, and cardiac output is much higher in adults who train aerobically than in sedentary adults.

•   **Blood pressure.** Older adults reach their peak cardiac output at a lower intensity of work than do younger adults (Brandfonbrener, Landowne, & Shock, 1955; Shephard, 1978a). Older adults' more rigid arteries resist the volume of blood the heart pumps into them. This resistance is even greater if the person has

Several methods can be used to assess a person's physiological responses to sustained activity requiring repetitive contraction of the large muscles. The most common activities used are cycling on an ergometer or walking or running on a treadmill. The effort asked of the individual can be submaximal or maximal. Measurements of aerobic power and capacity tend to be specific to the task performed (e.g., cycling, running), so caution must be used in comparing scores on different tasks. Young children have difficulty keeping a cadence during bicycle ergometer tests. They are also more likely than adults to make unnecessary movements during testing. In addition, they may be at risk of falling on a treadmill.

Aerobic exercise tests are usually graded; that is, they increase workload in stages. There is no standard protocol for any age group, but intensity should always be appropriate for the fitness level and size of those tested.

A common measure of fitness for endurance activities is maximal oxygen uptake, or maximal aerobic power, which is the maximum volume of oxygen the body can consume per minute (Heyward, 1991; Zwiren, 1989). The more efficiently a person's body uses oxygen (i.e., the less oxygen consumed for the same amount of work performed), the more fit the individual. Endurance exercise performance is too complex to be represented by any single measure, yet maximal oxygen uptake and endurance activity performance are highly correlated, making maximum oxygen uptake one of the preferred measures of endurance.

In a test assessing maximal oxygen uptake, you can measure or estimate the amount of oxygen consumed during activity. This score is also expressed as oxygen consumed per minute per kilogram of body weight. Maximal oxygen uptake is a common measure of endurance in studies of children and older adults because it can be estimated from a submaximal test, thus avoiding the need for exercise to exhaustion. Direct measures of oxygen use require more sophisticated and expensive equipment than is needed for estimates from submaximal tests.

atherosclerosis (the buildup of plaque on the artery walls). In turn, this resistance raises resting pulse pressure (the difference between systolic and diastolic blood pressure) and systolic blood pressure. Whether blood pressure increases or decreases during exercise also depends on the health of the cardiac muscle fibers and their ability to tolerate an increased workload. A lifestyle that includes regular physical activity is associated with lower systolic blood pressure (Reaven, Barrett-Connor, & Edelstein, 1991).

• **Blood flow and hemoglobin content.** For activity to be sustained, oxygen must be delivered to the working muscles by the blood. Peripheral blood flow is apparently well maintained in older adulthood. Hemoglobin is also maintained in older adulthood (Timiras & Brownstein, 1987), but the incidence of anemia increases in older adulthood. This condition is associated with reduced hemoglobin values.

Respiratory Structure and Function

Forced vital capacity is the maximum volume of air the lungs can expel after maximal inspiration.

Elasticity of the lung tissue and chest walls declines with aging (Turner, Mead, & Wohl, 1968). Therefore, older adults expend more effort in breathing than young adults. Of interest is the lung volume, especially the volume termed **forced vital capacity.** A large vital capacity reflects a large inspiratory capacity of the lungs and results in better alveolar ventilation. Because the greatest part of oxygen diffusion

Another measure of physiological response to prolonged exercise is maximal working capacity, which means the highest work, or exercise, load a person can tolerate before reaching exhaustion (Adams, 1973). Because this test requires maximal effort, it requires motivating individuals to work to exhaustion. Although it is unlikely, an individual may have a heart attack during such a test. For this reason this measure is not often used with children or older adults.

Other measures of endurance fitness are less common. For example, maximal cardiac output can be directly measured, but this test is difficult to administer because it requires intubation (inserting a tube into the body). Measuring an individual's electrocardiograph changes during exercise is of interest when studying adults (Heyward, 1991), but it does not apply very well to most children because its main purpose is to identify impaired heart function. Therefore, the preferred research measure of endurance fitness in children and older adults is maximal oxygen uptake for changes in aerobic power and adaptations to submaximal exercise efforts for changes in aerobic capacity.

Several research investigators attempted to identify field tests for children that estimate endurance nearly as reliably as when it is measured in a laboratory. Such field tests allow educators to measure aerobic performance without laboratory equipment. The investigators compared maximal oxygen uptake scores from laboratory tests with performance in 800 m, 1200 m, and 1600 m runs for 83 children in the first, second, and third grades. Performance on the 1600 m run was a better predictor of maximal oxygen uptake for boys and girls than performance on the 800 m or 1200 m runs. An average velocity score on the 1600 m run had a slightly higher correlation with maximal oxygen uptake than a total time score. We can conclude that a 1600 m run is a better field test of endurance in children than shorter runs. This test proved to have high test–retest reliability (Krahenbuhl, Pangrazi, Petersen, Burkett, & Schneider, 1978). In young trained runners, the correlation between maximal oxygen uptake and race time is high (Cunningham, 1990; Unnithan, 1993).

to the capillaries takes place at the alveoli (figure 15.4), better alveolar ventilation contributes to increased amounts of oxygen circulating in the blood and reaching the working muscles.

A decreased vital capacity with aging is well established; the average decrease is 4% to 5% per decade (Norris, Shock, Landowne, & Falzone, 1956; Shephard, 1987). The loss is more dramatic in smokers than in nonsmokers, and well-trained persons in their 40s are known to maintain the vital capacity of their 20s (Shephard, 1987).

The oxygen and carbon dioxide exchange in the lungs loses some efficiency with aging, and this decline is not offset by training (Dempsey, Johnson, & Saupe, 1990). Generally, though, the pulmonary systems of older adults do well at rest and during moderate activity. Moreover, the pulmonary system is not the major limiting factor in exercise capacity.

Changes in Muscle Mass

The decline in maximal oxygen uptake is probably related both to loss of muscle mass and the ability of muscles to use oxygen and to cardiovascular and respiratory changes. Maximal oxygen uptake measures the amount of oxygen delivered to and used by the muscles. So, the more muscle mass, the more likely maximal oxygen

KEY POINT
Cardiovascular factors are a greater limitation to older adults' aerobic performance than are pulmonary factors.

KEY POINT
Maximal oxygen uptake declines throughout adulthood, a trend that is related to a decrease in maximum heart rate and in muscle mass. Active older adults maintain an edge in maximal oxygen uptake over those who are sedentary.

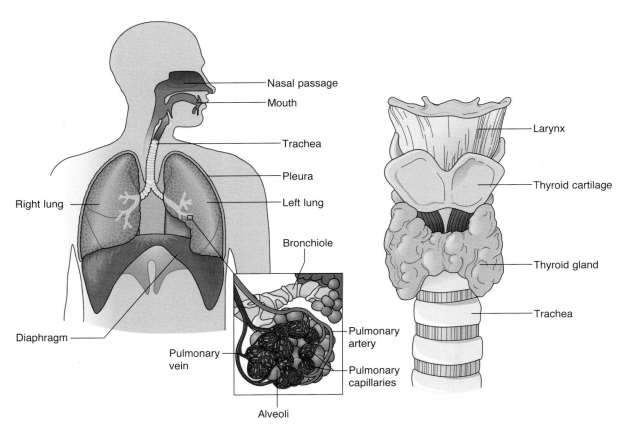

FIGURE 15.4   The respiratory system. Oxygen diffusion to the capillaries takes place at the alveoli, enlarged in the figure.

uptake is greater. In fact, when maximal oxygen uptake is related to the kilograms of muscle (rather than kilograms of body weight) in older adults, declines shrink from 60% to 14% in men and 50% to 8% in women (Spirduso, 1995). Thus, maintenance of muscle mass is a factor in minimizing the loss of endurance performance. The addition of adipose tissue with aging works against maintenance of maximal oxygen uptake.

The end result of cardiac and pulmonary changes and of the loss of muscle mass is that maximum exercise capacity and maximal oxygen uptake (whether absolute or relative to body weight) decline as an adult ages and the recovery period after vigorous activity lengthens. The results of both longitudinal and cross-sectional studies are plotted in figure 15.5, and a decline with advancing age is evident. A lifetime of negative environmental factors, such as smoking or poor nutrition, can contribute to or accelerate the changes. Conversely, a lifetime of exposure to positive environmental factors, such as healthful exercise, can better maintain endurance levels.

 If you were a personal trainer with older adult clients, what types of training activities would you plan in order to help them improve their aerobic performance?

Changes with growth and aging dramatically affect endurance performance throughout the life span. Various systems can constrain the potential for vigorous, sustained activity. It is important for everyone to have some knowledge of how the various systems influence aerobic activity because of the health implications of regular participation in aerobic activity. Moreover, educators and therapists must understand these influences thoroughly in order to promote training that yields significant health benefits.

Endurance Training

The result of aerobic training is predictable in adults. An adult improves maximal oxygen uptake by training at least 3 times a week for at least 20 min at an intensity of 60% to 90% of maximum heart rate. Stroke volume increases, and maximal cardiac output subsequently increases. Oxygen is better extracted from the blood at muscle sites. Maximal ventilation per minute rises. Inactive adults who begin training typically increase maximal oxygen uptake by 25% to 50% (Hartley, 1992). Therefore, appropriate training yields benefits. Let's consider whether the same is true for children.

Training Effect in Children

Children who begin an aerobic training program are continuing to grow, and, as noted earlier, maximal oxygen uptake increases with growth. Therefore, to know the effect of training in

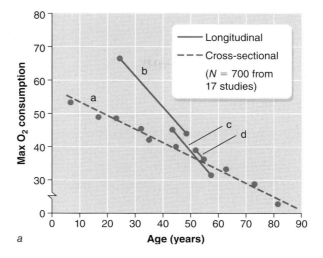

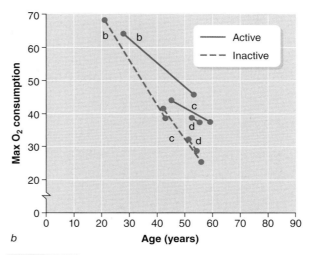

FIGURE 15.5 Maximal oxygen uptake declines as a person ages. *(a)* Cross-sectional studies and longitudinal studies show declines in adulthood. *(b)* The decline is not as rapid in active adults. The dotted lines represent the change in inactive adults and the solid lines represent the change in active adults. Data plotted are from *(a)* Dehn and Bruce (1972), *(b)* Dill et al. (1967), *(c)* Hollman (1965), and *(d)* Dehn and Bruce (1972) (all cited in Dehn & Bruce, 1972).

Reprinted, by permission, from B.A. Stamford, 1986, Exercise and the elderly. In *Exercise and sport sciences reviews*, Vol. 16, edited by K.B. Pandolf (New York: Macmillan), 344. © The McGraw-Hill Companies.

children, we must distinguish any increase in maximal oxygen uptake due to growth from that due to training. In research studies, this need for differentiation makes it absolutely necessary to include a control group that grows but does not train. Moreover, as noted in chapter 4, children mature at different rates. Comparing a group that contains many early maturers with a group that contains many late maturers can certainly bias an investigation of training effects. In fact, one research group noted that when they sought to compare inactive and active groups of children, late maturers more often fell into the inactive category (Mirwald, Bailey, Cameron, & Rasmussen, 1981). Thus, maturation level must be assessed in research studies.

Early studies of aerobic training in prepubescent children were equivocal. Consider the seven sample studies depicted in figure 15.6. Three found a significant increase in maximal oxygen uptake by the training group over the control group, and four found no significant difference after training. In a few longitudinal studies, training did not result in differences between active and inactive groups until the children reached peak height velocity (Kobayashi et al., 1978; Mirwald et al., 1981; Rutenfranz, 1986). In other words, training was not associated with a higher maximal oxygen uptake in preadolescents (beyond the increase due to growth), but it was in adolescents. This led Katch (1983) to propose the trigger hypothesis, which states that until the results of the hormones that initiate puberty are realized, the effects of aerobic training on maximal oxygen uptake are minimal at best.

Several factors could account for the lack of a training effect:

- Training effects may be reliant on hormonal responses.
- High activity rates in children before training may minimize the training effect.
- Research studies may have included too few children or may have used flawed research methods.
- Training intensity may have been insufficient for children (Rowland, 1989b).

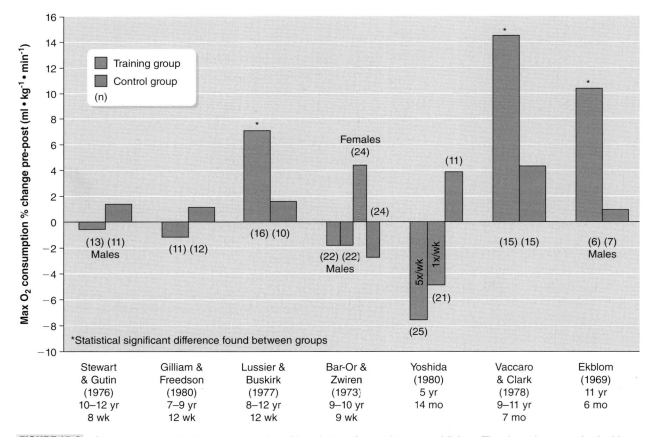

FIGURE 15.6   Changes in maximal oxygen uptake with training of prepubescent children. The three bars marked with an asterisk (*) indicate studies finding a statistically significant improvement over the control group. The other four studies found no significant differences after training.

- Maximal oxygen uptake may not be as useful a measurement of aerobic fitness in children as other measures (e.g., anaerobic threshold or ventilatory anaerobic threshold) (Armstrong & Welsman, 2007; Rowland, 1989a; Washington, 1989).

Aware of these possibilities, investigators more recently based their reviews on studies meeting certain criteria for research method and training intensity. Pate and Ward (1990) screened and then analyzed 12 studies; 8 of these found an increase in maximal oxygen uptake with training, though the mean increase was only 10.4%, compared with the control group increase of 2.7%. Similar analyses led some to conclude that appropriate aerobic training can lead to increases in maximal oxygen uptake of approximately 15% in children (Sady, 1986; Shephard, 1992; Vaccaro & Mahon, 1987).

Payne and Morrow (1993) reported from their meta-analysis of 23 studies that an average increase in fitness of less than 5% was found. Tolfrey, Campbell, and Batterham (1998) trained 26 children (boys and girls) matched to 19 control children for physiological maturation. The children trained 30 min per session 3 times per week for 12 weeks at nearly 80% of maximum heart rate. Habitual physical activity level and percentage body fat were considered in the analysis of the results, but the exercise-training group still did not improve in maximal oxygen uptake beyond the improvement also seen in the control group.

It is possible that research studies on the whole have not used training intensity levels that are sufficient to yield a training effect in children. However, exercise programs must not be so demanding as to be harmful, nor should they involve a level of activity that results in children disliking exercise. The overload principle is useful to follow with children. This principle calls for training with incrementally—not drastically—increased intensity or duration slightly beyond the individual's norm. The intensity or duration of each exercise bout is increased gradually over several weeks or months.

In contrast, adolescents after puberty respond to aerobic training much as adults do. Heart size and volume, total blood volume, total hemoglobin, stroke volume, and maximal cardiac output all increase in adolescents who receive training (Ekblom, 1969; Eriksson & Koch, 1973; Koch & Rocker, 1977; Lengyel & Gyarfas, 1979), whereas submaximal heart rate for a given level of exercise decreases (Brown, Harrower, & Deeter, 1972). Kobayashi et al. (1978) found a 15.8% increase in aerobic power with training between ages 14 and 17. A longitudinal study of males and females over the 15 years from ages 13 through 27 showed that those who reported being physically active had a 2% to 5% increase in aerobic fitness over those who did not (Kemper, Twisk, Koppes, van Mechelen, & Post, 2001).

Training is specific even in adolescents. Santos, Marinho, Costa, Izquierdo, and Marques (2012) noted that strength training in adolescent boys between 12 and 14 years did not improve aerobic capacity, but programs concurrently providing resistance and endurance training led to an improvement in both fitness components.

KEY POINT
Aerobic training yields small improvements, at best, in preadolescents but significant improvements after puberty.

 Imagine you are a physical education teacher serving on a districtwide committee charged with revising the physical education curriculum. How much activity that is characterized as aerobic training would you favor at each grade level from kindergarten through 12th grade? What about anaerobic-training activities? Would you advocate having high school students complete their physical education requirement as sophomores?

Training Programs in Adulthood

Earlier we reviewed the structural and functional changes that occur with aging in the cardiovascular and respiratory systems. We observed that maximal oxygen uptake declines with aging, even in those who train. However, we also noted that training and active adults had higher—even if declining with time—maximal oxygen uptakes than did sedentary adults (Hollenberg, Yang, Haight, & Tager, 2006) (figure 15.7). This finding provides a hint that training programs for adults yield benefits. Let's consider two groups: adults who maintain an active lifestyle and sedentary adults who take up training.

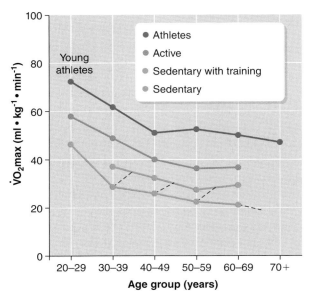

FIGURE 15.7 These average maximal oxygen uptake values for the adult years show that activity is associated with higher values, although all groups (active and inactive) experience decline. The dotted lines represent improvement in sedentary adults with training.

Reprinted by permission from Spirduso, Francis, and MacRae 2005.

First, evidence exists (Dehn & Bruce, 1972; Drinkwater, Horvath, & Wells, 1975; Kasch, Boyer, Van Camp, Verity, & Wallace, 1990; Shephard, 1978b; Smith & Serfass, 1981) that declines are not as dramatic in older adults who remain active as in those who become sedentary. Figure 15.5b shows that the decline in maximal oxygen uptake is steeper in inactive (dotted line) than in active (solid line) adults with advancing age. Vigorous training can even keep maximal oxygen uptake steady for a time in older adults (figure 15.7; Kasch & Wallace, 1976). Over a long period of time, prolonged training can sharply reduce the decline in maximal oxygen uptake. Kasch et al. (1990) observed only a 13% decline in men 45 to 68 years of age who maintained exercise training compared with an average loss of about 40% in nonexercisers.

Second, older adults can significantly increase their maximal oxygen uptake with a good training program (Posner, Gorman, Klein, & Woldow, 1986; Shephard, 1978b), even if they have undertaken little training earlier in their lives and even into their 70s (Hagburg et al., 1989; Stamford, 1973). Improvements ranged from 10% to 25% (Blumenthal et al., 1991; Shephard, 1987). These gains are not as high in absolute terms as those in younger people who begin training but are similar to those gains in the young in relative terms. Even low training intensity can be very effective for older adults early in their exercise program. Inactive older adults taking up aerobic training also improve in other strength and mobility tasks (Kalapotharakos, Michalopoulos, Strimpakos, Diamantopoulos, & Tokmakidis, 2006) and improve their blood lipids (Ring-Dimitriou et al., 2007).

What mechanisms are involved in the improvements in older adults with training? Undoubtedly, training maintains or improves muscle mass. As mentioned previously, more muscle mass is associated with higher maximal oxygen uptake. Fit older adults also have larger vital capacity than sedentary older adults (Shephard,

KEY POINT
Adults can benefit from aerobic training in order to minimize the decline in performance that would otherwise accompany aging.

1993). Information about the cardiovascular system is available from a case study of Clarence DeMar, who ran 12 miles a day throughout his life and competed in marathons at age 65. The autopsy performed after his death from cancer at age 70 showed well-developed cardiac muscle, normal valves, and coronary arteries two to three times the size normally seen (Brandfonbrener et al., 1955).

Although the benefits of endurance training even at low intensity are well established for the older adult, vigorous work can still overwhelm the diseased heart. Older adults with cardiovascular disease should participate in programs designed specifically for this population. The guiding principle in designing training programs for older adults as well as for children is a gradual increase in exercise intensity and duration.

 WEB STUDY GUIDE   Compare age group records for aerobic and anaerobic events and identify trends in performance among older adults in Lab Activity 15.2, Aerobic and Anaerobic Performance in Older Adulthood, in the web study guide. Go to www.HumanKinetics.com/LifeSpanMotorDevelopment.

Long-Term Training Effects

Despite the body's favorable response to training at any age, the question arises of whether active youths have an advantage over their sedentary counterparts in maintaining endurance into older adulthood. Ideally, researchers would assess this aspect of fitness through long-term longitudinal studies; however, the difficulties involved in obtaining longitudinal data (expense and subject attrition) make such research scarce.

In the absence of such research, consider a cross-sectional study conducted by Saltin and Grimby (1968) that measured the maximal oxygen uptake of three groups of men between ages 50 and 59. The men in the first group were nonathletes in their youth; those in the second group were former athletes but were now sedentary; and the men in the third group had been athletes in their youth and still maintained active lifestyles as older adults. The investigators had to rely on self-reports (rather than laboratory data) to determine the men's activity levels in youth. Even so, measures of maximal oxygen uptake yielded average values of 30, 38, and 53 ml·kg of body weight^{-1}·min^{-1} for the nonathletes, sedentary former athletes, and active adults, respectively.

More recently, Trudeau, Laurencelle, Tremblay, Rajic, and Shephard (1998) followed up with participants 20 years after their participation in a semi-longitudinal study. The treatment group in the original study took a 1 h specialized physical education class 5 times per week during their 6 years of elementary school. The control group received just 40 min of exercise per week during that time. As adults, women from the treatment group exercised 3 or more times per week more often than women from the control group. The men did not differ. Men and women from the treatment group more often self-reported their health to be very good to excellent.

Telama, Yang, Laakso, and Viikari (1997) also followed up on participants 9 and 12 years after they initially answered a questionnaire about their leisure activities (at the ages of 9, 12, 15, and 18 years). The correlations between youth and adult activity were low but significant. A line of longitudinal studies also shows that persistent participation in organized youth sports programs and competitions predicted physical activity levels in young adulthood (Telama, Yang, Hirvensalo, & Raitakari, 2006).

FIGURE 15.8 Endurance capacity is positively related to training, especially after puberty. Moreover, regular activity in childhood might predispose individuals to be more active in adulthood. Perhaps functional constraints such as a positive attitude toward exercise persist over the life span.

Despite the limitations of these studies, the evidence suggests that regular activity in childhood has positive lifelong benefits. Promoting an active lifestyle with children and youths could predispose them to be more active as adults (figure 15.8). Nevertheless, the most important factor for endurance is the individual's current activity level. At all ages, the capacity for prolonged, vigorous work tends to be transitory. People maintain (or improve) endurance if they are currently training for endurance; conversely, endurance capacity decreases when people discontinue their training programs.

 Think ahead to your own potential lifestyle 20 years from now. What is your plan for staying active? What physical activities do you plan to include in your life?

Effects of Disease on Endurance Performance

Diseases and disabilities can constrain endurance performance at any point in the life span. A detailed discussion of diseases and working capacity is beyond the scope of this text, but it is important to realize that cardiovascular, pulmonary, infectious, and neuromuscular diseases affect performance. An individual with such a disease possesses a unique set of structural constraints that affect physical performance. Therapists and educators must prescribe initial levels of activity based on these constraints and then constantly adapt activities as a disease progresses or rehabilitation brings about improvements.

Short-term infectious diseases, such as influenza, mononucleosis, and chicken pox, generally reduce an individual's working capacity (Adams, 1973) to varying degrees. It is important for a teacher, coach, or exercise leader to keep this in mind when monitoring performance. Individuals who are trying to maintain peak efficiency want to adhere to training schedules and performance levels even when they are ill, but this is an impractical goal.

 Imagine you are a physical education teacher with a student who has just returned to school after a 2-week illness. You are scheduled to begin fitness testing. What approach would you take with your student? Why?

Teachers, coaches, exercise leaders, doctors, nurses, therapists, and (when children are involved) parents should work as a team; every member should want to do his or her part to help the participant. Clearly, cooperation and communication are imperative. Activity may be beneficial in many cases, but it must never place the participant at increased risk. Those involved in the participant's exercise program, then, must plan the limits of activity carefully, set expectations accordingly, and monitor the participant closely.

Summary and Synthesis

Endurance for vigorous activities improves as the body grows. In addition, an individual can increase endurance after puberty by training, although the effects are transitory. A person must maintain training in order to preserve higher levels of endurance and reap the associated benefits.

After the adolescent growth spurt, sex differences in working capacity are apparent. The causes of these differences are still open to discussion, but body size, body composition, and hemoglobin levels are at least partially responsible. Recall our discussion of individual functional constraints in part V. Earlier in this chapter we saw how a myth influenced attitudes about children's training. Functional constraints might also be responsible for some of the sex and age group differences. Societal norms and expectations can constrain activity and training because some individuals are led to believe that such activity is inappropriate for their group. These attitudes are changing, but many people still do not undertake regular exercise. It remains to be seen whether recent exercise and fitness movements will have any effect on life span fitness in the 21st century.

 ## Reinforcing What You Have Learned About Constraints

TAKE A SECOND LOOK

Our discussion of cardiorespiratory endurance helps us appreciate the interaction between this component of physical fitness and the performance of motor skills. Endurance is necessary for the performance of many skills and physical activities of daily living. In addition, appropriate training for endurance supports growth and maintenance of the body's systems such that participants are in better overall health and enjoy a better quality of life. However, the availability of technology in westernized countries, including computers and gaming systems, tempts people to be more and more sedentary. Sedentary lifestyles at any age lead to a decline in the cardiac, respiratory, and vascular systems. This decline eventually results in a performance decrement and, with advancing age, greater risk of threats to good health. Other body systems, such as the neurologic system, also can suffer from a sedentary lifestyle, which in turn can lead to a reduced quality of life.

Other components of physical fitness include muscular strength and flexibility, and performance of many sport and everyday living activities depends on a minimal level of strength and flexibility. Chapter 16 examines these two fitness components, which interact with task and environmental constraints in giving rise to movements.

TEST YOUR KNOWLEDGE

1. How do anaerobic endurance and aerobic endurance change with growth in childhood? How do they change with aging?

2. Can prepubescent children improve anaerobic endurance with training? Aerobic endurance? Explain your answers.

3. What are the sex differences in anaerobic and aerobic endurance over the life span? To what factors might these differences be attributed?

4. At what points in the life span can individuals improve aerobic endurance with training? Do those who build higher endurance in youth realize a lifelong benefit? What types of studies best answer this question? Why?

5. How is anaerobic endurance measured? Aerobic endurance? What is the difference between power and capacity in the measurement of anaerobic and aerobic endurance?

6. How do infectious diseases affect endurance? What strategies are best followed when one begins training after an illness?

7. Do we know whether being active as a child or teen makes a difference in fitness levels in adulthood? On what do you base your answer?

8. How does maturity affect anaerobic and aerobic endurance in youth?

9. If you wanted to predict a youth's endurance level, would you base your prediction on age, size, maturity, or some combination of these? Why?

10. What factors tend to limit the aerobic endurance of older adults? Anaerobic endurance?

LEARNING EXERCISE 15.1

Testing Children and Teens for Endurance

Locate five research articles on endurance or aerobic performance in children and teens. You can use articles referenced in this text, perform an electronic search, or check a journal such as *Pediatric Exercise Science*. Once you have located the articles, read about the methods the authors used to conduct their research (typically described in a section titled "Methods"). Note the age and sex of the participants and summarize how endurance performance was tested. What was similar and what was different about how each set of researchers tested endurance? What accommodations, if any, were made for the ages of the participants?

16

Development of Strength and Flexibility

 CHAPTER OBJECTIVES

This chapter

- explores the relationship between muscle mass and strength and how these change in relation to each other over the life span,
- reviews the effects of strength training over the life span,
- describes changes in flexibility over the life span, and
- reviews the effects of flexibility training by individuals of any age.

Super Athletes

At the turn of the 21st century and shortly thereafter, the world was treated to exceptional performances by athletes in track and field, skiing, skating, baseball, and many other sports. As we moved to the middle of the first decade, however, reports surfaced that some of those athletes had used banned or illegal supplements. Many of these supplements, such as anabolic steroids, help athletes increase muscle mass quickly by allowing them to recover sooner from strenuous training. Because muscle mass is related to strength, these athletes gained a strength advantage over other competitors. The importance of strength, as well as flexibility, to performance of motor skills and tasks is widely recognized today, as we see by the risks some performers are willing to take in order to reach higher levels of strength and flexibility.

Strength and flexibility are obvious constraints to skilled performance; sometimes, in fact, skills can be performed only if one has sufficient strength. You might recall that we suspect leg strength is a rate limiter for infant standing. You also might know older adults who have difficulty climbing stairs after they have lost leg strength. Flexibility is also a necessity for many activities. Gymnasts and high jumpers work on their flexibility to perform skills. Senior golfers sometimes exhibit swings that reflect a loss of flexibility.

Today's coaches have come to realize that strength and flexibility are related. Athletes are at their best when they are strong *and* supple. Training that promotes increased muscle mass at the expense of flexibility puts athletes at risk of injury. Muscle balance is a goal of training today. Muscle strength should be built for all directions of joint movement (e.g., flexion and extension), and flexibility through the appropriate and full range of motion should be fostered. This chapter considers changes over the life span as well as the effects of training throughout the life span, first in strength and then in flexibility.

Development of Strength

As noted in chapter 4, muscle mass follows a sigmoid growth pattern, and this growth is largely the result of an increase in muscle fiber diameter. Sex differences are minimal until puberty, when boys add significantly more muscle mass than girls do, especially in the upper body. Loss of muscle is small from young adulthood until the age of 50, but thereafter the average loss can be pronounced. The loss is greater for sedentary individuals with poor nutrition.

Strength is the ability to exert force.

What about muscle **strength**? Does it simply parallel the changes in muscle mass? Strength-training programs are promoted for individuals of all ages. What effect does resistance training have on strength and muscle mass, especially before the adolescent growth spurt? What about in older adulthood, when muscle mass is typically lost?

These are important questions to answer. Many skills require a certain level of strength, such as the gymnastics skills performed on parallel bars. Some skills can be performed better with more strength, such as baseball batting. Even activities of daily living can become difficult without sufficient strength. Older adults who have lost much of their strength have difficulty with everyday tasks, such as getting out of the bathtub or climbing the stairs, and they are often at greater risk of falling.

The first step in answering these important questions about strength is to understand the relationship between muscle mass and strength. This section first describes the patterns of change for the average individual and then discusses the effects of training.

 If you were a therapist, what activities of daily living would you include in the clinic that might be difficult or even risky for an individual who has lost strength due to disease, disability, or aging?

Muscle Mass and Strength

The amount of force a muscle group exerts depends on the fibers (muscle cells) that are neurologically activated and on leverage (the mechanical advantage the muscle fibers gain based on where force is applied in relation to an axis of rotation). In turn, the fibers activated depend on the cross-sectional area of the muscle and on the degree of coordination in activating the fibers—that is, the nervous system's pattern and timing in innervating the various motor units to bring about the desired movement. The cross-sectional area of muscle increases with growth, which means that strength increases as muscles grow, but muscle mass is not the only factor in strength. Neurological factors are also involved, and neurological changes over the life span influence muscle strength. Therefore, we cannot assume that strength changes simply as muscle mass changes. Keeping this in mind, let's see how strength changes over the life span.

KEY POINT
Muscle strength is related to muscle size, but changes in strength do not always parallel changes in muscle size.

Developmental Changes in Strength

Strength is certainly one of the individual structural constraints that change with growth and aging. Changes in strength may be brought about by multiple influences on strength and resistance training, both in the long term and in the short term. Because an individual's strength level is a constraint that interacts with task and environmental constraints to permit or limit movements, strength levels change movements over the life span.

Preadolescence

Strength increases steadily as children grow older (figure 16.1) (Blimkie, 1989; Pate & Shephard, 1989). Boys and girls have similar strength levels until they are about 13 years old, although boys are very slightly stronger than girls of the same height during childhood (Asmussen, 1973; Blimkie, 1989; Davies, 1990; Parker, Round, Sacco, & Jones, 1990).

We know that muscle mass also increases steadily as children grow older, so how is strength related to muscle mass in childhood? Wood, Dixon, Grant, and Armstrong (2006) measured the elbow flexor strength, muscle size, and moment arm length (the perpendicular distance between the joint center or axis of rotation and the muscle tendon's point of attachment to the bone) of 38 boys and girls close to 9.6 years of age. The latter two values were assessed using magnetic resonance

Assessing Strength

Isotonic strength is the exertion of force against constant resistance through the range of motion at a joint.

Isokinetic strength is the exertion of force at a constant limb velocity through the range of motion at a joint.

Isometric strength is the exertion of force without a change in muscle length (i.e., without movement of a limb).

In strength assessments, individuals typically exert maximum force against resistance. They might move their limbs, as in an **isotonic** test (constant resistance, as in lifting a barbell) or **isokinetic** test (constant speed of movement, as with a Cybex machine), or they might exert force against an immovable resistance, as in an **isometric** test. For us to compare results between individuals, those conducting the assessment must report several kinds of information:

- The muscle group, such as knee flexors or elbow extensors
- The movement, such as knee flexion or elbow extension
- The speed of movement, usually in degrees per second

For isometric tests, the angle of the joint (in degrees) as force is exerted must also be recorded because a muscle group can exert different levels of force at different joint angles.

A common isotonic strength test is a 1-repetition maximum (1RM) lift of a free weight such as a barbell. As a limb moves through a range of motion, force production is maximal at one point and thus submaximal at other points. The 1RM test therefore indicates forces that can be sustained at the weaker ranges of joint motion. If an isokinetic exercise machine is used, movement speed is kept constant and the device automatically provides an adjusted counter force. A force–velocity curve is generated and the peak on that curve indicates the maximal strength achieved at the strongest joint angle. Because the 1RM test is difficult (and potentially dangerous) for novices, scales have been developed that estimate 1RM weight based on the maximum number of lifts at a given lower weight.

Several devices assess isometric strength. The spring-loaded dynamometer requires individuals to compress a handle, and their exertion is registered. Alternatively, the individual can pull on an anchored cable with a handle. A tensiometer is placed on the cable and registers the force of exertion. Dynamometers and tensiometers usually measure in Newtons, a measurement unit for force.

In school settings, functional tests of strength are often used with children. Among these are chin-ups, the flexed-arm hang, and rope climbing. Note that body weight is used as the resistance in these tasks, so body weight is a factor in performance levels. Some of these tasks also require skills, such as rope climbing, and the skill factor must be considered in interpreting test results.

imaging. The largest contribution to strength was the cross-sectional area of the elbow flexor muscles. In children, then, strength is greatly related to muscle mass. In fact, Barrett and Harrison (2002) found that children matched adults in the functional ability of muscle per unit of muscle volume, implying that muscle size plays a large factor in child–adult strength differences.

Other factors might be involved in strength levels. Consider the age at which individuals reach peak gains in muscle mass and strength. As noted in chapter 4, peak gain (the peak in the velocity curve) indicates the point of the fastest increase. If strength development directly follows muscle mass development, the peak gain in strength would coincide with the peak gain in muscle mass. In turn, teachers and coaches could predict children's strength levels by simply measuring their muscle mass, which can be estimated from weight measurements or by subtracting a child's estimated fat weight from body weight.

However, several studies indicate that these peak gains do not coincide with each other in most adolescents (Carron & Bailey, 1974; Jones, 1947; Stolz & Stolz, 1951). For example, Rasmussen, Faulkner, Mirwald, and Bailey (1990) conducted a longitudinal study with boys and found that peak muscle mass velocity occurred at an average age of 14.3 years but peak strength velocity occurred at 14.7 years. Tanner (1962) suggests that the typical sequence of peak muscle mass velocity followed by peak strength velocity probably reflects increasing hormone levels and their effect on the protein structure and enzyme systems of the muscle fibers. Thus, the endocrine system plays a role in strength increase with growth.

Another way to examine muscle growth and strength

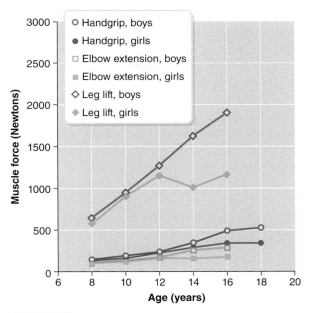

FIGURE 16.1 Development of isometric strength. Boys (open symbols) continue to steadily improve in isometric strength throughout adolescence whereas girls (filled symbols) tend to plateau. Graph is based on data accumulated by Shephard (1978b) for handgrip and on unpublished results of Howell, Loiselle, and Lucas (1966) for other measures.

Based on Shepard 1982.

development is to relate measures of muscle strength to various body sizes in children and determine whether strength increases at the same rate as body size. Asmussen and Heeboll-Nielsen (1955, 1956) took this approach in studying Danish children between ages 7 and 16 years. They assumed that body height could represent changes in body size, including body weight; in this age group, body weight is proportional to body height raised to the third power. Asmussen and Heeboll-Nielsen showed this was approximately true for their sample of Danish boys and girls. Because height measures could represent body size, they grouped the children into height categories by 10 cm intervals and measured them for isometric strength. Successive height groups demonstrated increasing muscle strength but at a rate greater than that of their increase in height.

Asmussen and Heeboll-Nielsen also divided boys of the same height into two age groups, one younger and one older by approximately 1.5 years. The older group showed greater arm and leg strength by about 5% to 10% per year of age. This experiment also demonstrates that strength is not related to muscle size alone; rather, neural influences are likely. These influences might include myelination of nerve fibers, improved muscle coordination (movement requires a contraction of some muscles and a coordinated relaxation of the muscle on the opposite aspect of the body), and improved extent of motor unit activation (Blimkie, 1989; Kraemer, Fry, Frykman, Conroy, & Hoffman, 1989; Sale, 1989). Only one of these neural influences—improved motor unit activation—has been examined experimentally. Blimkie (1989) found some support for the suggestion that older children can activate a greater proportion of motor units to exert force.

The studies mentioned thus far typically measured isometric strength directly with a cable tensiometer or a dynamometer. The benefit of measuring strength with this equipment is that the effects of skill, practice, and experience are minimized. However, these factors do influence the performance of sports skills, making studies of the development of functional muscle strength very useful.

Two skills that involve functional muscle strength are vertical jumping and sprinting. Practice and experience, as well as leg strength, influence children's performance on both tasks. Asmussen and Heeboll-Nielsen (1955, 1956) measured performance on these two skills in successive height groups of Danish children. They found that functional muscle strength, like isometric strength, increased at a faster rate than one would anticipate from muscle growth alone. Further, the rate of gain in functional muscle strength was even greater than the rate of gain in isometric strength, emphasizing again the role of neurological factors in improved muscle strength as children mature.

 WEB STUDY GUIDE   Plot data and analyze changes in functional strength in preadolescence in Lab Activity 16.1, Examining Trends in Strength Development, in the web study guide. Go to www.HumanKinetics.com/LifeSpan MotorDevelopment.

Adolescence and Young Adulthood

As noted in chapter 4, boys gain more muscle mass in adolescence than girls do, largely as a result of higher levels of androgen secretion. It is no surprise, then, that boys undergo a spurt of increased strength at about age 13. Girls continue a steady increase in strength during adolescence before reaching a plateau.

As a result of differential growth of muscle mass during adolescence, then, the average adult man is stronger than the average adult woman. Women can produce only 60% to 80% of the force that men can exert, although most of these differences can be attributed to differences in arm and shoulder strength rather than in trunk or leg strength (Asmussen, 1973). As noted in chapter 4, sex differences in muscle mass are more pronounced in the arms and shoulders than in the trunk and legs.

However, the average difference in body or muscle size accounts for only half of the difference in strength between men and women. Cultural norms probably play a role in the sex differences in strength. These norms, of course, begin to exert their influence very early in life. For example, Shephard (1982) noted the effect of repeating strength measures on naive boys and girls (i.e., boys and girls who have never been tested for strength). Whereas the boys showed no tendency to improve over three visits, the girls improved on each subsequent visit in almost every case and improved significantly on two of the eight strength measures (figure 16.2). It is possible that the task gained acceptability to the girls as they became more familiar with it. The boys may have been more used to all-out demonstrations of strength. Girls at that time were probably not encouraged to go all out and might even have been discouraged from doing so, which would have limited their experience in exerting strength. Neither should motivation be discounted as a major factor in strength measurement. Certainly, if Shephard had recorded only the first set of scores, he would have concluded that the sex differences in strength were much greater than what he found after comparing the third set of scores.

 If you were a coach or personal trainer of young girls, how might you work to overcome any stigmas associated with weight training in order to help them improve their strength?

Cultural norms can also influence strength differences between the sexes through habitual physical activity. That is, the traditional physical activities promoted to growing boys tend to provide long-term resistance exercise. Those promoted to girls do not. Daily physical activities that promote strength have a cumulative effect over the growing years, resulting in significant sex differences that cannot be attributed to muscle size alone.

Some research has hinted that sex differences exist in muscle fiber composition—that is, that men and women do not have the same proportions of type I (slow-twitch) and type II (fast-twitch) muscle fibers. If so, part of the sex differences in strength might be attributed to muscle fiber composition.

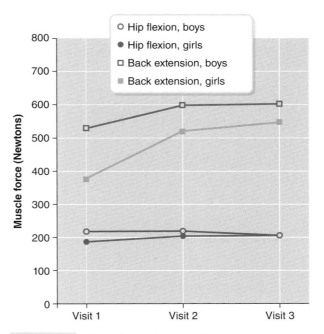

FIGURE 16.2 The effect of test repetition on muscle force measurement. When repeated visits were measured, girls improved on these strength measures whereas boys showed little or no change.

Based on Shepard 1982.

Animal studies indicate that muscle composition is related to isometric strength (see Komi, 1984, for a review). On the other hand, Davies, White, and Young (1983) could find no relationship between strength and muscle fiber composition in boys and girls 11 to 14 years of age. Much more research is needed on this topic.

After the growth period, increases in muscle mass are associated with resistance training. Some drugs used in conjunction with training can increase muscle mass at a rate greater than training alone, but most have unhealthy side effects. Electromyographic measurements of muscle activation in strength tasks show that improved strength in adults who are engaged in resistance training is related to improved neurological activation and increased muscle size. In fact, in the early weeks of training most strength improvements are related to neurological factors because muscle has not yet increased in size (Moritani & DeVries, 1980).

KEY POINT
Strength increases gradually throughout childhood; boys experience a spurt of increased strength in adolescence, whereas strength increases steadily in girls.

Middle and Older Adulthood

Strength levels generally are maintained throughout the 20s and 30s. For the average adult, strength declines thereafter. The decline is somewhat gradual at first. Shephard (1978b) placed the loss in the 50s at 18% to 20%. Shock and Norris (1970) measured a significant loss in arm and shoulder strength after age 65. Murray, Gardner, Mollinger, and Sepic (1980) reported a 45% loss of strength after age 65. Isometric strength (the ability to exert force against immovable resistance) and isotonic strength (the ability to exert force against movable resistance) both decline. The loss is particularly noticeable in the muscles of the upper leg.

 Imagine you are a physical education teacher. What activities not typically labeled "resistance training" might still improve leg strength? Upper body strength? Are any of these typically gender stereotyped?

TABLE 16.1   Summary of Strength Changes With Aging

Better maintenance	Greater decline
Muscles used in daily activities	Muscles used infrequently in specialized activities
Isometric strength	Dynamic strength
Eccentric contractions	Concentric contractions
Slow-velocity contractions	Rapid-velocity contractions
Repeated low-level contractions	Power production
Strength using small joint angles	Strength using large joint angles
Males' strength	Females' strength

Reprinted by permission from Spirduso 1995.

We see several trends in the overall decline of strength with aging; table 16.1, from Spirduso (1995), summarizes these trends. On the left are the better-maintained aspects of strength and on the right are the aspects that decline more in the general population.

These losses are what we would expect from the loss of muscle mass in older adulthood, yet the loss of strength might be larger than the loss of muscle mass. Young, Stokes, and Crowe (1985) found a 39% loss of strength but only a 25% loss in cross-sectional area in the quadriceps muscles of older men compared with younger men. Aniansson, Hedberg, Henning, and Grimby (1986) documented a 10% to 22% loss of strength (figure 16.3) but a 6% loss of muscle mass in the same muscle group over a 7-year span.

Thus, loss of muscle mass does not parallel loss of strength in older adulthood. Spirduso, Francis, and MacRae (2005) identified a number of factors, in addition to muscle atrophy, that can contribute to loss of strength with aging (figure 16.4). As illustrated, a decrease in activity, poor nutrition, and an increase in the likelihood of disease contribute to loss of strength either directly or through changes in the body systems. We have noted a change in the muscle system—muscle atrophy—but changes also occur in muscle fibers, possibly such that fibers are not as distinctly type I or type II with aging (Andersen, Terzis, & Kryger, 1999) and that type II fibers shrink in size.

The nervous system might be involved because of a loss of motor neurons in the spinal cord with aging, resulting in a loss of motor units (Green, 1986; Grimby, 1988). Other units reinnervate some of the fibers of the lost motor neurons, such that the number of fibers per motor neuron

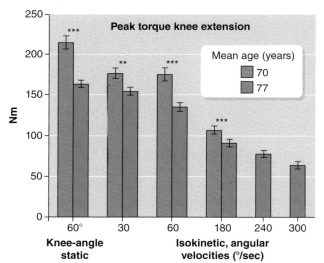

FIGURE 16.3 Changes in strength with aging. The average force (torque measured in Newton meters, Nm) exerted in a stationary knee position and at several speeds of knee extension decreased for 23 men over a 7-year interval. Changes are significant at the confidence levels of $p < .01$ (**) or $p < .001$ (***).

Reprinted by permission from Ariansson et al. 1986.

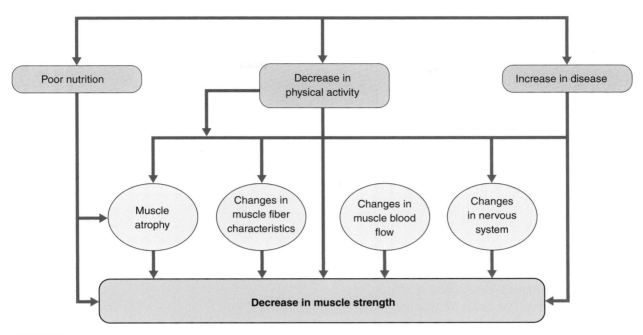

FIGURE 16.4   Factors contributing to the loss of muscle strength with aging.

Reprinted by permission from Spirduso, Francis, and MacRae 2005.

increases (Campbell, McComas, & Petito, 1973; Fitts, 1981). The result would be a loss of muscular coordination, especially fine motor coordination. The vascular system also might be involved in the loss of strength. The number of capillaries per muscle fiber seems to decline with aging, but this is almost assuredly related to a trend toward inactivity (Cartee, 1994). In older adults who undertake aerobic exercise, the number of capillaries actually increases and muscle blood flow improves.

As with so many other aspects of aging, it is difficult to distinguish whether loss of muscle mass and strength in older adults is related to aging of tissues or disuse. We know that strength is better maintained in frequently used muscles than in infrequently used muscles (Kauffman, 1985; Wilmore, 1991). Kallman, Plato, and Tobin (1990) demonstrated how variable the loss of strength is among older adults. They observed young, middle-aged, and older adults over a 10-year period. Many of the older adults lost *less* strength than middle-aged and young adults lost during the 10 years, and some lost no strength at all. This variability most likely reflects extrinsic factors among these adults, especially exercise and activity levels, reminding us that significant loss of strength with aging is not a foregone conclusion.

Strength and muscle mass share the same five general phases of change over the life span (early increase, steady advancement, adolescent spurt, maintenance in adulthood, possible decline in older adulthood), yet the timing of those changes can be distinct, as can the degree of change.

KEY POINT
Strength is maintained in adulthood. Gradual declines occur after the 30s and more notable declines begin in the 50s; losses are extremely variable among older adults.

Strength Training

An adult can increase muscle strength with strength training, which also results in a noticeable increase in muscle size. The effect is most noticeable in post-pubescent men; hence, circulating testosterone was initially considered the stimulus for such increases in muscle size. In the past, this view probably led many to think that resistance, or weight, training was of limited use to other groups. The thinking has changed dramatically. Numerous newspaper articles and television segments feature older adults who are taking up weight training. Resistance exercise has even become a part of curricula in elementary school physical education (figure 16.5). Rehabilitation programs focus on regaining strength after injury, even when the patient is not a professional athlete.

Strength is often an individual constraint in the performance of motor tasks. The strength level of an individual interacts with the task and environment either to permit a task or not or to influence how a movement is performed. If strength training can change an individual's level of strength in a relatively short time, then clearly it becomes a means to help individuals perform tasks. It can change the point at which strength becomes a rate limiter for a given task or skill. Educators and therapists can intervene to

FIGURE 16.5 Increasing muscle mass with growth—a structural constraint—leads to increased strength, but resistance training also increases strength over the life span.

change motor performance over a matter of weeks. Hence, we should take great interest in how strength training can change strength at any point in the life span. This section considers how strength training affects various age groups.

 If you were a therapist, why would restoring the strength of someone not participating in sport be as important as restoring the strength of an athlete after disease or injury?

Prepubescence

Research has documented that boys and girls as young as 6 or 7 years can increase their strength with a variety of resistance-training methods, including weights, pneumatic machines, hydraulic machines, and isometrics (figure 16.6) (de Oliveira & Gallagher, 1994; Duda, 1986; Falk & Tenenbaum, 1996; Sadres, Eliakim, Constantini, Lidor, & Falk, 2001; Sale, 1989; Weltman, 1989).

For example, Pfeiffer and Francis (1986) compared the strength of 14 prepubescent boys with that of a control group before and after a 9-week, 3-day-a-week training program. The boys trained on a Universal machine and with free weights, completing 3 sets of 10 repetitions in each session. Strength improved significantly in the young boys. In fact, the percentage increase was greater in the young boys than in the pubescent and postpubescent boys Pfeiffer and Francis also tested (figure 16.7). Others have confirmed that although postpubertal individuals gain more absolute strength with training, prepubertal individuals gain more strength

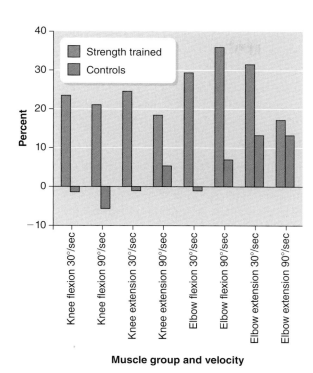

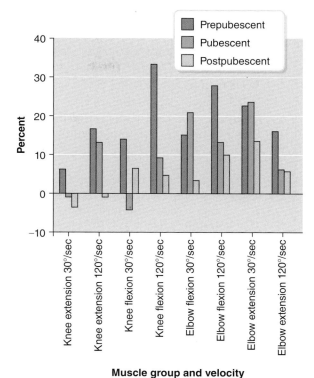

FIGURE 16.6 Muscle strength increases with training. Compared with their nontraining counterparts, prepubescent boys achieved larger relative increases in strength of four muscle groups at two speeds of movement.

Reprinted by permission from Malina, Bouchard, and Bar-Or 2004.

FIGURE 16.7 Percentage increases in strength with training. Prepubescent boys generally achieved larger relative increases in the strength of four muscle groups at two speeds of movement with 9 weeks of training than did pubescent or postpubescent boys.

Reprinted by permission from Malina, Bouchard, and Bar-Or 2004.

expressed as a percentage change from their starting strength (Sale, 1989). Faigenbaum, Milliken, Moulton, and Westcott (2005) considered whether low- or high-repetition-maximum resistance training is better. Although boys and girls increased their strength with either approach far more than a control group did, the high-repetition group demonstrated gains in muscle endurance and flexibility as well.

Several investigators found that increased muscle size did not accompany increased strength in prepubescents (Ramsay et al., 1990; Sale, 1989; Weltman et al., 1986). What, then, accounts for the strength increase? As noted previously, strength is related to muscle size and to the central nervous system's ability to fully activate muscles. Improvement in prepubescents likely results from their improved ability to exert force in the intended direction as they are better able to activate the agonist (contracting) muscles and coordinate the antagonist (lengthening) muscles (Sale, 1989). These neural factors probably account for much of the initial strength gain when males or females of any age group begin training.

Even if prepubescent children can improve their strength with training, does such training involve negative effects? Children's bones are still growing and could be susceptible to injury at both traction and pressure epiphyses. Weight training could potentially cause a single traumatic injury or chronic injury from repeated lifts. Also, some professionals who work with children are concerned that a loss of flexibility or even stature may accompany strength training. Several studies found no damage to bones or muscles in training prepubescents and recorded no

KEY POINT
Prepubescent children can increase strength with training, even without an accompanying increase in muscle size.

injuries (Rians et al., 1987; Servedio et al., 1985; Sewall & Micheli, 1986). In one study in which 27 prepubescent boys were observed over 2 years of a twice-weekly resistance-training program, only one minor injury occurred and there were no differences in height compared with a nontraining group (Sadres et al., 2001). Neither did researchers find loss of flexibility (Rians et al., 1987; Servedio et al., 1985; Sewall & Micheli, 1986; Siegel, Camaione, & Manfredi, 1989). However, all of the prepubescents in these studies were closely monitored. Educators should closely supervise weight-training programs for young children and insist that participants adhere strictly to guidelines (Sale, 1989).

 Imagine you are a middle school physical education teacher who is planning resistance-training activities. What are some important constraints to consider when implementing a training program for children? Think of individual structural and functional constraints as well as task and environmental constraints.

Adolescence

Developmentalists generally accept that strength training has beneficial effects for adolescents. Pfeiffer and Francis (1986) demonstrated that pubescent and postpubescent boys improved their strength with training. Other training methods yield the same result, including isometric training (Nielsen, Nielsen, Hansen, & Asmussen, 1980) and plyometric training (Steben & Steben, 1981). Tibana et al. (2012) noted that adolescent boys showed a higher recovery capacity between sets in a resistance-training session than did adult men.

After puberty, muscle **hypertrophy** can accompany regular strength training. As noted previously, adolescent boys add far more muscle mass than do adolescent girls during the growth spurt. Do the sexes also differ in their response to training? Cureton, Collins, Hill, and McElhannon (1988) placed young adult men and women on a weight-training program in which the resistance level was 70% to 90% of the individual's maximum. Men and women gained strength at identical levels in terms of percentage increase, but men gained more strength in terms of absolute increase for two of four tests. For example, men and women might increase 5%, but if the men were stronger at the start, their increase was greater in absolute terms. Both men and women experienced muscle hypertrophy in their upper arms, again by an identical percentage increase, although one measure yielded a greater absolute increase in men. After puberty, then, both improved coordination in recruiting the muscle units needed to exert force and muscle hypertrophy response to strength training appear to be similar in men and women in relative terms. Muscle hypertrophy is more noticeable in men in that a percentage increase of a larger muscle mass yields greater absolute dimensions.

Adolescents, like children, should be closely supervised when using weight training to improve strength. Their bones are still growing, and they are susceptible to a variety of musculoskeletal injuries (Risser & Preston, 1989). Performing Olympic-style lifts, in particular, can bring about back injuries (Jesse, 1977). Any activity that could possibly limit the ability to be active throughout life is of doubtful benefit to youths. Educators may want to take a cautious approach by starting adolescents with light resistance and scheduling progression in small increments. Close supervision is warranted because adolescents are susceptible to peer pressure and can easily be drawn into games of trying to outperform each other.

Year-to-year comparisons of strength measurements taken between ages 7 and 17 years show that the strongest children are not necessarily the strongest ado-

KEY POINT
Adolescents can increase strength and muscle mass with training.

lescents (Rarick & Smoll, 1967). The weakest 7-year-olds might be late maturers who eventually catch up to or pass their peers. Researchers have also found that children and adolescents who participate regularly in sport are stronger than those who do not (Bailey, Malina, & Rasmussen, 1978). This could be seen as proof that the training provided by sport participation develops strength. It should be noted, though, that young athletes are often more physiologically mature than nonathletes. Hansen, Klausen, Bangsbo, and Muller (1999) noted that the elite 10- to 12-year-old soccer players selected for the best teams were taller, leaner, and more mature than those not selected.

Middle and Older Adulthood

Young and middle-aged adults can maintain or even increase their strength through resistance training. Male soldiers improved push-up performance and leg power with just a 12-week resistance-training program (Kraemer et al., 2004). Even obese women not dieting increased their muscle strength with a 12-week training program (Sarsan, Ardic, Ozgen, Topuz, & Sermez, 2006). Women who had just gone through menopause improved muscle strength with a resistance-training program (Asikainen et al., 2006).

KEY POINT
Middle-aged and older adults can increase strength and muscle mass with training.

But what about older adulthood, when strength levels decline? Can older adults prevent or reverse losses in muscle mass and strength through training? Mayer et al. (2011) examined more than 1,500 articles published between 2005 and 2010 that addressed the effectiveness of resistance training in individuals over age 60 and concluded that older adults could increase their strength with training. This increased strength reflected an increase in muscle mass and an improved recruitment of motor units along with an increase in motor unit firing rate. Overall, these articles demonstrated that older adults could increase muscle mass by training at 60% to 85% of their maximum voluntary strength. Older adults could improve the rate of force development, but, just as with the young adults, this required a training intensity greater than 85%. Three to four training sessions per week yielded the best results.

 Imagine you are a recreation leader who would like to increase the participation of older adults in fitness classes—especially classes that would increase strength—at a recreation center. How would you promote participation to the area's citizens? What activities would you schedule? How would you minimize the risk of injury for participants?

Some professionals are reluctant to recommend resistance training to older adults, especially weight training with high-intensity resistance or isometric exercises. Their fear is that high pressures in the chest during contractions could resist blood flow and trigger cardiovascular or cerebrovascular catastrophes. Lewis et al. (1983) found little pressure difference between isometric and dynamic exercises; however, older adults at high risk for cardiac catastrophe or with osteoporosis (skeletal atrophy) or arthritis should train with light resistance and under the supervision of a knowledgeable professional. Mayer et al. (2011) found no evidence that older adults need to train at relatively lighter loads than young adults in order to avoid injury. Increases in strength were dependent on training at a fairly high intensity. Overall, older adults benefitted from and tolerated classic training regimens of 3 to 4 sets of about 10 repetitions at 80% of 1RM, done 3 times per week for 8 to 12 weeks.

KEY POINT
Resistance training is beneficial for increasing strength in preadolescence, adolescence, and young, middle, and older adulthood.

Summary of the Development of Strength

The typical pattern of strength change over the life span has five phases. In childhood, strength steadily increases. In adolescence, girls continue this steady increase but boys have a spurt of growth in strength. In the 20s and 30s, strength levels are relatively stable. After this, strength gradually declines until sometime in the 50s, when the loss becomes more dramatic.

This typical pattern can be changed by resistance training at any point in the life span. Parents, teachers, and therapists can change the movement that arises from the interaction of person, task, and environment by introducing resistance training to those in their care, thus changing an individual structural constraint.

Changes in strength tend to parallel changes in muscle mass. However, muscle mass is not the only factor involved in increased strength. Neurological factors play a large role; in fact, strength improvements in childhood with resistance training are largely related to neurological factors. Cultural norms probably also play a role in strength levels by influencing the habitual physical activities undertaken by individuals.

Although muscle strength is important for the performance of skills, so is suppleness, or flexibility. Individuals must be able to move through full ranges of motion and position their limbs to undertake movements in sport and dance as well as in daily living.

Development of Flexibility

Flexibility is the ability to move joints through a full range of motion.

Flexibility often benefits maximal performance. Limited flexibility is a factor in sport injuries and in restricted mobility; that is, flexibility can be a rate limiter. Limited flexibility also can influence the type and kind of activities that older adults can enjoy. Older adults whose strength and flexibility are severely limited must have help even to perform activities of daily living. Young athletes sometimes overlook this important aspect of physical fitness, emphasizing endurance and strength at the expense of flexibility. Exceptions to this generalization are dancers and gymnasts, who have long realized the importance of flexibility in their activities. Many young athletes are indifferent toward flexibility because they assume that young people are naturally supple and need no further flexibility training. People typically view lack of flexibility as a problem only for older adults, whose movement limitations are more readily apparent. Many of these generalizations are based on misconceptions about flexibility. This section describes first the pattern of change in flexibility for the average individual and then the effects of training and how it alters the typical pattern.

Developmental Changes in Flexibility

The range of motion possible at any joint depends on that joint's bone structure and on the soft tissues' resistance to movement. The soft tissues include muscles, tendons, joint capsules, ligaments, and skin. The belief that flexibility is related to limb length is incorrect. Habitual use and exercise preserve the elastic nature of the soft tissues, whereas disuse is associated with a loss of elasticity. To improve poor flexibility, a person must move the joint regularly and systematically through an increasingly larger range of motion to modify the soft tissues. Athletes, then, tend to increase the flexibility of joints they use in their sports, whereas laborers who spend much of their time in one posture may lose flexibility in some joints.

It is likely that people who do not exercise fully lose flexibility because everyday activities rarely require movement through a full range of motion. Thus, at any age, flexibility reflects the normal range of movement to which an individual subjects specific joints.

An important characteristic of flexibility is its specificity; that is, a certain degree of flexibility is specific to each particular joint. An individual can be relatively flexible at one joint and inflexible at another.

Childhood

Most of us can recall seeing an infant lie on his back and bring his feet nearly to his head. Or, we remember a toddler who can sit on the floor with her bent legs out to the side. We know from experience that infants and toddlers are very flexible. Most observations of children identify a decline in flexibility with advancing age.

After reviewing the information available in 1975, Clarke (1975) concluded that boys tend to lose flexibility after age 10 years and girls after age 12 years. For example, Hupprich and Sigerseth (1950) administered 12 flexibility measures to 300 girls aged 6, 9, 12, 15, and 18 years. Most of the flexibility measurements improved across the 6-, 9-, and 12-year-old groups but declined in the older groups (figure 16.8). Krahenbuhl and Martin (1977) found that flexibility in both boys and girls declined between ages 10 and 14, but Milne, Seefeldt, and Reuschlein (1976) reported that second graders in their study already had poorer flexibility than kindergartners. Factors that might be involved in this trend are the addition of muscle mass and the maturation of joint structures with growth, but more research on these topics is needed (Parker & James, 1985).

Some researchers are concerned that the sit-and-reach test reflects body proportions as well as flexibility because it measures flexibility relative to a point even with the feet. A small number of individuals with unusually long legs, short arms, or both are at a disadvantage. A modified sit-and-reach test corrects for limb length bias by measuring flexibility relative to an individual's fingertips when sitting straight up (Hoeger et al., 1990).

The sit-and-reach test has been used as the representative measure of flexibility in fitness test batteries. Norms developed in the National Children and Youth Fitness Study II project (Ross et al., 1987) for children aged 6 to 9 reflect generally stable sit-and-reach performance during childhood. In an extensive cross-sectional study of Flemish girls aged 6 to 18 years, the sit-and-reach scores of girls in the upper percentiles were stable until age 12 and then improved. The scores of girls in the lower percentiles declined from 6 to 12 years, improved somewhat in midadolescence, and then declined

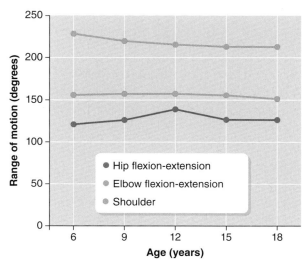

FIGURE 16.8 These three flexibility measures show that flexibility generally declines with advancing age, although range of motion in some joints might increase until approximately 12 years of age.

Adapted by permission from Hupprich and Sigerseth 1950.

Because flexibility is specific to a joint, one or two flexibility measures cannot accurately represent one's overall flexibility. To know the flexibility in a specific joint in a particular individual, it must be measured. Most flexibility measures are made with a goniometer, which is a protractor with two long arms. The axis of the goniometer is centered over the joint to be measured. The limb is positioned at one end of the range of motion, and one arm of the goniometer is aligned with it. The limb is moved to the other end of the range, and the second arm is aligned with it. The degrees between the two arms on the goniometer represent the range of motion at the joint.

Taking accurate flexibility measurements is not quite as easy as it sounds (Michlovitz, Harris, & Watkins, 2004). Starting and ending points are sometimes difficult to locate, and measurements often reflect the discomfort individuals are willing to endure to push themselves farther.

It is often impractical to give a battery of flexibility measures at various joints, especially if strength, endurance, and body composition are all being assessed at the same time. Fitness test batteries such as Physical Best (American Alliance for Health, Physical Education, Recreation and Dance, 1988), Fitnessgram (Meredith & Welk, 1999), and that used in the National Children and Youth Fitness Study II (Ross, Pate, Delpy, Gold, & Svilar, 1987) employ a single representative measure of flexibility. The sit-and-reach test (figure 16.9) was chosen because trunk and hip flexibility are thought to be important in the prevention and care of low back pain in adults (Hoeger, Hopkins, Button, & Palmer, 1990).

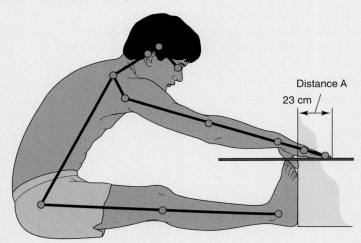

FIGURE 16.9 The sit-and-reach test. The individual sits with the feet against a box corresponding to the 23 cm point along the ruler. Upon reaching forward as far as possible, the individual receives a score of 23 cm plus or minus the distance reached measured at the fingertips (distance A).

Distance A
23 cm

again at 17 and 18 (figure 16.10). Thus, the range of scores was wider in successively older age groups (Simons et al., 1990). Belgian boys measured longitudinally improved their sit-and-reach performance from 12 to 18 years of age at a rate of about 1 cm per year (Beunen, Malina, Renson, & Van Gerven, 1988).

Generally, then, children maintain their sit-and-reach flexibility, whereas adolescents are able to improve their scores as they grow older. Some children and adolescents lose flexibility or improve very little. Abdominal strength might be a factor in sit-and-reach performance (Beunen et al., 1988) because individuals with strong abdominal muscles can pull the trunk forward to a greater degree of flexion. Performance might therefore be related to exercise and training, both for strength and for range of motion.

Girls as a group are usually more flexible than boys (Beunen et al., 1988; DiNucci, 1976; Phillips et al., 1955; Simons et al., 1990). This difference probably reflects the facts that stretching exercises are more socially acceptable for girls than are vigorous exercises and that higher proportions of girls than boys participate in gymnastics and dance, both of which emphasize flexibility. Participation in exercise programs emphasizing flexibility is a far better predictor of flexibility than is sex (figure 16.11).

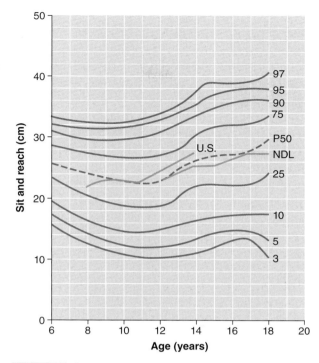

FIGURE 16.10 Changes in sit-and-reach test performance over age. Flemish girls at the upper percentiles maintained their flexibility during childhood and then improved in adolescence. Girls at the lower percentiles declined and then only slightly improved in midadolescence. The median scores of girls from the United States (U.S.) and the Netherlands (NDL) are superimposed on the graph.

Reprinted by permission from Simons et al. 1990.

FIGURE 16.11 Flexibility becomes more variable in adolescence as some individuals exercise and others become sedentary. It is unclear how the changing structural constraints of skeletal system growth and muscle system growth influence flexibility,

Researchers, then, document both declines and improvements in flexibility during the growing years. It is possible that because the bones grow in length and then stimulate muscles to grow in length, a temporary loss of flexibility occurs during growth, especially in early adolescence (Micheli, 1984), as muscle growth lags behind bone growth. However, it is not clear that this would result in a measurable decline in flexibility, even over a short period of time.

Although some changes might be particular to the joint or joints measured, overall it is apparent that children and adolescents can lose their flexibility if they do not train to maintain or improve it. Flexibility becomes more variable in groups of adolescents because some adolescents train whereas others abandon exercise programs and physical activities. Most of us think of arthritis as a disease of older adulthood, but approximately 1 out of every 250 children in the United States has a form of arthritis and associated joint pain. Expertise in treatment is required because the traditional adult therapy of steroids can stunt children's growth.

 Think about your own fitness regimen. Does it include activities that can maintain your flexibility over the next 30 or 40 years? Do you need to add to your personal workout plan?

 WEB STUDY GUIDE   Plot data and examine trends in flexibility over time in Lab Activity 16.2, Examining Trends in Sit-and-Reach Performance, in the web study guide. Go to www.HumanKinetics.com/LifeSpanMotorDevelopment.

Adulthood

Unfortunately, adolescence does not mark the end of a person's trend toward reduced flexibility. Holland, Tanaka, Shigematsu, and Nakagaichi (2002) reviewed the research literature on flexibility and older adults. From the mid- to late 20s, maximum range of motion declines; it does so faster in some joints than in others (Bell & Hoshizaki, 1981). For example, the decreases in spinal extension and shoulder flexion are relatively large compared with smaller decreases in hip extension and knee flexion (Einkauf, Gohdes, Jensen, & Jewell, 1987; Germain & Blair, 1983; Roach & Miles, 1991). Both upper and lower extremities showed declines in flexibility (Rikli & Jones, 1999).

Osteoarthritis is a degenerative, chronic disease of the joints.

KEY POINT
Flexibility declines in adulthood, especially in little-used joints.

Various factors contribute to decreases in flexibility, including degeneration of musculoskeletal and soft tissues as well as diseases, especially **osteoarthritis** and **osteoporosis**. Collagen increases and elastin degenerates with advancing age, and both of these changes lead to increased joint stiffness (Alnaqeeb, Al-Zaid, & Goldspink, 1984; Gosline, 1976). Disuse magnifies all of these changes, though we do not know how disuse influences the rate of decline. The research studies of range of motion in adulthood have used the cross-sectional design. Longitudinal studies would be needed to determine how much of the decline is due to age-related tissue change and how much is due to disuse. The learning exercise at the end of this chapter gives you an opportunity to observe flexibility in some older adults.

Flexibility Training

Researchers generally agree that both specialized stretch training and general exercise interventions moderately improve range of motion in older adults, including frail elderly persons. Munns (1981) formed two groups of 65- to 88-year-olds. One group served as a control and the other participated in a 1 h program of exercise and dance 3 times per week for 12 weeks. The exercising group improved significantly over the control group in all six of the flexibility measures taken. Germain and Blair (1983) documented improved shoulder flexibility in adults aged 20 to 60 who participated in a stretching program for shoulder flexion, and Brown and Holloszy (1991) even found a 35% improvement in hip flexion with 5 days of slow stretch and callisthenic training per week over 3 months. Low-impact aerobics, Tai Chi, rhythmic stretching, and general fitness interventions have all yielded improvements (Hubley-Kozey, Wall, & Hogan, 1995; Lan, Lai, Chen, & Wong, 1998; McMurdo & Rennie, 1993; Rikli & Edwards, 1991).

KEY POINT
An individual's flexibility decreases without training at any point in the life span, but specific training can reverse a loss of flexibility at any age.

Summary of the Development of Flexibility

The range of motion possible in a joint reflects a person's activity and training more than it reflects his or her age per se. Flexibility declines in the average adolescent and adult as a result of limited daily activity and lack of exercise. Flexibility training can bring about an improvement in the range of motion at any age. For many individuals, then, if flexibility limits a desired movement, appropriate training can change this structural constraint.

Summary and Synthesis

Muscle strength and flexibility are discussed separately in this chapter, but their interrelationship as individual structural constraints should be noted. Individuals can improve strength or flexibility at any time in the life span with an appropriate training program. Ideally, though, individuals train for both. Having strong muscles to move a joint in one direction such that the joint cannot move through its appropriate range in the opposite direction can limit movement just as much as a lack of strength can. Training for strength and flexibility is not just for athletes; to the contrary, if reasonable levels of strength and flexibility are not maintained, many movements needed for daily living can be difficult if not impossible. Therapists routinely help individuals regain lost strength and flexibility after accidents, injuries, and surgery.

Body composition is another component of fitness. A body composition that is high in lean muscle mass and low in fat tissue enhances cardiorespiratory endurance, is associated with increased strength, and permits flexibility as long as the muscles are balanced. Individuals can better maintain that body composition profile if they participate in endurance activities and resistance-training programs. Chapter 17 examines body composition more closely.

 Reinforcing What You Have Learned About Constraints

TAKE A SECOND LOOK

Being strong and flexible is an advantage to performance, whereas being weak and inflexible can limit performance. In other words, the musculoskeletal systems can be rate-limiting systems for movement. Training for strength and flexibility can be a healthy activity, and greater muscle mass can make a positive contribution to health. For example, greater muscle mass is associated with expending more calories and maintaining healthy body composition. Greater muscle mass is also associated with greater cardiovascular endurance. Yet, as we have seen so often, the musculoskeletal system does not function in isolation. Individuals who try to enhance their strength and flexibility training with drugs often risk damage to other systems, especially the endocrine system with the use of anabolic steroids. This fact reminds us that the interaction of all systems must be considered when examining the effect of changing a system to give rise to certain movements.

TEST YOUR KNOWLEDGE

1. How does the rate of increase in strength with growth compare with the rate of increase in muscle mass? How do the rates of decrease in strength and muscle mass compare in aging?
2. Can strength and flexibility improve with training? How?
3. How does flexibility change with growth and with aging?
4. What are the sex differences in the development of strength and flexibility in children and adolescents?
5. Consider the older adults in your society. Can you think of constraints (individual, environmental, and task) that might lead to a loss of strength in the older years?
6. How is maturation related to strength in children and teens?
7. What factors are involved in the loss of strength in older adulthood? What effect does resistance training have on these factors?
8. What factors are important to consider in assessing strength? In assessing flexibility?
9. How does the change in functional muscle strength compare with the change in isometric muscle strength during the growing years?
10. How can cultural norms differentially affect assessment of strength and flexibility of the sexes?

Learning Exercise 16.1

OLDER ADULT FLEXIBILITY

Observe the following in two or three older adults and report your findings.

1. When seated on the floor with his back against a wall, can the individual keep the knee of the extended leg flat on the floor as he draws the lower portion of his other leg up against the thigh?
2. Can she raise her arms overhead, fingers pointing to the ceiling, to be even with or behind the ears?
3. When standing facing you, can he keep his elbows tucked in and turn his palms to face you?
4. In a standing position, can she link her hands behind her back and raise them up away from her back to a level even with her waist?

Did the individuals pass or fail all four items? Ask individuals about their favorite activities and see if you can account for the maintenance of flexibility by matching body areas to those activities.

17

Development of Body Composition

 CHAPTER OBJECTIVES

This chapter

- reviews the effects of exercise on the body composition of children and youths through longitudinal research studies,
- notes any sex differences in the effects of exercise on body composition,
- examines the effects of exercise on body composition in middle and older adulthood, and
- discusses the recent increase in obesity in Western societies.

Obesity

It is difficult to pick up a few popular magazines or watch a few television talk shows without encountering concern over obesity. This has been true for a number of years. What has become more common lately are articles and segments about the growing number of children worldwide who are obese. For all the media attention, the trend has not been reversed. Of course, much of the concern surrounds the relationship between childhood and adulthood obesity; obese children are very likely to be obese adults. In fact, obese children are encountering health hazards previously seen only in adulthood. So, not only are obese children at risk of health problems at the present, they will be increasingly at risk as they move into adulthood. Many today even use the term *epidemic* for this trend of increasing childhood obesity.

Concern is ongoing about fitness and fatness, and rightly so. Alarming rates of obesity have prompted more attention to the roles of diet and exercise in body composition and to maintaining a healthy ratio of lean weight to fat weight at *all* points of the life span. Yet many do not understand the relationship of diet and exercise to body composition over the life span. This is valuable information, both for working in any professional role that involves diet and exercise and for one's personal well-being. It is imperative that professionals continue to teach key aspects of the relationship and advocate for opportunities for people of all ages to implement healthful practices.

Body mass can be divided into two types of tissue: **lean tissue**—which includes muscle, bone, and organs—and fat, or **adipose tissue**. The relative percentages of fat-free and fat tissues that make up the body mass give a measure of body composition. Many people care about body composition because it is related to appearance and it can influence individuals' feelings about themselves. Many societies value a lean body appearance. Obesity may contribute to a negative body concept and negative self-concept, thus making it difficult for an obese person to relate to others.

Aside from appearance, body composition is important in a variety of health issues:

- Higher proportions of lean body mass show a positive link to working capacity, and higher proportions of fat tissue show a negative link.
- Excess fat weight adds to the workload whenever the body is moved.
- Excess fat can limit an individual's range of motion.
- Obesity places a person at increased risk of suffering coronary heart and artery disease, stroke, diabetes, and hypertension.

Body composition is often related to success in executing motor skills; that is, it serves as a structural constraint. For individuals who are overweight, it can also serve as a functional constraint. A body composition high in muscle mass and low in adipose tissue contributes to optimal performance. The muscle mass can be used to exert force, and low adipose tissue means that a performer does not have extra weight to move, both of which constitute advantages in many physical activities. In contrast, a body composition that is high in adipose tissue can make it difficult to move the body, especially for extended times, and difficult to achieve certain body positions. So, in addition to the health repercussions, overweight can be a rate limiter to motor skills.

As noted in chapter 5, everyone has some fat tissue, which is needed for insulation, protection, and energy storage. Women need a certain level of fat tissue (approximately 12% of body weight) to support functions of reproduction. Only *excess* fat weight is negatively related to fitness and health. Attempts to reduce fat tissue to excessively low levels are equally a health concern.

Body Composition and Exercise in Children and Youths

Genetic and environmental factors affect body composition. People can manipulate two major environmental factors—diet and exercise—to manage the relative amounts of lean and adipose tissue in their bodies. Maintaining body composition is in part a matter of balancing the calories consumed against the metabolic rate and the amount of physical exertion. The metabolic rate is the amount of energy an individual uses in a given amount of time to keep the body functioning. Rates vary among individuals; some use more calories than others do just to keep the body running. The metabolic rate is under the control of various hormones, and it cannot be easily altered in the short term. In contrast, an individual can control exercise level on a daily basis. This discussion focuses on the relationship between body composition and exercise.

Because children are not biochemically identical to adults, dividing the body into fat and fat-free mass oversimplifies the changes in body composition that occur with growth. A more extensive breakdown, however, is beyond the scope of this text. This chapter considers what is known about the influence of exercise on fat and fat-free tissues in children and youths. This section considers the research of Jana Parizkova, much of which was published in the 1970s but which still constitutes a meaningful part of the little longitudinal work done on this topic. More recent cross-sectional, or short-term, studies are also considered.

 WEB STUDY GUIDE Evaluate changes in body mass index in a group of children over a period of 4 years in Lab Activity 17.1, Body Composition in Childhood, in the web study guide. Go to www.HumanKinetics.com/Life SpanMotorDevelopment.

The Parizkova Studies

Fat tissue increases rapidly during two periods: the first 6 months after birth and again in early adolescence. In girls, this increase continues throughout adolescence, whereas in boys the gain stops and may even reverse for a time. Muscle tissue also grows rapidly in infants, followed by a steady period of increase during childhood; it again increases rapidly during the adolescent growth spurt, more dramatically in boys than in girls. This typical pattern may be altered through either diet or exercise. Overeating results in excess fat weight, and starvation can lead to levels of fat so low that the body obtains energy by muscle wasting (breaking down muscle tissue to use as energy). Exercise, of course, burns calories, thus

Assessing Amounts of Body Fat

The amount of adipose tissue in the body can be measured in numerous ways. These measurements can be used directly to track changes with growth and aging, or they can be used to estimate the percentage of the body's weight that is fat. We also have several methods for measuring lean body mass; they allow an estimation of body fat as well:

- Measuring the thickness of the skin and underlying (subcutaneous) fat with skinfold calipers. The amount of total body fat can be estimated from skinfold measurements taken at specified sites. This is one of the most common ways of estimating fat weight, especially in children.

- Weighing a person underwater and contrasting that value with normal body weight. This method estimates body density and, subsequently, the proportion of lean versus fat weight. It is difficult to take this measurement on young children and adults who are afraid of being underwater.

- Analyzing the intensity of reemitted infrared light emitted by a probe into the biceps brachii muscle with a near-infrared interactance device. This is an easy measurement method to use with children but may not be as accurate as other methods (especially underwater weighing) (Smith et al., 1997).

- Measuring soft tissue composition with a dual-energy X-ray absorptiometer, which allows a direct measure of body density but requires expensive equipment (Steinberger et al., 2005; Sutton & Miller, 2006).

- Measuring air displacement (rather than water displacement) by air-displacement plethysmography. This measure requires a BodPod or Body Pod chamber but allows measurement of infants and obese individuals (Dioum, Gartner, Maire, Delpeuch, & Wade, 2005).

potentially altering a person's body composition. Resistance training can increase muscle mass, especially after puberty.

In cross-sectional and longitudinal studies, researchers have examined the relationship between exercise and body composition. Cross-sectional studies generally show that young athletes have lower proportions of body fat than do more sedentary children (Parizkova, 1973). However, it is impossible to determine from a cross-sectional study whether an active lifestyle results in leanness. (It could be the case that leaner children find activity easier and therefore adopt active lifestyles.) Longitudinal studies, then, are more valuable in the study of the interrelationships between activity levels and body composition.

Parizkova conducted a series of studies on body composition and activity levels of boys and girls in Czechoslovakia. The first study was cross-sectional and was one of the few studies to examine very young children; the remainder of the studies were longitudinal. In the cross-sectional study, Wolanski and Parizkova (1976; cited in Parizkova, 1977) compared skinfold measures in two groups of children aged 2 to 5 years. One group of children attended special physical education classes with their parents, whereas the other group did not participate in any type of physical-training program. Even at this young age, children in the physical education group had lower levels of subcutaneous fat.

Teenage Boys

In an extensive longitudinal study of teenage boys, Parizkova (1968a, 1977) divided nearly 100 boys into four groups by their activity level. Boys in the most active group (group I) were involved in basketball or track for at least 6 h a week. Boys in the least active group (group IV) participated only in unorganized and unsystematic activity. The boys in the other two groups had intermediate activity levels.

Parizkova first tested the boys at an average age of 10.7 years, then followed them in successive years until they were 14.7 years old. Over the 4 years, the children in the most active group significantly increased in body mass while their absolute level of fat weight remained the same; hence, the fat proportion of their total weight decreased. In contrast, the boys in the inactive group increased significantly in absolute fat weight. The two groups did not differ in initial amount of fat weight, but they differed at the end of the 4 years. In the active group, the increase in lean body mass *alone* accounted for the increase of body weight with growth (figure 17.1, *a* and *b*). Physical activity had a beneficial effect on body composition in these boys.

Parizkova (1972) then followed 41 of these boys for another 3 years, and the body composition trends of the first 4 years continued. The most active and least active groups differed in total weight by the time they reached age 16.7. The active group was heavier in total body weight because the boys' lean body mass was greater. The active boys had less total fat weight than the inactive boys, and their fat weight actually declined in some years. Parizkova determined that the groups did not differ in average skeletal age, so the differences noted in body composition cannot be attributed to maturational differences. He also noted that the boys maintained their relative position in the group in both distribution and absolute amount of subcutaneous fat. This means that the relative amount of fat weight and its pattern of distribution in the body were relatively stable over the years of the study.

Parizkova followed 16 of these 41 young men for yet another 6 years. Although this number was too small for a reliable analysis by activity level, Parizkova (1977) noted that percentage body fat declined in the group until age 21.7 years, then varied widely among individuals, probably reflecting changes in lifestyle. The

KEY POINT
In active teenage boys, increased body weight reflects increased lean body mass.

KEY POINT
Physical activity has a favorable effect on boys during the growing years in that it increases lean body mass and minimizes addition of fat weight.

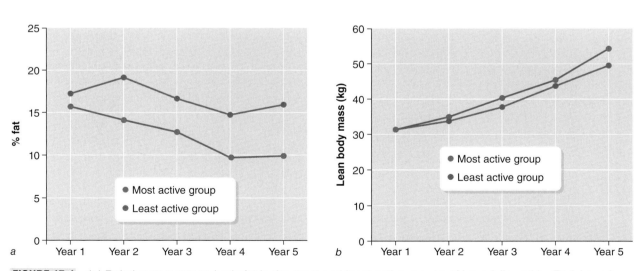

FIGURE 17.1 *(a)* Relative percentage body fat in the most and least active groups of boys followed by Parizkova from an average age of 10.7 years to 14.7 years. *(b)* Lean body mass of the same groups in Parizkova's study.

Reprinted by permission from Parizkova 1977.

Parizkova studies, then, indicate that physical activity has a favorable influence on boys' body composition during the growing years.

 If you were a high school principal, what implications would you see in the Parizkova study for the physical education curriculum at your school?

Teenage Girls

KEY POINT
Teenage girls in training can increase lean body mass and decrease subcutaneous fat, even when they eat more calories in response to training.

The growth of adipose and lean muscle tissue differs dramatically between the sexes during adolescence. Girls gain proportionately more fat than muscle compared with boys. Even so, the beneficial effect that activity has on body composition in boys also occurs in active girls. Over a span of 5 years, Parizkova (1963, 1977) studied 32 girls who belonged to a gymnastics school and 45 girls who were not engaged in any type of training. The girls were first measured at the age of 12 or 13 years. The gymnasts followed a regular yearly cycle of training in which they attended a rigorous camp in the summer, stopped training in the early fall, and resumed a heavy training schedule from October to December.

These cycles are shown (for 11 of the gymnasts) in figure 17.2 as black-outlined bars; the higher the bar, the more intense the training. Measurements of the girls' fat weight paralleled Parizkova's findings with boys. The gymnasts remained at the same level of subcutaneous fat during the 5 years, and the total skinfold thickness showed no trend, even though it increased or decreased for short periods. In

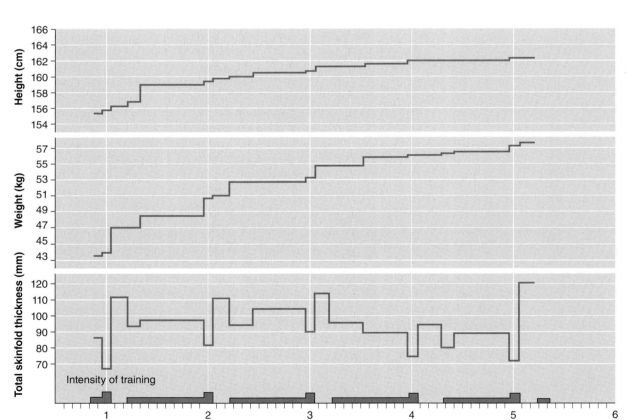

FIGURE 17.2 Changes in height, weight, and subcutaneous fat (sum of 10 skinfold measurements) in a group of regularly training female gymnasts (*n* = 11) during a 5-year period of varying intensity of training (see bottom scale).

Reprinted by permission from Parizkova 1977.

contrast, the control group gained a significant amount of fat weight. Height and body weight trends in the two groups were similar throughout the 5 years, so the differences were truly in body composition.

The cyclic nature of the gymnasts' training schedule provided information about their weight and skinfold thicknesses as they progressed through the various training phases. During periods of inactivity the gymnasts gained in both total body weight and skinfold thickness (including subcutaneous fat tissue), but during training they increased in total body weight while their skinfold thicknesses declined. (Note that in figure 17.2, total skinfold thickness goes down when the intensity of training goes up, and total skinfold thickness goes up when training stops for a time.) Total height and weight keep increasing with age. Therefore, the weight increases during the various activity periods resulted from changing ratios of fat and lean body weight. Parizkova also recorded the gymnasts' caloric intake and found that even though they consumed more calories during periods of intense training, fat deposits decreased and lean body mass increased.

 If you were a physical education teacher, what results from the Parizkova studies could you use to counsel your teenage girl students on diet and exercise?

Comparing Adolescent Boys and Girls

These longitudinal studies by Parizkova showed the same general relationship between body composition and activity in both boys and girls, but they did not allow direct comparison of the sexes. So Parizkova (1973, 1977) simultaneously followed 12 boys and 12 girls engaged in swimming training from ages 12 to 16. At age 12, the average height, weight, lean body mass, and fat weight of the two groups were about the same. Lean body mass values for the swimmers were higher than the average levels for teens not in training, which probably reflected the swimmers' previous training. By age 15, the boys were significantly taller, heavier, and leaner than the girls, but both sexes showed an increased proportion of lean body mass at the expense of fat weight over the first 3 years of training. Although higher in percentage fat than the boys, the girls did not gain as much fat as the typical nontraining adolescent girl. More research on this topic is necessary, especially to determine the length and intensity of training programs that have favorable results with girls. Tremblay, Despres, and Bouchard (1988) did not find a decline in fatness or a gain in lean body mass in girls after 15 weeks of intense training, although boys experienced significant changes in this period of time.

 How has your body composition changed throughout your life span? What do you think contributed to that change? How might you use your experience in working with others?

Short-Term Studies

Dollman, Olds, Norton, and Stuart (1999) compared more than 1,400 Australian children who were 10 and 11 in 1997 with a group measured in 1985. The 1997 children as a group were heavier and fatter, though slightly taller, than those in the 1985 group. They were also slower in the 1.6 km walk–run and 50 m sprint. These differences did not occur in the leaner and fitter children but rather in the one-fourth of the children who were fatter and less fit. Although it's not clear whether one decline caused the other (or whether something else caused both), being fatter coincided with poorer fitness performance. Olds and Dollman (2004) attempted to address the issue of whether poorer performance reflected increased fatness or decreased activity levels by further studying the children from the 1999 study. They matched participants in the two groups for fatness. The 1997 group was still slower in the 1.6 km walk–run, which suggests that decreased physical activity played a role in the decreased performance of the 1997 group.

The Muscatine Study is a longitudinal investigation of cardiovascular disease risk factors among the residents of Muscatine, Iowa. Participants were measured for fitness, body composition, blood pressure, heart mass, and maturation level in youth. Janz, Burns, and Mahoney (1995) reported on a 2-year follow-up with more than 120 children who were 10 years old at the first set of measurements. They found that increased systolic blood pressure was associated with increased body fatness and decreased physical fitness. Thus, the two factors coincided in a group approximately the same age as that observed by Dollman et al. (1999).

In summary, these investigations show that involvement in training programs favorably affects adolescents' body composition. Limited information suggests that the body composition of preschool children also benefits from activity. Although children and adolescents who engage in active training exhibit the general growth trend of increased weight, this increase represents the addition of relatively more lean body mass and less fat weight than in their nontraining peers. A person's higher caloric intake during training evidently increases lean body mass rather than fat stores.

It is possible for a person to carry training to an extreme wherein the body cannot meet the energy required for continued growth. This condition mimics starvation and can lead to loss of lean body mass and detrimental effects on growth (Lemon, 1989).

 If you were a teacher or a doctor, what would be your strategy for reversing the trend of declining fitness in today's youths?

Motor Skill and Fitness

The relationship between motor skill proficiency and level of physical fitness is of interest and has important implications for programming in childhood and adolescence. For example, if one is concerned about the trends toward increased overweight and declining fitness levels in youths, would the answer be to focus physical education programs solely on fitness activities, or would there be value in focusing on both developing motor skill proficiency and fitness activities? It's best to take a longitudinal approach for answers to this question.

Barnett, van Beurden, Morgan, Brooks, and Beard (2008) measured youths approximately 8 to 12 years old on fundamental motor skills and a shuttle run-type cardiorespiratory test. They then repeated the tests 5 years later. They found that some of the fundamental motor skills—interestingly, the object-control skills rather than locomotor skills—predicted adolescent cardiorespiratory fitness. This was true for both boys and girls. Perhaps the youths with good object-control skills were more likely to participate in physical activities. Hands (2008) took a similar approach but included children who were classified as either low or high in motor competence. She also repeated her measures every year for 5 years. The two competency groups were different in all measures (the high competency group was better) except body mass index, for which no difference was found.

The differences remained over the 5 years but widened on the shuttle run test for aerobic fitness and narrowed on a sprint run and a balance test. The children with low motor competency improved over the 5 years but never caught up with the children with high competency. Better motor skill was associated with greater cardiovascular endurance.

A study by Vedul-Kjelsås, Sigmundsson, Stendsdotter, and Haga (2011) is a reminder that self-perception in children is related to motor competence and physical fitness. They found this relationship in all aspects of self-perception measured by Harter's Self-Perception Profile for Children, social acceptance, athletic competence, physical appearance, and general self-worth. The authors suggested that these aspects of self-perception facilitate participation in physical activity.

In addition to longitudinal research, Rivilis, Hay, Cairney, Klentrou, Liu, and Faught (2011) recently reviewed 40 studies dealing with the relationship between motor proficiency and physical activity in children with developmental coordination disorder. Their overall conclusion was that poor motor proficiency is associated with high body composition, low cardiorespiratory fitness, lower strength and endurance, lower anaerobic capacity and power, and less physical activity. Flexibility was the only fitness component not clearly related to motor proficiency.

Generally, this research demonstrates that children with less motor proficiency are less fit. Of course, many fitness tests, especially cardiorespiratory fitness tests, require some level of motor skill. Better motor skill likely contributes to efficient test performance. Yet, this would be true in training as well. It appears that promoting the development of motor skill in youths can have a positive effect on fitness, and even children with low motor competency can improve over time on both skill and fitness measures.

Body Composition and Exercise in Adults

In middle age, the average adult loses fat-free body mass and gains fat such that body weight increases and the portion of body weight that is fat increases. Of particular concern is an accumulation of trunk fat, which is associated with increasingly poor cardiovascular health. In old age, fat-free body mass and fat mass decline. It is important to remember that this is the typical profile and that individuals are extremely variable. Also, obese individuals often die before reaching older adulthood, which can change average measurements taken on groups of older adults.

Exercise might favorably influence body composition in two ways: It could increase fat-free mass or decrease fat. The increase in fat-free mass could be an increase in muscle mass, an increase in bone density, or both. Some studies, discussed in this section, have tracked these changes in exercising adults.

Middle-aged and older adult athletes and regular exercisers tend to maintain their muscle and fat masses, and many compare favorably with younger adult populations (Asano, Ogawa, & Furuta, 1978; Kavanagh & Shephard, 1977; Pollock, 1974; Saltin & Grimby, 1968; Shephard, 1978b). However, we cannot assume from these observations that the same would be true of the population at large or of sedentary older adults who begin training. It is possible that healthier older adults are more able to be active and that what is being observed is good health status rather than the benefits of exercise. For this reason, it is important to longitudinally study older adults for exercise effects. The current number of longitudinal studies is tiny, however, so we often must rely on short-term studies for information.

Recent studies of changes in muscle mass with exercise have used computed tomography to document changes in muscle area. A study of men aged 60 to 72 (Frontera, Meredith, O'Reilly, Knuttgen, & Evans, 1988) and a study of men aged 86 to 96 (Fiatarone et al., 1990) reported increases in muscle area in the range of 4.8% to 11.4% after 12 and 8 weeks of training, respectively. Both type I and type II fibers increased. Other studies have found smaller changes (Forbes, 1992). It is clear that individuals are extremely variable. Fiatarone et al. (1990) reported on individual subjects who lost 8% of muscle area with training and subjects who gained 30% even though they trained the same number of weeks. These contradictions make it difficult to predict whether every older adult would see an increase in muscle mass with training.

Studies of young athletes have concluded that regular exercise promotes bone growth, but the few studies of older adults have reached conflicting conclusions. This difference might derive in part from weak research methods. Going, Williams, Lohman, and Hewitt (1994) point out that in some studies, the exercise program undertaken by the adults did not stress the body locations that were measured for bone density. Several studies of change in the bone mineral density of lumbar (lower back) vertebrae have shown improvements with weight training in premenopausal (Going et al., 1991; Lohman et al., 1992) and postmenopausal (Dalsky et al., 1988; Pruitt, Jackson, Bartels, & Lehnhard, 1992) women. Another study, however, reported a decline in bone mineral density (Rockwell et al., 1990). Researchers need to do much more work, especially on a wide range of older adults, and they need to determine the type, duration, and frequency of exercise that is helpful.

Schwartz et al. (1991) placed 15 men between 60 and 82 years of age on a 6-month endurance-training program. Their training intensity gradually increased so that eventually they were walking or jogging 45 min per session, 5 days per week, at 85% of heart rate reserve. Over the 6 months, their body fat decreased 2.3% and their waist circumferences decreased 3.4%. Although the loss of body fat overall was small, the loss of fat in specific trunk locations was more dramatic, which is significant because of the association between trunk fat and increased cardiovascular risk. Paillard, Lafont, Costes-Salon, Riviere, and Dupui (2004) found that a relatively short-term walking program of 12 weeks for men between 63 and 72 years of age brought about a decrease of fat weight. No increase occurred in lean body mass or bone mineral density, though, for an intervention of this length.

 Think about your own diet and fitness routines. Do you have habits that will keep your body composition similar to what it is now as you get older, or would a change be warranted?

Although more longitudinal research in the area of body composition and exercise is needed, there are clear indications that exercise has a favorable effect on body composition. Observation of those engaged in vigorous activity over the life span demonstrates at the very least that a decline in fat-free mass and an increase in fat mass is not a foregone conclusion for everyone.

 WEB STUDY GUIDE Measure skinfolds, height, and weight in Lab Activity 17.2, Comparing Body Composition Measures, in the web study guide. Go to www.HumanKinetics.com/LifeSpanMotorDevelopment.

Obesity

The prevalence of **obesity** is increasing around the world and in all age categories. Rates of obesity vary among countries; the prevalence is higher in industrialized nations. Increasing rates among the upper classes in developing countries, however, demonstrate the strong universal trend toward obesity (Kotz, Billington, & Levine, 1999; Rudloff & Feldmann, 1999). Various organizations and researchers use slightly different criteria to determine who is considered obese. The most common definition for adults is having a **body mass index (BMI)** of more than 30.0 (Kotz et al., 1999).

BMI is the ratio of body weight (kg) to height squared (m); normal is defined as the range from 18.5 to 24.9. This is a convenient measure to use in many settings because one needs only to be able to measure height and weight in order to calculate BMI. Yet body weight reflects both lean and adipose tissue, so the BMI might be misleading for some individuals with above-average lean muscle weight. This limitation should be kept in mind when reviewing research using the BMI measurement. It is challenging to define obesity for children because of ongoing growth, but one frequently used criterion is a weight-for-height measurement over the 95th percentile; another is a triceps skinfold over the 95th percentile (Rudloff & Feldmann, 1999).

Obesity is a concern at any point in the life span, yet chances are great that obese children will remain obese into adulthood, and obesity tends to be stable over young, middle, and older adulthood. Hence, there is a sense of urgency about addressing obesity in children even while recognizing its medical and social repercussions at any age.

In the United States about one-fourth of children and adolescents are obese, an increase of 54% in children and 39% in adolescents over 20 years (Rudloff & Feldmann, 1999). Parents often believe that their child's obesity is caused by a metabolic or thyroid disorder. In fact, these disorders account for less than 1% of obesity in children (Dietz & Robinson, 1993). What, then, is the typical cause?

Obesity is a good example of the interaction between genetic and extrinsic factors. Certainly genetic factors are related to obesity. BMI is highly correlated in twins, even if they are raised apart, but is poorly correlated in parents and adopted children. However, no single genetic factor is related to obesity in all individuals. Various factors under genetic influence include **basal metabolic rate**, dietary **thermogenesis**, appetite control and satiety, and lipid metabolism and storage (Rudloff & Feldmann, 1999).

The increase in obesity over the past several decades demonstrates the strong influence of extrinsic factors on obesity because genetic influences could not change the incidence rate so rapidly (Rosenbaum & Leibel, 1998). Increasing modernization reduces energy expenditure as laborious tasks are taken over by machines (figure 17.3). A Westernized diet, high in fat and sugar, is also a major factor in obesity (Kotz et al., 1999). Because genetic predispositions are fixed, manipulation of energy intake and expenditure is the most available means for altering body fatness during the life span.

Restricting caloric intake in children is challenging because sufficient energy must be provided to support growth. Overweight children typically do not eat large quantities. Rather, they have a small but daily caloric imbalance (Dietz & Robinson, 1993). A relatively modest adjustment of calories with good nutritional balance in diet can be very effective. However, reduced motor activity is a common

Obesity is most commonly defined as a body mass index of more than 30.0.

Body mass index (BMI) is the ratio of body weight (kg) to height squared (m); a normal index falls between 18.5 and 24.9.

Basal metabolic rate is the amount of energy needed to sustain the body's vital functions in the waking state.

Thermogenesis is the production of heat in the body.

KEY POINT
The trends in extrinsic factors that lead to obesity are problematic on two counts: People are less active, and diets increasingly consist of high levels of fat and sugar.

characteristic of obese children (Roberts, Savage, Coward, Chew, & Lucas, 1988), and increasing calorie expenditure through exercise has multiple benefits in altering body composition fat. First, it can offset the decrease in basal metabolic rate that accompanies caloric restriction. Second, it can promote the growth of muscle tissue, which requires more calories for maintenance than fat tissue requires (Bar-Or, 1993). This difference is significant because without exercise, 30% to 40% of the weight lost with caloric restriction in adults is from lean body mass (Harris, 1999); this is likely the trend with children, too.

Hesketh and Campbell (2010) reviewed 23 studies on interventions for preventing obesity in toddlers and young children up to 5 years of age. Most of the studies reviewed were conducted in preschool or child-care settings and home settings, and about half of the studies were done with disadvantaged participants. Researchers tended to use multiple modes of intervention, such as improved diet, increased physical activity,

FIGURE 17.3 It is increasingly common among individuals of all ages to devote considerable time to screened devices, such as computers, tablets, smart phones, and televisions. As a result, more people tend to be sedentary rather than active. These environmental and task constraints interact with body systems to create a downward health spiral: Lean body mass decreases, fat tissue increases, and the cardiovascular system develops increased risk for disease.

and reduced sedentary behavior. The nature of the intervention programs was varied and the success of the programs was mixed, but overall the studies demonstrated that interventions could positively affect obesity, especially if parents were involved.

A synthesis of reviews and meta-analyses (Khambalia, Dickinson, Hardy, Gill, & Baur, 2012) on obesity interventions in school-aged children suggested that intervention programs were more likely to yield a significant weight reduction in children if they were long term rather than short term. Additionally, programs tended to be successful if they combined improved diet, increased physical activity, and family involvement. Although the research conducted on intervention programs thus far has been helpful, more research is needed on programs that measure both weight-related outcomes and health-related outcomes.

It is well established that obese children do not perform as well as lean children do on a variety of physical fitness and motor skills tests. Malina et al. (1995) selected a group of Belgian girls between 7 and 17 years of age. At each age, the leanest 5% outperformed the fattest 5% on arm-strength and endurance tasks, trunk-strength tasks, the vertical jump, an agility shuttle run, and a balance task. Adolescent boys show the same performance differences (Beunen et al., 1983). On the other hand, participation in regular physical activity reduces fatness in obese

KEY POINT
Exercise is an important strategy in altering obesity because it expends calories and offsets a decrease in basal metabolic rate that accompanies caloric restriction.

children. Sasaki, Shindo, Tanaka, Ando, and Arakawa (1987) found that a 2-year program of daily aerobic activity significantly decreased skinfold thicknesses. Even short-term training programs of 10 weeks and 4 months yielded decreased body fat percentages in obese children between 7 and 11 years of age (Gutin, Cucuzzo, Islam, Smith, & Stachura, 1996; Gutin, Owens, Slavens, Riggs, & Treiber, 1997). Saavedra, Escalante, and Garcia-Hermoso (2011) conducted a meta-analysis of studies on the improvement of aerobic fitness in obese children. They found that programs that lasted more than 12 weeks and provided 3 sessions (more than 60 min per session) per week yielded better results. They also determined that programs focused on aerobic exercise had an effect on aerobic fitness whereas those that combined aerobic exercise with other exercise, especially strength training, did not, most likely because of the extended time spent in strength training. Korsten-Reck et al. (2007) demonstrated that a comprehensive intervention program for obese children brought about favorable changes in body composition, aerobic endurance, and motor ability tasks. These findings imply that activity programs might be relatively difficult for obese children, yet the benefits of regular activity can be significant. Well-designed programs are needed to set the workload appropriately for obese children.

 If you were a middle school physical education teacher, how might you intervene with your obese students to put them on a path toward improved health?

The incidence of obesity increases in men and women from age 20 to age 50 (Kotz et al., 1999; figure 17.4). Obesity puts individuals at risk for hypertension, cardiovascular disease, diabetes, gallstones, osteoarthritis, and some forms of cancer; hence, the obese are at greater risk of early mortality. In fact, a decrease in the prevalence of obesity in the 70s and 80s might reflect the shortened life span of the obese. The association of obesity and mortality is stronger among those whose increased fatness is particularly concentrated in the abdomen (Kotz et al., 1999).

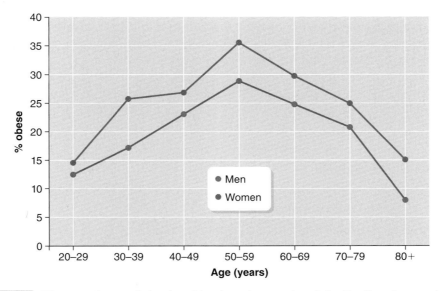

FIGURE 17.4 The prevalence of obesity with advancing age in adults. Declines in prevalence in later decades reflect the greater risk of early mortality in the obese; that is, declines reflect that many obese individuals died at younger ages than their nonobese counterparts.

Data from National Health and Nutrition Examination Survey III.

As at younger ages, genetic and extrinsic influences play a role in adult obesity, though the relative contributions of each can vary in an individual over the life span (Rosenbaum & Leibel, 1998). It is well known that activity levels are low among adults in Westernized countries. In the United States, less than one-fourth of adults regularly exercise at least 30 min per day, and 24% are sedentary. Of overweight adults, 41% of women and 33% of men are completely sedentary (Cowburn, Hillsdon, & Hankey, 1997). As with children and teens, a combination of caloric restriction and increased activity is the most effective strategy in altering body fatness among adults. Research studies show that progress is greater with a combination than with exercise alone or caloric restriction alone. Even a modest 10% loss of body weight can have a substantial benefit for cholesterol levels, fasting blood glucose levels, and blood pressure (Harris, 1999).

Summary and Synthesis

Body composition is an important component of physical fitness and is related to physical performance. Although body composition is related to genetic factors, the extrinsic factors of diet and exercise can greatly affect an individual's relative levels of fat and lean body mass. A person of any age who wishes to change his or her body fatness can manipulate both diet and exercise. Regular exercise can play a large and favorable role in altering body composition because it promotes muscle mass and an increase in basal metabolic rate. In turn, a body composition higher in lean mass and lower in fat mass makes exercise and physical performance easier.

 Reinforcing What You Have Learned About Constraints

TAKE A SECOND LOOK

The obesity issue highlights the interactive nature of the body's structural constraints and movement. Physical activity can alter the structural constraints over time and thus permit movements requiring fitness. In the case of obesity, being physically active contributes to reduction of body weight, thus making movement easier and more proficient. A lack of activity can alter the structural constraints over time. Not only is the body heavier, but the eventual effect on the body systems contributes to restriction of activities and movements, especially those requiring a certain level of fitness. Individuals can change their fitness levels and body composition with training, but age-related differences exist in the effect of training. Teachers, parents, coaches, therapists, and movers themselves must consider how the individual constraints related to the fitness systems interact with environment and task.

TEST YOUR KNOWLEDGE

1. How does regular participation in physical activity affect body composition in children and adolescents?

2. What are the sex differences in body composition? Does exercise affect the body composition of males and females similarly or differently? How so?

3. What are the best weight-management strategies for obese children?

4. What are the favorable effects of exercise on the body composition of older adults?

5. What negative effects does obesity have on children? On middle-aged and older adults?

6. How is body composition assessed? What are the advantages and disadvantages of specific techniques at various points in the life span?

LEARNING EXERCISE 17.1

Children and Obesity

The increase in the number of children around the world who are obese is of great concern to all of us. In the past few years this topic has received much attention in the popular press, and many people have tried to identify the causes and suggest interventions in order to reverse the trend. Conduct an Internet search and find three solutions that have been proposed to reverse the trend of increased obesity in children. Do the writers present evidence that would lead you to believe the solutions would work? Are you persuaded that there is one solution that would work, or do you believe that multiple solutions are necessary? Why?

Conclusion: Interactions Among Constraints

Applications to Movement

 CHAPTER OBJECTIVES

This chapter

- allows you to examine, all at one time, the individual, task, and environmental constraints and their interactions affecting an individual;
- encourages you to see each individual as unique;
- demonstrates how you can use the model to manipulate constraints for a specific educational or therapeutic purpose;
- gives you practice in structuring developmentally appropriate learning environments and designing developmentally appropriate learning tasks;
- provides a framework for charting constraints to both enhance developmentally appropriate teaching and track and assess progress; and
- provides case studies so that you have the opportunity to apply your knowledge of motor development to real-life situations.

The Paralympic Games

The following quote is from the official website of the 2004 Athens Paralympic Games: "The Paralympic Games is the top sports event in the life of every Paralympic athlete . . . . In the Paralympic Games, athletes engage in obstinate, noble, and sustained competition to achieve the highest sports distinction. Their efforts are guided and shaped by a unique strength and determination. Their strength and ability to overcome hardship becomes a shining flame, a pole of attraction for everyone who values sports as the highest expression of humanity."

The Paralympic Games have been held the same year as the Olympic Games since 1960 and in the same city since 1988. The London Games in 2012 were the largest to date, with 4,302 athletes from 164 countries competing in 21 sports. The events include, among others, four wheelchair sports, sitting volleyball, swimming, powerlifting, judo, and, of course, track and field.

What does this description of the Paralympics mean to you now that you have finished reading this text on life span motor development? We hope that you view Paralympians as people who have unique sets of constraints along with many others that are common to all humans. The structural and functional individual constraints of these Paralympians do not stop them from participating in physical activity at the highest levels. Their constraints allow them to move in activities of daily living and compete at a high level of athletics. These interacting constraints include high levels of strength (structural), strong motivation (functional), a supportive environment (sociocultural), and high-tech equipment (task), among others. Put these elements into the context of a sporting event and the results are elite, record-breaking athletes.

Years ago Paralympians might have been labeled disabled, just as special needs children once were. We hope that you now see individuals not as labels but rather as unique persons who possess unique combinations of individual functional and structural constraints. Those individual constraints interact with the environmental and task constraints to provide both possibilities and challenges in moving.

Not everyone can be—or wants to be—an elite athlete, but everyone moves constantly, every day. All movement occurs in a context and results from an interaction of constraints. Certain constraints may influence movement behavior more at a particular time than others do, and some can change drastically over the course of the life span. But all exist and interact, allowing movement to emerge. Why have we spent so much time emphasizing this point?

Throughout this text we use a developmental perspective in discussing the different types of constraints that affect motor development across the life span. To conceptualize how constraints work, we separate them into individual, environmental, and task constraints. It is important to realize, however, that although one type of constraint may be more influential at any given time, all are present and constantly interacting. In fact, something can act as a constraint only when it interacts with an individual in a movement context, which means that you must understand how constraints affect each other. At first glance, this may seem somewhat confusing. However, assessing the influence of constraints on each other is what we have been doing all along. Remember the girls' volleyball team discussed in chapter 4, where the younger players were taller than the older players? The significance of the story is related to individual constraints (height, strength, maturation), environmental constraints (the height of the net, the weight of the ball, sociocultural expectation of playing volleyball), and task constraints (rules of volleyball, the goal of a particular skill) all acting together. If any of the constraints are changed, motor development will change. For example, what if these girls were growing up in a country where volleyball was not as popular a sport?

Looking at the interaction of constraints is helpful in understanding life span motor development. The most important message of this text is that manipulating constraints can be useful in influencing movement and motor development (figure 18.1). Manipulating a constraint at any given time may produce a functional change in movement. However, in motor development, we are most concerned with changes in movements over time, particularly ones that become more permanent or structural. We emphasize this point: If short-term change in a constraint leads to a short-term change in the interaction among constraints, it can lead to long-term change in motor behavior. In other words, we can influence our own motor behavior and that of others by manipulating constraints to make them more developmentally appropriate. Isn't that the point of teaching and rehabilitation?

FIGURE 18.1 By manipulating task constraints—in this case, providing a prosthetic limb—a person with unique individual constraints can participate in many different physical activities in the same capacity as a person with typical individual constraints.

Using Constraints to Enhance Learning in Physical Activity Settings

In everyday life, people frequently modify constraints in order to change movements. These adjustments can enable movements that otherwise might have been difficult or impossible. For example, individuals using wheelchairs can perform activities of daily living more easily if their household appliances (e.g., sinks, stoves, and countertops) are scaled to their relative (seated) height. Sometimes without even thinking, an individual alters something in the relationships between himself or herself, the environment, and the task at hand. For example, we would probably slide a heavy book across the table and closer to us before picking it up rather than attempt to lift it at arm's length. Or consider children learning to play the violin: Because children have small hands and arms, music teachers often provide them with smaller instruments, scaled to their body size, so they can succeed in learning to play skillfully. These examples illustrate that modifying a task or environmental constraint can allow for a more developmentally appropriate, functional motor skill. For movement educators, it is important to consider all types of constraints and how they interact. As you might expect, interaction is a dynamic process and may result in a change in one or all of the interacting constraints. Movement educators, therefore, must attempt to manipulate constraints to allow their students or clients to perform skills more proficiently or to achieve a certain goal (Gagen & Getchell, 2004).

Physical educators often manipulate constraints when designing play experiences for students in their classes. Let's use the example of basketball. Thinking of Newell's triangle, imagine a child in a movement setting with the structural constraint of being short, the environmental constraint of the basket being high, and the task constraint of the goal of shooting the ball into the basket. Most of the situations in teaching and rehabilitation can be even more complicated than this. Let's adapt Newell's model by moving away from the triangle and using another shape to represent a larger number of relevant constraints. In figure 18.2, a hexagon is used to illustrate two structural constraints (being short and possessing moderate strength), two environmental constraints (a high basket and a large and heavy ball), and two task constraints (to shoot the ball through the basket and to use a one-hand set shot). Clearly, this combination of constraints is not likely to result in a movement of successfully shooting the basketball through a basket at the regulation height of 10 ft (3 m). Movement educators can adjust this play experience by altering one or more constraints.

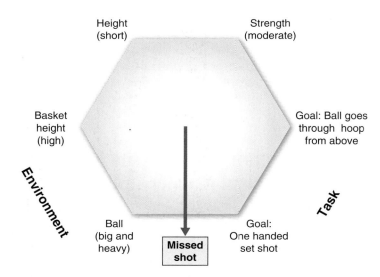

FIGURE 18.2 Using a hexagon instead of a triangle allows a model of constraints to represent more than one individual, environmental, and task constraint.

Theoretically, one can manipulate all constraints—individual, environmental, and task. Practically speaking and on a day-to-day basis, however, educators cannot change children's structural constraints. Over the course of a semester, individual constraints such as height and weight may change very little, and changing functional constraints such as fear or motivation may require longer time periods. Therefore, teachers must accept that individual constraints cannot be easily manipulated on a given day in the gym. However, by modifying environmental or task constraints, movement educators manipulate the *interactions* between the constraints and thereby facilitate change to allow and encourage more proficient or desired movements.

Returning to our basketball example, a teacher or coach realizes that the structural constraints cannot be changed in the short term and that the task constraints or goals can remain if adjustments are made to the environmental constraints. Figure 18.3 depicts the basket height. In the original scenario the hoop was at the standard 10 ft height, but if the teacher or coach lowers the hoop, the movement arising from the interaction of the constraints pictured might be the desired one. The teacher or coach could also provide a ball that is slightly smaller and somewhat lighter, making the desired movement even more likely to result from the interaction of these constraints (see figure 18.4). In addition, the children will be more successful, which will keep them engaged and excited about movement experiences.

Of course, structural constraints change over time and with growth, maturation, and experiences of individuals. Individuals get taller and stronger (see figure 18.5). As they do, basketball teachers and coaches can adjust the basket height, eventually to that established in rules for mature players, and can provide bigger and heavier basketballs until players again use a standard-size ball. Adjusting the environmental constraints in relation to the changes in structural constraints permits the same movement outcome. When teaching a learner over a time of growth and maturation,

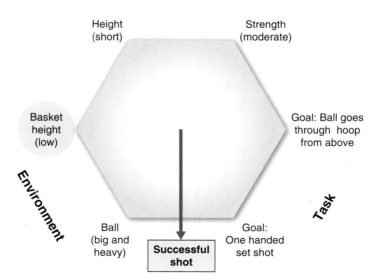

FIGURE 18.3 Changing one environmental constraint, basketball basket height, while the other constraints remain the same changes the interaction of this constraint with all the others.

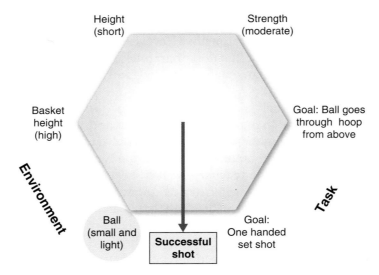

Individual (structural)

Height (short)   Strength (moderate)

Basket height (high)   Goal: Ball goes through hoop from above

Environment   Task

Ball (small and light)   Successful shot   Goal: One handed set shot

FIGURE 18.4 Changing the other environmental constraint, size and weight of the basketball, instead of changing basket height again changes the interactions among the constraints.

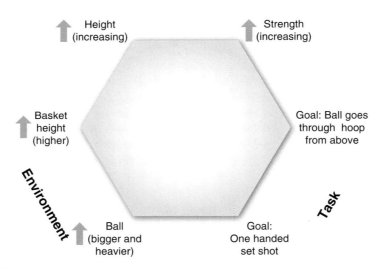

Individual (structural)

Height (increasing)   Strength (increasing)

Basket height (higher)   Goal: Ball goes through hoop from above

Environment   Task

Ball (bigger and heavier)   Goal: One handed set shot

FIGURE 18.5 Young persons' individual constraints clearly change with experience, growth, and maturation. This model represents an increase in height and an increase in strength. Teachers and coaches can change environmental constraints at a rate consistent with the change in individual constraints so that the movement outcome is the same. That is, the environmental constraints of basket height and ball size and weight are scaled up (e.g., moved toward regulation dimensions) as the individual constraints change. This way the movement will match the task goal of shooting a one-hand basketball set shot can be attained throughout the period of growth and maturation.

an instructor who keeps the environmental constraints developmentally appropriate permits the desired movement outside to arise from the interaction of all the constraints. If the instructor stubbornly maintains an environment intended for bigger and stronger movers, the movement outcome will be very different.

Therapists take a similar approach. They adapt environmental and task constraints to an individual's current structural constraints. As individuals improve by increasing their range of motion or strength, therapists adjust the constraints in concert. The relationship remains approximately the same among the constraints, but with small adjustments in environmental and task constraints, structural constraints that are limiting gradually improve to—or even surpass—the level before an injury or surgery.

In Paralympians, environmental and task constraints are often changed in concert with the athletes' structural constraints to permit the same sport movements that can be executed by other athletes. In archery, a bow can be adapted so that an individual missing an arm can draw the bow with his or her teeth. This is an adjustment to equipment. In sitting volleyball, adjustments are made to equipment and to the rules. The net is lowered to be slightly over 1 m high and the rules require that some part of a player's body between the buttocks and shoulders remain in contact with the floor when a ball is played. In other cases, a prosthetic, as an additional piece of equipment, allows a desired movement.

Constraints can also be adjusted to help push movers to different movement patterns. Recall the developmental sequence for upper arm action in the overhead throw. Imagine that a teacher observes many children in her class using a step 1 movement pattern: throwing with the elbow pointing downward rather than aligned with the shoulders. The teacher wants students to perform a throwing motion with an aligned upper arm. The teacher designs a task (i.e., structures a learning environment) that is more likely to result in a step 2 movement pattern (see figure 18.6). The instructor designs a game called "clean house" in which players throw small balls up and over a volleyball net until all of the balls in play are on the other team's side of the net. The teacher provides small balls that the children can throw with one hand and puts a volleyball net at a height that requires them to throw up and over but not so high that they cannot get balls to the other side. It is difficult to throw over the net with the elbow pointing down, so the environmental and task constraints encourage the children to use a movement pattern that brings the upper arm closer to parallel. This is another way that movement instructors can manipulate constraints in a developmentally appropriate way and encourage a new movement. With time, the new movement pattern becomes the preferred pattern for throwing.

 WEB STUDY GUIDE   Use the model of constraints to assess a playground space in Lab Activity 18.1, Assessing a Play Space, in the web study guide. Go to www.HumanKinetics.com/LifeSpanMotorDevelopment.

Structuring the Learning Environment

In this textbook, you have read about many developmental changes that occur across the life span. Movement educators should keep these changes in mind as they structure their learning environments. For example, it's easy to consider a gymnasium a static environment. However, factors such as wall color can influence how proficiently a child catches a ball. Remember, younger children have greater difficulty discriminating objects from the environment and benefit from more salient

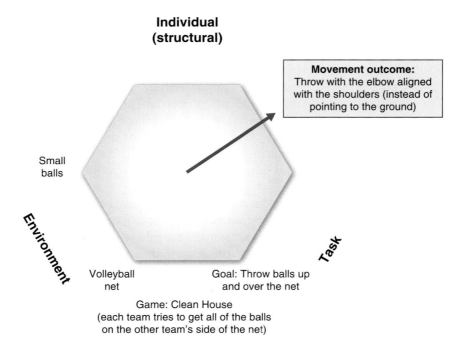

Individual (structural)

Movement outcome:
Throw with the elbow aligned with the shoulders (instead of pointing to the ground)

Small balls

Environment

Task

Volleyball net

Goal: Throw balls up and over the net

Game: Clean House
(each team tries to get all of the balls on the other team's side of the net)

FIGURE 18.6 The expanded model of constraints can help teachers and coaches identify ways to create a new movement outcome. In this figure the constraints are set to encourage young throwers to align the upper arm and elbow with the shoulders (arm step 2 in the throwing for force developmental sequence).

visual cues. To provide these cues, a physical educator can purchase equipment that is multicolored or distinct from the wall color. What if new equipment is not an option? Why not tape white paper to the wall as a backdrop? In a rehabilitation setting, the environment can be structured to be more ecologically valid, or more like the real world. The setting could be restructured to resemble a home or work environment, which would facilitate movement in that context.

When young children run at play, the running surface dictates how fast they run and how well they can remain on their feet. Long, clumpy grass presents different problems to running children than do blacktop playground surfaces or slippery tile gym floors. Weather is another environmental aspect that may influence activities. Running a mile on a hot, humid day, when breathing is difficult for most anyone, will be nearly impossible for some. Planning more strenuous activities for days when the temperature is cooler, the humidity is lower, and the air is clearer of pollen or pollutants (e.g., after a rain) will allow students to be more successful (Gagen & Getchell, 2004).

Let's not forget the sociocultural environment. When selecting activities and games, teachers can choose games that do not promote success based on sex, race, ethnicity, or socioeconomic status. For example, when activities are gender neutral, both boys and girls feel comfortable playing and succeeding. Some new games promote the same movement skills as traditional games but do not have particular sociocultural associations—team handball or sepak (a sport in which players kick a ball over a volleyball-type net) are examples. This approach opens opportunities to children who otherwise might not participate in a more traditional American sport that has been stereotyped. Different types of environmental constraints influence the structure of the learning environment. Manipulating the environment—or at

KEY POINT
More proficient movement might emerge when environmental and task constraints are adjusted for an individual's structural and functional constraints.

the very least, being mindful of its influence—will allow movement educators in many fields to create a setting that promotes movement proficiency.

Designing the Learning Task

No matter what the setting, movement educators *design* learning and rehabilitation tasks. The model of constraints provides a methodical means for designing the tasks. Consider how the interaction of relevant constraints encourages particular movement skills, keeping in mind that making changes can make skills easier or more difficult to achieve. How do the goals and rules of the task, as well as the equipment used in a task, interact with students' unique individual constraints in the class environment to allow the children to perform a desired, successful movement?

Task goals are the behavioral outcomes of the lesson. Teachers choose the goal of a task to encourage certain desired movements. Consider the task of throwing a ball. How a child throws depends on the goal of the task: to throw the ball as far as possible, as high as possible, as accurately as possible, or as quickly as possible. The throwing movements that result from each of these different task goals will differ substantially.

If children are young, small, or not very strong, some task goals are developmentally inappropriate and will not result in the practice of good throwing technique. For example, competitive games such as "pickle" (a game that simulates a baseball runner caught between two bases while two throwers attempt to get the runner "out") encourage children to throw quickly but may inhibit the use of appropriate throwing technique. When children focus on competition, they may simply pick up the throwing objects and use any method to propel them in the interest of speed. This does not encourage children to set their feet and use an appropriate backswing or aiming technique, nor does it promote correct use of all the body parts that should be sequentially involved in applying force and direction to the throw. In this example, then, if the task goal is proficient throwing technique, competitive games should be avoided with young children.

Movement educators can carefully manipulate the task goals so that children achieve an intended skill without being conscious of the intent. If a teacher places large pieces of paper against a wall and asks her students to "make the biggest noise possible," the students will throw harder without any potentially negative comparisons with their classmates for not throwing as far as another child. In this case, throwing harder without throwing farther will often encourage children to use better technique; throwers will get feedback from the noise of the paper targets as the balls hit them, but the students need to control the throw in order to hit the target. The game "clean house" described previously is an example of encouraging a specific movement by using a manipulation of a learning task in the form of a game rather than direct instruction.

Teachers can also modify the rules of a task to elicit a desired movement behavior. Teachers often modify games (change the rules) to encourage different movements or levels of participation. Playing three-on-three soccer on small fields is a game modification that allows shorter, more controlled kicking and receiving of the ball and more participation by each child, thus changing the focus of the game from running and chasing to movement technique. Playing volleyball with rules that allow the ball to bounce once will often give children the time to move into a better striking position, thus allowing them to use more appropriate striking technique. Requiring three passes before a shot in basketball promotes team play and cooperation. Such modifications can also be made so that children with disabilities can participate with their typically developing peers (Getchell & Gagen, 2006). For example, volleyball can be played from a seated position similar to the Paralympic sport, allowing for the inclusion of children who have a disability involving the lower limbs (e.g., certain types of cerebral palsy or spina bifida). The game can be enjoyable for a class of students, even those capable of playing "stand up" volleyball!

Body scaling is a relatively easy way to manipulate task constraints by modifying the equipment and play spaces in proportion to the physical size or strength of the movers. Movement educators and rehabilitation specialists often scale equipment and play spaces to assist movers who have smaller stature or less strength. Bats, rackets, golf clubs, and balls designed for women are often smaller and lighter than those designed for men, and those designed for children are smaller and lighter still. Soccer fields and base paths for children's leagues are often shortened to better match the shorter legs of younger children. Shorter volleyball nets and 6- and 8-foot basketball standards are thought to promote more effective ball skills in younger performers (Chase, Ewing, Lirgg, & George, 1994; Davis, 1991). Thus, when teaching, coaching, or rehabilitating people, movement educators should very carefully think through the process of choosing equipment to match physical size and strength. Smaller balls that fit into smaller hands are easier to throw, *but* larger balls are easier to catch (Payne & Koslow, 1981). Therefore, the overall goal of the task (e.g., throwing or catching) must always be kept in mind.

Let's consider the example of a striking task for children, that of batting a ball. A range of bat characteristics must be considered in relation to the child: the weight of the bat (the child's strength interacting with gravity to allow her to swing the bat using correct technique), the length of the bat (the child's ability to judge where the barrel of the bat will be relative to the ball and his own body), the grip size of the bat (so that the child's hands can fit around the grip to hold it well), and perhaps the size of the barrel of the bat (a wider barrel provides more surface area and perhaps a greater chance of contacting the ball). Certain choices can allow the child to swing the bat easily, whereas other choices can lead to difficulty in swinging it. A good bat choice for very young children might be lightweight with a small grip, and short but with a wider barrel. When educators work with a group of children, they should expect a wide range of size, strength, and maturation levels. Providing bats with a wide range of characteristics gives each child the opportunity to select a bat that he or she can succeed with (Gagen & Getchell, 2004, 2006).

Ecological Task Analyses: Charting Constraints to Enhance Developmentally Appropriate Teaching

Imagine that you are coaching for the first time a volleyball team made up of 10-year-olds. Height, weight, and skill level vary widely in the group. How do you approach coaching this team? You could simply teach the skills they need to learn by showing them the "correct" form, then making them practice over and over again. This approach might or might not provide results over the long run, but it will probably prove to be frustrating or boring for all involved. Is there a better way to teach motor skills?

By using ecological task analysis (Burton & Davis, 1996; Davis & Broadhead, 2007; Davis & Burton, 1991), you can create developmentally appropriate lesson plans and assess movement ability. In general, a task analysis is exactly what it sounds like—an analysis of how a particular task or skill is accomplished, focusing on critical components that influence movement. This analysis is usually performed by a teacher, therapist, or coach who is interested in developing motor proficiency in children performing the task or skill. Once a task analysis is developed, it can be used as a guide to help advance motor performance in that task in small, sequential steps.

When someone uses traditional task analysis to teach or coach, he compares the movement pattern of an individual with the "correct" form; in that way, traditional task analysis provides an error model. Each person moves somewhere on the continuum of incorrect to correct. The instructor teaches skills by interceding in the production of the skill wherever it deviates from the ideal performance and correcting that portion of the movement.

What could be improved in this approach to teaching movement skills? For one thing, the traditional task analysis doesn't account for the different individual constraints each person might have. Second, no real consideration is given to the ways in which the environmental and task constraints might act in conjunction with individual constraints. Ecological task analysis, in contrast, does both of these things. The term *ecological* is a nod to the theoretical overview from which it was developed, the ecological perspective (see chapter 2). As we have discussed throughout this text, the ecological perspective acknowledges that action does not happen in a vacuum; rather, movement is influenced by the mover's environment as well as the goals and rules of the task. Ecological task analysis acknowledges the confluence of constraints and uses them to the advantage of the teacher or coach so that a developmentally appropriate, or skill-level-appropriate, challenge can be provided to students (Newell & Jordan, 2007). Furthermore, each person moves on a developmental continuum, which enhances the current ability of the performer rather than labels it as correct or incorrect.

Creating a Developmentally Appropriate Ecological Task Analysis

Burton and Davis (1996) outline four steps involved in creating an ecological task analysis. The initial step involves establishing the task goal through structuring the environmental constraints. Next, the movement educator should allow the mover to solve the movement task in a variety of ways. In other words, don't provide one "solution" to the movement task (e.g., "Throw like this"); instead, let the mover pick from a variety of available movements. In the next step, which comes into play after the individual moves, the educator manipulates the mover, environment, or task in a way that allows more proficient movement to emerge. Finally, the movement educator should provide instruction to assist in a more proficient performance.

What does a movement educator do as a first-time teacher who has never attempted to make a constraints-based task analysis? Here is a practical method of working through the process using a constraints perspective. Essentially, teaching any given skill involves three steps. Begin by considering the most important individual constraints related to that skill. Of course, there may be many, but try to narrow the list to the two or three that seem most important or influential. Consider the skill of kicking a ball. Three important individual constraints include balance (an individual must balance on one foot while striking the ball with the other), coordination (an individual must sequence and time the action within and between legs), and strength (an individual must strike the ball with sufficient power). Now consider ways to change the environment or task to make the skill easier or more difficult in relation to the individual constraints. This is the basis of the constraints-based task analysis. If coordination is an important individual constraint to kicking, what changes can be made to the task to make it easier or more difficult? How about changing the movement of the ball? Kicking a stationary ball is easier, and kicking a moving ball is more difficult. This change in task constraint is also related to balance. To account for strength, changing the distance to be kicked changes the individual–task constraint interaction.

To develop an ecological task analysis, systematically scale environmental and task constraints to accommodate individual constraints in a developmentally appropriate manner. To summarize, the process is as follows:

- Pick out a skill or task to teach.
- Determine the individual constraints that are most important for this skill.
- Pick several environmental or task constraints for this particular task that can be manipulated in relation to each individual constraint.
- For each environmental or task constraint, determine a practical range (from easy to hard) for the learner. When scaling, keep in mind that small changes in a constraint can lead to large changes in performance.

The finished product is an ecological task analysis for a particular skill (figures 18.7 and 18.8). There are two ways to use your task analysis. First, you can use it to structure lesson plans or teaching progressions. If an individual or group has difficulty with the task as initially designed, the task analysis suggests changes in task and environmental constraints to make the challenge more appropriate. As individuals progress in skill level within a particular profile, the task analysis suggests ways to make the task more difficult by scaling up one or more of the constraints. This keeps the task interesting, rewarding, and challenging for learners. Individuals are more likely to succeed when a new challenge is slightly more difficult than what they can achieve easily, so it is best to be conservative in the number of constraints made more difficult at any one time. Building success on success through small

Factors	Size of the object being thrown	Distance object must be thrown	Weight of the object being thrown	Accuracy required of the throw	Speed at which target being thrown at is moving	Acceleration and deceleration characteristics of the target being thrown at	Direction in which target being thrown at is moving
Simple	Small	Short	Light	None	Stationary	No movement	No movement
			Moderately light	Little	Slow	Steady speed	Left to right of thrower
							Right to left of thrower
	Medium	Medium					
Complex				Moderate	Moderate	Decelerating	Toward thrower
	Large	Long	Heavy	Much	Fast	Accelerating	Away from thrower

FIGURE 18.7 General task analysis for throwing behavior.

Reprinted by permission from Herkowitz 1978.

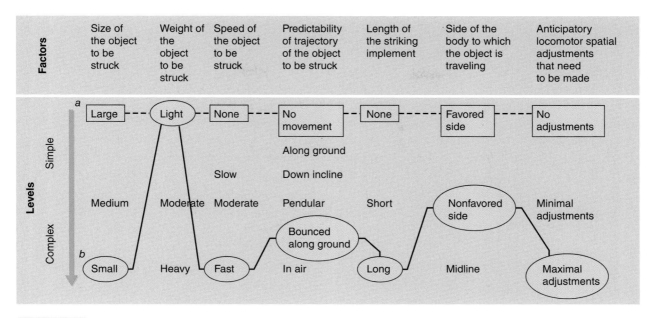

FIGURE 18.8   General task analysis for striking behavior. *(a)* Profile of a general task analysis for a relatively simple striking task (dotted line). *(b)* Profile of a general task analysis for a relatively complex striking task (solid line).
Reprinted by permission from Herkowitz 1978.

steps in difficulty contributes to confidence. Varying combinations of constraints also creates many practice activities, which keeps the learning process interesting and challenging.

How do the model of constraints and ecological task analysis relate to one another? Imagine that the columns of a task analysis chart represent various constraints and show how each constraint could be scaled for a particular individual or group of individuals with a common characteristic. Figure 18.9 illustrates this relationship. The constraints placed on the hexagonal model can be entered as column headings on a task analysis chart. The easiest relevant level of a constraint can be written at the top of the column, the most difficult relevant level at the bottom of the column, and intermediate levels in between. The tasks analysis chart helps an individual identify changes to the constraints that scale to the other constraints so that the desired movement outcome arises from their interaction.

The ecological task analysis also provides a way to standardize a test environment so performers can easily be compared with each other (or with themselves on different occasions). In this case, select a particular profile and set up an assessment environment accordingly. Using these standard task and environmental constraints, assess students' developmental levels for that skill within that profile. This approach allows for a more systematic assessment between students and over a set period of time.

In many programs, instructors or therapists are held accountable for the progress of learners and patients. Task analysis charts can provide a written record of how an initial developmentally appropriate task was progressively made more difficult. It can indicate the combination of constraints that yielded a successful performance outcome, perhaps to some criterion such as four out of five attempts, at a particular point in time. If instructors and therapists prepare the task analysis chart ahead, they can quickly circle the constraints for a successful performance. Charts can be completed for individuals or groups and can both suggest an adjustment based on

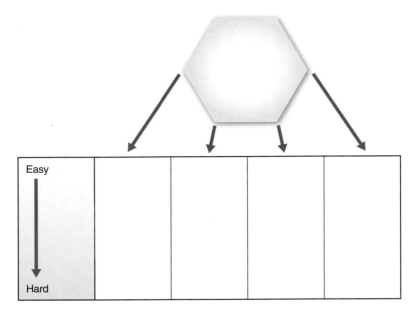

FIGURE 18.9   A hexagonal model of constraints can be converted to an ecological task analysis table by using the constraints as column headings. The levels along the continuum of change for each constraint are then entered into the table in order from easy (at the top of the column) to difficult (at the bottom of the column).

performance and document the performance for a specific combination of levels of constraints.

Interacting Constraints: Case Studies

By manipulating constraints we can make immediate, short-term, and long-term changes in motor development and behavior. Often, knowing what changes to make is simply an issue of understanding the varying degrees of influence exerted by different constraints. Sometimes, even small changes in one constraint will allow a wide variety of behaviors to emerge. For example, providing an infant with support can account for both strength and posture, allowing for many different upright movements. With this in mind, read the following case studies; try to determine the most important constraints and what you can change to allow certain motor behaviors to appear. After identifying the constraints to be changed, analyze how these constraints interact with one another (if they do) and whether the interaction helps achieve the goal or works against it.

Case Study A: Gender Typing of Physical Activities

You are the movement educator for a class of 25 fourth graders. During your first class, you attempt to teach gymnastic skills. The boys in your class show an obvious dislike for the activities, and one exclaims, "Gymnastics is for girls!" What can you do to modify the task so that the children learn the skills you want but are not put off by gender typing?

Case Study B: Older Adults

AB is a 76-year-old man who recently lost his spouse of 45 years. He lives in a suburb of a large metropolitan area. Since the death of his spouse, AB has not gone on the daily strolls they used to take together. He is losing strength and flexibility, and his arthritis is flaring up. How can you reintroduce physical activity into AB's life?

Case Study C: Teaching Fundamental Motor Skills

You are coaching an under-10-year-old soccer team. You've noticed a wide diversity of individual constraints (height, weight, skill level) among the players. How can you make practices challenging for all the players?

Case Study D: Cerebral Palsy

You are teaching an 11th-grade physical education class. In your class is an individual with cerebral palsy. He can walk, but he has some muscle spasticity and rigidity. You would like your class to participate in an activity or game in which everyone can be equally involved without having to change or modify the rules. What kind of activity could you play?

Case Study E: Middle-Aged Adults

CW is a 50-year-old woman who plays doubles on a tennis team. Women from their 20s to their 60s participate in this tennis program. CW weighs about 15 pounds more than she did in her 20s, but she does walk for a half hour each day. CW's team has one match per week and one practice per week for 8 months of the year. The top teams qualify for a series of playoffs—district, sectional, then national—in which the winning team advances to the next level. CW's team lost in the semifinals of the sectional tournament last year and has established the goal of getting to and winning the finals of the sectional tournament for the upcoming year. CW wants to be a major contributor to the team's success. What constraints could prove to be a challenge to CW's success, and how would you recommend that she address those constraints?

Case Study F: Age Grouping

MF was born in July, just before the cutoff date for her parents to be able to delay school entry for a year. Therefore, she is the youngest girl in her elementary school class. A youth sports program is available at the school, and children participate with their grade level. This means that MF is one of the youngest players on her team every year and for every sport. MF listens to her coach and works hard in practices, but she doesn't have the coordination required to be among the better performers in her elementary school years. If you were MF's parent, how would you talk with her about her youth sports experiences? On which constraints would your conversation center?

Case Study G: Grade-Level Expectations

You are a physical education teacher about to start a new school year, and you have just received documents identifying the grade-level expectations for each of the six levels of physical education classes you teach. Grade-level expectations indicate what skills or knowledge a student should have upon completing a particular grade. What tools could you use to ensure that your students progress to the expected level by the end of the school year? A sample grade-level expectation for the fifth grade is "Demonstrate ability to follow rules, cooperate with teammates, and apply a simple strategy in a variety of sport-specific lead-up games." How could you use the tools you identified to plan a sequence of activities over the year to achieve this expectation?

 WEB STUDY GUIDE   Apply the model of constraints to examine the interaction of players in a soccer game in Lab Activity 18.2, Examining Constraints in a Context: Soccer, in the web study guide. Go to www.HumanKinetics.com/LifeSpanMotorDevelopment.

Summary and Synthesis

The challenge confronting motor developmentalists, teachers, coaches, and parents is to tailor goals and expectations to individual capabilities and characteristics. Optimal motor development is likely related to the degree to which practice opportunities and insightful instruction are matched with individual constraints. It is complex and time consuming to individualize motor development goals and instruction in most institutional settings, but findings from motor development research at various stages of the life span point in this direction. Continued research and observation of motor development will undoubtedly yield a better understanding of developmental processes, but our task remains to find ways of using our knowledge to foster optimal motor development in every individual.

Reinforcing What You Have Learned About Constraints

TAKE A SECOND LOOK

The Paralympic Games are an excellent example of a program that changes task and environmental constraints in conjunction with individual structural constraints to provide an appropriate challenge for those who would like to compete. Individuals with disabilities can be tested at the highest level by competing with and against like individuals. People with disabilities affecting their locomotion can play wheelchair basketball or sitting volleyball. Individuals with the use of only one arm can hold a bowstring with their teeth to compete in archery. An important realization for all of us is that although Paralympic athletes might have obvious and permanent disabilities, all of us have individual characteristics that can influence our ability to move in a certain way. Those characteristics might exist because we are still growing, because we are aging, because we are injured, because we lack confidence in our ability, or because we don't have much experience with an activity. Whatever the reason, adapting environmental and task constraints to those individual constraints can allow us to move in a way that is enjoyable and healthful.

TEST YOUR KNOWLEDGE

1. How might a teacher or coach use either a model of constraints or an ecological task analysis to design a sequence of lesson or practice plans?

2. How might a teacher or community program leader use a model of constraints or an ecological task analysis to allow for the involvement of a disabled child in a group activity?

3. How might a teacher, coach, or program leader use a model of constraints or an ecological task analysis to develop individualized instruction plans?

4. Teachers are charged with providing a challenging learning task for students whose physical growth and maturation status, level of coordination, and expe-

rience with a task vary. How could a teacher use a model of constraints to plan four stations of varying difficulty levels for the class?

LEARNING EXERCISES

The case studies in "Interacting Constraints" serve as the learning exercises for chapter 18.

APPENDIX
Skinfold, Body Mass Index, and Head Circumference Charts

Skinfolds (mm)   Boys

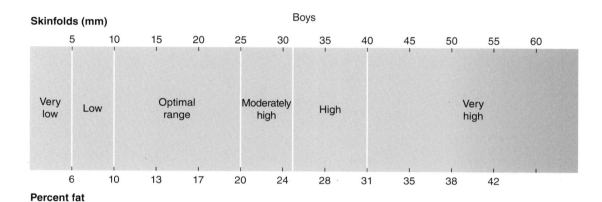

Percent fat

FIGURE A.1 Calf plus triceps skinfolds: boys.

Skinfolds (mm)   Girls

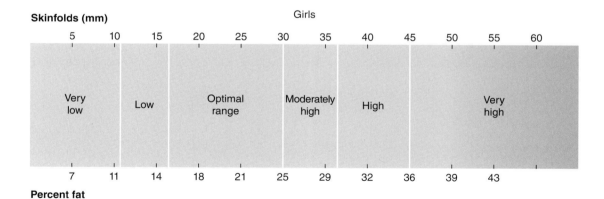

Percent fat

FIGURE A.2 Calf plus triceps skinfolds: girls.

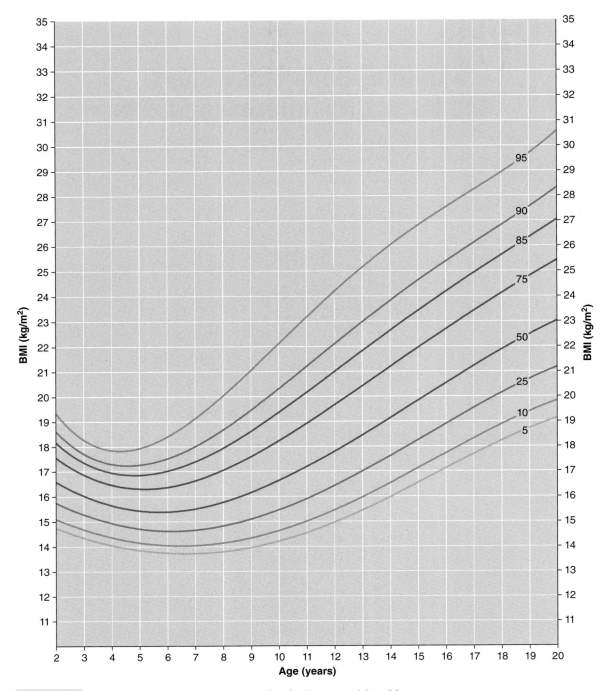

FIGURE A.3a Body mass index for age percentiles for boys aged 2 to 20 years.

Adapted from CDC 2000.

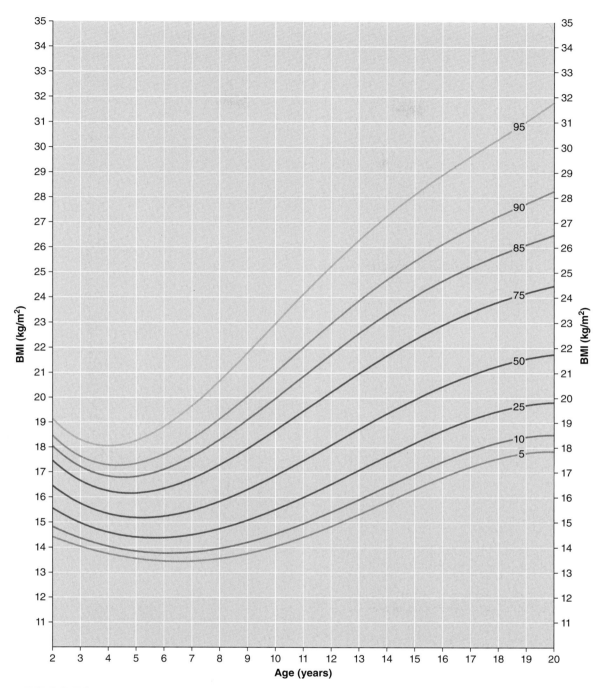

FIGURE A.3b Body mass index for age percentiles for girls aged 2 to 20 years.

Adapted from CDC 2000.

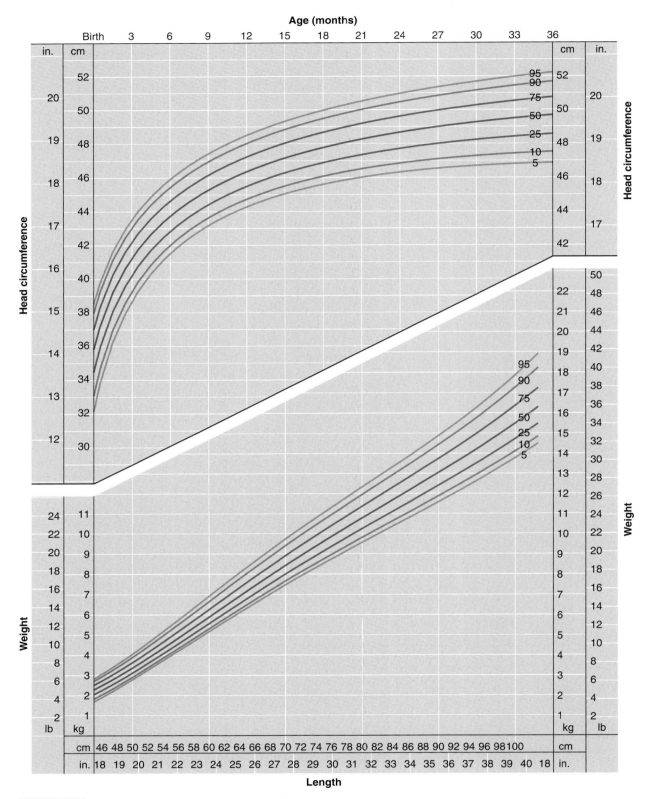

FIGURE A.4a Head circumference-for-age and weight-for-length percentiles for boys, birth to 36 months.

Adapted from CDC 2000.

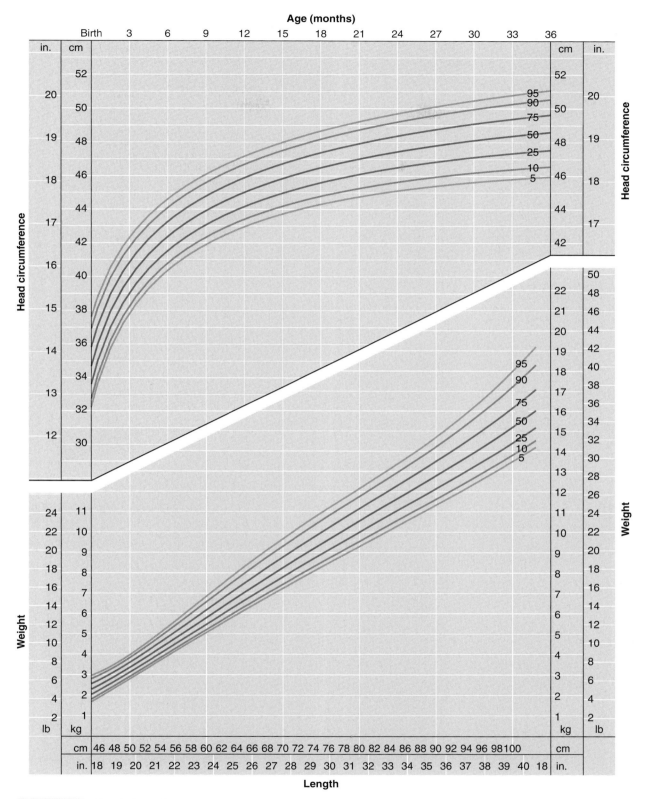

FIGURE A.4b Head circumference-for-age and weight-for-length percentiles for girls, birth to 36 months.

Adapted from CDC 2000.

References

Abernethy, B., Wood, J.M., & Parks, S. (1999). Can the anticipatory skills of experts be learned by novices? *Research Quarterly for Exercise and Sport, 70,* 313–318.

Acosta, V., & Carpenter, L.J. (2008). Women in intercollegiate sport: A longitudinal, national study. Thirty one year update (1977–2008). Available: www.acostacarpenter.org.

Adams, F.H. (1973). Factors affecting the working capacity of children and adolescents. In G.L. Rarick (Ed.), *Physical activity: Human growth and development* (pp. 80–96). New York: Academic Press.

Adolph, K. (1997). Learning in the development of infant locomotion. *Monographs of the Society for Research in Child Development, 62*(3), 1–162.

Adolph, K., Vereijken, B., & Denny, M. (1998). Learning to crawl. *Child Development, 69,* 1299–1312.

Adolph, K., Vereijken, B., & Shrout, P.E. (2003). What changes in infant walking and why. *Child Development, 74*(2), 475–497.

Adolph, K.E., & Berger, S.A. (2006). Motor development. In W. Damon & R. Lerner (Series Eds.) & D. Kuhn & R.S. Siegler (Vol. Eds.), *Handbook of child psychology: Vol. 2. Cognition, perception, and language* (6th ed.) (pp. 161–213). New York: Wiley.

Adolph, K.E., Eppler, M.A., & Gibson, E.J. (1993). Crawling versus walking in infants' perception of affordances for locomotion over sloping surfaces. *Child Development, 64,* 1158–1174.

Adolph, K.E., & Robinson, S.R. (2013). The road to walking: What learning to walk tells us about development. In P. Zelazo (Ed.), *Oxford handbook of developmental psychology* (Vol. 1, pp. 403–443). New York: Oxford University Press.

Adrian, M.J. (1982, April). *Maintaining movement capabilities in advanced years.* Paper presented at the American Alliance for Health, Physical Education, Recreation and Dance, Houston.

Allen, M., & Alexander, G. (1994). Screening for cerebral palsy in preterm infants: Delay criteria for motor milestone attainment. *Journal of Perinatology, 14,* 190–193.

Alnaqeeb, M.A., Al-Zaid, N.S., & Goldspink, G. (1984). Connective tissue changes and physical properties of developing and aging skeletal muscle. *Journal of Anatomy, 189*(4), 677–689.

American Alliance for Health, Physical Education, Recreation and Dance. (1988). *Physical best.* Reston, VA: Author.

Ames, C. (1992). Classroom: Goals, structures, and student motivation. *Journal of Educational Psychology, 84,* 409–414.

Andersen, J.L., Terzis, G., & Kryger, A. (1999). Increase in the degree of coexpression of myosin heavy chain isoforms in skeletal muscle fibers of the very old. *Muscle and Nerve, 22,* 449–454.

Aniansson, A., Hedberg, M., Henning, G.B., & Grimby, G. (1986). Muscle morphology, enzymatic activity and muscle strength in elderly men: A follow-up study. *Muscle and Nerve, 9,* 585–591.

Arabadjis, P.G., Heffner, R.R., & Pendergast, D.R. (1990). Morphologic and functional alterations in aging rat muscle. *Journal of Neuropathology and Experimental Neurology, 49,* 600–609.

Armstrong, N., & Welsman, J.R. (2007). Aerobic fitness: What are we measuring? *Medicine and Sport Science, 50,* 5–25.

Armstrong, N., Welsman, J.R., & Kirby, B.J. (1997). Performance on the Wingate Anaerobic Test and maturation. *Pediatric Exercise Science, 9,* 253–261.

Asano, K., Ogawa, S., & Furuta, Y. (1978). Aerobic work capacity in middle- and old-aged runners. In F. Landry & W.A.R. Orban (Eds.), *Proceedings of the International Congress of Physical Activity Sciences: Vol. 4. Exercise physiology.* Quebec: Symposia Specialists.

Ashmead, D.H., Clifton, R.K., & Perris, E.E. (1987). Precision of auditory localization in human infants. *Developmental Psychology, 23*(5), 641–647.

Asikainen, T.M., Suni, J.H., Pasanen, M.E., Oja, P., Rinne, M.B., Miilunpalo, S.I., et al. (2006). Effect of brisk walking in 1 or 2 daily bouts and moderate resistance training on lower-extremity muscle strength, balance, and walking performance in women who recently went through menopause: A randomized, controlled trial. *Physical Therapy, 86,* 912–923.

Aslin, R.N., & Shea, S.L. (1990). Velocity thresholds in human infants: Implications for the perception of motion. *Developmental Psychology, 26*(4), 589–598.

Asmussen, E. (1973). Growth in muscular strength and power. In G.L. Rarick (Ed.), *Physical activity: Human growth and development* (pp. 60–79). New York: Academic Press.

Asmussen, E., & Heebøll-Nielsen, K. (1955). A dimensional analysis of physical performance and growth in boys. *Journal of Applied Physiology, 7,* 593–603.

Asmussen, E., & Heebøll-Nielsen, K. (1956). Physical performance and growth in children: Influence of sex, age, and intelligence. *Journal of Applied Physiology, 8,* 371–380.

Assaiante, C. (1998). Development of locomotor balance control in healthy children. *Neuroscience and Biobehavioral Reviews, 22*(4), 527–532.

Assaiante, C., & Amblard, B. (1995). An ontogenetic model for the sensorimotor organization of balance control in humans. *Human Movement Science, 14*, 13–43.

Assibey-Mensah, G. (1998). Role models and youth development: Evidence and lessons from the perceptions of African-American male youth. *Western Journal of Black Studies, 21*, 242–252.

Åstrand, P. (1976). The child in sport and physical activity: Physiology. In J.G. Albinson & G.M. Andrew (Eds.), *Child in sport and physical activity* (pp. 19–33). Baltimore: University Park Press.

Åstrand, P.O., & Rodahl, K. (1986). *Textbook of work physiology.* New York: McGraw-Hill.

Atkinson, J., & Braddick, O. (1981). Acuity, contrast sensitivity, and accommodation in infancy. In R. Aslin, J. Alberts, & M. Peterson (Eds.), *Development of perception* (pp. 245–277). New York: Academic Press.

Ay, L., Hokken-Koelega, A.C.S., Mook-Kanamori, D.O., Hofman, A., Moll, H.A., Mackenbach, J.P., et al. (2008). Tracking and determinants of subcutaneous fat mass in early childhood: The Generation R study. *International Journal of Obesity, 32*, 1050–1059.

Ay, L., Jaddoe, V.W.V., Hofman, A., Moll, H.A., Raat, H., Steegers, E.A.P., et al. (2011). Foetal and postnatal growth and bone mass at 6 months: The Generation R study. *Clinical Endocrinology, 74*, 181–190.

Ayres, A.J. (1966). *Southern California sensory-motor integration tests.* Los Angeles: Western Psychological Services.

Ayres, A.J. (1969). *Southern California perceptual-motor tests.* Los Angeles: Western Psychological Services.

Ayres, A.J. (1972). *Southern California sensory-motor integration tests manual.* Los Angeles: Western Psychological Services.

"Babies driving their own robots." *Science Daily,* November 11, 2007. Available: www.sciencedaily.com/releases/2007/11/071109211510.htm.

Bachman, J.C. (1961). Motor learning and performance as related to age and sex in two measures of balance coordination. *Research Quarterly, 32*, 123–137.

Bailey, D.A., Malina, R.M., & Rasmussen, R.L. (1978). The influence of exercise, physical activity, and athletic performance on the dynamics of human growth. In F. Falkner & J.M. Tanner (Eds.), *Human growth* (Vol. 2, pp. 475–505). New York: Plenum Press.

Baldwin, K.M. (1984). Muscle development: Neonatal to adult. In R.L. Terjung (Ed.), *Exercise and sport science reviews* (Vol. 12, pp. 1–19). Lexington, MA: Collamore.

Bandura, A. (1986). *Social foundations of thought and action: A social cognitive theory.* Englewood Cliffs, NJ: Prentice Hall.

Banerjee, R., & Lintern, V. (2000). Boys will be boys: The effect of social evaluation concerns on gender-typing. *Social Development, 9*(3), 397–408.

Bar-Or, O. (1983). *Pediatric sports medicine for the practitioner.* New York: Springer-Verlag.

Bar-Or, O. (1993). Physical activity and physical training in childhood obesity. *Journal of Sports Medicine and Physical Fitness, 33*(4), 323–329.

Bar-Or, O., Shephard, R.J., & Allen, C.L. (1971). Cardiac output of 10- to 13-year-old boys and girls during submaximal exercise. *Journal of Applied Physiology, 30*, 219–223.

Bard, C., Fleury, M., Carriere, L., & Bellec, J. (1981). Components of the coincidence-anticipation behavior of children aged 6 to 11 years. *Perceptual and Motor Skills, 52*, 547–556.

Bard, C., Fleury, M., & Gagnon, M. (1990). Coincidence-anticipation timing: An age-related perspective. In C. Bard, M. Fleury, & L. Hay (Eds.), *Development of eye-hand coordination across the life span* (pp. 283–305). Columbia: University of South Carolina Press.

Barela, J.A., Jeka, J.J., & Clark, J.E. (1999). The use of somatosensory information during the acquisition of independent upright stance. *Infant Behavior and Development, 22*(1), 87–102.

Barnett, L.M., van Beurden, E., Morgan, P.J., Brooks, L.O., & Beard, J.R. (2008). Does childhood motor skill proficiency predict adolescent fitness? *Medicine and Science in Sports and Exercise, 40*, 2137–2144.

Barrett, K.R. (1979). Observation for teaching and coaching. *Journal of Physical Education and Recreation, 50*, 23–25.

Barrett, T.M., Davis, E.F., & Needham, A. (2007). Learning about tools in infancy. *Developmental Psychology, 43*, 352–368.

Barrett, U., & Harrison, D. (2002). Comparing muscle function of children and adults: Effects of scaling for muscle size. *Pediatric Exercise Science, 14*, 369–376.

Barsch, R.H. (1965). *Achieving perceptual-motor efficiency.* Seattle: Special Child.

Bartlett, D. (1997). Primitive reflexes and early motor development. *Journal of Developmental and Behavioral Pediatrics, 18*, 151–157.

Bayley, N. (1936). The development of motor abilities during the first three years. *Monographs of the Society for Research in Child Development, 1*(1), 1–26.

Bayley, N. (1969). *Manual for the Bayley Scales of Infant Development.* New York: The Psychological.

Beck, M. (1966). *The path of the center of gravity during running in boys grades one to six.* Unpublished doctoral dissertation, University of Wisconsin, Madison.

Bell, R., & Hoshizaki, T. (1981). Relationships of age and sex with joint range of motion of seventeen joint actions in humans. *Canadian Journal of Applied Sport Sciences, 6*, 202–206.

Bennett, S., Button, C., Kingsbury, D., & Davids, K. (1999). Manipulating visual informational constraints during practice enhances the acquisition of catching skill in children. *Research Quarterly for Exercise and Sport, 70*(3), 220–232.

Bergenn, V.W., Dalton, T.C., & Lipsett, L.P. (1992). Myrtle B. McGraw: A growth scientist. *Developmental Psychology, 28*, 381–395.

Bergstrom, B. (1973). Morphology of the vestibular nerve: II. The number of myelinated vestibular nerve fibers in man at various ages. *Acta Oto-Laryngologica, 76*, 173–179.

Berliner, D.C. (1986). In pursuit of the expert pedagogue. *Educational Researcher, 15*, 5–13.

Bertenthal, B., Campos, J., & Barrett, K. (1984). Self-produced locomotion: An organizer of emotional, cognitive and social development in infancy. In R. Emde & R. Harmon (Eds.), *Continuities and discontinuities in development* (pp. 175–210). New York: Plenum Press.

Bertenthal, B., & von Hofsten, C. (1998). Eye, head, and trunk control: The foundation for manual development. *Neuroscience and Biobehavioral Reviews, 22*(4), 515–520.

Bertenthal, B.I., & Bai, D.L. (1989). Infants' sensitivity to optical flow for controlling posture. *Developmental Psychology, 25*, 936–945.

Bertenthal, B.I., & Campos, J.J. (1987). New directions in the study of early experience. *Child Development, 58*, 560–567.

Bertenthal, B.I., Rose, J.L., & Bai, D.L. (1997). Perception-action coupling in the development of visual control of posture. *Journal of Experimental Psychology: Human Perception and Performance, 23*(6), 1631–1643.

Beunen, G., & Malina, R.M. (1988). Growth and physical performance relative to the timing of the adolescent spurt. *Exercise and Sport Sciences Reviews, 16*, 503–540.

Beunen, G., Malina, R.M., Ostyn, M., Renson, R., Simons, J., & Van Gerven, D. (1983). Fatness, growth and motor fitness of Belgian boys 12 through 17 years of age. *American Journal of Physical Anthropology, 59*, 387–392.

Beunen, G., Malina, R.M., Renson, R., & Van Gerven, D. (1988). *Adolescent growth and motor performance: A longitudinal analysis of Belgian boys*. Champaign, IL: Human Kinetics.

Bigelow, B., Tesson, G., & Lewko, J. (1996). *Learning the rules: The anatomy of children's relationships*. New York: Guilford Press.

Birch, L.L. (1976). Age trends in children's timesharing performance. *Journal of Experimental Child Psychology, 22*, 331–345.

Bird, A.M., & Williams, J.M. (1980). A developmental-attributional analysis of sex-role stereotypes for sport performance. *Developmental Psychology, 16*, 319–322.

Birren, J.E. (1964). The psychology of aging in relation to development. In J.E. Birren (Ed.), *Relationships of development and aging* (pp. 99–120). Springfield, IL: Charles C Thomas.

Blakemore, J.E.O., & Centers, R.E. (2005). Characteristics of boys' and girls' toys. *Sex Roles, 53*, 619–633.

Blimkie, C.J.R. (1989). Age- and sex-associated variation in strength during childhood: Anthropometric, morphological, neurologic, biomechanical, endocrinologic, genetic, and physical activity correlates. In C.V. Gisolfi & D.R. Lamb (Eds.), *Youth, exercise, and sport* (Vol. 2, pp. 99–164). Indianapolis: Benchmark Press.

Blumenthal, J.A., Emergy, C.F., Madden, D.J., Coleman, R.E., Riddle, M.W., Schniebolk, S., et al. (1991). Effects of exercise training on cardiorespiratory function in men and women >60 years of age. *American Journal of Cardiology, 67*, 633–639.

Boff, K.R., Kaufman, L., & Thomas, J.P. (Eds.). (1986). *Handbook of perception and human performance*. New York: Wiley.

Boothby, J., Tungatt, M., & Townsend, A. (1981). Ceasing participation in sports activity: Reported reasons and their implication. *Journal of Leisure Research, 13*, 1–14.

Bornstein, M.H. (1985). Habituation of attention as a measure of visual information processing in human infants: Summary, systematization, and synthesis. In G. Gottlieb & N.A. Krasnegor (Eds.), *Measurement of audition and vision in the first year of postnatal life: A methodological overview* (pp. 253–300). Norwood, NJ: Ablex.

Bower, T.G.R. (1977). *A primer of infant development*. San Francisco: Freeman.

Bower, T.G.R., Broughton, J.M., & Moore, M.K. (1970). The co-ordination of visual and tactual input in infants. *Perception and Psychophysics, 8*, 51–53.

Brandfonbrener, M., Landowne, M., & Shock, N.W. (1955). Changes in cardiac output with age. *Circulation, 12*, 557–566.

Branta, C., Haubenstricker, J., & Seefeldt, V. (1984). Age changes in motor skill during childhood and adolescence. In R.L. Terjung (Ed.), *Exercise and sport science reviews* (Vol. 12, pp. 467–520). Lexington, MA: Collamore.

Brodkin, P., & Weiss, M.R. (1990). Developmental differences in motivation for participation in competitive swimming. *Journal of Sport and Exercise Psychology, 12*, 248–263.

Brouwer, W.H., Waterink, W., Van Wolffelaar, P.C., & Rothengartter, T. (1991). Divided attention in experienced young and older drivers: Land tracking and visual analysis in a dynamic driving simulator. *Human Factors, 33*, 573–582.

Brown, B., Frankel, G., & Fennell, M. (1990). Hugs or shrugs: Parental and peer influences on continuation of involvement in sport by female adolescents. *Sex Roles, 20*, 397–412.

Brown, B.A. (1985). Factors influencing the process of withdrawal by female adolescents from the role of competitive age group swimmers. *Sociology of Sport Journal, 2*, 111–129.

Brown, C.H., Harrower, J.R., & Deeter, M.F. (1972). The effects of cross-country running on pre-adolescent girls. *Medicine and Science in Sports, 4*, 1–5.

Brown, M., & Holloszy, J.O. (1991). Effects of a low-intensity exercise program on selected physical performance characteristics of 60- to 71-year-olds. *Aging—Clinical and Experimental Research, 3*(2), 129–139.

Brundage, C.L. (1983). *Parent/child play behaviors as they relate to children's later socialization into sport.* Unpublished master's thesis, University of Illinois, Urbana–Champaign.

Bruner, J.S. (1970). The growth and structure of skill. In K.J. Connolly (Ed.), *Mechanisms of motor skill development* (pp. 63–94). London: Academic Press.

Bruner, J.S. (1973). Organization of early skilled action. *Child Development, 44,* 1–11.

Bruner, J.S., & Koslowski, B. (1972). Visually pre-adapted constituents of manipulatory action. *Perception, 1,* 3–12.

Brustad, R.J. (1988). Affective outcomes in competitive youth sport: The influence of intrapersonal and socialization factors. *Journal of Sport and Exercise Psychology, 10,* 307–321.

Buchanan, J.J., & Horak, F.B. (1999). Emergence of postural patterns as a function of vision and translation frequency. *Journal of Neurophysiology, 81*(5), 2325–2339.

Bull, D., Eilers, R., & Oller, K. (1984). Infants' discrimination of intensity variation in multisyllabic stimuli. *Journal of the Acoustical Society of America, 76,* 13–17.

Burnett, C.N., & Johnson, E.W. (1971). Development of gait in childhood, part II. *Developmental Medicine and Child Neurology, 13,* 207–215.

Burton, A.W. (1999). Hrdlicka (1931) revisited: Children who run on all fours. *Research Quarterly for Exercise and Sport, 70,* 84–90.

Burton, A.W., & Davis, W.E. (1996). Ecological task analysis: Utilizing intrinsic measures in research and practice. *Human Movement Science, 15,* 285–314.

Bushnell, E.W. (1982). The ontogeny of intermodal relations: Vision and touch in infancy. In R. Walk & H. Pick (Eds.), *Intersensory perception and sensory integration* (pp. 5–36). New York: Plenum Press.

Bushnell, E.W. (1985). The decline of visually guided reaching during infancy. *Infant Behavior and Development, 8,* 139–155.

Bushnell, E.W., & Boudreau, J.P. (1993). Motor development and the mind: The potential role of motor abilities as a determinant of aspects of perceptual development. *Child Development, 64,* 1005–1021.

Bushnell, I.W.R. (1998). The origins of face perception. In F. Simion & G. Butterworth (Eds.), *The development of sensory, motor and cognitive capacities in early infancy: From perception to cognition* (pp. 69–86). Hove, UK: Psychology Press.

Bushnell, I.W.R., Sai, F., & Mullin, J.T. (1989). Neonatal recognition of the mother's face. *British Journal of Developmental Psychology, 7,* 3–15.

Butcher, J. (1983). Socialization of adolescent girls into physical activity. *Adolescence, 18,* 753–766.

Butcher, J. (1985). Longitudinal analysis of adolescent girls' participation in physical activity. *Sociology of Sport Journal, 2,* 130–143.

Butterworth, G., & Hicks, L. (1977). Visual proprioception and postural stability in infancy. *Perception, 6,* 255–262.

Butterworth, G., Verweij, E., & Hopkins, B. (1997). The development of prehension in infants: Halverson revisited. *British Journal of Developmental Psychology, 15*(2), 223–236.

Campbell, A.J., Robertson, M.C., Gardner, M.M., Norton, R.N., & Buchner, D.M. (1999). Falls prevention over 2 years: A randomized controlled trial in women 80 years and older. *Age and Ageing, 28,* 513–518.

Campbell, A.J., Robertson, M.C., Gardner, M.M., Norton, R.N., Tilyard, M.W., & Buchner, D.M. (1997). Randomised controlled trial of a general practice programme of home based exercise to prevent falls in elderly women. *British Medical Journal, 315,* 1065–1069.

Campbell, D., & Eaton, W. (2000). Sex differences in the activity level of infants. *Infant and Child Development, 8,* 1–17.

Campbell, M.J., McComas, A.J., & Petito, F. (1973). Physiological changes in aging muscles. *Journal of Neurology, Neurosurgery, and Psychiatry, 36,* 174–182.

Campenni, C.E. (1999). Gender stereotyping of children's toys: A comparison of parents and nonparents. *Sex Roles, 40,* 121–138.

Carnahan, H., Vandervoort, A.A., & Swanson, L.R. (1998). The influence of aging and target motion on the control of prehension. *Experimental Aging Research, 24*(3), 289–306.

Carr, G. (1997). *Mechanics of sport.* Champaign, IL: Human Kinetics.

Carron, A.V., & Bailey, D.A. (1974). Strength development in boys from 10 through 16 years. *Monographs of the Society for Research in Child Development, 39,* 4.

Cartee, G.D. (1994). Aging skeletal muscle: Response to exercise. *Exercise and Sport Sciences Reviews, 22,* 91–120.

Centers for Disease Control and Prevention. (2007). Healthy People 2010. Available: www.cdc.gov/nchs/hphome.htm.

Cerella, J. (1990). Aging and information-processing rate. In J.E. Birren & K.W. Schaie (Eds.), *Handbook of the psychology of aging* (3rd ed., pp. 201–221). New York: Academic Press.

Cerella, J., Poon, L.W., & Williams, D.M. (1980). Age and the complexity hypothesis. In L.W. Poon (Ed.), *Aging in the 1980s.* Washington, DC: American Psychological Association.

Chase, M.A., Ewing, M.E., Lirgg, C.D., & George, T.R. (1994). The effects of equipment modification on children's self-efficacy and basketball shooting performance. *Research Quarterly for Exercise and Sport, 65*(2), 159–168.

Chase, W.G., & Simon, H.A. (1973). Perception in chess. *Cognitive Psychology, 4,* 55–81.

Chen, L.-C., Metcalfe, J.S., Jeka, J.J., & Clark, J.E. (2007). Two steps forward and one back: Learning to walk affects infants' sitting posture. *Infant Behavior and Development, 30,* 16–25.

Chi, M.T.H. (1978). Knowledge structures and memory development. In R.S. Siegler (Ed.), *Children's thinking: What develops?* (pp. 73–105). Hillsdale, NJ: Erlbaum.

Chi, M.T.H. (1981). Knowledge development and memory performance. In M.P. Friedman, J.P. Das, & N. O'Connor (Eds.), *Intelligence and learning* (pp. 221–229). New York: Plenum Press.

Chi, M.T.H., & Koeske, R.D. (1983). Network representation of a child's dinosaur knowledge. *Developmental Psychology, 19,* 29–39.

Chiesi, H.L., Spilich, G.J., & Voss, J.F. (1979). Acquisition of domain related information in relation to high and low domain knowledge. *Journal of Verbal Learning and Verbal Behavior, 18,* 257–273.

Chugani, H.T., & Phelps, M.E. (1986). Maturational changes in cerebral function in infants determined by 18FDG positron emission tomography. *Science, 231,* 840–843.

Clark, J.E. (1982). Developmental differences in response processing. *Journal of Motor Behavior, 14,* 247–254.

Clark, J.E. (1995). On becoming skillful: Patterns and constraints. *Research Quarterly for Exercise and Sport, 66,* 173–183.

Clark, J.E. (2005). From the beginning: A developmental perspective on movement and mobility. *Quest, 57,* 37–45.

Clark, J.E., & Phillips, S.J. (1985). A developmental sequence of the standing long jump. In J. Clark & J. Humphrey (Eds.), *Motor development: Vol. 1. Current selected research* (pp. 73–85). Princeton, NJ: Princeton Book.

Clark, J.E., & Phillips, S.J. (1993). A longitudinal study of intralimb coordination in the first year of independent walking. *Child Development, 64,* 1143–1157.

Clark, J.E., Phillips, S.J., & Petersen, R. (1989). Developmental stability in jumping. *Developmental Psychology, 25,* 929–935.

Clark, J.E., & Whitall, J. (1989a). What is motor development? *Quest, 41,* 183–202.

Clark, J.E., & Whitall, J. (1989b). Changing patterns of locomotion: From walking to skipping. In M.H. Woollacott & A. Shumway-Cook (Eds.), *Development of posture and gait across the life span* (pp. 128–151). Columbia: University of South Carolina Press.

Clark, J.E., Whitall, J., & Phillips, S.J. (1988). Human interlimb coordination: The first 6 months of independent walking. *Developmental Psychobiology, 21,* 445–456.

Clarke, H.H. (Ed.). (1975). Joint and body range of movement. *Physical Fitness Research Digest, 5,* 16–18.

Clarkson-Smith, L., & Hartley, A.A. (1990). Structural equation models of relationships between exercise and cognitive abilities. *Psychology and Aging, 5,* 437–446.

Clifton, R.K., Muir, D.W., Ashmead, D.H., & Clarkson, M.G. (1993). Is visually guided reaching in early infancy a myth? *Child Development, 64,* 1099–1110.

Clifton, R.K., Perris, E.E., & Bullinger, A. (1991). Infants' perception of auditory space. *Developmental Psychology, 27*(2), 187–197.

Clouse, F. (1959). *A kinematic analysis of the development of the running pattern of preschool boys.* Unpublished doctoral dissertation, University of Wisconsin, Madison.

Coakley, J. (1998). *Sport in society: Issues and controversies* (6th ed.). Madison, WI: McGraw-Hill.

Cobb, K., Goodwin, R., & Saelens, E. (1966). Spontaneous hand positions of newborn infants. *Journal of Genetic Psychology, 108,* 225–237.

Colcombe, S., & Kramer, A.F. (2003). Fitness effects on the cognitive function of older adults: A meta-analytic study. *Psychological Science, 14,* 125–130.

Colcombe, S.J., Erickson, K.I., Raz, N., Webb, A.G., Cohen, N.J., McAuley, E., et al. (2003). Aerobic fitness reduces brain tissue loss in aging humans. *Journal of Gerontology: Series A: Biological Sciences and Medical Science, 55,* 176–180.

Colcombe, S.J., Erickson, K.I., Scalf, P.E., Kim, J.S., Prakash, R., McAuley, E., et al. (2006). Aerobic exercise training increases brain volume in aging humans. *Journal of Gerontology: Series A: Biological Sciences and Medical Sciences, 61A,* 1166–1170.

Colcombe, S.J., Kramer, A.F., Erickson, K.I., Scalf, P., McAuley, E., & Cohen, N.J. (2004). Cardiovascular fitness, cortical plasticity, and aging. *Proceedings of the National Academy of Science, 101,* 3316–3321.

Colcombe, S., Wadwha, R., Kramer, A., McAuley, E., Scalf, P., Alvarado, M., et al. (2005). *Cardiovascular fitness training improves cortical recruitment and working memory in older adults: Evidence from a longitudinal fMRI study.* Presented at the *Annual Meeting of the Cognitive Neuroscience Society,* New York.

Colling-Saltin, A.S. (1980). Skeletal muscle development in the human fetus and during childhood. In K. Berg & B.O. Eriksson (Eds.), *International congress on pediatric work physiology: Children and exercise IX* (pp. 193–207). Baltimore: University Park Press.

Comery, T.A., Shah, R., & Greenough, W.T. (1995). Differential rearing alters spine density on medium-sized spiny neurons in the rat corpus striatum: Evidence for association of morphological plasticity with early response gene expression. *Neurobiology of Learning and Memory, 63*(3), 217–219.

Comery, T.A., Stamoudis, C.X., Irwin, S.A., & Greenough, W.T. (1996). Increased density of multiple-head dendritic spines on medium-sized spiny neurons of the striatum in rats reared in a complex environment. *Neurobiology of Learning and Memory, 66*(2), 93–96.

Connolly, K.J., & Elliott, J.M. (1972). The evolution and ontogeny of hand function. In N. Blurton-Jones (Ed.), *Ethological studies of child behavior* (pp. 329–383). Cambridge: Cambridge University Press.

Contreras-Vidal, J.L., Teulings, H.L., & Stelmach, G.E. (1998). Elderly subjects are impaired in spatial coordination in fine motor control. *Acta Psychologica, 100,* 25–35.

Coopersmith, S. (1967). *The antecedents of self-esteem.* San Francisco: Freeman.

Corbetta, D., & Bojczyk, K.E. (2002). Infants return to two-handed reaching when they are learning to walk. *Journal of Motor Behavior, 34*(1), 83–95.

Corbetta, D., & Mounoud, P. (1990). Early development of grasping and manipulation. In C. Bard, M. Fleury, & L. Hay (Eds.), *Development of eye-hand coordination across the life span* (pp. 188–216). Columbia: University of South Carolina Press.

Corbetta, D., & Thelen, E. (1996). The developmental origins of bimanual coordination: A dynamic perspective. *Journal of Experimental Psychology: Human Perception and Performance, 22*, 502–522.

Corso, J.F. (1977). Auditory perception and communication. In J.E. Birren & K.W. Schaie (Eds.), *Handbook of the psychology of aging* (pp. 535–553). New York: Van Nostrand Reinhold.

Cotman, C.W., & Berchtold, N.C. (2002). Exercise: A behavioral intervention to enhance brain health and plasticity. *Trends in Neurosciences, 25*, 295–301.

Cowburn, G., Hillsdon, M., & Hankey, C.R. (1997). Obesity management by lifestyle strategies. *British Medical Bulletin, 53*(2), 389–408.

Craig, C.H., Kim, B., Rhyner, P.M.P., & Chirillo, T.K.B. (1993). Effects of word predictability, child development, and aging on time-gated speech recognition performance. *Journal of Speech and Hearing Research, 36*, 832–841.

Craik, R. (1989). Changes in locomotion in the aging adult. In M.H. Woollacott & A. Shumway-Cook (Eds.), *Development of posture and gait across the life span* (pp. 176–201). Columbia: University of South Carolina Press.

Cratty, B.J. (1979). *Perception and motor development in infants and children* (2nd ed.). Englewood Cliffs, NJ: Prentice Hall.

Crossman, E.R.F.W., & Szafran, J. (1956). Changes with age in the speed of information intake and discrimination. *Experientia, 4(Suppl.)*, 128–135.

Crowell, J.A., & Banks, M.S. (1993). Perceiving heading with different retinal regions and types of optic flow. *Perception and Psychophysics, 53*, 325–337.

Cumming, R.G. (1990). Calcium intake and bone mass: A quantitative review of the evidence. *Calcified Tissue International, 47*, 194–201.

Cunningham, L.N. (1990). Relationship of running economy, ventilatory threshold, and maximum oxygen consumption to running performance in high school females. *Research Quarterly for Exercise and Sport, 61*, 369–374.

Cureton, K.J., Collins, M.A., Hill, D.W., & McElhannon, F.M. (1988). Muscle hypertrophy in men and women. *Medicine and Science in Sports and Exercise, 20*, 338–344.

Curtis, J.E., & White, P.G. (1984). Age and sport participation: Decline in participation with age or increased specialization with age? In N. Theberge & P. Donnelly (Eds.), *Sport and the sociological imagination* (pp. 273–293). Fort Worth: Texas Christian University Press.

Dalsky, G.P. (1989). The role of exercise in the prevention of osteoporosis. *Comprehensive Therapy, 15*, 30–37.

Dalsky, G.P., Stocke, K.S., Eshani, A.A., Slatopolsky, E., Lee, W.C., & Birge, S.J. (1988). Weight-bearing exercise training and lumbar bone mineral content in postmenopausal women. *Annals of Internal Medicine, 108*, 824–828.

Damasio, A.R. (1989). The brain binds entities and events by multiregional activation from convergence zones. *Neural Computation, 1*, 123–132.

Davies, B.N. (1990). The relationship of lean limb volume to performance in the handgrip and standing long jump tests in boys and girls, aged 11.6–13.2 years. *European Journal of Applied Physiology, 60*, 139–143.

Davies, C.T.M., White, M.J., & Young, K. (1983). Muscle function in children. *European Journal of Applied Physiology, 52*, 111–114.

Davis, C.I. (1991). The effects of game modification on opportunities to respond in elementary volleyball classes. *Dissertation Abstracts International, 52*(2), 465.

Davis, W.E., & Broadhead, G. (Eds.) (2007). *Ecological task analysis and movement*. Champaign, IL: Human Kinetics.

Davis, W.E., & Burton, A.W. (2007). Ecological task analysis: Translating movement behavior theory into practice. *Adapted Physical Activity Quarterly, 8*, 154–177.

Dehn, M.M., & Bruce, R.A. (1972). Longitudinal variations in maximum oxygen intake with age and activity. *Journal of Applied Physiology, 33*, 805–807.

de Jonge, L.L., van Osch-Gevers, L., Willemsen, S.P., Steegers, E.A.P., Hofman, A., Helbing, W.A., et al. (2011). Growth, obesity, and cardiac structures in early childhood: The Generation R study. *Hypertension, 57*, 934–940.

Dekaban, A. (1970). *Neurology of early childhood*. Baltimore: Williams & Wilkins.

Delacato, C.H. (1959). *Treatment and prevention of reading problems*. Springfield, IL: Charles C Thomas.

Delacato, C.H. (1966). *Neurological organization and reading*. Springfield, IL: Charles C Thomas.

Demany, L., McKenzie, B., & Vurpillot, E. (1977). Rhythmic perception in early infancy. *Nature, 266*, 718–719.

Dempsey, J.A., Johnson, B.D., & Saupe, K.W. (1990). Adaptations and limitations in the pulmonary system during exercise. *Chest, 97*(3 Suppl.), 81S–87S.

de Oliveira, A.R., & Gallagher, J.D. (1994, August). *Strength training in children: A meta-analysis*. Paper presented at the meeting of the North American Society for Pediatric Exercise Medicine, Pittsburgh.

de Onis, M., Garza, C., Victora, C.G., Onyango, A.W., Frongillo, E.A., & Martines, J, (2004). The WHO Multicentre Growth Reference Study: Planning, study design, and methodology. *Food Nutrition Bulletin, 25*, S15–S26.

de Onis, M., Onyango, A.W., Borghi, E., Siyam, A., Nishida, C., & Siekmann, J. (2007). Development of a WHO growth reference for school-aged children and adolescents. *Bulletin of the World Health Organization 2007, 85*, 660–667.

DeOreo, K., & Keogh, J. (1980). Performance of fundamental motor tasks. In C.B. Corbin (Ed.), *A textbook of motor development* (2nd ed., pp. 76–91). Dubuque, IA: Brown.

DeOreo, K., & Wade, M.G. (1971). Dynamic and static balancing ability of preschool children. *Journal of Motor Behavior, 3,* 326–335.

DeOreo, K.L., & Williams, H.G. (1980). Characteristics of kinesthetic perception. In C.B. Corbin (Ed.), *A textbook of motor development* (2nd ed., pp. 174–196). Dubuque, IA: Brown.

Diamond, A. (2000). Close interrelation of motor development and cognitive development and of the cerebellum and prefrontal cortex. *Child Development, 71,* 44–56.

Dietz, W.H., & Robinson, T.N. (1993). Assessment and treatment of childhood obesity. *Pediatric Review, 14,* 337–343.

DiLorenzo, T., Stucky-Ropp, R., Vander Wal, J., & Gotham, H. (1998). Determinants of exercise among children: II. A longitudinal analysis. *Preventive Medicine, 27,* 470–477.

DiNucci, J.M. (1976). Gross motor performance: A comprehensive analysis of age and sex differences between boys and girls ages six to nine years. In J. Broekhoff (Ed.), *Physical education, sports, and the sciences.* Eugene, OR: Microform.

Dioum, A., Gartner, A., Maire, B., Delpeuch, F., & Wade, S. (2005). Body composition predicted from skinfolds in African women: A cross-validation study using air-displacement plethysmography and a black-specific equation. *British Journal of Nutrition, 93,* 973–979.

DiPietro, J.A. (1981). Rough and tumble play: A function of gender. *Developmental Psychology, 17,* 50–58.

DiSimoni, F.G. (1975). Perceptual and perceptual-motor characteristics of phonemic development. *Child Development, 46,* 243–246.

Dittmer, J. (1962). *A kinematic analysis of the development of the running pattern of grade school girls and certain factors which distinguish good from poor performance at the observed ages.* Unpublished master's thesis, University of Wisconsin, Madison.

Dollman, J., Olds, T., Norton, K., & Stuart, D. (1999). The evolution of fitness and fatness in 10- to 11-year-old Australian schoolchildren: Changes in distribution characteristics between 1985 and 1997. *Pediatric Exercise Science, 11,* 108–121.

Dorfman, P.W. (1977). Timing and anticipation: A developmental perspective. *Journal of Motor Behavior, 9,* 67–80.

Doty, D. (1974). Infant speech perception. *Human Development, 17,* 74–80.

Drillis, R. (1961). The influence of aging on the kinematics of gait. *The geriatric amputee, NAS-NRC publication 919,* 134-145.

Drinkwater, B.L., Horvath, S.M., & Wells, C.L. (1975). Aerobic power of females, age 10–68. *Journal of Gerontology, 30,* 385–394.

Drowatzky, J.N., & Zuccato, F.C. (1967). Interrelationship between static and dynamic balance. *Research Quarterly, 38,* 509–510.

Duche, P., Falgairette, G., Bedu, M., Fellmann, N., Lac, G., Robert, A., et al. (1992). Longitudinal approach of bioenergetic profile in boys before and during puberty. In J. Coudert & E. Van Praagh (Eds.), *Pediatric work physiology: Methodological, physiological and pathological aspects* (pp. 43–45). Paris: Masson.

Duda, J.L., & Tappe, M.K. (1988). Predictors of personal investment in physical activity among middle-aged and older adults. *Perception and Motor Skills, 66,* 543–549.

Duda, J.L., & Tappe, M.K. (1989a). Personal investment in exercise among middle-aged and older adults. In A.C. Ostrow (Ed.), *Aging and motor behavior* (pp. 219–238). Indianapolis: Benchmark Press.

Duda, J.L., & Tappe, M.K. (1989b). Personal investment in exercise among adults: The examination of age and gender-related differences in motivational orientation. In A.C. Ostrow (Ed.), *Aging and motor behavior* (pp. 239–256). Indianapolis: Benchmark Press.

Duda, M. (1986). Prepubescent strength training gains support. *The Physician and Sportsmedicine, 14,* 157–161.

Duijts, L., Jaddoe, V.W.V., Hofman, A., & Moll, H.A. (2010). Prolonged and exclusive breastfeeding reduces the risk of infectious diseases in infancy. *Pediatrics, 126,* e18.

Dunham, P. (1977). Age, sex, speed and practice in coincidence-anticipation performance of children. *Perceptual and Motor Skills, 45,* 187–193.

DuRandt, R. (1985). Ball catching proficiency among 4-, 6-, and 8-year-olds. In J.E. Clark & J.H. Humphrey (Eds.), *Motor development: Current selected research* (pp. 35–44). Princeton, NJ: Princeton Book.

Earles, J.L., & Salthouse, T.A. (1995). Interrelations of age, health, and speed. *Journal of Gerontology: Psychological Sciences, 50B,* P33–P41.

Eaton, W.O., & Enns, L.R. (1986). Sex differences in human motor activity level. *Psychological Bulletin, 100,* 19–28.

Eaton, W.O., & Keats, J.G. (1982). Peer presence, stress, and sex differences in the motor activity levels of preschoolers. *Developmental Psychology, 18,* 534–540.

Ebihara, O., Ikeda, M., & Miyashita, M. (1983). Birth order and children's socialization into sport. *International Review of Sport Sociology, 18,* 69–89.

Ebrahim, S., & Rowland, L. (1996). Towards a new strategy for health promotion for older women: Determinants of physical activity. *Psychology, Health and Medicine, 1*(1), 29–40.

Einkauf, D.K., Gohdes, M.L., Jensen, G.M., & Jewell, M.J. (1987). Changes in spinal mobility with increasing age in women. *Physical Therapy, 67,* 370–375.

Eisenberg, N., Welchick, S.A., Hernandez, R., & Pasternack, J.F. (1985). Parental socialization of young children's play: A short-term longitudinal study. *Child Development, 56,* 1506–1513.

Eitzen, D.S., & Sage, G.H. (2003). *Sociology of North American sport* (7th ed.). Madison, WI: WCB McGraw-Hill.

Ekblom, B. (1969). Effect of physical training on oxygen transport system in man. *Acta Physiologica Scandinavica Supplementum, 328,* 1–76.

Elkind, D. (1975). Perceptual development in children. *American Scientist, 63,* 533–541.

Elkind, D., Koegler, R., & Go, E. (1964). Studies in perceptual development: Whole-part perception. *Child Development, 35,* 81–90.

Elliott, C.B., Whitaker, D., & Thompson, P. (1989). Use of displacement threshold hyperacuity to isolate the neural component of senile vision loss. *Applied Optics, 28,* 1914–1918.

Elliott, R. (1972). Simple reaction time in children: Effects of incentive, incentive shift, and other training variables. *Journal of Experimental Child Psychology, 13,* 540–557.

Erickson, K.I., Colcombe, S.J., Wadhwa, R., Bherer, L., Peterson, M.W., Scalf, P.E., et al. (2007). Training-induced plasticity in older adults: Effects of training on hemispheric asymmetry. *Neurobiology of Aging, 28,* 272–283.

Eriksson, B., & Koch, G. (1973). Effect of physical training on hemodynamic response during submaximal exercise in 11–13 year old boys. *Acta Physiologica Scandinavica, 87,* 27–39.

Eriksson, B.O. (1972). Physical training, oxygen supply and muscle metabolism in 11 to 15 year old boys. *Acta Physiologica Scandinavica Supplementum, 384,* 1–48.

Eriksson, B.O. (1978). Physical activity from childhood to maturity: Medical and pediatric considerations. In G. Landry & W.A.R. Orban (Eds.), *Physical activity and human well-being.* Miami, FL: Symposia Specialists.

Espenschade, A.S. (1947). Development of motor coordination in boys and girls. *Research Quarterly, 18,* 30–44.

Espenschade, A.S., Dable, R.R., & Schoendube, R. (1953). Dynamic balance in adolescent boys. *Research Quarterly, 24,* 270–274.

Eston, R.G., Robson, S., & Winter, E. (1993). A comparison of oxygen uptake during running in children and adults. *Kinanthropometry IV,* 236–241.

Ewart, C.K., Stewart, K.J., Gillilan, R.E., & Kelemen, M.H. (1986). Self-efficacy mediates strength gains during circuit weight training in men with coronary artery disease. *Medicine and Science in Sports and Exercise, 18,* 531–540.

Exton-Smith, A.N. (1985). Mineral metabolism. In C.E. Finch & E.L. Schneider (Eds.), *Handbook of the biology of aging* (2nd ed., pp. 511–539). New York: Van Nostrand Reinhold.

Fagard, J. (1990). The development of bimanual coordination. In C. Bard, M. Fleury, & L. Hay (Eds.), *Development of eye-hand coordination across the life span* (pp. 262–282). Columbia: University of South Carolina Press.

Fagot, B., & Leinbach, M. (1996). Gender knowledge in egalitarian and traditional families. *Sex Roles, 32,* 513–526.

Fagot, B., Leinbach, M., & O'Boyle, C. (1992). Gender labeling, gender stereotyping, and parenting behaviors. *Developmental Psychology, 28*(2), 225–230.

Fagot, B.I. (1978). The influence of sex of child on parental reactions to toddler children. *Child Development, 49,* 459–465.

Fagot, B.I. (1984). Teacher and peer reactions to boys' and girls' play styles. *Sex Roles, 11,* 691–702.

Fagot, B.I., & Leinbach, M.D. (1983). Play styles in early childhood: Social consequences for boys and girls. In M.B. Liss (Ed.), *Social and cognitive skills: Sex roles and children's play* (pp. 93–116). New York: Academic Press.

Faigenbaum, A.D., Milliken, L., Moulton, L., & Westcott, W.L. (2005). Early muscular fitness adaptations in children in response to two different resistance training regimens. *Pediatric Exercise Science, 17,* 237–248.

Falgairette, G., Bedu, M., Fellmann, N., Van Praagh, E., & Coudert, J. (1991). Bio-energetic profile in 144 boys aged from 6 to 15 years. *European Journal of Applied Physiology, 62,* 151–156.

Falgairette, G., Duche, P., Bedu, M., Fellmann, N., & Coudert, J. (1993). Bioenergetic characteristics in prepubertal swimmers. *International Journal of Sports Medicine, 14,* 444–448.

Falk, B. & Tenenbaum, G. (1996). The effectiveness of resistance training in children. A meta-analysis. *Sports Medicine, 22,* 176–186.

Farley, C. (1997). Just skip it. *Nature, 394,* 721–723.

Feltz, D.L., & Petlichkoff, L. (1983). Perceived competence among interscholastic sport participants and dropouts. *Canadian Journal of Applied Sport Sciences, 8,* 231–235.

Fiatarone, M.A., Marks, E.C., Ryan, N.D., Meredith, C.N., Lipsitz, L.A., & Evans, W.J. (1990). High-intensity strength training in nonagenarians. *Journal of the American Medical Association, 263,* 3029–3034.

Fieandt, K.V., Huhtala, A., Kullberg, P., & Saarl, K. (1956). *Personal tempo and phenomenal time at different age levels* (Report no. 2). Helsinki: Psychological Institute, University of Helsinki.

Fitts, R.H. (1981). Aging and skeletal muscle. In E.L. Smith & R.C. Serfass (Eds.), *Exercise and aging: The scientific basis* (pp. 31–44). Hillside, NJ: Enslow.

Fleg, J.L. (1986). Alterations in cardiovascular structure and function with advancing age. *American Journal of Cardiology, 57,* 33C–44C.

Flegal, K.M., Carroll, M.D., Kuczmarski, R.J., & Johnson, C.L. (1998). Overweight and obesity in the United States: Prevalence and trends, 1960–1994. *International Journal of Obesity, 22,* 39–47.

Forbes, G.B. (1992). Exercise and lean weight: The influence of body weight. *Nutrition Reviews, 50,* 157–161.

Forssberg, H., & Nashner, L. (1982). Ontogenetic development of postural control in man: Adaptation to altered support and visual conditions during stance. *Journal of Neuroscience, 2,* 545–552.

Fox, K.R., & Corbin, C.B. (1989). The physical self-perception profile: Development and preliminary validation. *Journal of Sport and Exercise Psychology, 11,* 408–430.

Franck, H., Beuker, F., & Gurk, S. (1991). The effect of physical activity on bone turnover in young adults. *Experimental and Clinical Endocrinology, 98,* 42–46.

Frankenburg, W.K., & Dodds, J.B. (1967). The Denver Developmental Screening Test. *Journal of Pediatrics, 71,* 181–191.

French, K.E., Nevett, M.E., Spurgeon, J.H., Graham, K.C., Rink, J.E., & McPherson, S.L. (1996). Knowledge representation and problem solution in expert and novice youth baseball players. *Research Quarterly for Exercise and Sport, 67*(4), 386–395.

French, K.E., & Thomas, J.R. (1987). The relation of knowledge development to children's basketball performance. *Journal of Sport Psychology, 9,* 15–32.

Frontera, W.R., Meredith, C.N., O'Reilly, K.P., Knuttgen, H.G., & Evans, W.J. (1988). Strength conditioning in older men: Skeletal muscle hypertrophy and improved function. *Journal of Applied Physiology, 64,* 1038–1044.

Frostig, M., Lefever, W., & Whittlesey, J. (1966). *Administration and scoring manual for the Marianne Frostig Developmental Test of Visual Perception.* Palo Alto, CA: Consulting Psychologists Press.

Gabel, R.H., Johnston, R.C., & Crowninshield, R.D. (1979). A gait analyzer/trainer instrumentation system. *Journal of Biomedical Engineering, 12,* 543–549.

Gabell, A., & Nayak, U.S.L. (1984). The effect of age on variability of gait. *Journal of Gerontology, 39,* 662–666.

Gagen, L., & Getchell, N. (2004). Combining theory and practice in the gymnasium: "Constraints" within an ecological perspective. *Journal of Physical Education, Recreation and Dance, 75,* 25–30.

Gagen, L., & Getchell, N. (2006). Using "constraints" to design developmentally appropriate movement activities for early childhood education. *Early Childhood Education Journal, 34,* 227–232.

Gagen, L., & Getchell, N. (2008). Applying Newton's apple to elementary physical education: An interdisciplinary approach. *Journal of Physical Education, Recreation, and Dance, 79,* 43–51.

Gagen, L.M., Haywood, K.M., & Spaner, S.D. (2005). Predicting the scale of tennis rackets for optimal striking from body dimensions. *Pediatric Exercise Science, 17,* 190–200.

Gallagher, J.D., & Thomas, J.R. (1980, April). *Adult-child differences in movement reproduction: Effects of kinesthetic sensory storage and organization of memory.* Paper presented at the annual convention of the American Alliance for Health, Physical Education, Recreation and Dance, Detroit.

Galloway, J.C. (2004). The emergence of purposeful limb movement in early infancy: The interaction of experience, learning and biomechanics. *Journal of Human Kinetics, 12,* 51–68.

Geerdink, J.J., Hopkins, B., Beek, W.J., & Heriza, C.B. (1996). The organization of leg movements in preterm and full-term infants after term age. *Developmental Psychobiology, 29,* 335–351.

Germain, N.W., & Blair, S.N. (1983). Variability of shoulder flexion with age, activity, and sex. *American Corrective Therapy Journal, 37,* 156–160.

Gesell, A. (1928). *Infancy and human growth.* New York: Macmillan.

Gesell, A. (1954). The ontogenesis of infant behavior. In L. Carmichael (Ed.), *Manual of child psychology* (2nd ed.). New York: Wiley.

Gesell, A., & Amatruda, C.S. (1949). *Gesell Developmental Schedules.* New York: Psychological.

Getchell, N., & Gagen, L. (2006). Interpreting disabilities from a "constraints" theoretical perspective: Encouraging movement for *all* children. *Palaestra, 22,* 20–53.

Getchell, N., & Roberton, M.A. (1989). Whole body stiffness as a function of developmental level in children's hopping. *Developmental Psychology, 25,* 920–928.

Getman, G.N. (1952). *How to develop your child's intelligence: A research publication.* Lucerne, MN: Author.

Getman, G.N. (1963). *The physiology of readiness experiment.* Minneapolis: P.A.S.S.

Gibson, E.J., Riccio, G., Schmuckler, M.A., Stoffregen, T.A., Rosenberg, D., & Taormina, J. (1987). Detection of the traversability of surfaces by crawling and walking infants. Special issue: The ontogenesis of perception. *Journal of Experimental Psychology: Human Perception and Performance, 13*(4), 533–544.

Gibson, E.J., & Walk, R.D. (1960). The "visual cliff." *Scientific American, 202*(4), 64–71.

Gibson, J.J. (1966). *The senses considered as perceptual systems.* Boston: Houghton Mifflin.

Gibson, J.J. (1979). *An ecological approach to visual perception.* Boston: Houghton Mifflin.

Giuliano, T., Popp, K., & Knight, J. (2000). Football versus Barbies: Childhood play activities as predictors of sport participation by women. *Sex Roles, 42,* 159–181.

Goggin, N.L., & Keller, M.J. (1996). Older drivers: A closer look. *Educational Gerontology, 22,* 245–256.

Goggin, N.L., & Stelmach, G.E. (1990). A kinematic analysis of precued movements in young and elderly participants. *Canadian Journal on Aging, 9,* 371–385.

Going, S.B., Lohman, T., Pamenter, R., Boyden, T., Houtkooper, L., Ritenbaugh, C., et al. (1991). Effects of weight training on bone mineral density in premenopausal females. *Journal of Bone and Mineral Research, 6,* S104.

Going, S.B., Williams, D.P., Lohman, T.G., & Hewitt, M.J. (1994). Aging, body composition, and physical activity: A review. *Journal of Aging and Physical Activity, 2,* 38–66.

Goldfield, E.C., & Michel, G.F. (1986). The ontogeny of infant bimanual reaching during the first year. *Infant Behavior and Development, 9,* 81–89.

Goodale, M.A. (1988). Modularity in visuomotor control: From input to output. In Z. Pylyshyn (Ed.), *Computational processes in human vision: An interdisciplinary perspective* (pp. 262–285). Norwood, NJ: Ablex.

Goodman, L., & Hamill, D. (1973). The effectiveness of the Kephart Getman activities in developing perceptual-motor and cognitive skills. *Focus on Exceptional Children, 4,* 1–9.

Goodnow, J.J. (1971a). Eye and hand: Differential memory and its effect on matching. *Neuropsychologica, 9,* 89–95.

Goodnow, J.J. (1971b). Matching auditory and visual series: Modality problem or translation problem? *Child Development, 42,* 1187–1201.

Goodway, J.D., & Branta, C.F. (2003). Influence of motor skill intervention on fundamental motor skill development of disadvantaged pre-school children. *Research Quarterly for Exercise and Sport, 74,* 36–46.

Goodway, J.D., Crowe, H., & Ward, P. (2003). Effects of motor skill instruction on fundamental motor skill development. *Adapted Physical Activity Quarterly, 30,* 298–314.

Gosline, J.M. (1976). The physical properties of elastic tissue. In D.A. Hull & D.S. Jackson (Eds.), *International review of connective tissue research* (Vol. 7, pp. 184–210). New York: Academic Press.

Gould, D., Feltz, D., Horn, T., & Weiss, M.R. (1982). Reasons for attrition in competitive youth swimming. *Journal of Sport Behavior, 5,* 155–165.

Gould, D., Feltz, D., & Weiss, M.R. (1985). Motives for participating in competitive youth swimming. *International Journal of Sport Psychology, 6,* 126–140.

Granrud, C.E., Yonas, A., Smith, I.M., Arterberry, M.E., Glicksman, M.L., & Sorknes, A.C. (1984). Infants' sensitivity to accretion and deletion of texture as information for depth at an edge. *Child Development, 55,* 1630–1636.

Grassi, B., Cerretelli, P., Narici, M.V., & Marconi, C. (1991). Peak anaerobic power in master athletes. *European Journal of Physiology, 62,* 394–399.

Green, H.J. (1986). Characteristics of aging human skeletal muscles. In J.R. Sutton & R.M. Brock (Eds.), *Sports medicine for the mature athlete* (pp. 17–26). Indianapolis: Benchmark Press.

Greendorfer, S.L. (1976, September). *A social learning approach to female sport involvement.* Paper presented at the annual convention of the American Psychological Association, Washington, DC.

Greendorfer, S.L. (1977). Role of socializing agents in female sport involvement. *Research Quarterly, 48,* 304–310.

Greendorfer, S.L. (1979). Childhood sport socialization influences of male and female track athletes. *Arena Review, 3,* 39–53.

Greendorfer, S.L. (1983). Shaping the female athlete: The impact of the family. In M.A. Boutilier & L. Sangiovanni (Eds.), *The sport woman* (pp. 135–155). Champaign, IL: Human Kinetics.

Greendorfer, S.L. (1992). Sport socialization. In T.S. Horn (Ed.), *Advances in sport psychology* (pp. 201–218). Champaign, IL: Human Kinetics.

Greendorfer, S.L., & Brundage, C.L. (1984, July). *Sex differences in children's motor skills: Toward a cross-disciplinary perspective.* Paper presented at the 1984 Olympic Scientific Congress, Eugene, OR.

Greendorfer, S.L., & Ewing, M.E. (1981). Race and gender differences in children's socialization into sport. *Research Quarterly for Exercise and Sport, 52,* 301–310.

Greendorfer, S.L., & Lewko, J.H. (1978). Role of family members in sport socialization of children. *Research Quarterly, 49,* 146–152.

Greenough, W.T., Black, J.E., & Wallace, C.S. (1987). Experience and brain development. *Child Development, 58,* 539–559.

Greenough, W.T., Wallace, C.S., Alcantara, A.A., Anderson, B.J., Hawrylak, N., Sirevaag, A.M., et al. (1993). Development of the brain: Experience affects the structure of neurons, glia, and blood vessels. In N.J. Anatasiow & S. Harel (Eds.), *At-risk infants: Interventions, families, and research* (pp. 173–185). Baltimore: Brookes.

Grimby, G. (1988). Physical activity and effects of muscle training in the elderly. *Annals of Clinical Research, 20,* 62–66.

Grodjinovsky, A., Inbar, O., Dotan, R., & Bar-Or, O. (1980). Training effect on the anaerobic performance of children as measured by the Wingate Anaerobic Test. In K. Berg & B.O. Eriksson (Eds.), *Children and exercise IX* (pp. 139–145). Baltimore: University Park Press.

Gutin, B., Cucuzzo, N., Islam, S., Smith, C., & Stachura, M.E. (1996). Physical training, lifestyle education, and coronary risk factors in obese girls. *Medicine and Science in Sports and Exercise, 28,* 19–23.

Gutin, B., Owens, S., Slavens, G., Riggs, S., & Treiber, F. (1997). Effects of physical training on heart period variability in obese children. *Journal of Pediatrics, 130,* 938–943.

Gutteridge, M. (1939). A study of motor achievements of young children. *Archives of Psychology, 244,* 1–178.

Gygax, P.M., Wagner-Egger, P., Parris, B., Seiler, R., & Hauert, C.-A. (2008). A psycholinguistic investigation of football players' mental representations of game situations: Does expertise count? *Swiss Journal of Psychology, 67,* 85–95.

Hagburg, J.M., Allen, W.K., Seals, D.R., Hurley, B.F., Ehsani, A.A., & Holloszy, J.O. (1985). A hemodynamic comparison of young and older endurance athletes during exercise. *Journal of Applied Physiology, 58,* 2041–2046.

Hagburg, J.M., Graves, J.E., Limacher, M., Woods, D.R., Leggett, S.H., Cononie, C., et al. (1989). Cardiovascular responses of 70- to 79-year-old men and women to exercise training. *Journal of Applied Physiology, 66,* 2589–2594.

Hall, S.J. (2006). *Basic biomechanics* (5th ed.). Dubuque, IA: McGraw-Hill.

Halverson, H.M. (1931). An experimental study of prehension in infants by means of systematic cinema records. *Genetic Psychology Monographs, 10,* 107–286.

Halverson, L.E. (1983). *Observing children's motor development in action.* Paper presented at annual convention of the American Alliance for Health, Physical Education, Recreation and Dance, Eugene, OR.

Halverson, L.E., Roberton, M.A., & Langendorfer, S. (1982). Development of the overarm throw: Movement and ball velocity changes by seventh grade. *Research Quarterly for Exercise and Sport, 53,* 198–205.

Halverson, L.E., & Williams, K. (1985). Developmental sequences for hopping over distance: A prelongitudinal screening. *Research Quarterly for Exercise and Sport, 56,* 37–44.

Hands, B. (2008). Changes in motor skill and fitness measures among children with high and low motor competence: A five-year longitudinal study. *Journal of Science and Medicine in Sport, 11,* 155–162.

Hand Transplant. (2014). Available: www.handtransplant.com /ThePatients/MatthewScott.

Hannaford, C. (1995). *Smart moves: Why learning is not all in your head.* Arlington, VA: Great Ocean.

Hansen, L., Klausen, K., Bangsbo, J., & Muller, J. (1999). Short longitudinal study of boys playing soccer: Parental height, birth weight and length, anthropometry, and pubertal maturation in elite and non-elite players. *Pediatric Exercise Science, 11,* 199–207.

Hansman, C.F. (1962). Appearance and fusion of ossification centers in the human skeleton. *American Journal of Roentgenology, 88,* 476–482.

Harris, J.E. (1999). The role of physical activity in the management of obesity. *Journal of the American Osteopathic Association, 99*(4), S15–S19.

Harrison, T.R., Dixon, K., Russell, R.A., Bidwai, P.S., & Coleman, H.N. (1964). The relation of age to the duration of contraction, ejection, and relaxation of the normal human heart. *American Heart Journal, 67,* 189–199.

Harter, S. (1978). Effectance motivation reconsidered: Towards a developmental model. *Human Development, 21,* 34–64.

Harter, S. (1981). A model of intrinsic mastery motivation in children: Individual differences and developmental change. In W.A. Collins (Ed.), *Minnesota Symposium on Child Psychology* (Vol. 14, pp. 215–225). Hillsdale, NJ: Erlbaum.

Harter, S. (1985). *Manual for the self-perception profile for children.* Denver: University of Denver.

Harter, S., & Pike, R. (1984). The pictorial scale of perceived competence and social acceptance for young children. *Child Development, 55,* 1969–1982.

Hartley, A.A. (1992). Attention. In F.I.M. Craig & T.A. Salthouse (Eds.), *The handbook of aging and cognition* (pp. 3–49). Hillsdale, NJ: Erlbaum.

Hasselkus, B.R., & Shambes, G.M. (1975). Aging and postural sway in women. *Journal of Gerontology, 30,* 661–667.

Haubenstricker, J.L., Branta, C.F., & Seefeldt, V.D. (1983). *Standards of performance for throwing and catching.* Paper presented at the annual conference of the North American Society for Psychology of Sport and Physical Activity, Asilomar, CA.

Haubenstricker, J.L., Seefeldt, V.D., & Branta, C.F. (1983, April). *Preliminary validation of a developmental sequence for the standing long jump.* Paper presented at the American Alliance for Health, Physical Education, Recreation and Dance, Houston.

Hausler, R., Colburn, S., & Marr, E. (1983). Sound localization in subjects with impaired hearing: Spatial discrimination and discrimination tests. *Acta Oto-Laryngologica (Suppl.), 40C,* 6–62.

Hawn, P.R., & Harris, L.J. (1983). Hand differences in grasp duration and reaching in two- and five-month old infants. In G. Young, S. Segalowitz, C.M. Carter, & S.E. Trehub (Eds.), *Manual specialization and the developing brain* (pp. 331–348). New York: Academic Press.

Haywood, K., & Trick, L. (1990). Changes in visual functioning and perception with advancing age. *Missouri Journal of Health, Physical Education, Recreation and Dance,* 51–73.

Haywood, K.M. (1977). Eye movements during coincidence-anticipation performance. *Journal of Motor Behavior, 9,* 313–318.

Haywood, K.M. (1980). Coincidence-anticipation accuracy across the life span. *Experimental Aging Research, 6*(3), 451–462.

Haywood, K.M. (1982). Eye movement pattern and accuracy during perceptual-motor performance in young and old adults. *Experimental Aging Research, 8,* 153–157.

Haywood, K.M. (1989). A longitudinal analysis of anticipatory judgment in older adult motor performance. In A.C. Ostrow (Ed.), *Aging and motor behavior* (pp. 325–335). Indianapolis: Benchmark Press.

Haywood, K.M., Greenwald, G., & Lewis, C. (1981). Contextual factors and age group differences in coincidence-anticipation performance. *Research Quarterly for Exercise and Sport, 52,* 458–464.

Haywood, K.M., & Williams, K. (1995). Age, gender, and flexibility differences in tennis serving among experienced older adults. *Journal of Aging and Physical Activity, 3,* 54–66.

Haywood, K.M., Williams, K., & VanSant, A. (1991). Qualitative assessment of the backswing in older adult throwing. *Research Quarterly for Exercise and Sport, 62,* 340–343.

Heaney, R.P. (1986). Calcium, bone health, and osteoporosis. *Journal of Bone and Mineral Research, 4,* 255–301.

Hecaen, H., & de Ajuriaguerra, J. (1964). *Left-handedness: Manual superiority and cerebral dominance.* New York: Grune & Stratton.

Hecox, K. (1975). Electro-physiological correlates of human auditory development. In L.B. Cohen & P. Salapatek (Eds.), *Infant perception: Vol. 2. From sensation to cognition* (pp. 151–191). New York: Academic Press.

Held, R. (1985). Binocular vision: Behavioral and neuronal development. In J. Mehler & R. Fox (Eds.), *Neonate cognition: Beyond the blooming buzzing confusion* (pp. 37–44). Hillsdale, NJ: Erlbaum.

Held, R. (1988). Normal visual development and its deviations. In G. Lennerstrand, G. Von Noorden, & E. Campos (Eds.), *Strabismus and amblyopia* (pp. 247–257). London: Macmillan.

Held, R., & Hein, A. (1963). Movement-produced stimulation in the development of visually guided behavior. *Journal of Comparative and Physiological Psychology, 56,* 872–876.

Helfer, K.S. (1992). Aging and the binaural advantage in reverberation and noise. *Journal of Speech and Hearing Research, 35,* 1394–1401.

Hellebrandt, F.A., & Braun, G.L. (1939). The influence of sex and age on the postural sway of man. *American Journal of Physical Anthropology, 24*(Series 1), 347–360.

Hellmich, N. (1999, November 15). Aging Americans settle up in size. *USA Today,* p. 6D.

Heriza, C.B. (1986). *A kinematic analysis of leg movements in premature and fullterm infants.* Unpublished doctoral dissertation, University of Southern Illinois, Edwardsville.

Herkowitz, J. (1978). Developmental task analysis: The design of movement experiences and evaluation of motor development status. In M.V. Ridenour (Ed.), *Motor development* (pp. 139–164). Princeton, NJ: Princeton Book.

Hesketh, K.D., & Campbell, K.J. (2010). Interventions to prevent obesity in 0-5 year olds: An updated systematic review of the literature. *Obesity, 18,* S27–S35.

Heyward, V.H. (1991). *Advanced fitness assessment and exercise prescription* (2nd ed.). Champaign, IL: Human Kinetics.

Hickey, T.L., & Peduzzi, J.D. (1987). Structure and development of the visual system. In P. Salapatek & L.B. Cohen (Eds.), *Handbook of infant perception: From sensation to perception* (pp. 1–42). New York: Academic Press.

Higginson, D.C. (1985). The influence of socializing agents in the female sport-participation process. *Adolescence, 20,* 73–82.

Hoeger, W.W.K., Hopkins, D.R., Button, S., & Palmer, T.A. (1990). Comparing the sit and reach with the modified sit and reach in measuring flexibility in adolescents. *Pediatric Exercise Science, 2,* 155–162.

Hogan, P.I., & Santomeir, J.P. (1984). Effect of mastering swim skills on older adults' self-efficacy. *Research Quarterly for Exercise and Sport, 55,* 294–296.

Hohlstein, R.E. (1982). The development of prehension in normal infants. *American Journal of Occupational Therapy, 36,* 170–176.

Holland, G.J., Tanaka, K., Shigematsu, R., & Nakagaichi, M. (2002). Flexibility and physical functions of older adults: A review. *Journal of Aging and Physical Activity, 10,* 169–206.

Hollenberg, M., Yang, J., Haight, T.J., & Tager, I.B. (2006). Longitudinal changes in aerobic capacity: Implications for concepts of aging. *Journal of Gerontology Series A: Biological Sciences and Medical Sciences, 61,* 851–858.

Holtzman, R.E., Familant, M.E., Deptula, P., & Hoyer, W.J. (1986). Aging and the use of sentential structure to facilitate word recognition. *Experimental Aging Research, 12,* 85–88.

Hopkins, B., & Ronnqvist, L. (1998). Human handedness: Developmental and evolutionary perspectives. In F. Simion & G. Butterworth (Eds.), *The development of sensory, motor and cognitive capacities in early infancy: From perception to cognition* (pp. 191–236). Hove, UK: Psychology Press.

Horak, F.B., & MacPherson, J.M. (1995). Postural orientation and equilibrium. In J. Shepard & L. Rowell (Eds.), *Handbook of physiology* (pp. 252–292). New York: Oxford University Press.

Horak, F.B., Nashner, L.M., & Diener, H.C. (1990). Postural strategies associated with somatosensory and vestibular loss. *Experimental Brain Research, 82,* 167–177.

Horn, T.S. (1985). Coaches' feedback and changes in children's perceptions of their physical competence. *Journal of Educational Psychology, 77,* 174–186.

Horn, T.S. (1986). The self-fulfilling prophecy theory: When coaches' expectations become reality. In J.M. Williams (Ed.), *Applied sport psychology: Personal growth to peak performance* (pp. 59–73). Mountain View, CA: Mayfield.

Horn, T.S. (1987). The influence of teacher–coach behavior on the psychological development of children. In D. Gould & M.R. Weiss (Eds.), *Advances in pediatric sport science: Vol. 2. Behavioral issues* (pp. 121–142). Champaign, IL: Human Kinetics.

Horn, T.S., & Hasbrook, C.A. (1986). Information components influencing children's perceptions of their physical competence. In M.R. Weiss & D. Gould (Eds.), *Sport for children and youths* (pp. 81–88). Champaign, IL: Human Kinetics.

Horn, T.S., & Hasbrook, C.A. (1987). Psychological characteristics and the criteria children use for self-evaluation. *Journal of Sport Psychology, 9,* 208–221.

Horn, T.S., & Weiss, M.R. (1991). A developmental analysis of children's self-ability judgments in the physical domain. *Pediatric Exercise Science, 3,* 310–326.

Howard, B., & Gillis, J. (2007). *Participation in high school sports increases again.* Indianapolis: National Federation of State High School Associations.

Howell, M.L., Loiselle, D.S., & Lucas, W.G. (1966). *Strength of Edmonton schoolchildren.* Unpublished manuscript, University of Alberta Fitness Research Unit, Edmonton, Alberta.

Howell, M.L., & MacNab, R. (1966). *The physical work capacity of Canadian children.* Ottawa: Canadian Association for Health, Physical Education and Recreation.

Howze, E.H., DiGilio, D.A., Bennett, J.P., & Smith, M.L. (1986). Health education and physical fitness for older adults. In B. McPherson (Ed.), *Sport and aging* (pp. 153–156). Champaign, IL: Human Kinetics.

Hrdlicka, A. (1931). *Children who run on all fours: And other animal-like behaviors in the human child.* New York: Whittlesey House.

Hubley-Kozey, C.L., Wall, J.C., & Hogan, D.B. (1995). Effects of a general exercise program on passive hip, knee, and ankle range of motion of older women. *Topics in Geriatric Rehabilitation, 10,* 33–44.

Hughes, S., Gibbs, J., Dunlop, D., Edelman, P., Singer, R., & Chang, R.W. (1997). Predictors of decline in manual performance in older adults. *Journal of the American Geriatrics Society, 45,* 905–910.

Hupprich, F.L., & Sigerseth, P.O. (1950). The specificity of flexibility in girls. *Research Quarterly, 21,* 25–33.

Inbar, O., & Bar-Or, O. (1986). Anaerobic characteristics in male children and adolescents. *Medicine and Science in Sports and Exercise, 18,* 264–269.

Isaacs, L.D. (1980). Effects of ball size, ball color, and preferred color on catching by young children. *Perceptual and Motor Skills, 51,* 583–586.

Isaacs, L.D. (1983). Coincidence-anticipation in simple catching. *Journal of Human Movement Studies, 9,* 195–201.

Ivry, R.B. (1993). Cerebellar involvement in the explicit representation of temporal information. In P. Tallal, A.M. Galaburda, R.R. Llinas, & C. von Euler (Eds.), *Temporal information processing in the nervous system: Special reference to dyslexia and dysphasia* (pp. 214–230). New York: New York Academy of Sciences.

Ivry, R.B., & Keele, S.W. (1989). Timing functions of the cerebellum. *Journal of Cognitive Neuroscience, 1,* 136–152.

Jackson, T. (1993). *Activities that teach.* Cedar City, UT: Red Rock.

Jackson, T. (1995). *More activities that teach.* Cedar City, UT: Red Rock.

Jackson, T. (2000). *Still more activities that teach.* Cedar City, UT: Red Rock.

Jagacinski, R.J., Greenberg, N., & Liao, M. (1997). Tempo, rhythm, and aging in golf. *Journal of Motor Behavior, 29*(2), 159–173.

Jagacinski, R.J., Liao, M.J., & Fayyad, E.A. (1995). Generalized slowing in sinusoidal tracking in older adults. *Psychology and Aging, 10,* 8–19.

Janz, K.F., Burns, T.L., & Mahoney, L.T. (1995). Predictors of left ventricular mass and resting blood pressure in children: The Muscatine study. *Medicine and Science in Sports and Exercise, 27*(6), 818–825.

Jensen, J. (2005). The puzzles of motor development: How the study of developmental biomechanics contributes to the puzzle solutions. *Infant and Child Development, 14*(5), 501–511.

Jensen, J.L., Thelen, E., Ulrich, B.B., Schneider, K., & Zernicke, R.F. (1995). Adaptive dynamics of the leg movement patterns of human infants: III. Age-related differences in limb control. *Journal of Motor Behavior, 27,* 366–374.

Jesse, J.P. (1977). Olympic lifting movements endanger adolescents. *The Physician and Sportsmedicine, 5,* 60–67.

Johansson, G., von Hofsten, C., & Jansson, G. (1980). Event perception. *Annual Review of Psychology, 31,* 27–63.

Johnsson, L.G., & Hawkins, J.E., Jr. (1972). Sensory and neural degeneration with aging, as seen in microdissections of the inner ear. *Annals of Otology, Rhinology, and Laryngology, 81,* 179–193.

Jones, H.E. (1947). Sex differences in physical abilities. *Human Biology, 19,* 12–25.

Jouen, F. (1990). Early visual-vestibular interactions and postural development. In H. Bloch & B.I. Bertenthal (Eds.), *Sensory-motor organization and development in infancy and early childhood* (pp. 199–215). Dordrecht, the Netherlands: Kluwer.

Jouen, F., Lepecq, J.C., Gapenne, O., & Bertenthal, B.I. (2000). Optical flow sensitivity in neonates. *Infant Behavior and Development, 23*(3–4), 271–284.

Kalapotharakos, V.I., Michalopoulos, M., Strimpakos, N., Diamantopoulos, K., & Tokmakidis, S.P. (2006). Functional and neuromotor performance in older adults: Effect of 12 wks of aerobic exercise. *American Journal of Physical Medicine and Rehabilitation, 85,* 61–67.

Kallman, D.A., Plato, C.C., & Tobin, J.D. (1990). The role of muscle loss in the age-related decline of grip strength: Cross-sectional and longitudinal perspectives. *Journal of Gerontology: Medical Sciences, 45,* M82–M88.

Kane, E.W. (2007). "No way my boys are going to be like that!": Parents' responses to children's gender. *Gender Society, 20,* 149–176.

Karpovich, P.V. (1937). Textbook fallacies regarding the development of the child's heart. *Research Quarterly, 8,* 33–37. (Reprinted in 1991 in *Pediatric Exercise Science, 3,* 278–282.)

Kasch, F.W., Boyer, J.L., Van Camp, S.P., Verity, L.S., & Wallace, J.P. (1990). The effects of physical activity and inactivity on aerobic power in older men (a longitudinal study). *The Physician and Sportsmedicine, 18,* 73–83.

Kasch, F.W., & Wallace, J.P. (1976). Physiological variables during 10 years of endurance exercise. *Medicine and Science in Sports, 8,* 5–8.

Katch, V.L. (1983). Physical conditioning of children. *Journal of Adolescent Health Care, 3,* 241–246.

Kauffman, T.L. (1985). Strength-training effect in young and aged women. *Archives of Physical Medicine and Rehabilitation, 65,* 223–226.

Kauranen, K., & Vanharanta, H. (1996). Influences of aging, gender, and handedness on motor performance of upper and lower extremities. *Perceptual and Motor Skills, 82*, 515–525.

Kavanagh, T., & Shephard, R.J. (1977). The effect of continued training on the aging process. *Annals of the New York Academy of Sciences, 301*, 656–670.

Kawai, K., Savelsbergh, G.J.P., & Wimmers, R.H. (1999). Newborns and spontaneous arm movements are influenced by the environment. *Early Human Development, 54*(1), 15–27.

Keele, S.W., & Ivry, R. (1990). Does the cerebellum provide a common computation for diverse tasks? A timing hypothesis. *Annals of the New York Academy of Sciences, 608*, 179–211.

Kellman, P.J., & Arterberry, M.E. (1998). *The cradle of knowledge: Development of perception in infancy.* Cambridge, MA: MIT Press.

Kelly, J.R. (1974). Socialization toward leisure: A developmental approach. *Journal of Leisure Research, 6*, 181–193.

Kemper, H.C.G., Twisk, J.W.R., Koppes, L.L.J., van Mechelen, W., & Post, G.B. (2001). A 15-year physical activity pattern is positively related to aerobic fitness in young males and females (13–27 years). *European Journal of Applied Physiology, 84*, 395–402.

Kenshalo, D.R. (1977). Age changes in touch, vibration, temperature, kinesthesis, and pain sensitivity. In J.E. Birren & K.W. Schaie (Eds.), *Handbook of the psychology of aging* (pp. 562–579). New York: Van Nostrand Reinhold.

Kenyon, G.S., & McPherson, B.D. (1973). Becoming involved in physical activity and sport: A process of socialization. In G.L. Rarick (Ed.), *Physical activity: Human growth and development* (pp. 301–332). New York: Academic Press.

Kephart, N.C. (1964). Perceptual-motor aspects of learning disabilities. *Exceptional Children, 31*, 201–206.

Kephart, N.C. (1971). *The slow learner in the classroom* (2nd ed.). Columbus, OH: Merrill.

Kermoian, R., & Campos, J.J. (1988). Locomotor experience: A facilitator of spatial cognitive development. *Child Development, 59*, 908–917.

Khambalia, A.Z., Dickinson, S., Hardy, L.L., Gill, T., & Baur, L.A. (2012). A synthesis of existing systematic reviews and meta-analyses of school-based behavioural interventions for controlling and preventing obesity. *Obesity Reviews, 13*, 214–233.

Kidd, A.H., & Kidd, R.M. (1966). The development of auditory perception in children. In A.H. Kidd & J.L. Rivoire (Eds.), *Perceptual development in children* (pp. 113–142). New York: International Universities Press.

Kinsbourne, M. (1988). Sinistrality, brain organization and cognitive deficits. In D.L. Molfese & S.J. Segalowitz (Eds.), *Brain lateralization in children: Brain implications* (pp. 259–280). New York: Guilford.

Kinsbourne, M. (1997). The development of lateralization. In H.W. Reese & M.D. Franzen (Eds.), *Biological and neuropsychological mechanisms: Life span developmental psychology* (pp. 181–197). Hillsdale, NJ: Erlbaum.

Kinsella, K., & Velkoff, V.A. (2001). *An aging world: 2001* (U.S. Census Bureau, Series P95/01-1). Washington, DC: U.S. Government Printing Office.

Kisilevsky, B.S., Stach, D.M., & Muir, D.W. (1991). Fetal and infant response to tactile stimulation. In M.J.S. Weiss & P.R. Zelazo (Eds.), *Newborn attention: Biological constraints and the influence of experience* (pp. 63–98). Norwood, NJ: Ablex.

Klausner, S.C., & Schwartz, A.B. (1985). The aging heart. *Clinical Geriatric Medicine, 1*, 119–141.

Kline, D.W., Culham, J., Bartel, P., & Lynk, L. (1994). Aging and hyperacuity thresholds as a function of contrast and oscillation rate. *Canadian Psychology, 35*, 14.

Klint, K.A., & Weiss, M.R. (1986). Dropping in and dropping out: Participation motives of current and former youth gymnasts. *Canadian Journal of Applied Sport Sciences, 11*, 106–114.

Knudson, D. (2007). *Fundamentals of biomechanics.* New York: Springer-Verlag.

Kobayashi, K., Kitamura, K., Miura, M., Sodeyama, H., Murase, Y., Miyashita, M., et al. (1978). Aerobic power as related to body growth and training in Japanese boys: A longitudinal study. *Journal of Applied Physiology, 44*, 666–672.

Koch, G., & Rocker, L. (1977). Plasma volume and intravascular protein masses in trained boys and fit young men. *Journal of Applied Physiology, 43*, 1085–1088.

Koivula, N. (2000). Gender stereotyping in televised media sport coverage. *Sex Roles, 41*, 589–604.

Komi, P.V. (1984). Physiological and biomechanical correlates of muscle function: Effects of muscle structure and stretch-shortening cycle on force and speed. In R.L. Terjung (Ed.), *Exercise and sport science reviews* (Vol. 12, pp. 81–121). Lexington, MA: Collamore.

Konczak, J. (1990). Toward an ecological theory of motor development: The relevance of the Gibsonian approach to vision for motor development research. In J.E. Clark & J.H. Humphrey (Eds.), *Advances in motor development research* (Vol. 3, pp. 201–224). New York: AMS Press.

Korsten-Reck, U., Kaspar, T., Korsten, K., Kromeyer-Hauschild, K., Box, K., Berg, A., et al. (2007). Motor abilities and aerobic fitness of obese children. *International Journal of Sports Medicine, 28*, 762–767.

Kotz, C.M., Billington, C.J., & Levine, A.S. (1999). Obesity and aging. *Clinics in Geriatric Medicine, 15*(2), 391–412.

Kraemer, W.J., Fry, A.C., Frykman, P.N., Conroy, B., & Hoffman, J. (1989). Resistance training and youth. *Pediatric Exercise Science, 1*, 336–350.

Kraemer, W.J., Vescovi, J.D., Volek, J.S., Nindl, B.C., Newto, R.U., Patton, J.F., et al. (2004). Effects of concurrent resistance and aerobic training on load-bearing performance and the Army Physical Fitness Test. *Military Medicine, 169*, 994–999.

Krahenbuhl, G.S., & Martin, S.L. (1977). Adolescent body size and flexibility. *Research Quarterly, 48,* 797–799.

Krahenbuhl, G.S., Pangrazi, R.P., Petersen, G.W., Burkett, L.N., & Schneider, M.J. (1978). Field testing of cardio-respiratory fitness in primary school children. *Medicine and Science in Sports, 10,* 208–213.

Krahenbuhl, G.S., Skinner, J.S., & Kohrt, W.M. (1985). Developmental aspects of maximal aerobic power in children. *Medicine and Science in Sports and Exercise, 13,* 503–538.

Kuczaj, S.A., II, & Maratsos, M.P. (1975). On the acquisition of front, back, and side. *Child Development, 46,* 202–210.

Kuffler, S.W., Nicholls, J.G., & Martin, A.R. (1984). *From neuron to brain* (2nd ed.). Sunderland, MA: Sinauer.

Kugler, P.N., Kelso, J.A.S., & Turvey, M.T. (1980). On the concept of coordinative structures as dissipative structures: I. Theoretical lines of convergence. In G.E. Stelmach & J. Requin (Eds.), *Tutorials in motor behavior* (pp. 3–47). New York: North-Holland.

Kugler, P.N., Kelso, J.A.S., & Turvey, M.T. (1982). On the control and coordination of naturally developing systems. In J.A.S. Kelso & J.E. Clark (Eds.), *The development of movement control and coordination* (pp. 5–78). New York: Wiley.

Kuhn, D. (2000). Does memory development belong on an endangered topic list? *Child Development, 71,* 21–25.

Kuhtz-Buschbeck, J.P., Stolze, H., Boczek-Funcke, A., Joehnk, K., Heinrichs, H., & Illert, M. (1998). Kinematic analysis of prehension movements in children. *Behavioural Brain Research, 93,* 131–141.

Kuo, A.D., & Zajac, F.E. (1993). Human standing posture: Multi-joint movement strategies based on biomechanical constraints. *Progress in Brain Research, 97,* 349–358.

Laidlaw, R.W., & Hamilton, M.A. (1937). A study of thresholds in appreciation of passive movement among normal control subjects. *Bulletin of the Neurological Institute, 6,* 268–273.

Lan, C., Lai, J.S., Chen, S.U., & Wong, M.K. (1998). 12-month tai chi training in the elderly: Its effects on health fitness. *Medicine and Science in Sports and Exercise, 30*(3), 345–351.

Landahl, H.D., & Birren, J.E. (1959). Effects of age on the discrimination of lifted weights. *Journal of Gerontology, 14,* 48–55.

Langendorfer, S. (1980). *Longitudinal evidence for developmental changes in the preparatory phase of the overarm throw for force.* Paper presented at the annual convention of the American Alliance for Health, Physical Education, Recreation and Dance, Detroit.

Langendorfer, S. (1982). *Developmental relationships between throwing and striking: A prelongitudinal test of motor stage theory.* Unpublished doctoral dissertation, University of Wisconsin, Madison.

Langendorfer, S. (1987). Prelongitudinal screening of overarm striking development performed under two environmental conditions. In J.E. Clark & J.H. Humphrey (Eds.), *Advances in motor development research* (Vol. 1, pp. 17–47). New York: AMS Press.

Langendorfer, S. (1990). Motor-task goal as a constraint on developmental status. In J.E. Clark & J.H. Humphrey (Eds.), *Advances in motor development research* (Vol. 3, pp. 16–28). New York: AMS Press.

Langendorfer, S., & Roberton, M.A. (2002). Individual pathways in the development of forceful throwing. *Research Quarterly for Exercise and Sport, 73,* 245–256.

Langley, D.J., & Knight, S.M. (1996). Exploring practical knowledge: A case study of an experienced senior tennis performer. *Research Quarterly for Exercise and Sport, 67*(4), 433–447.

Larsson, L. (1982). Physical training effects on muscle morphology in sedentary males at different ages. *Medicine and Science in Sports and Exercise, 14,* 203–206.

Leavitt, J. (1979). Cognitive demands of skating and stickhandling in ice hockey. *Canadian Journal of Applied Sport Science, 4,* 46–55.

Lee, D.N., & Aronson, E. (1974). Visual proprioceptive control of standing in human infants. *Perception and Psychophysics, 15,* 529–532.

Lee, M., Liu, Y., & Newell, K.M. (2006). Longitudinal expressions of infant's prehension as a function of object properties. *Infant Behavior and Development, 29,* 481–493.

Lefebvre, C., & Reid, G. (1998). Prediction in ball catching by children with and without a developmental coordination disorder. *Adapted Physical Activity Quarterly, 15*(4), 299–315.

Leme, S., & Shambes, G. (1978). Immature throwing patterns in normal adult women. *Journal of Human Movement Studies, 4,* 85–93.

Lemon, P.W.R. (1989). Nutrition for muscular development of young athletes. In C.V. Gisolfi & D.R. Lamb (Eds.), *Perspectives in exercise science and sports medicine: Vol. 2. Youth, exercise, and sport* (pp. 369–400). Indianapolis: Benchmark Press.

Lengyel, M., & Gyarfas, I. (1979). The importance of echocardiography in the assessment of left ventricular hypertrophy in trained and untrained school children. *Acta Cardiologica, 34,* 63–69.

Lenoir, M., Musch, E., Janssens, M., Thiery, E., & Uyttenhove, J. (1999). Intercepting moving objects during self-motion. *Journal of Motor Behavior, 31*(1), 55–67.

Levy, G.D. (2000). Gender-typed and non-gender-typed category awareness in toddlers. *Sex Roles, 41,* 851–873.

Lew, A.R., & Butterworth, G. (1997). The development of hand–mouth coordination in 2- to 5-month-old infants: Similarities with reaching and grasping. *Infant Behavior and Development, 20*(1), 59–69.

Lewis, M. (1972). Culture and gender roles: There is no unisex in the nursery. *Psychology Today, 5,* 54–57.

Lewis, S.F., Taylor, W.F., Bastian, B.C., Graham, R.M., Pettinger, W.A., & Blomqvist, C.G. (1983). Haemodynamic responses to static and dynamic handgrip before and after autonomic blockage. *Clinical Science, 64*, 593–599.

Lewko, J.H., & Ewing, M.E. (1980). Sex differences and parental influences in sport involvement of children. *Journal of Sport Psychology, 2*, 62–68.

Lewko, J.H., & Greendorfer, S.L. (1988). Family influences in sport socialization of children and adolescents. In F.L. Smoll, R.A. Magill, & M.J. Ash (Eds.), *Children in sport* (3rd ed., pp. 287–300). Champaign, IL: Human Kinetics.

Lewkowicz, D.J., & Marcovitch, S. (2006). Perception of audiovisual rhythm and its invariance in 4- to 10-month-old infants. *Developmental Psychobiology, 48*, 288–300.

Lexell, J. (1995). Human aging, muscle mass, and fiber type composition. *Journal of Gerontology Series A: Biological and Medical Sciences, 50*, 11–16.

Lexell, J., Henriksson-Larsen, K., Wimblad, B., & Sjostrom, M. (1983). Distribution of different fiber types in human skeletal muscles: Effects of aging studies in whole muscle cross-sections. *Muscle and Nerve, 6*, 588–595.

Lexell, J., Taylor, C., & Sjostrom, M. (1988). What is the cause of ageing atrophy? Total number, size, and proportion of different fiber types studied in whole vastus lateralis muscle from 15- to 83-year-old men. *Journal of Neurological Sciences, 84*, 275–294.

Lindquist, C., Reynolds, K., & Goran, M. (1998). Sociocultural determinants of physical activity among children. *Preventive Medicine, 29*, 305–312.

Lipsitz, L.A. (1989). Altered blood pressure homeostasis in advanced age: Clinical and research implications. *Journal of Gerontology: Medical Sciences, 44*, M179–M183.

Liss, M.B. (1983). Learning gender-related skills through play. In M.B. Liss (Ed.), *Social and cognitive skills: Sex roles and children's play* (pp. 147–166). New York: Academic Press.

Lloyd, B., & Smith, C. (1985). The social representation of gender and young children's play. *British Journal of Developmental Psychology, 3*, 65–73.

Lockman, J.J. (1984). The development of detour ability during infancy. *Child Development, 55*, 482–491.

Lockman, J.J. (2000). A perception-action perspective on tool use development. *Child Development, 71*, 137–144.

Lockman, J.J., Ashmead, D.H., & Bushnell, E.W. (1984). The development of anticipatory hand orientation during infancy. *Journal of Experimental Child Psychology, 37*, 176–186.

Lohman, T.G., Going, S.B., Pamenter, R.W., Boyden, T., Houtkooper, L.B., Ritenbaugh, C., et al. (1992). Effects of weight training on lumbar spine and femur bone mineral density in premenopausal females. *Medicine and Science in Sports and Exercise, 24*, S188.

Lohman, T.G., Roche, A.F., & Martorell, R. (Eds.). (1988). *Anthropometric standardization reference manual*. Champaign, IL: Human Kinetics.

Long, A.B., & Looft, W.R. (1972). Development of directionality in children: Ages six through twelve. *Developmental Psychology, 6*, 375–380.

Lorber, J. (1994). Believing is seeing: Biology as ideology. *Gender and Society, 7*, 568–581.

Lowrey, G.H. (1986). *Growth and development of children* (8th ed.). Chicago: Year Book Medical.

Loy, J.W., McPherson, B.D., & Kenyon, G. (1978). *Sport and social systems*. Reading, MA: Addison-Wesley.

Lutman, M.E. (1991). Degradations in frequency and temporal resolution with age and their impact on speech identification. *Acta Oto-Laryngologica (Suppl.), 476*, 120–126.

Lynch, A., & Getchell, N. (2010). Using an ecological approach to understand perception, cognition, and action coupling in individuals with Autism Spectrum Disorder. *International Public Health Journal, 2*(1), 7–16.

Lyons, J., Fontaine, R., & Elliott, D. (1997). I lost it in the lights: The effects of predictable and variable intermittent vision on unimanual catching. *Journal of Motor Behavior, 29*(2), 113–118.

Madden, D.J., Whiting, W.L., & Huettel, S.A. (2005). Age-related changes in neural activity during visual perception and attention. In R. Cabeza, L. Nyberg, & D. Park (Eds.), *Cognitive neuroscience of aging: Linking cognitive and cerebral aging* (pp. 157–185). New York: Oxford University Press.

Maehr, M.L. (1984). Meaning and motivation. In R. Ames and C. Ames (Eds.), *Research on motivation in education* (Vol. 1, pp. 115–144). New York: Academic Press.

Mally, K.K., Battista, R.A., & Roberton, M.A. (2011). Distance as a control parameter for place kicking. *Journal of Human Sport and Exercise, 6*(1), 122–134.

Malina, R.M. (1978). Growth of muscle tissue and muscle mass. In F. Falkner & J.M. Tanner (Eds.), *Human growth: Vol. 2. Postnatal growth* (pp. 273–294). New York: Plenum Press.

Malina, R.M., Beunen, G.P., Claessens, A.L., Lefevre, J., Vanden Eynde, B., Renson, R., et al. (1995). Fatness and fitness of girls 7 to 17 years. *Obesity Research, 3*, 221–231.

Malina, R.M., & Bouchard, C. (1991). *Growth, maturation, and physical activity*. Champaign, IL: Human Kinetics.

Malina, R.M., Bouchard, C., & Bar-Or, O. (2004). *Growth, maturation, and physical activity* (2nd ed.). Champaign, IL: Human Kinetics.

Maloney, S.K., Fallon, B., & Wittenberg, C.K. (1984). *Aging and health promotion: Market research for public education, executive summary* (Contract no. 282-83-0105). Washington, DC: Public Health Service, Office of Disease Prevention and Health Promotion.

Marcon, R., & Freeman, G. (1999). Linking gender-related toy preferences to social structure: Changes in children's letters to Santa since 1978. *Journal of Psychological Practice, 2*, 1–10.

Marques-Bruna, P., & Grimshaw, P.N. (1997). 3-dimensional kinematics of overarm throwing action of children age 15 to 30 months. *Perceptual and Motor Skills, 84*, 1267–1283.

Marshall, W.A., & Tanner, J.M. (1969). Variations in pattern of pubertal changes in girls. *Archives of Disease in Childhood, 44,* 291–303.

Marshall, W.A., & Tanner, J.M. (1970). Variations in the pattern of pubertal changes in boys. *Archives of Disease in Childhood, 45,* 13–23.

Martorell, R., Malina, R.M., Castillo, R.O., Mendoza, F.S., & Pawson, I.G. (1988). Body proportions in three ethnic groups: Children and youth 2–17 years in NHANES II and HHANES. *Human Biology, 60,* 205–222.

McAuley, E. (1994). Physical activity and psychosocial outcomes. In C. Bouchard & R. Shephard (Eds.), *Physical activity, fitness, and health: International proceedings and consensus statement* (pp. 551–568). Champaign, IL: Human Kinetics.

McAuley, E., Kramer, A.F., & Colcombe, S.J. (2004). Cardiovascular fitness and neurocognitive function in older adults: A brief review. *Brain, Behavior, and Immunity, 18,* 214–220.

McBeath, M.K., Shaffer, D.M., & Kaiser, M.K. (1995). How baseball outfielders determine where to run to catch fly balls. *Science, 268,* 569–573.

McBride-Chang, C., & Jacklin, C. (1993). Early play arousal, sex-typed play and activity level as precursors to later rough-and-tumble play. *Early Education and Development, 4,* 99–108.

McCallister, S., Blinde, E., & Phillips, J. (2003). Prospects for change in a new millennium: Gender beliefs of young girls in sport and physical activity. *Women in Sports and Physical Activity Journal, 12,* 83–109.

McCarty, M.E., & Ashmead, D.H. (1999). Visual control of reaching and grasping in infants. *Developmental Psychology, 35,* 620–631.

McCaskill, C.L., & Wellman, B.L. (1938). A study of common motor achievements at the preschool ages. *Child Development, 9,* 141–150.

McClenaghan, B.A., & Gallahue, D.L. (1978). *Fundamental movement: A developmental and remedial approach.* Philadelphia: Saunders.

McComas, A.J. (1996). *Skeletal muscle: Form and function.* Champaign, IL: Human Kinetics.

McConnell, A., & Wade, G. (1990). Effects of lateral ball location, grade, and sex on catching. *Perceptual and Motor Skills, 70,* 59–66.

McDonnell, P.M. (1979). Patterns of eye-hand coordination in the first year of life. *Canadian Journal of Psychology, 33,* 253–267.

McGinnis, P. (2005). *Biomechanics of sport and exercise* (4th ed.). Champaign, IL: Human Kinetics.

McGraw, M. (1935). *Growth: A Study of Johnny and Jimmy.* New York: Appleton-Century-Crofts.

McGraw, M.B. (1943). *The neuromuscular maturation of the human infant.* New York: Columbia University Press.

McKenzie, B.E., & Bigelow, E. (1986). Detour behavior in young human infants. *British Journal of Developmental Psychology, 4,* 139–148.

McLeod, P., & Dienes, Z. (1993). Running to catch the ball. *Nature, 362,* 23.

McLeod, P., & Dienes, Z. (1996). Do fielders know where to go to catch the ball or only how to get there? *Journal of Experimental Psychology: Human Perception and Performance, 22*(3), 531–543.

McManus, A.M., Armstrong, N., & Williams, C.A. (1997). Effect of training on the aerobic power and anaerobic performance of prepubertal girls. *Acta Paediatrica, 86,* 456–459.

McMurdo, M.E., & Rennie, L. (1993). A controlled trial of exercise by residents of old people's homes. *Age and Ageing, 22,* 11–15.

McPherson, B.D. (1978). The child in competitive sport: Influence of the social milieu. In R.A. Magill, M.J. Ash, & F.L. Smoll (Eds.), *Children in sport: A contemporary anthology* (pp. 219–249). Champaign, IL: Human Kinetics.

Mayer, F., Scharhag-Rosenberger, F., Carlsohn, A., Cassel, M., Müller, S., & Scharhag, J. (2011). The intensity and effects of strength training in the elderly. *Deutsches Ärzteblatt International, 108,* 359-364.

McPherson, B.D. (1983). *Aging as a social process: An introduction to individual and population aging.* Toronto: Butterworths.

McPherson, B.D. (1986). Sport, health, well-being and aging: Some conceptual and methodological issues and questions for sport scientists. In B. McPherson (Ed.), *Sport and aging* (pp. 3–23). Champaign, IL: Human Kinetics.

McPherson, B.D., Marteniuk, R., Tihanyi, J., & Clark, W. (1980). The social system of age group swimmers: The perceptions of swimmers, parents, and coaches. *Canadian Journal of Applied Sciences, 5,* 143–145.

McPherson, S.L. (1999). Tactical differences in problem representations and solutions in collegiate varsity and beginner female tennis players. *Research Quarterly for Exercise and Sport, 70*(4), 369–384.

McPherson, S.L., & Kemodle, M. (2007). Mapping two new points on the tennis expertise continuum: Tactical skills of adult advanced beginners and entry-level professionals during competition. *Journal of Sports Science, 25,* 945–959.

Meltzoff, A.N., & Borton, R.W. (1979). Intermodal matching by human neonates. *Nature, 282,* 403–404.

Meredith, M.D., & Welk, G.J. (1999). *Fitnessgram test administration manual* (2nd ed.). Champaign, IL: Human Kinetics.

Mero, A., Kauhanen, H., Peltola, E., Vuorimaa, T., & Komi, P.V. (1990). Physiological performance capacity in different prepubescent athletic groups. *Journal of Sports Medicine and Physical Fitness, 30,* 57–66.

Messick, J.A. (1991). Prelongitudinal screening of hypothesized developmental sequences for the overhead tennis serve in experienced tennis players 9–19 years of age. *Research Quarterly for Exercise and Sport, 62,* 249–256.

Messner, M., Duncan, M., & Jensen, K. (1993). Separating the men from the girls: The gendered language of televised sports. *Gender and Society, 7,* 121–137.

Metcalfe, J.S., McDowell, K., Chang, T.Y., Chen, L.-C., Jeka, J.J., & Clark, J.E. (2005). Development of somatosensory-motor integration: An event-related analysis of infant posture in the first year of independent walking. *Developmental Psychobiology, 46,* 19–35.

Michaels, C.F., & Oudejans, R.R.D. (1992). The optics and actions of catching fly balls: Zeroing out optical acceleration. *Ecological Psychology, 4,* 199–222.

Michel, G.F. (1983). Development of hand-use preference during infancy. In G. Young, S. Segalowitz, C.M. Carter, & S.E. Trehub (Eds.), *Manual specialization and the developing brain* (pp. 33–70). New York: Academic Press.

Michel, G.F. (1988). A neuropsychological perspective on infant sensorimotor development. In C. Rovee-Collier & L.P. Lipsitt (Eds.), *Advances in infancy research* (Vol. 5, pp. 1–37). Norwood, NJ: Ablex.

Michel, G.F., & Goodwin, R.A. (1979). Intrauterine birth position predicts newborn supine head position preferences. *Infant Behavior and Development, 2,* 29–38.

Michel, G.F., & Harkins, D.A. (1986). Postural and lateral asymmetries in the ontogeny of handedness during infancy. *Developmental Psychobiology, 19,* 247–258.

Micheli, L.J. (1984). Sport injuries in the young athlete: Questions and controversies. In L.J. Micheli (Ed.), *Pediatric and adolescent sports medicine* (pp. 1–9). Boston: Little, Brown.

Michlovitz, S.L., Harris, B.A., & Watkins, M.P. (2004). Therapy interventions for improving joint range of motion: A systematic review. *Journal of Hand Therapy, 17,* 118–131.

Milani-Comparetti, A. (1981). The neurophysiologic and clinical implications of studies on fetal motor behavior. *Seminars in Perinatology, 5,* 183–189.

Milani-Comparetti, A., & Gidoni, E.A. (1967). Routine developmental examination in normal and retarded children. *Developmental Medicine and Child Neurology, 9,* 631–638.

Milne, C., Seefeldt, V., & Reuschlein, P. (1976). Relationship between grade, sex, race, and motor performance in young children. *Research Quarterly, 47,* 726–730.

Milner, A.D., & Goodale, M.A. (1995). *The visual brain in action.* New York: Oxford University Press.

Mirwald, R.L., & Bailey, D.A. (1986). *Maximal aerobic power: A longitudinal analysis.* London, Ontario: Sport Dynamics.

Mirwald, R.L., Bailey, D.A., Cameron, N., & Rasmussen, R.L. (1981). Longitudinal comparison of aerobic power in active and inactive boys aged 7.0 to 17.0 years. *Annals of Human Biology, 8,* 405–414.

Molen, H.H. (1973). *Problems on the evaluation of gait.* Unpublished doctoral dissertation, Free University, Amsterdam.

Mook-Kanamori, D.O., Durmus, B., Sovio, U., Hofman, A., Raat, H., Steegers, E.A.P., et al. (2011). Fetal and infant growth and the risk of obesity during early childhood: The Generation R study. *European Journal of Endocrinology, 165,* 623–630.

Moritani, T., & DeVries, H.A. (1980). Potential for gross muscle hypertrophy in older men. *Journal of Gerontology, 35,* 672–682.

Morris, G.S.D. (1976). Effects ball and background color have upon the catching performance of elementary school children. *Research Quarterly, 47,* 409–416.

Morrongiello, B.A. (1984). Auditory temporal pattern perception in 6- and 12-month-old infants. *Developmental Psychology, 20,* 441–448.

Morrongiello, B.A. (1986). Infants' perception of multiple-group auditory patterns. *Infant Behavior and Development, 9,* 307–320.

Morrongiello, B.A. (1988a). The development of auditory pattern perception skills. In C. Rovee-Collier & L.P. Lipsitt (Eds.), *Advances in infancy research* (Vol. 6, pp. 135–172). Norwood, NJ: Ablex.

Morrongiello, B.A. (1988b). Infants' localization of sounds along the horizontal axis: Estimates of minimum audible angle. *Developmental Psychology, 24*(1), 8–13.

Morrongiello, B.A., & Clifton, R.K. (1984). Effects of sound frequency on behavioral and cardiac orienting in newborn and five-month-old infants. *Journal of Experimental Child Psychology, 38,* 429–446.

Morrongiello, B.A., Fenwick, K.D., Hillier, L., & Chance, G. (1994). Sound localization in newborn human infants. *Developmental Psychology, 27*(8), 519–538.

Morrongiello, B.A., Trehub, S.E., Thorpe, L.A., & Capodilupo, S. (1985). Children's perceptions of melodies: The role of contour, frequency, and rate of presentation. *Journal of Experimental Child Psychology, 40,* 279–292.

Morrow, D., & Leirer, V. (1997). Aging, pilot performance, and expertise. In A.D. Fisk & W.A. Rogers (Eds.), *Handbook of human factors and the older adult* (pp. 199–230). San Diego: Academic Press.

Munns, K. (1981). Effects of exercise on the range of joint motion in elderly subjects. In E.L. Smith & R.C. Serfass (Eds.), *Exercise and aging: The scientific basis* (pp. 149–166). Hillside, NJ: Enslow.

Murphy, G.L., & Wright, J.C. (1984). Changes in conceptual structure with expertise: Differences between real-world experts and novices. *Journal of Experimental Psychology: Learning, Memory, and Cognition, 10,* 144–155.

Murray, M.P., Drought, A.B., & Kory, R.C. (1964). Walking patterns of normal men. *Journal of Bone and Joint Surgery, 46A,* 335–360.

Murray, M.P., Gardner, G.M., Mollinger, L.A., & Sepic, S.B. (1980). Strength of isometric and isokinetic contractions. *Physical Therapy, 60,* 412–419.

Murray, M.P., Kory, R.C., Clarkson, B.H., & Sepic, S.B. (1966). Comparison of free and fast speed walking patterns of normal men. *American Journal of Physical Medicine, 45*, 8–24.

Murray, M.P., Kory, R.C., & Sepic, S.B. (1970). Walking patterns of normal women. *Archives of Physical Medicine and Rehabilitation, 51*, 637–650.

Nanez, J., & Yonas, A. (1994). Effects of luminance and texture motion on infant defensive reactions to optical collision. *Infant Behavior and Development, 17*, 165–174.

Napier, J. (1956). The prehensile movements of the human hand. *Journal of Bone and Joint Surgery, 38B*, 902–913.

Naus, M., & Shillman, R. (1976). Why a Y is not a V: A new look at the distinctive features of letters. *Journal of Experimental Psychology: Human Perception and Performance, 2*, 394–400.

Nelson, C.J. (1981). *Locomotor patterns of women over 57.* Unpublished master's thesis, Washington State University, Pullman.

Nevett, M.E., & French, K.E. (1997). The development of sport-specific planning, rehearsal, and updating of plans during defensive youth baseball game performance. *Research Quarterly for Exercise and Sport, 68*(3), 203–214.

Newell, K.M. (1986). Constraints on the development of coordination. In M.G. Wade & H.T.A. Whiting (Eds.), *Motor development in children: Aspects of coordination and control* (pp. 341–361). Amsterdam: Nijhoff.

Newell, K., & Jordan, K.M. (2007). Task constraints and movement organization: A common language. In W. Davis & B.D. Broadhead (Eds.), Ecological task analysis and movement (pp. 5-23). Champaign, IL: Human Kinetics.

Newell, K.M., Scully, D.M., McDonald, P.V., & Baillargeon, R. (1989). Task constraints and infant grip configurations. *Developmental Psychobiology, 22*, 817–832.

Newell, K.M., Scully, D.M., Tenenbaum, F., & Hardiman, S. (1989). Body scale and the development of prehension. *Developmental Psychobiology, 22*, 11–13.

Nielsen, B., Nielsen, K., Hansen, M.B., & Asmussen, E. (1980). Training of "functional muscle strength" in girls 7–19 years old. In K. Berg & B.O. Eriksson (Eds.), *Children and exercise IX* (pp. 69–78). Baltimore: University Park Press.

Nielsen, J.M., & McPherson, S.L. (2001). Response selection and execution skills of professionals and novices during singles tennis competition. *Perceptual and Motor Skills, 93*, 541–555.

Nilsson, L. (1990). *A child is born.* New York: Delacorte Press.

Nordlund, B. (1964). Directional audiometry. *Acta Oto-Laryngologica, 57*, 1–18.

Norris, A.H., Shock, N.W., Landowne, M., & Falzone, J.A. (1956). Pulmonary function studies: Age differences in lung volume and bellows function. *Journal of Gerontology, 11*, 379–387.

Northman, J.E., & Black, K.N. (1976). An examination of errors in children's visual and haptic-tactual memory for random forms. *Journal of Genetic Psychology, 129*, 161–165.

Nougier, V., Bard, C., Fleury, M., & Teasdale, N. (1998). Contribution of central and peripheral vision to the regulation of stance: Developmental aspects. *Journal of Experimental Child Psychology, 68*, 202–215.

Nyhan, N.L. (1990). Structural abnormalities. *Clinical Symposia, 42*(2), 1–32.

Oettingen, G. (1985). The influence of the kindergarten teacher on sex differences in behavior. *International Journal of Behavioral Development, 8*, 3–13.

Olds, T., & Dollman, J. (2004). Are changes in distance-run performance of Australian children between 1985 and 1997 explained by changes in fatness? *Pediatric Exercise Science, 16*, 201–209.

Olson, P.L., & Sivak, M. (1986). Perception-response time to unexpected roadway hazards. *Human Factors, 28*, 91–96.

Orlick, T.D. (1973, January/February). Children's sport: A revolution is coming. *Canadian Association for Health, Physical Education, and Recreation Journal*, 12–14.

Orlick, T.D. (1974, November/December). The athletic drop-out: A high price for inefficiency. *Canadian Association for Health, Physical Education, and Recreation Journal*, 21–27.

Oudejans, R.R.D., Michaels, C.F., Bakker, F.C., & Dolne, M.A. (1996). The relevance of action in perceiving affordances: Perception of catchableness of fly balls. *Journal of Experimental Psychology, 22*(4), 879–891.

Paillard, T., Lafont, C., Costes-Salon, M.C., Riviere, D., & Dupui, P. (2004). Effects of brisk walking on static and dynamic balance, locomotion, body composition, and aerobic capacity in ageing healthy active men. *International Journal of Sports Medicine, 25*, 539–546.

Pargman, D. (1997). *Understanding sport behavior.* Englewood Cliffs, NJ: Prentice Hall.

Parish, L.E., & Rudisill, M.E. (2006). HAPPE: Promoting physical play among toddlers. *Young Children, 61*(3), 32.

Parish, L.E., Rudisill, M.E., & St. Onge, P.M. (2007). Mastery motivational climate: Influence on physical play heart rate and intensity in African American toddlers. *Research Quarterly for Exercise and Sport, 78*, 171–178.

Parizkova, J. (1963). Impact of age, diet, and exercise on man's body composition. *Annals of the New York Academy of Sciences, 110*, 661–674.

Parizkova, J. (1968a). Longitudinal study of the development of body composition and body build in boys of various physical activity. *Human Biology, 40*, 212–225.

Parizkova, J. (1968b). Body composition and physical fitness. *Current Anthropology, 9*, 273–287.

Parizkova, J. (1972). Somatic development and body composition changes in adolescent boys differing in physical activity and fitness: A longitudinal study. *Anthropologie, 10*, 3–36.

Parizkova, J. (1973). Body composition and exercise during growth and development. In G.L. Rarick (Ed.), *Physical activity: Human growth and development* (pp. 97–124). New York: Academic Press.

Parizkova, J. (1977). *Body fat and physical fitness*. The Hague, the Netherlands: Nijhoff.

Parker, A.W., & James, B. (1985). Age changes in the flexibility of Down syndrome children. *Journal of Mental Deficiency Research, 29*, 207–218.

Parker, D.F., Round, J.M., Sacco, P., & Jones, D.A. (1990). A cross-sectional survey of upper and lower limb strength in boys and girls during childhood and adolescence. *Annals of Human Biology, 17*, 199–211.

Pate, R.R., & Shephard, R.J. (1989). Characteristics of physical fitness in youth. In C.V. Gisolfi & D.R. Lamb (Eds.), *Youth, exercise, and sport* (Vol. 2, pp. 1–46). Indianapolis: Benchmark Press.

Pate, R.R., & Ward, D.S. (1990). Endurance exercise trainability in children and youth. In W.A. Grana, J.A. Lombardo, B.J. Sharkey, & J.A. Stone (Eds.), *Advances in sports medicine and fitness* (Vol. 3, pp. 37–55). Chicago: Year Book Medical.

Patrick, H., Ryan, A.M., Alfeld-Liro, C., Fredricks, J., Hruda, L., & Eccles, J. (1999). Adolescents' commitment to developing talent: The role of peers in continuing motivation for sports and the arts. *Journal of Youth and Adolescence, 28*, 741–763.

Patriksson, G. (1981). Socialization to sports involvement. *Scandinavian Journal of Sports Sciences, 3*, 27–32.

Payne, V.G. (1982). Simultaneous investigation of effects of distance of projection and object size on object reception by children in grade 1. *Perceptual and Motor Skills, 54*, 1183–1187.

Payne, V.G., & Koslow, R. (1981). Effects of varying ball diameters on catching ability of young children. *Perceptual and Motor Skills, 53*, 739–744.

Payne, V.G., & Morrow, J.R. (1993). Exercise and VO$_2$max in children: A meta-analysis. *Research Quarterly for Exercise and Sport, 64*, 305–313.

Peiper, A. (1963). *Cerebral function in infancy and childhood*. New York: Consultants Bureau.

Pennell, G. (1999). Doing gender with Santa: Gender-typing in children's toy preferences. *Dissertation Abstracts International, 59-8(B)*, 4541.

Perlmutter, M., & Nyquist, L. (1990). Relationships between self-reported physical and mental health and intelligence performance across adulthood. *Journal of Gerontology: Psychological Sciences, 45*, P145–P155.

Perrin, P.P., Jeandel, C., Perrin, C.A., & Bene, M.C. (1997). Influence of visual control, conduction, and central integration on static and dynamic balance in healthy older adults. *Gerontology, 43*, 223–231.

Pew, R.W., & Rupp, G. (1971). Two quantitative measures of skill development. *Journal of Experimental Psychology, 90*, 1–7.

Pfeiffer, R., & Francis, R.S. (1986). Effects of strength training on muscle development in prepubescent, pubescent, and postpubescent males. *The Physician and Sportsmedicine, 14*, 134–143.

Phillips, M., Bookwalter, C., Denman, C., McAuley, J., Sherwin, H., Summers, D., et al. (1955). Analysis of results from the Kraus-Weber test of minimum muscular fitness in children. *Research Quarterly, 26*, 314–323.

Piaget, J. (1952). *The origins of intelligence in children*. New York: International Universities Press.

Pick, A.D. (Ed.). (1979). *Perception and its development: A tribute to Eleanor J. Gibson*. Hillsdale, NJ: Erlbaum.

Pick, H.L. (1989). Motor development: The control of action. *Developmental Psychology, 25*, 867–870.

Piek, J.P., & Gasson, N. (1999). Spontaneous kicking in full term and preterm infants: Are there leg asymmetries? *Human Movement Science, 18*, 377–395.

Piek, J.P., Gasson, N., Barrett, N., & Case, I. (2002). Limb and gender differences in the development of coordination in early infancy. *Human Movement Science, 21*, 621–639.

Piéraut-Le Bonniec, G. (1985). Hand-eye coordination and infants' construction of convexity and concavity. *British Journal of Developmental Psychology, 3*, 273–280.

Pollock, M.L. (1974). Physiological characteristics of older champion track athletes. *Research Quarterly, 45*, 363–373.

Pomerance, A. (1965). Pathology of the heart with and without failure in the aged. *British Heart Journal, 27*, 697–710.

Ponds, R.W., Brouwer, W.H., & Van Wolffelaar, P.C. (1988). Age differences in divided attention in a simulated driving task. *Journal of Gerontology: Psychological Sciences, 43*, P151–P156.

Pope, M.J. (1984). *Visual proprioception in infant postural development*. Unpublished doctoral dissertation, University of Southampton, Highfield, Southampton, UK.

Posner, J.D., Gorman, K.M., Klein, H.S., & Woldow, A. (1986). Exercise capacity in the elderly. *American Journal of Cardiology, 57*, 52C–58C.

Power, T.G. (1985). Mother- and father-infant play: A developmental analysis. *Child Development, 56*, 1514–1524.

Power, T.G., & Parke, R.D. (1983). Patterns of mother and father play with their 8-month-old infant: A multiple analyses approach. *Infant Behavior and Development, 6*, 453–459.

Power, T.G., & Parke, R.D. (1986). Patterns of early socialization: Mother- and father-infant interactions in the home. *International Journal of Behavioral Development, 9*, 331–341.

Prader, A., Tanner, J.M., & von Harnack, G.A. (1963). Catch-up growth following illness or starvation: An example of developmental canalization in man. *Journal of Pediatrics, 62*, 646–659.

Prohaska, T.R., Leventhal, E.A., Leventhal, H., & Keller, M.L. (1985). Health practices and illness cognition in young, middle aged, and elderly adults. *Journal of Gerontology, 40*, 569–578.

Pruitt, L.A., Jackson, R.D., Bartels, R.L., & Lehnhard, H.J. (1992). Weight-training effects on bone mineral density in early postmenopausal women. *Journal of Bone and Mineral Research, 7,* 179–185.

Pryde, K.M., Roy, E.A., & Campbell, K. (1998). Prehension in children and adults: The effects of size. *Human Movement Science, 17*(6), 743–752.

Purhonen, J., Kilpelainen-Lees, R., Valkonen-Korhonen, M., Karhu, J., & Lehtonen, J. (2005). Fourth-month-old infants process own mother's voice faster than unfamiliar voices: Electrical signs of sensitization in infant brain. *Cognitive Brain Research, 24,* 627–633.

Raag, T. (1999). Influences of social expectations of gender, gender stereotypes, and situational constraints on children's toy choices. *Sex Roles, 41*(11/12), 809–831.

Raag, T., & Rackliff, C.L. (1998). Preschoolers' awareness of social expectations of gender: Relationships to toy choices. *Sex Roles, 38*(9/10), 685–700.

Rabbitt, P. (1965). An age decrement in the ability to ignore irrelevant information. *Journal of Gerontology, 20,* 233–238.

Ramsay, D.S. (1980). Onset of unimanual handedness in infants. *Infant Behavior and Development, 3,* 377–386.

Ramsay, D.S. (1985). Infants' block banging at midline: Evidence for Gesell's principal of "reciprocal interweaving" in development. *British Journal of Developmental Psychology, 3,* 335–343.

Ramsay, D.S., Campos, J.J., & Fenson, L. (1979). Onset of bimanual handedness in infants. *Infant Behavior and Development, 2,* 69–76.

Ramsay, J.A., Blimkie, C.J.R., Smith, K., Garner, S., MacDougall, J.D., & Sale, D.G. (1990). Strength training effects in prepubescent boys. *Medicine and Science in Sports and Exercise, 22,* 605–614.

Rarick, G.L., & Smoll, F.L. (1967). Stability of growth in strength and motor performance from childhood to adolescence. *Human Biology, 39,* 295–306.

Rasmussen, R.L., Faulkner, R.A., Mirwald, R.L., & Bailey, D.A. (1990). A longitudinal analysis of structure/function related variables in 10–16 year old boys. In G. Beunen, J. Ghesquiere, T. Reybrouck, & A.L. Claessens (Eds.), *Children and exercise* (pp. 27–33). Stuttgart: Verlag.

Ratey, J.J. (2001). *A user's guide to the brain: Perception, attention, and the four theaters of the brain.* New York: Vintage Books.

Ratey, J.J. (2008). *Spark.* New York: Little, Brown.

Reaburn, P.R.J., & Mackinnon, L.T. (1990). Blood lactate response in older swimmers during active and passive recovery following maximal sprint swimming. *European Journal of Applied Physiology, 61,* 246–250.

Reaven, P.D., Barrett-Connor, E., & Edelstein, S. (1991). Relation between leisure-time physical activity and blood pressure in older women. *Circulation, 83,* 559–565.

Reith, K.M. (2004). *Playing fair: A Women's Sports Foundation guide to Title IX in high school and college sports.* East Meadow, NY: Women's Sports Foundation.

Rians, C.B., Weltman, A., Cahill, B.R., Janney, C.A., Tippett, S.R., & Katch, F.I. (1987). Strength training for prepubescent males: Is it safe? *American Journal of Sports Medicine, 15,* 483–489.

Rikli, R.E., & Busch, S. (1986). Motor performance of women as a function of age and physical activity level. *Journal of Gerontology, 41,* 645–649.

Rikli, R.E., & Edwards, D.J. (1991). Effects of a 3 year exercise program on motor function and cognitive speed in older women. *Research Quarterly for Exercise and Sport, 62*(1), 61–67.

Rikli, R.E., & Jones, C.J. (1999). Functional fitness normative scores for community-residing older adults, ages 60–94. *Journal of Aging and Physical Activity, 7,* 162–181.

Ring-Dimitriou, S., von Duvillard, S.P., Paulweber, B., Stadlmann, M., Lemura, L.M., Peak, K., et al. (2007). Nine months aerobic fitness induced changes on blood lipids and lipoproteins in untrained subjects versus controls. *European Journal of Applied Physiology, 99,* 291–299.

Risser, W.L., & Preston, D. (1989). Incidence and causes of musculoskeletal injuries in adolescents training with weights [Abstract]. *Pediatric Exercise Science, 1,* 84.

Rivilis, I., Hay, J., Cairney, J., Klentrou, P., Liu, J., & Faught, B.E. (2011). Physical activity and fitness in children with developmental coordination disorder: A systematic review. *Research in Developmental Disabilities, 32,* 894–910.

Roach, K.E., & Miles, T.P. (1991). Normal hip and knee active range of motion: The relationship to age. *Physical Therapy, 70,* 656–665.

Roberton, M.A. (1977). Stability of stage categorizations across trials: Implications for the "stage theory" of overarm throw development. *Journal of Human Movement Studies, 3,* 49–59.

Roberton, M.A. (1978a). Longitudinal evidence for developmental stages in the forceful overarm throw. *Journal of Human Movement Studies, 4,* 167–175.

Roberton, M.A. (1978b). Stages in motor development. In M.V. Ridenour (Ed.), *Motor development: Issues and applications* (pp. 63–81). Princeton, NJ: Princeton Book.

Roberton, M.A. (1984). Changing motor patterns during childhood. In J.R. Thomas (Ed.), *Motor development during childhood and adolescence* (pp. 48–90). Minneapolis: Burgess.

Roberton, M.A. (1988). The weaver's loom: A developmental metaphor. In J.E. Clark & J.H. Humphrey (Eds.), *Advances in motor development research* (Vol. 2, pp. 129–141). New York: AMS Press.

Roberton, M.A. (1989). Motor development: Recognizing our roots, charting our future. *Quest, 41,* 213–223.

Roberton, M.A., & DiRocco, P. (1981). Validating a motor skill sequence for mentally retarded children. *American Corrective Therapy Journal, 35,* 148–154.

Roberton, M.A., & Halverson, L.E. (1984). *Developing children: Their changing movement.* Philadelphia: Lea & Febiger.

Roberton, M.A., & Halverson, L.E. (1988). The development of locomotor coordination: Longitudinal change and invariance. *Journal of Motor Behavior, 20,* 197–241.

Roberton, M.A., & Konczak, J. (2001). Predicting children's overarm throw ball velocities from their developmental levels in throwing. *Research Quarterly for Exercise and Sport, 72,* 91–103.

Roberton, M.A., & Langendorfer, S. (1980). Testing motor development sequences across 9–14 years. In D. Nadeau, W. Halliwell, K. Newell, & G. Roberts (Eds.), *Psychology of motor behavior and sport—1979* (pp. 269–279). Champaign, IL: Human Kinetics.

Roberts, S.B., Savage, J., Coward, W.A., Chew, B., & Lucas, A. (1988). Energy expenditure and intake in infants born to lean and overweight mothers. *New England Journal of Medicine, 318,* 461–466.

Rockwell, J.C., Sorensen, A.M., Baker, S., Leahey, D., Stock, J.L., Michaels, J., et al. (1990). Weight training decreases vertebral bone density in premenopausal women: A prospective study. *Journal of Clinical Endocrinology and Metabolism, 71,* 988–992.

Rosenbaum, M., & Leibel, R.L. (1998). The physiology of body weight regulation: Relevance to the etiology of obesity in children. *Pediatrics, 101*(3S), 525–539.

Rosenhall, V., & Rubin, W. (1975). Degenerative changes in the human sensory epithelia. *Acta Oto-Laryngologica, 79,* 67–81.

Ross, J.G., Pate, R.R., Delpy, L.A., Gold, R.S., & Svilar, M. (1987). New health-related fitness norms. *Journal of Physical Education, Recreation and Dance, 58,* 66–70.

Rotstein, A., Dotan, R., Bar-Or, O., & Tenenbaum, G. (1986). Effect of training on anaerobic threshold, maximal power, and anaerobic performance of preadolescent boys. *International Journal of Sports Medicine, 7,* 281–286.

Rowland, T.W. (1989a). Oxygen uptake and endurance fitness in children: A developmental perspective. *Pediatric Exercise Science, 1,* 313–328.

Rowland, T.W. (1989b). On trainability and heart rates. *Pediatric Exercise Science, 1,* 187–188.

Rowland, T.W. (1996). *Developmental exercise physiology.* Champaign, IL: Human Kinetics.

Rowland, T.W. (2012). Inferior exercise economy in children: Perpetuating a myth? *Pediatric Exercise Science, 24,* 501–506.

Roy, E.A., Winchester, T., Weir, P., & Black, S. (1993). Age differences in the control of visually aimed movements. *Journal of Human Movement Studies, 24,* 71–81.

Royce, W.S., Gebelt, J.L., & Duff, R.W. (2003). Female athletes: Being both athletic and feminine. *Athletic Insight, 5,* 1–15.

Rudel, R., & Teuber, H. (1971). Pattern recognition within and across sensory modalities in normal and brain injured children. *Neuropsychologia, 9,* 389–400.

Rudloff, L.M., & Feldmann, E. (1999). Childhood obesity: Addressing the issue. *Journal of the American Osteopathic Association, 99*(4), S1–S6.

Rudman, W. (1986). Life course socioeconomic transitions and sport involvement: A theory of restricted opportunity. In B. McPherson (Ed.), *Sport and aging* (pp. 25–35). Champaign, IL: Human Kinetics.

Ruff, H.A. (1984). Infants' manipulative exploration of objects: Effects of age and objects' characteristics. *Developmental Psychology, 29,* 9–20.

Rutenfranz, J. (1986). Longitudinal approach to assessing maximal aerobic power during growth: The European experience. *Medicine and Science in Sports and Exercise, 15,* 486–490.

Saavedra, J.M., Escalante, Y., & Garcia-Hermoso, A. (2011). Improvement of aerobic fitness in obese children: A metal-analysis. *International Journal of Pediatric Obesity, 6,* 169–177.

Sadres, E., Eliakim, A., Constantini, N., Lidor, R., & Falk, B. (2001). The effect of long-term resistance training on anthropometric measures, muscle strength, and self-concept in pre-pubertal boys. *Pediatric Exercise Science, 13,* 357–372.

Sady, S.P. (1986). Cardiorespiratory exercise in children. In F. Katch & P.F. Freedson (Eds.), *Clinics in sports medicine* (pp. 493–513). Philadelphia: Saunders.

Safar, M. (1990). Aging and its effects on the cardiovascular system. *Drugs, 39*(Suppl. 1), 1–18.

Sale, D.G. (1989). Strength training in children. In G.V. Gisolfi & D.R. Lamb (Eds.), *Perspectives in exercise science and sports medicine: Vol. 2. Youth, exercise and sport* (pp. 165–222). Indianapolis: Benchmark Press.

Salkind, N.J. (1981). *Theories of human development.* New York: Van Nostrand.

Salthouse, T.A. (1984). Effects of age and skill in typing. *Journal of Experimental Psychology, 113,* 343–371.

Saltin, B., & Grimby, G. (1968). Physiological analysis of middle-aged and old former athletes: Comparison with still active athletes of the same ages. *Circulation, 38,* 1104–1115.

Santos, A.D., Marinho, D.A., Costa, A.M., Izquierdo, M., & Marques, M.C. (2012). The effects of concurrent resistance and endurance training following a detraining period in elementary school students. *Journal of Strength & Conditioning Research, 26,* 1708-1716.

Sapp, M., & Haubenstricker, J. (1978, April). *Motivation for joining and reasons for not continuing in youth sport programs in Michigan.* Paper presented at the annual convention of the American Alliance for Health, Physical Education, Recreation and Dance, Kansas City, MO.

Sarsan, A., Ardic, F., Ozgen, M., Topuz, O., & Sermez, Y. (2006). The effects of aerobic and resistance exercises in obese women. *Clinical Rehabilitation, 20,* 773–782.

Sasaki, J., Shindo, M., Tanaka, H., Ando, M., & Arakawa, K. (1987). A long-term aerobic exercise program decreases the obesity index and increases the high density lipoprotein cholesterol concentration in obese children. *International Journal of Obesity, 11,* 339–345.

Scanlan, T.K. (1988). Social evaluation and the competition process: A developmental perspective. In F.L. Smoll, R.A. Magill, & M.J. Ash (Eds.), *Children in sport* (3rd ed., pp. 135–148). Champaign, IL: Human Kinetics.

Scanlan, T.K., & Lewthwaite, R. (1986). Social psychological aspects of competition for male youth sport participants: IV. Predictors of enjoyment. *Journal of Sport Psychology, 8*, 25–35.

Scanlan, T.K., Stein, G.L., & Ravizza, K. (1988). An in-depth study of former elite figure skaters: II. Sources of enjoyment. *Journal of Sport and Exercise Psychology, 11*, 65–83.

Schellenberger, B. (1981). The significance of social relations in sport activity. *International Review of Sport Sociology, 16*, 69–77.

Schmidt, R., & Lee, T. (2014). *Motor control and learning: A behavioral emphasis* (5th ed.). Champaign, IL: Human Kinetics.

Schmidt, R., & Wrisberg, C. (2014). *Motor learning and performance (5th ed.)*. Champaign, IL: Human Kinetics.

Schmuckler, M.A. (1997). Children's postural sway in response to low- and high-frequency visual information for oscillation. *Journal of Experimental Psychology: Human Perception and Performance, 23*(2), 528–545.

Schultz, S.J., Houglum, P.A., & Perrin, D.H. (2000). *Assessment of athletic injuries (p. 347)*. Champaign, IL: Human Kinetics.

Schwanda, N.A. (1978). *A biomechanical study of the walking gait of active and inactive middle-age and elderly men.* Unpublished doctoral dissertation, Springfield College, Springfield, MA.

Schwartz, R.S., Shuman, W.P., Larson, V., Cain, K.C., Fellingham, G.W., Beard, J.C., et al. (1991). The effect of intensive endurance exercise training on body fat distribution in young and older men. *Metabolism, 40*, 545–551.

Seefeldt, V., Reuschlein, S., & Vogel, P. (1972). *Sequencing motor skills within the physical education curriculum.* Paper presented at the annual convention of the American Association for Health, Physical Education, and Recreation, Houston.

Seils, L.G. (1951). The relationship between measures of physical growth and gross motor performance of primary grade school children. *Research Quarterly, 22*, 244–260.

Servedio, F.J., Barels, R.L., Hamlin, R.L., Teske, D., Shaffer, T., & Servedio, A. (1985). The effects of weight training using Olympic style lifts on various physiological variables in prepubescent boys [Abstract]. *Medicine and Science in Sports and Exercise, 17*, 288.

Sewall, L., & Micheli, L.J. (1986). Strength training for children. *Journal of Pediatric Orthopedics, 6*, 143–146.

Shaffer, D.M. (1999). Navigating in baseball: A spatial optical tracking strategy and associated naïve physical beliefs. *Dissertation Abstracts International: Section B. The Sciences and Engineering, 59*, 4504.

Shaffer, D.M., & McBeath, M.K. (2002). Baseball outfielders maintain a linear optical trajectory when tracking uncatchable fly balls. *Journal of Experimental Psychology: Human Perception and Performance, 28*, 335–348.

Shakib, S., & Dunbar, M.D. (2004). How high school athletes talk about maternal and paternal sporting experiences. *International Review for the Sociology of Sport, 39*(3), 275–299.

Sheldon, J.H. (1963). The effect of age on the control of sway. *Gerontologia Clinica, 5*, 129–138.

Shephard, R.J. (1978a). *IBP Human Adaptability Project synthesis: Vol. 4. Human physiological work capacity.* New York: Cambridge University Press.

Shephard, R.J. (1978b). *Physical activity and aging.* Chicago: Year Book Medical.

Shephard, R.J. (1981). Cardiovascular limitations in the aged. In E.L. Smith & R.C. Serfass (Eds.), *Exercise and aging: The scientific basis* (pp. 19–29). Hillsdale, NJ: Enslow.

Shephard, R.J. (1982). *Physical activity and growth.* Chicago: Year Book Medical.

Shephard, R.J. (1987). *Physical activity and aging* (2nd ed.). London: Croom Helm.

Shephard, R.J. (1992). Effectiveness of training programs for prepubescent children. *Sports Medicine, 13*, 194–213.

Shephard, R.J. (1993). Aging, respiratory function, and exercise. *Journal of Aging and Physical Activity, 1*, 59–83.

Shirley, M.M. (1931). *The first two years: A study of twenty five babies.* Minneapolis: University of Minnesota Press.

Shirley, M.M. (1963). The motor sequence. In D. Wayne (Ed.), *Readings in child psychology.* Englewood Cliffs, NJ: Prentice Hall.

Shock, N.W., & Norris, A.H. (1970). Neuromuscular coordination as a factor in age changes in muscular exercise. In D. Brunner & E. Jokl (Eds.), *Physical activity and aging* (pp. 92–99). Baltimore: University Park Press.

Shuleva, K.M., Hunter, G.R., Hester, D.J., & Dunaway, D.L. (1990). Exercise oxygen uptake in 3- through 6-year-old children. *Pediatric Exercise Science, 2*, 130–139.

Shumway-Cook, A., & Woollacott, M. (1985). The growth of stability: Postural control from a developmental perspective. *Journal of Motor Behavior, 17*, 131–147.

Sibley, B.A., & Etnier, J.L. (2003). The relationship between physical activity and cognition in children: A meta-analysis. *Pediatric Exercise Science, 15*, 243–256.

Siegel, J.A., Camaione, D.N., & Manfredi, T.G. (1989). The effects of upper body resistance training on pre-pubescent children. *Pediatric Exercise Science, 1*, 145–154.

Siegler, R.S., & Jenkins, E.A. (1989). *How children discover new strategies.* Hillsdale, NJ: Erlbaum.

Simoneau, J.A., & Bouchard, C. (1989). Human variation in skeletal muscle proportion and enzyme activities. *American Journal of Physiology, Endocrinology, and Metabolism, 257*, E567–E572.

Simons, J., Beunen, G.P., Renson, R., Claessens, A.L.M., Vanreusel, B., & Lefevre, J.A.V. (1990). *Growth and fitness of Flemish girls: The Leuven growth study.* Champaign, IL: Human Kinetics.

Sinclair, C. (1971). Dominance pattern of young children: A follow-up study. *Perceptual and Motor Skills, 32,* 142.

Sinclair, C.B. (1973). *Movement of the young child: Ages two to six.* Columbus, OH: Merrill.

Singleton, W.T. (1955). *Age and performance timing on simple skills: Old age and the modern world* (Report of the Third Congress of the International Association of Gerontology). London: Livingstone.

Skinner, B.F. (1938). *The behavior of organisms. An experimental analysis.* New York: Appleton-Century.

Skrobak-Kaczynski, J., & Andersen, K.L. (1975). The effect of a high level of habitual physical activity in the regulation of fatness during aging. *International Archives of Occupational and Environmental Health, 36,* 41–46.

Slater, A., Mattock, A., & Brown, E. (1990). Size constancy at birth: Newborn infants' responses to retinal and real size. *Journal of Experimental Child Psychology, 49*(2), 314–322.

Smith, A.B. (1985). Teacher modeling and sex-types play preferences. *New Zealand Journal of Educational Studies, 20,* 39–47.

Smith, D.B., Johnson, G.O., Stout, J.R., Housh, T.J., Housh, D.J., & Evetovich, T.K. (1997). Validity of near-infrared interactance for estimating relative body fat in female high school gymnasts. *International Journal of Sports Medicine, 18,* 531–537.

Smith, E.L. (1982). Exercise for the prevention of osteoporosis: A review. *The Physician and Sportsmedicine, 3,* 72–80.

Smith, E.L., Sempos, C.T., & Purvis, R.W. (1981). Bone mass and strength decline with age. In E.L. Smith & R.C. Serfass (Eds.), *Exercise and aging: The scientific basis* (pp. 59–87). Hillside, NJ: Enslow.

Smith, E.L., & Serfass, R.C. (Eds.). (1981). *Exercise and aging: The scientific basis.* Hillside, NJ: Enslow.

Smith, M.D. (1979). Getting involved in sport: Sex differences. *International Review of Sport Sociology, 14,* 93–99.

Smith, R.E., Smoll, F.L., & Curtis, B. (1979). Coach effectiveness training: A cognitive-behavioral approach to enhancing relationship skills in youth sport coaches. *Journal of Sport Psychology, 1,* 59–75.

Smoll, F.L., & Smith, R.E. (1989). Leadership behaviors in sport: A theoretical model and research paradigm. *Journal of Applied Social Psychology, 19,* 1522–1551.

Smoll, F.L., & Smith, R.E. (2001). Conducting sport psychology training programs for coaches: Cognitive-behavioral principles and techniques. In J.M. Williams (Ed.), *Applied sport psychology: Personal growth to peak performance* (4th ed., pp. 378–400). Mountain View, CA: Mayfield.

Smyth, M.M., Katamba, J., & Peacock, K.A. (2004). Development of prehension between 5 and 10 years of age: Distance scaling, grip aperture, and sight of the hand. *Journal of Motor Behavior, 36,* 91–103.

Smyth, M.M., Peacock, K.A., & Katamba, J. (2004). Changes in the role of sight of the hand in the development of prehension in childhood. *The Quarterly Journal of Experimental Psychology A: Human Experimental Psychology, 57A,* 269–296.

Snyder, E.E., & Spreitzer, E. (1973). Family influences and involvement in sports. *Research Quarterly, 44,* 249–255.

Snyder, E.E., & Spreitzer, E. (1976). Correlates of sport participation among adolescent girls. *Research Quarterly, 47,* 804–809.

Snyder, E.E., & Spreitzer, E. (1978). Socialization comparisons of adolescent female athletes and musicians. *Research Quarterly, 79,* 342–350.

Sonstroem, R. (1997). Physical activity and self-esteem. In W. Morgan (Ed.), *Physical activity and mental health* (Series in health psychology and behavioral medicine, pp. 127–143). Washington, DC: Taylor & Francis.

Spetner, N.B., & Olsho, L.W. (1990). Auditory frequency resolution in human infancy. *Child Development, 61,* 632–652.

Spilich, G.J., Vesonder, G.T., Chiesi, H.L., & Voss, J.F. (1979). Text processing of individuals with high and low domain knowledge. *Journal of Verbal Learning and Verbal Behavior, 18,* 275–290.

Spirduso, W.W. (1975). Reaction and movement time as a function of age and physical activity level. *Journal of Gerontology, 30,* 435–440.

Spirduso, W.W. (1980). Physical fitness and psychomotor speed: A review. *Journal of Gerontology, 35,* 850–865.

Spirduso, W.W. (1995). *Physical dimensions of aging.* Champaign, IL: Human Kinetics.

Spirduso, W.W., Francis, K.W., & MacRae, P.G. (2005). *Physical dimensions of aging* (2nd ed.). Champaign, IL: Human Kinetics.

Spreitzer, E., & Snyder, E. (1983). Correlates of participation in adult recreational sports. *Journal of Leisure Research, 15,* 28–38.

Sprynarova, S., & Reisenauer, R. (1978). Body dimensions and physiological indications of physical fitness during adolescence. In R.J. Shephard & H. Lavallee (Eds.), *Physical fitness assessment* (pp. 32–37). Springfield, IL: Charles C Thomas.

Stadulis, R.I. (1971). *Coincidence-anticipation behavior of children.* Unpublished doctoral dissertation, Columbia University, New York.

Stamford, B.A. (1973). Effects of chronic institutionalization on the physical working capacity and trainability of geriatric men. *Journal of Gerontology, 28,* 441–446.

Stamford, B.A. (1988). Exercise and the elderly. In K.B. Pandolf (Ed.), *Exercise and sport sciences reviews* (Vol. 16, pp. 341–379). New York: Macmillan.

Steben, R.E., & Steben, A.H. (1981). The validity of the strength shortening cycle in selected jumping events. *Journal of Sports Medicine and Physical Fitness, 21,* 1–7.

Stein, B.E., & Meredith, M.A. (1993). *The merging of the senses.* Cambridge, MA: MIT Press.

Stein, B.E., Meredith, M.A., & Wallace, M.T. (1994). Development and neural basis of multisensory integration. In D.J. Lewkowicz & R. Lickliter (Eds.), *The development of intersensory perception: Comparative perspectives* (pp. 81–105). Hillsdale, NJ: Erlbaum.

Steinberger, J., Jacobs, D.R., Jr., Raatz, S., Moran, A., Hong, C.-P., & Sinaiko, A.R. (2005). Comparison of body fatness measurements by BMI and skinfolds vs. dual energy X-ray absorptiometry and their relation to cardiovascular risk factors in adolescents. *International Journal of Obesity, 29,* 1346–1352.

Sterritt, G., Martin, V., & Rudnick, M. (1971). Auditory-visual and temporal-spatial integration as determinants of test difficulty. *Psychonomic Science, 23,* 289–291.

Stevenson, B. (2007). Title IX and the evolution of high school sports. *Contemporary Economic Policy, 25,* 486–505.

Stine, E.L., Wingfield, A., & Poon, L.W. (1989). Speech comprehension and memory through adulthood: The roles of time and strategy. In L.W. Poon, D.S. Rubin, & B.A. Wilson (Eds.), *Everyday cognition in adulthood and later years* (pp. 195–221). Cambridge, UK: Cambridge University Press.

Stodden, D.F., Fleisig, G.S., Langendorfer, S.J., & Andrews, J.R. (2006). Kinematic constraints associated with the acquisition of overarm throwing. Part I: Step and trunk actions. *Research Quarterly for Exercise and Sport, 77,* 417–427.

Stolz, H.R., & Stolz, L.M. (1951). *Somatic development of adolescent boys.* New York: Macmillan.

Stones, M.J., & Kozma, A. (1989). Age, exercise, and coding performance. *Psychology and Aging, 4,* 190–194.

Strohmeyer, H.S., Williams, K., & Schaub-George, D. (1991). Developmental sequences for catching a small ball: A prelongitudinal screening. *Research Quarterly for Exercise and Sport, 62,* 257–266.

Sutherland, D. (1997). The development of mature gait. *Gait and Posture, 6*(2), 162–170.

Sutherland, D.H., Olshen, R., Cooper, L., & Woo, S. (1980). The development of mature gait. *Journal of Bone and Joint Surgery, 62A,* 336–353.

Sutherland, R., Pipe, M., Schick, K., Murray, J., & Gobbo, C. (2003). Knowing in advance: The impact of prior event information on memory and event knowledge. *Journal of Experimental Child Psychology, 84,* 244–263.

Sutton, R.A., & Miller, C. (2006). Comparison of some secondary body composition algorithms. *College Student Journal, 40,* 791–801.

Swanson, R., & Benton, A.L. (1955). Some aspects of the genetic development of right-left discrimination. *Child Development, 26,* 123–133.

Sweeting, T., & Rink, J.E. (1999). Effects of direct instruction and environmentally designed instruction on the process and product characteristics of a fundamental skill. *Journal of Teaching in Physical Education, 18,* 216–233.

Swingley, D. (2005). 11-month-olds' knowledge of how familiar words sound. *Developmental Science, 8,* 432–443.

Szafran, J. (1951). Changes with age and with exclusion of vision in performance at an aiming task. *Quarterly Journal of Experimental Psychology, 3,* 111–118.

Tanner, J.M. (1962). *Growth at adolescence* (2nd ed.). Oxford, UK: Blackwell Scientific.

Tanner, J.M. (1975). Growth and endocrinology of the adolescent. In L.I. Gardner (Ed.), *Endocrine and genetic disease of childhood and adolescence* (2nd ed., pp. 14–63). Philadelphia: Saunders.

Teeple, J.B. (1978). Physical growth and maturation. In M.F. Ridenour (Ed.), *Motor development: Issues and applications* (pp. 3–27). Princeton, NJ: Princeton Book.

Telama, R., Yang, X., Hirvensalo, J., & Raitakari, O. (2006). Participation in organized youth sport as a predictor of adult physical activity: A 21-year longitudinal study. *Pediatric Exercise Science, 17,* 76–88.

Telama, R., Yang, X., Laakso, L., & Viikari, J. (1997). Physical activity in childhood and adolescence as predictor of physical activity in young adulthood. *American Journal of Preventive Medicine, 13,* 317–323.

Temple, I.G., Williams, H.G., & Bateman, N.J. (1979). A test battery to assess intrasensory and intersensory development of young children. *Perceptual and Motor Skills, 48,* 643–659.

Thelen, E. (1979). Rhythmical stereotypies in normal human infants. *Animal Behaviour, 27,* 699–715.

Thelen, E. (1981). Kicking, rocking, and waving: Contextual analysis of rhythmical stereotypies in normal human infants. *Animal Behaviour, 29,* 3–11.

Thelen, E. (1983). Learning to walk is still an "old" problem: A reply to Zelazo. *Journal of Motor Behavior, 15,* 139–161.

Thelen, E. (1985). Developmental origins of motor coordination: Leg movements in human infants. *Developmental Psychobiology, 18,* 1–22.

Thelen, E. (1995). Motor development: A new synthesis. *American Psychologist, 50,* 79–95.

Thelen, E. (1998). Bernstein's legacy for motor development: How infants learn to reach. In M. Latash (Ed.), *Progress in motor control* (pp. 267–288). Champaign, IL: Human Kinetics.

Thelen, E., Corbetta, D., Kamm, K., Spencer, J.P., Schneider, K., & Zernicke, R.F. (1993). The transition to reaching: Mapping intention and intrinsic dynamics. *Child Development, 64,* 1058–1098.

Thelen, E., & Fisher, D.M. (1983). The organization of spontaneous leg movements in newborn infants. *Journal of Motor Behavior, 15,* 353–377.

Thelen, E., Kelso, J.A.S., & Fogel, A. (1987). Self-organizing systems and infant motor development. *Developmental Review, 7,* 37–65.

Thelen, E., Ridley-Johnson, R., & Fisher, D.M. (1983). Shifting patterns of bilateral coordination and lateral dominance in the leg movements of young infants. *Developmental Psychobiology, 16,* 29–46.

Thelen, E., & Ulrich, B.D. (1991). Hidden skills: A dynamic systems analysis of treadmill stepping during the first year. *Monographs of the Society for Research in Child Development, 56*(1, Serial no. 233).

Thelen, E., Ulrich, B.D., & Jensen, J.L. (1989). The developmental origins of locomotion. In M.H. Woollacott & A. Shumway-Cook (Eds.), *Development of posture and gait across the life span* (pp. 25–47). Columbia: University of South Carolina Press.

Thomas, J.R. (1984). *Motor development during childhood and adolescence.* Minneapolis: Burgess.

Thomas, J.R., French, K.E., Thomas, K.T., & Gallagher, J.D. (1988). Children's knowledge development and sport performance. In F.L. Smoll, R.A. Magill, & M.J. Ash (Eds.), *Children in sport* (3rd ed., pp. 179–202). Champaign, IL: Human Kinetics.

Thomas, J.R., Gallagher, J.D., & Purvis, G.J. (1981). Reaction time and anticipation time: Effects of development. *Research Quarterly for Exercise and Sport, 52,* 359–367.

Thomas, J.R., Thomas, K.T., & Gallagher, J.D. (1981). Children's processing of information in physical activity and sport. *Motor Skills: Theory Into Practice Monograph, 3,* 1–8.

Tibana, R.A., Prestes, J., Nascimento, D.D.A., Martins, O.V., DeSantana, F.S., & Balsamo, S. (2012). Higher muscle performance in adolescents compared with adults after a resistance training session with different rest intervals. *Journal of Strength & Conditioning Research, 26,* 1027-1032.

Timiras, M.L., & Brownstein, H. (1987). Prevalence of anemia and correlation of hemoglobin with age in a geriatric screening clinic population. *Journal of the American Geriatrics Society, 35,* 639–643.

Timiras, P.S. (1972). *Developmental physiology and aging.* New York: Macmillan.

Tolfrey, K., Campbell, I.G., & Batterham, A.M. (1998). Aerobic trainability of prepubertal boys and girls. *Pediatric Exercise Science, 10,* 248–263.

Tomkinson, G.R., Hamlin, M.J., & Olds, T.S. (2006). Secular changes in anaerobic test performance in Australasian children and adolescents. *Pediatric Exercise Science, 18,* 314–328.

Tomkinson, G.R., & Olds, T.S. (2007). Secular changes in pediatric aerobic fitness test performance: The global picture. *Medicine and Sport Science, 50,* 46–66.

Tomkinson, G.R., Olds, T.S., Kang, S.J., & Kim, D.Y. (2007). Secular trends in the aerobic fitness test performance and body mass index of Korean children and adolescents (1968–2000). *International Journal of Sports Medicine, 28,* 314–320.

Trehub, S.E., Bull, D., & Thorpe, L.A. (1984). Infants' perception of melodies: The role of melodic contour. *Child Development, 55,* 821–830.

Trehub, S.E., & Hannon, E.E. (2006). Infant music perception: Domain-general or domain-specific mechanisms? *Cognition, 100,* 73–99.

Tremblay, A., Despres, J.P., & Bouchard, C. (1988). Alteration in body fat and fat distribution with exercise. In C. Bouchard & F.E. Johnston (Eds.), *Fat distribution during growth and later health outcomes* (pp. 297–312). New York: Liss.

Trevarthen, C. (1974). The psychobiology of speed development. In E.H. Lenneberg (Ed.), *Language and brain: Developmental aspects. Neurosciences Research Program Bulletin* (Vol, 12, pp. 570–585). Boston: Neurosciences Research Program.

Trevarthen, C. (1984). How control of movement develops. In H.T.A. Whiting (Ed.), *Human motor actions: Bernstein reassessed* (pp. 223–261). Amsterdam: North-Holland.

Troe, E.J.W.M., Raat, H., Jaddoe, V.W.V., Hofman, A., Looman, C.W.N., Moll, H.A., et al. (2007). Explaining differences in birthweight between ethnic populations. The Generation R study. *BJOG, 114,* 1557–1565.

Trudeau, F., Laurencelle, L., Tremblay, J., Rajic, M., & Shephard, R.J. (1998). A long-term follow-up of participants in the Trois-Rivieres semi-longitudinal study of growth and development. *Pediatric Exercise Science, 10*(4), 366–377.

Tun, P.A., & Wingfield, A. (1993). Is speech special? Perception and recall of spoken language in complex environments. In J. Cerella, J. Rybash, W. Hover, & M.L. Commons (Eds.), *Adult information processing: Limits on loss* (pp. 425–457). San Diego: Academic Press.

Turner, J.M., Mead, J., & Wohl, M.E. (1968). Elasticity of human lungs in relation to age. *Journal of Applied Physiology, 35,* 664–671.

Turner, P., & Gervai, J. (1995). A multidimensional study of gender typing in preschool children and their parents: Personality, attitudes, preferences, behavior, and cultural differences. *Developmental Psychology, 31*(5), 759–779.

Turner, P., Gervai, J., & Hinde, R.A. (1993). Gender-typing in young children: Preferences, behaviour and cultural differences. *British Journal of Developmental Psychology, 11*(4), 323–342.

U.S. Department of Health and Human Services, Centers for Disease Control and Prevention, National Center for Chronic Disease Prevention and Health Promotion. (1996). *Physical activity and health: A report of the Surgeon General.* Atlanta: Author.

Ulrich, B.D., Thelen, E., & Niles, D. (1990). Perceptual determinants of action: Stair-climbing choices of infants and toddlers. In J.E. Clark & J.H. Humphrey (Eds.), *Advances in motor development research* (Vol. 3, pp. 1–15). New York: AMS Press.

Unnithan, V.B. (1993). *Factors affecting submaximal running economy in children.* Unpublished doctoral dissertation, University of Glasgow, Glasgow, Scotland.

Vaccaro, P., & Mahon, A. (1987). Cardiorespiratory responses to endurance training in children. *Sports Medicine, 4*, 352–363.

Valentini, N.C., & Rudisill, M.E. (2004a). An inclusive mastery climate intervention and the motor development of children with and without disabilities. *Adapted Physical Activity Quarterly, 21*, 330–347.

Valentini, N.C., & Rudisill, M.E. (2004b). Effectiveness of an inclusive mastery climate intervention on the motor skill development of children. *Adapted Physical Activity Quarterly, 21*, 285–294.

Valentini, N.C., & Rudisill, M.E. (2004c). Motivational climate, motor-skill development and perceived competence: Two studies of developmentally delayed kindergarten children. *Journal of Teaching in Physical Education, 23*, 216–234.

Valentini, N.C., Rudisill, M.E., & Goodway, J.D. (1999). Incorporating a mastery climate into elementary physical education: It's developmentally appropriate. *Journal of Physical Education, Recreation and Dance, 70*, 28–32.

Van der Fits, I.B.M., & Hadders-Algra, M. (1998). The development of postural response patterns during reaching in healthy infants. *Neuroscience and Biobehavioral Reviews, 22*(4), 521–525.

van der Kamp, J., Savelsbergh, G.J.P., & Davis, W.E. (1998). Body-scaled ratio as a control parameter for prehension in 5- to 9-year-old children. *Developmental Psychology, 33*(4), 351–361.

Van Duyne, H.J. (1973). Foundations of tactical perception in three to seven year olds. *Journal of the Association for the Study of Perception, 8*, 1–9.

Van Hof, P., van der Kamp, J., & Savelsbergh, G.J.P. (2008). The relation between infants' perception of catchableness and the control of catching. *Developmental Psychology, 44*, 182–194.

Van Praagh, E., Fellmann, N., Bedu, M., Falgairette, G., & Coudert, J. (1990). Gender difference in the relationship of anaerobic power output to body composition in children. *Pediatric Exercise Science, 2*, 336–348.

van Rooij, J.C.G.M., & Plomp, R. (1992). Auditive and cognitive factors in speech perception by elderly listeners. III: Additional data and final discussion. *Journal of the Acoustical Society of America, 91*, 1028–1033.

Vedul-Kjelsås, V.I., Sigmundsson, H., Stendsdotter, A.-K., & Haga, M. (2011). The relationship between motor competence, physical fitness and self-perception in children. *Child: Care, Health, and Development, 38*, 394–402.

Vercruyssen, M. (1997). Movement control and speed of behavior. In A.D. Fisk & W.A. Rogers (Eds.), *Handbook of human factors and the older adult* (pp. 55–86). San Diego: Academic Press.

Vereijken, B., & Thelen, E. (1997). Training infant treadmill stepping: The role of individual pattern stability. *Developmental Psychobiology, 30*, 89–102.

Verret, L., Trouche, S., Zerwas, M., & Rampon, C. (2007). Hippocampal neurogenesis during normal and pathological aging. *Psychoneuroendocrinology, 32*(Suppl. 1), S26–S30.

Victors, E. (1961). *A cinematographical analysis of catching behavior of a selected group of seven and nine year old boys.* Unpublished doctoral dissertation, University of Wisconsin, Madison.

von Hofsten, C. (1982). Eye–hand coordination in the newborn. *Developmental Psychology, 18*, 450–461.

von Hofsten, C. (1984). Developmental changes in the organization of pre-reaching movements. *Developmental Psychology, 3*, 378–388.

von Hofsten, C. (1990). Early development of grasping an object in space-time. In M.A. Goodale (Ed.), *Vision and action: The control of grasping* (pp. 65–79). Norwood, NJ: Ablex.

von Hofsten, C., Kellman, P., & Putaansuu, J. (1992). Young infants' sensitivity to motion parallax. *Infant Behavior and Development, 15*(2), 245–264.

von Hofsten, C., & Spelke, E.S. (1985). Object perception and object-directed reaching in infancy. *Journal of Experimental Psychology: General, 114*(2), 198–212.

Vouloumanos, A., & Werker, J.F. (2007). Listening to language at birth: Evidence for a bias for speech in neonates. *Developmental Science, 10*, 159–164.

Wade, M.G. (1980). Coincidence-anticipation of young normal and handicapped children. *Journal of Motor Behavior, 12*, 103–112.

Walk, R.D. (1969). Two types of depth discrimination by the human infant. *Psychonomic Science, 14*, 253–254.

Walk, R.D., & Gibson, E.J. (1961). A comparative and analytical study of visual depth perception. *Psychological Monographs: General and Applied, 75*(15), 1.

Wallace, C.S., Kilman, V.L., Withers, G.S., & Greenough, W.T. (1992). Increases in dendritic length in occipital cortex after 4 days of differential housing in weanling rats. *Behavioral and Neural Biology, 58*(1), 64–68.

Warren, R., & Wertheim, A.H. (1990). *Perception and control of self-motion.* Hillsdale, NJ: Erlbaum.

Warren, W.H. (1984). Perceiving affordances: Visual guidance of stair-climbing. *Journal of Experimental Psychology: Human Perception and Performance, 10*, 683–703.

Washington, R.L. (1989). Anaerobic threshold in children. *Pediatric Exercise Science, 1*, 244–256.

Wattam-Bell, J. (1996a). Visual motion processing in one-month-old infants: Preferential looking experiments. *Vision Research, 36*(11), 1671–1677.

Wattam-Bell, J. (1996b). Visual motion processing in one-month-old infants: Habituation experiments. *Vision Research, 36*(11), 1679–1685.

Weisner, T., Garnier, H., & Loucky, J. (1994). Domestic tasks, gender egalitarian values and children's gender typing in conventional and nonconventional families. *Sex Roles, 30*(1/2), 23–54.

Weiss, M.R. (1993). Psychological effects of intensive sport participation on children and youth: Self-esteem and motivation. In B.R. Cahill & A.J. Pearl (Eds.), *Intensive participation in children's sports* (pp. 39–69). Champaign, IL: Human Kinetics.

Weiss, M.R., & Barber, H. (1996). Socialization influences of collegiate male athletes: A tale of two decades. *Sex Role, 33,* 129–140.

Weiss, M.R., & Ebbick, V. (1996). Self-esteem and perceptions of competence in youth sports: Theory, research and enhancement strategies. In O. Bar-Or (Ed.), *Encyclopedia of sports medicine: Vol. 6. The child and adolescent athlete* (pp. 3364–3382). Oxford, UK: Blackwell Scientific.

Weiss, M.R., & Horn, T.S. (1990). The relation between children's accuracy estimates of their physical competence and achievement-related characteristics. *Research Quarterly for Exercise and Sport, 61,* 250–258.

Weiss, M.R., & Knoppers, A. (1982). The influence of socializing agents on female collegiate volleyball players. *Journal of Sport Psychology, 4,* 267–279.

Weiss, M.R., McAuley, E., Ebbeck, V., & Wiese, D.M. (1990). Self-esteem and causal attributions for children's physical and social competence in sport. *Journal of Sport and Exercise Psychology, 12,* 21–36.

Welford, A.T. (1977a). Causes of slowing of performance with age. *Interdisciplinary Topics in Gerontology, 11,* 23–51.

Welford, A.T. (1977b). Motor performance. In J.E. Birren & K.W. Schaie (Eds.), *Handbook of the psychology of aging* (pp. 450–496). New York: Van Nostrand Reinhold.

Welford, A.T. (1977c). Serial reaction times, continuity of task, single-channel effects, and age. In S. Dornic (Ed.), *Attention and performance VI* (pp. 79–97). Hillside, NJ: Erlbaum.

Welford, A.T. (1980). Motor skill and aging. In C.H. Nadeau, W.R. Halliwell, K.M. Newell, & G.C. Roberts (Eds.), *Psychology of motor behavior and sport—1979* (pp. 253–268). Champaign, IL: Human Kinetics.

Welford, A.T., Norris, A.H., & Shock, N.W. (1969). Speed and accuracy of movement and their changes with age. *Acta Psychologica, 30,* 3–15.

Weltman, A. (1989). Weight training in prepubertal children: Physiological benefit and potential damage. In O. Bar-Or (Ed.), *Biological issues* (Vol. 3, pp. 101–130). Champaign, IL: Human Kinetics.

Weltman, A., Janney, C., Rians, C.B., Strand, K., Berg, B., Tippitt, S., et al. (1986). The effects of hydraulic resistance strength training in prepubertal males. *Medicine and Science in Sports and Exercise, 18,* 629–638.

Weuve, J., Kang, J.E., Manson, J.E., Breteler, M.M.B., Ware, J.H., & Grodstein, F. (2004). Physical activity, including walking, and cognitive function in older women. *Journal of the American Medical Association, 292,* 1454–1461.

Whitall, J. (1988). *A developmental study of interlimb coordination in running and galloping.* Unpublished doctoral dissertation, University of Maryland, College Park.

Whitall, J., & Getchell, N. (1995). From walking to running: Using a dynamical systems approach to the development of locomotor skills. *Child Development, 66,* 1541–1553.

White, B.L., Castle, P., & Held, R. (1964). Observations on the development of visually directed reaching. *Child Development, 35,* 349–364.

WHO Multicentre Growth Reference Study Group. (2006). Reliability of motor development data in the WHO Multicentre Growth Reference Study. *Acta Paediatrica* (Suppl. 450), 47–55.

Wickens, C.D. (1974). Temporal limits of human information processing: A developmental study. *Psychological Bulletin, 81,* 739–755.

Wickstrom, R.L. (1983). *Fundamental motor patterns* (3rd ed.). Philadelphia: Lea & Febiger.

Wickstrom, R.L. (1987). Observations on motor pattern development in skipping. In J.E. Clark & J.H. Humphrey (Eds.), *Advances in motor development research* (Vol. 1, pp. 49–60). New York: AMS Press.

Wiegand, R.L., & Ramella, R. (1983). The effect of practice and temporal location of knowledge of results on the motor performance of older adults. *Journal of Gerontology, 38,* 701–706.

Wigmore, S. (1996). Gender and sport: The last 5 years. *Sport Science Reviews, 5*(2), 53–71.

Wijnhoven, T.M.A., de Onis, M., Onyango, A.W., Wang, T., Bjoerneboe, G.E.A., Bhandari, N., et al. (2006). Assessment of gross motor development in the WHO Multicentre Growth Reference Study. *Food and Nutrition Bulletin, 25,* 37–45.

Wild, M. (1937). *The behavior pattern of throwing and some observations concerning its course of development in children.* Unpublished doctoral dissertation, University of Wisconsin, Madison.

Wild, M. (1938). The behavior pattern of throwing and some observations concerning its course of development in children. *Research Quarterly, 9,* 20–24.

Williams, H. (1968). *Effects of systematic variation of speed and direction of object flight and of age and skill classification on visuo-perceptual judgments of moving objects.* Unpublished doctoral dissertation, University of Wisconsin, Madison.

Williams, H. (1973). Perceptual-motor development in children. In C. Corbin (Ed.), *A textbook of motor development* (pp. 111–148). Dubuque, IA: Brown.

Williams, H. (1983). *Perceptual and motor development.* Englewood Cliffs, NJ: Prentice Hall.

Williams, H. (1986). The development of sensory-motor function in young children. In V. Seefeldt (Ed.), *Physical activity and well-being* (pp. 104–122). Reston, VA: American Alliance for Health, Physical Education, Recreation and Dance.

Williams, K., Goodman, M., & Green, R. (1985). Parent–child factors in gender role socialization in girls. *Journal of the American Academy of Child Psychiatry, 24,* 720–731.

Williams, K., Haywood, K., & VanSant, A. (1990). Movement characteristics of older adult throwers. In J.E. Clark & J.H. Humphrey (Eds.), *Advances in motor development research* (Vol. 3, pp. 29–44). New York: AMS Press.

Williams, K., Haywood, K., & VanSant, A. (1991). Throwing patterns of older adults: A follow-up investigation. *International Journal of Aging and Human Development, 33,* 279–294.

Williams, K., Haywood, K., & VanSant, A. (1993). Force and accuracy throws by older adult performers. *Journal of Aging and Physical Activity, 1,* 2–12.

Williams, K., Haywood, K., & VanSant, A. (1996). Force and accuracy throws by older adults: II. *Journal of Aging and Physical Activity, 4*(2), 194–202.

Williams, K., Haywood, K., & VanSant, A. (1998). Changes in throwing by older adults: A longitudinal investigation. *Research Quarterly for Exercise and Sport, 69*(1), 1–10.

Willoughby, D.S., & Pelsue, S.C. (1998). Muscle strength and qualitative myosin heavy chain isoform mRNA expression in the elderly after moderate- and high-intensity weight training. *Journal of Aging and Physical Activity, 6,* 327–339.

Wilmore, J.H. (1991). The aging of bones and muscle. In R.K. Kerlan (Ed.), *Sports medicine in the older adult* (pp. 231–244). Philadelphia: Saunders.

Wilmore, J.H., & Costill, D.L. (1999). *Physiology of sport and exercise (2nd ed.).* Champaign, IL: Human Kinetics.

Winter, D.A. (1983). Biomechanical motor patterns in normal walking. *Journal of Motor Behavior, 15,* 302–330.

Winterhalter, C. (1974). *Age and sex trends in the development of selected balancing skills.* Unpublished master's thesis, University of Toledo, Toledo, OH.

Witelson, S.F. (1987). Neurobiological aspects of language in children. *Child Development, 58,* 653–688.

Witherington, D.S., Campos, J.J., Anderson, D.I., Lejeune, L., & Seah, E. (2005). Avoidance of heights on the visual cliff in newly walking infants. *Infancy, 7,* 285–298.

Wolff, P.H., Michel, G.F., Ovrut, M., & Drake, C. (1990). Rate and timing precision of motor coordination in developmental dyslexia. *Developmental Psychology, 26,* 349–359.

Women's Sports Foundation. (2000). *Women's sport and fitness facts & statistics.* Available: www.womenssports foundation.org/binary-data/WSF_article/Pdf_file/106.pdf.

Wood, J.M., & Abernethy, B. (1997). An assessment of the efficacy of sports vision training programs. *Optometry and Vision Science, 74,* 646–659.

Wood, L.E., Dixon, S., Grant, C., & Armstrong, N. (2006). Elbow flexor strength, muscle size, and moment arms in prepubertal boys and girls. *Pediatric Exercise Science, 18,* 457–469.

Woollacott, M., Debu, B., & Mowatt, M. (1987). Neuromuscular control of posture in the infant and child. *Journal of Motor Behavior, 19,* 167–186.

Woollacott, M., Shumway-Cook, A.T., & Nashner, L.M. (1982). Postural reflexes and aging. In J.A. Mortimer (Ed.), *The aging motor system* (pp. 98–119). New York: Praeger.

Woollacott, M., Shumway-Cook, A.T., & Nashner, L.M. (1986). Aging and posture control: Changes in sensory organization and muscular coordination. *International Journal of Aging and Human Development, 23,* 97–114.

Woollacott, M.H. (1986). Gait and postural control in the aging adult. In W. Bles & T. Brandt (Eds.), *Disorders of posture and gait* (pp. 326–336). New York: Elsevier.

Woollacott, M.H., Shumway-Cook, A., & Williams, H. (1989). The development of posture and balance control in children. In M.H. Woollacott & A. Shumway-Cook (Eds.), *Development of posture and gait across the life span* (pp. 77–96). Columbia: University of South Carolina Press.

Woollacott, M.H., & Sveistrup, H. (1994). The development of sensorimotor integration underlying posture control in infants during the transition to independent stance. In S.P. Swinnen, J. Massion, & H. Heuer (Eds.), *Interlimb coordination: Neural, dynamical and cognitive constraints* (pp. 371–389). San Diego: Academic Press.

World Health Organization. (1998). *Obesity: Preventing and managing the global epidemic. Report of a WHO consultation on obesity.* Geneva: Author.

World Health Organization Expert Subcommittee on the Use and Interpretation of Anthropometry in the Elderly. (1998). Uses and interpretation of anthropometry in the elderly for the assessment of physical status report to the Nutrition Unit of the World Health Organization. *The Journal of Nutrition, Health, and Aging, 2,* 15–17.

Wright, C.E., & Wormald, R.P. (1992). Stereopsis and aging. *Eye, 6,* 473–476.

Yamaguchi, Y. (1984). A comparative study of adolescent socialization into sport: The case of Japan and Canada. *International Review for Sociology of Sport, 19*(1), 63–82.

Yekta, A.A., Pickwell, L.D., & Jenkins, T.C.A. (1989). Binocular vision, age and symptoms. *Ophthalmic and Physiological Optics, 9,* 115–120.

Young, A., Stokes, M., & Crowe, M. (1985). The size and strength of the quadriceps muscles of old and young men. *Clinical Physiology, 5,* 145–154.

Zaichkowsky, L.D., Zaichkowsky, L.B., & Martinek, T.J. (1980). *Growth and development: The child and physical activity.* St. Louis: Mosby.

Zelazo, P.R. (1983). The development of walking: New findings and old assumptions. *Journal of Motor Behavior, 15,* 99–137.

Zelazo, P.R., Zelazo, N.A., & Kolb, S. (1972a). "Walking" in the newborn. *Science, 176,* 314–315.

Zelazo, P.R., Zelazo, N.A., & Kolb, S. (1972b). Newborn walking. *Science, 177,* 1058–1059.

Zimmerman, H.M. (1956). Characteristic likenesses and differences between skilled and non-skilled performance of the standing broad jump. *Research Quarterly, 27,* 352.

Zwiren, L.D. (1989). Anaerobic and aerobic capacities of children. *Pediatric Exercise Science, 1,* 31–44.

Index

About the Authors

Kathleen M. Haywood, PhD, is a professor and associate dean for academic programs at the University of Missouri at St. Louis, where she has researched life span motor development and taught courses in motor behavior and development, sport psychology, and biomechanics. She earned her PhD in motor behavior from the University of Illinois at Urbana-Champaign in 1976.

Haywood is a fellow of the National Academy of Kinesiology and the Research Consortium of the Society for Health and Physical Education (SHAPE). She is also a recipient of SHAPE's Mabel Lee Award. Haywood has served as president of the North American Society for the Psychology of Sport and Physical Activity and as chairperson of the Motor Development Academy of SHAPE.

Haywood is also the coauthor of four editions of *Archery: Steps to Success* ? of *Teaching Archery: Steps to Success*, published by Human Kinetics. She resi Saint Charles, Missouri, and in her free time enjoys fitness training, ter og training.

Nancy Getchell, PhD, is an associate professor at the University of Delaware in Newark. For nearly 30 years, Getchell has investigated developmental motor control and coordination in children with and without disabilities. She teaches courses in motor development, motor control and learning, research methods, and women in sport.

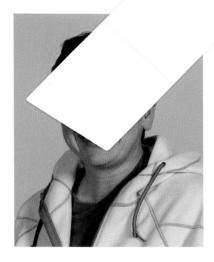

Getchell is a professional member of the North American Society for the Psychology of Sport and Physical Activity, the International Society of Motor Control, and the International Society for Behavioral Nutrition and Physical Activity. She is a research fellow for the Research Consortium of the American Alliance for Health, Physical Education Recreation and Dance (AAHPERD). From 2005 to 2009, Getchell served as editor for the Growth and Motor Development section of *Research Quarterly for Exercise and Sport*. Getchell has also served as the chairperson of the AAHPERD Motor Development and Learning Academy.

Getchell obtained her PhD from the University of Wisconsin at Madison in 1996 in kinesiology with a specialization in motor development. In 2001, Getchell was the recipient of the Lolas E. Halverson Young Investigators Award in motor development.

Getchell resides in Wilmington, Delaware, where she enjoys hiking, geocaching, and bicycling.